CW01096104

The Equine Tapestry

The Equine Tapestry

Horse Breeds, Their History and Their Colors

Volume I - Draft and Coaching Breeds

Lesli Kathman

Blackberry Lane Publishing

Dedication

to my husband, Alan, for his unfailing love and support,
and
to my companions in mayhem, Joanie and Sarah —I finished mine; now it is your turn

First published in 2012 by:
Blackberry Lane Publishing
4700 Lone Tree Court
Charlotte, NC 28269 USA
www.horsecolor.info

Copyright © 2012 by Lesli Kathman

All rights reserved. No part of this publication may be reproduced, stored in a retrieval system or transmitted in any form or by any means, electronic, mechanical, photocopying, recording or otherwise, without the prior written permission of the author.

ISBN 978-0-6155-1149-8

Cover images by:
Clydesdale mare and foal: Kim Bjorgo
Appaloosa Sport horse mare: Cindy Bellamy
Highland stallion: Neil Jones
Pinto pony gelding: Lesli Kathman

"Nature uses only the longest threads to weave her patterns, so that each small piece of her fabric reveals the organization of the entire tapestry."

– Richard Feynman

Contents

Appendixes

Preface

"I wish someone would have told them that is *not* a proper Walking Horse color."

That was the comment made by a woman to her shopping companion at the World Champion tack shop in Shelbyville, Tennessee. The shop sits across from the Calsonic Arena, and the women where there—just as I was—for the annual Walking Horse Celebration. The speaker was referring to a tobiano-spotted figurine of a Tennessee Walking Horse made by Breyer Animal Creations.

Breyer is a popular manufacturer of model horses. As someone who works in the equine collectibles industry, I understand the market pressures that encourage the production of eye-catching and unusual colors. It is likely that the speaker would have considered a solid black horse more accurate. Unfortunately for Breyer, their business success depends upon selling multiple copies of the same sculpture. The key to doing this is color variety, and there is not a lot of variety in a solid black.

That demand for variety was how I first became interested in horse color. My customers want figurines with realistic, detailed and truly unique coloration. The added challenge is that they also want these things within what is accurate for a given breed. As a result I have, like many artists in my industry, become a student of breeds and their lesser-known colors. That was, in fact, why I was standing in line at World Champion Horse Equipment. I had come to retrieve a copy of the newly published *Echo of Hoofbeats*, a detailed history of the Walking Horse breed. I was excited because the book was said to contain rare photographs of some of the foundation horses. I knew from stud book records that many of those foundation horses had white patterns, and I hoped that the photographs would help me determine what kind they had.

I found it amusing that two people could be so concerned about all the questionable "painted" horses turning up in their breed while a stack of books holding historical photographs of that very thing sat just a few feet away. But I also wondered how many ardent fans of the different breeds had lost sight of the real stories behind their chosen breeds. Color, arguably one of the first things we notice about an individual horse, is woven through those stories. To tell the history of color in the different breeds is to tell a large part of their stories.

Horse color has always been subject to changing fashions, and we are arguably in the midst of one of those changes now. It is my hope that this book will help set those changes in the larger context of the history of the different breeds, and the story of the domestic horse as a whole.

Lesli Kathman
March 2012

Acknowledgements

This is a book that has been more than thirty years in the making. That is how long I have been collecting images of horses with unusual colors, patterns or markings. I have spent much of that time in agricultural and sporting libraries, or in breed association basements, pouring over old magazines and show catalogs, stud books and registry records. In more recent years, much of that work has shifted to combing online databases and photo archives. That has also opened up what was once a more solitary pursuit to one that involves connections with a large network of people interested in horse breeds and their colors, as well as the owners and breeders of the horses. This book is richer for their many contributions, and listing them all would require an additional volume to this already large set of books.

I do want to express my deep appreciation for the many people involved in horse color research. Dr. Phillip Sponenberg opened my eyes to a more organized way of looking at the subject with his original book *Horse Color*. Over time the work of others has added to my understanding, including J. K. Wiersema, Reiner Geurts, Carole Knowles-Pfeiffer, Jeanette Gower, Henriette Arriens, Rebecca Bellone, Sheila Archer, and Carolyn Shepard. I have been blessed to get to know some of these people on a more personal basis, and the ability to discuss ideas about horse color with others who love the same obscure subject is a great blessing.

Many of the breeds covered in this particular volume are rarely seen outside their native countries, and I am indebted to a number of individuals who graciously shared their knowledge of them. J. K. Wiersema deserves much of the credit for the exhaustive information on the Gelderlander and especially the Groninger. His work on horse color, done in a time before molecular studies filled in some of the pieces of the puzzle, was remarkably insightful. His son, Frans, was extremely generous with his father's research materials and the Dutch breed chapters are far more complete for his assistance. Thomas Armbruster was invaluable for understanding the Black Forest Horse, and moreover is one of the most delightful horsemen I have had the pleasure to meet. Barbara Hofmanová provided crucial information about the rare and historical colors of the Kladruber. Matuez Kaca answered my many questions about the Polish Coldblood. His pictures and his blog entries were a consistent source of inspiration while I was working on the heavy horse section. Leah Patton is one of the few Americans to import a Mulassier, and her insight into that breed was extremely helpful. Caroline Jones provided information on the Suffolk as it is currently bred in the United Kingdom, which was helpful to contrast with how the horses are bred here in America.

Breed registry staff also provided invaluable assistance. In some cases, they supplied the images that appear in the breed sections. Often they gave the names of breeders and historians that could answer my questions. Owners of the horses were also extremely helpful, and often gave background information on family tendencies, or details about their coloring that were not obvious from photographs. This was particularly true of Lucy Philp, who provided information about the Bald Eagle line of splashed white horses. Joanne Abramson of Pacific Pintos was another wonderful resource. Her commitment to test and photograph all her horses for the benefit of those who study color was a godsend, as were her encouraging words about writing books that do not neatly fit into a particular subject category. There are many more, too numerous to mention, that have taken my calls and were generous with their time while they answered what must have sometimes seemed like really odd questions. In return, I have tried to keep in mind that while these horses are of academic interest to those of us who find color fascinating, to their owners they are often beloved companions.

In addition to the owners, many photographers freely shared their work for this book. A comprehensive list can be found at the back of this book, but special gratitude is due Claudia Dispa, Christine Sutcliffe, Cindy Evans and Martina Vannelli, each of whom allowed me free access to their extensive files. I cannot thank them, and the other photographers who participated, enough for what they have added to this work. Thanks also go to the library and museum staff who helped me locate some of the historical images that appear in this book.

Mention must also be made of the groups originally intended as the target for this work, which are the artists and collectors that make up the equine collectibles industry. It is an community defined by a consuming interest in all things equine, across the entire spectrum of breeds, disciplines and historical eras. Having spent most of my professional life there, I could not help but be influenced by this. Furthermore, it is a community that encourages the open sharing of information. That is how I began writing and speaking about horse color. Sometimes questions others ask provide more opportunity for learning than the answers you could give. My experiences there have encouraged me to look at color in new ways, and given me invaluable lessons about how complex information can be presented in an approachable way.

I am also grateful to the many owners and showers who have allowed me to take pictures—sometimes seemingly odd pictures!—of their horses. For everyone who posed a horse, or moved to an area with better lighting, or invited me to their homes and farms to get more pictures, I am in your debt. I am especially grateful to everyone involved at Horse Shadow Run. Many of the horses there make an appearance in this book in some fashion. It is also true that without Melanie Dortschy and Savannah Sheldon, my own pony would have cheerfully reverted back to the wild while I sat staring at page spreads and proof copies. Both women represent what is best about the people who make horses central to their lives.

And finally I would like to acknowledge the constant support and sacrifice of my friends and family. My husband Alan was always able to strike the right balance between unconditional support and stubborn insistence that I actually complete this project. This book could never have been finished without him. My sons, Brandon and Matthew, were equally encouraging, even if they did believe the story might be improved by the inclusion of a few zombies. My parents, Tom and Chris Jeffreys, also gave their support. Few children can say that, when explaining that they intended to make a career of art, and art centered around horses no less, their parents were enthused about their prospects. Mine were, and I remain forever grateful for that. I am also grateful to Joanie Berkwitz, Kim Bjorgo, Melissa Gaulding, Elaine Lindelef, and Sarah Minkiewicz-Breunig. In various ways each has served as a sounding board and provided valuable insights, and I consider myself fortunate to call them friends.

Introduction

This book began as a set of charts designed to answer questions artists might have about the colors that were accurate for a given breed. I had a fascination with horse color which was reflected in my own artwork, and over the years I had collected extensive reference material to answer those kinds of questions. The charts became a living document; when new information came to light, updates were made. Eventually I expanded the charts to include historical colors once present, but that were no longer found, in each breed. Unlike breeders, artists are not restricted to breeds as they are, but can instead choose to depict horses as they once were, so the charts needed to reflect the history of each breed.

As the scientific understanding of equine coat color progressed, the charts became increasingly complex. As time passed I found the format, with only so much space and so many categories, limited. I began to think about producing a supplemental booklet to explain the information contained within the charts. Such a booklet would allow me to elaborate on the reasons why I chose, for example, to categorize a color as suspected rather than confirmed. Charts are great for presenting a lot of information in a small space, but they are not good for nuance. But mostly I yearned to tell the background stories. How did this color come into the breed? How was it lost? Why is this a preferred color but that is not? Has it always been so?

And so this project was born. Looking back, it is hard to believe that what I thought would be a small book with only the most basic information—little more than a booklet, really—could turn into such an undertaking. Yet the more I researched, and the more I wrote, the more I realized that much of the information about breeds and colors was not readily available, even to people with a strong interest in the subject. It seemed worthwhile to set it all down in one place, even if it meant that my little project began to take on rather daunting proportions.

This all took place while great strides were being made towards unlocking some of the mysteries behind the more complex pinto and appaloosa patterns. As the breeds and their information grew, so did the opening section about the colors. Brief explanatory paragraphs and occasional photographs were replaced with complete chapters and elaborate pattern example charts. I did not intend to write a book about identifying colors. Given the limitations of black and white printing, I felt that was a book that needed to wait for more reliable, affordable color options to become available. Still, more information was necessary if readers were going to make sense of the patterns found (or not found) in each breed.

The end result was a four-volume series, the first of which is the book you are holding. Three more are planned to complete the set.

How the Volumes are Structured

The scope of the subject required that the book be split into several volumes. The most logical way to do this was to group the breeds by general types and include a few related groups in each volume. This proved to be challenging, as classifying breeds can be highly controversial. Even where no controversy exists, there are those breeds that could arguably fit in more than one group. There are even breeds that have their own stud book sections that spread across multiple categories. As a result, the groupings are somewhat arbitrary. Often the final groupings were based as much on shared history and overlapping stories as they were on body type or current usage.

I have begun the series with the draft and coaching breeds. I have chosen to start there in part because they, along with the racing breeds that make their appearance in the final volume, were the first breeds to have stud books, and so are among the oldest of the formalized breeds. From a practical standpoint, this is also the smallest group of breeds, which made it easier to fit them into the same volume as the background information on the colors and patterns.

Three more volumes are intended to follow this one. The next volume will cover ponies and small horses. That book will also cover some of the primitive breeds, since they often overlap with the ponies. That will be followed the by Spanish horses and their New World descendants. Here in the United States, that will include our stock horses and the southern gaited breeds. Finally the series will wrap up with the riding and sport breeds. Some of the light drafts and the trotting breeds, which got bumped from this volume as the page count grew, will also make their appearance in that last volume.

It is my hope that by presenting this information in a series of books, I will be able to include new information as it becomes available. Future volumes will have a section for new developments in color research, and also for any additional information or corrections to the previous volumes. Every effort has been made to ensure that the information within is accurate, but a project of this size is bound to contain errors. I encourage anyone who has corrections, or even just additional information, to send it to the address found on the inside cover for inclusion in subsequent volumes.

How this Book is Structured
This first volume is divided into three sections. The first is a brief overview of how the concept of "breed" evolved, and a look at the different systems used by registries. Color in any given breed is limited by what is present in the gene pool, and by what is accepted as legitimate. For that reason, the systems used by the registries are an import part of understanding breed colors.

The second section contains descriptions of the different colors and patterns. Although not a comprehensive guide for identification, this section is designed to give a basic framework for understanding the colors and patterns mentioned in the breed entries. Although the genetic mechanisms involved are briefly discussed (when they are known), the focus in the section is on the visual nature of the colors and patterns, and not the technical aspects of the mutations that create them. More detailed discussions of some of the rarer colors, and the less common variations, appear in the chapters on the breeds where they are known to occur.

Finally the last part is the breed entries. In this volume there are the coaching breeds and the

heavy drafts, with each breed covered in a separate chapter. The breed chapters open with the structure of the stud book and an estimate of the current population. Current colors are then covered, followed by historical colors. Each breed chapter closes with a look at eye color and markings. Each breed has a summary section located near opening page for quick reference. The information in the breed chapters is also summarized in the charts in Appendix E. For those familiar with the original color charts from the "Possibilities" articles, these follow a similar format.

The appendixes offer further information on both breed formation and the history of horse color. There is also a section for breed resources and a fairly extensive bibliography for those interested in further exploration of the topics presented here.

Some Conventions Used Throughout the Book
One of the challenges in writing this book was to include as much information as possible without making the text necessarily complex. For that reason a few conventions have been adopted.

Horses
The names of horses appear is small caps. Because it is often helpful to set a horse in context of the history of the breed, foaling year is included whenever it is known. Typically this follows in parenthesis after the initial mention of the horse by name. When horse names are used to describe families or sire lines, they are not capitalized. Registration numbers are included when the conventions of the breed include them as are part of the name. Otherwise registration numbers are only included when multiple horses were registered with the same name (a surprisingly common occurrence in the early years of many registries).

Color Names
For consistency and simplicity, I have chosen to use the scientific names for colors whenever they are available. When not available, I have tried to use the most common English term. When foreign color names are mentioned, they appear in italics. A more comprehensive dictionary of foreign color

names can be found in Appendix C. When they can clarify a situation, the symbols for the specific alleles are included in parenthesis. When the official allele symbols are different from the testing symbols, such as the newly identified splashed white patterns, I have used the testing symbols since they are likely to be more familiar to owners and breeders. For patterns that have, or are believed to have, multiple forms that have no individual names, I have used the numerical notations (sabino-1, pattern-1) when speaking specifically about the forms that have been formally identified. The one exception is for splashed white-1, which is usually referred to in the text as classic splash.

Illustrations

Three basic horse outlines were used for all the patterning diagrams: a small pony, a trotting mare, and a larger walking gelding. The drawings were not intended to represent any particular breed or type, but rather to serve as a generic canvas for the different patterns. Sometimes the visual similarities between patterns are easier to see without the distraction of any obvious breed type. The choice of which outline to use for each illustration was random, though the pony appears least often because I did not anticipate how much his long coat would obscure pattern details.

All the sample patterns were taken directly from real horses. Within the limits of cell-shaded illustration and black and white printing, their body colors have been faithfully duplicated. That is, a flaxen chestnut splashed white horse will have a medium body color and a lighter mane and tail. The specific horses used are detailed in the back of the book after the photo credits.

Breed Formation

The connection between breed and color has a long history. Writing in 1841, naturalist Colonel Hamilton Smith divided horses by what he believed to be their ancestral colors. In his system, all breeds could be divided into the Bay Stock, the White or Grey Stock, the Black Stock, the Dun or Tan Stock, and the Tangum or Piebald Horse. Kladruby nad Labem, one of the oldest continuously operating stud farms, still refers to the Old White and the Old Black breeds, as the Kladrubers were originally known. Centuries later, color is still closely tied to breed identity.

Breed Formation

When Colonel Smith wrote *The Natural History of Horses*, the selective breeding of domestic animals was still a recent innovation. While claims of ancient origins are almost universal among breed registries—even crossbreds are frequently marketed as recreating some ancient type—the concept of standardized breeds with publicly recorded pedigrees and governing registries is a relatively modern one. Few stud books date back before the turn of the last century. It is also a concept that, while it radically changed horse breeding in most western countries, has yet to be universally adopted.

To explore the history of breeds and their colors, it is important to understand how landraces evolved into standardized breeds. A landrace is a group of animals bred in a region to suit a specific purpose, but without written records or a codified standard. While landraces can still be found in some parts of the world, the western horse world is dominated by standardized breeds. This change came about in several ways.

Royal and Clerical Studs

The earliest efforts to improve horses through systematic breeding were stud farms established by princes, noblemen and monasteries. The oldest of these still operating is the Einsiedeln Stud in Switzerland, which was established by Benedictine monks in 934 AD. Among the better known are the Kladruby National Stud in the Czech Republic, the Royal Frederiksborg Stud in Denmark and the Lipica Stud Farm in Slovenia, all founded in the sixteenth century. Many of these early stud farms began with Spanish, Italian and Oriental horses.

Although private records were often kept, many of these were lost during wars and political upheav-als, leaving gaps in the recorded ancestry of what are otherwise very old breeds. But perhaps more importantly, pedigrees were not used to guarantee purity of blood. Such a concept would have been foreign to breeders of that time, all of whom practiced what would now be considered cross-breeding. This changed somewhat over time, especially as the eastern breeds and their traditions took on more importance, but the original approach would seem rather eclectic to modern horsemen accustomed to purebred registries. Horses from different places, and with different backgrounds, were frequently exchanged. Experimental crosses were common.

At times this flexibility has been used to expand the range of colors in a breed. An example of this is DOLLY (1834), a tobiano mare of English breeding used at Lipica. Although the stud had not used outcross blood for some time, and had not used

The Imperial Stud at Kladruby nad Labem was founded by the Holy Roman Emperor Maximilian II in 1562, and it one of the oldest continuously operating stud farms in Europe. Both the farm and the Kladruber breed were designated as Czech national landmarks in 2002.

English horses in the past, the Empress Elizabeth of Austria had a fondness for piebald horses. The last known descendant of DOLLY was born in 1913, and sold to the Schumann Circus, but for a brief time royal whim ensured that tobiano was (once again) a legitimate color for Lipizzans. DOLLY is a relatively modern example, but her inclusion reflected the historical way royal studs operated.

When the European monarchies were abolished, most royal studs became state or national studs. Only a few remain actively involved in the breeding of horses, and fewer still produce breeds unique to their institution.

State Studs and Government Control
State stud farms began to appear soon after the formation of royal stud farms. These facilities were owned by the government, but their purpose was to provide well-made stallions to local farmers, and thereby raise the overall quality of the horses of a region. This gave rulers a reliable source for remounts, and kept the money generated from the enterprise within their own borders. Louis XIV of France is often credited with forming the first state stud farms by royal decree in 1665, though some noblemen, like Johann XVI of Oldenburg, has already pioneered the practice of offering stallions to their tenant farmers.

In the late seventeenth and early eighteenth centuries regional governments began taking measures to improve the quality of their horses through the control and licensing of breeding stallions. In 1688, the Prince-Archbishop of Salzburg issued an order that mare owners must use government stallions. Ostfriesia in northwestern Germany began holding stallion inspections in 1715. Oldenburg followed in 1755, and by 1820 rules regarding the use of approved stallions were made mandatory in Germany.

Just as with the royal studs, the horses were strongly associated with their place of origin. Indeed, the vast majority of breeds take their names from the region where they were first bred. This reflects the state involvement in the development of breeds for various purposes, but it also can be explained by prevailing ideas about the influence of environment on foals. At the time, it was widely

> PROPOSALS
> FOR *PUBLISHING BY SUBSCRIPTION,*
> IN MAY NEXT,
> THE GENERAL STUD-BOOK,
> OR,
> Pedigrees of Horses,
> FROM
> THE COMMENCEMENT OF RACING IN
> ENGLAND, TO THE PRESENT TIME;
> ON AN IMPROVED PLAN.
> By the *AUTHOR* of the *INTRODUCTION.*
>
> CONDITIONS.
>
> I. THE Work to be printed on a fine wove paper, and neatly bound in calf, price to Subscribers, 12s. 6d.—Also, on common paper, and in boards, price to Subscribers, 7s. 6d.
>
> II. THE Subscription to close on the First of March, 1793; when the work will be put to press, and the prices advanced to Non-subscribers.
>
> III. THE money to be paid at the time of subscribing, and the books to be forwarded to the Subscribers, as they shall direct.
>
> MUCH pains have been taken to make this work as correct and as extensive as possible, and from the general approbation the late publication experienced, and the many additions and alterations now making, from the best authorities, the Publisher has every reason to hope, that THE GENERAL STUD-BOOK will be found exceedingly useful.
>
> SUBSCRIPTIONS received by J. WEATHERBY, Jun. No. 7, *Oxenden-Street, London*; Mr. WEATHERBY, *Newmarket*; and Mr. RHODES, *York.*

This advertisement for the General Stud-Book appeared in the 1791 Racing Calendar. Believed to be the first public stud book for horses, the first volume was sent to subscribers in 1793.

believed that the land, and particularly the nature of the soil, contributed to the qualities of the horses bred in a region. Absent a general understanding of the contribution each parent made to the offspring, this idea continued to influence the formation of breeds into the early twentieth century, until it was replaced by the modern understanding of genetics.

When armies mechanized and horses lost their central role in military campaigns, many countries found it difficult to justify maintaining government stud farms. Some became historical and cultural sites, while others were disbanded or became private entities. France and Germany are notable for their continued commitment to providing stallions through state-owned stud farms, but even there the programs are greatly reduced in scale. Many European countries still maintain a measure of control over breeding stock, particularly stallions, though now it is primarily for economic rather than military reasons. This level of state involvement in breeding decisions is often surprising to American breeders, but it has a long history in these countries.

General Stud Books

The eighteenth century was a time of dramatic changes in agriculture, particularly in England. Credit for introducing selective breeding is often given to Robert Bakewell, a Leicestershire tenant farmer. He pioneered the use of inbreeding, then called "in-and-in", as a way of ensuring desired traits, and of hiring breeding males to the public. Although his own breeding programs primarily focused on sheep and cattle, and his horses had little long-term influence, his idea of maintaining records and breeding "like to like" had a profound impact on livestock breeding. His Dishley Society, formed to maintain the purity of his line of Leicester sheep, also served as a template for later breed associations.

It was during this time that James Weatherby began work on his *General Stud-Book*, a collection of the pedigrees of English race horses compiled from racing calendars and sales reports. He offered his book by subscription in the 1791 Racing Calendar, and published the first volume in 1793. It was not Weatherby's original intention to define the Thoroughbred as a breed, but to address the problem of pedigree fraud in racing. It was the *Coates Herd Book for Shorthorn Cattle*, published in 1822, that shifted the focus to breed standardization. The idea soon spread, and public pedigree records quickly became tied to the process of standardizing breeds.

Breeders in the United States were among the early adopters. In 1829, John Stuart Skinner began publishing the *American Turf Register*, a periodical that contained the pedigrees and performance records of American racing stock. He was soon followed by Patrick Nisbett Edgar, who published the *American Race Turf Register* in 1833. Although

only one volume was published, Edgar's register is still considered relevant because it documented many of the foundation horses of the Quarter Horse. It also provided much of the information used in later stud books.

What began as an effort to create a public record of racehorses and their pedigrees spread, and a number of farm periodicals began publishing pedigrees. Daniel Linsley published *Morgan Horses: A Premium Essay* in 1857, which included more than 200 stallions of Morgan breeding. He continued to solicit pedigrees which were published in the *Vermont Stock Journal* until the project was taken over by Joseph Battell in 1884. John H. Wallace published *Wallace's American Stud Book* in 1867. That book contained a supplemental section for trotting horses, which were gaining popularity at the time. It proved more popular than the main section, and in 1871 he published the first *American Trotting Register*, which became the stud book for the American Standardbred. Around the same time, Colonel Sanders Dewees Bruce used the more familiar *General Stud-Book* format for his *American Stud Book* in 1873. His books proved more popular than the one by Wallace, at least within the racing community, and served as the basis for the American Thoroughbred stud books.

Although now largely replaced by online databases, printed stud books were the standard for British and American breed registries in the early part of the twentieth century.

Not long after, public stud books began to appear for a number of draft and coaching breeds both in Europe and America. They were soon followed by pony and saddle breeds, until they became something expected for any formal breed. Most were published as periodicals, yearly in the case of most British stud books, but much more irregularly in other countries. This continued until the middle of the twentieth century, when printing costs began to rise and interest in the actual books began to wane. Printed stud books are now rare outside of Britian, but the information once contained in them is still collected and preserved in computerized databases.

Registries, Societies and Associations
Although maintaining a stud book is thought of as the purpose of a registry, at the time standardized breeds were taking shape stud books were primarily the work of individuals. Governing bodies formed somewhat later. Wallace published his *Trotting Register* in 1871, but the National Association of Trotting Horse Breeders was not formed for another eight years. In the United Kingdom, many pony breeds were recorded in their own section of the Polo Pony Stud Book decades before they had a governing breed society. By the early twentieth century, though, most registries had acquired control of the stud book for their breed. For the older stud book breeds, this was the typical pattern of development.

Privately held stud books meant that the editor decided what was legitimately part of the breed, including color. If a compiler held an opinion about a given color—both Wallace and Battell, for instance, appear to have had a certain admiration for dun—then those views determined the inclusion (or exclusion) of horses of that color. When registries took over that role, groups of breeders made those decisions. That is the most typical arrangement for breeds in the twenty-first century; registries set the rules that govern stud book entry. Registries have become so central to breed identity that most horsemen, particularly American horsemen, do not think in terms of entry in a stud book but rather in terms of eligibility for registration.

In their role as final arbiter of what is or is not part of the breed, registries set the parameters for what colors are included. Sometimes this is done intentionally by making certain colors or patterns a condition for inclusion. Another approach is to write color specifications into the rules that govern the show ring. This tactic is less absolute, because it does not bar less desirable colors from inclusion in the gene pool, but show ring success does tend to shape breeding decisions.

Registries also determine color variety indirectly through the structure of the stud book. If the book is closed to outside blood, then barring new mutations only those colors already within the breed are possible. If outcrosses are permitted, then the colors in the accepted outcross breeds become possibilities. Using inspections or grading schemes, new colors can be intentionally introduced.

Breeds without Registries or Stud Books
In most western countries, it is registries that determine the structure of the stud book, and by extension, which colors are found within the breed. That is not universal, however, and there are recognized breeds that do not have public stud books or registries, or do not have these in the same sense that American horsemen might find familiar.

Included in this group are some of the breeds that originated in the old royal and state studs. The Kladruber and the Lipizzan are good examples of this, as are some of the breeds of the former Soviet Union. Others are landraces in countries that never adopted the British and American stud book system, but that were nonetheless bred for a consistent type or purpose. Sometimes these breeds have been intentionally bred in purity, while others remain isolated because there is little economic incentive to bring in foreign horses, or to export the local stock to outside countries.

Another way that breeds were formed was through geographical isolation. Here populations of horses were cut off from outside influences, either intentionally or unintentionally, and develop in relative isolation. Perhaps the best-known example of this kind of breed is the Icelandic, which originated with Norse and Celtic horses brought by the people who settled the island. Importation ended in 982 AD, cutting the breed off from outside influences. Horses on the island are, by definition, purebred Icelandics. Like the Icelandic, such breeds are often found on islands, but other remote areas can produce the same result.

Because outside influences are restricted, colors and patterns are limited just as they are with formalized breeds. Depending on the circumstances, it is possible that colors have been even more effectively limited. While the immediate ancestry of these kinds of breeds is not recorded, their isolation from other breeding groups often creates interesting combinations (and sometimes the absence of combinations). For that reason, these breeds can provide helpful clues about the interaction between colors.

Stud Book Structure

There are a number of different systems that are used by registries. It is fair to say that no registry has ever used just one; systems tend to evolve over time. Even the most restrictive closed registry had to start with some kind of inspection process for foundation stock, and registries that have never had some kind of grading scheme or outcross program are relatively rare.

Blood Purity

The concept of blood purity as a condition of registration is perhaps the most common understanding of stud book structure among animal fanciers, probably because most are familiar with kennel clubs, where it is the norm. The value placed on pedigree over individual merit, in twentieth century America in particular, is another reason that many see breeds as synonymous with blood purity.

In a stud book based on blood purity, males and females are identified and determined to be "pure" representatives of a breed. This may have been based on oral traditions, or it may be a consensus that the horse represented the true breed. Once a large enough foundation population of both genders is identified and registered, the books are then closed to any horses that do not have two registered parents. The end result is a breed where the individual animals trace back in all lines to recognized foundation horses.

While this structure is often assumed, and is often used as the baseline for defining something as a breed (as opposed to a crossbred or mongrel), in horses it is not a common system. There are breeds that are well-known for using blood purity, such as the Arabian, but most either do not currently have a closed stud book or they have not always had one.

Pure blood stud books are among the few where colors can often be definitively ruled as absent in the gene pool. Because every individual in the pedigree, male and female, trace back to identified animals, their is not a lot of ambiguity in regards to the range of possible colors. Barring mutations, what was present at the start is what is possible now.

Top-Crossing

Many stud books now considered closed were originally built on a system known as top-crossing. In top-crossing, the focus is on the male ancestors. The name comes from the fact that in western pedigrees, the stallions' names appear in the top squares. Because selective breeding grew from the practice of using royal and state studs to improve local mares, many of the earliest stud books only recorded stallions. Mares, when they were included, were deemed to be suitable by virtue of their sires. From this came the idea that a sufficient number of crosses to acceptable males qualified a horse as purebred. Most often three or four generations of these crosses were considered enough.

The Indian Marwari is a good example of a breed with a recognizable type that is not yet governed by a registry or stud book. This is not unusual in Eastern or Asian breeds.

With top-cross breeds, the first stud book is often a retrospective volume that contains the stallions that have won acclaim as sires of the desired type of horse. Retrospective volumes often contain horses that lived generations earlier, as well as their most accomplished descendants. In that way, contemporary breeding animals (also usually stallions) could be said to be pure, as they already had the necessary three or four generations of acceptable crosses. Mares were also added, also using the top-cross criteria, until there were enough of both genders to close the books.

Top-crossing was extremely common in breeds that were already well-established, with a number of recognized male families, in an area. Top-crossing was also used when demand rose for a type not found in a region. This was the case with the earliest draft breeds imported into the United States, where there had not previously been a heavy horse breed. The first volume of the American French Draft stud book contained 882 stallions and 164 mares. Obviously a strictly pure breeding program was not practical with a ratio of one mare to every six stallions.

It is harder to speak definitively about the colors that are, and that have been, present in breeds that once utilized a top-cross system. Typically unusual or undesirable colors were eventually eliminated, and color variety tended to narrow over time. Even so, the lack of complete documentation on the mares involved at the early stages opens the door for less common colors. In cases where colors are recessive, or can be mistaken for something that is accepted, this can give expected results.

Inspected Stock
Some stud books have programs that allow new stock to be inspected for inclusion in an established stud book. In the early stud books, this was most often used to increase the number of mares, particularly when a type or a section did not have a viable number of horses. Usually these mares, once inspected and deemed suitable, were considered fully registered. In some stud books, they were not granted full registration status, but were closer to fully registered than the mares in a grading scheme.

In modern breeds, inspections tend to serve a slightly different purpose. There are those breeds, most notably some of the warmbloods, where the inspection processes determines whether or not a horse can be included in the breeding pool. In these cases, pedigree and blood purity can mean far less than in traditional stud books. Although many western horsemen associate inspection procedures with quality control, unless diversity is seen as a virtue, these systems also tends to tightly restrict color as well as type.

Grading Schemes
Grading schemes are really just a more modern version of top-crossing, only they are typically enacted in response to a crisis, and are usually viewed as a temporary measure. Like top-crossing, they vary in the number of generations required before the resulting foals are considered purebred, though three- and four-crosses are the most common. Grading schemes were particularly common in the British native pony breeds following the

Fully Registered Offspring	Purebred sire	Purebred grandsire	Purebred great-grandsire
			Purebred great-granddam
		Purebred granddam	Purebred great-grandsire
			Purebred great-granddam
	Dam	Purebred grandsire	Purebred great-grandsire
			Purebred great-granddam
		Granddam	Purebred great-grandsire
			Great-granddam (upgrade stock)

Figure 1. A typical upgrading scheme

devastation of the World Wars. Often it is assumed that the mares being upgraded are purebred stock that were not registered due to hardship, or at least are closely related to the purebred horses.

Grading systems have a variety of names depending on the country. In the United States such sections of the stud book are sometimes called an appendix or tracking register to avoid negative connotations. (In the United States, "grade" means an unregistered horse of unknown breeding.) In the Netherlands, the section is usually called a helpbook (*hulpboek*). Whatever the name, the purpose is to expand the genetic base through the inclusion and "breeding up" of mares.

Grading schemes have had a resurgence in popularity in recent years, largely due to increased awareness of the issues surrounding genetic diversity in endangered breeds. For that reason, grading registers are often used to retain mares (rarely stallions) that have the right pedigree, but do not meet all the requirements for full registration. Often that missed requirement is related to color or markings.

Outcrossing
Some registries permit outcrossing to specified breeds for the purposes of improving the existing stock. Though the use of Thoroughbred and Arabian outcrossing is common in many warmblood breeds, registry-sanctioned outcrossing is perhaps most common in the United States. It is often associated with the "color" breeds like the Appaloosa and the Paint, but it is common across a wide range of American pony and riding breeds.

Outcrossing allows colors present in one breed to migrate to the other. In many of the breeds where color is considered a definitive characteristic, it is controlled by registry or show regulations so that undesirable colors do not cross over along with the desirable traits, or if they do, they are not rewarded in the show ring.

Recent Changes
Because registries have traditionally had the power to exclude horses from a breed, their decisions can have a big impact on the business of breeding. Unregistered horses represent an economic loss for their owners—at times a significant one. In recent years, some American breeders have used that fact to challenge registries in court using anti-trust laws, claiming such policies unfairly restrict trade. This has caused many registries to relax their rules, particularly in regards to cosmetic issues like color. This has not meant that non-traditional colors are no longer penalized in the show ring, but it has meant that they are less likely to be denied entry in the stud book.

A similar situation has arisen in European countries where horses are required to have a passport, most of which are issued through registries. To comply with these regulations, some breed organizations have created stud book sections for horses that might otherwise be denied registration. Because perceptions about genetic diversity are changing more rapidly in parts of Europe, it is not surprising that many of these new sections have provisions that allow them to operate much like a grading register.

These new legal considerations come as fashion has once more changed, and the demand for unusual colors and eye-catching patterns has risen significantly. This shift has also come as new technologies allow breeders to not only prove the parentage of horses that have unconventional coloring, but in many cases to explain how the parents produced the color in the first place. Horses that in the past might have been sold into obscurity (if they were lucky) are more likely to be used for breeding, and in the process, contribute to a greater understanding of coat color genetics.

Not everyone views these changes as a positive development. There is concern among those who value traditional coloring that horses will be bred in trendy colors without regard for more practical qualities like soundness, ability and temperament. But even so, knowledge of both breed histories and genetic mechanisms enable breeders to make informed choices, regardless of the colors they prefer.

Color Descriptions

Basic Coat Colors

Pigmented hair on horses is either red or black. This applies to the hair on the body and the points: mane, tail, and lower legs. Horses are either red with red points (chestnut), or black with black points (black) or red with black points (bay or brown). The wide variety of horse coat colors are all built from the four basic colors. No matter how exotic a horse's color may appear, under it all he will always one of these base colors. Likewise, each modified color has a chestnut, black, bay and brown version.

Chestnut

Chestnut horses are all-over red in color. The shade can vary from a pale blonde to a deep chocolate brown, with the most common a medium shade of red. The point color can be lighter than the body (flaxen chestnut) or a few shades darker (tostado). In rare instances, the mane and tail may be gray.

Inheritance

Although the idea that all horses are one of four basic colors is simple, the genes that produce those colors are more complicated. That is because there is not a chestnut gene, or a bay gene. Instead there are two genes, Extension and Agouti, that combine to create the different base colors.

The first of these, Extension, determines whether or not the horse can produce black pigment. For that reason, it is sometimes referred to as the black gene or the black factor. Horses that have the dominant form of Extension (*E*) can produce black pigment, while horses that have the recessive form (*e*) cannot produce black and are red. Extension can be thought of as the gene that determines whether a horse is chestnut (*ee*) or one of the black-based colors (*Ee* or *EE*).

Chestnut horses have the second gene, Agouti, so they carry the instructions for some combination of black, bay, and brown. Without black hairs, however, it has no effect. Studies have shown that chestnuts carrying black do not look different from those carrying bay or brown, so the Agouti status cannot be determined just by looking at the horse; it requires testing.

Because chestnut is recessive, the color can appear unexpectedly from non-chestnut parents. Likewise, two chestnut parents can only produce chestnut foals.

History and Breed Distribution

The chestnut allele (*e*) was identified in the remains of a Romanian wild horse from the Copper Age. The horse was not chestnut, but carried the gene. The earliest chestnut was a domestic horse in Siberia in 3000 BC. The color spread rapidly after domestication, with 28 percent of Bronze Age samples testing positive for the mutation. Interestingly enough, it was not found in the Iberian Peninsula until the Middle Ages.

Chestnut is widespread throughout the equine population. Among the rare cases where it is not found, or is found only rarely, are the primitive European breeds, including many of the British mountain and moorland ponies. In those breeds, its presences is sometimes viewed as proof of eastern influence.

Chestnut is one of the basic coat colors, and one of the most common colors found among horses.

Black

Just as a chestnut has uniformly red hair, black horses have uniformly black hair. Some black horses have a warmer, more muted tone, and some fade in the summer months, but even then the hair is not truly red. The best test to determine whether a horse is black is to look at the muzzle and the fold of the stifle. If those are black, and not red or tan, then the horse is black and not brown or dark bay.

Inheritance
Where chestnut horses have the recessive form of Extension and can only make red pigment, black horses have the dominant version that makes black pigment possible. That is why the three colors that depend on the dominant allele of Extension (E)—black, bay and brown—are sometimes referred to collectively as the black-based colors. That is also why the dominant form of Extension is sometimes called the "black factor" and the recessive form the "red factor."

Extension turns on the black pigment, and the second gene, Agouti, determines where the black

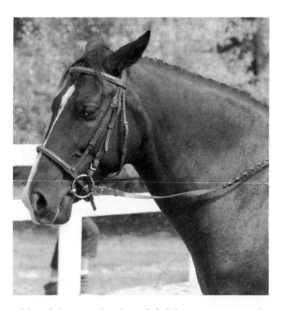

Although her coat has been faded from exposure to the sun, the muzzle on this black mare is the same dark color as her body. That is what makes her different from a brown horse, which would have a tan or reddish muzzle.

pigment will go. Black horses have the recessive form of Agouti (*a*), which results in a horse that is all-over black. The other forms of Agouti, which are all dominant to the black color, restrict black pigment to specific areas of the body.

Because the black color is recessive, bay and brown horses can carry it. Likewise, two black horses should never produce a bay or brown foal. The complication is that the initial gene that turned on the black pigment, Extension, is dominant. So while the placement of the black (over the entire horse) is recessive, the ability to make the black pigment in the first place is dominant. Black horses are recessive to bay and brown, but all three are dominant to chestnut, so two black parents can produce a chestnut foal.

History and Breed Distribution
Black is the earliest known color mutation. It was common among the wild horses of the Iberian Peninsula between 5500 and 4950 BC. Among the samples tested, half the horses were black and an additional 25 percent carried the allele. Black is also found among the eastern European wild horses between 4350 BC and 3100 BC. It is thought that the color flourished in response to changes in the environment that increased the tree cover where the horses lived.

Black is still relatively common among older Spanish breeds like the Sorraia and the Asturcón. It is also quite common in some of the rustic European horses including the Mérens, Fell, Dales, and Bardigiano. Many of these breeds bear a strong resemblance to the Friesian, which is uniformly black. Black is also common among the British mountain and moorland breeds, and among the heavy drafts.

Black was also popular during the Baroque era, so is common in breeds like the Kladruber, Lipizzan, Murgese and Noriker, which were developed during that period. It is less common among the other light breeds, particularly those developed using the Arabian and English Thoroughbred where the color has traditionally been rare. Black is slightly more common in some of the American gaited breeds, particularly the Tennessee Walking Horse and the Mountain Pleasure breeds.

Bay and Brown

The other two black-based colors are bay and brown. Because brown can be difficult to distinguish from the darkest shades of bay without a test, and because owners and breeders have not consistently separated out browns when describing their horses, in the breed chapters of this book bay and brown are treated as one color. Genetically they are two separate colors. In fact, it is theorized that there are actually three different colors that should be included in this group: bay, wild bay and brown.

Bay
Bay horses have red bodies and black points. Just as with the chestnuts, the red hair can vary in shade from red-blonde to a dark chocolate brown. With traditional bays, the black areas are the mane, tail, and legs. Most bays also have some degree of countershading along the topline and on the front of the face. They also tend to have dark ear tips and darker hair around the muzzle than chestnuts.

Wild Bay
Wild bays are very similar to ordinary bays in that they have red bodies, but the black points are more limited. Sometimes the ankles are black and there is little more than dark smudging on the joints of the upper part of the leg. On others even the ankles have only a minimal amount of black smudging. The mane and tail are black, but body color is sometimes mixed at the dock of the tail or the base of the mane. The Dutch refer to this as having a "bloom on the tail." Most wild bays tend towards the lighter shades of red, and are less countershaded than the typical bay.

Brown
Where wild bay horses have very limited amounts of black, brown horses have black hair that has extended onto the body so that the only red areas left are the muzzle, the area around the eyes, and the undersides of the body. The amount and intensity of red, particularly on the body, can vary, with the darkest horses showing no more than a slight reddish tone on the muzzle and the fold of the stifle.

Bay horses have black points, which include the mane, tail and legs. This mare is a wild bay, where the lower legs have dark shading on the joints, but are not completely black.

In the United Kingdom, brown horses are sometimes called black and tans. In the United States, they are often called seal brown.

Inheritance

As with black, bay horses have the dominant version of the Extension gene (E) that makes black pigment possible. For this reason, bay is referred to as one of the black-based colors. The difference between bay and true black is in the second gene that controls base color, Agouti.

Bay horses have the dominant form of Agouti (A). Where the recessive form allows unrestricted (all-over) black pigment, the dominant form restricts black to the points, leaving the remainder of the coat red.

Because bays have the dominant form of both genes that color base color (E and A), bay is dominant to both chestnut and black. Because the necessary recessives for the other two colors are each on one of those genes, it is possible for a bay horse to carry both black (a) and chestnut (e). That is also why a bay horse can be born from a chestnut and black cross. The black parent has the necessary dominant Extension (the 'black factor') and a chestnut can carry the dominant Agouti (A) instructions hidden behind a coat that has no black to restrict. Bays have the potential to produce any of the three basic colors, and can be produced by any combination except chestnut to chestnut.

The other two forms of dominant Agouti, brown and wild bay, differ only in their effectiveness in

The pronounced black and tan coloring of this Polish Coldblood stallion is often called seal brown. Horses with this type of coloring usually carry an allele of Agouti called brown, or A^t.

restricting the black pigment. Wild bay, which has only minimal color on the points, restricts the black pigment more strongly than traditional bay. Conversely brown, which is predominantly black, is less effective at restricting the color. A commercial test for brown, which has the symbol A^t, is available. Wild bay, which is usually written A^+, has not been formally identified so its position as an Agouti allele is still a theory.

The relationship between the three dominant Agouti alleles is not clear. It has been theorized that they are dominant to one another according to the strength with which they can restrict the black pigment. That would mean that wild bay is dominant to bay, which in turn is dominant to brown. This theory does not appear to hold up in practice, however, with studies by both W. S. Anderson (1912) and Henriette Arriens (2009) showing that brown parents routinely produce both bay and brown offspring. The situation is further complicated by the similarity between very dark bay and brown, and the inconsistent use of the term in stud book records.

History and Breed Distribution

Bay, or rather bay dun, is believed to have been the ancestral color of horses. Although it is not yet possible to reliably test for dun, the Agouti test did confirm that the oldest remains were indeed bay. Wild horses in the late Pleistocene were uniformly bay. By the Copper Age, the horses were evenly split between bay and black.

In modern times, the popularity of the color benefited from its association with the English Thoroughbred. In his book *The Origin and Influence of the Thoroughbred Horse* (1905), Professor Ridgeway echoes some of the ideas first presented by Colonel Hamilton Smith about the superiority of the "Bay Stock."

> "But as increase of speed is gradually rendering the English thoroughbred a purely Bay Stock, and as from the earliest times of which we have any record the Libyan horse has been not only the swiftest horse known, but also has been of a bay colour, we are justified in concluding that his bay colour is as fundamental a characteristic as his speed, and that it is due not to artificial selection, but to natural specialisation."

Although few modern horsemen subscribe to these outdated theories about ancestral root stock based on color, Ridgeway was certainly in the mainstream for his time. Because bay and other dark colors were so closely associated with quality (and speed), it is not surprising that so many of the breeds established during the late nineteenth and early twentieth century were predominantly bay. Many of the most popular breeds used for improving local stock during that time—Thoroughbreds, Cleveland Bays, Oldenburgs, and Hackneys—were primarily bay or brown. Bay was also not uncommon in the other popular improvement breed, the Arabian.

Bay is still very common in riding and sport breeds, especially those that descend from the blood-horse breeds. It is also common in ponies, including the British mountain and moorland breeds and some of the primitive European ponies like the Gotland. Bay is also common in European drafts, particularly those that were influenced by the Brabant and the Ardennes. In those breeds, the wild bay variant is also common. In the United States, it is common in the Morgan, Standardbred, Saddlebred and Quarter Horse breeds.

Modifiers

There are a number of modifiers that make subtle alterations to the basic color of the horse. The modification is not so great that the horse is considered a separate color, but these factors often change the shade enough that two horses that are genetically the same base color can look quite different.

Mealy

The mealy pattern is familiar to anyone who has seen stylized images of ancient cave paintings, where the horse has a red-brown topline and creamy white undersides. It is a pattern closely associated with the last remaining wild horse, the Przewalski, and primitive breeds like the Exmoor and Gotland Ponies. It is likely that the modifier was found in the earliest horses.

The pattern is characterized by a light underbelly, chest and buttocks, as well as a pale patches around the eyes and muzzle. The latter is sometimes called a mealy mouth. Mealy is visible on both chestnut and bay horses, though it tends to be more pronounced on bays. It is often paired with wild bay, though there are mealy bays with fully black points. Mealy chestnuts often have markedly lighter manes, tails and lower legs.

The prevailing idea is that the mealy pattern does not affect black horses. At one time it was theorized that seal brown horses were genetically black with the mealy pattern. Because seal browns have tan markings in the same areas that are pale on a mealy bay, this is not an unreasonable assumption. However, tests have shown that seal brown horses have the dominant form of Agouti (A), and so cannot be black.

Sooty

Horses that have a mixture of black hairs are said to be sooty. In bay and brown horses, sootiness tends to take a very specific countershaded pattern, with the darkest areas concentrated on the neck and saddle area and paler areas on the poll and down the jugular groove (see photo on page 26). Often there is pronounced dappling.

This same countershaded pattern is not seen in dark chestnut horses. Liver and black chestnut horses, which are presumed to be sooty chestnuts, have a body color that is more uniformly dark. The points can vary, with dark smudging on the joints and black hairs mixed in the mane and tail. Lighter or more truly red colors are sometimes seen on the lower legs or mane and tail. Vivid dappling is rare, and is more often seen in pale, dusty chestnuts than in the horses that fall in the copper or red shades. Sooty palominos can show the same kind of dappling and areas of light and dark that are seen in sooty bays. Other palominos are uniformly dark, much like the liver chestnuts, and some have dark hairs that concentrate on the lower legs, making them easy to mistake for buckskin silver.

It is possible for a horse to be both mealy and sooty. These horses have the pale undersides of the mealy pattern, but have an overlay of black hairs in the darker areas. Dappling is not uncommon.

The inheritance of sootiness is not well understood. A recent study of colors in the Freiberger breed suggested that the darker shades of bay and chestnut were recessive, but it is thought that sootiness may be only one of many factors that influence the shade of the base colors.

Flaxen

When horsemen speak of flaxen points, they are typically speaking of the point color of chestnut horses. Flaxen chestnuts have manes and tails that

The difference between a standard chestnut and a mealy chestnut can be seen in the pale cream undersides of the Belgian in the foreground. This type of coloring is common in heavy draft breeds.

Flaxen manes on bays are occasionally seen in some of the Nordic breeds. This does not appear to be connected to silver, since the legs and tail remain undiluted.

are lighter than their body color. In some breeds, notably the heavy drafts, the lower legs are also paler than the body. The difference in shade between the points and the body can vary, with some horses showing dramatic contrast and others showing only a little. Manes and tails can also be mixed chestnut and flaxen, or even chestnut, flaxen and black. The latter tends to give the mane a gray or silver appearance. Such horses are sometimes mistaken for bay silvers, though the manes on gray-maned chestnuts are usually more evenly mixed, while the manes on bay silvers have dark roots and pale ends.

Flaxen is often described as a single recessive gene, but it is more likely that the range of color seen in the manes and tails of chestnut horses is the result of a number of genetic factors. In addition to the gene responsible for flaxen points, it is likely that individual shade and the mealy pattern play a role in some horses.

Flaxen chestnuts are widespread throughout the equine population, with the notable exception of the Thoroughbred, where the trait is rare. Particu-

larly dramatic flaxens are common in many of the draft and pony breeds. When paired with the mealy pattern, the resulting color—called blonde sorrel in America—is sometimes mistaken for palomino.

Flaxen-Maned Bays

There are rare instances of flaxen manes on bay horses. These horses do not have the diluted legs of a bay silver, and often the tail does not affected, or is not affected to the same extent as the mane. The trait appears in many of the same breeds as wild and mealy bay, but it is not clear if it is related to those variations. It does tend to run in families, so probably has a genetic cause.

Some bays have silvering in the mane or tail. These are often less dramatic than the flaxen-maned bays, with fewer white or flaxen hairs. Like the flaxen manes on bays, it also runs in families, though because it is more subtle it is sometimes overlooked.

Gulastra Plume

Flaxen tails on bay or black horses are sometimes referred to as Gulastra's Plume. GULASTRA himself was an ordinary chestnut with a self-colored mane and tail, but Arabian breeders often credit him with having produced the trait. Outside the Arabian breed, it is sometimes called silvertail. Typically the tail is flaxen or mixed flaxen and silver with a darker core. It is more pronounced when the horse is young, and often darkens or disappears with age.

The exact cause of the trait is not known. It is more often seen in breeds where sabino markings are common, particularly those that have very ragged or roany edges. Clydesdales and Welsh Ponies and Cobs have the trait in fairly high numbers. The connection is not absolute, however. In Thoroughbreds and some of the warmblood breeds, silver tails are seen without extensive white markings.

Dilutions

Dilutions are modifiers that make the base color of the horse paler. With some dilutions, the skin and eyes are also affected. There are five dilution genes that can be identified by testing: dun, cream, silver, champagne and pearl. There is one additional dilution, mushroom, that is known to occur but the mutation responsible has not yet been identified. There are also instances of black horses that are visibly diluted, but that do not test for any known dilution.

Dun

Dun lightens both red and black pigment on the body, while leaving the points close to the original base color. The body of a chestnut horse turns some shade between a dusty red to reddish-tan. These are called red duns. Bays have a similar body color to the red duns, though the countershading of the bay base color often makes the color look more muted or dusty. Bay horses with the dun dilution are most often called yellow duns or zebra duns. The latter refers to the various forms of striping common to duns, which are often more pronounced on bay duns.

Black horses have their body color lightened to a shade between warm slate gray and pale dove gray. In America black duns are called grulla, though in much of Europe they are called mouse. Grullas that have a brownish cast are often assumed to have a brown base color rather than black. Grullas that have a cooler, paler blue tone are sometimes called silver grullas, though this terminology can be confusing for horsemen familiar with the silver dilution.

Whatever the final body color, all duns have a distinct dorsal stripe that begins at the top of the tail and continues up to the mane. This is sometimes called a lineback or an eel stripe, and its presence on a horse with a pale body color is considered the primary indicator that the horse is a dun.

Dun Factors or Primitive Markings

In addition to the dorsal stripe and the dark points that are found on all dun horses, most have one or more primitive marks, also known as dun factors. The following is a list of dun factors, starting with the most common and ending with the more rare variations.

Leg Barring: Most duns have some degree of striping on the backs of their knees and forearms, and again on their hocks and the insides of the leg above the hock joint. Yellow duns are particularly inclined to very pronounced leg barring, while barring on red duns is often more subtle.

Face Mask: Duns often have a dark facial mask that covers the front of their face and extends down the nasal bones towards the nose. On some horses, the entire head is a few shades darker than the body.

Ear Tips and Lining: When viewed from behind, the last third of a dun ear is darker than the body color. Some duns have a secondary band of dark color in between that dark tip and the base of the ear. Viewed from the front, the outer edge is outlined with a darker color.

Dramatically frosted manes and tails, like those on this Highland Pony stallion, are common in duns. Buckskins occasionally have frosted manes and tails, but not as often as the dun dilutes.

Darker ear rims are not a trait exclusive to duns, but most duns have it.

Shoulder Stripe or Shadow: Duns often have a dark line that crosses the dorsal stripe at the shoulders. On some duns, there is not a defined line as much as there is a just an area of darker shading. On others, there are broad triangles on either side of the dorsal stripe, coming to a point inside the shoulder area.

Frosting: Dun manes and tails typically have a dark core that looks like an extension of the dorsal stripe. The hairs to either side are often a few shades paler than the body color, which gives the mane and sides of the tail a frosted appearance. This is different from the kind of frosting seen on some buckskins (see the tail of the buckskin on page 24), which are the result of the cream dilution turning the red guard hairs white.

Mottling: Although this goes by the same name as the appaloosa skin characteristic, when used to describe duns it means a collection of small spots usually located on the upper portions of the legs. They are a shade or two darker than the body color, and are smaller and more crisply defined than reversed dapples.

Cobwebbing: Cobwebs are a group of fine lines that begin under the forelock and extend around the forehead, forming a pattern that resembles a spider's web.

Brindling: Occasionally dun horses have random areas of striping or brindling. This happens most often on the hips or the shoulders, and unlike the other dun factors is not always symmetrical.

With all the dun factors, it is helpful to think of dun as preventing the color from being diluted in the areas where the factors are found. So the dorsal stripe on a bay is a deep red, while the leg barring is black where a bay would have black shading, but red in those areas that would have been red. In this way, dun factors are not an addition to the coat, but rather areas where the original color is preserved.

That resistance to diluting is apparent when dun is combined with other dilutions. Dun cannot fully preserve the original base color in those areas, but it does hamper the ability of the other dilutions to take the color away. Even the palest double-diluted creams will have dun factors that are a few shades darker than their body color.

It has been speculated that horses that carry the sooty modifier have more pronounced dun factoring. Because duns do not typically show sooty dappling, it may be that dun redirects the sooty pattern to the dun factors, effectively intensifying the contrast between the primitive markings and the body color.

Inheritance and Testing

Dun is a dominant gene, so a dun horse will always have a dun parent, and will descend in an unbroken line from dun ancestors. Heterozygous duns will produce duns 50 percent of the time, while homozygous duns will have 100 percent dun foals.

Because dun dilutes all base colors equally, it does not hide or skip generations. It is possible to overlook dun on chestnut horses, especially those that do not show much contrast between the body and the point color. This happens more often in breeds where dun is uncommon, or where the difference between dun and cream is poorly understood. When studying old records that use the term dun for all dilutes, the general rule of thumb is that if the color skips generations through black or brown horses, it is likely cream, and if it skips generations through chestnut is it more likely lineback dun.

Among modern horses it is more likely that breeders will incorrectly identify a horse as dun than overlook a horse that is dun. In Britain, buckskin is called dun, and that tradition persists in many of the pony breeds. In some cases the horse's appearance is confusing. Usually these horses are buckskins with a countershaded dorsal stripe. Countershaded stripes have a softer edge than the dorsal stripe on a dun, but the difference is subtle.

The mutation responsible for dun has not been identified, though it has been mapped to a specific chromosome. A zygosity test is available which uses nearby markers to determine if a horse is homozygous for dun, but it is not reliable for Iberian breeds like the Lusitano and the Pura Raza Espanola. It is not known if horses from these breeds have a different mutation, or if they merely have different markers.

History and Breed Distribution

Although it is not yet possible to test ancient remains for dun, it is believed to be part of the original coloring of horses prior to domestication. The last known wild horses, the Tarpan and the Przewalski Horse, were both uniformly dun, as are the remaining wild asses. Prehistoric cave paintings are believed to portray mealy bay dun horses.

Because dun was believed to be a sign of reversion to the original wild type, it captured the interest of many early naturalists, including Charles Darwin, who wrote about the color in *The Origin of Species*. Darwin rejected Colonel Hamilton Smith's theory of aboriginal color breeds based on the wide range of body types, and the geographical spread, of horses with primitive markings. He wrote of his suspicions about the ancestral color of domestic horses.

> "In the horse we see this tendency strong whenever a dun tint appears—a tint which approaches to that of the general colouring of the other species of the genus. The appearance of the stripes is not accompanied by any change of form or by any other new character... For myself, I venture confidently to look back thousands on thousands of generations, and I see an animal striped like a zebra, but perhaps otherwise very differently constructed, the common parent of our domestic horse"

Even today dun is most common in primitive breeds where outcrosses to Arabians and Thoroughbreds were not widely used. Primitive European ponies like the British Shetland, Icelandic, and Highland Pony are sometimes dun, while Fjords are uniformly dun. It is also common in the rustic ponies of eastern Europe, including the Huzul and the Konik, and is still found in some of the unimproved breeds of Russia. With the exception of the Felin Pony, it is less common among the improved pony breeds, though there are rare dun Welsh Ponies and American Shetlands.

There is one remaining line of duns in the Caspian, and it is still found in the Kathiawari of India. Many of the native Indonesian ponies are also dun.

Dun is believed to have been present in the original Turkoman horses, though it is not known if it can still be found in the Akhal-Teke.

Dun is common in the Poitevin Mulassier, but it is otherwise rare in draft and coaching breeds, as well as the European warmbloods. It is more common in North and South American breeds with a strong Spanish influence, including Quarter Horses, Criollos, Campolinas, Pasos, Spanish Mustangs and Carolina Marsh Tackies. It is found only rarely among the American gaited breeds.

While the prevalence of dun in New World Spanish breeds like the Criollo and the Campolina suggests that the color was once common in the horses that originated in the Iberian Peninsula, it is quite rare in the modern Lusitano and Pura Raza Espanola. The Sorraia is uniformly dun, but like the other Iberian horses it is not clear that theirs is the same mutation seen in other dun breeds. The Sorraia stallion ALTAMIRO had an inconclusive zygosity test, despite the fact that he appears dun and presumably comes from a uniformly dun breed.

Although the width can vary along the length of the topline, the dorsal stripe of a dun is characterized by its clearly defined edge.

Cream

Although the dun dilution was probably the color of the earliest horses, the cream dilution is arguably more familiar to most Americans because of its connection with the popular palomino coloring. In addition to palomino, cream produces buckskin, smoky black, cremello, perlino and smoky cream.

Palominos and Buckskins

A single copy of the cream gene turns red pigment to yellow or gold, but does not affect black pigment. That means that a chestnut horse, which is entirely red, becomes a yellow horse. Called *isabella* in many countries, the most common English term is palomino. A bay horse has its red body lightened to yellow, but retains its black points. Although often called dun in the United Kingdom, in American where lineback duns are common the color is called buckskin.

Cream dilutes tend to have a clearer, brighter tone than dun dilutes. The color is also more truly yellow, and less of a dusty tan. The shade can vary from a creamy white to a deep golden. Palominos and buckskins lack the clearly defined dorsal stripe of the lineback dun, though some buckskins are countershaded in a way that suggests a dorsal stripe. Some individual palomino and buckskin horses have lighter brown eyes, although most are dark-eyed.

Buckskins and many palominos have dark skin. Some palominos have skin with a purplish cast or even fine pink and lavender speckles. This is usually most visible inside the thighs, on the genitals, under the tail and inside the ears. The skin around the eyes and muzzle tend to remain dark and the overall impression is still that the horse is dark-skinned.

Another distinctive aspect of this particular dilution is the tendency to develop dapples. Many palomino and buckskin horses develop pronounced seasonal dapples, particularly in the late summer and fall months, before becoming paler for the winter. This is often attributed to the presence of the sooty pattern, which tends to produce dramatic dappling on both palominos and buck-

skins, but the effect can be seen in creams that have clear body colors as well.

Smoky Blacks

Black horses that inherit the cream gene are called smoky black. Because a single cream gene does not usually alter black pigment, these horses are not always immediately identifiable as cream dilutes. In some breeds, smoky black horses appear faded in color, or may be more prone to sunfading, but in others they look no different than ordinary blacks.

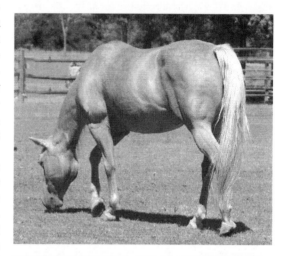

A single cream gene dilutes the red hair, turning chestnut into palomino (top) and bay into buckskin (bottom). Note that the black points of the buckskin remain unaffected.

Double-Diluted Creams

One copy of the cream dilution does not significantly alter the black pigment, nor does it affect the pigment in the skin or eyes. That changes when a horse inherits two copies of cream. With two cream genes, both red and black hair are diluted to a pale cream or buff. The skin is also diluted to pink and the eyes to a pale blue. Neither the skin nor the eyes are truly colorless. Compared to the skin of a white-born horse, the skin of a double-diluted cream will appear a few shades darker. The eyes, while often paler than those of a blue-eyed pinto, often have a slight greenish cast.

It is sometimes possible to tell the base color of a double-diluted cream by the shade of the body and the points. Areas that would have been black, such as the mane and tail of a bay, can retain a little more color than the areas that had been red. This is not foolproof, however, since some perlinos and smoky creams are the same all-over cream as a cremello.

Inheritance and Testing

Because many horsemen are familiar with the idea that two palomino horses can produce a blue-eyed cream, the cream dilution is a good color to use when explaining the concept of incomplete dominance. With incompletely dominant genes, one copy produces an intermediate expression while two copies produces the full effect. In the case of cream, one copy of the dilution results in a horse that has yellow instead of red hair. Two copies bleach out the color of the hair, skin and eyes.

Because cream is dominant, palomino, buckskin and smoky black horses will always have at least one cream parent. Cremellos, perlinos and smoky creams will always have two cream parents, and will in turn produce cream offspring 100 percent of the time. Smoky black horses complicate the picture though, because the presence of one cream gene in black horses is not always obvious. A single cream gene can also be difficult to see on brown or extremely sooty horses. For that reason cream can appear to hide in breeds where black, brown or sooty horses are common.

In the past cream was assigned to the C-locus, which is also known as the albino locus due to its association with red-eyed albinos in other animals.

Two copies of the cream gene bleaches most of the color from the horse, regardless of the pigment color. Double-diluted creams have pink skin and pale blue eyes.

This has contributed to the mistaken impression that double-diluted creams are albinos. Research has since shown that the mutation responsible for cream occurred at the MATP-locus. Despite the error, use of the symbol *C* for cream (and pearl, the other allele at the same location) is traditional and has not changed.

There is a commercially available test for identifying cream dilutes. There are no known health issues connected with cream, though blue-eyed creams remain unpopular with many horsemen. Awareness that the horses are not albinos, and that they are reliable producers of palominos and buckskins has led to greater acceptance, but there are still organizations that ban or restrict their registration.

History and Breed Distribution

The cream dilution was already present during the Iron Age. Of the fourteen horses found in the Scythian burial mound at Arzan, two were buckskin. Another buckskin was found among the horses excavated from Olon-Kurin-Gol in the Altai Mountains. Cream dilutes are still seen among the horses of Mongolia, but it is not known if the color originated there. The remains found at these ceremonial sites have not proven to be a genetically isolated group, so their diverse origins leave open the possibility that colors found there may have originated somewhere else.

Wherever the mutation first occurred, cream horses appear throughout art and literature. Because cream dilutes are often referred to as yellow or golden, it is not always clear whether or not a written reference is to dun, cream or even pearl horses. Images and descriptions of deep golden horses with dark eyes and white manes and tails have the most value, since that combination is not produced by either dun or pearl. Unambiguous palomino images are found in Persian paintings and in Chinese paintings and pottery.

During the Baroque and Romantic eras, when many painters paid particular attention to coat color details, cream dilutes were frequent subjects. The von Hamilton brothers, Johann Georg and Philipp Ferdinand, both included them in multiple paintings. One of the best known of these, *The Imperial Stud with Lipizzaner Horses*, features a golden palomino mare at the center of the composition. James Ward has a team of blue-eyed creams in his work *The Triumph of the Duke of Wellington*. That painting, along with his portrait of King George III's stallion ADONIS, suggest that at least for a while the cream dilution was part of the Royal Hanoverian White and Cream breeds. George Stubbs also used palominos and cremellos in his images of horses battling big cats.

Pale horses became popular during the seventeenth and eighteenth centuries, and a number of studs, like those at Oldenburg, Berberbeck, Herrenhausen, and Kinsky, became known for producing them. Breeding records suggest that it is likely that many of these were cream dilutes. This is supported by accounts of yellow horses with white manes and tails, and also by the presence of *hermelin* (ermine) horses in the production records. This color is also referred to as *weißisabell* (white isabella), so probably denotes blue-eyed creams. The Lipizzaner stallion TOSCANELLO, foaled in 1780, is recorded as *hermelin*. Bred to three different bay mares, he produced three 'dun' (*falb*) foals. Around that same time, a number of ermine-colored horses appear in the early records of the Reiß Stud in Salzburg, which also had isabellas and duns.

Pale horses, including palominos, fell out of favor with the rising influence of the Arabian and the English Thoroughbred in the late nineteenth

Sooty, when paired with cream, often produces very vivid dappling. This sooty palomino pony shows the pale jugular groove that is a hallmark of the sooty pattern.

century. Dilutes, including creams, could still be found in rare occasions among the mares, but the color was lost in most European stud book breeds by the early twentieth century. The notable exceptions were the stud books for ponies, though even there the mistaken association of blue-eyed creams with albinism tended to limit the popularity of the color. This was less true in the New World breeds, particularly in North America, where both palominos and buckskins were viewed favorably, and where the color was preserved at least in low levels in most breeds.

Today the cream dilution is found in a wide variety of breeds. It is particularly common among the pony breeds, from Welshes and Connemaras in the United Kingdom to the Icelandic and Gotland Ponies in the Nordic countries. It is also frequently found among horses of Spanish descent, probably because the color was popular during the time that breeding group has its greatest influence. It is less common among the heavy drafts and those breeds heavily influenced by the Thoroughbred, but it can be found in eastern breeds like the Akhal-Teke and the Barb. Although some controversy exists about its historical presence in the Arabian horse, the cream dilution was not present among the stock used by western breeders involved in formalizing the Arabian breed.

Silver

The silver dilution can be thought of as the opposite of the cream dilution. Where one copy of cream dilutes red pigment and leaves the black pigment unaltered, silver dilutes the black pigment and leaves the red unaltered. Where cream turns red pigment yellow, silver turns black pigment to a color somewhere between silvery flaxen and a deep mocha brown.

It is that darkest shade that causes breeders of Rocky Mountain Horses, where the color tends towards the darker shades, to call the color chocolate. In Australia, it is called taffy. Both terms are perhaps more descriptive than the traditional silver, which was the name given the color by Shet-

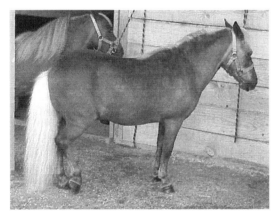

The silver gene dilutes black hair, turning black into black silver (top) and bay into red silver (bottom). Note that the body of the bay, which is red, remains unaffected.

land Pony breeders in the early twentieth century. Those breeders called the color silver dappled chestnut, or just silver dapple. At the paler end of the spectrum, the color could appear to be a cooler, more silvery version of chestnut, and vivid dappling was a feature of the color in that breed. Unfortunately in many other breeds where silver is found, the color is neither dappled nor particularly silver, which can lead to confusion.

Black Silvers

Black horses with the silver gene show the most dramatic change. The body color of these horses can range from nearly black through dark chocolate, and on down to a pale "dead grass" shade. Compared to a chestnut or a palomino, the color has a distinctly cool tone. The mane and tail are diluted more strongly than the body, changing to pale flaxen or silvery with darker roots. The area nearest the hoof is usually lighter than the body color, and the cannons are often mottled with light areas.

As their name suggests, silvers can be intensely dappled. This is not progressive like that of a grey horse, though the amount of dappling and the level of contrast on a single individual can vary from season to season. The location of the dappling is somewhat different from dappling caused by greying or the sooty gene, tending to be more concentrated along the belly and up the sides of the horse.

Many black silvers have a dark mask. This usually includes the forehead and extends to the area around the eyes, and down the nasal bones to the muzzle. Masks are most noticeable on the lighter silver dapples, but they do appear on even the darkest shades.

Silvers often have striped hooves. Evidence from the Icelandic suggests that this trait may be universal in silver foals, but that it becomes less pronounced or disappears with age. Many silvers are born with white or very pale eyelashes, which also tend to darken with age.

Red or Bay Silver

Bay horses with the silver dilution are called red silvers, though some prefer the term bay silver to avoid confusion with chestnuts that carry silver.

With bays, the most obvious change is in the mane and tail, which become flaxen. In some horses, this can be quite extreme, with the mane and tail nearly white, while in others it can be a far more subtle. The manes on silver dilutes tend to darken with age, and this appears to be particularly true for bay and brown silvers. Aged red silvers sometimes have predominantly dark manes with flaxen ends, though typically the forelock will remain quite pale. The legs are also affected, though the extent varies from horse to horse. Usually the leg is reddish nearest the body, and changes to nearly black are the knees and hocks, and finally becomes flaxen closest to the hoof. Often the back sides of the lower legs will be flaxen, or dappled flaxen.

The end result is a horse that does not look exactly like a chestnut, because he has oddly dark legs, nor does he look exactly like a bay because he has a flaxen mane and tail. While many horseman cannot identify the color by name, most will recognize that they do not look quite right to be either bay or chestnut.

Brown Silver

Dark bay and brown silvers are easy to misidentify as liver chestnuts, even by those familiar with the dilution. That is because the best indicator that a horse is dark chestnut is a dark brown coat with a reddish cast. Black hair diluted by the silver gene has a cool tint without a trace of red. When silver is added to a brown horse, which is mostly black with more limited areas of red hair, the effect can easily be mistaken for liver chestnut. The best clue the horse is actually a brown silver is that the red areas fall where they might be expected on a bay or brown horse, usually the muzzle, undersides, buttocks, and girth area. The back of the hock, where the black points transition to red, is another area that gives away the presence of brown.

Chestnut Carrying Silver

Just as black horses can hide the cream gene without showing any effects, because they have no red hair to dilute, so chestnut horses hide the silver dilution. Unlike smoky creams, though, chestnuts with the silver dilution have never been shown to look any different. They do not necessarily have

Dark facial masks are sometimes seen on the paler, vividly dappled varieties of black silver.

flaxen manes and tails, nor do they have mixed black and silver hairs in their manes and tails. Unless a chestnut has produced a silver dilute, the only way to know a chestnut carries silver is to test.

Inheritance and Testing

Silver is a dominant gene, so a silver horse will always have a silver parent, and will descend in an unbroken line from silver ancestors. Heterozygous silvers will produce silvers 50 percent of the time, while homozygous silvers will have 100 percent silver foals.

What can cause confusion is that silver cannot be seen on chestnut horses. Silver can also be missed on an older horse. Because the manes and tails of silvers darken with age, it is possible for an aged silver to be mistaken for a black or bay horse with a weathered mane and tail. Both situations can make it seem as though silver appears randomly, though genetic testing would reveal the true picture.

There is a commercially available test for identifying silver dilutes. Like mutations in other species that map to PMEL17, silver is associated with eye defects. Multiple congenital ocular anomalies (MCOA) was originally thought to be limited to the Rocky Mountain Horse, but a 2011 study showed that it was also present in the older, unrelated Icelandic breed. Although vision is not impaired in heterozygous silvers, homozygous horses are affected. For that reason, researchers have recommended that silver to silver crosses be avoided.

History and Breed Distribution

For many years it was believed that the silver gene was a mutation that occurred in 1886, with the birth of the American Shetland mare TROT. The color was popularized by her grandson CHESTNUT, who was a particularly striking silver dapple. Within a few generations, the American Shetland—which was then at the height of its popularity—became overwhelmingly silver. This contributed to the impression that it was color unique to the Shetland Pony breed.

The color was not unique to Shetlands, or even to ponies, and it was much older. The oldest documented silver was found among the horses buried during the Iron Age at Arzan in the Altai Mountains of Siberia. It is also present in the Icelandic, which is been isolated from outside influences since 982 AD. There is even some evidence that *Equus lambei*, an extinct species from the Ice Age, may have had coloring that closely resembled red silver.

In the United States the color is still heavily associated with the Shetland Pony. Because of their close relation to the Shetland, both the Miniature Horse and the German Classic Pony have a fairly high incidence of silver. It is also the preferred color in both the Rocky Mountain Horse, where the color is known as chocolate, and the Comtois Draft, where it is called *bai crins laves* (bay with a flaxen mane and tail).

Outside of those breeds, it is an uncommon color with a fairly widespread distribution. Among the ponies it is found in low numbers in Welsh Ponies, Australian Ponies, Highland Ponies, and Nordlands. It is present, although quite rare, in most of the American riding breeds, including the Quarter Horse, Morgan, Saddlebred, Missouri Foxtrotter and Tennessee Walking Horse. Other light breeds that have silver include the Dutch warmblood and coaching breeds and the Australian Stock Horse. It is also found in a number of the European heavy draft breeds, including the Ardennes and the Breton.

There has been some controversy over whether or not the dilution was ever present in either the Arabian or the Iberian breeds. Red silver horses of a distinctly Spanish type appear in at least two seventeenth century illustrations of *carousels*, which were elaborate equestrian ballets popular France. This suggested that the color was present at least at some point, but many felt that it had been lost over time. More recently, at least one Pura Raza Espanola mare tested positive for the dilution, so while rare it is still a part of the Spanish gene pool.

The situation with the Arabian is less clear. Bay Arabians are sometimes found with flaxen tails, which are known in the breed as Gulastra's Plume. There have also been Arabians with chocolate bodies and very pale manes and tails, including the famous mare ROSE OF SHARON. Both the flaxen-tailed bays and the white-maned liver chestnuts can look a great deal like silvers, but to date no Arabians have tested positive for the dilution. It is possible that one may yet be found, but it seems more likely that the Arabian has a number of colors that closely mimic silver.

Because the colors that result from the silver gene are often quite dark, and only subtly different from bay, black and liver chestnut, few breeds discriminate against them for registration purposes. They are frequently misidentified, but are not typically denied papers due to their color. Therefore it is not uncommon to find silver dilutes in breeds where they were previously not known to exist.

Champagne

Champagne is unlike cream and silver in that it dilutes both red and black pigment. It is unlike dun, silver and heterozygous cream in that it dilutes both the hair, the skin and the eyes. Red hair gets diluted to a light gold, and black hair to a silvery chocolate brown. The skin is diluted to a freckled pink, and the eyes to hazel or amber.

Chestnuts with the champagne gene are called gold champagnes. They have gold bodies and pale manes and tails. Bay horses with the champagne gene are called amber champagnes. They have the same golden body as the gold champagnes with a brown mane and tail. Although they are genetically bay, many amber champagnes do not have darker legs or, if they do, there is far less contrast with the body than the mane and tail. Black horses with the champagne gene are called classic champagnes. Their body color is difficult to describe, because it is not truly a brown nor is it a silver-grey. It is sometimes compared to the color of a Weimaraner dog. The mane and tail, like those of the amber champagnes, are chocolate. Brown horses with the champagne gene are called sable champagnes, though without a genetic test it can be difficult to distinguish them from classic champagnes.

Most adult champagnes have skin with a distinctive lavender undertone and darker freckling.

The reversed dapples on this amber champagne Paint mare are typical of the dilution. Her skin is particularly pale for a champagne, and may darker slightly with age.

There are abundant dark freckles on a lighter background, rather than the occasional pink flecks on a darker background seen on the lighter palominos. Amber, sable and classic champagnes tend to have slightly darker skin than gold champagnes.

Champagnes have a distinctive iridescent sheen that gives them a slight metallic look. They lack countershading, even on the black-based colors, and are one even tone from topline to belly. They do not appear to get sooty dapples, although reversed dapples are common and sometimes quite dramatic.

Another thing that sets champagnes apart is that they are born with relatively dark fur that lightens with the adult coat. In contrast, their skin is more clearly pink at birth and then begins to develop freckles after a few months. The eyes begin as bright blue and darken to amber by the end of the first year.

Champagne with Cream
The presence of the cream gene enhances the dilution of the champagne gene. As a group these colors are often called ivory champagnes, although using the champagne name with cream is also common: gold cream, amber cream, sable cream and classic cream. Ivory champagnes typically have paler hair and eyes than regular champagnes. This is most noticeable in gold creams, which often resemble cremellos with darker, more freckled skin and eyes that are closer to green or gold.

Inheritance and Testing
Champagne is a dominant gene, so a champagne horse will always have a champagne parent, and will descend in an unbroken line from champagne ancestors, though they may not be identified as such in older pedigrees. Heterozygous champagnes will produce champagnes 50 percent of the time, while homozygous champagnes will have 100 percent champagne foals. Homozygous champagnes are generally lighter than heterozygous champagnes, but the difference is not significant.

Champagne is visible on all four basic colors, so it cannot hide. It is possible to find horses misidentified as champagne. Because the color has been well-publicized in recent years, it is more often that non-champagnes are incorrectly called champagne. This can happen with palominos that have lighter skin as well as with homozygous pearls. Some double-diluted creams darken enough with exposure to sun that they could be mistaken for ivory champagnes.

Where doubt exists, there is a commercially available test that identifies the champagne mutation. There are no known health problems associated with the dilution.

History and Breed Distribution
One of the assumptions made by researchers in the twentieth century was that the brown allele (*b*) was involved in horse color. Brown in this context is unrelated to the color of the same name. In genetic terms brown is an altered form of black pigment common in many different mammals. Probably the most familiar animal with this type of mutation is the chocolate Labrador Retriever. Many of the early papers on horse color focused on identifying the equivalent brown color in horses. Because brown is recessive, the assumption—later disproved and replaced with Extension—was that chestnut horses were brown (*bb*).

When *Horse Color* was published in 1983, it included pictures of two horses that were theorized to have recessive brown (*bb*). It was thought that both also had a single copy of the cream gene. The first was the Saddlebred stallion SO PROUDLY WE HAIL, called a pink-skinned palomino. The second was a grade pony referred to as lilac dun. Pink-skinned palominos were the focus of a lot of attention in the Golden Saddlebred community during the 1930s and 1940s, but at the time there did not seem to be mention of horses with the same odd color as the pony.

That changed in the early 1990s with a handful of advertisements for the Tennessee Walking Horse CHAMPAGNE LOOK. In those ads, his owner described the stallion and asked if readers knew what color he was. She called the color champagne, and it was strikingly similar to the lilac dun pony. At first the connection between his color and the pink-skinned palominos was not obvious, even though it had already been drawn in Sponenberg's book. CHAMPAGNE LOOK was homozygous

for black (*EE*), so he did not produce pink-skinned palominos (gold champagnes). Researchers began looking, and more unusual horses came to light. The theory that the horses carried the recessive brown gene (*bb*) was dropped in favor of one that proposed a new dilution named for CHAMPAGNE LOOK and his family.

One of the early discoveries was the classic champagne Saddlebred JONQUIL, pictured in a 1929 issue of *Saddle & Bridle*. Her stud book entry listed her as dun, which was not a term commonly used in the Saddlebred community. Contemporary accounts almost always made mention of her odd color, just as they had for CHAMPAGNE LADY DIANE, the dam of CHAMPAGNE LOOK. Another was the very prolific Walking Horse stallion BARKER'S MOONBEAM. Assumed to have been a palomino, conversations with people who had known the stallion revealed that, while registered as "yellow", his points had been chocolate and his eyes green. These horses and others reinforced the idea that there was a another dilution, separate and unrelated to cream, in horses.

In 2000, the International Champagne Horse Registry (ICHR) was formed. It was the first organization to register horses based on the presence of a specific genetic mutation. It was also the first to take full advantage of the internet, maintaining a publicly accessible, online stud book with photos and pedigrees. This, along with detailed identification guides, helped raise awareness of the color. It proved very effective in locating not only champagnes, but other previously unidentified dilutions.

Champagne has since been found in most of the gaited breeds of the American South, including the Saddlebred, Walking Horse, Foxtrotter, and the Mountain Pleasure breeds. It is also present in the American stock horse breeds and the Miniature Horse. It is the signature color of the American Cream Draft. Because the oldest recorded lines are all found in the Saddlebred and the Tennessee Walking Horse, it is believed the original mutation may have occurred in the American South sometime in the early nineteenth century and spread from there. Because it is not found in European or South American breeds, it is not believed to have originated with the Spanish horses.

Pearl

Pearl is sometimes called a "new" dilution, though the designation refers to when it was discovered rather than when it first occurred. Pearl existed long before it was properly identified; it is a newly identified dilution that is relatively rare and probably quite old.

Like champagne, pearl dilutes the hair, skin and eyes. Red hair turns a color that ranges from pale straw to a rich apricot, while black hair changes to a color somewhere between silvery taupe and pale milk chocolate. The overall effect is warm in tone, and there is a slight sheen to the coat. On bay and black pearls, the points are often a shade or two darker than the body. Unlike gold champagnes, chestnut pearls usually have self-colored manes and tails.

Most pearls have skin that is a dusky lavender color with faint freckling, which makes them easy to mistake for champagnes. Usually the freckles are more subtle than those on a champagne, giving the impression of skin that is stippled and uneven in color, rather than specifically freckled. There does seem to be a fair bit of individual variation, just as there is among champagnes, so it many not always be possible to tell the difference simply by looking at the skin alone.

Pearls are often born with blue eyes that darken with maturity. The final color can range from a pale hazel to a chestnut brown. Although the number of identified pearls is still relatively small, there does seem to be a correlation with eye color and base coat. Chestnut pearls are more likely to have eyes that fall in the hazel-green spectrum, while the black-based colors tend towards light brown eyes. Some of the lightest chestnut pearls have eyes the same golden tan as the coat.

At least one suspected pearl horse shows signs of being a sooty as well as a pearl. Oro Mafioso, an Iberian stallion in Russia, has countershading and dappling in a pattern consistent with sooty.

Pearl Carriers

To be pearl, a horse must have two copies of the pearl gene. Horses that only carry pearl have ordinary, undiluted coats. It has been reported that some pearl carriers in the American stock horse breeds have slightly diluted skin under their tails, similar to what is sometimes seen on palominos. This has not been reported in the Iberian carriers, though that may be because most of the American pearl carriers are chestnuts, while chestnut is still relatively rare among Spanish horses in Europe.

Pearl with Cream

Alone a single copy of the pearl dilution does not alter the coat. When paired with a single copy of the cream dilution, however, the result is a horse that looks a lot like a double-dilute cream. The biggest difference is the eye color, which tends to have less blue and more green or gold tones. Like the paler chestnut pearls, many have eyes of a similar shade to their body.

Inheritance and Testing

Pearl is believed to be an allele of cream, and is sometimes described as a weaker version of that dilution. Whereas cream is an incomplete dominant, pearl is recessive. Horses that carry one copy of pearl are not diluted; only homozygous pearls are diluted. When bred to non-pearls, homozygous pearls have 100 percent undiluted pearl carriers. Like other recessive colors, when bred together, homozygous pearls breed true.

When pearl is paired with cream, the pearl gene magnifies the dilution of the cream gene. Cremellos and perlinos, which are homozygous for cream, cannot also carry pearl. Because cream and pearl occupy the same location, the horse can only have two creams, two pearls or one cream and one pearl. Cream pearls can only give one of the two dilutions, either pearl or cream, to each of their offspring.

There is a commercially available test for identifying the pearl mutation. There are no known health problems associated with the dilution.

History and Breed Distribution

The discovery of the pearl dilution is closely tied to the work of Carolyn Shepard and the International Champagne Horse Registry (ICHR). Because the mission of the champagne registry was to include only those horses thought to have the champagne gene, horses were screened both on appearance and parentage. Champagne is dominant, so horses submitted for registration were expected to have at least one champagne parent. In 2001, a Paint mare, Barlnk Peaches N Cream, was submitted for registration. She closely resembled a gold champagne, but she came from two chestnut parents. More unexplained dilutes, including horses that resembled double-diluted creams, were found and the color became known as the Barlink Factor.

Around the same time, an unusual Lusitano colt named Majodero R was garnering quite a bit of attention within the community of horse color researchers. Majodero R looked like a perlino, but he had only one cream parent. When tested, he proved to have a single copy of the cream dilution.

In 2006, scientists isolated the mutation for the Barlink Factor, which they called apricot. Carol Shepard tested Majodero R's half-sister Guindaleza R, and confirmed that the mutation in the pseudo-perlino Iberian horses and the Barlink Factor were the same. The name apricot was dropped in favor of pearl, which was the term already in use by Spanish and Portuguese breeders.

To date pearl has been found primarily in Iberian breeds, or breeds known to have descended from Spanish horses. It Europe it is present in both the Pura Raza Espanola and the Lusitano. In the Americas it is found in Quarter Horses, Paint Horses and Peruvian Pasos. In Paint Horses, the pearl gene is believed to be more common than the better-known champagne dilution, due to the popularity of the stallion Barlink Macho Man. As a pearl carrier, he would have given the gene to roughly half of his 393 registered foals. As of 2009, his descendants included twenty-seven cream pearls and seven homozygous pearls.

Because the two Spanish groups have not been crossed in modern times, the pearl dilution is assumed to predate the colonization of the Americas. The term pearl was used to describe horses at some of the royal studs of the seventeenth century, but it is not clear if there was any distinction between this and the color called ermine, or how each was used relative to the different combinations of cream and pearl. Given that consistency of terminology is a struggle in the twenty-first century, it seems unlikely that names for colors were more precise then.

The notable exception to the obvious Spanish connections among pearls is the Gypsy Horse, where horses have tested positive. Because Gypsy Horses are a landrace without recorded ancestry, it is certainly possible that Iberian horses were used recently to obtain the pearl gene. The other interesting possibility is that the color came from the remnants of the Hanoverian Creams, some of which were used by Garrard Tyrwhitt-Drake at his Cobtree Manor Stud. It is this author's suspicion that the Hanoverian Creams probably carried the pearl dilution. If that is the case, then the Creams would be the one known source for pearl among the horses in the British Isles.

Pearl Terminology

Because the pearl dilution is newly identified, there is no single accepted terminology for the different combinations. In this book, *pearl* is used to describe diluted horses whose pale color is soley the result of the pearl gene. *Red pearls* are chestnut horses that are homozygous for pearl, while *bay pearls* and *black pearls* are used for bay and black homozygous pearls. Heterozygous pearls are simply noted as *pearl carriers*.

Other writers prefer to use terms like *red pearl* for the carriers, and insert the word homozygous or double, as in *red homozygous pearl* or *red double pearl*, for the visibly diluted horses. A small percentage still use the term *apricot* for homozygous chestnut pearls.

Horses that have both the pearl and the cream dilution are called *cream pearls*. The different base colors are indicated with the name of the cream dilution involved: *palomino pearl*, *buckskin pearl* and *smoky black pearl*. These are used more uniformly than the names for the homozygous pearls.

Other Dilutions

Because it is possible to test for all the base colors and a wide range of known dilutions, it is easier to identify new dilutions. Whenever a horse appears to be one color, but tests show that it is something else, and none of the existing dilution genes are present, it is reasonable to suspect that there is new dilution.

Mushroom

The dilution called mushroom was identified when Shetland Ponies suspected of being black silver were shown to be genetically chestnut. Before there was a specific test for silver, testing for the black factor was used as a way to confirm the presence of silver. Horses that appeared to be liver chestnut, but that tested as black, were assumed to be carrying silver. Even before tests found that the mushroom ponies were chestnut, they were atypical for suspected silvers. Instead of being dark liver with a white manes and tails, which is the form of chestnut most often mistaken for black silver, the ponies were a dull, undappled version of the taupe or dead grass shade seen in the lightest silvers. Like silvers, and indeed like most diluted forms of black, there was no reddish cast to the coat. It seems certain that while they are chestnuts, they are a much-altered form of it.

So far the color, which is suspected to be recessive, has been limited to a specific family of Shetland Ponies in the United Kingdom. Because the color goes back to the earliest British stud books, the responsible mutation may predate the formation of the Shetland breed. If that is the case, it may be possible to find the dilution in other breeds, particularly the other mountain and moorland pony breeds.

Light Black or *Globrunn*

In recent years there have been a number of horses that have obviously diluted coats, but test negative for any of the known dilution genes. Most have tested positive for black, so they are often referred to collectively as light blacks. In Iceland, the palest black horses are called *globrunn*. Many of these are just faded smoky blacks, but others are unusually pale even for that color combination. Because the circumstances surrounding light blacks vary, it is quite likely that the group includes a number of different genetic causes. It is also possible that some breeds have modifiers that allow a single cream gene to more effectively dilute black hair.

Light black horses are similar in tone to the diluted black color found on some appaloosas. They might be mistaken for a dusty liver chestnut, though the tone of the coat ranges more towards bronze than red or gold. The paler light blacks are a soft milk chocolate color. Most have golden or amber eyes, and many have lavender or purplish skin. Others are faded to a color very like the browner versions of grulla. These tend to have very pale inner ears that are lined around the edge with dark chocolate, but they lack the dorsal stripe or primitive marks of a true grulla.

The light blacks that have appeared in breeds that do not have any of the common dilution genes, like the Arabian and the Dutch Draft, are reported to have been born with very pale skin, hair and eyes. The horses have then developed more pigment in all three, until they were chocolate brown with amber eyes. It seems likely that, unless each instance is a unique mutation, that this type of light black has a recessive mode of inheritance.

In some breeds, horses that could be described as light black or *globrunn* may be black horses with a combination of the cream and silver dilutions. Smoky black silvers are often an unusual shade of milk chocolate with skin that has a purplish rather than a blue-gray cast. As foals they are born with blue or gray-green eyes that darken to amber. Smoky black silvers often have less contrast between their body color and their manes and tails, which makes them less recognizable as silver dilutes.

White Hairs

Some of the most common modifiers are those that add white hairs to the base color of the horse. Of these, the most familiar are grey and roan. In the past the terms grey and roan were used interchangeably, even though the two modifiers are unrelated and work quite differently. This still occurs in countries where one or both are uncommon. There are also additional modifiers that add white hairs that are unrelated to either grey or roan.

Grey

Because it is so common, grey is often included with the basic colors. This is misleading because grey is not a color, but rather a progressive loss of color. All grey horses are also chestnut, black, bay or brown, in addition to being grey. Greys are born one of those base colors and, over time, the original dark hairs are replaced with white. The gene affects the pigment in the hair and not the skin, so grey horses retain the black skin they were born with, which makes them easy to distinguish from horses that are truly white.

The Greying Process
Foals are usually born a few shades lighter than they will be as adults, but grey foals are an exception; typically they are darker than a non-grey foal of the same base color. This is the reason for the saying among Percheron breeders that "blacks are born grey, and greys are born black". In addition to being born unusually dark, another sign that a foal will eventually turn grey is the presence of a light grey ring around each eye. These are sometimes called goggles.

Greys turn progressively lighter each time they shed out. The rate at which a grey loses color varies with each individual, although many breeds have been selected for a certain rate of change. Percherons, for example, have been bred over time for a slow rate of greying, and tend to stay dappled the longest. Some of the Baroque breeds like the Lipizzans and Kladrubers were specifically bred to turn white completely and rapidly. The base color will also affect the apparent rate of greying, since it takes fewer white hairs to make a pale color seem white than it would with a dark color.

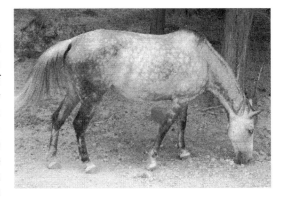

Grey horses progressively lighten with age, so the attractive dappled color on this mare is only temporary. Within two years of this picture, she was almost entirely white with only smudges of color on her knees and hocks.

Just as with the speed of change, the areas that lighten first or remain darkest longest will vary somewhat among individuals, but there is a common pattern for the progression. The first place to lighten is usually the face, with the exception of the forehead and nasal bones, which often develop an irregular, splotchy pattern, and the lower edge of the cheeks. Also typical in the early stages are white hairs in the tail, especially the tip, and a paler ring around the coronet. After that, the white will begin to show up at the jugular groove of the neck behind the throatlatch (the same area that remains light in the sooty pattern), on the chest and between the front legs, behind the elbows and along the flank.

At this point, if the horse is destined to dapple these will begin to appear on the sides, shoulders and neck. The dappling will become progressively more vivid and widespread, while the areas that greyed first remain the lightest. The dappling spreads to the limbs in irregular blotches up the cannon bone. The insides of the legs will be lighter and more blotchy than the outsides. The forearms and stifles will often have erratic lines of white hairs, sometimes called spider veins. The light areas spread and the dapples fade until the horse seems mostly white, with the knees, hocks and hindquarters remaining darkest longest.

Not all greys develop dapples, however. Some horses get progressively lighter without going through the dappled phase. Individuals with this type of progression are sometimes called iron greys. Other greys only develop faint dappling in limited areas. The tendency to dapple, and to dapple vividly, runs in families so it is assumed to have some genetic component. Whatever the individual variation, grey is progressive, so each stage is only a temporary state until the horse is white.

Manes and Tails
The manes and tails usually lighten along with the coat, but this is largely influenced by the original color of the horse. Colors noted for light manes and tails, such as flaxen chestnuts and silver dapples, will have manes and tails that appear white quite early, while colors with black manes and tails will lighten much more slowly. Base colors with pale body colors and darker manes and tails, such as buckskins and duns, will seem to keep very dark

As grey horses age, some develop the small dark flecks known as fleabites. Fleabites vary in size and density, with some families known for producing particularly large or particularly abundant flecks.

manes and tails long after their bodies are white. Some rare greys keep a dark mane and tail regardless of their original color. There are also breeds where the base color is very dark, such as the Percheron, yet horses develop very pale manes early in the greying process.

Fleabiting
Some greys develop small flecks of color called fleabites throughout their coat. Most develop fleabiting on the face and forehand after those areas have turned white, or nearly so, but it is possible for a horse to begin getting fleabites before they have finished dappling. The last areas of the body to turn completely white are often the hindquarters and the legs, so fleabites may not appear there until later.

The size and density of the fleabites varies with each individual. Fleabites do tend to increase as the horse ages, with the pattern stabilizing at some point. Some breeds like the Arabian are known for intense fleabiting patterns. Like vivid dappling, this is a trait that runs in families. Often these horses can appear quite dark, but the pattern does not extend to the mane and tail, which remain white.

Blood Marks
Blood marks are irregular areas of dark hair that appear on some greys. Blood marks can develop at any time, and may increase in size as the horse ages. Although they can appear on any breed, many associate the markings with Arabians, where they are called bloody shoulders, although they do not appear exclusively on the shoulders. Some blood-marked horses, like the Arabian stallion AL NAHR MONTEGO, are so extensively patched that they could be mistaken for a pinto.

Chubari or Tetrarch Spots
Some greys will develop large, oblong white spots in their coat. This resembles a reversed leopard pattern, but it is not related to appaloosa spotting. As horses with this pattern grey further, the spots eventually blend in with the rest of the coat and disappear. Because it is a transient pattern, it does not currently have a formal name, although some authors have used the term chubari, which is one of the older British terms for a leopard patterned

horse. Thoroughbred breeders describe such horses as having Tetrarch Spots, after the Thoroughbred stallion famous for them.

Depigmentation
Greys that have completed the greying process look white, but their dark skin gives them a slightly grey or bluish cast. Darkly pigmented skin is what separates a white grey horse from one that was born white. True whites have a creamy, pinkish cast from their underlying pink skin. Pink skin is also be visible around the muzzle, eyes, ears and genitals of a white horse, while those areas are charcoal gray on grey horses.

Some greys begin to lose this skin pigment along with the pigment in their hair. This depigmentation is fairly common in some breeds, particularly those bred for early and complete greying. This is discussed in more detail in the chapter on skin pigmentation.

Inheritance and Testing
Grey is a simple dominant. With the exception of those white patterns that leave little or no colored areas, if it is inherited the effect—the progressive lightening of the coat—will be visible. Grey does not hide in a breed for generations and crop up unexpectedly; the grey gene will lighten the horse no matter what other colors, modifiers or patterns are present.

For this reason, a grey horse will always have at least one grey parent, and will descend in an unbroken line from grey ancestors. A heterozygous grey horse will produce 50 percent grey foals. Homozygous greys produce 100 percent grey foals. Homozygous greys are believed to grey earlier and turn more completely white than heterozygous greys. It is also believed that only heterozygous greys develop fleabites.

There is a commercially available test for identifying grey. Greys have an increased risk for melanoma, which was a tendency first documented in 1903. Between 70 and 80 percent of grey horses over the age of 15 years develop benign melanomas. The rate of malignant melanomas is lower. Homozygous greys appear to be at higher risk than heterozygous greys for developing melanomas.

History and Breed Distribution
The scientists that identified the mutation responsible for greying reported that all grey horses trace back to a common ancestor believed to have lived more than 2,500 years ago. It is their belief that the white Persian horses mentioned by the Greek historian Herodotus were most likely greys.

Because grey is so closely associated with the Arabian and other related breeds, the mutation is widely suspected to have eastern origins. Some late nineteenth and early twentieth century writers insisted that the grey color came to the Arabian through outside blood, perhaps from the Turkoman or North African horses. This argument was based on the popular belief that blood horses were properly bay. There was also a tendency at the time to equate uniformity of color with blood purity, and conflate color with breed. Despite this, the public perception was that the grey color was proof of eastern influence, and the prevalence of the color in Arabians supported that assumption.

Many of the modern breeds where grey is common have known or suspected Arabian influence. These include a number of Spanish and French breeds, as well as the mountain and moorland ponies, particularly the Welsh Pony. The association is not exclusive, however. Grey is found in breeds, like the Icelandic and the Nordland Pony, where there is no recent connection to the Arabian.

Grey is also a color that has been the subject of changing fashion. Grey never enjoyed the same popularity in England that it did in France, and it became extremely unpopular there during the Edwardian era. It was not in high demand in the United States, so it is uncommon in most American breeds, though it can be found in small numbers in the Quarter Horse, Standardbred, Morgan and most of the southern gaited breeds.

Dark-Headed Roan

Like grey, roan is a modifier that adds white hairs to the base color, but unlike grey, roan horses do not turn progressively lighter as they age. Roan horses are born roan or they shed out to roan when they lose their foal coat, and they remain roan throughout their lives. Roan is also different from grey in that only the body is affected, while the head, legs, mane and tail remain dark.

Roans can be identified by the absence (either partial or complete) of white hairs on the head, and for this reason they are sometimes called dark-headed roans. A darker head is a good indicator that a horse is roan and not grey, because the head is among the first areas to lighten during the greying process. Roans also have an area on their upper forelegs where the white hairs begin, which gives the dark area above the knee a distinctive upside-down V-shape. That shape is a reliable sign that the horse is true roan, and not one of the other patterns that feature roaning like rabicano or sabino.

Another trait that characterizes true roans is roaning that is fairly uniform in shade, without areas that are conspicuously light or dark. Although it is evenly mixed, the percentage of white hair does vary. Some horses have a great deal of white in the coat, contrasting sharply with their dark heads and points. Other more lightly roaned horses will appear quite dark overall, with less contrast between their body and points. This has more to do with individual variations than it does with age. It is also common for roans to turn darker in the winter, and to appear lighter after the winter coat has been shed. Hormonal changes and aging are also thought to cause some roans to darken. Roans are not typically dappled, but they can have reversed dapples. Reverse dapples have centers that are darker than the surrounding coat instead of lighter.

The dark head gives the color its name, both in English (dark-headed roan) as well as many European countries (*testa di moro, mohrenkopf, moorkop*). Because the term roan is often used as a catch-all by horsemen to describe any horse with white hairs in the coat, this specific pattern of

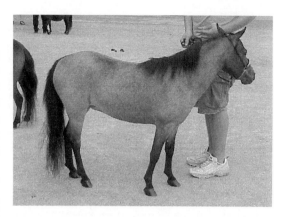

The gene responsible for dark-headed roan is closely linked to the gene that determines whether the base color is black-based (bay, brown or black) or red-based (chestnut). The means that this bay roan Miniature horse is more likely to produce bay roans and non-roan chestnuts than chestnut roans and non-roan bays.

roaning is also called classic or true roan to separate it from other unrelated roaning patterns.

Because the background color is still very apparent on roans, even those with a high percentage of white hairs, they are usually described in a way that indicates the base color. Roan on black is called blue roan, while roan on bay is red roan. Chestnut roans are called strawberry roans, although there are some who used red roan to mean either chestnut or bay roan.

Frosty Roan
Some roans have a dark head and dark legs, but their mane and tail are mixed with white hairs. Others have white hairs on the face as well as in the mane and tail. These roans are sometimes called frosty roans. Because the frosty roan pattern occurs most frequently in those breeds where roan is relatively common, such as the Ardennes and the Brabant, some have theorized that it may be a variation of roan, or perhaps a modifier of the original pattern, and not a separate gene.

Inheritance and Testing
Roan is a dominant gene, so all roan horses will have one roan parent and will trace back through an unbroken line of roan parents. Roan cannot hide for generations, but it is prone to being mis-

identified. Some of this comes from the tendency to confuse grey and roan, or to use roan as a generic term for anything with white hairs. It is also possible to find dark roans registered by their base color with no mention of the roan hairs, or with just the notation that they have white ticking.

Roan was once believed to be lethal in its homozygous form, though this has been called into question in recent years with several tested homozygous roan stallions in the Quarter Horse. Additional homozygous horses have been identified in the Criollo and the Tennessee Walking Horse. Earlier researchers had found Belgian Brabant stallions that appeared to be homozygous using production records. The theory that roan was a homozygous lethal came from a study that showed roan parents produced two roan foals for every non-roan. Were roan not lethal, the expected ratio would be three roan foals to every non-roan. Lethal genes have a 2:1 ratio because the homozygotes are lost early in pregnancy. The reason behind the discrepancy in the initial study is not known.

Roan is part of a linkage group with Extension and Tobiano. Linked genes are located close together and are more often inherited as a set than separately. Because Extension determines whether a horse is black-based or red-based, roan is linked to the base color. That means that black-based roans are more likely to produce other bay and black roan foals, while chestnut roans are more likely to produce more chestnut roans. When a bay roan is bred to a chestnut, the resulting foals are more likely to be bay roan or chestnut, and only rarely bay or chestnut roan.

The mutation responsible for roan has not been identified, but it has been mapped to a specific chromosome. A zygosity test is available which can determine if a horse is homozygous for roan.

History and Breed Distribution
Dark-headed roan is difficult to track through historical records because roan has been used to describe a number of unrelated colors, including grey and sabino. It is known that black and black roan Neapolitans were favored for producing ceremonial carriage horses during the Baroque era.

Roans appear in artwork from that time period, although they are less common than the pintos and appaloosas. The dark-headed roan Norikers and Italian Murgese are descendants of these horses.

Today true roan is found in a wide variety of breeds and types, but outside the Ardennes, Brabant and some of the related draft breeds, it is relatively rare even in the breeds where it is found. Among the pony breeds, it is probably most common in Welsh Ponies, but it is also found in small numbers in most of the mountain and moorland breeds as well as in the Icelandic. In the riding breeds, it is present in very small numbers in some of the European warmbloods, Hackneys and Finnhorses. It is slightly more common in the North and South American breeds, including the Criollo, Mangalarga, Paso Fino, Quarter Horse, Standardbred and most of the southern gaited breeds.

One group where roan is notably absent are the majority of the eastern breeds. Dark-head roan does not exist is the Arabian. Arabians registered as roan are invariably rabicanos, sabinos or a combination of those two patterns. A single Thoroughbred stallion, Catch A Bird, is suspected as the source of a novel roan mutation. His offspring, and other rare instances of horses that look roan but that have solid parents, suggest that there may be multiple variations of roan.

Although the pattern is called dark-headed roan, some individuals show some degree of roaning on the cheeks and even the area between the muzzle and the eyes.

White Ticking

White hairs can be found on many otherwise solid colored horses. Such horses are said to be ticked with white, or to have roaning in the coat. The latter can be confusing since roan is a very specific pattern of white hairs as well as a general term for white hairs in the coat, regardless of the cause.

Ticking is more common in chestnuts, particularly clear red chestnuts, though it does occur on black-based colors. Ticking is unrelated to white patterning or markings, though many of the sabino patterns produce a similar effect.

Some horses are so extensively ticked that they could be mistaken for true roan. What distinguishes them is that the white hairs are sprinkled throughout the coat and include the face, mane and tail. Most importantly, these horses lack the clear definition between their unroaned legs and face that are seen on most dark-headed roans. Many come from breeds or families where dark-headed roan is not known to occur, and have solid, unroaned parents.

Rabicano
Rabicano is a form of white ticking that concentrates on the flanks and top of the tail. Unlike true roans that have evenly mixed white hairs on the body, rabicanos have roaning that is concentrated on the flank. The most minimally marked rabicanos only show some white ticking on the fold of the stifle, while more extensively marked rabicanos often show lighter roaning on the throat, chest and between their hind legs. With these horses, the roaning on the flanks is quite pronounced and forms light and dark bands along the sides, giving the horse a brindled look. Another telling characteristic of rabicano is the presence of white hairs at the dock of the tail. This can be as subtle as a few white hairs on either side of the tail, or in some cases the entire top of the tail can be white. Often the white hairs split down the center of the tail, forming bands to either side and giving rise to the name coon tail.

It is likely that some of the sabino patterns mimic both the flank roaning and white hairs at the dock of the tail. Rabicano is not thought to

be involved in adding white markings to the face or legs. In fact, many rabicanos are solid or very minimally marked. For that reason, it can be difficult to confirm the presence of rabicano in specific breeds, especially those where sabino is common.

In breeds where both rabicano and sabino are found, there have been individuals who have typical sabino markings on the legs and face, and more densely ticked flanks than are typical for unmarked rabicanos. Such horses fit the theory that sabino boosts the expression of other white patterns. Breeding these horses to relatively solid, unroaned mates should result in the two patterns segregating, with some foals having the rabicano pattern and others having sabino markings.

There are horses that have pronounced flank roaning but that lack the brindled effect that is common in rabicanos. These horses typically have blazes, and while they lack leg markings, they tend to occur in breeds or families where sabino is common. For that reason, they are discussed on page 80 in the section for other white pinto patterns. It is possible, however, that this type of pattern is related to rabicano or one of the other types of white ticking, rather than sabino.

Frosty
In frosty horses, the white hairs are concentrated over the bony areas of the hips, spine, neck and shoulders. As with rabicano, there are often white hairs at the tailhead. The tail usually lacks the

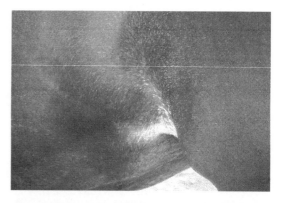

White ticking is often concentrated on the fold of the stifle, and spreads out from there upward to the flanks and downward to the area between the hind legs.

banding found in rabicanos and is called a squaw tail. Some breeders report that the manes and tails get whiter with age.

Frosty horses are often found in breeds and families where roan is present, which suggests the two colors may be related. There may also be a connection with the frosty roan form of dark-headed roan. It is also possible that all three—dark-headed roan, frosty and frosty roan—are just differing expressions of the same mutation.

Inheritance and Testing

White ticking has not yet been the studied using modern molecular analysis. There are older Dutch studies that report on the percentages of registered horses with white ticking or white hairs in the coat, as well as a few that look at the number of offspring that inherited the trait. One of these involving Dutch Draft horses, where the trait was common, found that ticked stallions produced 48 percent ticked foals. This would be consistent with a dominant mode of inheritance. Other smaller studies had similar findings. What is not known is whether or not the horses in the studies were marked with white, and therefore possibly ticked due to a sabino pattern, or if the ticking was caused by a factor like rabicano, which is unrelated to markings.

Unfortunately using stud book records is problematic, both because white ticking is inconsistently reported, and because the different causes for white hairs (if indeed there are different causes) are not yet fully understood. Isolating the mutation for dark-headed roan, as well as progress on some of the sabino patterns, could answer some of the questions about the white ticking patterns.

History and Breed Distribution

White ticking can occur in almost any breed, though it is more often noted in breeds where white markings are minimal. In breeds that have markings, white hairs are rarely included in descriptions unless the ticking is pronounced, even though it is likely that white hairs are present. More extensively ticked horses are sometimes recorded as roan. For that reason, white ticking can be very difficult to trace through historical records.

Although not as common as white ticking on the flanks, ticking can cover the entire body of the horse. Unlike a true dark-headed roan, heavily ticked horses like this have white hairs on the face, manes and tails and lack the upside-down V-marks on the fronts of their forelegs.

The use of the word rabicano has a long tradition. In Spanish it translates to "white tail", and was used as early as 1495 as the name of the supernatural horse ridden by Argalia, one of Charlemagne's knights in the romantic poem *Orlando Innamorato*. The French version of the word, *rubican*, appears in a 1673 French-English dictionary with the definition, "white hairs that be scattered here and there upon the coats of some coloured horses." Later French writers encourage owners to indicate the intensity and location of the white hairs, so that a horse might be "very rubican on the back and neck" or "slightly rubican on the flanks." Even so, many dictionaries indicate that the word most commonly referred to white hairs on the flanks.

Because it is closely associated with the breed, rabicano is sometimes called Arabian roan. It is also seen in Thoroughbreds and breeds where Thoroughbreds are used. It is suspected to have been the true color of IRISH BIRDCATCHER, who was said to have gray hairs on his flanks and a white tail. His sire, SIR HERCULES, was a black horse with a white tail top and enough white hairs on his flanks that he was sometimes described as "black or grey". In addition to being black, SIR HERCULES was marked with only a star, so was probably not a sabino.

Hackneys display a number of different types of white ticking and roaning, including rabicano. The Dutch Harness Horse also has occasional white ticking due to the influence of both the Gelder-

lander and the Hackney. A small percentage of early Friesians were ticked with white, though whether they had a true rabicano pattern or just a sprinkling of white hairs is not known. The trait was eliminated from the Friesian gene pool in the middle of the twentieth century.

Flank roaning is also present in some Spanish horses, though often their roaning is the type that is paired with white face markings, and may actually be a type of sabino pattern. The frosty pattern is also found in horses of Spanish descent, particularly Spanish Mustangs and Quarter Horses. It is also seen on rare occasions in the Tennessee Walking Horse. If frosty is related to the frosty roan variation of dark-headed roan, then it would also be found in the Ardennes and Brabant, and somewhat less frequently in the Poitevin Mulassier.

Other Patterns of White Hair

In addition to roaning and ticking there are a handful of more exotic patterns of white hairs found in horses. These are different from the pinto patterns in that they do not involve underlying pink skin, and many develop with age. All are relatively rare, and have not been the focus of formal studies.

Lacing

Lacing is a network of fine white lines that mark off rectangular patches along the horse's back. It is often called giraffe spotting for its resemblance to the pattern on that animal. In veterinary literature, it is called *reticulated leukotrichia*. It is a progressive pattern which often begins as a scattering of white hairs along the spine, and then spreads outward across the back, forming more distinctly white lines until the reticulated pattern is obvious. When clipped, the dark rectangles can appear lighter at the center, similar to condition dappling. In rare instances, the pattern appears as an outline of paler color, rather than true white. This is sometimes called shadow lacing.

Lacing is believed to be caused by a crusting and subsequent shedding of the skin, after which the hairs grow back white. Many owners, however, have noted that their horse developed the pattern without showing any sign of skin problems. Because lacing is known to occur more frequently in certain breeds and bloodlines, the condition is thought to have a genetic component

Much of the scientific research on lacing has focused on Quarter Horses, but it is also common in certain strains of Shetlands and Miniature Horses. It has also been noted in Arabians, Morgans, and Standardbreds.

Marbling (Non-Appaloosa)

Because it also creates a pale outline around darker spots, marbling is also referred to as giraffe spotting. Marbling is different from lacing in that the outlines are broader and softer, so that the horse looks far more like it has reverse dapples rather than a network of crisp white lines. Marbling is not centered on the back like lacing, but rather tends to concentrate on the sides of the horse. The pattern is thought to be progressive, though the typical time frame involved is not known. Many marbled horses have blazed faces, which has led to speculation that the pattern may be part of the sabino complex.

White Striping

Horses are occasionally born with irregular white striping. Unlike chimeric brindles, the stripes are often uneven and asymmetrically placed on the horse. It is thought that these markings are the

This unusual Saddlebred mare has a roaning pattern very similar to dark-headed roan, but has no roan horses in her background. Her mane hairs are variegated dark to white and back to dark at the roots.

result of errors during fetal development, and are probably not inheritable.

Because such occurrences are random, they can happen in any breed. Among the horses known to have white stripes, there are PINTA, the black warmblood filly pictured in *Equine Color Genetics*, VIDA LOCA, a bay Dutch Warmblood mare, and DA REMOTE CONTROL, a bay Half-Arabian mare. In all three mares, the white striping was found on only one side of the body.

Another famous case of white striping was the Thoroughbred stallion CATCH A BIRD. Because he went on to produce a number of dark-headed roan foals, it is believed that CATCH A BIRD was the source of a new roan mutation. It may be that the same disruption that produced the roan mutation could also be responsible for the odd striping.

Spanish Greys

Recently two Pura Raza Espanola full brothers, COMICO IV and COMICO VI, were found to have an unusual form of greying. Because the bodies of the two horses remained dark well past maturity, they were initially suspected of having an unusual form of rabicano. The white hairs on both horses have increased significantly over time, which would not be expected with rabicano or any of the other forms of white ticking. In some ways the areas where the white hairs have appeared—the face, the jugular groove, the lower legs—are a little like those of an ordinary grey, but the character is quite different. Instead of concentrating on the lower part of the face, the greying on the Comico horses was concentrated on the forehead and along the top of the poll, as well as down the jugular groove. Greying also concentrated on the lower legs, with extensive mottling up the cannons. White hairs also appeared at the dock, which is what caused many to assume rabicano was involved. The white at the dock looks different from rabicano, though, appearing more starkly white and extending in a point towards the croup.

Similar patterns of greying have since been found in at least one family of Mangalarga Marchadors, and a crossbred mare in Spain. Further studies are necessary to determine whether the horses carry a modified version of grey, or a separate mutation that produces a similar effect.

Fungus Spots

There have been rare instances where horses had large, irregular patches of white. The general outline of the white spots is rounded, but they are much larger and vary more in size than those commonly referred to as Birdcatcher spots. Unlike most white patterns, the patches do not follow the pattern of hair growth or pigment migration during fetal development. The loss of pigment appears to only involve the hair and not the underlying skin, although some horses with the condition have also displayed facial depigmentation.

Though the pattern has not been the focus of scientific study, it is widely believed that such spots are the result of a fungal infection or other skin disorder. Many horses that develop the spots have colored hair return in the same areas, giving the pattern a more muted appearance. The World Champion Saddlebred SIMPLY STRIKING is a well-known example of this type of spotting.

Pinto Patterns

At the present, there are six formally identified pinto patterns: tobiano, splashed white, frame overo, sabino, dominant white and manchado. Each is separate and distinct, with a unique appearance and mode of inheritance. Of those six, sabino is actually a catch-all term for a number of white patterns that are genetically separate. For that reason, it is likely that the number of pinto patterns will increase as more mutations are identified.

The visual differences between these patterns are best understood in terms of point of origin, pattern progression and areas of exclusion. The point of origin is where the white first appears on minimally marked animals. Pattern progression is the direction those white areas spread on more extensively marked animals. (It should be noted that pattern progression in pintos applies to groups of horses showing varying amounts of white, and not the individual horse itself since, generally speaking, pinto patterns are fixed from birth and do no change with age.) The areas of exclusion are those parts of the coat that resist white and remain dark on horses with the maximum expression of the pattern. Differences between the points of origin, pattern progression and the areas of exclusion are what make it possible to tell one pattern from another.

Tobiano

Tobiano is the most familiar of the pinto patterns, and is the easiest for most people to identify. That may explain why the common grouping of patterns into tobiano and overo is in fact grouping horses into tobiano and all the pinto patterns that are not tobiano. Even in countries where pinto patterns are not common, the default term for pinto often refers to tobiano.

Tobianos look like white horses that have large, rounded areas of color. Their face markings tend to be conservative, much like those found on solid horses, and the eyes are typically dark. Tobianos almost always have four white legs and the white on their body will usually cross over their necks, back or croup. The borders of the colored areas are rounded and well defined, though the placement of many spots in one area can make the white areas appear jagged. Even in the wildest tobiano pattern it is usually possible to see how roundish spots grew together to form the pattern. That is why the German and Dutch names for the pattern—*plattenshecke* and *platenbont*—translate to plate-spotting; the large colored areas are shaped like plates.

Although most tobianos do look like they have dark spots on a white background, the pattern can still be understood in terms of where the white starts on minimally-marked horses (the point of

With its large round spots on a white background, the tobiano is one of the easiest pinto patterns to recognize. It is also one of the most widely distributed pinto patterns.

origin), where it progresses as individuals have increasing amounts of white patterning (pattern progression), and finally the areas that retain color even when the horse is primarily white (areas of exclusion).

Points of Origin
On tobianos, white originates on the legs and to a slightly lesser degree along the topline. That is, minimal tobianos with white legs and little or no white on the topline are far more typical than those with a white topline and little or no leg white. Usually all four legs are white to some degree, though this is not an absolute rule. On the

Figure 2. *The tobiano pattern originates on the legs and the topline, and merges on the sides of the horse to create what looks like a white horse with large, circular patches of color.*

topline, the most common places for white to start are the withers, the croup, and the base of the tail.

Pattern Progression

The most minimally marked tobianos have socks or stockings. When viewed in profile, the markings on the hind legs often come to a point on the side of the leg. This is different from sabinos, where the stockings usually extend up the front of the leg. There will typically be a small patch of white on either the lower neck or the withers. There may also be a small amount of white on the croup or at the base of the tail, which will turn the top of the tail white, or at least partially white.

In horses with a little more patterning, the white at the withers will spread along the topline, eventually joining with the white on the croup or tail. As the pattern progresses, the white tends to flow down from the topline towards the white on the legs, and the rounded nature of the colored areas becomes more obvious.

When a tobiano horse is about 50 percent white, the pattern takes on the classic appearance of a colored head and chest and large spots on the flanks or hindquarters. This seems to be the norm that the pattern gravitates towards, as many tobianos are marked this way.

When the pattern becomes more extensive, more of the body becomes white, until the only color left is the head and possibly a small area on the chest or hindquarters. It is likely that this is the most extreme expression of this pattern, and that it is as far as it will progress without the influence of other white patterns.

Areas of Exclusion

Tobianos have a strong tendency to retain color on their heads. That includes the front of the head, forelock and ears. Tobianos also tend to keep some amount of color on the tip of their tail.

Homozygotes

Horses with two copies of the tobiano mutation are not more extensively white, and are in most respects not very different from horses that have only one. The one exception is that homozygous tobianos often have smaller spots, known as cat tracks or ink spots, in the white areas of the pat-

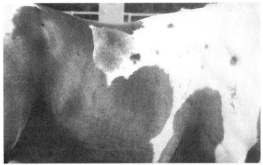

Homozygous tobianos often have smaller spots of color known as cat tracks or ink spots (top). Tobianos can also have spots or areas of spots that are roaned (bottom). This is also more common in homozygotes.

tern. These can vary in number from just a few to numerous, overlapping spots. Ermine spots are also typical, as are colored patches around the front and back chestnuts. The tendency towards particularly heavy cat tracks and ermine spots does appear to run in certain tobiano families.

Another quirk of homozygous tobiano patterns is the tendency towards random areas of roaning. Sometimes it is an entire spot, and sometimes it is just a section of a spot. (See the Paint Horse on page 180 for a particularly striking example of the latter.)

Behavior with Other Colors and Patterns

Tobiano can be thought of as overriding the instructions of most other patterns. In this way it operates a bit like a mask of white that was dropped over the top of whatever other colors were present. If the horse is dun, for instance, the dorsal stripe will end where the white from the tobiano begins.

If the horse is an appaloosa, that pattern will appear only in the colored areas left behind by the tobiano pattern.

Because the head retains color even when the pattern is quite extensive, tobianos with face white beyond a star are often assumed to carry one or more of the overo mutations and are called toveros. White on the face may not prove the presence of an overo pattern in the case of homozygous tobianos, which show a high incidence of face white. This is true even in breeds where conservative face markings, or no markings at all, are more typical. Until more patterns are definitively identified, however, it is hard to know if the additional tobiano gene is responsible, or if all tobianos with face markings are in fact toveros.

When paired with some of the sabino patterns, the tobiano pattern can change in two ways. The first is that white pattern area spreads in such a way that the colored areas look slightly smaller, but are more plentiful. The end result still looks like tobiano, but the pattern is more complex in outline. This is consistent with the "sabino boost" observed in appaloosas, where the sabino increases the white areas of a leopard or blanket pattern, while making the spots smaller. The second change seen in some sabino-tobianos is in the outline of the pattern. Instead of simply overlapping a ragged or lacey sabino pattern over the top of the colored areas, the ragging or lacing is redirected to the outline of the tobiano pattern. This can be as subtle as soft roaning along the edges of the dark spots, or more pronounced ragged or scalloped areas.

Inheritance and Testing

Tobiano is a simple dominant. For that reason, all tobianos will have at least one tobiano parent, and an unbroken line of tobiano ancestors behind that parent. Unlike many of the overo patterns, tobiano does not go undetected for generations. It is possible for a minimally marked tobiano, where just the legs are white, to be mistaken for a solid horse, but it would be extremely unusual for such a horse to consistently produce white legs and no body white. The one known exception are a handful of Nordic pony breeds which show a propensity for minimized patterns, but even in those breeds there

This tovero pony has both types of sabino alterations to his pattern. This most obvious is the ragged edge of his pattern, but sabino has also broken the larger dark areas into smaller patches of color.

are a mix of minimal and typical pattern expressions. (The unusual nature of tobiano in the Nordic breeds will be discussed in more detail in the upcoming volume on ponies.)

There is a commercially available test for identifying tobianos. There are no known health issues connected to the pattern, and homozygous tobianos are viable. It is possible then to develop a program of true-breeding tobianos. This, along with the consistent nature of the pattern, has made tobiano a popular choice among breeders of colored horses.

History and Breed Distribution

Tobiano is a very old color mutation. When equine archaeological samples were tested, only sabino-1 proved to be older. The first sample to test positive for tobiano was a single individual believed to have lived in Eastern Europe during the Bronze Age. Samples were also found in China, Mongolia and Siberia dating to the early Iron Age. Even before it was possible to test ancient remains for colors, the presence of tobiano in the Icelandic—a breed isolated since the tenth century—suggested the color was old.

The pattern was popular throughout the seventeenth and eighteenth centuries, and can be seen in numerous paintings made during the Baroque period. Caravaggio placed a buckskin tobiano behind Saint Paul in *Conversion on the Way to Damascus*, and Ruebens had a bay tobiano pegasus in his *Perseus Liberating Andromeda*. By the latter part of the nineteenth century, at the dawn of the stud book era, the color had fallen out of favor. Writing about color and markings of domestic animals for the American Association for the Advancement of Science in 1881, W. M. Brewer sums up the situation:

> "Formerly spotted horses were fashionable, as they still are among barbarous or semi-barbarous peoples, and indeed among people of our civilization in regions where horse-stealing is also fashionable, but spotted horses are now so unfashionable in the older states that it is not easy to find a sufficiently large number for extensive generalizations."

Other writers from the same period made similar observations about the difficulty in finding spotted horses in large enough numbers to study. It was still possible to see evidence of its earlier popularity further back in some pedigrees, but by the early twentieth century tobiano was rarely seen in pedigreed horses.

This began to change in America in the 1950s and 1960s with the formation of the Pinto Horse Association and the American Paint Horse Association. The trend spread from there to Europe, reflecting the rise in popularity of unusual colors and patterns of all kinds by the end of the twentieth century.

The tobiano pattern is found in a wide range of breeds and body types, from ponies to riding horses to heavy drafts. Some early writers attributed the color in Shetlands to a Scandinavian influence, perhaps because the other breed known at the time to be tobiano was the Icelandic. There is no real concentration of tobianos in the Nordic breeds, or in any particular region. The Marwari of India and the Campolina of Brazil, both of which have the pattern, are pretty far removed both from the North Atlantic and the Nordic pony type. Modern distribution of the color probably has far more to do with the dictates of fashion, and the effect that had on the selection of breeding stock, than with the area the color originated.

Although the distribution of the pattern is pretty wide, one notable absence is the Arabian, which is not thought to have ever had the pattern. In the early twentieth century, there was a widespread image of the Arabian as tobiano-spotted. This perception is often blamed on circuses, which invariably claimed exotic origins for their animals. Even so, some of the earliest stud books have pedigrees that include "spotted Arabians." It is hard to know just how many of these spotted horses may have been tobiano, since the mid-nineteenth century marked the time when American breeders began to use spotted to mean pinto rather than appaloosa, as British English speakers still do. Undoubtedly some were tobianos, but not Arabians in the modern sense. In 1978, breed historian Michael Bowling wrote:

> "A brisk trade in spotted horses of low degree was carried out with the claim that they were Arabians. When the Arabian Horse Registry was founded in 1908, it was felt to be a good idea to disassociate the genuine article."

Whether tobiano was part of the ancient middle eastern gene pool is not currently known, but changes in fashion ensured that for most of the older breeds with closed stud books, the pattern was effectively excluded.

Naturalists in the early nineteenth century believed that "piebald" was the natural coloring of the wild horses of Tibet, which they called Tangums. This 1841 illustration suggests that at least some of the Tangums were tobianos.

Frame Overo

(Lethal White Overo)

In the latter part of the twentieth century, as pinto patterns gained popularity in American, it became common to see rules for distinguishing tobianos from overos. Tobianos, the rules asserted, had white that crossed the back, while overos did not. Tobianos had white legs, while overos had one or more dark legs. Overos had dark tails, while tobianos had mixed tails.

It is rare to see articles that talk about these rules now. There is greater awareness that overo is not a specific pattern, but rather a group of patterns, and that within that group there are quite a few that routinely break one or more of the accepted overo rules. There is a pattern, however, that does conform to the rules: frame overo.

While tobianos look like white horses with rounded spots of color, frame overos look like colored horses with torn white patches. Instead of conservatively marked faces, they have conservatively marked legs. Their leg markings resemble those of a solid horse. Their face markings, on the other hand, tend to be more extensive, and the eyes are sometimes blue. The spots are generally concentrated on the sides of the horse, most often the neck and barrel. These spots often look like large pieces of torn paper, though in some horses they have a more intricate, lacey outline.

Like tobiano, the points of origin and the way frame overo tends to progress on the most minimal to the most extensive individuals is pretty consistent. At moderate levels of expression, and when it is not obscured by tobiano or the other overo patterns, frame is one of the easier overo patterns to identify.

Points of Origin

White on frame overos originates on the face, the broad side of the neck, and the barrel. The primary point of origin appears to be the face.

Pattern of Progression

Although the points of origin for frame include the neck and sides of the horse, not all frames have white on the body or even unusual markings on

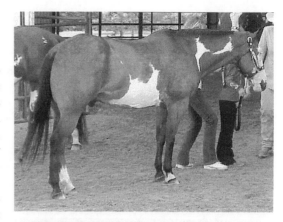

In the frame overo, white originates on the broad sides of the neck and the barrel, as well as the face (top). Unless one of the other pinto patterns are present, the legs are dark (bottom). Both horses show the dark moutache marking that many frame overos have.

the face. Horses with no more than a small star have tested positive for frame, and in some families frame overos with broad blazes but no body white are common. This type of minimal patterning, particularly when it involves a gene that causes damage when it is homozygous, is sometimes called cryptic.

Among frame overos that do have some kind of visible patterning, minimally-marked horses tend to have unusually wide face markings. While the face markings on sabinos tend to spread over the nose and wrap over the lips and under the jaw, the white on a frame overo spreads horizontally across the face in the area between the eye and the corner of the mouth, giving the impression that the white is moving out from the forehead towards the cheeks, rather than down the front of the face and under the nose. In fact, the nose area, which sabino markings cover, often remains as a dark moustache. There may also be a small spot of white on either the side of the neck or body.

In horses with a little more patterning, the spots on the neck or body might be a bit larger. As the pattern progresses, the white on the neck will often join with the white on the body, although the area between the two sections tends to be irregular rather than truly fused. This increase in white usually occurs on both sides of the horse. More so then the other overo patterns, frame tends to progress in a roughly symmetrical fashion. While not identical to each other, the two sides will have a similar percentage and placement of white.

Some frames have narrow patches of white on the upper portion of their front legs, just under the chest. Others get a narrow strip that angles over the hip. It is unusual for the pattern to cross the outer edges of the body—the colored frame around the pattern—when the horse is viewed in profile. The exception is the middle of the neck, where the white pattern sometimes extends far enough to touch the midline and turn a section of the mane white.

At its most extreme expression, frame will cover the hindquarters and most of the body, leaving the lower legs, the ears and only a narrow band of color along the midline. It is likely that this is the most extreme expression of this pattern, and that it is as far as it will progress without the influence of other white patterns.

Although most frame overos with visible patterning have broad white faces, it is possible to get a moderate amount of white on the neck and sides, and only have a star or snip. In those cases the face markings do tend to be larger than average, and may be slightly irregular in placement or shape.

Areas of Exclusion

Frame overo is a pattern that is as much characterized by the areas that remain dark as where it places the white. None of the other patterns common in North America leave the legs dark. Other areas that tend to retain color are the ears and the topline extending down to include the tail and the backs of the hind legs above the hocks.

Behavior with Other Colors and Patterns

When paired with the tobiano pattern, frame may be visible only in the form of broad white on the face. Because face markings on frames vary, though, and because tobiano often places white in

These three frame overo horses show the frame overo pattern's strong tendency to leave the topline, tail and backs of the upper legs dark, even when other overo patterns are present.

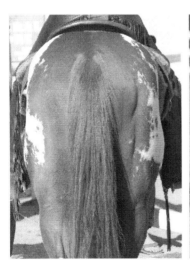

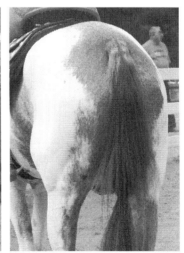

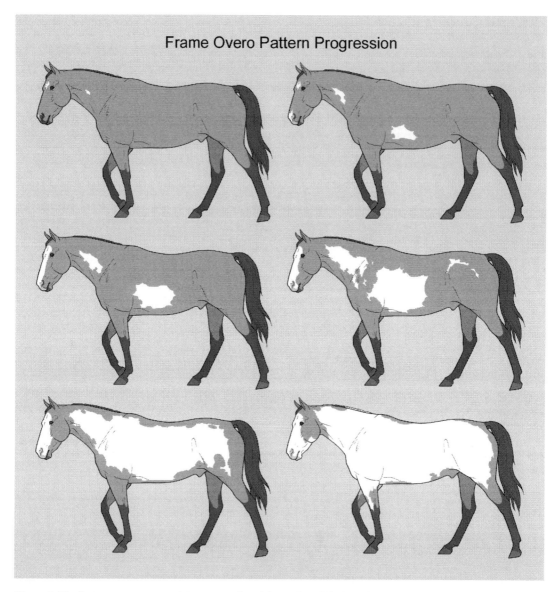

Frame Overo Pattern Progression

Figure 3. The frame overo pattern originates on sides of the neck and the barrel, and merges on the shoulders. In more extensive horses, the white extends to the hindquarters, leaving a dark outline when the horse is viewed in profile.

the areas of the body where frame would normally be visible, many frame-tobiano combinations are cryptic.

When paired with the other overo patterns, frame overo quickly loses the dark legs, and the overall effect is usually a much whiter horse. Frame does tend to keep a dark tail and dorsal area. On more moderately marked overos, espe-

cially sabinos, one of the best clues that frame is involved is the presence of larger areas of opaque white on the broad side of the neck. White tends to be most opaque where a pattern originates, so a sabino (which often does not have very large areas of opaque white anyway) will usually be whitest on the underside of the jaw, and progressively less white as the pattern moves further from that point. Since frame originates on the sides of the neck, white that is most intense there, and that becomes less opaque towards the outer edges of the neck, is a sign the horse may carry a copy of the frame mutation.

At least some of the sabino patterns appear to change the character of the frame pattern itself without adding white to the legs. These horses have what looks like a pure frame pattern, but the outline is lacey and the area on the shoulder where the two white sections connect may be extensively ticked and roaned. The Paint mare SUGAR IN MY TE is a good example of this type of combination.

Inheritance and Testing

Although it was long assumed to be recessive, frame overo is a dominant gene with a variable range of expression. All frame overos have at least one frame overo parent, and an unbroken line of frame ancestors. The minimal, and in some cases cryptic, nature of the pattern can make it seem that the pattern appears spontaneously, but the horses still have the mutation for frame.

Frame is also a homozygous lethal, so all living frame overos are heterozygous. That means a frame overo will produce its own pattern 50 percent of the time. Frame overos with high color production rates carry additional patterns along with frame, since each heterozygous pattern represents a separate 50 percent chance for white patterning. A horse with three different patterning genes would then have a 87.5 percent chance of giving his foals some kind of white pattern. The chance of inheriting the specific frame pattern, however, would still be 50 percent.

Homozygous frames have Lethal White Overo Syndrome (LWOS). The foals are born white or nearly white with blue eyes, and initially appear healthy, but die within a few days. The mutation responsible for frame is on the EDNRB gene. With just one mutated copy, the single non-mutated EDNRB can compensate and perform the tasks needed for normal development. Pigmentation is disrupted, but the horse is otherwise healthy. Homozygous frame overos do not have that non-mutated gene to compensate, and one of the other tasks of that particular gene, the final formation

of the colon, never occurs and the resulting foal cannot survive.

This situation mirrors what is believed to happen with some of the other homozygous lethal colors. Without at least one normal gene to compensate, the foal is not viable. What makes frame overo different is that the condition does not end the pregnancy early. For example, dominant white is assumed to be lethal based on the functions of the genes, and on the fact that no homozygous dominant whites have been identified, but there is no foal. The loss is thought to occur very early in fetal development. Lethal White Overo foals are born, and even seem healthy at first, though they are typically euthanized to prevent suffering. The situation is heartbreaking for everyone involved.

While other patterns, and many combinations of patterns, can produce all-white foals, only frame overo is associated with LWOS. For that reason, ethical breeders test for frame if there is even a remote possibility that the horse could be a carrier.

History and Breed Distribution

To date no ancient samples have tested positive for frame, nor is it present in any of the older isolated populations. Because the confirmed instances of the pattern are limited to New World breeds, it

Horses with more than one overo pattern often have a higher percentage of white on the body. This can make it harder to identify the specific patterns contributing to the final appearance of the horse. Frame is suspect when large areas on the neck and barrel are clear white.

Horses with frame overo patterns are often seen in late nineteenth and early twentieth century photos of Native Americans, suggesting that the pattern was already widespread by that time.

is widely believed to be a more recent mutation. There are images of what appear to be frame overo patterns, including one in a seventeenth-century Ottoman hunting manual. Dr. Phillip Sponenberg has reported seeing horses that appear to have the frame pattern among feral herds in Ethiopia. It is possible then that the pattern originated elsewhere, but was later lost in most Old World populations.

Wherever the mutation originated, the pattern has been widespread in North America for some time. Frame patterns are visible in many of the images taken of Native Americans in the late nineteenth and early twentieth century. It was also found occasionally among the saddle horses of Kentucky during the same time, and is still present, if only rarely, in most of the southern gaited breeds.

Frame overo was common among American pintos, and that was particularly true among the stock horses that were used to establish the American Paint Horse. Just as some registries for solid breeds used an outline to define the area of allowable white, pinto registries often used a mirror image (see page 293) to define the area where a minimal amount of white had to be found. Frame overo was attractive to breeders because the pattern tended to place white in the right areas for foals to qualify for regular papers. Horses with the frame pattern were also more likely to have colored legs, and many horsemen believed that dark hooves are more durable than white ones.

There are also at least two lines of frame overo in the American Shetland, though it is presumed to be the result of outcrossing to American ponies and not one of the colors present among the original imports. The pattern is also present in the Miniature Horse, which shares some bloodlines with the American Shetland. A handful of Thoroughbreds have the frame pattern, though like the Shetland Ponies the original source for the pattern is not clear.

Paint Horses, which are still the primary source for the pattern, have been widely exported in the last few decades, so the pattern can be found outside North America. In the Australian Stock Horse, a descendant of the Paint Horse ADIOS AMIGOS, WATCH THE DUCO, had the pattern. A son of the Paint stallion BLUE MAX was exported to the United Kingdom and was used by the Louella Stud to produce sport horses. Paint Horses are also popular in Germany, and a number of frame overos have been exported there. It is possible that descendants of these horses may one day spread the frame overo to the local horse population, making it possible to find frame overos without a recorded connection to American imports.

Classic Splashed White
(Splashed White-1)

If frame overo was what American pinto breeders had in mind when formulating the rules for identifying overos, then it is pretty clear that the classic splashed white pattern was not. There is hardly an overo rule that the pattern does not break. The legs are all white, the outline is smooth, the tail is partially white and the white crosses the back more often than not.

With the exception of the white face and the blue eyes, classic splash follows more of the tobiano rules, which is why horses with the pattern are often mistaken for toveros. Yet even though classic splashes looks a bit like toveros, many recognize that they do not look quite right for that pattern combination either.

It is understandable that breeders did not take splashed white into account. A lot less was known about white patterning genes, and splashed white was quite rare compared to tobiano, frame and the various types of sabinos. It is also incompletely dominant, so only the homozygous horses had a form of the pattern that made them immediately recognizable as pintos.

The pattern was first described by the Finnish researcher Valto Klemola in a 1931 paper on dominant and recessive spotting in horses. Because the heterozygous horses did not have a spotted phenotype, he proposed the name splashed white for what he believed was a recessive form of spotting. He contrasted the pattern with the more common dominant spotting (now called tobiano). His theory fell out of favor in the late twentieth century when a 1994 study showed that, contrary to popular belief, overos were dominant. It is not known if any splashed white horses were included in that particular study, which analyzed the production records of thirteen different Paint stallions. Splashed white was not common in Paints at that time, so it is quite possible that most of the stallions had some combination of frame and sabino patterns.

In 2012, Klemola's pattern was formally identified as splashed white-1 (*SW1*). The same study found three additional mutations at either the same gene (MITF) or another gene (PAX3) that

performed a similar function in pigmentation. Because the newer splashed white patterns operate differently, they are included in a separate chapter.

Points of Origin (Heterozygotes)
The classic form of splashed white originates on the forehead, the nose, and the feet, particularly the hind feet. The typical markings on a heterozygous classic splash are a star and snip and short hind socks. Blue eyes and blue segments in the eyes do occur in the heterozygotes, but only intermittently.

Although these are the points where white originates, heterozygous splashes do not always have white in those areas. In some of the pony breeds,

The Morgan mare Journey's Made to Order is a good example of the classic splash pattern produced by two copies of the splashed white-1 (SW1) gene. Her heterozygous parents were more minimally marked.

That parents of JOURNEY'S MADE TO ORDER (pictured on the preceding page) each had a blue eye. Her dam JOURNEYS RUMOR HASIT (top) has a comet and two white feet, while her sire ADIELS SNICKER ZIP (bottom) has a star, snip and four white feet. Both horses are typical of horses that are heterozygous for splashed white-1.

and so far testing, though still its early stages, has supported that theory.

As the pattern progresses, the white tends to travel upward towards the topline, crossing the croup and turning the tail white, or crossing the back to form a band around the midsection. Horses with this kind of banded pattern are the ones most likely to be mistaken for toveros. White also spreads under the chest and along the underside of the neck to join with the white on the head.

In the more extensively white patterns, the entire body from just behind the forehand to the end of the tail will be white, while the shoulders and neck remain colored. In some horses the white on the face can spread over the ears, until the horse is white from nose to mid-neck. On rare occasions, some portion of the face will retain color, usually over one side of the face, though the eyes are still blue. Classic splash is often very asymmetrical, so it is not unusual to find one side has more extensive white patterning than the other.

Areas of Exclusion
Even in the most extensively white horses, classic patterns tend to retain some color along the top of the neck and shoulders. Unlike most other pinto patterns, classic splashes do not necessarily retain color on their ears.

Behavior with Other Colors and Patterns
As is often the case, the presence of the sabino pattern tends to boost the amount of white. Classic splashed patterns are slightly whiter on average in breeds that have sabino than in breeds that do not. The difference is even more noticeable in the horses that have only one copy of splashed white-1 (*SW1*). Instead of ordinary white markings, the heterozygous horses are much more likely to have what is often thought of as the "moderate" expression of splashed white: white face, blue eyes, stock-

they often have a lot less, and there have been at least two horses that have tested positive for one copy of the mutation that have no white markings whatsoever. The amount of white on the heterozygotes does not have any bearing on the horse's ability to produce a loud classic pattern if bred to another classic splash.

Pattern of Progression (Homozygotes)
Without another pattern to boost the amount of white, the heterozygous horses have what look like ordinary white markings, if they have markings at all. The homozygous horses have the classic splash pattern, which is sometimes called obvious splash because it has such a distinctive appearance. Prior to the identification of the mutation responsible, the classic pattern was used to confirm the presence of splashed white in a breed or bloodline.

Even at the minimal end of its expression, horses with the classic pattern are very white. All four legs, the face, the end of the tail and a significant portion of the belly are white. It is believed that all homozygous classic splashes have two blue eyes,

ings and belly white. Some forms of sabino alter the edges of the classic splash pattern, making them look more lacey.

When paired with tobiano, classic splash can skew the tobiano pattern in unusual ways. Many of the horses that look like classic splashes, but that have oddly placed patches of color on their face are tobianos with the splashed white pattern. Horses with this combination are also quite prone to medicine hat markings where the colored patch only partially covers the ears. Tobianos with color that extends unusually far on the neck, or that have color along the topline that comes down in front of the hip in a point are also suspected of carrying a copy of the classic splash pattern.

Inheritance and Testing

Classic splashed white is incompletely dominant. One copy of the gene results in a horse with what look like ordinary markings, though some individuals are unmarked. Two copies produce the very distinctive classic splashed white pattern.

Because the heterozygous horses do not always look different from a horse with ordinary markings, the classic pattern can appear unexpectedly. Although the minimally-marked classic splashes will always have a splashed white parent, and horses with the full-blown pattern will always have two, the parents may not necessarily be recognized as splashes until they produce the classic pattern. This is especially true in breeds that lack the white patterning genes that tend to boost the amount of white. In breeds where sabinos are common, the heterozygous splashes can be easier to identify because they are more likely to have large white face and leg markings and blue eyes.

There is a commercially available test for identifying horses that have the splashed white-1 (*SW1*) mutation. Unlike the other known splashed white mutations, classic splash is not lethal. It is associated with a higher incidence of deafness, but formal studies have not been done to determine the frequency. Classic splash is a mutation of the MITF gene, which is also associated with white patterning and increased rates of deafness in dogs.

There is at least one splashed white family that has a roany version of the classic pattern that does

not test positive for splashed white-1. These horses all trace to the Australian Paint Horse stallion BALD EAGLE.

History and Breed Distribution

Although it was not yet possible to test the samples for splashed white when the original study on ancient colors was done, it is quite likely that classic splash is an old mutation. It dates back to at least 982 AD, since it is found among the Icelandic horses which have been isolated from outside crosses since that time.

The horses in the Klemola study all descended from one Finnish draft stallion, EVERSTI (1876). Klemola observed the pattern in Norwegian, Danish and Swedish horses and believed that it originated in the native breeds of Northern Europe. It is found in many of the Nordic breeds, including the Døle-Gudbrandsdal, North Swedish, Coldblooded Trotter, Gotland Pony and Icelandic. It is also found in some of the oldest strains of the Welsh Mountain Pony. It is also found in American Shetlands and Miniature Horses, which may have gotten the pattern either from the original Scottish ponies, or outcrosses to Welsh Ponies.

A photo exists of an obvious splash stallion in East Prussia (fifth horse in Figure 4), dated just be-

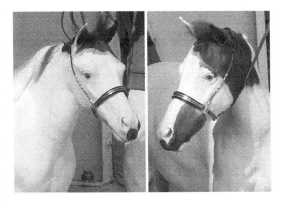

The classic splashed white pattern sometimes covers one or both ears. Small dark spots on the muzzle (sometimes called "kissy spots") are not typical of classic splash, but larger dark patches on the lower face are occasionally seen. Although some homozygous splashes have some color on the head, this appears to be more common in horses that have both classic splash and tobiano.

Homozygous Splash Overo Patterns

Figure 4. The horses pictured here are all believed to be homozygous for the splashed white-1 mutation. Prior to the advent of testing, the presence of this type of pattern in a breed was used to confirm the presence of splashed white. The newer splashed white mutations do not appear to progress much further than the pattern in the lower right corner.

fore the end of World War II. At least one line of splashed white Trakehners has since tested positive for splashed white-1. There is speculation that the color may trace to the Thoroughbred Blair Athol (1861), who had a wide blaze. To date, no Thoroughbreds with the full, classic pattern have been identified. It remains to be seen if any test positive for the original (*SW1*) mutation.

The Arabians that have been tested were negative for this form of splashed white, and the only eastern breeds where unmistakable classic patterns have been found are the Kathiawaris and Marwaris of India. One blue-eyed tovero mare was tested (see page 9), but came back negative for the classic splash mutation (*SW1*), so another splashed mutation may be involved.

Classic splash is present in low numbers in most of the American breeds, including Morgans, Saddlebreds, Foxtrotters, Paints, Appaloosas and Quarter Horses. In stock horses, the most common source for the classic pattern is OLD FRED, particularly through his great-granddaughter PLAUDETTE, who had extremely successful descendants in all three stock horse breeds. There are other suspected classic splash lines, many of them tracing back to OLD BILLY, who was the great-grandsire of OLD FRED. One of the best-known classic splash Paint stallions, GAMBLING MAN, traces back in multiple lines to both OLD FRED and OLD BILLY.

Classic splash is less common among the South American horses, though a few Puerto Rican Pasos have had what looks like the classic pattern. Because the research into both classic splash and the other splashed white mutations is ongoing, and because many horses with very white faces, or with blue eyes test negative, it is quite likely that there are more splash mutations. While the two newly identified splashed white mutations appear to produce only the most minimal end of the classic splash pattern themselves, unidentified mutations might prove to have a different range of expression. For that reason, horses with a classic pattern, but that do not belong to breeds or families that have tested positive for classic splash (*SW1*) may later prove to have a different splashed mutation.

Other Splash Patterns

When the long-awaited test for splashed white was announced, the fact there were multiple mutations took many by surprise. Sabino has long been assumed to be polygenic, but splashed white was widely considered to be a single pattern.

The study found four different mutations, and with many horses testing negative it seems likely that still more will be identified. At the moment though, the known splashed white patterns consist of one very old mutation that is rare but relatively broadly distributed, two modern mutations that are limited to a single breeding group, and one individual believed to be sterile.

Splashed White-2
The splashed white-2 mutation is believed to have originated with the Quarter Horse mare KATIE GUN. Although she was not affected by the mutation herself, at least two of her sons, COLONELS SMOKINGUN (Gunner) and SPOOKS GOTTA GUN have produced foals that tested positive. With sixteen registered foals, many with splashed white traits, it is possible that other sons and daughters carry the mutation. Katie was also heterozygous

Horses with the two newer splashed white mutations, SW2 and SW3, often have patterns similar in appearance to this mare. Both mutations are believed to have originated in the American stock horse breeds.

for classic splash (*SW1*), so some of her offspring inherited both mutations. COLONEL SMOKINGUN has produced descendants with both types of patterns. Deafness in the family has also been widely reported.

The splashed white-2 mutation does not appear to produce the high levels of body white seen in the classic splash pattern (Figure 4), even when paired with one copy of splashed white-1. Most splashed white-2 horses have extensive white on the face, blue eyes, and stockings. The one horse in the study that was homozygous for classic splash and heterozygous for splashed white-2 was entirely white and deaf.

Unlike the other splashed white patterns, which are located on the MITF gene, splashed white-2 is located on PAX3. Based on similar mutations in other animals, and the known function of the PAX3 gene, it is believed that splashed white-2 is a homozygous lethal. No homozygous horses have been identified and it is assumed that they are lost early during pregnancy.

Splashed White-3
Less is known about the third splashed white mutation. It was found in a single Paint mare and her daughter. The daughter also carried one copy of the classic splash mutation (*SW1*) and was completely white, while the mother had a white head, blue eyes, four stockings and a white belly. Although the mare was not identified by name, researchers indicated her mutation was rare. Like classic splash and the macchiato pattern, it was caused by a mutation to the MITF gene, but unlike classic splash it was believed that the pattern was semi-lethal in its homozygous state. Similar mutations in mice result in microphthalmia (small, damaged eyes) in homozygotes.

Macchiato
Researchers retained the name being used by breeders, macchiato, for the fourth splashed white mutation identified in the study. The source for the mutation was the 2008 Freiberger stallion APACHE DU PEUPE. As the name might suggest, in addition to adding white patterning and blue eyes, the mutation diluted his bay coat to a pale coffee color. Although his is the first known mutation in horses

*This filly (top) and colt (bottom) come from the Austra-
lian Bald Eagle line of Paint Horses. Although horses from
this family frequently have patterns that closely resemble
homozygous classic splash horses, they test negative for
the three known splash mutations.*

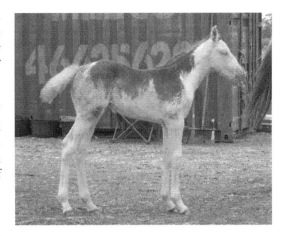

that was both a pattern and a dilution, some MITF
mutations in human beings have been associated
with pale hair and eyes, piebald patches and deafness. Although he has blue eyes, the pattern on
APACHE more closely resembles those on some of
the dominant white and patchy sabinos.

Bald Eagle Splash

In her book *Horse Color Explained*, Jeanette
Gower described a family of splashed white Paint
Horses that originated with the stallion BALD
EAGLE. The horses have what appear to be classic
splash patterns, or in some cases very roany versions of the classic splash pattern, but the mode
of inheritance suggests that the pattern is dominant rather than incompletely dominant. Breeders believe the pattern is a lethal dominant, and
that deafness is common. Several horses from this
line have been tested, and are negative for all the
known splashed white patterns. It is thought that
they carry a splashed white pattern that has not
yet been identified.

Some horses from the Bald Eagle line have been
described as somewhat diluted in color. Other
horses with splashed white phenotypes, but that
test negative for the current patterns, have also appeared to be lighter than would be typical for their
base color, though not as dramatically diluted as
the horse with the macchiato mutation.

Other Splashed White Patterns

Because many splash tests have come back negative, some breeders have concluded that the tests
are inaccurate. They are accurate for what they
test, but they are likely incomplete. Like sabino

and dominant white, it is possible that only a frac-
tion of the patterns in this group have been found.
Some of the horses that test negative, like the Bald
Eagle Paint Horses, probably have mutations that
simply have not yet been identified. Because the
research team intends to examine these cases more
closely, it is likely that in the future the group of
testable splash patterns will be more complete.

It is also quite possible that the splash pattern
has been over-diagnosed, particularly among horses with blue eyes. Research into dominant white
and the sabino patterns may shed more light on the
differences between the three pattern categories, as
well as the specific patterns within each group.

Sabino-1

Much like overo, sabino is more accurately understood as a pattern category than as a single pattern.
Taken as a group, the sabino patterns are the most
common type of spotting in horses. What they have
in common is that they are an exaggeration of the
face and leg markings found on solid horses, but
beyond that generalization they show a great deal
of variation. Some sabinos are patchy, with distinct
areas of white and colored hair. Some have patterns
with ragged edges but very little roaning, while others are heavily roaned and ticked with no distinct

*Horses with one copy of the sabino-1 gene display the sa-
bino pattern, with sabino roans being the most common
expression (top). Horses with two copies of sabino-1 are
born white (bottom).*

areas of dark and white. Their range of expression
is one of the things that makes them so interesting,
and also what makes studying them challenging.

The Incompletely Dominant Sabino
Although it is widely accepted that there are many
different sabino patterns, to date only one has been
formally identified. Because it was the first, it was
given the name sabino-1. The expectation is that
there will be more patterns in the series, all numbered in the order of their discovery.

Sabino-1 is the only pattern in the group identifiable with a test, but in many ways it is atypical for
sabino. The most obvious difference is that it is incompletely dominant. Horses with one copy of sa-
bino-1 have a sabino pattern. Horses with two copies of sabino-1 are white. Those white horses have
led to confusion in two different ways. In the past,
homozygous sabino-1 horses have been mistaken
for dominant whites. The distinction between the
two patterns still confuses many horsemen.

The other mistake was to view the horses as the
whitest end of a continuum of varying expression
of the sabino pattern—as "maximum sabinos".
They do represent the whitest form taken by a
sabino pattern, but they are not simply the upper
limit of a pattern that ranges from "marked with
white" to "entirely white", any more than cremellos
are the upper limit to a series of successively lighter
palominos. This is why sabino-1 does not lend itself well to a pattern progression chart. The heterozygous horses are suspected to have a limited
range of expression unless other patterns are present, and the homozygotes do not vary significantly.

Points of Origin (Heterozygotes)
As with other sabinos, the white originates on the
face and under the jaw, on the legs and under the
belly, favoring the area close to the girth. White on
the leg can be very asymmetrical, and disconnected patches of white are not uncommon. Roaning is
consistently present on the entire body, including
the mane and the tail.

Pattern of Progression (Heterozygotes)
The most minimally marked sabino-1 horses have
some white on the face and roan hairs. Most will

have some white on the legs, but there are horses that have tested positive for the pattern that have unmarked legs.

In horses that have a little more patterning, the white tends to spread over the face, widening across the forehead, but narrowing somewhat below the eyes and wrapping around the nose and under the jaw. The legs are more likely to be white, though the placement of the white can be quite erratic. There may be white on the belly and girth, and the roaning is often more pronounced.

Once the pattern has reached the point that the white has spread in multiple patches on the body, the hind legs are almost always white. Often all four are white, though on horses with particularly irregular patterns the white does not always include the lower leg or hoof. The body may be extensively roaned and appear quite pale.

After this stage, it is unclear just how far the pattern will progress without the presence of other white modifiers. There are sabino-1 horses that have flecks of clear white, particularly across the hindquarters, that mimic the direction of the hair growth. On some horses, the white flecks connect to form a lacey network, or grow larger until the coat has a faintly swirly appearance. The Tennessee Walking Horse stallion PUSHER'S COAT OF COLOR is a good example of this type of pattern. Others have extensive white, but the border between the white and the roaned areas is soft and indistinct.

Some have theorized that sabino-1 horses with extensive white or more distinct patches carry additional sabino patterns, or perhaps a dominant white mutation. It is also possible that they carry smaller modifying genes that boost existing white patterns. Because many of the breeds that have sabino-1 have other patterning genes, the upper limit for sabino-1 by itself is not known.

Areas of Exclusion (Heterozygotes)
Even if the more extensively marked sabino-1 horses are carrying one of the other white patterns, the pattern has a strong tendency to retain color on the ears, the poll, and along the spine. The area around the eyes, and the eyes themselves, also tend to remain dark.

Homozygotes (Sabino Whites)
Horses with two copies of the sabino-1 mutation are born white with pink skin. All tested homozygous sabino-1 horses have had patterns that were at least 90 percent white. The vast majority are close to pure white, with only a few small spots of pigment on the ears, around the eyes, or down the front of the neck. Those that do have some color have faint roan areas on the poll and ears, along the spine, and in the mane or tail.

Most sabino whites have dark eyes, though blue eyes do occur. In Tennessee Walking Horses, where the sabino-1 pattern was once the predominant color, a portion of the white-born Walking Horses had one or both eyes blue. It is also possible that the blue eyes, like the more vivid white patches, were due to an additional pattern or modifier.

Behavior with Other Colors and Patterns
When paired with tobiano, sabino-1 tends to break the colored areas of the tobiano pattern apart. The result is a very distinctive torn-tissue look to the colored areas. Aside from the white on the face, the placement of the dark areas of the tobiano pattern are not greatly altered, but the color inside those areas is ragged and patchy. Johann Georg von Hamilton's famous painting *The Piebald Stallion at the Eisgruber Stud* captures the tobiano-sabino-1 combination quite faithfully.

When paired with frame overo, sabino-1 often gives a more extensively white pattern, because it tends to add the white legs that the frame pattern lacks. It also will add roaning to the colored areas, though the contrast between the dorsal area, which both patterns tend to exclude, and the rest of the pattern is greater than in sabino-1 horses without frame.

It is possible to get a heterozygous sabino-1 horse that is visually indistinguishable from an all-white homozygote by combining patterns. Because these combined patterns often include either frame or splashed white, the horses are more likely than true homozygous sabino-1 horses to have blue eyes.

Inheritance and Testing
Sabino-1 is an incompletely dominant gene. Horses that have one copy of the mutation have a sa-

bino pattern, and horses that have two copies are white. Although the homozygotes are born white, the color is unrelated to Lethal White Overo Syndrome; sabino white horses have no health issues.

Horses that have one copy of the sabino-1 gene will produce sabinos 50 percent of the time. Crossing two sabino-1 horses will produce 50 percent sabinos, 25 percent solids and 25 percent sabino white. When bred to solids, sabino whites produce sabinos 100 percent of the time. Bred together, sabino whites produce 100 percent white foals.

This is the essential difference between sabino-1 and dominant white. Both mutations produce white horses, but one is homozygous for an incompletely dominant gene, and one is heterozygous for a gene that is lethal when homozygous. As viable homozygotes, sabino whites could be used to develop a true-breeding population of white horses. As a homozygous lethal, dominant white could not.

Their ability to produce color is different, too. The sabino white will, when bred to solids, produce nothing but sabinos. What he cannot do, though, is produce another white, unless he is bred to another sabino-1 horse. The dominant white, when bred to solid mates, will produce 50 percent whites (defined loosely, as will be explained in the next chapter) and 50 percent solids. What he cannot do is produce 100 percent white.

There is a commercially available test for identifying sabino-1. Because most horses with the sabino pattern are not believed to carry sabino-1, many breeders interested in color opt not to test for it. Absent test results, sabino roans that consistently produce white foals, or populations that have a mix of sabino roan and white horses, are often assumed to have sabino-1.

History and Breed Distribution
The other big difference between sabino-1 and dominant white is the origin of the pattern. The sabino-1 mutation first appeared sometime between 2500 and 3000 BC, making it the oldest identified pinto patterning gene. The first known sabino-1 was found at the Tartas-1 burial site in western Siberia. The gene was also found in later Bronze Age samples, one from Lchasen in Armenia and a second from Miciurin in Moldova. Modern sabino-1 horses carry that same mutation, passed down through the ages. The identified dominant white families are all modern mutations.

Although sabino-1 has been a part of the equine population for close to five millennium, it is quite limited in its distribution. It is notably absent among the primitive pony breeds, even those that originated in the areas where the pattern was first found. Even in breeds where it is found, it is often a minority color. It is likely that once fashions changed, the flashy, irregular markings (never mind a reputation for producing white foals!) would have caused many sabinos to be culled from breeding programs. Yet even during the Baroque period when color was fashionable, sabino-1 horses do not seem to have had a major impact.

The one time the color enjoyed a brief surge of popularity was during the formation of the Tennessee Walking Horse. There the pattern traces back to Roan Allen, and his influence ensured that for the first few decades at least, most horses in the stud book had the gene. From the Walking Horse it spread to many of the other American gaited breeds. There is good reason to believe the original Copperbottom horses had sabino-1, which might explain its presence in many of the American breeds. In Europe, the pattern was common in Drenthe, and from there spread to the Groninger. It is still found on rare occasions in European warmbloods. It is also suspected to be present in the Marwaris of India, which have both sabino roans and white-borns. It is also found in Gypsy Horses, though like many breeds with sabino roans, there are also horses that look like heterozygous sabino-1 horses, but that test negative for the pattern.

Dominant White

Dominant white is the second pinto pattern, after sabino-1, that can produce a truly white foal. Like sabino-1, it tends to be the subject of a lot of confusion. Part of the problem is the name, which only accurately describes some of the horses that have the mutation. It is also the case that it is impossible to speak about dominant white as a single color. Dominant white is really a group of mutations, each slightly different, that all produce a white or somewhat-white horse.

It is those not-quite-white horses that create problems, because the ones that are not white often have patterns that are visually indistinguishable from what has traditionally been called sabino. Indeed, when the first handful of dominant white mutations were identified, some color enthusiasts were quite vexed that they were not added to the sabino series as sabino-2 through sabino-5. Even now, many owners of horses from known dominant white families, especially those prone to a spotted expression, prefer to call their horses sabino because it requires less explanation. In the case of breeding stallions, the name sabino often gives mare owners a more accurate impression of the type of patterns the horse is likely to produce.

There are eleven dominant white mutations described in peer-reviewed papers. It is believed that more have been identified, but these have not yet been published. Beyond those eleven founders and their families, there are more horses that, by the circumstances of their own birth and their production records, are believed to be dominant whites. There are many more historical instances that also fit the profile. Each represents a separate, unique mutation with a slightly different range of expression.

Range of Expression
There are dominant white families that consistently produce all-white coats. One of the older American white lines, OLD KING, was known for producing uniformly white offspring. The Camarillo White Horses, which were the fourth identified dominant white family (*W4*), also tend to be very white. Other families, like that of the

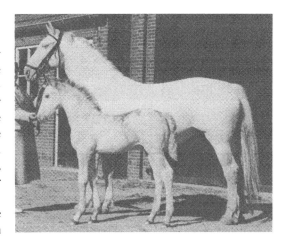

The Groninger mare SNEEUWWITJE and her filly MARMORA by the Friesian stallion LUTSEN. Because SNEEUWWITJE produced white foals like MARMORA from solid sires, it is thought that she was a dominant white mutation. Had she been a sabino white (homozygous for sabino-1), all her foals from solid mates should have been sabino.

Thoroughbred PUCHILINGUI (*W5*), produce patterns very similar to patchy sabinos (Figure 6 on page 75). Quite a few of the founders, including PUCHILINGUI and the Icelandic mare THOKKADIS VOM ROSENHOF, look like sabino roans. Some dominant whites are born with colored hairs that fade as the horse matures, leaving ghost spots on the skin under the white hair. Although each family has a tendency to throw a certain type of pattern, it seems possible to get the fully white horses from each family, even if it is more rare in some than in others. Likewise, all dominant whites appear to throw at least some percentage of broken-colored foals.

This tendency to throw a mix of both white and pinto offspring has caused frustration for breeders trying to produce pure white horses. If dominant white can be thought of as an attempt to block pigment from migrating to its proper place during fetal development, then it can be said that it is not always very effective; the barrier is often pretty leaky. When that happens, the resulting horse is spotted rather than white. In almost every account of white breeding programs, there is mention of the tendency to throw spotted patterns along with

The name dominant white is somewhat misleading, because many horses with dominant white mutations look like sabinos. This Thoroughbred stallion, SATO, comes from a dominant white family (W5) that is known for producing horses with this type of pattern.

the whites. Some German writers have preferred the term *weißgeborener scheck*, or white-born pinto, to reflect that reality.

Eye Color

Dominant whites are sometimes called dark-eyed whites, which helps differentiate them from the nearly white blue-eyed creams. Dark eyes have also been used to make the point that these horses are not albinos. Yet a reading of historic accounts and early studies, as well as a study of current examples, makes it clear that many of the horses have or had blue or partially blue eyes. This is true even of horses believed to have carried the original mutations. Founders (or suspected founders) known to have blue eyes include:

SNEEUWWITJE
1952 Groninger mare, white, both eyes blue

MONT BLANC II
1963 Thoroughbred stallion, white, partial blues

CLARENCE STEWART
1977 Thoroughbred stallion, white, both eyes blue

GRAND ESPOIR BLANC
1984 Thoroughbred stallion, white, both eyes blue

THOKKADIS VOM ROSENHOF
2003 Icelandic mare, sabino roan, one eye blue

VERY WHITE DU VALLON
2007 Ardennes stallion, white, both eyes blue

Because blue eyes are found with some consistency in both the founders and the descendants, even in otherwise solid or minimally-marked breeds, it seems likely that dominant white can produce blue eyes independent of other white patterns, even if dark eyes are more typical.

Inheritance and Testing

Dominant white is, as its name suggests, a dominant gene. Dominant white horses give the mutation to 50 percent of their offspring. The percentage that are actually white may be much lower, but half will have some kind of white patterning.

Dominant white is believed to be a homozygous lethal. In the past, this was supported by color production ratios that suggested the homozygotes were lost early during fetal development, and also by the fact that even in concentrated white breeding programs there were no examples of true-breeding horses. When the mutations were mapped, it became clear that most, if not all, homozygous dominant white mutations would not be viable because the function of the KIT gene would be compromised.

Heterozygous dominant whites produce like other dominant colors. Where dominant white is different from other dominant genes is the expectation that one of the parents will also have the color. Color mutations are extremely rare, and most patterned horses are the present-day descendants of a founding horse that lived hundreds if not thousands of years ago. Had records been kept that far back, the pedigree would show at least one line of continuous descent (sometimes called the color line by those who research the incidence of color in different breeds or families) back to the original mutation. Dominant whites are different in that the type of mutation that produces them occurs far more often. Of the eleven identified dominant whites families, all have founders born in the last hundred years, and the majority have founders born in the last thirty years. Because this type of mutation happens with surprising frequency, dominant whites do not necessarily have generations of dominant white ancestors. In fact, the spontaneous occurrence of a white foal from completely ordinary parents is considered strong evidence of a new dominant white mutation.

Because dominant white mutations are all slightly different, there is not one dominant white test—there are eleven. It is possible to test for those eleven mutations, though most of the families are too small for the tests to be profitable. Those tests cannot determine if an unexpected white foal is a new dominant white mutation, though. For that reason, most new occurrences of spontaneous white foals are presumed to be dominant whites because they fit the profile.

History and Breed Distribution

The specific nature of the current dominant white tests make it difficult to trace the dominant white mutation back to antiquity. Older references to white horses offer little guidance, since sabino-1, which can produce a white horse, and the cream dilution, which produces a horse that could be described as white, are both old mutations. Grey is likewise suspected to be quite old, and many scholars suspect that some of the white horses in historical accounts were aged greys.

Stud books provide the best resource for tracking color mutations, since it is possible to examine colors and often the markings in a pedigree, but few stud books date back further than the late nineteenth century. For much of that time, there was a strong selection bias for dark, conservatively-marked horses. Instances of spontaneous whites were probably under-reported.

The one group where dominant white foals were more consistently documented is the Thoroughbred, where white foals have long been considered a novelty. The earliest known instance was a colt called White Cross, born in Tennessee in 1896. An unrelated white filly, called Woher?, was born in Germany in 1925. Although these and other instances attracted some attention at the time, it

was the three white foals born in 1963 that were widely reported outside the racing community. The first two were half-siblings, War Colors and White Beauty. Their sire KY Colonel, said to have been an extensively marked chestnut, is thought to have been the founder, and theirs is the second identified mutation (*W2*). The last of the three foals was the French colt Mont Blanc II. Others followed, including Glacial and Miasmic in Australia, both daughters of Milady Fair. Her pattern, and those of some of the offspring of the white Thoroughbreds, could be described as sabino roan. The fact that many of these hors-

Genes versus Mutations

Because white-born horses occur spontaneiously from ordinary parents, dominant white is widely understood to be a mutation. Because white morphs are common in a wide variety of animals, it fits the mental image most people have of a mutated color.

Other colors are more often referred to as genes. A horse might be said to have the cream gene or the tobiano gene. This gives the impression that these colors are somehow different from something like dominant white, but they are not. The "cream gene" is actually just a mutation—a very old mutation—to the MATP gene. All horses, and many other animals (including human beings) have the MATP gene. Only cream-diluted horses have that particular mutation to it.

The term gene is often used in non-technical discussions of color, because it is less confusing and because mutation tends to have a negative connotation in popular culture. It is more accurate, though, to say mutation. The two terms are used interchangeably in this book.

es seemed to produce broken colors was known even then, and it was not unusual to come across comments about "albino" Thoroughbreds carrying "overo". Most breeders chose to highlight the appearance of white foals, and downplay the connection to pintos.

There were also instances of white-born foals in Arabians and Standardbreds, though they did not seem to get as much attention in the press. White-born foals in the draft breeds were far more rare, even though many Clydesdales and a smaller portion of Shires have sabino roan patterns almost identical to those seen on some dominant whites. Spontaneous whites have also been relatively rare in the pony breeds. White foals are born in the American Shetland Pony, but it is likely that most of these are homozygous for sabino-1. The Tennessee Walking Horse and its related breeds are often white at birth, but since one of the founder

stallions had sabino-1, they are usually assumed to have that mutation and not dominant white.

Dominant white mutations can occur in breeds where sabino-1 is found. That was the case with SNEEWWITJE, a Groninger mare born in 1952. She was identified by the Dutch researcher J. K. Wiersema as a horse that did not fit the mode of inheritance he saw in the other white-born Groningers. His theory that the majority were sabinos, and that SNEEWWITJE had a dominant white pattern has since been proven correct.

In recent years the instances of new (presumed) dominant white mutations have risen considerably. White foals have been born to unpatterned parents in the Standardbred, Holsteiner, Ardennes, Haflinger, Icelandic and Finnhorse. The rate at which new dominant white mutations occur is not currently known, but evidence suggests that it is significantly higher than previously expected.

Manchado

Manchado is one of the most distinctive, and yet least understood of the formally identified pinto patterns. It is usually classified as a type of overo, though in many ways it visually resembles some of the appaloosa patterns. That is because small, rounded spots are abundant inside the white areas of the pattern. There is no connection to leopard complex, though, and a closer inspection shows these horses do not look quite right for appaloosas.

The pattern is quite unique and extraordinarily rare. Because of this, generalizations about manchado are by necessity based on a small number of individuals. Even so, there are some consistent characteristics.

Points of Origin
Manchado patterning is unusual in that the white originates along the topline. Body white in the other overo patterns originates on the underside of the horse, or in the case of frame overo, on the broad sides of the horse. The only other pinto pattern that originates along the topline is tobiano.

Manchado does share the topline origin with tobiano, but the precise location on that topline is a little different. Manchado favors the entire length of the neck rather than the withers as a starting point. For that reason, minimally marked manchados often appear to have an unusual concentration of white patterning along their neck compared to other patterns.

The white at the other end of the topline is similarly shifted from the tobiano, so that it appears to originate at the tailhead rather than the top of the croup. Although the extent does vary, significant white on the tailhead appears to be a feature of the manchado pattern.

Perhaps most unusual of all is the involvement of the forelock area and ears. So far all the known manchados have appeared to have some amount of white in these areas, and many have extensive amounts. Typically there are round spots inside this white as well, though smaller in scale than those found on the body. Although it is hard to tell for certain from limited photographs, on some individuals it appears that the white patterning be-

tween the ears continues down the front of the face to merge with a blaze or bald face marking.

Pattern of Progression
Manchado starts along the topline, concentrated primarily in the area between the ears and withers, and again at the tailhead. From the top of the neck it tends to spread downward towards the chest, and from there back towards the middle of the body. From the tailhead it spreads along the dorsal area and down under the tail towards the inner thighs and genitals. In more extensively marked horses, the hindquarters are included in the patterning, until it merges with the patterning on the forehand.

Throughout the interior of the white areas there are rounded spots of widely varying sizes. Often these spots run together, cluster and overlap, creating irregular patches alongside the smaller round spots. Some individuals also have patches that do not appear to be clusters of round spots so much as irregular blocks of body color. Sometimes these patches are of significant size. This gives the pattern a more chaotic, and less regular, appearance than the typical leopard or blanketed appaloosa.

Areas of Exclusion
If manchado is like tobiano in that the white originates along the topline, it is unlike tobiano—and very like frame overo—in that the white patterning avoids the legs. Even when there is extensive patterning on the body, it usually ends somewhere above the hocks on the hind legs and above the knees or fetlocks o the front legs. Some manchados have white markings on the legs, but these look much like the leg markings seen on the average horse. That contrasts with the wilder nature of the rest of their pattern, so that often these look as if they were added on separately, rather than an extension of the pattern itself.

Aside from the forelock and ears, the head also tends to remain dark. This appears to be true even when the horse is extensively patterned. There have been manchados with white face markings, and even a few with broad white on their faces, but like the leg markings these look as if they have been added by some other factor.

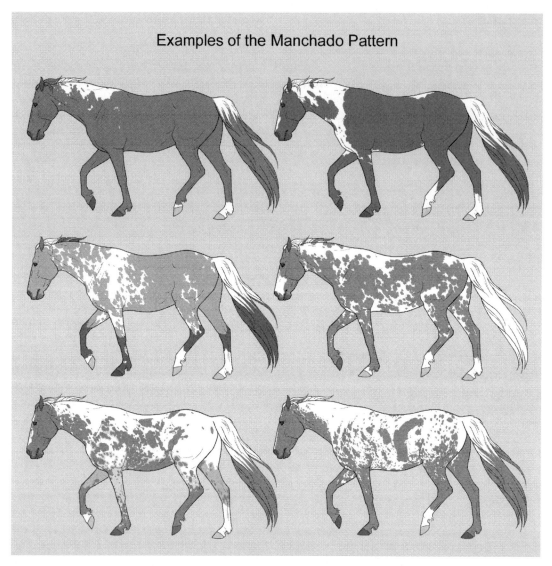

Examples of the Manchado Pattern

Figure 5. These examples of the manchado pattern were taken from the following horses (left to right, starting at the top): Gepera Lagarto, Anglo-Normand; unknown Criollo; Payanca Pinturita, Criollo; Greenmeadows Prince Charly, Hackney; Royal Manchado, Thoroughbred; Trabag, Arabian. All were bred in Argentina.

The other area that retains color even when the horse is extensively marked is the tail end. Like the patterning on the front of the face, this can be more difficult to determine conclusively from photographs than from direct observation. Staining of a white tail can give the impression that the tail end is dark, but in most cases the manchados have tails that have a significant amount of dark hair that contrasts quite sharply with the bordering white hairs.

Behavior with Other Colors and Patterns
With so few individuals to study, it is difficult to known just how manchado might interact with other colors and patterns. So far the pattern has occurred on chestnut, bay and brown base colors,

and at least one has also had the dun dilution. A black manchado has not been identified, but this could be due to the relatively rarity of that base color combined with the rarity of the pattern. Chestnut manchados have been the most common, but that may be due to base color frequencies in the breeds where manchado has been found. The most extensively marked manchados have all been chestnut, which would be consistent with the way other white patterns work, but it should be noted the most minimal pattern was also found on a chestnut.

With so few individuals to compare, it is hard to know how the other patterning genes might interact with the manchado pattern. So far all the horses have had some degree of ordinary white markings, but none have had an immediately identifiable pattern besides manchado. There has been at least one sabino horse that has some of the characteristics of the manchado pattern, including the densely clustered round spots on the white background and the very white tailhead.

Inheritance

Just as there are too few horses to get a clear picture of the full range for the pattern or its interactions with other patterns, the exact mechanism behind the pattern is not known. Because the pattern has cropped up in members of the same family, but has done so only sporadically, it is suspected to be the result of a recessive gene.

History and Breed Distribution

The first horse with the manchado pattern to garner widespread attention was the loudly marked Argentinian Arabian mare, TRABAG. She was pictured in the Lady Wentworth book *The World's Best Horse* (1958) in a chapter on palomino and parti-coloured horses. Although belly-spotted Arabians were not unheard of at the time, her pattern stood out as distinctly odd.

For many with an interest in horse color, TRABAG remained a singular individual until 2002 when an image of a "leopard appaloosa" Hackney mare began to circulate on the internet. That mare was LA BARRANCOSA ECLAT, and it was clear that she had some variation of the same pattern as

TRABAG. ECLAT and her grandson GREENMEADOWS PRINCE CHARLY proved that TRABAG's pattern was not a one-time occurrence.

Although awareness of manchado is relatively recent, evidence suggests that the pattern is an older mutation. In his book *Overos Manchados*, Alberto Martin Labiano gives the history of six purebred manchado horses in five separate breeds. The earliest horse was foaled in 1946 and the most recent in 1993. Because the five breeds are not closely related, it is assumed that the pattern dates back to a time before their populations were separated.

That distribution, restricted to a single country, was perhaps the most puzzling aspect of the pattern. So far all known manchados have occurred within Argentina, yet within that country the pattern has been found across a wide cross-section of breeds: Arabian, Thoroughbred, Anglo-Norman, Criollo, Hackney and Polo Pony. With such a seemingly unrelated grouping, some have wondered if the pattern might be due to environmental rather than genetic factors.

It seems more likely that the isolation is due to the founder effect, rather than something strange about the environment of Argentina. A founder effect occurs when a population starts with a relatively small breeding group, and unusual qualities

This sabino Pato Pony has some of the characteristics of a manchado, including the clustered dark spots inside the white markings and the white tailhead. The clustered spots are much smaller, and much denser, than is typical for a manchado. This may be one way that sabino interacts with manchado.

in those ancestors are amplified in the new population, even as they become rare or are lost entirely to the larger population. Late nineteenth-century literature is full of references to colored horses being bred for the Argentinian market. This would have increased the chance that rare and unusual horses might end up there.

It is also true that the breeds where it has occurred are not as disparate as one might think. Breeds are more distinct from one another now, but that was not the case as recently as a hundred years ago. With the possible exception of the Arabian, almost every Argentinian breed where manchado individuals have occurred began with top-crossing stallions on local mares. If a color was in the local mare population, and was not intentionally bred out, then it could spread across a wide group of breeds. If the gene occurred only rarely, as might happen with a recessive, it might go unnoticed by many breeders until an unexpected individual appeared. If the breed was already known for white patterning, which could be true for some strains of Hackneys and Criollos at least, then such horses might not draw much attention.

Other White Patterns

As this book has been written, the understanding of white patterning is once again being revised. Twenty years ago, most American horsemen understood white patterns in terms of tobiano and overo. That was expanded to tobiano, frame overo, sabino, and splashed white, and more recently dominant white and manchado were added. Those pattern names are more widely used by owners and breeders, just as it has become clear that there are still more patterns.

The ability to study color mutations at the molecular level has given researchers unprecedented abilities to separate out colors that look quite similar, but are genetically different. Genetic testing made it possible to separate out and name the new dilutions, many of which mimic older colors or even one another. Because breeders seeking a certain kind of coat color or pattern are likely to assemble a group of horses that have any genetic combination that might produce it, different genes that produce similar colors are often found in the same population. Mixed together in a group, they can appear to all be one thing (palomino) with individual variations (pink skin or pumpkin skin or dark skin). Technology can do what visual identification cannot, by drawing the line between what is individual variation and what is an entirely separate color.

Closer, more thoughtful observation of white patterns produced the current categories. What is happening now is that technology is drawing new lines between things that look alike, but that are genetically quite distinct. Even though this process is still in the very early stages, it is clear that there are more than just six pinto patterns. There are already eleven different dominant white patterns (and those are just the ones with names) and four different splashed white patterns. The chance that there are a large number of white patterns is quite high.

Specific Patterns and Pattern Groups
Among the six named pinto patterns, there are patterns that have a single, defined cause. Tobiano and frame overo are known to each be a single pattern. Manchado is assumed to be a single pattern,

This Quarter Horse mare is a good example of the flashy white type of sabino patterning. This is one of the most common forms of white patterning in horses, and is found across a wide range of breeds and body types.

though its rarity makes conclusions provisional. The other three patterns, sabino, splashed white and dominant white, are not really single patterns so much as they are pattern categories. Just as overo was once a category for all patterns not tobiano, these patterns are categories for those things that are not tobiano, frame overo or manchado.

This can make attempts to describe those patterns in general terms difficult. Just as the old rules for overos did not always apply because some patterns in the category fit the rules better than others, so describing sabinos as if they are one thing is problematic, because there are patterns within the group that do not fit the parameters as well as others. Just as Paint and Pinto breeders defined overo primarily by the frame pattern that was familiar (and desirable) to them, aspects attributed to sabino patterns as a whole may only reflect the most common versions. When more is known about the separate patterns that make up the sabino group, it may be necessary to move some patterns into different categories.

At this time, there are more pintos with patterns that cannot be formally identified by a test than pintos with patterns that can. Most of the undefined patterns are considered a type of sabino. More than any other pattern, sabino has become the catch-all term for not only the patterns that fit its profile, but for any other patterns of white that

The pattern on this gelding is more ragged and irregular than the mare on the facing page. He also has extensive roaning throughout his coat which has softened the edges of his pattern.

do not quite fit the other categories. For lack of a better term (many of these pattern varieties have no specific name), sabino is used here, though it is quite possible that some of the patterns will prove to be unrelated.

These are all groupings based on phenotype, which is the outward appearance of the horse. As the situation with sabino roan and some of the dominant white mutations has shown, sometimes horses with the same phenotype can be the product of completely different genes. It is, however, a place to start. It also provides at least some guidelines for the later chapters of this book, because not all breeds that have sabino patterned horses have all the different types.

Flashy White Sabinos

At its most basic, sabino appears to be an amplification of ordinary face and leg markings. It takes the white on the face and pulls it down across the chin, and in some cases wraps it under the jaw. It takes the leg markings and pulls them upward towards the body. This has led to the question of whether there is a difference between markings and the sabino pattern. Current studies seem to suggest that there is a marking gene that is separate from the sabino patterning genes. Certainly there are breeds and bloodlines that have moderate white markings, but that do not produce excessive white, or do so only rarely. But it does appear that there is a connection between markings and this type of pattern.

In addition to making ordinary markings more flashy, this type of sabino does put white on the body, though it is most often seen in patches on the belly. Viewed in profile, it is sometimes visible along the bottom line of the horse, though its origin tends to be ventral rather than on the sides of the horse. White hairs are often sprinkled through the coat, though they tend to only be visible upon close inspection. From a distance, horses with this type of pattern do not usually appear roany. Small amounts of white hairs at the base of the tail are also not uncommon, though it is not usually as pronounced as the coon tails seen on rabicanos.

Like ordinary markings, this type of sabino has a strong connection with the chestnut base color. It is certainly possible to find bay and even black horses that fit the flashy white description, but it is far more common in chestnuts, particularly clear red chestnuts.

Compared to the other forms of sabino, flashy white horses have a cleaner, more distinct edge to their markings, especially when viewed at a bit of a distance. But perhaps more importantly, this type of pattern does not appear to spread far up on the body. This is helpful for breeds like the Quarter Horse, where flashy white markings are popular, but excessive white is considered a fault, because many horses with the pattern are going to fall within the accepted range of white. It might be a challenge if the goal is to reliably produce loud pintos in a breed that has no other patterning genes.

Flashy white sabinos are the most common type of sabino, and can be found in a wide range of breeds. They are particularly common in the Arabian, especially those that trace back to the Crabbet Park breeding program. Its presence in many of the European warmbloods and improved ponies can be credited to the influence of either Arabians or Thoroughbreds. It is present in most of the American breeds, though it is relatively rare in the Morgan and Standardbred. It is also present in some of the South American Spanish breeds, including the Criollo, Paso Fino and the Mangalarga, but quite rare in the Old World Spanish breeds. It is believed to be absent in many of the primitive pony breeds, including the British Shetland and the Icelandic.

Unbalanced Sabinos

White markings on the face and legs tend to correlate, so that horses with flashy white markings on the face are more likely to have matching white on the legs. That is not necessarily true of white patterns. Because tobiano places white on the legs but not the face, and frame places white on the face but not the legs, mismatched markings often serve as a clue that one of those white patterns is involved. Because sabino is an unpredictable pattern, the white on the face and legs do not always match. In some breeds, the mismatch is consistent and tends to take a fairly specific form.

Unbalanced sabinos have a strong resemblance to minimal tobianos in that they have minimal white on the face and high white markings on the legs. On horses that have white on the legs and not the face, it would be relatively easy to mistake one for a tobiano (see page 137). The fact that the unbalanced pattern, like the flashy white pattern, has relatively clean edges adds to the impression these horses could be tobianos.

Once the pattern spreads closer to the body, it may extend from the front or hind legs onto the body. On others, the body white originates on the belly much like it might on a flashy white sabino, though the white areas can be quite broad. These larger areas of opaque, unroaned body white paired with only moderate amounts of face white also tends to register as tobiano with a lot of observers, but the origin of the white is ventral and

the progression is towards the topline, rather than dorsal progressing down towards the legs (see Figure 13). Although unbalanced sabinos can have large areas of body white, that does seem to be the upper limit for that particular type of pattern. Most have just a star and high stockings, and even the loudest only have white covering approximately 35 percent of the body.

This is not a common form of sabino. Most breeds where it is found have some connection to the Hackney, where it is relatively common. It is also fairly common in the Akhal-Teke, though white on the body is far less common in that breed.

Ragged Sabinos

Although flashy white sabinos sometimes have disconnected patches of white, particularly on the knees, their markings still tend to fall in expected areas. There are some sabinos, however, that have markings that are far less predictable. This is especially noticeable on the legs, where a horse might have a small patch near the hoof that stops, then continues in a much larger patch on the upper leg. Sometimes the white does not get near the hoof, or it might travel in an irregular line down the side of one leg. White still originates in much the same areas as other sabinos, but it tends to break apart into irregular pieces that are then placed erratically within those areas.

Ragged sabinos also tend to be significantly more roany than flashy white sabinos, though this is not usually extensive enough over the entire body that the horse might be classified as a sabino roan. Instead the roaning and ticking tends to cluster around the markings, which already have a more irregular ragged edge than the previous two sabino patterns. Bay and black ragged sabinos are more likely than flashy white or unbalanced sabinos to have a flaxen tail.

Ragged sabinos appear to have a top limit of body white, though like their markings this tends to be broken apart and roany. There is a significant overlap between this group and the next category, the patchy sabino, with ragged sabinos showing less contrast and fewer areas of pure, unflecked white.

Ragged sabinos are more common in breeds that have a wide range of sabino patterning, like

The irregular white patches and ticking on the legs of this horse are typical of the ragged type of sabino pattern. Often with this type of white patterning, the larger areas of white skew in unexpected directions.

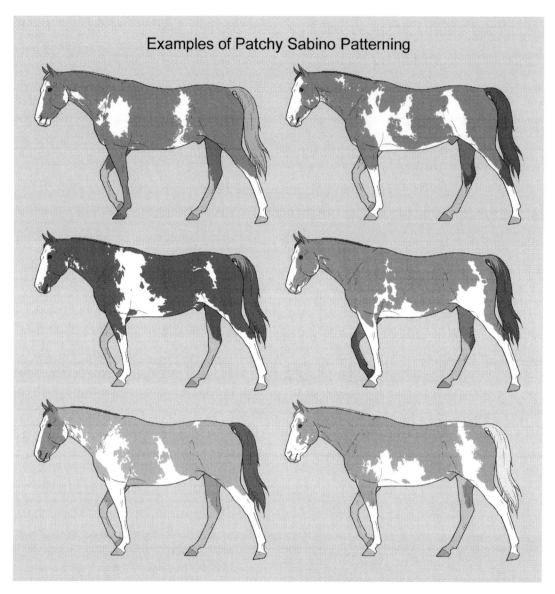

Figure 6. Patchy sabinos have broader areas of white on the sides of the body than flashy white sabinos, and often have a variable quality to the pattern with areas that are ticked, patched, roaned or smooth-edged. The breeds shown here are (left to right, starting at the top) two Arabians, two Criollos, and a Tennessee Walking Horse. The last horse is the dominant white pictured on page 66, and is included here to show just how visually similar the patterns are.

the Clydesdale, Paint Horse, and the Tennessee Walking Horse.

Patchy Sabinos

There are breeding groups that have sabino markings where the amount of white, even on chestnut horses, remains fairly moderate. Horses do get white patches on the belly and occasional patches on the body, but large areas of white spread across the body are quite unusual. This seems to suggest that some other factor may come into play that either produces more white than ordinary sabino, or that amplifies the sabino white much like flashy sabino amplifies ordinary markings.

Horses in this group do look like sabinos. The white on the face tends to spread in much the same way, and like sabino the legs are often—but not uniformly—white. The white on the hind legs tends to travel along the front of the leg towards the stifle and the white on the body originates from the belly and spreads upward. The white on the body, however, is often far more irregular in outline, much like the markings on the ragged sabino. Often there are broad areas of unticked white on the shoulders, barrel or hindquarters, surrounded by smaller patches and ticks. Unlike the previous three patterns, the white often reaches the topline and even can cross it.

Horses with this type of pattern sometimes appear unexpectedly among ordinary sabinos, and then proceed to produce similarly patterned offspring. This is particularly noticeable in some Arabian families where flashy white chestnuts were crossed (and often inbred) for generations without producing much more than occasional belly spots. In 1979, the loud chestnut sabino stallion RAFFONS ABIDA (Figure 7) was born to two flashy white parents. His sire had thirty-nine registered foals. Most had flashy markings on the face and legs, just as did the majority of his ancestors. Two had smaller belly spots, which was also typical for his family; a small percentage of the flashy white horses would

usually have some white on the belly. The amount of white on ABIDA was far from typical. Yet in his limited career at stud, he produced nine purebred foals with similar levels of body white. Some of the foals that were not loudly patterned had odd and erratic markings, even for a sabino.

There have been other instances of extensively marked horses appearing and then producing loud foals with surprising consistency. Because these horses attract the attention of those interested in producing colored Arabians, they are often crossed on horses that are themselves flashy white sabinos. The interesting question is why these horses appear so rarely from two flashy white sabinos, if the two patterns have the same cause.

Some have speculated that patchy sabinos are in fact dominant white mutations. Figure 6, which shows five patchy white sabinos and one dominant white, illustrates why this is a reasonable theory. Horses from the dominant white families that are prone to sabino, rather than white, expressions look virtually indistinguishable from patchy sabinos. The patchy sabinos certainly resemble that particular dominant white more than they resemble a typical flashy white sabino.

The difference between them is that even though some dominant white families tend to produce sabino-like patterns, they still have some percentage

Two Types of Patterns that Resemble Splashed White

Figure 7. Horses with high stockings and very white undersides (left) are often identified as splashed white, though they lack blue eyes. White-faced horses with stockings (right) also tend to be identified as splashed white, but like the white-dipped horses many never produce the type of classic pattern seen in the figure on page 58.

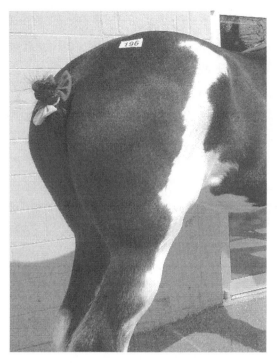

White-dipped horses often have white that extends upward from the front of the hindquarter towards the topline. This is part of what gives patterns like this one a splash-like appearance, since classic splash often crosses the topline between the croup and the neck.

white are less distinctive. The Freiberger stallion that carried the original macchiato mutation has a pattern quite similar to patchy sabino.

His pattern also looks a great deal like the dominant white horse in Figure 6. The Freiberger had blue eyes, which might be expected in a splashed white, but not all splashed white horses have blue eyes. Heterozygous classic splashes are only intermittently blue-eyed. Historic records as well as a number of modern instances point to the conclusion that dominant whites can also have blue eyes. Both loudly marked Arabians and Clydesdales are more prone to blue eyes than any of the other sabino patterns.

It does seem likely that something other than, or in addition to, the original sabino pattern recently arose in some Arabians lines. A similar type of pattern is found in a large number of Clydesdales, as well as Criollos. Because there is considerable overlap between the appearance of these patchy sabinos, some dominant whites and some splashed whites, the only way to sort them out may be an examination at the molecular level. This might not necessarily shed light on whether the horses were sabinos or dominant whites, since those are thought to both occur on KIT, but it could provide answers about splashed white, which are not located on KIT.

of foals that are white. Some breeds where patchy sabinos are common, like the Clydesdale, are notable for the absence (or at least extreme rarity) of white foals.

The other theory that has been offered, at least in the case of some of the patchy sabino Arabians, is that the horses are splashed whites. RAFFONS ABIDA has been described in a number of articles as a splashed white. To date no Arabians have tested positive for the classic splashed pattern (*SW1*), and none of the suspected horses ever produced a classic splash pattern, even when inbred. Clear classic splash patterns have not been found in the Clydesdale, even though crosses between patchy sabinos are quite common.

It is possible that patchy sabinos have previously unidentified splashed white mutations. While the classic splashed pattern is difficult to mistake for something else, the other known forms of splashed

White-Dipped and White-Faced Sabinos
While RAFFONS ABIDA could be classified as a patchy sabino, he also illustrates how that category overlaps with a type of pattern that is often mistaken for splashed white. These horses have extensive white on their legs and belly, which gives the impression they are splashed whites. Often the white spreads up the hind leg and over the hip. When the white on the hind leg ends before it reaches the body, it often has a squared-off top rather than the peaked outline of a flashy white sabino. Although the outline of the white area is often more irregular than that of a splashed white, the white itself tends to form a large, connected piece along the belly, which is quite similar to splashed white.

What makes these horses different from true splashes is that they lack to broad white face and the blue eyes. From the shoulders down they are dipped in white much like a splash, particularly the newer splash mutations. If the body is disregarded, and just the head is analyzed, they look far more like an ordinary flashy white or perhaps a patchy sabino. Because the researchers that identified the currently known splashed white mutations used extensive white on the face and blue eyes as a selection criteria when searching for the gene, it seems unlikely that horse with these white-dipped patterns are splashed whites.

The second type of pattern does fit that criteria, and some of the horses that have it may later prove to have a splashed white mutation. Unlike the white-dipped sabinos, these horses are white-faced, often quite dramatically so. The head is white from just in front of the ears down to the bottom of the cheek, just as is seen in some of the newer splashed white mutations (*SW2* and *SW3*). The legs are often white, and there may be some white on the belly, but horses with this type of pattern invariably lack the extensive body white associated with the classic splash pattern. When searching for the original splashed white pattern (classic splash, which was later identified as splashed white-1), these types of horses proved to be frustrating dead-ends, because they did not seem to produce a classic pattern. They did consistently reproduce their own white-faced pattern, which is something that, as an incomplete dominant, classic splash does not do.

Like the patchy and the white-dipped sabinos, these white-faced horses often appear suddenly in breeds or families that are known to have white markings, or even flashy white sabino, but where this type of marking is not expected. Because splashed white, like dominant white, is now known to have multiple mutations, several of which are quite recent, it seems quite possible that at least some of these white-faced horses have some type of splash mutation, rather than a form of sabino. If that is the case, tests should show that they have a mutation at the MITF or PAX3 genes, rather than KIT.

White-dipped sabinos can be found in many of the breeds where sabino is common and where white on the body is not restricted. White-faced sabinos are more rare, with recent instances in the Arabian, Thoroughbred, and the Gelderlander. Some Clydesdales and Shires resemble white-faced sabinos, though they tend to have a little more white on the body.

Stippled Sabinos

Many sabinos have a sprinkling of white hairs in their coat. This might not always be visible in photographs, because the body color looks solid from a distance. Some sabinos seem to take this characteristic, and the white tailhead, a bit further. Instead of a faint sprinkling of silver hairs, the colored areas look like they fell victim to a lot of white overspray. Instead of white hairs, the horse has larger flecks of white concentrated on the belly, flanks, barrel and between the legs. Often the white that wraps under the jaw merges with the flecking at the throat, and the hind legs merge with the white on the flanks.

There is a lot of overlap between the white ticking patterns and sabino, and often sabinos

This young Clydesdale is typical of the white-faced type of patterning. Unlike the classic splash pattern, which usually produces an entirely white face, horses like this often have "mascara" around the eyes and dark patches on the lips. In its homozygous form, classic splash (SW1) rarely leaves any color on the face.

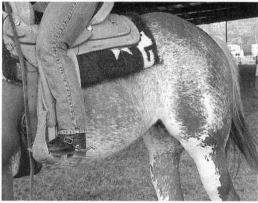

Although often identified as rabicano, stippled sabinos tend to have a more densely flecked, whiter appearance than the typical rabicano. Often the flecking merges with the markings on the legs (bottom).

with any kind of flank roaning or white hairs at the tailhead are identified as sabino-rabicanos. It seems likely that at least in some breeds, many of these horses are just sabinos because they do not breed like horses that have two patterns. A sabino-rabicano should produce some portion of sabinos without rabicano patterning, and rabicanos without sabino patterning. When the two traits, flashy markings and white ticking, do not segregate in the offspring, it seems likely that they are part of the same pattern.

Stippled sabinos, however, may truly be sabino-rabicanos. When paired with other patterns, sabino will often provide a boost to whatever white

patterning is already there. On appaloosas, sabino tends to increase the white patterning, though it usually does so at the expense of some of the spots. Stippled sabinos look like someone took the rabicano pattern and gave it a boost, then added typical sabino markings on top of it. Most stippled sabinos occur in breeds like the Arabian and the Paint Horse, where both sabinos and rabicanos are common.

False-Roan
Sabino shares a lot of characteristics with rabicano, which makes identification of rabicano dependent on the absence of markings. When ticked horses have sabino markings, and many horses with white ticking and white tailheads do, the question becomes whether or not the horses are rabicanos with white markings, rabicanos with sabino, or sabinos that mimic rabicano.

At its most minimal, this type of sabino does look a lot like rabicano. The flanks are roaned and the tailhead is frosted, but the horse has a blaze. The placement of the roaning is also a bit different from that of the rabicano. Instead of originating at the fold of the stifle and radiating from there towards the ribs, the roaning is more dispersed across the hindquarters, with the lightest area running from the fold of the stifle to the hip. Sometimes the roaning looks uneven, with small, slightly darker patches (see page 214) mixed with lacey flecks. Sometimes the blaze is roaned, or has small spots of color inside, but most stop short of the chin.

The most extensive versions of this type of pattern could be mistaken for roan, except that the horse is uniformly roaned from nose-to-toes, or at least almost-to-toes. Some have slightly less roaning on the legs, though the pronounced upside-down V-mark of the true roan is absent.

Visually these horses might appear to be the maximum expression of one of the white ticking patterns, or perhaps a form of frosty roan, but they tend to appear in sabino families with no history of roan. They are also invariably some shade of chestnut, though that may be due to the base coat possibilities in the breeds or families rather than the genetic limits of the pattern. Sabino-1 horses with very minimal patterns can have a similar all-over roan look, and can be found in bay or black base colors. The breeds where sabino-1 is most often found have a high percentage of black-based horses, so that might explain the difference.

False-roan sabinos are found in some of the draft breeds, including the American Belgian. They occur rarely in the Black Forest Horse, where they are often descendants of FREYER, the stallion line developed using a Freiberger outcross. More minimal forms are often found in the New World Spanish breeds. The Mangalarga Paulista stallion CALIFA DO SHEIK has this type of pattern, as do many in his family.

Sabino Roan

While the false-roan sabinos could be easily mistaken for rabicanos or even true roans because of their unmarked legs, most heavily roaned sabinos have white legs. Horses with this type of pattern have much more uneven roaning than the false-roans, which gives them a slightly splotchy or streaked look. The area of deepest color tends to be the hindquarters and the ears, poll and forelock. On some sabino roans, the palest areas are more clearly defined, while others have a much softer transition from light to dark. Many have a mix of the two, with more clearly defined white in some areas (often the hindquarters) and more muted roaning in others.

This type of pattern is often called sabino roan, but like sabino itself, the term is a catch-all for what are visually similar, but genetically different, patterns. The lesson to be drawn from the sabino roan phenotype is that different mutations, with entirely

False-roan sabinos are distinguishable from classic roans by their more uneven, ticked body coloring and their white face and leg markings. Note the typical contrast on tops of the legs of the true roan horse in front. The horse behind him has uniform roaning down the legs, as well as a blaze that wraps around his chin, making it likely that he is a sabino roan.

different patterns of inheritance, can look the same. The patterns on the dominant white founders PU-CHILINGUI and THOKKADIS FRA ROSENHOF look much like those found on many of the descendants of the sabino-1 Tennessee Walking Horse THE PUSHER CG. They also look like those on the sabino roan Arabian HAAP SNOWY RIVER and quite a few Clydesdales, even though those breeds are not believed to carry sabino-1. As a group, most sabino roans that have sabino-1 tend to have more even roaning and less contrast than dominant whites or unidentified sabino roans, but there are atypical individuals in all three groups.

There is also a fair bit of overlap between the more contrasted sabino roans and the patchy sabinos, and the sabino roans that do not yet test positive for one of the identified patterns have a lot in common with patchy sabinos. Like the patchy sabino pattern, sabino roans are not necessarily found in every breed that has flashy white markings or even body spots. They do seem to appear in breeds that already have sabino markings of some variety, but it appears to be a separate pattern and not part of the natural range of sabino itself. It is tempting to imagine that they may be still more instances of dominant white mutations, but like patchy sabinos they do not often produce white-born offspring. It would also be expected, if large numbers of horses in breeds like the Clydesdale were dominant whites, that there would be noticeable reductions in fertility due to the early fetal loss of the homozygotes. The other possibility is that new sabino mutations, like dominant white, are surprisingly common.

History and Breed Distribution

Horses with flashy white markings can be found in artwork throughout history, and it is likely at least some of these patterns are quite old. What is perhaps more interesting is that so many breeds have seen a dramatic increase in the amount of

This young Criollo has a very typical sabino roan pattern. This kind of patterning is very common among horses that test positive for sabino-1, but it is also seen in some dominant white horses as well as horses that do not test positive for any patterns that can currently be identified.

white markings and patterns. Some of this can be attributed to the fact that unusual colors and patterns are highly desirable, so mutations are much more likely to be retained and used by breeders. The opportunities for a stallion like RAFFONS ABIDA, born more than thirty years ago, and a present-day mutation like PUCHILINGUI or COLONELS SMOKINGUN, are quite different. But even where flashy markings are not especially sought, the overall levels of white have increased.

As more patterns are formally identified, it may be possible to trace their history more precisely. At the moment many of these flashier horses do not have testable patterns, and the overlap between the different patterns makes it increasingly difficult to state with absolute confidence which patterns can, and which patterns cannot, be found in the different breeds.

Appaloosa Patterns

Appaloosa patterns are not the result of a single gene, but rather a group of genes that work together in a variety of ways to produce the different kinds of spotting patterns. That complexity alone would make understanding appaloosa patterns a challenge, but many of the component parts are themselves incompletely dominant. So there are several genes, and some of those genes have more than one outcome.

Therefore it is helpful to think of these components as the ingredients in a recipe. The recipes for each of the appaloosa patterns require a base, and then additional ingredients that change the flavor of the pattern. That base, the gene that makes all the appaloosa patterns possible, is called leopard complex (Lp). No matter what the final pattern, all appaloosas start with that base mutation. That is the mutation that gives the horse those traits most often thought of as appaloosa characteristics, and that sets the stage for all the other appaloosa patterns. Those other patterns are the result of separate genes, known as patterning genes, that modify leopard complex.

Leopard Complex
(Varnish Roan)

The term leopard complex is somewhat misleading because the mutation is not directly responsible for the leopard pattern. The name leopard complex refers to the group, or complex, of patterns that include leopard spotting. North American horsemen tend to refer to the group of patterns generically as appaloosa, after the American breed of the same name, while in Britain those same patterns are called spotted. The historical term, however, was leopard, or in some countries, tiger.

The gene is named for the group of patterns made possible by its presence, rather than the specific color it produces. Had it been named for the resulting color, it would have been the varnish roan gene. Without the additional patterning genes (without the other ingredients in the recipe), a horse with leopard complex will be varnish roan.

Like grey, varnish roan is a progressive color. Varnish roan foals are born dark and lighten in a distinctive pattern as they age. Typically a varnish roan will be lightest on the hindquarters, often with some small spots on the hips, which are usually more densely pigmented than the body. Aside from the spots, the darkest areas appear along the high points of the body—the points of the hip and elbow, the outer edge of the barrel, the nasal bones, the ears—and the legs. The dark area on the front of the face often forms a distinctive V along the nasal bones, and there is another dark V

Without the other patterning genes, leopard complex (Lp) results in the color commonly called varnish roan, or appaloosa roan.

formed by the edges of the jaw on the underside of the head.

The leopard complex gene is what gives the horse appaloosa characteristics: mottled skin, striped hooves and white sclera. It has often been stated that appaloosas will always have these three things, and that is true, though they are not always strongly expressed. But appaloosas do have them to some degree because all appaloosa patterned horses are, genetically at least, varnish roans.

Mottled Skin
Horses with the leopard complex gene have mottled skin. This is visible on the muzzle, udder, sheath, and anus. In some individuals, it can in-

clude the insides of the ears and the skin around the eyes. Like the roaning, mottling is progressive and develops as the horse matures. It is variable in extent, with some horses only showing a few spots of pink skin around the lips or genitals, while others have extensive mottling over the entire face.

Mottling also varies in appearance. Most appaloosas give the impression of a dark-skinned horse with smaller areas of unpigmented (or less intensely pigmented) skin. More rarely, the horse can appear to have pink skin with dark speckles. In general appaloosa mottling has more contrast than the freckling on a champagne, and has larger, more irregular spots. The scale of the spots tends to be larger than the depigmentation seen on grey horses, but smaller than the patches on depigmented non-greys. (See page 113 for images of depigmentation for comparison.)

Striped Hooves

The hooves on the colored legs of an appaloosa are striped. These are not found on the hooves of legs that have white markings, so an appaloosa with four white feet would not have striped hooves—or at least he would not have stripes that were caused by leopard complex. Ermine spots and some of the sabino patterns can cause a horse to have striped hooves. Silver dilutes and even some palomino and chestnut horses have striped hooves, although many of these do not have the bold contrast that the appaloosa hooves have. Because other colors can have striped hooves, the presence of striping without any of the other appaloosa characteristics is not considered proof that a horse has the leopard complex gene.

Visible Sclera

Most horses have color that fills the exposed area of the eye, so that the whites of the eyes are only visible when the horse is looking to the back or the front. Appaloosas have white that is visible in both corners of the eye, regardless of the direction they are looking. This is sometimes called a ring eye, or a human eye. While it is consistently seen in horses with appaloosa patterns, it is not unique to them. Visible sclera is sometimes seen in horses with pinto patterns, particularly with sabinos. For that reason, some appaloosa registries do not accept white sclera as proof of appaloosa patterns when it is accompanied by large white face markings.

Color Shifting

Although it is not considered one of the official characteristics of leopard complex, many appaloosas have an odd pewter-brown coloring that does not look quite like chestnut, even liver chestnut, and yet is not truly black. This is sometimes referred to as color shifting or bronzing. Tests confirm that the horses have black pigment, but the color has been altered. Legs that show the bronzing effect lack the red tones of a true chestnut, and lack the contrast and mottling seen with black silver. They are similar in tone to the black dilution known as *globrunn*.

It is not known why black pigment shifts in tone in some appaloosas but not others. It can be found in all the breeds that have leopard complex, though it does seem more common in black appaloosas than in bays.

Homozygotes

Leopard complex is an incompletely dominant gene, so horses with two copies look different from horses with one copy. From a patterning standpoint, the most significant difference is that the presence of the second copy of leopard complex

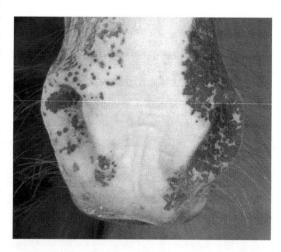

Appaloosa mottling can look like dark spots on pink skin, or pink mottles on dark skin.

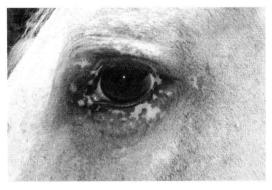

The leopard complex gene also produces the appaloosa characteristics of striped hooves, skin mottling and visible sclera (eye whites). Because all appaloosas carry the leopard complex gene, all display these characteristics to some degree.

erases the spots, or at least the vast majority of them. The change is not as noticeable on varnish roan horses, which tend to have smaller spots that are only revealed as the horse roans. The effect does make a big difference with the patterning genes, which would otherwise produce larger, contrasting spots. For those horses, two copies of the leopard complex gene changes a leopard to a fewspot and a blanket pattern to a snowcap. For horses that do not have one of the additional patterning genes, but that have two copies of the leopard complex gene, the varnish pattern develops much like it does in horses with just one copy, though the roaning does not reveal darker spots as it progresses.

The other visible difference in horses that are homozygous for leopard complex is that their colored legs have shell-colored hooves. Where the colored legs of a heterozygous appaloosa have hooves that are primarily dark with intermittent pale streaks, on homozygous appaloosas those same hooves would be primarily light with a few dark streaks. Homozygous appaloosas are also

more prone to extensive skin mottling than those that are heterozygous, although this does vary in individual horses.

Interactions with Other Patterns
On its own, leopard complex produces what is essentially a progressive pattern of roaning. The horses can be subtly spotted (see the horse on page 83), assuming they have only one copy of the gene, but they do not have the kind of contrast considered so desirable by appaloosa breeders. To get the more dramatic patterns, appaloosas need additional patterning genes. Patterning genes take the diffused white from leopard complex and amplify and organize it.

The patterning genes that are specific to leopard complex are discussed in more detail in the following chapters. What has been most interesting about current appaloosa research is just how many genes do interact with leopard complex. Not only are there larger pattern genes, those responsible for leopards and blankets, but there are probably other genes that alter the final pattern in more subtle ways. It may be that some of the pinto genes (most likely some of the sabinos) can function as pattern genes for leopard complex.

The important thing to remember, though, is that underneath any patterning, appaloosas are all varnish roans. Because the horse is really a varnish roan, he will have the traits that go with that. Just as a bay horse that has begun to turn grey can still show signs that he was originally a bay, so leopard and blanketed appaloosas still show signs of their base pattern. They have the striped hooves, visible sclera and the mottled skin. And where the pattern leaves large areas of body color, those will eventually lighten just like the body of a unpatterned varnish roan.

Inheritance and Testing
Varnish roan is produced by an incompletely dominant gene. Horses with one copy can have dark spots that do not roan over time, while horses with two copies have patterns without spots. Both heterozygotes and homozygotes develop the varnish roan pattern over time. Varnish roan appaloosa horses will always have at least one appaloosa par-

Two copies of the leopard complex gene eliminate the dark spotting caused by the pattern genes, leaving the patterned areas very white. Homozygous appaloosas with a blanket pattern, like this gelding, are called snowcaps while homozygous leopards are called fewspots.

ent. Horses that are homozygous for leopard complex produce appaloosa offspring 100 percent of the time, but the type of appaloosas produced is dependant on the patterning genes present in the parents.

The mutation for leopard complex has been mapped to TRPM1, but there is not yet a commercially available test. In its homozygous form, the gene causes Congenital Stationary Night Blindness (CSNB). That means that all homozygous varnish roans, and all fewspot and snowcap appaloosas, are night blind. This condition is present at birth and is not progressive. Horses with the condition are blind in low light situations, but have normal vision in the daylight.

It is also believed that appaloosas of all kinds are more prone to Equine Recurrent Uveitis (ERU), which is a chronic inflammation of the inside of the eye. In the past it was believed to be tied to phases of the moon, and was called moon blindness. This is unfortunate because it leads to confusion with Congenital Stationary Night Blindness. Unlike that disease, uveitis is not inherited. The

most popular theories involve various types of infections, but it is not known why appaloosas are more susceptible.

There have been instances of a cryptic varnish roan. The color can be obscured by other genes that add white hairs, like true roan and grey. Greying adds additional challenges because it can also result in mottled skin. The rate and amount of roaning also varies, so a horse that roans very late and only a minimal amount may be mistaken for a non-appaloosa. However, most unexpected appaloosas are born to varnish roan parents that were misidentified as true roan.

History and Breed Distribution
Breeders have long maintained that cave paintings on the walls of Pech Merle, made 25,000 years ago, depict appaloosa patterned horses. Many historians believed the spots on the horses were symbolic in nature, rather than a realistic portrayal of coat color. In 2010, analysis of remains from the Pleistocene Era showed that the leopard complex mutation was present in four of the ten Western European samples. Two more horses with the mutation were identified in Ukrainian samples from the Copper Age. That makes leopard complex the oldest pattern, at least among those that have been tested, and the only pattern to date that has been found in horses prior to domestication.

It is not known if any of the wild horses had additional patterning genes, since those cannot yet be identified by testing. All that is currently known is that the wild horses had the leopard complex mutation, so they would have at least been varnish roans. The horses that tested positive were all heterozygous. That is not surprising in a wild population, since the night-blind homozygotes would be at a disadvantage. The advantage to the heterozygotes is less clear, though it has been speculated that it provided camouflage in snowy environments. The color was not found among Asian samples from the same time period.

Although appaloosa patterns appear in artwork throughout the Middle Ages up through the Early Modern period, the patterns fell out of favor in the nineteenth century. Because leopard complex is visible even when no patterning genes are present, it was possible to select against it quite effectively. The mutation survived primarily in isolated pockets. Two of the European remnants were the Danish Knabstrupper and the Austrian Noriker. These two breeds have a historical connection to the old Baroque appaloosas. In some breeds, like the Welsh Mountain Pony, leopard complex was masked by grey or roan and survived in small numbers even after it was banned by the registry.

Horses with the appaloosa spotting patterns were also preserved in the Altai Mountains of Siberia, in Uzbekistan, and at the Michałów Stud in Poland. Malopolskis from the Michałów Stud gave the pattern to both the Wielkopolski and the Felin Pony. There is also a strain of appaloosas in the Swedish Gotland Pony, though the color did not originate there. Gotlands are interesting in that they only have leopard complex. The patterning genes once found in the appaloosa strain were lost, and the only other white patterning gene found in the population is classic splashed white.

Appaloosa patterns were also found in the American west. This was the population that Claude Thompson sought to preserve when he formed the Appaloosa Horse Club of America in 1938. Leopard complex was also present in some of the foundation Quarter Horse families, and many of the influential stallions during the forma-

tion of the Appaloosa breed were crop-out Quarter Horses. Like the remnants of the pattern in the Welsh Mountain Pony, many of the varnish roan mares that carried leopard complex were mistaken for roan or grey. At least one line of appaloosa Tennessee Walking Horses also came through roan or grey mares. Appaloosa patterns are also present in some of the newer breeds where unusual colors are prized, such as the American Miniature and the Gypsy Horse.

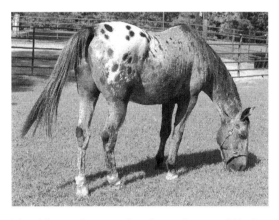

This older appaloosa was born bay with a spotted blanket. The leopard complex gene has caused his body color—those areas that are not white pattern or dark spots—to roan as he has aged.

Leopard

(Pattern-1)

Leopard complex gives a horse the varnish roan pattern and the appaloosa characteristics. What leopard complex can not do, at least not on its own, is add dense white patterning or dramatic spotting to the horse. The louder, highly contrasted patterns so sought after by breeders are the result of other genes that work with the leopard complex gene. Those modifying genes are called patterning genes. Patterning genes change leopard complex, which is essentially a progressive roaning pattern, into something that produces white patterning.

For many appaloosa breeders, the most important of these patterns is leopard or, as it is called in some parts of Europe, tiger. If leopard complex is the base ingredient in every appaloosa recipe, then leopard is the most popular flavor. For as long as people have selected horses for spotted coats, this particular variation has been considered the most desirable. This is the pattern most past studies have focused on, and it has been central in the work done by the Appaloosa Project, which is the research group that identified the leopard complex mutation.

A leopard is an otherwise white horse that is covered with round, colored spots. Unlike the varnish pattern, which is progressive, the white patterning and the spots are present at birth. Leopard patterning is believed to be responsible for most appaloosas that have appaloosa patterning on more than 60 percent of their body.

The amount of patterning on a leopard is affected by a number of factors. Horses that are homozygous for the leopard pattern (but not for leopard complex) have white patterning and spotting over their entire body. This is sometimes called a nose-to-toes leopard. Heterozygous horses have slightly less patterning. There is also a gender bias, with mares having 15 percent less patterning on average than stallions or geldings. The black-based colors also suppress patterning, so bay and black appaloosas tend to have less white than chestnuts. It is also believed that minor genes can boost patterning. The result is a fairly wide range of expression from the one pattern gene.

Near-leopards, also called suppressed leopards, often roan out to a pattern that looks closer to the nose-to-toes horses, though often the outlines of the spots on the forehand are less crisp and distinct than those on the hindquarters.

Suppressed Leopards

Although the image most horsemen have of a leopard is a white horse with dark spots, not all horses with the leopard pattern look like leopards. Some have what is known as a suppressed pattern. Appaloosa breeders call horses with this type of pattern near-leopards. The leopard pattern can actually be suppressed a little further than what most would call a near-leopard, until it is more like a blanket in size.

Even the smallest suppressed leopard patterns do not look quite like ordinary blanket patterns. Sheila Archer, the coordinator for the Appaloosa Project, likens a suppressed pattern to a shrunken sweater, where the original design is all there, but it covers a much smaller area. That is a very helpful image for understanding the difference between a true blanket and a leopard pattern suppressed down to blanket size. The spots that would have covered the horses's body are still there, but they are compressed into a smaller area. And like a sweater that is now a few sizes too small, the design looks a little stretched. Suppressed leopards tend to have smaller, more numerous spots that are slightly enlongated in shape when compared with the spots on an ordinary leopard.

To some extent, the suppression is somewhat temporary. Whatever white patterning is present on an appaloosa at birth does not change. That is part of what makes true nose-to-toes leopards so appealing, because they do not lose contrast with age. That is not true for the parts of the pattern that do not have white patterning or spots. The forehand of a bay blanketed appaloosa, for instance, will not stay bay. Over time, the bay areas roan out, until the horse is a varnish roan with a blanket (see page 87). On a suppressed leopard, the colored areas roan out in a pattern much like the leopard the horse was meant to be. The spots are often more roaned and less distinct that a horse that was born a leopard, but it does provide a clue that the horse is probably carrying the leopard pattern, and not one of the smaller patterning genes.

This tendency to revert back to the leopard pattern despite the suppression is most visible on the face. Blanketed or near-leopard appaloosas that have spotting on their faces are more likely carrying the leopard pattern gene. Given enough time, they will probably roan out to something that looks a little more like a leopard.

Interactions with Leopard Complex - Fewspots
With one copy of leopard complex (varnish roan) to activate the leopard pattern, the horse is covered to a greater or lesser degree with white patterning and colored spots. Unfortunately if the horse inherits a second copy of leopard complex, it comes back through and erases all the spots. The horse still gets to keep the white patterning, but it will have few if any colored spots. Horses like this are called fewspots.

By definition a leopard patterned horse is heterozygous for leopard complex, and a fewspot is homozygous for leopard complex. The lack of spots does not indicate whether or not the horse is carrying one or two copies of the leopard pattern itself, though. Instead, pattern-1 controls the extent of the pattern. One copy of the leopard pattern (*PATN1*) produces a slightly smaller pattern than two copies. With fewspots, the spotting from those patterns is no longer there, but the white patterning is. The fewspots that are homozygous for the pattern as well as for varnish roan are whiter because they had a larger pattern prior to the removal of the spots. Those that are heterozygous have more color on places like the ears, the lower legs and the area behind the front leg, because those areas were

colored (but not spotted) before the second leopard complex removed the spotting. Although the all-white horses might look more like dominant whites than appaloosas, they are the one color that will always produce a leopard from a solid mate.

Interactions with Other Patterns
It is believed a lot of different factors can either increase or descrease the patterning on appaloosas, which helps explain why breeders see so much variation even among close relatives. This particular area of study touches on some of the same questions that arise about interactions between markings and some types of white patterning, which is part of what makes the research into appaloosa patterns so fascinating.

It is known that at least some types of sabino interact with the leopard pattern. Sabino tends to boost the levels of white patterning, and it tends reduce or erode colored areas, and that is exactly what happens to leopards that inherit typical sabino markings. The horses do not lose their spots entirely like those that are homozygous for leopard complex. Instead the white areas are bigger, effectively making the spots smaller and more widely spaced. Like sabino itself, the effect tends to be

The nose-to-toes version of the leopard pattern seen on this Knabstrupper gelding is widely seen as the most desirable of the appaloosa patterns. Producing it requires that a single copy of leopard complex (Lp) be paired with two copies of the leopard pattern (pattern-1).

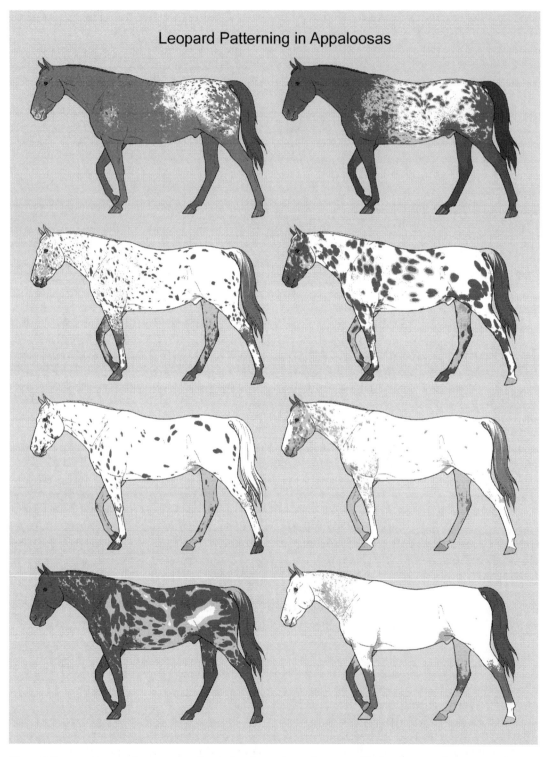

Figure 8. Pattern-1 can produce a range of leopard and near-leopard patterns. The last horse is a homozygous fewspot.

most pronounced in horses with a chestnut base color, but it does affect all appaloosas. The easiest way to identify leopards that have been altered by sabino is to look at the face, which often has enough dark skin and thin hair that the typical sabino blaze can be seen.

Mismarks

Some leopards have an irregular patch where the coat has reverted to the base color. More extensive patching is sometimes mistaken for a pintaloosa pattern, but the appaloosa patterns change the colored areas of a pinto, not the white. The patches are called mismarks, and like mismarks of white on a solid horse, they are believed to be somatic. Mismarks do not roan out like the rest of the colored areas of an appaloosa, so they often become more noticeable as the horse ages.

Inheritance and Testing

The gene responsible for the actual leopard pattern is called pattern-1 (*PATN1*). Although its location has not been published, researchers have stated that pattern-1 is located on a different gene and is inherited separately from leopard complex. Pattern-1 is dominant, but is only activated in the presence of the leopard complex gene. If a horse with the leopard complex gene inherits a copy of pattern-1, some degree of leopard patterning will be visible. A varnish roan cannot, therefore, carry a hidden leopard pattern. Solid horses can hide the pattern, because they lack the leopard complex gene necessary to activate the pattern.

It is possible to get a horse that is homozygous for pattern-1, and that horse will pass the patterning gene to all its offspring. But because a leopard must be heterozygous for leopard complex or it will not have spots, it will only give the gene necessary to activate pattern-1 to half its offspring. So while each foal will inherit a copy of pattern-1, only the half that get leopard complex will actually be leopards.

Although pure white fewspot appaloosas are not often considered desirable as indivduals, they produce 100 percent leopards from solid mates, because they are homozygous for both the genes necessary for the leopard pattern. It would not be possible to develop a program of true-breeding

leopards, because the desired pattern requires that the horse be heterozygous for leopard complex (*Lp*), but a population that was homozygous for pattern-1 (*PATN1*) would certainly increase the odds that when appaloosas were produced, they had the more desirable type of pattern.

There is not yet a test available for pattern-1, so the only way to determine that a leopard is homozgyous is to analyze the pedigree and the production records. There are no known health problems associated with pattern-1.

History and Breed Distribution

Tests have shown that the base for the appaloosa patterns, leopard complex (*Lp*), was present in horses prior to domestication. This proved that the spots on the horses in cave paintings were not symbolic. What is still not known is whether or not the artists were depicting the kinds of subtle spots seen on varnish roans, or if the horses really were as loudly patterned as they appear. Because it is not yet possible to test for pattern-1, that question remains unanswered.

Horses with more obvious leopard patterns appear in Chinese artwork in the Iron Age. Leopard patterns were painted on some of the horses found in the mausoleum for the Chinese Emperor Qin Shi Huang, best known for his Terra Cotta Army. Many versions of Beatus of Liebana's *Commentary on the Revelation*, first published in 786 AD, include leopards among the horses. In one particularly striking example from 1086 AD, Christ is pictured astride a small-spotted leopard while two of his companions ride horses with more pronounced patterns. Leopards are also common in Persian miniatures from the thirteenth century.

While leopards were obviously valued during that time, their true heyday was the Early Modern period, particularly the seventeenth and eighteen centuries. Black, black roan, grey, white and very pale dilutes were generally sought out as ceremonial carriage horses (*galakarossiers*), but leopard appaloosas were believed to be suitable for riding, and particularly for the higher level schooling that was fashionable among nobility at the time. Numerous paintings and engravings from the time depict appaloosa patterns in meticulous detail, and leopards and near-leopards were the prevailing patterns.

Breeders of the horses that have the closest connections to the appaloosas from the Baroque era, the Knabstrupper and the Noriker, still have a strong preference for horses with leopard pattern, and the nose-to-toes, or "full tiger", pattern in particular. In the American Appaloosa, leopard patterns are somewhat less common than horses with blanket patterns, but there have always been breeders that have specialized in producing them. The leopard pattern is also found in the Polish and Russian appaloosa breeds, and to a lesser extent Miniatures and Gypsy Horses. It has also been lost in some breeds, like the Gotland Pony. The founding stallion in that breed was a black leopard Arabian/Knabstrupper cross named KHEDIVEN. A few ponies still have the leopard complex gene, but pattern-1 appears to have been lost over time.

The fact that pattern-1 is not visible without the leopard complex also raises interesting questions. When appaloosa patterns fell out of favor, it would have been easy to select away from horses with the leopard complex, especially in breeds that had neither roan or grey, since the color is visible. Patterning genes would have been another matter, because they are not visible unless the horse also has leopard complex. No doubt the genes were often lost when horses that had appaloosa patterns were not used for breeding, but if any of their solid descendants were used, the possibilty is there that the pattern genes were preserved.

In much of Europe and America, appaloosas were culled in the eighteenth century, but there are intriguing cases in the stud books of the late nineteenth century. At least one leopard patterned stallion was included in the *American Stallion Register*. ALEXANDER was a black leopard foaled in 1822 and said to be a Spanish horse. At least two of his sons, GRAY EAGLE and BENEDICT MORRILL, were included in the first volume of the *Morgan Horse Register*. BENDICT MORRILL had descendants in both the Morgan and Standardbred stud books, but like many horses that were used at stud in the time period just before the widespread use of stud books, it is quite possible that some portion of his descendants were entered into stud books as horses with no recorded background, or with incomplete backgrounds. This may have also been true of ALEXANDER as well. Morgans and Standardbreds are not breeds most people would consider testing for hidden leopard patterning genes, but the remote possibilty is there for them, and probably for a lot of other breeds.

If finding a hidden gene for leopard patterning is a remote possibility for a Morgan, how much more likely is it for breeds like the Frederiksborg and the Lipizzan, which have much closer ties to the Baroque leopards? When it is possible to test for pattern-1, and for other appaloosa patterning genes, it may prove that while appaloosas were only preserved in a handful of modern breeds, a remnant of their coloring survived in far more of them than expected.

Other Appaloosa Patterns

Appaloosa breeders have traditionally divided patterned horses with spots into three categories: leopard, near-leopard and blanket. Those were visual categories, and they are useful for describing how much white patterning is present on the horse. They do not have a direct one-to-one relationship with the genetic categories. Depending on a number of variables, the gene responable for leopard patterning (*PATN1*), can produce all three types of patterns.

Horses with the leopard gene (*PATN1*) can have the blanket pattern, but not all horses with blanket patterning have the leopard gene. There are families of appaloosas that produce white patterns, but those patterns remain within the 20 to 60 percent range. Their patterns tend to look a bit different from the type of blanket that comes from suppressing the leopard pattern. There are usually fewer spots, and they are larger and more widely spaced. On some horses, the blanket looks less like a partial leopard pattern than it does lacey patches of white on the hindquarters. Others have almost as much white patterning as a near-leopard, but the spotting has the same differences that the smaller patterns have.

There is a temptation say there is a blanket gene responsible for this type of appaloosa patterning, and call it pattern-2. However, the situation with the smaller patterns is more complicated. Traits that are the result of multiple genes are said to be polygenic. Within the context of polygenic traits, some genes are referred to as large-effect, and others as small-effect. Appaloosa patterns, which require the leopard complex and some kind of patterning gene, are polygenic. Leopard patterning is a large-effect gene for appaloosa patterning. It is thought that blanket patterns (at least those not created by suppressing leopard patterning) are caused by some number of small-effect genes.

There are probably multiple small-effect genes that work together to produce blanket patterns, which is why, like sabino, there is so much variation. That variation can be seen by comparing the patterns in Figure 8 with those in Figure 9. Leopards do vary, but those variations are primarily about quantity, scale and spacing. Blanket patterns can differ from one another in those ways, but even when two blanket appaloosas have similar levels of white patterning and even similar numbers of spots, the pattern can have a completely different character.

Appaloosas with a large number of these small-effect genes can have significant white patterning. It is likely that the horses that fall closer to the 60 percent patterning range, but that do not have the leopard pattern (*PATN1*), probably have a high number of these small-effect genes.

Sabino as a Patterning Gene

Although sabino is known to give the white areas of an existing pattern a boost, leopard complex may be able to use sabino—or at least some forms of sabino—as patterning genes. It is not unusual to see appaloosas with sabino markings that also have frosty white patterns, usually centered around the hips, reminiscent of sabino ticking. The more extensive patterns resemble a loose colletion of lacey patches on the hindquarters and back. Most of these patterns do not have very pronounced spotting, though that is typical of other appaloosa patterns that have been altered by sabino. Horses with this kind of pattern are frequently

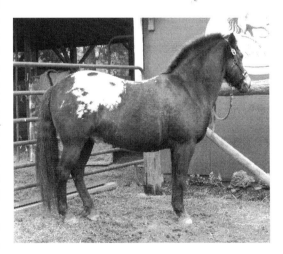

It is thought that additional pattern genes exist that work with leopard complex to create the variety of smaller, non-leopard patterns seen in appaloosas. This blanket-marked gelding is a good example of that kind of patterning.

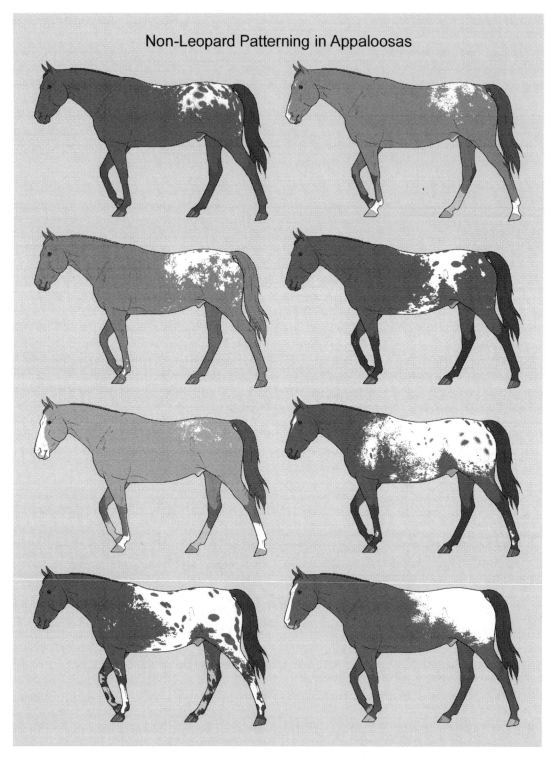

Figure 9. Other patterning genes create blanket and hip spotting. The last horse is a homozygous snowcap.

chestnut, which tends to promote the expression of the sabino patterns.

Because it is not possible to test for either the small-effect appaloosa patterning genes or for most of the sabino patterns, the limits of the patterning possible with just sabino is not known. It does not appear that sabino creates large patterns with wide areas of opaque white, but then sabino rarely does that as a pinto pattern. It may be that even the very minimal frosty hip patterns need some kind of appaloosa patterning present.

Interactions with Leopard Complex
Varnish roan is progressive, but it does not affect either the white patterning or the colored spots. Horses born with those will keep them unless they have the actual grey (*G*) gene. A leopard pattern, made up primarily of white patterning and dark spots, will not change much with age. Blanket patterns are different because some portion of the horse is not patterned. Varnish roan will not change the blanket or the spots, but the rest of the horse will roan out over time, and the contrast with the pattern will be greatly reduced (see page 87). Blanket patterns, at least in the way they are most often pictured, are a temporary phase.

Just as with leopards, horses with the a blanket pattern and one copy of leopard complex are spotted. Horses with two copies of leopard complex still have the white patterning, so they have a blanket, but they lose the spots. Horses with this type of pattern are called snowcaps. Like other horses that are homozygous for leopard complex, they have shell-colored hooves, which are often more noticeable on a snowcap where some or all of the legs may be dark.

Snowcaps can be difficult to identify by sight alone, because other factors can greatly reduce the amount of spotting inside a blanket. Just as sabino can boost the white on a leopard, it does the same thing to blanket patterns. Appaloosas patterns on dark-headed roans can also be mistaken for snowcaps or even fewspots, because the area where the spots would be is already roaned, and it appears the leopard complex may have an additive effect that makes the roan areas paler than usual. The grey gene (*G*) can also erase spots. There are also

patterns that do not appear to be be spotted, not because the spots were removed, but because they were not part of the pattern in the first place. Some of the sabino-influenced patterns do not seem to include spots, or have only small ones. All of these patterns are referred to as false-snowcaps, or in the case of leopards, false-fewspots. Sometimes it is possible to tell a horse is not a snowcap when they have a striped hooves on dark legs. White on the face and legs is another clue that the horse has sabino rather than a second copy of leopard complex.

Snowflakes and Snowballs
The varnish roan pattern progresses in slightly different ways on each horse. Sometimes appaloosas

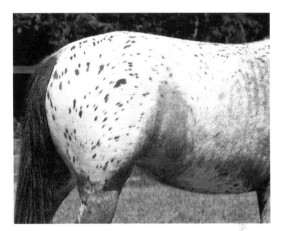

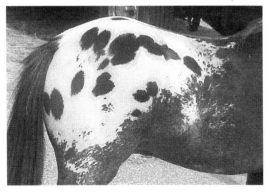

Suppressed leopard patterns (top) are often mistaken for blanket patterning (bottom). When the expression of pattern-1 is restricted, the spots tend to be smaller, more abundant and more closely spaced than those of a true blanket pattern.

that are roaning out develop round white spots as well as white hairs as the varnish pattern progresses. There are also some horses that develop this type of snowflaking in a much more exaggerated fashion, so that the horse appears to have a normal appaloosa pattern with a layer of overlapping white spots over the top. This may be related to the rare instances of progressive Birdcatcher spots, which is itself often mistaken for appaloosa patterning. It also may just be a modification of the varnish pattern. Appaloosas that have extensive snowflake markings are sometimes called marbled. A similar type of snowflaking is sometimes seen on appaloosas that inherit the grey (G) gene. The unusual marbled pattern on the crop-out appaloosa Welsh Mountain Pony, WIGGS LEGEND, was probably due to the presence of grey, since his sire TWYFORD MILO was grey.

Another rare variation are the larger white spots called snowballs. Unlike snowflakes, which are progressive, snowball spots are part of the pattern at birth and do not change, although they often fade as the surrounding coat roans. These are much larger, and more diffused and soft-edged, than snowflakes. They do not follow the direction of the coat, and literally look like the horse was hit was a large snowball. The Appaloosa stallion WHISTLE BRITCHES had several large snowball spots across his withers and barrel.

Inheritance and Testing

In the past, one of the popular theories about the inheritance of appaloosa patterns was that the heterozygotes had blankets, while the homozygotes were leopards. That theory has proven to be too simplistic, though there is a grain of truth to it. Horses with the larger patterning gene, pattern-1, can have a partial pattern, and they are more likely to have that smaller version of the leopard pattern if they have only one copy of pattern-1 than if they have two. It is not known if any of the small-effect appaloosa patterns have a similar mode of inheritance, though it is certainly possible.

There are not yet formal tests for the small-effect appaloosa patterns, nor have they been studied to the same extent that the leopard pattern has. Horse with smaller appaloosa patterns can still be tested for leopard complex, which is helpful for identifying snowcaps and false-snowcapes, but determining the actually patterning genes that may be present is still a combination of pedigree analysis and guesswork based on phenotype.

History and Breed Distribution

Appaloosas with blanket patterning appear in artwork around the same time as the leopard patterns. Because many of the earliest images are stylized, it is difficult to determine if the artists were painting horses that were truly blanketed or were suppressed leopards. A blanketed horse painted on silk during the Ming Dynasty has the moderately spaced spots that are typical of a blanket pattern, but he also has the spotted patches on the shoulder and neck that are often signs of a suppressed leopard. During the Baroque period, when many equestrian artists focused on the nuances of patterns, there are clear blanket patterns. But perhaps the best evidence that the smaller effect appaloosa

The Appaloosa Project

In 2000, Sheila Archer wrote about the genetics behind appaloosa patterning in a paper titled "A Puzzle Worth Solving". That grew into a research initiative to better understand appaloosa genetics. In 2003, the gene that carried the base mutation was found, and by 2010 it was possible to test horses for the presence of the leopard complex.

The Appaloosa Project has been involved in discoveries that have implications for all forms of white patterning in horses. They have also pioneered an approach to genetic research the involves partnerships with enthusiasts, artists, breeders and scientists, while also directing a great deal of energy towards education. The "puzzle worth solving" produced an approach to research worth duplicating.

patterns are an old variation is the fact that they are present in a wide range of breeds.

Blanket patterns are often associated with the American Appaloosa. This is understandable since there have always been a high proportion of blanketed appaloosas in the Appaloosa breed, especially compared to other spotted breeds like the Noriker and the Knabstrupper. Of the first twenty Appaloosas inducted into the Hall of Fame, only four have leopard patterns, and only one, SUNDANCE F-500, has a nose-to-toes pattern. The rest have various types of blankets. Many of the appaloosa crop-out Quarter Horses had blanket patterns, and horses with Quarter Horse blood also brought the sabino pattern.

Although some of the smaller appaloosa patterns are less common outside of the Appaloosa breed, they are not unique to New World appaloosas. At least one mare with a small blanket was pictured in an early Pinzgauer stud book, and a chestnut with a frosty blanket, OLD THOR (1847), was one of the founders of the Knabstrup. When the Egemosegård Stud was formed and the Knabstrupper was revived following World War II, one of the two stallions, MAX BODILSKER, had a blanket pattern. Although leopards are more common, blanketed Knabstruppers can still be found.

Both the Polish warmblood breeds, the Malopolski and the Wielkopolski, have individuals with blanket patterns. The smaller patterns are

Some of the pinto patterning genes are known to alter the appearance of appaloosa patterns. When paired with leopard complex, some may also play a role in creating certain kinds of appaloosa patterns.

rare in the Noriker, which has historically been selected for the leopard pattern, but they do exist. Blanket patterns can also be found in the British Spotted Pony, though like many other European appaloosa breeds, the leopard pattern is more common.

Back in the New World, blanket patterns are found among the Spanish Mustangs and the Pony of the Americas, as well as in the Miniature Horse. Miniatures, which have such a wide range of patterns and modifiers, present the opportunity to study unusual combinations of large and small-effect appaloosa patterns along with the white patterning caused by the pinto genes.

Pintaloosas

There are two ways to categorize horses as pinta-loosas. The first is to decide that all horses that car-ry both leopard complex and one or more of the pinto patterning mutations are pintaloosas, which is certainly accurate. The second option is to re-serve the name pintaloosa for those horses that the average horseman would recognize as having both types of patterns. At the moment, the latter approach is more common.

Many of the pinto patterns, in their more mini-mal forms of expression, are not obvious even to experienced observers. Since these horses can go unnoticed among solid horses, it is reasonable to expect that a number of appaloosas, if they come from populations where those genes are found, also have these types of patterns. Using this defini-tion, a pretty sizable percentage of American Ap-paloosas would technically be pintaloosas. For in-dentification and registration purposes, however, they are just appaloosas.

Minimally expressed patterns complicate the situation with pintaloosas, but the real issue is the line between a pinto patterning gene and an appaloosas patterning gene. As mentioned in the previous chapter, the leopard complex gene ap-pears able to incorporate some forms of pinto patterning into its patterns. Pintaloosas, then, can be said to be those horses that have leopard com-plex and one of the pinto patterns that it is not able to co-opt for its own patterning. Again, be-cause pintaloosas are categorized based on visual rather than genetic identification, this is the ac-tual approach, even if it has not necessarily been thought out as such.

Tobianos

The most common type of visual pintaloosa is the combination with tobiano. It is the image most peo-ple have when they think of a pintaloosa pattern.

One of the things that makes tobiano pintaloo-sas so easy to identify is that the tobiano pattern, which is already among the easiest pinto patterns to identify, is unaltered. The horse looks like a to-biano that has had its colored areas swapped out for an appaloosa pattern.

The majority of the tobiano pintaloosas are var-nish roans. The more contrasted appaloosa pat-terns do occur in combination with tobiano, but they are less common. It is likely that this is be-cause most pintaloosas are randomly bred, rather than a genetic factor like gene linkage. Contrast-ing patterns like leopards and blankets can be lost in appaloosa breeding programs if crosses are not planned to maximize their preservation.

Tobianos with extensive cat tracks, and horses that have belton patterning (see page 116) are sometimes mistaken for pintaloosas. This comes from the erroneous idea that appaloosa patterns, particularly the leopard pattern, add dark spots to a white background. While that might seem logical, the spots from the appaloosa patterns do not spread over onto the tobiano pattern because the appaloosa patterning genes do not add dark spots to white, but rather alters varnish roan into a spotted pattern. Appaloosa patterns are an al-teration of a colored area, not a white area. That is why appaloosas have striped hooves on their colored feet, but not on the feet that have white leg markings.

Splashed White

The other pattern that does not appear to be al-tered by leopard complex is splashed white, or more specifically classic splash (*SW1*). Because the other two identified splashed white patterns are recent mutations, their interaction with appaloosa patterns is not yet known.

Many splashed white pintaloosas, which are sometimes called splashaloosas to differentiate them from the better-known tobiano pintaloosas, are not immediately recognizable as pintos. Hors-es with just one copy of the classic splash gene are often only minimally marked, but the horses that also have sabino patterning are more likely to have extensively white faces and blue eyes. That is why pintaloosas that have white faces, high stockings and belly white often have the frosty hip blankets. The same sabino pattern responsible for boosting the amount of white from the splash pattern is also working in conjunction with leopard complex to create a frosty blanket on the the hindquarters. Al-though many recognize this type of pattern as a pintaloosa, it often falls within the range of what is acceptable to appaloosa registries.

The pintaloosas that are homozygous for splashed white are not usually registerable with appaloosa registries. Like the tobiano pintaloosas, their white pinto patterning is unaltered, but the colored areas show the appaloosa patterning. Unlike the tobiano pattern, however, the classic splash pattern tends to take color away from the hindquarters, where varnish roaning is often first visible. White also covers the areas where the appaloosa characteristics are found: the face, the hooves and the areas under the tail. This makes it difficult to tell if young classic splash crop-outs have also inherited the leopard complex.

Frame Overo
Appaloosa patterns do not appear to interact with frame. There have been a few Appaloosas that have what look like pure frame patterns superimposed over their appaloosa patterns. At least one is a leopard with the large spots that are typical of an appaloosa that does not have white face or leg markings. This would suggest that leopard complex does not interact, or does so only minimally, with the frame pattern. There are relatively few identified frame pintaloosas, however, so any conclusions about them should be considered provisional.

Inheritance and Testing
Although the pinto and appaloosa patterns can work together, they are caused by different genes, each inherited separately. Because they are separate, pintaloosas can produce pintos, appaloosas and other pintaloosas. The exact possibilities depend on the individual patterns and whether the horse is homozygous for them, but each different pattern represents a separate genetic chance. The foal of a tobiano with a blanket pattern, for example, would get one chance for tobiano, one chance for the leopard complex, and one chance for the pattern responsible for the blanket. Pintaloosas are limited to producing the types of patterns they have, so a horse that is both tobiano and varnish roan cannot produce a true leopard, because that particular combination does not have the gene for leopard patterning (*PATN1*).

It is possible to test for leopard complex and a handful of the pinto patterns, but the majority of pinto patterns remain unidentified. Pintaloosas are vulnerable to any of the health problems associated with their pinto pattern or with leopard complex, but the combination of the patterns does not create any new health issues.

History and Breed Distribution
Even during the Baroque period, when both tobianos and appaloosas were at the height of their popularity, tobiano pintaloosas are notably absent from paintings and engravings. This is somewhat surprising since the two colors were both considered desirable for haute école. Sabino-influenced leopard patterns are also missing. It may be that this was intentional, since keeping herds separated according to color has a long history at European state studs.

It is likely that unintentional mixing of appaloosas and pintos occured, particularly in programs seeking to produce true white horses. Horses that are homozygous for leopard complex and for pattern-1 are often very white, and can be mistaken for white-born pintos. Accounts from the

The combination of tobiano and leopard complex is one of the most readily identifiable forms of pintaloosa, and also one of the most common. This mare has a large snip, white chin and two partially blue eyes, so probably carries one of the overo patterns in addition to tobiano.

Frederiksborg Stud suggest that this happened, as does confusion over whether the Lipizzan founder PLUTO was white-born, a fewspot appaloosa, or a white grey.

In modern times, the practice of keeping the two types of patterns separate has been nearly universal, even in breeds where broken colors were considered desirable. From the start, both the American and the British Shetland registries forbid the registration of ponies with appaloosa patterns. American color breed registries invariably banned the use of breeding stock that exhibited a different pattern than the one they promoted.

In the Appaloosa breed, the splashed white pattern has been present from the earliest days of the registry. The most influential source for the pattern is the Hall of Fame stallion BRIGHT EYES BROTHER. His unregistered dam, PLAUDETTE, had the classic splash pattern, and his line was known to produce occasional crop-outs with the classic pattern. There were other early sires that had facial markings that suggested that they, too, carried the splashed white pattern, including HANDS UP and his Hall of Fame son HIGH HAND.

The tendency of these lines, and others, to throw undesirable white has long been controversial among Appaloosa breeders. Officially, the Appaloosa Horse Club will not register horses that have "Pinto or Paint breeding" or that have undesirable white markings. This was complicated by recent changes in the Quarter Horse registry, which meant that it was possible to have an Appaloosa with grandparents that were dual-registered with the Paint Horse registry. It was ruled that such horses were eligible, provided that the Quarter Horse parent did not have the notation for undesirable white on his registration papers. This ruling would effectively control the introduction of obvious pintaloosas through outcrossing to colored Quarter Horses, but it does leave open the possibility of introducing some of the white patterning genes, particularly frame overo and splashed white, which can be present in horses that appear quite minimally marked with white.

Because tobiano is shunned by many breeders of Colonial Spanish horses, tobiano pintaloosas are not common in that group. There have been appaloosa Spanish Mustangs that have tested positive for frame overo, including the stallion DUNSMOKE MAVERICK. Because frame overo is a New World mutation, it is unlikely that many appaloosas outside the United States carry it. Even within the American breeds, it is rare.

In Danish Knabstruppers, horses with "distinctly piebald or skewbald markings" are ineligible for grading, though just what constitutes a distinct pinto marking is open to interpretation. Even horse color researchers do not all agree upon that topic. Stallions with blue eyes are also ineligible for grading, which would tend to minimize (but not necessarily eliminate) the splashed white pattern.

Pintaloosas are readily accepted by the American Miniature and the Gypsy Horse. The most common combination in both breeds is with the tobiano pattern, though frame overo and splashed white combinations are found in Miniatures. In Miniatures, one of the leading sires, ORION LIGHT VANT HUTTENEST, was a black near-leopard with the tobiano pattern. A number of his successful sons, including BREWERS ORION COMMANDER and XENON LIGHT VANT HUTTENEST, were pintaloosas. Another breed where tobiano pintaloosas have been accepted is the Felin Pony, which was developed in Poland as a colorful pony for children.

There is at least one tobiano pintaloosa in the Noriker. One of the interesting aspects of the reintroduction of the tobiano pattern into the breed (discussed more thoroughly in the chapter on Norikers) is that a leopard appaloosa stallion, GRUNDNER VULKAN, was used in the program and produced the primary tobiano stallions, GAUNER VULKAN and LOTTO VULCAN. Since neither has a visable appaloosa pattern, they did not inherit leopard complex (*Lp*), but it is possible they or their descendants carry a hidden copy of their sire's leopard patterning (*PATN1*) gene.

Markings and Distinctive Traits

With the increasing awareness that many white patterns have a variable range of expression (and often multiple forms!), the line between white markings and white patterning has become very uncertain. This book was written with the assumption that there is a separate genetic mechanism that creates ordinary white markings on the face and legs, as well as a handful of pinto patterning genes that can also produce horses with what look like ordinary markings. Although a number of extremely detailed statistical analyses have been done on white markings, there are still many unanswered questions and understanding is still in the early stages.

In addition to white markings, there are characteristics that are not usually extensive enough to be considered a separate color, but that are often thought of as identifying traits in individual animals. Like white markings, many of these traits are only partially understood.

Face and Leg Markings

White markings on the face and legs are common among domestic horses. On the face this can range from a sprinkling of white hairs on the forehead to a head that is completely white. The legs can have as little as a small spot of white on the heel, or white that extends all the way to the body. The typical amount of white varies between breeds, and even between different bloodlines within the same breed.

Some factors are known to have an impact on white markings. Chestnut horses have significantly more white on average than bays, which in turn have slightly more white than black horses. Because of this, black-based colors, and black in particular, are said to be resistant to white markings. The hind legs are more likely to be white than the front legs, and there is slightly more white to the left side of the horse than the right. In some breeds, there is a gender bias in markings.

White face markings on horses originate in four different places: the forehead, the bridge of the nose, the nose, and the chin. The corresponding markings are the star, strip, snip, and chin spot. Studies have shown that of the markings on the face itself (discounting the chin), the most common solitary marking was the star, while the least common was the snip. White on the nose is far more common on horses that already have white in one of the other areas. At least one study showed that with chestnut horses, the second-most common marking after a star was a blaze.

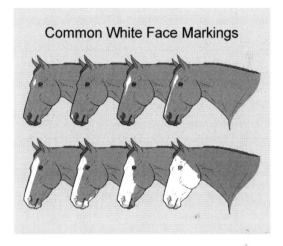

Common White Face Markings

Figure 10. From left to right, starting at the top: star, snip, comet, and a strip or narrow blaze. The markings on the second row are closely associated with white patterning genes. The first two are typical of the sabino patterns, the third of frame overo and the last of splashed white.

White markings on the legs consistently originate from the hoof. Front legs are more likely to be marked with white if at least one of the hind legs is also white. Leg markings tend to correlate with white markings on the face. Horses that have extensively white on the face are far more likely to have white on the legs than horses that have solid faces. This is not an absolute rule, especially in populations where pinto patterns are found, and there are populations that are notable for their deviation from this. Haflingers, for example, often have blazes, but rarely have white on the legs. At

Sabinos often have white that travels down the face, over the muzzle and then under the jawline. Note that this gelding also has a colored spot over his eye set inside his blaze.

the same time it is not unusual to find Akhal-Tekes or Hackneys with four white legs and only a small star or even a solid face.

Although there are consistent tendencies, the genetic mechanisms behind markings are not clear. Because two parents with markings can produce a foal without white, and two unmarked parents can produce a foal with markings, it is assumed that multiple genes are involved. The prevailing theory is that there is one major gene, probably recessive, that increases the likelihood that the horse will have white markings. It is thought to be located on KIT (the same genetic site as sabino-1 and the dominant white mutations), which would explain the tendency for chestnut horses to have more extensive markings, since Extension (the red/black gene) is located nearby.

Random Chance

It is likely that multiple genes have a role in white markings, but they are only part of the picture. Using mathematical models to analyze markings in the Arabian breed, C. M. Woolf found the genetic influence on the amount of white to be around 77 percent. That finding suggests that horses with the same genetic makeup might have significantly different markings.

The truth of this has become more obvious with the advent of cloning. Cloned animals carry the same genetic instructions as the original, yet they show surprising variation in white patterning. One of the more striking instances of this is the Quarter Horse gelding GILLS BAY BOY (Scamper) and his clone CLAYTON. Scamper has a hind sock and a solid face, while his clone has two hind socks and a broad broken blaze that extends to the inside edge of both nostrils and the bottom of the upper lip.

The difference between the two outcomes is often attributed to environmental factors, such as conditions or events during pregnancy. This does not take into account the third factor, which is random chance. The scientific term for this is *stochastic events*. White markings have a genetic basis, but just which part of the face and limbs have pigment depends, at least to some degree, on random chance.

Markings and Patterns

Understanding the genetics of white markings is complicated by the fact that there are pinto patterns that also put white on the face and legs. At the more minimal end of their expression, the sabino and splashed white patterns put white on the face and legs. Frame can do this to the face, and tobiano can add leg markings. Indeed, in some of the pony breeds, the presence of white on the feet may be the only sign that tobiano is present.

For some of these patterns, notably the sabino group, the line between the pattern and white markings is still unclear. It is quite possible that at least some sabino patterns have a relationship with ordinary markings. Others, like heterozygous classic splash, produce markings that can be difficult to distinguish from ordinary markings. It is quite likely that past studies of white markings included horses with a mix of true markings and those caused by various white patterning genes, which could help explain why no clear pattern of inheritance emerged.

Because multiple factors are involved in the production of white markings, including random chance, it is not always possible to predict the nature and extent of white markings in future offspring. It can be surprisingly difficult to determine which genetic mechanism caused markings on adult horses. There are, however, some tendencies that can be used as clues.

Face markings have the most variability, and so often provide the most information. Blazes that extend down the face towards the nose and chin, and then wrap under the jaw, are typical of the sabino patterns. A bald face that widens across the area between the muzzle and the cheek is more typical of frame overo. White that covers the entire head, sometimes called a paperface, is typical of the splashed white patterns. Broad, angular or off-set stars or snips are common in heterozygous classic splashes.

Legs white has less variation, but there are clues in the way the markings rise towards the body. Hind socks or stockings that come to a point in the front of the leg are associated with the sabino patterns. Dramatic differences in the height of a leg marking, either between the front and the back or the inside and the outside of the leg are also common in sabinos. Hind stockings that rise to a point on the outside of the leg are more typical of tobianos.

Those are tendencies, but there is a lot more to learn about both ordinary markings and the patterns that put white on the face and legs. Until the different patterns can be identified and their boundaries understood, they will continue to complicate the picture.

Whole-Coloured and Solid

Distinctions must be made between the two ways in which horses are commonly said to be a solid color. In the stricter sense, a solid horse is one that does not have white markings on the face or legs. In Britain these types of horses are often called whole-coloured. Solid is also used to describe a horse that does not have a pinto or appaloosa pattern. This second type of solid might have ordinary white markings. Solid, in this sense, means the horse is not visibly patterned.

From a genetic standpoint, it might be more accurate to offer five basic categories:

1) Horses that are unmarked and lack the ability to make white markings
2) Horses that are unmarked but carry some genetic factor that could create white markings
2) Horses that have ordinary white markings
3) Horses that have white markings on the face and legs caused by one of the pinto patterns
4) Horses that have white markings on the face and legs that are caused by some combination of marking and pinto genes

Using the stricter definition, only the first two groups would be considered solid, though horses from the second group might occasionally produce offspring marked with white. Using the second definition, all five categories would be considered solid, though only the first three—horses without marking genes and horses with only ordinary white markings—might be reliable producers of solids. Horses in the second two categories might produce a mix of solid and pinto offspring.

For breeders seeking to produce whole-coloured horses, the usual approach is to strictly limit the amount of white to a small star on the forehead. Registries sometimes go as far as to specify a maximum diameter for stars. This appears to be quite effective in keeping horses free from white markings, but it is not foolproof. The fact that there is that second group that are unmarked but that carry the ability to produce markings means that two unmarked parents can produce a foal with white

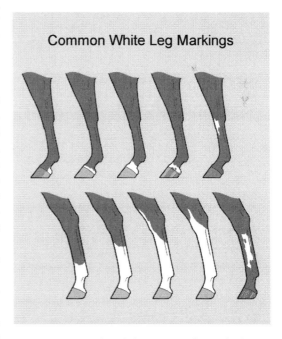

Figure 11. From right to left, starting at the top: heel, coronet, ankle, ermine spots, knee patch, sock, stocking, stocking typical of sabino, stocking typical of tobiano, lightning marks seen on some appaloosas.

markings. This does occur on rare occasions in otherwise whole-coloured breeds. The result can be particularly dramatic if the two whole-coloured parents are bay or black, and the foal is chestnut. In breeds where strict selection for unmarked horses has been practiced, and where the population is small or highly inbred, there is a greater chance that the white marking carriers have been eliminated.

For the purposes of this book, horses that have no white on the head or legs are referred to as unmarked or whole-coloured. Horses that are not thought to carry one of the white patterning genes, but that may or may not have ordinary white markings, are referred to as solid.

Markings Specific to Patterns

At the current level of understanding, predicting patterns based solely on markings is a bit like try-

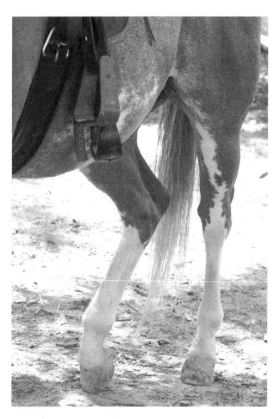

Stockings on sabinos often end in a point on the front of the hind leg, or travel up the gaskin towards the stifle. Irregular or roaned edges are common. (The same horse is pictured on page 73 and 102.)

ing to read tea leaves, and it is wise to be skeptical that traits are exclusively tied to one pattern when so much is still unknown. However, there are a handful of markings that are more likely to be specific to certain patterns, or at least specific to horses with some kind of pattern.

Lightning Marks

One of the clearest examples of markings unique a specific pattern are what appaloosa breeders call lightning marks. These are irregular areas of white on the dark legs of an appaloosa. They are unusual because unlike standard leg markings, they do not originate at the hoof. Most are found on the sides of the cannons between the knee and the pastern, though the placement can slip up or down somewhat. When viewed in profile, the outer edge of the leg typically remains dark much like the body is outlined on a frame overo. Lightning markings often have a torn, irregular outline, and may have smaller spots set inside the white area. It may be that lightning marks are an incomplete form of the white that normally covers the leg of an appaloosa, while leaving dark triangles to the front of the coronet and a dark "zipper" up the back of the leg.

Knee and Stifle Patches

The disconnected patches of white found on the knees and stifles are probably specific to certain types of sabino patterns. Knee patches are most often found at the front of the knee and tend to have ragged, angular edges. Separate patches of white are less common on the fronts of the hocks or stifles, but do occur.

Chin Spots

Markings on the lower lip and chin have been of special interest to researchers. In 1936, Blunn and Howell conducted a study of white markings in the Arabian Horse that suggested white on the face had a dominant mode of inheritance, while white on the chin was recessive. They found that when crossing chin spot to chin spot, fourteen of the twenty-one foals had a chin spot. The remaining seven were believed to have been inaccurately recorded. Under-reporting of chin spots in stud book records is common, but the assumption did dismiss one-third of what was already a small sample set. Later studies have found the situation with white that extends over the chin to be more complex.

White that extends to the lower lip or chin is closely associated with white patterns, particularly those in the sabino group. Whether white chins are exclusive to pinto patterns, and cannot occur as part of ordinary white markings, is not known. What is interesting is that while it seems possible to breed horses with blazes, even rather broad ones, and still maintain consistently dark legs, once the face white extends to the lower lip it becomes much harder to keep the white off the legs. The leg white is not necessarily extensive, but most horses that have readily observable white on the chin have at least one white foot.

Suppressors

In addition to factors that add white markings to the horse, there are factors that limit the amount of white. Black-based colors are believed to suppress the expression of white. It has even been shown that horses that are homozygous for the black gene (*EE*) have less white than horses that carry chestnut. The recessive form of Agouti, *a*, is thought to suppress white markings further, so that black horses have less white than bays.

In addition to the base color, some researchers have speculated about the possibility of a separate "white suppressor" gene. It is already believed that there are small-effect genes that add to the whiteness of horses with markings and patterns, so it is not much of a leap to imagine that there are factors that might have the opposite effect. Such genes could explain the variation in levels of white on parents and foals, and the tendency in some breeds for patterns to remain more minimally expressed.

When considering the possibility of white suppressors, those breeds that have not been specifically selected for solid colors, but are nonetheless conservatively marked are of particular interest. It is sometimes said that breeds like the British Shetland, the Icelandic and the Gotland Pony lack the sabino gene, and that does seem to be true. What is perhaps more interesting is that they appear to lack ordinary markings unless they inherit one of the white patterning genes. In the British Shetland, ponies with white legs are invariably minimally

Although the top horse looks like he has a small star and a large snip, the irregular outlines suggest that he has a blaze that has been partially obscured by several large overlapping spots of color. The Criollo mare below is a more dramatic example of occluding spots, with a large patch obscuring all but the outermost edges of her white face marking. Horses like this are sometimes said to be badger-faced.

Completely dark legs on tobianos are rare. Although this gelding appears to have a dark right front foreleg, there is a small amount of white on the heel only visible from behind. White suppressor genes are suspected in breeds where dark-legged tobianos are common.

spots merge into one continuous band around the coronet, giving the horse a completely dark hoof. Other horses have ermine spots that look more like angular patches than small, round spots.

On tobianos, ermine spotting is usually part of the cat tracking seen in homozygous horses. The cause of ermine spots on ordinary markings is not known. Most horses with ermine spots do not have corresponding spots on their face markings, nor do the spots tend to spread far up the leg. The possibility that horses with the rarer all-over ermine spots might have a different pattern is discussed in the section about Belton patterning.

On the face, color is sometimes added back in the form of occluding spots. These are the patches that overlap white face markings. In its most minimal form, an occluding spot can take the form of a round patch of color inside a blaze. Sometimes the spot is offset so that it overlaps part of the white, giving the marking an irregular or broken outline. Many horses that have broken blazes appear to have occluding spots that bisect the original white marking. In their most extreme form, occluding spots can cover most of the forehead down to the nose, so that all that is left of the original face marking is an irregular outline of white. Horses with this type of marking are sometimes said to be badger-faced. Badger markings are occasionally seen on horses with an otherwise white head, which gives the impression that the normal order of a dark head with a white blaze has been reversed. In her book *Horse Color Explained*, Jeanette Gower has a particularly striking example of a sabino roan Clydesdale with this type of badger marking.

marked tobianos. (This is not necessarily true of ponies bred outside of the British Isles, particularly those in America, where outside blood has expanded the range of colors and patterns.) The situation is similar with the Icelandic. It is not known if the minimal nature of their patterns is connected to the absence of markings, or of sabino, or if there is a separate gene that encourages color at the expense of white markings.

Occluding Spots

In addition to genes that suppress white markings, there appear to be factors that can add color back again in the form of spots or patches. The most familiar of these are the ermine spots that are sometimes found on horses with white leg markings. Ermine spots are often concentrated around the coronary band, where they result in a particolored hoof. On some homozygous tobianos, the ermine

History and Breed Distribution

In mammals, the appearance of white markings on the extremities is closely tied to domestication. One of the most cited studies on this topic is Dmitry Belyaev's program to breed a more docile Silver Fox. Within eight generations, white markings appeared. Though other traits now associated with domestication appeared in later generations, white markings were the first. Forty years later, the domesticated fox population had approximately 12,400 white-marked foxes for every 100,000 animals. This represented a 1,646 percent increase over the incidence of white markings in the wild population. What makes these numbers particularly interesting is that the foxes were only selected for tameness; no other factor was considered. The presence of white markings in domestic horses is often attributed to selection for the trait, but the Russian experiment suggests that just selecting for tameness might produce a similar result.

Even so, it is likely that ancient horses were selected for distinctive markings. It is known that some of the white patterns were present among early horses, and the fact that they were included in ceremonial burials suggests that they were valued. White patterns were certainly valued in Early Modern period, which is the earliest period for which there is a great deal of visual evidence. In the last two centuries, however, western horse breeders have largely focused on controlling or eliminating white markings and patterns. Fashions changed, and conservatively markings and the ability of a breeding horse to reduce white became highly prized.

It is not surprising then that many registries adopted "white rules" that specified the amount and the location of white markings. The most common limitation for the face was an area created by drawing a line from the furthest corner of the eye to the corner of the mouth, and then down to the chin, or the entire head from the front of the ear to the back of the cheek. On the legs, the lines were typically drawn at the knees and hocks, or midway between those joints and the body.

Many of these rules have been eliminated in recent years. In the United States, a legal challenge to the American Quarter Horse Association position on registering embryo transfer horses resulted in a ruling that the measure violated Texas anti-trust laws. To protect itself from similar lawsuits by owners of horses denied registration for having excessive white, the rules limiting white markings were dropped. Many smaller registries followed suit. In Europe, similar problems arose from the requirement that registries provide horses with

The white legs of some pintos have such dense ermine spotting that the entire hoof is dark. This is most often seen in homozygous tobianos.

passports, and some registries responded by establishing appendix registers to record off-color horses.

There has also been growing awareness of the issue of depleted genetic diversity in rare breeds, which has led some registries to relax rules that deal with cosmetic issues like markings. Although solid horses, or those with more conservative markings are still considered preferable, horses that might previously have been denied inclusion in the stud books can now be incorporated into breeding programs so long as they are bred in such a way that the white is not perpetuated.

Meanwhile is some breeds where markings are not limited, there has been a clear trend towards increased levels of white. This was shown in the study of markings in the Freiberger, which has seen a doubling in the size and number of white markings in the last thirty years, despite a general preference for more conservative markings. Even without a formal study, browsing through old livestock publications with images of breeds like Shires and Clydesdales, the difference in the amount of white is striking. While fashion has changed once again, and flashy markings and patterns are popular, the increase points to the likelihood that there are additive factors involved. If that is the case, a thorough understanding of the mechanisms involved would be extremely valuable for those seeking to minimize the amount of white.

Eye Color

The majority of horses have dark brown eyes. Foals are sometimes born with smoky blue eyes that darken to brown. Although it is less common, adult horses can have light brown, yellow, hazel or blue eyes. Pale eyes are closely associated with dilutions, and bright blue eyes with some of the pinto patterns. Also, in rare instances, horses can have hazel or golden eyes that appear to be unrelated to any coat color or pattern.

Diluted Eyes

Some of the dilutions lighten the color of the eyes. In general, the pale eyes of a diluted horse are warmer in tone than those associated with the pinto patterns. They are also more prone to shifts in color as the horse matures. This is the group of eye colors with the widest variations in tone and shade, so it is possible to find horses that stray somewhat from what is typical for their coat color.

Heterozygous Creams

Most horses with one copy of the cream gene have dark eyes, but a few have eyes that are light brown. Typically these are not green or even golden eyes, but still noticeably lighter than a normal brown eye. Cream foals, particularly palominos, are often born with blue or dusky blue eyes, though these tend to be darker and change much more rapidly to brown than the blue eyes on champagne foals. Creams that also have the silver dilution are often born with dusky gray-blue or gray-green eyes that darken to light brown or brown at maturity.

Homozygous Creams

As the name blue-eyed cream suggests, horses with two copies of the cream gene have blue eyes. Although the eyes are blue, they are a more muted shade than the blue eyes seen on pintos. When the two are compared side by side, those on the blue-eyed creams have a creamy golden cast that makes them appear neutral to almost green-blue, whereas those on the pintos are an icy blue. It is not unusual to see darker blue, green, gold or even light

brown striations in the eyes of a blue-eyed cream. Many also have a slightly darker green-gold band around the outside of the iris.

Although the eyes of double-diluted creams are warmer tone, the overall impression is still that the eye is blue. Eyes that appear more truly gold or green are a good clue that the horse may be a double-dilute, but that the second dilution is something other than cream. Most often the second dilution is pearl or champagne.

Champagnes

Champagnes are born with bright blue eyes that darken to amber or light brown. The eyes on champagne foals are more truly blue in appearance than those on single-dilute cream foals. The blue begins to turn golden after a few months, shifting through a hazel-green color until reaching the adult color of amber or light brown.

Champagnes that have the cream dilution are also born with blue eyes, but they tend to retain the blue color longer. These shift from blue to green to amber, though some remain blue or blue-green. The lighter adult colors are more common on those with a chestnut base (gold cream champagnes) than those that are black-based. The

Horses homozygous for the cream gene, like this cremello, have pale blue eyes, and are sometimes referred to as blue-eyed creams (BEC).

black-based cream champagnes are more likely to have amber eyes as adults.

Pearl
Because pearl is recessive, horses with just one copy of the gene have ordinary dark eyes. Homozygous pearls have golden or light brown eyes. As with the champagnes, homozygous pearls on a chestnut base color often have paler eyes than those on black-based colors.

Cream pearls, which are horses that have one copy of pearl and one copy of cream, have paler eyes than the homozygous pearls. The color can be very similar to that of a blue-eyed cream, but generally cream pearl eyes are closer to a green-gold or golden tan. This can give cream pearls a somewhat monochromatic appearance, since their eye color is often close in color to their coat.

Light Black
One of the features of light black horses is that they have pale eyes. In color the eyes often resemble the light brown seen in some cream dilutes, though others are somewhat lighter and closer to golden. Some light black horses are said to have been born blue-eyed. The light black Arabian mare Lira II (1964) was reported to have been glass-eyed at birth, though by six months her eyes were golden. Because the color is rare and not well understood, it is not clear if this is typical, but it is similar to what occurs in other dilutions.

Blue Eyes
In horses, bright blue eyes are associated with the white patterning genes. Although blue eyes can be found on horses with very little facial white, their appearance is considered a sign that one of the pinto patterns is present. To date, no "blue-eyed gene" that is independent of white patterning has been identified in horses.

Blue eyes can occur when the area around the eye is colored. (Conversely, dark eyes can occur when the area around the eye is entirely white.) Horses can have one or both eyes blue, or just portions that are blue. Horses with partially blue eyes are sometimes said to have bicolored eyes. The small sections of blue are called segments.

It is sometimes said that certain patterns, usually the splashed white patterns, produce eyes that are a deeper shade of blue. Lorna Howlett, in the *Complete Book of Ponies*, describes the blue eyes associated with the splash pattern as being a "deep forget-me-not blue" that was quite distinct from a colorless wall-eye. The lack of comprehensive tests for the many different pinto patterns make it difficult to determine whether or not the shade of blue varies between them. It is true that the color is quite different from the blue seen on double-diluted creams. The difference is particularly striking on the rare occasion that a blue-eyed cream has an eye with a segment of blue caused by pinto patterning.

Splashed White
The patterns most closely associated with blue eyes are the group known as splashed white. Splashed whites are more consistently blue-eyed than any of the other pinto patterns. Within that group, however, the regularity of blue eyes varies.

The oldest of the splashed white patterns, classic splash (*SW1*), is an incomplete dominant. In that pattern, heterozygous horses are occasionally blue-eyed. In breeds where markings are minimal or completely absent, like the Gotland Pony, it is uncommon to find a heterozygous horse with a blue eye. When other patterns are present, blue eyes occur more often. The homozygous horses, however, appear to be uniformly blue-eyed. Even when the colored area has extended across the eyes, horses with the classic (homozygous) pattern have had two blue eyes.

The horses that have the Australian splashed white pattern, which originated with the stallion Bald Eagle, consistently have two blue eyes. The two more recent splashed white mutations, *SW2* and *SW3*, often have blue eyes, though both occurred in the Paint Horse breed where other forms of white patterning are common.

In addition to the Bald Eagle horses, there have been other horses that were expected to test positive for splash that did not. Many have blue eyes, and it is thought that many will prove to have splash mutations beyond the three that are currently identified.

Frame Overo

Frame overo is the other pattern that is often associated with blue eyes. Blue eyes do not occur quite as frequently in frame overos as they do in splashed whites, but they are not uncommon. In some breeds like the Miniature Horse, where the frame pattern tends to be very minimal, they can indicate the need to test for Lethal White Overo Syndrome (LWOS). This is particularly true when the horse has broad face white, blue eyes, and four dark legs.

Dominant White

Although dominant white is sometimes referred to as "black-eyed white" in older literature, perhaps to distinguish it from blue-eyed cream, not all dominant white horses are dark-eyed. The Groninger mare originally studied by Wiersema, Sneeuwwitje, had two blue eyes, as does the suspected dominant white Ardennes stallion Very White du Vallon. The founder of the eighth white family (*W8*), the Icelandic mare Thokkadis vom Rosenhof, has two partially blue eyes. Two of the formally identified dominant white families, those of R Khasper (*W3*) and Puchilingui (*W5*), have produced blue eyes and partially blue eyes. The Japanese Thoroughbred Shirayukihime, suspected to be a dominant white, has at least two sons with blue or partially blue eyes.

This is consistent with reports of occasional blue eyes among the Frederiksborg Whites and

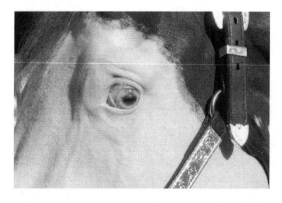

Blue eyes are most closely associated with the splashed white patterns, but the do occur in frame overos, dominant whites and sabinos.

the horses of later European studs that were involved in breeding white-born horses. It is possible that the blue eyes came from other white pattern mutations, but the fact that they appear consistently across a broad range of breeds, particularly among the founders, does suggest that their blue eyes may be a (less common) part of the pattern itself.

Sabino

Even more so than the dominant white patterns, the sabino patterns tend to result in dark-eyed horses. They can have blue eyes, but it is not yet known if the cause is the sabino pattern or some other pattern working with sabino. Certainly many of the sabino patterns, when paired with splashed white, appear to increase the chances of having blue eyes. There have also been a number of homozygous sabino-1 horses that had one or two blue eyes. Whether sabino-1 or any of the other sabino patterns can cause blue eyes on their own is an open question that probably will not be answered until a more comprehensive set of pinto tests are available.

Other Causes

Although horse color is much better understood than it was even just ten years ago, there are still a lot of unknowns. Blue eyes and their relationship with the different patterning genes is one of those unknowns. It is not uncommon to hear someone make the assertion that all horses with blue eyes are splashes or frames, and that a blue eye is proof of the presence of one of those two patterns. It is certainly true that those two patterns are known to produce blue eyes, but a clear link between a trait and a specific pattern does not prove an absolute and exclusive relationship. The fact that one pattern consistently produces blue eyes does not mean that other patterns cannot produce blue eyes, or that there could never be a separate, unrelated gene for blue eyes. It is too early, and there are still too many questions, to be sure what can—and what cannot—cause blue eyes.

It is clear that a surprising number of blue-eyed pintos have tested negative for both frame overo and the three separate splashed white tests, even though many of those horses were marked in such a way that their owners expected that they were splashed white. It is likely that there are additional splashed white mutations that have not yet been identified, and that some of these horses may later test positive for those. This may help answer the question of whether or not the other white patterns, or even an independent gene for blue eye coloring, can produce blue eyes. If there are blue-eyed pintos who do not have any changes at the two sites where splashed white mutations have been found, then it would be a strong argument for the idea that other patterns might also produce blue eyes.

Hazel and Tiger Eyes

Golden eyes, called tiger eyes, are known to occur in certain strains of Puerto Rican Paso Finos. Horses with the tiger eyes have normal, undiluted coats, which would suggest that it may be a mutation that only changes the color of the eyes. That would be unique in horses, which have not yet been shown to have a gene that alters eye color without changing the coat. Initial studies have indicated that the trait is recessive, and work is being done to isolate the mutation responsible.

Certain strains of Highland Pony are also known for having golden or hazel eyes. Like the Pasos, the eye color does not appear to be connected to any of the dilutions. A modern example is the stallion Torrin of Croila. He has pale golden eyes, but is an otherwise fully pigmented dark bay. There are a number of historical accounts of golden or hazel eyes in the breed, including the West Highland mare used in Professor Ewart's zebra hybrid experiments. Mulatto was said to be jet black with golden eyes. Her owner, Lord Arthur Cecil, believed that this combination was typical of the ponies from the Island of Rhum. Lord Cecil purchased many of these ponies, all said to be black with hazel eyes, to use for improvement of the New Forest Pony. There

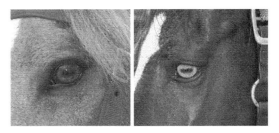

Some cream dilutes, like the silver buckskin (top left), have light or golden brown eyes. More rarely horses can have yellow "tiger" eyes (top right) or hazel eyes (bottom). Tiger eyes are the subject of a current study.

are also early accounts of hazel or golden eyes in both the Exmoor and the Welsh Pony.

It is not known if the tiger eyes in the Paso Finos and the hazel eyes in Highland Ponies are the result of the same gene, or if they are two separate but similar traits. Should the current research result in a test, that question could be answered.

Skin Pigmentation

In most instances, horses have dark skin unless the area has a marking or a white pattern, in which case the underlying skin is pink. A tobiano, for instance, would have dark skin under his colored spots, and pink skin under the white patterning. A handful of colors and conditions are the exceptions to this rule.

Dilutions

Some of the dilutions lighten the skin as well as the coat. Even those dilutions thought of as having dark skin, like single-dilute creams and silvers, can have skin that is not fully pigmented. Palominos often have skin that, upon closer examination, is not fully dark. This is not usually visible on the face of adult palominos, but on the parts of the body that have little or no hair, the skin may look purplish with tiny flecks of pink. Some chestnuts that carry pearl have been reported to have similar skin. Black silvers that inherit a single copy of the cream dilution can also have this type of skin, although theirs is often visible on the face as well as the rest of the body.

Champagne and homozygous pearls have more obviously diluted skin. Both are born with pink skin which darkens to a dusky lavender. As the horse matures, freckles begin to appear. Adult champagnes tend to have abundant, more clearly defined freckles. Adult pearls have less contrast

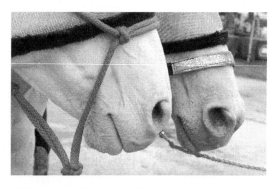

Although cremellos and perlinos are thought of as having pink skin, it is not the same clear pink that is found under white markings. The horse in the foreground is a white-faced pinto, and the horse behind him is a cremello.

between their freckles and the rest of their skin, which gives them a stippled rather than a freckled appearance. Older champagnes can be freckled to the extent that they also appear stippled, but the freckles give the skin a slightly deeper color.

Double-diluted creams are often said to be pink-skinned, but the skin is not the same unpigmented pink that is seen in the white areas of a pinto. There is some pigment present, which is obvious when one is standing beside a predominantly white pinto. If very pale champagnes and pearls can be said to have skin that is dusky lavender, blue-eyed creams have skin that is dusky pink. Most lack the freckling that is seen in champagnes and pearls, but there are double-diluted creams that have faint freckling, particularly on the face. This is more common in horses that spend a lot of time exposed to the sun, but there are also some individuals that are darker than average.

The skin on an ivory champagne typically falls somewhere in between blue-eyed creams and champagnes, but they and the atypical cremellos and perlinos illustrate just how difficult it can be to identify the different dilutes by skin color alone. It is often just one clue in determining which dilution genes are present, and sometimes the only way to be sure is to test.

Appaloosa Skin

Mottled skin is a well-known characteristic of appaloosas. This can cause horses that have one of the colors or conditions that produce variegated skin—champagne, pearl, greying, vitiligo—to be mistakenly identified as appaloosas. It is helpful to remember that while all appaloosas have some degree of speckled skin, not all horses with speckled skin are appaloosas. Often the character of the mottling makes the cause obvious, but there are quite a few depigmented greys that have skin that would be hard to distinguish from appaloosa mottling, and pale appaloosas with primarily pink skin that could be mistaken for dilutes.

Although appaloosas are known for having mottled skin, what may be more surprising is how often the horses have dark skin. Many loud appaloosa patterns have underlying dark skin. Near-leopards with small, closely-spaced spots can have

Loss of pigment happens more rarely among non-greys than greys, though when it does the patches are often larger. The ring around the eye is typical of the condition.

entirely dark skin (see the top image on page 94). Some nose-to-toes leopards have predominantly dark skin on the head and forehand, but have pink skin on the hindquarters in the form of a blanket pattern. That is why many leopards have faces that resemble those of a grey horse with dark spots superimposed, but have hindquarters that look like dark spots on a truly white background.

Depigmentation in Greys

In addition to a loss of pigment in the hair, some greys progressively lose skin pigment as well. In its most minimal form, this can begin with fine mottling around the edges of the lips and up the fleshy part of the nose. Often there are similar markings on the genitals and under the tail. There also might be fine specks of pink skin on the body, visible when the horse is wet.

These pink specks increase with age, travelling up the face along the tear bone and around the eye. Inside the ears is another common location. Over time the pink specks begin to merge until there are larger areas of pink.

Depigmentation is more prevalent in breeds like the Lipizzan and the Boulonnais, which have been selected for early and complete greying. Stallions tend to have more extensive pigment loss than mares, and some families are more prone than others. In breeds where skin depigmentation is common, making an occasional cross to a non-grey is believed to reduce pigment loss, which suggests that heterozygous greys may be less susceptible.

Depigmentation in Non-Greys

Occasionally horses that are born fully pigmented progressively lose color in irregular patches on the face, and particularly around the eyes and mouth. The most common name is vitiligo, though it is also known as Pinky Syndrome or Arabian Fading Syndrome. The problem is a cosmetic one and does not harm the horse. The reason the affected horses lose pigment is not known.

Horses with vitiligo have distinct patches of pink skin. The scale of the patches are usually larger than those found in depigmented greys, and more clearly pink than the mottling on most appaloosas. The most distinctive aspect of this kind of depigmentation is the ring around the eye, which often gives the horse a goggle-eyed look.

Pigment loss is common on the faces and undersides of greys. Because this is found in a higher frequency in some breeds and among some families, it is believed to have a genetic component.

Other Distinctive Marks

There are a number of other distinctive marks or patterns that occur in horses that defy easy categorization. Some of these are quite rare, which makes research challenging. As a result, the causes for many of these traits are poorly understood.

Bend Or Spots

Bend Or spots are patches of dark hair that are sometimes found on chestnuts or horses that have a chestnut base color. Most Bend Or spots look sooty rather than truly black. They are most often seen on the hindquarters, particularly the hips, but they can occur anywhere. The size varies, but most are similar in scale to the spots seen on appaloosas. That is why horses with abundant Bend Or spots resemble a leopard appaloosa with a red or yellow background in place of the white.

Palominos seem particularly inclined to have abundant Bend Or spotting. This is particularly interesting because Bend Or spots have a sooty appearance, and palominos are also prone to the more dramatic forms of sooty dappling. It may be that Bend Or spots are one way that the sooty pattern expresses on a chestnut horse, or that there is some relationship between the two modifiers.

Bend Or spots are named for the Thoroughbred stallion Bend Or, who had them and was prone to producing them. Interestingly, Bend Or was a chestnut with random white spots in addition to the darker ones. His ancestor, Comus, also had both white and dark spots, which might explain why some horsemen use the term Bend Or spots to refer to random spotting on solid horses, whether white or black.

Birdcatcher Spots

Random white spots on a solid horse are known as Birdcatcher spots. The spots get their name from a nineteenth century racehorse known as Irish Birdcatcher, but the original Birdcatcher did not have the markings that eventually took his name. With white ticking on his flanks and a white tailhead, he was most likely a rabicano.

Birdcatcher spots are most often seen on chestnut horses and develop some time during adult-

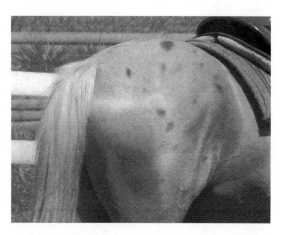

Sooty patches on the body of chestnut-based horse are known as Bend Or spots, for the Thoroughbred racehorse that was known to have them. Extensive Bend Or spotting covering the entire body occur more frequently on palominos.

hood. They tend to be small, round and clearly white (not roan). Some horses lose them over time, while others acquire more, but the pattern is not truly progressive in that horses do not become more spotted with each change of coat.

There is a rare pattern of white spotting that is often identified as Birdcatcher spotting that does appear to be progressive. Horses with this type of pattern acquire white spots which increase over time. More extensively spotted individuals can look very similar to the more mottled varnish roan appaloosas, though they lack the other appaloosa characteristics. Unlike Birdcatcher spots, the spots on these horses are not an opaque white and are less distinct in outline. The cause is not known, but it does not appear to be related to traditional Birdcatcher spotting. It may be that this type of pattern is involved in some of the appaloosas that have round white spotting, since horses with it might have been included in appaloosa breeding programs under the assumption that they were appaloosas of some kind. At least one Thoroughbred with this type of pattern, Pelouse's Queen, was used in the Money Creek Ranch appaloosa breeding program.

It is possible that this second form of Birdcatcher spotting is related to, or is simply another form of, the fungal spots discussed in the chapter on white hair patterns. There have been claims that a fungal infection was responsible for the pattern on PELOUSE'S QUEEN, though the source of that information is not known. Breeders are inclined to attribute unexpected white hair to fungal infections or reactions to shampoos or fly repellents, though the author is unaware of formal studies on the condition

Brindling

Brindle horses have attracted a lot of attention in recent years, and a number of breeders have sought to develop lines of true-breeding brindles. Unfortunately the most distinctive form of brindling comes from a condition known as chimerism. A chimera, as the name suggests, is an organism that are created by the fusion of two separate individuals during embryonic development. Such animals have two separate sets of genetic material, just as two fraternal twins would have, mixed together in the same body. In horses, this condition can result in a brindled coat pattern similar to the Blaschko's Lines seen on the skin of human chimeras. The different stripes of color represent the colors of the two original horses, which is why chimeric brindles show so much variation in stripe color. A fusion of two chestnut horses might produce only a subtle contrast in the striping pattern, while the combination of a roan with a non-roan might produce faintly white stripes. Because they have more than one set of genetic material, modern chimeric brindles can be identified by testing. Well-known historical incidences of brindling that look similar to chimeric brindling, like the Noriker stallion NORBERT or the Arabian mare ROSSLETTA, remain open to speculation.

There have been brindles that were not chimeras, though they are much more rare. One of the most striking examples is the bay brindle mare BRENDA BATTY ATTY. Because BATTY ATTY produced at least one daughter with a similar pattern, some kind of genetic brindle is suspected. Most non-chimeric brindles have not shown a lot of contrast, or have only shown a brindled texture. It is thought that sootiness may play a role in more vivid brindles. Dun is another color that may be involved, though BATTY ATTY was a dark bay or brown horse with no dorsal stripe or dun factors.

White striping can look like brindling, but is typically limited to one side of the horse. Brindled marks on duns can also be asymmetrical. Although there has been speculation that a gene for brindling might have a partial expression, the horses with these markings are not known to have produced full-bodied brindling.

Mosaics

Chimeric brindles occur when two separate horses fuse together. Mosaics are single horses that have two different sets of genetic instructions due to an error during development. The most common type of mosaic in horses are those with irregular patches of black and chestnut. The Icelandic mare MILJON FRA GRUND and the Paint stallion STETSON'S MR. BLUE are two examples of mosaic horses. Like the chimeric brindles, mosaics are the result of a somatic mutation, and cannot reproduce their own color.

Mismarks

Mismarks are patches of white that do not correspond with any markings or white patterns. Mismarks tend to be found on unexpected parts of the body, like a hip or the barrel, on an otherwise solid or minimally marked horse. Mismarks often have underlying dark skin. Colored mismarks occur on patterned horses. Some leopard appaloosas have colored patches that are not part of their regular spotting patterns, and tobianos sometimes have what look like a colored sock on an otherwise nor-

Brindle in horses is not well-understood. Some are chimeras, but others appear to have sooty or dun markings that have been redirected into striping.

mal white tobiano leg. Most mismarks are probably somatic mutations, and not something that the horse is likely to pass along to offspring.

Bleach Spots
Some horses have an oddly diluted or roaned patch on their coat. In some cases the hair itself is paler than the rest of the coat, while in other it is the presence of white hairs. Some bleached spots made up of white hairs have a more intensely white outer ring, much like the water ring created by dropping solvent on paint. The cause for both types of bleach spots is not known.

Calicos
The colored areas on some buckskin and palomino tobianos are patched with red and yellow, much like the pattern on a calico cat. This happens when the cream gene fails to activate in random areas of the coat, leaving the hair the original red color. To date it has only been noted in tobianos, and only in a limited number of breeds. Unlike the calico pattern in cats, it is not linked to gender and so is found in both males and females.

Belton Patterning
Tobiano cat tracks and leopard patterning are the two most common causes for small spots of color on a white background. There are rare cases of horses that have a similar type of spotting inside their white markings, or inside the white areas of their pinto pattern, but that are not homozygous tobianos or leopard appaloosas. In these horses, the spotting is reminiscent of the kind of spotting seen in some piebald dogs, where it is called ticking. In English Setters, which have been selected for the pattern, it is called *belton*.

Although rare, some horses have dark ticking or spotting within their white markings similar to those seen on belton patterned dogs.

Unlike cat tracking, which tends to form irregular shapes that cluster around the existing tobiano patches, belton patterning is distributed more evenly across the body. Some individuals have more dense spotting inside the face markings, which is similar to the belton pattern in dogs, but quite unlike cat tracking in tobianos. It is also unlike appaloosa patterning in that the appaloosa patterns, when paired with pinto, alter the colored areas and not the white.

Like many of the rare color variants, belton patterning has not been formally studied and little is known about what causes it.

Breeds

Coaching Breeds

The nineteenth century was the golden age of carriage driving. Countries began to pave roads and the Industrial Revolution made is possible to mass-produce carriage parts, while a growing middle class provided a ready market for fashionable teams. The concept of a public breeding record in the form of a formal stud book was also beginning to gain support, and the coaching breeds were among the first to be organized. Elegant coach horses like the Cleveland Bay, the Hackney and the Oldenburg were in high demand and were exported in large numbers. Many were used to improve local stock for carriage and light agricultural work, but they were also among the first to be adversely affected by the rise of the automobile. Some countries took their coaching breeds and refashioned them into sport horses, laying the foundation for the modern warmblood. Almost too late it was realized that the original type of horse was at risk. Most of the breeds in this section have conservation plans in effect to preserve the breeding stock that remains.

Alt-Oldenburg

Origin: Lower Saxony in Germany

The Oldenburg was one of the best-known breeds at the turn of the last century and served as the foundation for many of the European coaching breeds. Like a lot of the closely related breeds, the Oldenburg transitioned to a lighter riding type after World War II, mostly using an infusion of Thoroughbred blood. Since that time, the Oldenburg has become one of the most liberal of the European stud books in terms of recognizing and utilizing horses from other breeding programs. In recent years there has been renewed interest in preserving the original type, which is called the Alt-Oldenburg.

Stud Book

The Oldenburg is unusual among European warmbloods in that it was initially developed by private breeders within the region rather than at a State Stud. The improvement of horses began during the seventeenth century when Count Johann XVI of Oldenburg brought in Turk, Neapolitan, Andalusian, Frederiksborg and Friesian stallions for his tenant farmers to use. His successor, Count Anton Günther, built on that foundation and the resulting horses were in demand throughout much of Europe.

Stallion inspections, which had started in neighboring Ostfrisia in 1715, had spread to Oldenburg by 1755. In 1820, a law was enacted requiring that stallions be approved for breeding, which effectively made the inspections mandatory. A stud book recording approved breeding stock was created in 1861. It took time—and further restrictions on the use of unrecorded stallions—for breeders to recognize its value, so the first volume of the stud book was not published until 1893. The book contained a section for current breeding stock and another for those animals accepted as ancestors of the breed.

From the start the Oldenburg and the neighboring East Friesian were closely related, both sharing common founder animals and exchanging breed-ing material. The two were separated by the Horse Breeding Act of 1897, which created one society for the horses of Oldenburg and one for the horses of Ostfrisia. From that point forward, all breeding animals in Oldenburg, male and female, were required to be registered in the stud book.

In the meantime, two registries were established in the United States, where Oldenburgs were known as German Coach Horses. The German, Hanoverian and Oldenburg Coach Horse Association was formed in 1892, and was promptly followed by the rival Oldenburg Coach Horse Association. The first registry published two volumes of its stud book, but the breed did not find lasting favor in the United States. By the mid-1920s, both organizations had failed.

The original coaching type also fell out of favor in Germany and over time horses were selected for sport rather than for coach work. In the 1980s a group sought to preserve the original heavier Oldenburg that existed before World War II, prior to the widespread use of Thoroughbred and Anglo-Arabian outcrosses. The group used some of the

Summary

Current colors: Black and brown are the most common. Bay, chestnut and grey are also found in smaller numbers. A light black mare was born in 2004.

Historical Colors: In the seventeenth century the Oldenburg Stud was known for the variety of colors found there, particularly white and diluted colors. After the formation of the stud book, there were a few true roan Oldenburgs. There was also a smoky cream stallion, but he was primarily used to breed Groningers.

Markings/patterns: Historically the breed had minimal markings, but there is more variety among the current horses.

Eye color: The eyes are usually dark, although some of the horses from the cream line had pale golden eyes.

remaining mares of the older type, as well as East Friesians, to form the Ostfriesen and Alt-Oldenburg. A stud book was established in 1986 and the breed was recognized in 1988. The stud book is partially closed, with some crosses of Silesian, Saxon-Thuringia, Groninger and even Dutch Harness Horse blood used to expand the limited gene pool.

More recently an effort has been made to unite what is left of the old European coaching breeds in one stud book as the International Heavy Warmblood. The registry was founded in 1994 and accepts Alt-Oldenburg, Groninger, Silesian and East Friesian horses into its main stud book. There are also separate sections for Gelderlanders and Dutch Harness Horses that have been bred using classic lines. For all three sections, mares must have at least 75 percent classic breeding, and stallions must have at least 87.5 percent classic breeding. The reasoning behind the International Heavy Warmblood is that the included breeds were formed using the same foundation stock, and that combining their limited numbers provides the best chance for perpetuating the classic coaching type.

Population

There are currently 25 approved stallions and 190 mares in the stud book of the Breeding Association for the East Friesian and Alt-Oldenburg Horse. There is also a small group of horses of the older type that have been preserved within the Danish Oldenburg population.

Colors

Black and seal brown are colors long associated with heavy warmbloods, particularly the Oldenburg. Writers in the nineteenth century invariably comment about the Oldenburg being consistently bay, black or seal brown. The first volume of the Oldenburg stud book shows that bay was the most common color, accounting for 60 percent of the stallions and 78 percent of the mares. This disparity between the genders reflects a general truth about breeding populations, which is that the colors of the mares tend to reflect the breed as it is (and recently was), and the stallions tend to reflect where it is that breeders wish to go. A mare of an

This unnamed Oldenburg stallion from the late nineteenth century was pictured in <u>Das Buch vom Pferde</u> by Graf C. G. Wrangel (1895). The breed became considerably heavier in the early twentieth century.

unfashionable color can always be matched with a stallion of a more favorable color, but stud owners know that a stallion of an unpopular color will book few mares. In the case of the Oldenburg, the foundation stock utilized in the early nineteenth century was largely bay, but the direction breeders wished to go was towards the darker colors the breed would eventually become known for having. This meant that while 60 percent of the stallions in the foundation section of the first volume were bay and 29 percent were brown, in the later years covered by the book the proportion was closer to 48 percent bay and 38 percent brown. Meanwhile black, which had accounted for only 3 percent of the earlier stallions, rose to a little over 10 percent among the later foundation stallions. Discounting the posthumous ancestors in the foundation section, stud book entries in the first volume show the stallion population almost uniformly brown or black, with only a handful of bays.

Today the predominant color of the East Friesian and Alt-Oldenburg is darker still, with the most common color being black. Of the twenty-five stallions approved by the registry for breeding in 2011, sixteen are black and seven are seal brown. The browns are very dark with mealy points, which suggest that they are brown (A^t) rather than dark bay (A).

Chestnut

There is one chestnut stallion among those currently approved for the breed. Frieso (1996) is by the chestnut Dutch Harness Horse stallion Fortissimo, who is himself out of two black parents. Fortissimo traces back in all lines to the Gelderlander stud book, which in turn trace back to East Friesians and Oldenburgs. That makes his breeding a little unusual among modern Dutch Harness Horses, which usually have fairly recent Hackney Horse outcrosses. Frieso's dam, Daisy, is a Danish Oldenburg. Frieso is unusual for a chestnut in that he has very little face white—just a small crescent star and a snip—while sporting three socks. His sire was a more typically marked sabino, with a broad blaze that covered his muzzle, a white chin and four high stockings.

Another chestnut, Joviaal (1991), was approved for a single season in 2009 and left sixteen foals. He is a very dark chestnut, almost black, with a broad blaze and four stockings. He is a Dutch Harness Horse with an outcross to the Hackney Cambridge Cole in the third generation.

Chestnut was present in the original Oldenburg, although it was always rare. There is also some confusion about the chestnut coloring and one of the founding stallion lines. Some modern writers have referred to the stallions Staeve (1806) and his sons Neptun (1821) and Thorador I (1823) as chestnuts. Perhaps some of this confusion comes from the writings of Graf C. G. Wrangel, who wrote about the color found in this line in his book *Die Rassen des Pferdes*, published in 1908. There he describes Staeve as being *kastanienbraun*. *Braun* is the German word for the color brown, and the specific term for bay, just as the English word brown can mean either the color brown or a specific color in horses. When horses are said to be *braun*, modifiers are typically added to the front that describe the shade of bay. So *rotbraun* is a red bay, *dunkelbraun* is a dark bay, and *hellbraun* is a light bay. The problem with *kastanienbraun* is that it has two meanings. The word *kastanien* means chestnut, so following the German naming conventions for horse colors, this would be chestnut bay. That is, a bay horse where the red areas are chestnut brown in color. But *kas-*

tanienbraun is often translated literally to mean a horse that is a dark brownish red, or chestnut. To add to the confusion, the Dutch form of the word, *kastanjebruin*, does mean chestnut.

Wrangel describes Staeve as *kastanienbraun*, which is the term that appears in his stud book entry. Wrangel also writes about the likelihood that Staeve was a "scion of the old Cleveland race." In fact, elsewhere in the same book he uses *kastanienbraun* to refer to the coloring of the Cleveland Bay. Staeve was an English import and given his type that does seem to be a logical conclusion regarding his possible background. If that is true, it seems unlikely that he would actually be chestnut. Quality horses of the wrong color were sometimes shipped where their coloring was not an issue—the Jutland founder Oppenheim was rumored to have been an unwanted chestnut Shire—but it seems that mention might have been made of this fact where it so. Wrangel's use of the word to describe the coloring of the Cleveland Bay suggests that in this case the term was used to describe a specific shade of bay.

His son Neptun, who is also sometimes referred to as having been chestnut, was registered as *rotbraun*, or red bay. His other son, Thorador I, is also registered as *kastanienbraun*, though oddly enough he is more often referred to by later writers as bay. The Neptun son Marten has also been called chestnut, but he was registered as *rotbraun*. An engraving in the Wrangel book also shows him to have been a bay horse. The Thorador son Hubertus and his son Acibiades are likewise entered in the studbook as red bay (*rotbraun*) rather than the chestnut they are sometimes said to have been.

There were true chestnuts entered in the ancestor section, but they were not direct descendants of Staeve and his sons. Most traced back to Hanoverians. In the main stud book, however, there were no chestnut stallions and only a handful of chestnut mares. Chestnuts did appear occasionally in later years and were sometimes used at stud. One example is the successful stallion Gardist (1901). He came from two brown parents, but traced on both sides of his pedigree to the Young Duke of Cleveland, who had produced multiple chestnut foals. Euto (1909) was another. Both his parents were chestnut, and both traced

The brown RUTHARD *(1890) was considered to be one of the finest stallions of his era. He epitomized the ideal coach horse, right down to his unmarked brown coat.*

back multiple times to the Hanoverian AGAMEM-NON. Chestnuts were not popular for the coaching trade, however, so the preference remained for dark bays and browns.

Grey

Although there were grey horses included among the ancestors of the Oldenburg, they do not seem to have had a long-term impact on the breed. By the time horses were registered in the main section, only one grey stallion remained, ROLAND (1890). His dam traced her coloring back to the stallion LEO (1821), given number twelve in the ancestor section. By the early 1900s the color is believed to have been lost. In this respect the Oldenburg is different from the East Friesian, where the grey coloring persisted far longer and grey stallions had more influence.

In 2010 a grey stallion, IDANO (2006), was approved for breeding by the Association for the Breeding of East Friesian and Alt-Oldenburg Horses. He is unrelated to the greys in the original Oldenburg stud books, but instead gets the color from his grey Silesian sire, INDYGO. INDYGO is a grandson of the grey Saxon stallion EIDAM, who was leased by the Polish government in the 1980s. EIDAM is often credited with returning the grey

coloring to the Silesian breed, although there are other grey lines. One of them is INDYGO's other grandsire, the Thoroughbred ORKISZ, who traces his color back to THE TETRARCH. To date INDYGO has produced only greys, though he has too few offspring to yet know if he is homozygous.

Light Black

In 2004 a pale-skinned, pale-eyed foal with white eyelashes was born. Her sire was the black GLÜCKSBURG (1997) and her dam was the dark bay GUNJA (1999) by the black LORD II. The filly, named GAJA, darkened to a pale chocolate color as she matured. When initial tests came back showing that she was homozygous for black, it was assumed that she carried the silver dilution even though it was not evident in either parent. Prior to the development of a test for silver, testing for the red gene was often used as a de facto test for silver; if a chocolate-colored horse came back genetically black rather than red, he was assumed to be a silver. When the test for the actual silver mutation was available, it showed that GAJA was not a silver, nor did she carry any other known dilution.

Horses like GAJA have been called light black. Such horses differ from summer blacks, which are born dark and fade with exposure to the sun. Light blacks are born taupe-colored with pinkish skin and pale eyes. Skin, eyes and coat all darken with age, though not to a true black color. Because many have come from seemingly ordinary parents, it is assumed that the color is recessive. If that is the case, then both the sire and the dam of GAJA would have to be carriers. The other possibility is that GAJA is herself a mutation.

Historical Colors

Although the shift to a uniformly dark coloring was already well underway when the Oldenburg stud book was first published, the foundation laid by Anton Günther, the Count of Oldenburg, was far more colorful. Count Günther ruled Oldenburg from 1603 until 1667, which was a time when horses of unusual colors were at the height of their popularity. One seventeenth-century writer praised the extent of Count Günther's stables, including more than seventy high-quality stallions brought from Naples, Spain, Turkey, Poland and the Tartars, all with colors "so different that a horseman is likely never to see their match elsewhere." Another biographer praised the Count's talent for predicting the color of an unborn foal, saying that he had the ability to unlock the secret nature of the horse.

Among the colors mentioned as part of Count Günther's herd were dapple greys, yellows with black manes and tails, isabellas, tigers and horses that were "pearl colored." This last one is of particular note because pearl is the name given to the newly identified dilution found primarily in horses of Spanish descent. It is not known if the earlier pearl color, which is noted as having been popular at the time, was in fact the same, or if it was something else entirely. In *Die Beurteilung des Pferdes* (1922), Ulrich Duerst includes it among the shades of isabella (palomino), and indicates that the color was sometimes called ermine. Ermine was a term also used for what modern horsemen would call cremello.

Although Count Günther's property reverted to the Danish crown after his death, some of the less common colors may have persisted among the mares of that region into the eighteenth and even early nineteenth century. Because the foundation of the nineteenth-century Oldenburg was primarily recorded in terms of top-crosses, the color of the mares used is open to speculation. What is clear is that few colors beyond bay, brown and black survived past the formation of the stud book.

Roan

Older German stud books do not usually differentiate between grey or roan horses; both are entered as *schimmel*. There is one distinctive term, however, that is sometimes used to signify that a horse is a true roan. That is *mohrenkopf*, which translates as "the Saracen's head"—a less culturally sensitive version of the English dark-headed roan. *Mohrenkopf* was specifically used to designate dark-headed black roans, which suggests that in Germany at least, roan was more often linked to the black gene rather than the red gene.

There was at least on true roan Oldenburg entered in the foundation stud book. That was HEROS (1818), listed as *blauschimmel, mohrenkopf.*

That is, blue roan with a dark head. Nothing is said of his background so it is impossible to know the source of his coloring. He did leave a roan daughter, EFFY (1836), who in turn produced the roan GALATHA, but the line appears to die out after that.

Dilutes

It is clear that some of the original horses owned by the Count of Oldenburg were dilutes. The Count was fond of giving his horses as gifts, and among the records of those donations it is noted that in 1648 he gave seven dun-colored horses with black manes and tails to the Duke of Orange. The following year he gave six cream-colored mares to the King of Denmark and a dun-colored horse to the Count of the Pfalz. In 1658, he made a gift of a team of six cream horses to the young Empress of Vienna, which she used to pull the State Coach. Around that same time, the Duke of Newcastle wrote that the Oldenburg horses of Queen Christine of Sweden were "broad in the chest and loins, upstanding, with well formed heads and necks, cream coloured, with white tails and manes." He stated that the Queen had given some of them to the King of Spain, and that they were "verily a kingly present, worthy of both giver and receiver."

It was not the blood of Günther's horses that produced the one known cream line of Oldenburgs, however. The color of the founder mare WALLY, registered as dark isabella, came from her dam THUSNELDA, who was said to be a descendant of the golden horses of Hanover. Had the mare come from the same program that produced the famed Hanoverian Creams, it might prove an interesting piece of the puzzle in trying to determine the exact color of those horses. That is because while it is clear that the WALLY family carried cream, she also appeared to carry something else that lightened the color of her eyes. WALLY was said to be golden-eyed, as were her female descendants in an unbroken line down to the smoky black stallion RHEINFELD (1938). Golden eyes were a feature noted by some observers who saw the Hanoverian Creams. Rheinfeld was used exclusively in the Netherlands for breeding Groningers, so did not leave any Oldenburg offspring. (RHEINFELD is discussed at greater length in the chapter on Groningers.)

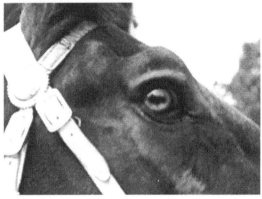

The smoky black Oldenburg stallion RHEINFELD had unusually pale eyes. Some cream dilutes have light eyes, but his were closer to the shade of yellow called tiger eye. His dam, granddam and great-granddam had yellow eyes.

There are two other mares in the ancestor section of the first stud book that may have been dilutes of some kind. The first of these is the most interesting because her color is described in such a way that it is pretty clear that the dilute she carried was dun. That is OLIVE (1842), registered as *lehmfuchs*, which means clay-chestnut, with an eel stripe. Her sire was the chestnut Thoroughbred CHERSIDAMAS, and her dam was a daughter of the bay STAEVE grandson HEROS. It is likely this unnamed mare, and her mother before her, were the source for the dun coloring.

The second mare, RHEA (1847) is likewise recorded as *lehmfuchs*, though if she had a dorsal stripe it was not noted when she was registered. In her case, both parents were recorded in the same ancestor register that she was. Her dam, BRÜNETTE 33, is registered as red bay, which is the most common designation in the Oldenburg stud book. Her sire, BRILLANT 63, is registered as hellbraun, which is light bay. In addition to the clay-colored RHEA, he has another daughter registered as light chestnut. It may be that the family was simply prone to lighter, yet not truly diluted, shades of otherwise ordinary coloring. It is also possible that the family carried one of the dilutions.

There was also one stallion, ALBION (1867), that was registered as golden bay with a dorsal stripe. His sire was brown and his dam was bay, so it seems unlikely that he carried a dilution. Smoky black horses are sometimes registered as brown, so on rare occasions cream dilutes come from pedigrees with nothing but brown horses. That would not be the pedigree of a yellow dun horse, though, since a brown or bay horse would show the dilution and not be registered as brown or bay. ALBION had a number of descendants that were registered as light or golden bay, though as with the mare RHEA that could have been nothing more than the tendency to throw lighter shades that were typical in a breed more inclined towards the darker shades of bay.

Eye Color

The line originating with the mare WALLY II was known for consistently producing golden eyes. The last of that line, the smoky black stallion RHEINFELD, was used for breeding Groningers and it appears that whatever mutation may have been responsible for the trait, it was lost with him.

Aside from the family of WALLY, there is no indication that blue or light-colored eyes have occurred in the Oldenburg since Anton Günther's time. There are Alt-Oldenburgs with disproportionately large snips, which are sometimes seen as a sign that a splash mutation is present, but to date those horses have not produced as if they carried splashed white. To this author's knowledge, none have produced blue eyes. It seems more likely that these horses carry some version of the sabino, perhaps dampened by modifiers that restrict the expression of white above and beyond what the breed's black-based base colors would already do.

Markings

The present-day Alt-Oldenburg displays more white on average than the Oldenburgs of the early nineteenth century. Among the twenty-five approved Alt-Oldenburg stallions, almost half have three or more white feet. Seven have full blazes, while two more have large snips. Only four have unmarked faces, and only two have four dark legs. This is different from the original Oldenburg, which was noted for the absence of markings. Wrangel writes that the stallion STAEVE was well-received because he reduced markings when bred to local mares with blazes and white feet. Fashion had changed for coach horses, and darker unmarked horses were desired. This is noticeable in the first stud book, where blazes and white feet are still seen in the ancestor section, which includes horses foaled as far back as 1806, but are not seen in the stud book section for living animals, which had registrations composed primarily of horses born between 1888 and 1890.

Cleveland Bay

Origin: England

The Cleveland Bay is one of the oldest of the British breeds, having been developed in the seventeenth century from a landrace known as the Chapman Horse. Originally bred as a coach horse, it contributed to the development of many of the draft and coaching breeds, including the Jutland, Oldenburg and Hanoverian.

Stud Book

The Cleveland Bay has existed in its modern form since the early nineteenth century. The Cleveland Bay Horse Society was founded in 1883 and the first stud book, a retrospective volume listing stallions foaled prior to 1880, was published in 1884. An American registry, the Cleveland Bay Horse Society of America, was organized a year later and published its first stud book in 1889.

The original stud book required that stallions have three top-crosses and mares have two top-crosses. A competing registry with less restrictive policies, the Yorkshire Coach Horse Society, was established in 1886. Although some Cleveland Bays were double-registered as Yorkshire Coach Horses, the two societies remained largely antagonistic until 1938 when they were merged. The American registry accepted horses from either stud book.

The breed suffered heavy losses during the first World War when Cleveland Bays were used as both cavalry mounts and artillery haulers. As a result, a special register was opened for mares of Cleveland type. Their filly foals from registered stallions were eligible for full registration. At the same time two sons of the Yorkshire Coach Horse BREASTON PRINCE (1900) were admitted to the stud book by a special resolution. The addition of the Yorkshire Coach horses was extremely controversial at the time, and the Grading Register was only slightly less so. The Grading Register still exists, and is more widely accepted as necessary given the inbred nature of the remaining Cleveland Bay population.

Population

There are thought to be less than 550 purebred Cleveland Bays worldwide. The Rare Breed Survival Trust estimates that there are fewer than 300 breeding mares left. The Cleveland Bay is listed as Critical with both British Rare Breeds Survival Trust and the American Livestock Breeds Conservancy. The breed has pioneered the use of SPARKS (Single Population Analysis & Record Keeping System), a computer program originally designed to help manage captive breeding programs of endangered species in zoos, to preserve the genetic diversity within the breed.

Colors

The Cleveland Bay is uniformly bay. At one time the breed standard specified a preference for red bays, then called bright bays. While that is no longer part of the official standard, it is still a preference among many breeders. Red and clear bay are favored, followed by dark bay and then lighter bay. The legs are to be completely black, with any red tones on the lower legs considered a fault. Red

Summary

Current colors: The breed is uniformly bay. Legs are fully black without red hairs on the lower legs. Gray in the mane and tail are occasionally seen and are permitted.

Historical colors: There is some evidence that dun was once present. Gray was present in the Yorkshire Coach Horse, but the color was gone before that stud book was merged with the one for the Cleveland Bay.

Markings/patterns: A small star is permissible, but most are completely unmarked. No white is permitted on the legs.

Eye color: The eyes are dark.

Restrictions: Horses born chestnut or that have excessive white are entered in the stud book, but are noted as being mismarked.

hairs on the lower legs have traditionally been attributed to chestnut Thoroughbred blood. While legs that are not completely filled with black may indeed come from Thoroughbred outcrosses, there is no evidence that breeding to chestnuts in itself reduces the amount of black on the legs of bays. Sooty dappling is seen in some individuals, but it is not as common as clear bay.

The breed standard also states that gray hairs in the mane and tail are not considered a fault, as they are associated with certain strains. The trait was visible in the stallion HAWTHORNE HERO, whose picture appeared in one of the early stud books. His tail was dark grey in a photograph of him as a young horse, but a photo of him as an older stallion shows what looks like a uniformly black tail. It may be that the trait is similar to the Gulastra plume seen in some Arabian strains; visible when the horse is a young adult, but lost with age.

Chestnut Cleveland Bays are occasionally born. At one time these horses were entered in the Grading Register, even though they were purebred. In 2005 the rules were changed, and all purebred Cleveland Bays are entered in the main stud book. Those that are chestnut, or that have excessive white, are noted as being mismarked on official registry documents—papers, passports and stud book entries—but can still be used for breeding.

At least one stallion, TYNEDALE ST. JULIAN (1971), is a known chestnut carrier. He produced the purebred liver chestnut mare KATIE DE NEUFVILLE (1992). It is likely that there are others, but the stigma of producing a chestnut keeps many from registering the foals when they occur. It has long been rumored that chestnut and mismarked Cleveland Bays have been entered into the stud book of the Irish Draught Horse.

Historical Colors

Dun

At one time, some Cleveland Bays were pale and had what sound like dun factors. True dun might seem unlikely in a breed that has bay in the name, but there were individuals that were both lighter in body color and had dorsal stripes and leg barring.

The Yorkshire Coach stallion BREASTON PRINCE *was once blamed for the appearance of a cream Cleveland Bay. There is considerable question about whether or not the foal,* LUCIFER, *was in fact cream. If he was, as a bay* BREASTON PRINCE *could not have been the cause.*

In the first volume of the *Journal of the Royal Agricultural Society*, published in 1840, J. B. Lloyd gives a description of the Cleveland Bay that states that the breed is "bay—either light or dark—with black legs, clear of hair, and black zebra-like stripes on the arm and above the hock are sometimes seen. These are known as the black points, and are supposed to denote especial purity of breeding." This description is repeated in the first volume of the stud book, published in 1884, with the following clarification:

> "An erroneous idea prevails in some places that only the light golden bay is admissible. No greater mistake can exist, as many of the purest and best bred horses have been dark in colour."

W. C. A. Blew, in *Light Horses: Breeds and Management* (1898), also mentions the black points (which would be called dun factors today) when describing the color of the Cleveland Bay. He states that zebra-like stripes on the legs and a mark down the back had long been a characteristic of the Cleveland Bay, but that at the time of the writing they had become rare. He notes the similarity of the black points to those on fallow dun ponies, where the lightest horses were the "most strongly marked" with the black points. He dismisses the popular theory that this peculiarity in Cleveland Bays was introduced by the Scandinavian horses used by the Saxons and Danes during their conquest of the British Isles, based on the belief that crosses with such poor quality animals could never produce something with the quality found in Cleveland Bays. He favored the idea that the color was a sign of reversion to an earlier wild ancestor. His descriptions, and the comparison to the Scandinavian breeds, add to the likelihood that the horses really were linebacked duns.

This type of coloring was present in one of the early founders, POMFRET'S VOLUNTEER (1824). VOLUNTEER was a big prize winner in his day, and was described as a "singularly handsome horse, light bay in colour, and perfectly clear of white." The first volume of the stud book indicates that he had what Mr. Lloyd had called black points, but that modern horsemen would call leg barring, "very distinctly marked", along with a dorsal stripe. These were said to be frequently found among his immediate descendants.

POMFRET'S VOLUNTEER had a half-brother, also called VOLUNTEER, that stood at stud in the 1830s. He was described as a light bay with a black mark down his back. It was said his owner sold him after five years of service because, while he produced excellent action and soundness, many of his foals were light bays with "fawny legs." At the time buyers were looking for more deeply pigmented horses, so a stallion known to produce lighter colors was unlikely to attract many mares.

The subject of pale coloring came up again a hundred years later, when Sir Alfred Pease tried to register LOCKRYS DAIZIE (1916). The twenty year-old mare was purebred, but it was proposed that she be placed in the Grading Register rather than the main stud book. At question was her 1937 colt LUCIFER, who some breeders felt was cream instead of bay. They pointed to his color as proof of the outside blood from his Yorkshire Coach grandsire, BREASTON PRINCE. His owner argued that light bay was a traditional color for the breed. LUCIFER and his dam were granted full registration status, and LUCIFER can still be found modern

pedigrees. It seems likely that he was simply light bay, since there is no indication that he had cream or dun foals.

This leaves open the question whether or not VOLUNTEER was a dun. Distinctly marked leg barring and a dorsal stripe, paired with a light body color, do argue for the possibility. The fact that these things were passed along regularly to his offspring makes another strong argument, as does the fact that other relatives had them and also passed them along. It is true, however, that ordinary bays can have dorsal stripes. Whatever VOLUNTEER and his family were, both the lighter coloring and the leg barring appear to have been lost over time.

Grey

Although the Cleveland Bay has always been some shade of bay, the Yorkshire Coach Horse, which was later merged with the Cleveland Bay, was less restrictive. Greys were still found in reasonably high numbers in the 1850s, including two grey stallions, DUNCAN GREY and ROBIN GREY. In 1856, six of the twenty-eight entries in the coaching classes at the largest show in Cleveland were grey. This was no longer true by the end of the century, when greys were no longer found in the Yorkshire horses. Contemporary writers attribute this to the prepotency of the bay coloring in the

Not long ago, a mare like this one would have been placed in the Grading Register, despite being purebred. To preserve diversity in this endangered breed, horses with excessive white markings are now entered in the stud book with the notation that they are mismarked.

Cleveland Bays, which was thought to be stronger than any color crossed with it. It is not surprising that breeders of that era would have gotten that impression since the typical Cleveland Bay would have been homozygous for both Agouti (*AA*) and Extension (*EE*). Crossed with either chestnuts (*ee*) or blacks (*aa*), the outcome would have been bay foals every time. This would not have been true for grey crosses, since the grey gene is separate from the genes that govern base color inheritance. It is true that the foals from greys crossed with Cleveland Bays would all be bay, but on average half of them would also turn grey over time. It is unlikely that the grey Yorkshire Coach Horses died out because they never had grey foals; it is likely that such foals were sold down the road without mention of their background.

Eye Color

There is no evidence that there have ever been Cleveland Bays with light or blue eyes. Given the minimal nature of their white markings, it seems unlikely that the patterns known to produce blue eyes were ever present in the gene pool.

Markings

Cleveland Bays should be unmarked. A white star no bigger than a 50 pence piece is permissible and is seen occasionally, but anything larger is considered a mismark. When the breed was first standardized, slightly more white was admissible. Horses could have a small star and a few white hairs on the heel. A complete absence of white was always the preference, however, and many of the foundation stallions were particularly prized for their ability to eliminate white markings in their offspring.

On rare occasions horses are born with more white on the face. In the past these horses were denied registration, but concerns about loss of rare genetic material prompted the registry to change this policy. For a while mares with excessive white that were otherwise typical of the breed had been accepted into the Grading Register, and their correctly marked female offspring were eligible for regular registration. In 2005, that policy was changed and mismarked purebreds were included in the main register with the notation that they were mismarked.

Dutch Harness Horse
Tuigpaard

Origin: Netherlands

The Dutch Harness Horse is a subgroup within the Dutch Warmblood that is bred as a fine carriage horse. The emphasis on action at the trot, as well as extensive outcrossing, has resulted in a horse that greatly resembles the English Hackney. Although it shares many of the same bloodlines as the Gelderlander and even bears the name the Gelderlander once used (*Tuigpaard*), it is a separate breed.

Stud Book
The Royal Warmblood Horse Studbook of the Netherlands (KWPN) was formed in 1969 with the merger of the Gelderlander and Groninger stud books. The book is divided into sections, one of which is for the *Tuigpaard*, or Dutch Harness Horse.

Because the bloodlines for the Dutch Harness Horse were so limited, efforts were made to expand the gene pool with outside stallions. The first of these were the Hackney stallions BROWN'S LIBERTY LIGHT and MARFLEET RAFFLES. Both were approved for breeding when the stud book was formed. Another Hackney, CAMBRIDGE COLE, was added in 1977 and had a great deal of influence. Hackney stallions are still occasionally approved for breeding. In the early 1990s, two American Saddlebreds were also approved for breeding. To qualify for registration, Dutch Harness horses may have no more than 62.5 percent Saddlebred or Hackney blood.

There is also a separate section for Classic Tuigpaard horses in the International Heavy Warmblood stud book. Horses qualify if they have no recent outcrosses to Hackneys or Saddlebreds.

Population
The Tuigpaard section of the Dutch stud book is small, with less than 2,000 mares and 40 approved stallions. There are six additional stallions in North America, and one in Germany.

Colors
The most common color in the Dutch Harness Horse is chestnut. Of the forty approved stallions, almost half are this color. Although German coach horse breeders traditionally favored plain brown horses, chestnut has long been a popular color for harness horses in the Netherlands. It was the prevailing color of the Gelderlander, a breed instrumental in the formation of the Dutch Harness Horse. Chestnut Dutch Harness Horses are deeply pigmented in color, typically with self-colored manes and tails. Dark chestnut is not uncommon, and occasionally they are found in a nearly-black shade known as *koffievos*. The influential stallion HOOGHEID (1966) was said to have been this color.

In close second is the color bay. This was the color of the Gelderlander OREGON (1950), a stallion found in almost all Dutch Harness Horse pedigrees. Thirteen of the forty approved stallions are bay. As with the chestnuts, the coloring on the bays tends towards the deeper tones; mealy bay and wild bay do not appear to be part of the gene pool. The last of the common colors is black, with six approved stallions. Most black stallions trace to WATERMAN (1980) or the Gelderlander PYGMALION (1974). The popular chestnut stallion MANNO (1994) also carries black.

Summary

Current colors: Chestnut is the most common color, followed by bay and black. Grey is less common, and true roan, cream and silver are rare.

Historical colors: As a relatively new breed, the colors have not changed significantly over time.

Markings/patterns: Sabino is very common, with flashy white and unbalanced patterns the most common forms. White ticking can also be found. Body spots are less common, but are not penalized when they occur. Tobiano could be introduced through the other KWPN sections.

Eye color: The eyes are dark.

Although not as common as chestnut, bay or even black, there are grey Dutch Harness Horses. One of the most successful in recent years is the stallion VICTORY (2002), the 2004 Dutch National Harness Champion. His coloring came from his grey grandsire, BATELLO (1983), whose color traces back to the great East Friesian stallion, TELLO.

The TELLO line is also responsible for the grey mare KORIENE (1969). Her most famous descendant, her great-grandson FORTISSIMO, did not inherit her coloring, but she produced the grey stallion DOBAS (1985), who was used in the 1990s. Two of her grey daughters, AKORIENE (1982) and ULKORIENE (1978) were also used for breeding.

Another successful grey line comes from the mare CHARLIE (1984). Her color traces back to ANOUSCHKA, a mare registered in an auxiliary section of the stud book known as the helpbook. CHARLIE produced the grey geldings LAMOER and GLAMOER, who are often shown as a team. LAMOER was the 2005 KWPN Horse of the Year. Their full sister NOESKA, and half-sisters HANOESCA and INOESKA, are all grey.

Sabino

Most Dutch Harness Horses have sabino markings. Blazes and stockings are typical, and belly spotting is sometimes seen. Among the stallions, FABRICUS (1987), GRAAF WOUTER (1988), KOWALSKI (1992), SAFFRAAN (1999), and UDO (2001) all have body-spotting, although none is especially extensive.

SAFFRAAN and KOWALSKI are both examples of unbalanced sabinos. SAFFRAAN has four stockings, with the right front to the knee and the left front well above the knee. He also has a long, narrow white stripe on his right side just beyond his ribs, yet his face is marked only with a star, a small strip offset on the nasal bone and a small snip. KOWALSKI has four white feet and a mark on his left barrel and no apparent face white. Both are descendants of the Hackney stallion CAMBRIDGE COLE (1971), who appears in the pedigrees of many of the Harness Horses with these types of markings.

There is a link between white on the legs and white on the face. A horse with a lot of leg white will usually have a lot of white on the face as well. Most of the time the presence of high white on the legs with little or no face white is a good indicator that the horse is carrying a very minimal version of the tobiano pattern. This is not the case with Dutch Harness Horses, where the same kind of marking combination can be found in horses with sabinos in their background, but no tobianos. This may be due to the widespread use of Hackneys to

Two Dutch Harness Horses showing very different sabino patterns. The horse at the top has the flashy white version of the pattern typical of the Gelderlander. It is the most common form of sabino in the Dutch Harness Horse. The bottom horse has a pattern typical of horses that carry the sabino-1 mutation, which was once more closely associated with the Groninger.

expand the genetic diversity of the breed, since the same kind of markings are often seen there.

Unbalanced sabino markings are not exclusive to horses with recent Hackney crosses. One of the most influential early sires of Gelderlanders, DOMBURG (1916) was marked in this way, as was his son AMBURG. In markings, DOMBURG was very similar to his grandsire CICERO II, a black Holsteiner. What does seem different is that the more recent sabinos are more often belly-spotted, but that may well be due to the higher incidence of sabino in the breeding population. The widespread use of Oldenburgs and Groningers would have meant that DOMBURG was probably being crossed on more conservatively marked mares, whereas the similarly-marked Dutch Harness stallions of the current era are more often paired with mares that have more extensive white markings.

Stippled sabinos are also seen in Dutch Harness Horses, and are also likely to have Hackney breeding. One of the most dramatic of these is the brown stallion MONEYMAKER (1994). MONEYMAKER is dark enough that he could easily be mistaken for black, with three high stockings and a sock, a broken blaze and heavy roaning on his flanks. There is also the Hackney stallion MOROCCO FIELD MARSHALL, recently approved for breeding. He is a dark chestnut with a large star, four stockings and very pronounced flank roaning. Flank roaning, while not yet common among the Dutch Harness Horses, is fairly common in Dutch Hackneys.

There have also been a few sabino roans as well as a few patchy sabinos. One of the more extensively marked is the black sabino mare, PAULA (1997). PAULA was imported to the United States, where she has produced other patchy sabino foals from a variety of sires of different breeds. PAULA's sire HEINEKE is a black sabino of the ordinary flashy variety, but her maternal grandsire, ALCHIMIST, was referred to as a bay overo, and was said to have thrown surprising colors and markings. At least one of his foals, the stallion HERMELIJN (1989), was born white, so ALCHIMIST may have carried either sabino-1 or a dominant white mutation. He does not have a clear line to any of the known sabino-1 families in the Netherlands, but

it is quite possible that there are other lines not yet identified; it is easy enough for the pattern to hide among the other types of sabino. It may be that PAULA carries the sabino-1 pattern through her grandsire, but just happens to show less roaning and more contrast than is typical for sabino-1.

Roan

True, dark-headed roan is present in at least one line of the Dutch Harness Horse represented by the successful black roan gelding ZOMOOI (2004). His color goes back to the black roan Gelderlander mare, IKKER I (1921). IKKER was registered as bay roan with a gray mane and tail. She had six recorded foals: three chestnut, two blue roans and one registered simply as roan. This pattern of roan segregating with the black and bay offspring was consistent throughout this family, which suggests that the roan was linked to black rather than red.

The roan foals of IKKER I were all daughters: CANELIA (1938), HYACINT (1943) and JIKKER (1945). All were registered as Gelderlanders. The first of these, CANELIA, was recorded as blue roan with a dark head (*moorkop*). She produced two non-roan foals, neither of which were used in breeding.

The second roan IKKER I daughter, HYACINT, was registered as blue roan. All three of her foals were black roan, though only her daughter TYACINT (1954) was used for breeding. TYACINT was registered as black with white hairs, so she may have been darker in coloring than the average roan. TYACINT produced one black roan daughter, JOLANDA (1968), who was entered into the harness horse section of the Dutch Warmblood stud book. JOLANDA's roan granddaughter, SINY (1993), is being used in a Groninger breeding program. Another granddaughter, KAMILLE, produced the bay roan ROSWITHA, dam of ZOMOOI.

IKKER's last roan daughter, JIKKER, was used in sport horse breeding rather than harness horses and did not pass on her coloring.

Cream

In 1991, the palomino American Saddlebred stallion DENMARK'S GOLDEN PLAYBOY (1986) was exported to the Netherlands. He was the 1990

World Champion Five-Gaited Stallion prior to his exportation, a fact that might come as a surprise to those who think of him as a warmblood sire. Once in the Netherlands he was approved for breeding Dutch Harness Horses under the name HOL-LAND'S GOLDEN BOY. He was used through 1995, but was rejected when he did not produce the desired movement in his foals. He was then exported to Germany and died shortly afterwards from an allergic reaction to penicillin.

PLAYBOY was a dark sooty palomino with a white mane and tail, marked with a star and three socks. His coloring, which was not present in the Dutch Harness Horse at the time, was considered a factor in his approval. His official KWPN report reads, "The enrichment of the color palette is also a consideration." Although he was not used for a long period, he left 105 foals, including two approved palomino sons, KENTUCKY BOY and MODERN. Another palomino son, KAARELTJE (1994), was exported back to America where he was successfully shown in dressage under the name KALAMINO.

Silver

The approved stallion GOYA (1988) was a bay silver. GOYA died young and left few offspring, but he has at least one daughter, LAGOYA, that has been tested and shown to carry the silver mutation. GOYA was a great-grandson of IREGON, a bay silver Gelderlander. The line from IREGON to GOYA was through two chestnut mares, his dam and granddam, so it was hidden until his dam was bred to GOYA's bay sire, WILHELMUS.

Other silvers have appeared in both the Dutch Harness Horse and the Dutch Warmblood that are not related to IREGON, or that have a line to IREGON that clearly could not have carried the color. Silver can hide behind chestnut for generations, just as cream can hide behind black, because the horse lacks the pigment that would reveal the dilution. That makes it possible for the silver mutation to hide in some portion of the predominantly chestnut Gelderlander population. Silver cannot hide on a horse that is genetically black or bay, however, so if a silver horse traces back to another silver through a bay or

Breed Context Can Be Important

Horsemen often assume that color in their breed is somehow different from color in other breeds. This is usually a mistake, as there is no "Arabian black" or "Quarter Horse chestnut." On the whole, color genes behave pretty consistently throughout the equine population.

There are, however, times when breed does influence color. This is particularly true of patterns, where modifiers are believed to alter the distribution and character of the white areas. The two horses above are a good example. The larger horse has the kind of unbalanced sabino patterning found in Dutch Harness Horses. The pony, with the same star and high socks, has the kind of minimized tobiano patterning seen in Shetlands. The two causes are quite different, but the end result is visually similar, so without knowing the breed it would be hard to tell the two apart.

The founder effect, where a small group of ancestors have a great deal of influence on a breed, can ensure that atypical expressions of patterns like these become common in a particular breed. Similarly, oddities in pattern expression can often point to relationships between breeds, like the Hackney with the Dutch Harness Horse, or the Shetland and the American Miniature.

black ancestor, then the color could not have come from that line.

That is the case with the bay silver mare ZHANNA B (2006). Although not tested, there is little question that she is a bay silver. Her owner has said that her dam BONNY, an ordinary red chestnut, has thrown other oddly-colored foals like ZHANNA. BONNY does trace back to the bay silver IREGON, but she does so through his popular grandson PYGMALION. A Dutch Harness Horse sire of purely Gelderlander lines, PYGMALION was black, so he could not have carried the silver mutation. If he had the mutation, he would have been a black silver. The silver mutation BONNY carried must have come from her mother, ULRIKE.

ULRIKE is a daughter of OCTAVIAAN and a great-great-granddaughter of NELSON, both chestnuts suspected of carrying the silver mutation. OCTAVIAAN descends in an unbroken line of chestnuts back to NELSON and from there back to the mare EFENKA (1940). EFENKA was registered as *bruinvos*, or bay chestnut. She could not have been a true chestnut however, because she had a bay filly, JEFENKA, from the chestnut stallion ERIBO. JEFENKA was not used in breeding, but her chestnut sister ICOBA was, and produced the sire NELSON.

NELSON was a Gelderlander, as were his sons and daughters, but like many Gelderlanders from his era, his lines continue primarily through the Dutch Harness Horse and the Dutch Warmblood. He has a number of silver Dutch Warmblood descendants that will be discussed in the upcoming volume on the riding breeds.

Eye Color
Dutch Harness Horses appear to have had uniformly dark eyes. Because sabino markings are widespread in the population, it is possible that there are blue-eyed individuals; however it would be an exception rather than a regular occurrence.

Markings
Almost all Dutch Harness Horses are marked with white to some degree, and most have flashy markings. Because of the influence of the Hackney, many of the horses have unbalanced markings, with minimal white markings on their faces and more extensive white on their legs. Horses with all four legs dark are particularly uncommon, just as they are with the closely related Gelderlander. Spots are sometimes seen on the belly, though large body marks are uncommon.

East Friesian

Origin: Ostfriesland, Germany

Although the name might cause confusion for some American horsemen, this breed is unrelated to the more familiar Dutch Friesian. The East Friesian was one of the breeds collectively known in early twentieth-century America as German Coach Horses. The goal was to produce a horse large enough to pull a carriage, yet with more style and refinement than a true draft horse. The East Friesian stud book explains it in this way: "The object of the breed is to produce a strong, noble and docile coach horse, which will develop quickly, and can be put to light agricultural work in its third year, in order to refund a part of its cost of rearing."

The breed was influential during the formation of many of the modern warmbloods, but like many coaching breeds it was almost lost to outcrossing. In recent years the breed, along with the closely related Alt-Oldenburg, was saved from extinction by a group of preservation breeders.

Stud Book

The East Friesian region has the distinction of being one of the first to utilize *keuring*. The Prince of Ostfriese began evaluating the suitability of stallions in 1715. The German state did not follow suit and mandate stallion inspections for another hundred years.

The registry for East Friesian horses was formed in 1869, and the first East Friesian stud book was published in 1893. In 1923, the stud books were closed to outcrossing. In 1975, the East Friesian lost its status as a separate breed. East Friesian stallions were replaced with Hanoverians, Trakehners, Thoroughbreds and Arabians. East Friesian mares that had produced warmblood foals were absorbed into the Hanoverian stud book.

In 1986, an organization was formed to preserve the remaining East Friesian and Alt-Oldenburg horses. Because the gene pool was small, horses from breeds developed using East Friesian blood were utilized: the Silesian Heavy Warmblood, the Saxony-Thuringia Warmblood, the Danish Oldenburg and the Groninger. Since then two Dutch Harness Horse stallions with a high percentage of East Friesian and Groninger blood have also been added.

More recently an effort has been made to unite what is left of the old European coaching breeds in one stud book for the International Heavy Warmblood. The organization was formed in 1994 and accepts Alt-Oldenburg, Groninger, Silesian and East Friesian horses into its main stud book.

Population

There are currently 25 stallions and 190 mares in the stud book of the Breeding Association for the East Friesian and Alt-Oldenburg Horse.

Colors

The East Friesian was a little less uniform in color than its close relative the Oldenburg, but it was still primarily a dark breed. In the first volumes of the East Friesian stud book, bay and brown were most common, accounting for 75 percent of stallions and 71 percent of mares. Black was the second largest group, making up 17 percent of the stallions and 18 percent of the mares. Chestnut and grey or roan made up most of the remaining registrations. The prevalence of bay and brown was probably due to the widespread use of Cleveland

Summary

Current colors: Black and brown are the most common colors, followed by bay. Chestnut and grey are rare. The current grey line did not originate with the East Friesian.

Historical colors: One of the most influential East Friesian sire lines was grey, but it continues in other breeds. Roan was once present, and chestnut was once much more common.

Markings/patterns: Historically the breed had slightly more white than its close relative the Oldenburg, but excessive white is not considered typical.

Eye color: The eyes are dark.

Bays and Yorkshire Coaching Horses in the mid-nineteenth century.

Fifty years later, in the early twentieth century, the portion of chestnuts had risen dramatically so that among the stallions it accounted for 28 percent of the population. Bay and brown made up 54 percent, while black stayed close to the original proportion of 16 percent. This was largely due to the popularity of the chestnut stallions EDELSTEIN and GOLDMAN.

Today, however, the predominant color of the East Friesian and Alt-Oldenburg is black. Of the twenty-five stallions approved by the registry for breeding in 2011, sixteen are black and seven are seal brown. There is one chestnut and one grey stallion as well. (For more information about these, please see the section on the Alt-Oldenburg.)

Historical Colors

While bay and brown were the predominant colors of the East Friesian, the breed retained some variety a little longer than the Oldenburg.

Grey

Grey was once found in some of the best the breed had to offer, but the lines that existed in the original East Friesian were lost or absorbed into other warmblood breeds. The most notable of these was that of the stallion TELLO (1903). His color can be traced back to the first volume of the East Friesian stud book and the stallion CLENEAS (1882). CLENEAS is entered as *blauschimmel*, or blue-grey. His granddaughter, CLEMENTIA, is registered in the second volume as a grey with a blaze and a white hind foot. TELLO was her only registered foal.

TELLO produced the grey stallion TAPPER (1914). When TAPPER was crossed with his half-sister's grey daughter COLAKIND, he produced two influential daughters, TRUDA and COLANDE. Both were grey and both were registered as East Friesians. When bred to the TELLO son THEO (also a grey), TRUDA had a daughter, KATINKA, who went on to become a *preferant* mare in the Groninger breed. Meanwhile TRUDA's sister, COLANDE, was bred to THEO and produced a grey stallion, also named TELLO. (Early Dutch breeders often recycled names after several generations, which can cause confusion.) Unlike KATINKA, the second TELLO remained in the East Friesian stud book. He was also approved for use in the Drenthe and Frie-

The Association for the Breeding of East Friesian and Alt-Oldenburg was established to preserve horses like this team of black East Friesians.

sian (Book B) stud books. Having been linebred to the original TELLO, he was homozygous for grey.

The breeding career of the second TELLO spanned twenty-three years and his influence—and coloring—extends to many of the modern warmblood breeds. Several of his female descendants continued his line in the Dutch Warmblood. Among Dutch Harness Horses, his great-granddaughter produced the grey stallion BATELLO, who is the great-grandsire of VICTORY. The TELLO granddaughter, AYA (1943), when crossed with the TRUDA great-grandson RINKO, produced the homozygous grey stallion TELLOBLUT. He was registered as an East Friesian, but his branch of this family was subsequently absorbed into the Hanoverian breed.

The original TELLO did his part in perpetuating the grey coloring, too. His East Friesian great-grandson LANDESSOHN (1927) was particularly successful. The grey Gelderlander stallion PATRICK traces his color back to GEOLOOG (1965), who is a great-great grandson of LANDESSOHN. (This is a different LANDESSOHN from the Oldenburg of the same name, who was brown.)

The East Friesian stallion MUSSOLINI was an influential stallion in the Netherlands. He was approved for breeding Groningers, Gelderlanders, and Friesians (Book B).

Roan
Like Oldenburg breeders, early East Friesian breeders used the term *schimmel* for both greys and roans. Whether they were mostly grey or mostly roan, the designation was relatively common with fifty-four entries in the first two stud books.

Although it was likely less common than grey, dark-headed roan was originally found among the German coaching breeds. In the American translation of *Our Domestic Animals* (1907) by Gos de-Voogt, there is a photo of a two year-old roan mare labeled "Blue-white mare (German Coach Horse)." Her specific breed is not given, though elsewhere in the text several Oldenburgs are specifically identified, which suggests she was something other than an Oldenburg. The Oldenburg horse would have been familiar to most American readers, but many of the other heavy warmbloods of the area would simply have been called a German Coach Horse. At that time that designation would have included the East Friesian, as well as breeds that are now considered lighter warmbloods like Hanoverians

and Holsteiners. Whatever the roan mare's breed, the interchanging of bloodlines between the different coaching breeds meant that a color found in one might well appear in another.

The roan color did appear in the East Friesian in at least two instances. The first was the bay roan MUSSOLINI (1925). Although he was a purebred East Friesian, MUSSOLINI was approved for use in the Drenthe, Friesian (Book B), Gelderlander and Groninger studbooks. He was primarily used to produce Groningers, and appears to have left no East Friesian descendants.

The other was the black roan MOOR (1936). Like MUSSOLINI, he was registered as an East Friesian and came from registered East Friesian parents. His sire, LORDMAJOR, was also a black roan. MOOR was approved for use in the Groninger stud book, where he was rated as a premium stallion. All his known offspring were Groningers.

Dilutes
There was a single mare registered as yellow. That was BLONDINE, foaled in 1872. She is listed as having parents that were both East Friesian horses, but no names are given. She is recorded with two previous foals, both brown, but nothing more is heard of her or them beyond that single entry. With so little information, the exact nature of her color can only be guessed.

Another mare named BLONDINA appears in the second volume. She is registered as a chestnut with a dorsal stripe. It is not clear if she was a red dun, though her name does suggest that she might have been paler than a typical chestnut.

Others

There were a number of horses in the early East Friesian stud books that were described as having white hairs on the flanks, or white hairs in the tail. Because many of these had no other markings mentioned, or had only small amounts of white, the rabicano pattern may have been present. It is also possible that the horses had white ticking like that found in some lines of Suffolks, or that they had the type of flank roaning seen in some lines of Hackneys. That latter seems possible given that Hackneys were being widely used for breeding in Ostfrisia during that time period, and Hackney blood is mentioned in many early stud book entries.

One unusual entry is for the stallion called, perhaps descriptively, STEINBUTT (1877). He was registered as chestnut, and was noted as having shaded black spots on his loins. He may have had abundant Bend Or spots, though more dramatic versions of that trait are more often seen on palominos than on chestnuts. Another horse from the same volume that has a similar description is MEISTER I (1878). He is registered as red bay with large black spots on his flank.

Eye Color

East Friesians appear to have uniformly dark eyes. Some East Friesians have been moderately marked with white, so it is possible that blue-eyed individuals might occur, but none have yet been noted.

Markings

While many of the original East Friesians had the same kind of minimal markings seen in the Oldenburg, the breed did have more white on average than the Oldenburg. In the early days of the stud book, almost a third of the horses were unmarked. By the middle of the twentieth century, almost all East Friesians had some degree of white. Most were only moderately marked, but flashy blazes and stockings were seen in some horses, from early stallions like the chestnut SULTAN (1904) to later stallions like the black ARTIST (1960). In general the chestnuts were more extensively marked, but markings that extended to the body have never been typical, even on chestnuts.

Frederiksborg White
(Extinct)

Origin: Denmark

The white horses of the Royal Frederiksborg Stud were bred during the seventeenth, eighteenth and early nineteenth centuries as coach horses for the European royal houses. The breed died out after the stud was dispersed, but the horses have long held the interest of those involved in horse color research.

Stud Book
The Frederiksborg Stud, like most royal studs, kept records of its breeding stock, and the records that date after 1840 are complete and very detailed. This kind of resource is rare among the older European studs, as many lost records to fires or military conflicts.

Population
Although the breed known as the Frederiksborg still exists, the White Horses of Frederiksborg are considered to be extinct. The last white horse at the stud died in 1865, and by 1871 the stud itself was dissolved. (The modern Frederiksborg will be discussed in the upcoming volume on light breeds.)

Colors
The Frederiksborg Stud was founded by King Frederick II in 1562 using primarily Neapolitan and Spanish blood. It was his great-grandson, King Frederick III (1648-1678) who brought the first known white horses to the stud: a white horse from Württemberg and another from Russia. Not much information remains about the influence of those early horses, and it does not appear that white horses were the primary focus of the stud until after the Duchy of Oldenburg passed from Count Anton Günther to the Danish crown in 1667.

By 1672 the stud had assembled a herd of pale mares with the goal of breeding milk-white horses. It is believed that some of the mares were the descendants of Anton Günther's famed grey stallion KRANICH and so were probably white-greys.

Because the Oldenburg Stud was famous for producing pale colors, often referred to as pearl and ermine in nineteenth-century descriptions, it is also likely that some of the mares were dilutes of some kind. Those mares were crossed with an Oldenburg stallion, JOMFRÜEN, who was said to have been born white. (In some documents JOMFRÜEN is called JUNGFRAU.)

After JOMFRÜEN, a Turkish stallion was used. He was described as *fliegenschimmel*, which is a term more commonly used now to mean a fleabitten grey, but at that time was also used for leopards that has very small, numerous spots. The Frederiksborg Stud was known for producing leopards as well as white-born horses, so it is possible that the horse was carrying some type of appaloosa pattern. The white-borns of the Frederiksborg stud are often associated with the leopard breeding program, and it appears that the two were intermingled at various times. The Turkish stallion produced several white mares as well as a stallion, SULTAN, said to have his sire's coloring. When the white mares were crossed with SULTAN, the result was two white-born stallions, LA TRUITE (1694) and PEARL (1699). Neither left a surviving stallion line, but their daughters remained in the breeding herd.

An outside stallion from Ploen in Holstein-Schleswig, MIGNON (1690), was added next. There

---

Summary

The Frederiksborg White has been extinct since the late nineteenth century.

Historical colors: The Frederiksborg Stud began with white grey horses, but became best known for producing true white horses.

Markings/patterns: The history of the Frederiksborg White Stud suggests that the horses were most likely dominant whites, though some may have been greys, dilutes or few-spot appaloosas.

Eye color: The eyes were typically dark, although some horses were reported to have blue eyes. Blue eyes occur occasionally in dominant whites.

are differing accounts of his coloring. He is often referred to as white-born, but in his article "Heredity Factors in White Horses at Frederiksborg Stud", Wriedt indicates that he was a fading grey. Whatever his true coloring, all subsequent white stallions at Frederiksborg trace back to him.

Mignon has surviving descendants among the modern Frederiksborg, though none are grey or white-born. Interestingly enough, one of his descendants is Pluto (1765), one of the foundation stallions of the Lipizzan. Although often referred to simply as white, many breed historians believe that Pluto was white-born. Some suspect him to have been a white-born appaloosa, which certainly would have been possible since the Frederiksborg mare band contained descendants of Sultan. It is also possible that Pluto was dominant white, or grey, or perhaps a combination of all three.

A descendant of Mignon, Le Beau (1728), was added in 1735. His white sons, Le Gentil II (1736) and Magnifique (1737), were his primary successors. A white full brother, Le Badin, was also used. A nineteenth-century scholar of the history of the Frederiksborg Stud, Professor Harald Goldschmidt, explained that with each generation, grey horses were reintroduced because such a low percentage of white horses were produced. They tended to revert, he said, back to black, or to white, gray and black. J. Jensen, in his book *Det Kongelige Frederiksborgske Stutteris Historie*, writes that dark spots were not rare on the skin of white-born horses. In his 1912 dissertation on horse color, Adolph Richard Walther shared a letter from the former breeding director at Herrenhaus on the subject of the white-born foals at that royal stud. The director indicated that the white horses came from brown pintos with a mixture of Arabic blood, as well as a stallion from the Frederiksborg stud, and that these horses in turn produced a number of pintos. Walther classified the white-born horses as a form of pinto and went so far as to suggest that the color might more accurately be called *weißgeborener scheck,* or white-born pinto.

This mix of white and partially white offspring looks a lot like the situation with modern dominant white horses. Just as Walther noted with the term *weißgeboren*, the name dominant white is

The Frederiksborg White stallion Hother, foaled in 1838. His maternal grandsire, Pegasus, was recorded as yellow, so it is clear that even in the latter years of the Stud, diluted colors were being used along with the whites.

misleading, because not all dominant white horses look white. Many individual horses with the dominant white mutation have a mixture of white and colored areas. Perhaps it was this feature of the dominant white pattern that made the production of pure white horses so elusive for Frederiksborg. The tendency to produce broken colors appears to vary among the modern dominant white families, with some more inclined to white expressions and others more inclined towards roany or patchy expressions. This could explain why some stallions were credited with improving the white coloring; their form of the mutation was inclined to whiteness compared to the stallions that threw more mixed coloration.

It also might explain why other colors, particularly grey, were often used to improve the breed. Prior to a modern understanding of genetics, breeding for color was approached a bit like mixing paint. That is, adding a color like the desired end result was thought to move the program closer. So the black horses—and the black patches—were corrected by breeding to lighter colors in hopes of moving closer to true white. That meant crossing white-born stallions to grey mares selected for early and clear greying (that is, not inclined to get dapples or fleabites), as well as to diluted mares. This would have seemed like progress, since a horse patched with grey or with a dilute color would appear more nearly white. The downside would be that by adding both grey and one or more dilutions, identifying the horse's true color would become harder, and predicting outcomes would be even more difficult.

The fact that so many of the horses were not entirely white also suggests that the Frederiksborg horses did not carry the other pattern known to produce white-born foals, which is sabino-1. Horses that are homozygous for sabino-1 are also born white, and in many breeds these horses are more consistently white in appearance than the dominant whites. Had that pattern been utilized, there would have been pintos from the first crosses, but the production of white-born foals would increase as the carriers were bred to each other or to the all-white homozygotes. Crosses between two sabino whites (*Sb1Sb1*) would have bred true, which would eventually lead to a herd that predictably produced white-born foals. The fact that this did not happen over the long history of the Frederiksborg and Herrenhausen Studs suggests that dominant white, and not sabino-1, was involved.

While the presence of sabino-1 appears unlikely, it is possible that some of the white stallions used were few-spotted leopards. Not only was Sultan likely a leopard, but at one time appaloosa patterns were also bred at the Frederiksborg Stud. Horses that are homozygous for both the leopard complex and the leopard pattern can look white-born, and it is clear that some of the white horses of Frederiksborg had this kind of coloring. Crossing such horses with greys would also increase the chances that the adult horses would look white. It would also lead to very some surprising results, but, just as with the grey and dilute crosses, the results of these crosses would also look like progress towards bleaching out the color.

The other indicator that the Frederiksborg horses were dominant white is that in the later years the stud struggled with fertility issues, especially among the mares. This was not reportedly a problem during the formation of the stud, but became an issue when the white horses began to be crossed

Frederiksborg White Time Line

1562 The Royal Frederiksborg Stud is founded with white grey horses.

1603 Anton Günther succeeds his father as the Count of Oldenburg and seeks to restore the stud to its former glory. He has a particular fondness for white and cream-colored horses.

1667 The Duke of Oldenburg dies without an heir, and the duchy and ownership of its white horses revert to Denmark.

1675 The white-born Oldenburg stallion Jomfrüen is used at Frederiksborg.

1714 Electress Sophia's son becomes King George I. He brings the white horses of Hanover to England. They are later joined by a breed of cream-colored horses.

1727 The white Barb stallion Auguste is used at Memsen in Hanover.

1735 A white Turkish stallion, Le Beau, is used at the Frederiksborg Stud. His sire line, though not his color, remains part of the modern Frederiksborg.

1746 The white Frederiksborg stallion Le Blanc is used at Memsen.

1840 Only four white mares remain at Frederiksborg. The white stallion Frederiksborg is sent to Herrenhausen.

1862 The last white stallion, Loke, is born at the Frederiksborg stud.

1871 By order of the King of Denmark, the Frederiksborg stud is closed. The stallion Loke is among the horses sold.

1895 The last white-borns are put down at Herrenhausen, reportedly due to infertility.

together. In the past writers have attributed the decline in fertility to the effects of inbreeding, but dominant white is theorized to be a homozygous lethal, with mares aborting the non-viable embryos early in the pregnancy.

The last of the Le Beau sire line was Superbe, foaled in 1764. The sire line of his brother, Le Badin, continued into the nineteenth century, but difficulty in obtaining the pure white coloring and changing tastes took their toll. Those buying horses wanted the more refined type produced by Thoroughbred crosses. In 1840, the Frederiksborg Stud was reorganized and only four white mares were retained: F (1827), Thyra (1830), Svanhvide (1835) and Pasta (1835). The last white stallion was Loke, foaled in 1862. He was sold in 1871 when the stud was dissolved. White horses continued to be bred alongside the Royal Creams at Herrenhausen, but by 1895 these too were gone.

Eye Color

When talking about pink-skinned horses, eye color takes on a special importance because it is one of the factors that can be used to differentiate between white-born pintos and the palest dilutions. Homozygous creams and pearls have blue, green or golden eyes, whereas dominant white and homozygous sabino-1 horses more often have dark eyes, with occasional instances where one or both eyes are blue.

Unlike the closely related Hanoverian Creams, there is no real disagreement about the eye color of the Frederiksborg Whites. There are no reports of pink or red eyes; those closest to the Frederiksborg breeding program consistently reported that red-eyed albinos were never seen among the Whites. In his 1924 paper "Hereditary Factors in the White Horses of the Frederiksborg Stud", Wriedt frequently refers to the white horses at Frederiksborg and Herrenhausen as black-eyed. He also notes that Jensen, whose research he drew heavily upon, stated that there were also blue eyes in the Frederiksborg Whites, along with the more usual dark eyes. That description of a breed with predominantly dark eyes, along with occasional blue eyes, is consistent among the historical accounts. This is also consistent with the eye colors in modern dominant white families, which are most typically black but can be blue or partially blue.

Friesian

Origin: Friesland, Netherlands

With their elegant appearance, high action and uniformly black coats, the Friesian is one of the most identifiable of the modern breeds. The Friesian is thought to be one of the oldest fixed types, and probably influenced most of the Northern European trotting breeds as well as the Dales, Fell and Mérens.

Stud Book

Horses resembling the Friesian are known to have existed in the Netherlands since at least the thirteenth century. The breed was first mentioned by name in a document in 1544. The *Friesch Paarden-Stamboek* (FPS) was established in 1879 and has recorded the history of the breed up until the present time.

From the beginning, the breed was threatened. It is often stated that the Friesian was almost lost to crossbreeding. This gives an inaccurate impression to many modern horsemen, particularly Americans, who are familiar with the use of outcross blood to improve or alter an existing breed. That is because the modern concept of horse breeding centers around a registry devoted to a specific breed, which then administers the stud book. In much of late nineteenth-century Europe, horse breeding was closely tied to a specific place, which is why so many horse breed names are actually geographic places. The *Friesch Paarden-Stamboek* began as a record of the horses of the Dutch province of Friesland. In the years prior to the formation of the stud book, that had primarily been the Friesian, but the horses of the region were in transition. Heavier East Friesians and Oldenburgs, known as Bovenlanders, had become popular with farmers who thought they were more practical than the showy Friesian.

It would be more accurate than to say that the original breed was almost lost to a competing breed. It is true that the Bovenlander was itself a crossbreed, but it was not a crossbred Friesian. That is, Friesian breeders were not using East Friesian and Oldenburg horses to alter the older

Friesian. Instead, Friesians were being replaced by them. This changing preference was reflected in the actions of the International Agricultural Exchange in Amsterdam, which pronounced the original Friesian unsuitable for the production army horses. The majority of horses selected by the army were Oldenburgs.

Initially there were two sections in the Friesian stud book: Book A for the original Friesian and Book B for the Bovenlander. From 1883 until 1896, the stud book also accepted horses from Groningen and Drenthe into Book B. For that brief time, the name of the breed was changed to the Inland Horse, but that was dropped when the Groningen and Drenthe horses split to form their own studbook.

In 1907 the sections for Friesians and the Bovenlanders were combined into a single stud book. Demand still favored the heavier East Friesian and Oldenburg type, so the Bovenlander prevailed in the merged stud book. In the six years

Summary

Current colors: The breed is uniformly black, which has always been the preferred color. Occasional chestnuts are born, though recent rules requiring stallions to be tested for the red gene will prevent that in the future.

Historical Colors: At one time there were bay, chestnut, roan and grey mares. Silver and cream are suspected to have once been present in low numbers. White ticking was once present in some strains. For a while the stud book for the Friesian also included a section for the Bovenlander, which were more colorful, but they were a different breed than the Friesians.

Eye color: The eyes are dark.

Restrictions: Horses that are born chestnut are entered into the Foal Book but cannot advance to the main stud book. Stallions that carry chestnut can no longer be approved for breeding. The only allowed marking is a small white star. White hairs on the body, legs or tailhead are not permitted.

that followed, no purebred Friesian stallions were approved for breeding, and only three aged stud book stallions remained. This led to the formation of the Friesian Horse Society by breeders interested in preserving the original type. At their request, the stud book was once again divided in 1915, with Book A for the Friesians and Book B for the upland breeds. In 1942 the upland horses left the Friesian stud book and merged with the Groninger Studbook to form the North-Netherlands Warmblood Horse Studbook (NWP). (See the entry for Groningers.) From 1943 forward, the *Friesch Paarden-Stamboek* was exclusively devoted to Friesians.

The breed was depleted enough that an auxiliary stud book, known as a helpbook, was used to record mares without documented pedigrees that otherwise had the correct type. The helpbook was discontinued in 1978 and the stud book was closed. Stallions testing was also instituted at that time, and continues into the present.

Population

The Dutch Foundation for Rare Animal Breeds (*Stichting Zeldzame Huisdierrassen*) reports that there are 20,000 mares and 90 stallions. Approximately 6,000 foals are born annually. The American Livestock Breeds Conservancy estimates there to be close to 9,000 Friesians in the United States, and officially classifies the breed as Recovering, although the unusually high levels of inbreeding within the breed are still viewed with concern.

Colors

The Friesian breed is known for being uniformly black. Black has been a requirement for admission into the stud book since 1918, but it was the traditional color of the breed long before the rule was adopted. Provincial stallion regulations stated a preference for black as early as 1849.

Because the gene for red is recessive, chestnut Friesians are occasionally born. The red gene was present in the original Friesian stock, though it was never common. From 1880 until 1908 the rate of chestnuts among the mares was just over 1 percent. At least one of the mare line originators, DA-VIDJI (1892), was chestnut. Chestnut mares were

still recorded up until 1918, though their numbers had dropped below 0.5 percent.

Although the stud book was eventually closed to any but black horses, the red gene was present in the population so it was just a matter of time before it resurfaced. Two that came to widespread attention were born in the Netherlands in 1991. In the eight years that followed, seven more born. After analyzing the numbers and finding that the incidence of the red gene was likely to increase dramatically over time, the registry began screening for carriers in 1998 as part of the stallion approval process. Stallions born after 2007 must test negative for the presence of the red gene in order to be approved for breeding. Because a chestnut must inherit the red gene from both parents, this means that the color will eventually be eliminated from the breed, once the stallion carriers that were approved prior to testing pass away.

In *The Horse-World of London*, published in 1893, the author speaks of the black horses from the "flats of Holland" used in the funeral trade. An estimated 700 of these horses, often called Flemish Blacks, worked in London at the time.

Typical Friesian Book B Pedigrees

Olympus 447 B	Olivier *Oldenburg*	Coco - *Oldenburg*	Enno - *Oldenburg*
			Calma - *Oldenburg*
		Erna - *Oldenburg*	Monac - *Oldenburg*
			Erechta - *Oldenburg*
	Doornroos *Groninger*	Xerxes II - *Groninger*	Xerxes - *East Friesian*
			Schwarza - *Groninger*
		Netti - *Groninger*	Cicero II - *Holsteiner*
			Achima - *Groninger*

Lurida FPS 4590 B	Mussolini *East Friesian*	Grumbach III - *East Friesian*	Grumbach II - *East Friesian*
			Loni - *East Friesian*
		Elfleda I - *East Friesian*	Thronherr - *East Friesian*
			Elfleda - *East Friesian*
	Mutine *Groninger*	Guntbert - *Oldenburg*	Gunther - *Oldenburg*
			Elisa - *Oldenburg*
		Grille - *Groninger*	Gregor - *Oldenburg*
			Grille - *Oldenburg*

Kerea FPS 4210 B	Tellobloed *East Friesian*	Tapper - *East Friesian*	Tello - *East Friesian*
			Treja - *East Friesian*
		Xanitta - *East Friesian*	Thronherr - *East Friesian*
			unrecorded
	Estalla FPS 3978 B	Wilhard - *Oldenburg*	Esmarch - *Oldenburg*
			Offiziose II - *Oldenburg*
		Wolda - FPS 3821 B	Matador II - *Oldenburg*
			Kata - unrecorded background

Askaria FPS 3687 B	Regulus *Groninger*	Wilfried - *Oldenburg*	Edelmann - *Oldenburg*
			Donau III - *Oldenburg*
		Joke - *Groninger*	Martinus - *East Friesian*
			Zeoliete - *Groninger*
	Johanni *Groninger*	Angelo - *Oldenburg*	Elimar - *Oldenburg*
			Askarie II - *Oldenburg*
		Abeltje - *Groninger*	Xerxes II - *Groninger*
			unrecorded

Figure 12. This random sampling of pedigrees from the early twentieth century comes from Book B of the Friesch Paarden-Stamboek (FPS). Note that while they are in fact crossbreds, they are not crossbred Friesians.

Modern red carriers trace back to the stallion FREARK 218 (1960) or his maternal half-brother YSBRAND 238 (1969). Their dam, TYPIES, traces back on both sides of her pedigree to the stallion PRESIDENT 123 (1913). PRESIDENT was black, but it is known that he produced a chestnut foal in 1920. His male descendants known to carry the red gene include:

LAES 278	(1975-2004)
DIEDERT 288	(1982, disapproved)
JILLIS 301	(1985)
WICHER 334	(1991-2003)
ATSE 342	(1992, disapproved)
ABE 346	(1992)

Both DIEDERT 288 and ATSE 342 were disapproved for breeding, so only ABE 346 and JILLIS 301 remain. JILLIS is twenty-six years old, and ABE is nineteen. Once they have retired from breeding, it is unlikely that another chestnut Friesian will be born from fully approved parents.

One of the most publicized chestnut Friesians is the stallion RAMON, also known as FIRE MAGIC, imported to the United States from the Netherlands in 1997. He is very dark red in color with a self-colored mane and tail. He is often described as a registered Friesian, which is true. Foals born to purebred Friesian parents are registered in the Foal Book, but those that do not meet the breed standard—which would include horses that are a color other than black as well as those with excessive white—cannot advance to the main stud book.

The registry position on the testing and elimination of the red gene has not been without controversy. While many breeders have expressed concerns that the breed keep its traditional black color, the Friesian population suffers from a number of genetic disorders, including dwarfism and hydrocephalus. Although tests are not yet available, both conditions are thought to be the result of recessive genes, so a horse producing either a dwarf or a hydrocephalic foal is by definition a carrier. Some have questioned the strict removal of a cosmetic defect like color while these kinds of debilitating conditions are not subject to similar restrictions. It may be that this decision will have to be revisited, especially if attempts to develop tests for dwarfism

Colorful Book B Stallions

Pintos

Hellas   f. 1928   black tobiano
sire: Gerhard, black Oldenburg
dam: Annie, tobiano Bovenlander   *FPS*

Koekoek   f. 1923   black tobiano
sire: Griedel, brown Groninger
dam: Arama I, tobiano Groninger   *FPS, NSTg*

Primo   f. 1928   grey sabino-1
sire: Guntbert, brown Oldenburg
dam: Jesselina, sabino Groninger   *FPS, NSTg*

Greys

Tello   f. 1927   grey
sire: Theo, grey East Friesian
dam: Colande, grey East Friesian   *FPS, DPS*

Bart   f. 1931   grey
sire: Landessohn, grey East Friesian   *FPS,*
dam: Jadea, bay Groninger   *Sgrt, GrPS*

Tellobloed f. 1922   grey
sire: Tapper, grey East Friesian
dam: Xanitta, East Friesian   *FPS, DPS*

Roan

Mussolini f. 1925   bay roan
sire: Grumbach, East Friesian   *FPS, DPS,*
dam: Elfleda, East Friesian   *GrPS, NSTg*

Bovenlanders were not subject to the same color restrictions as the Friesians. While the majority of the stallions in Book B were black or brown, other colors were found in smaller numbers. Stud books that approved the stallion for breeding are noted to the right.

and hydrocephalus are successful. With such an inbred population, breeders may have to consider the trade-offs between further narrowing a limited gene pool, which testing and culling will do, and utilizing imperfect individuals to retain a level of diversity. In this regard they would be in good company, as registries like the Cleveland Bay and the Mountain Pleasure Horse find they must relax their positions on undesirable coloring in order to retain the health of their breeding population.

Light Black

Like many black horses, Friesians often bleach when exposed to sunlight. When this happens, the legs typically remain black. For that reason, faded black horses can be mistaken for dark bay or brown. There has been one unusual gelding, NICO (1996), that had a faded body color with dark points and a dark head, even when kept in the shade. At times his coat had a decidedly yellowish cast, though his head remained dark. At his palest, he had a dark countershaded dorsal stripe much like a false-dun buckskin.

There have also been a few Friesians that were born a permanent liver brown. Unlike the typical sun-faded black with black coloring on the legs, these horses have liver red coloring that extends to the hoof. One, the stallion MONTE (2004), was tested and proved to be genetically black (*EEaa*) just like ordinary Friesians. Visually he looks like a very dark liver chestnut. His sire HESSEL is a true black, but his dam MINNIE W was said to have a similar color to MONTE.

Light black occurs in other breeds, most notably some of the primitive pony breeds. Icelandic breeders call the color *globrunn*. The light black Friesians can look somewhat similar, except that they have ordinary dark eyes whereas light blacks in other breeds usually have light brown or golden eyes.

Historical Colors

Although black was the traditional and officially preferred color from the start, prior to the 1918 rule the mares in the stud book were more varied in color. From 1880 until 1895, the mare population was 75 percent black, 20 percent bay or brown, 3 percent grey or roan and 1 percent chestnut. That is 174 bay, 29 grey or roan and 11 chestnut mares. From 1895 until 1908, the percentages were 83 percent black, 15 percent bay or brown, 1 percent chestnut and just over 0.5 percent grey or roan: 46 bay, 4 chestnut and 2 gray or roan mares. From 1908 until the black rule was put in place in 1918, the population was 94 percent black, 6 percent bay or brown and less than 0.5 percent chestnut. Grays and roans had disappeared, and there were just fourteen bay mares and one chestnut mare.

Although black was the preferred color, there were five bay stallions approved. These were the red bay stallions DAVID 11 (1877) and KEIZER 18 (1882) and the dark bay stallions MINISTER THORBECKE 34 (1883), BRUNO 38 (1884), and RADBOUD 67 (1886). RADBOUD was the last non-black stallion given a breeding approval. MINISTER THORBECKE 34 and RADBOUD 67 had unknown dams, which were most likely the source for their color. BRUNO 38 had a bay dam, AALTJE 174. In 1928 the last non-black Friesian, the light brown helpbook mare NELLY 90H, was admitted.

Ticked or Roaned

Although the early stud books had a total of thirty-one mares registered as *schimmel* it is not known if the mares were grey or roan. Both colors were found in the nearby Bovenlander, though grey was more common. It is also possible that the mares were heavily ticked rather than truly roan or grey.

In *Hair Colour in the Horse*, Reiner Geurts states that white ticking once occurred in 2.5 percent of the Friesian population. At least one stallion, DE JONGE FLORIS (1886), is noted in the stud book as having white hairs in his coat, but it is likely that in many other instances white hairs went unmentioned in the formal records. That is true of the stallion most often associated with roaning. Although he is registered as black with no markings, CRE-

The black tobiano HELLAS was registered as number 441 in Book B of the Friesch Paarden-Stamboek. He was by a black Oldenburg stallion and out of a pinto Bovenlander mare. His offspring can be found in the Groninger, Gelderlander and Friesian stud books.

MER (1923) was a roaned horse who passed on the trait to many of his descendants, including his son PLUTUS (1935). Although not true, dark-headed roans, Friesians of this line were said to be ticked with white hairs throughout their bodies. CREMER was rejected for breeding in 1936, in part because he regularly produced roaning, but also because he was believed to carry the same dwarfing mutation as his sire, US HEIT. (It should be said that it is not thought that the dwarf mutation is exclusive to this sire line, though it is among those clearly linked.) CREMER was still used for breeding unregistered stock, and his blood returned to the breed though his female descendants when the Breeding Committee determined that he and ELIUS 138 were all that was left of the PRINS 109 sire line, and that his was one of the few lines without crosses to the stallion FRISO 117. Although there are no male-line CREMER descendants, he can still be found on the female side of the pedigree, and it is said that the roaning still occurs upon occasion, causing some foals from this line to be denied entry in the main section of the stud book.

Frosted Manes

The stallion GRAAF ADOLF 21 (1880) was described as being black with white hairs in the mane and tail. He was used at stud, leaving behind four approved sons and twenty-seven daughters, but his male line did not continue. According to their stud book entries, his sons were all solid blacks without white hairs of any kind.

Silver

Dutch color researcher J. K. Wiersema believed that the silver present in the Gelderlander and Groninger breeds may have originally come from Friesian mares. He lists eleven mares from the early Friesian stud books with descriptions that could fit horses carrying the silver dilution.

SNEL 75	f.1878	Dapple chestnut
DE NETTE 111	f.1877	Dark chestnut, light colored mane and tail
JOHANNA 244	f.1878	Dapple chestnut, blaze, white mane and tail
MARIE 697	f.1878	Dapple chestnut, white mane and tail

EMMA 827	f.1888	Dapple chestnut, blaze, almost white mane and tail
SOPHIE 847	f.1885	Dapple brown
ANNA 877	f.1888	Dark chestnut, gray mane and tail
CORRIE 1046	f.1898	Dirty chestnut, light mane and tail
VOSJE 1050	f. 1898	Dirty chestnut, white mane and tail
MARIE 2783	f. 1909	Dirty chestnut, white mane and tail
FLORA 17H	f.1910	Dirty chestnut, gray mane and tail

Reiner Geurts, in his dissertation on the colors and markings in the Friesian horse, also mentions a handful of *zweetvos* (dirty chestnut) and dappled chestnut stallions presented for approval in 1901.

WILLIAM	f.1896	Dirty chestnut
FRANS	f.1898	Dapple chestnut
SIGFRIED	f.1891	Dapple chestnut
ALEXANDER	f.1898	Dapple chestnut

The use of the term "dappled chestnut" is interesting because that was the term used by many late nineteenth- and early twentieth-century American

This unidentified black silver Friesian mare was photographed by the Dutch color researcher J. K. Wiersema. In the late nineteenth century, a number of Friesian mares were registered as dappled chestnut.

breeders to describe silver dapple Shetland Ponies. It makes sense because black silver looks more like chestnut than like black or bay, and because ordinary chestnuts, unlike bays, do not tend to display very striking dappling. Even with bays and buckskins, owners rarely mention the presence of dappling, but dappling on a seemingly chestnut horse might well be unusual enough to be mentioned on a registry application.

Without photos or more detailed production records, this is all speculation. If the color was present, it would have been lost once breeders began selecting for black. Silver would have been particularly attractive had it been retained. American breeders of Shetland Ponies were quick to realize that the cross that gave the best contrast and the most vivid dappling was a non-fading, jet black. With many jet black Friesians, that highly sought-after version of the silver coloring would likely be easy to obtain, and one can only imagine the results would be quite striking.

Other Dilutes
In addition to the potential silvers, Wiersema also mentions a mare that could have been a cream dilute. That was VOSJE 60 (1876), listed as *geel voskleurig*, or yellow-colored chestnut. He included her among the potential silvers, but it is difficult to imagine someone using the term yellow when describing the very cool tones of a typical silver. It is also possible that VOSJE was just a pale mealy chestnut. Either mutation—the cream dilute or the mealy factor—would be considered unusual in modern Dutch horses.

There were two mares recorded prior to 1895 that were entered as *geelbruin*, or yellow bay. Another three mares from the same time period were entered as light bay. Four of the black mares were entered as *vaalzwart*, or pale black. Just as with VOSJE, it may be that the horses were lighter shades of ordinary colors, or they may have carried a dilution that was later lost when the breed tightened its color requirements.

Tobiano
Because there were a handful of tobianos in Book B, it is sometimes said that there were once tobiano Friesians. This overlooks the fact that the horses in

Book B were not only genetically unrelated to the horses is Book A, but were of a very different type. Most were not Friesians in the sense that modern horsemen would understand the term. Confusion about this prompted the Friesian registry to take out an advertisement clarifying the registration status of the unlicensed tobiano stallion NICO VAN FRIESLAND (1957) in 1965. NICO was not registered with the *Friesch Paarden-Stamboek*, but the few tobiano stallions that were would more accurately be called Groningers than Friesians.

There were two black pinto mares in Book A, EMMA 2501 (1905) and EMMA 2977 (1908). Neither mare had a recorded pedigree, though Emma 2977 was said to have been of Friesian breeding. This kind of limited background information was not unusual for the mares entered in the stud book during the restoration of the breed, regardless of their color. As for the color of the two mares, it is not known with certainty what patterns the mares carried, though the term used in the stud book, *bont*, often refers to tobiano. The line to EMMA 2501 did not continue, but EMMA 2977 had five registered foals, including a son, COLIJN 135 (1923), by the stallion PAULUS 121. He was registered as a solid black with no markings, so he did not inherit his mother's pattern. He left behind one daughter in the regular stud book, and one in the helpbook, before he was disapproved for breeding in 1927. If EMMA produced tobiano offspring, they were not recorded. Rules requiring that the offspring of off-colored mares be black without significant white markings would have eliminated them from consideration.

Eye Color
There is no evidence that there were ever purebred Friesians with pale or blue eyes. From the start, the Friesian was a breed with minimal amounts of white, and even the Bovenlanders which were included in the stud book for a time were conservatively marked and not known to produce blue eyes. The strict limitations on white markings would insure that the pinto patterns linked to blue eyes would not have continued into the present population, even if they had once been present. Unlike the faded or light black horses occasionally seen in other breeds, which sometimes have light

brown or amber eyes, light black Friesians have had dark eyes.

Markings

The only accepted white marking is a small star no larger than 1.25 inches in diameter. Small white spots on the soles of the feet are permitted, but no white is allowed on the leg or the hoof wall. Stallions presented for inspection may be denied approval even if they have permissible white markings. Markings on the body, including roaning or ticking, and white hairs at the base of the tail are not permitted.

Although the 1849 Provincial Council rules that established black as a preferred color also specified restrictions on markings that were similar to those currently in place, many of the mares and even a few stallions used to rebuild the breed had white markings. During the period from 1880 until 1895, 30 percent of the black mares and 36 percent of the bay mares had white face markings. The percentages were even higher among the chestnuts, where 73 percent had white on the face, and the greys and roans, where 79 percent did. White markings on the legs were much less common, appearing on only 3 percent of the black mares and 8 percent of the bay mares. The percentage jumps considerably with the chestnuts, where 18 percent of the mares had white on the legs, but it is the grey and roan mares that were the most consistently marked. Among those mares 52 percent had white leg markings, which suggests that a significant portion of the mares in this category may have been sabino roans. True roans and greys are not more prone to white markings than other colors.

Among the likely sabinos was the mare Emma 4, foaled in 1873 and registered in the first volume of the stud book. She was described as black with roaned hairs, a small blaze, and white hind feet. There was also at least one stallion, Bles 101 (1891), with a blaze and two white feet. Horses like Emma and Bles were exceptions, though, and it is quite possible that none of these horses would have been included in the initial stud books had the breed not been so depleted in numbers.

Today it is rare to see stallions with even the small star that is permitted. It is rumored that foals are occasionally born with white markings on the face or even the feet. These kinds of markings disqualify a horse from the main stud book, but they can be entered in the foal book, just as chestnut horses can. The stigma involved makes it likely that their occurrence is under-reported.

Breeders often link the appearance of unexpected white markings with the presence of the red gene, and there is some scientific basis for that. Black is known to restrict white markings. This can be seen by comparing the base colors and the marking percentages among the early Friesian mares. Horses that are homozygous for black (*EE*), as is true for most Friesians, are less likely to be marked with white than horses that carry chestnut (*Ee*). It may be that Friesians carry some of the factors that ordinarily might produce small white markings on the face and legs, but their black coloring prevents them from having an effect. When only one black gene is present, the prevention is slightly less effective. This could also explain why some of the chestnut Friesians have white markings, including blazes, even though their parents were unmarked blacks.

Gelderlander

Origin: Gelderland, Netherlands

The Gelderlander is a heavy warmblood originally developed as a high-class carriage horse. It is more stylish and has a lighter build than the closely related Groninger.

Stud Book

The original stud book for the Gelderlander was the *Gelderlander Paarden Stamboek* (GPS), which was founded in 1890. A rival stud book, the *Nederlands Stamboek Tuigpaard* (NSTg), was later established and for a short time the GPS was dormant. The breeding direction of the NSTg changed from producing elegant carriage horses to a heavier warmblood in 1925, utilizing Oldenburg outcrosses much like the Groninger stud book. This caused a split and a group broke off and restarted the Gelderlander studbook for horses of the original lighter type. The two reunited in 1939 and formed the *Vereeniging tot bevordering van de Landbouwtuigpaardenfokkerij in Nederland* (VLN). There were two designations in the VLN: the Gelderlander type (Sgldt) and the Groninger type (Sgrt).

In 1964 the VLN set up a preliminary stud book for crosses with Thoroughbreds. The original idea was that the descendants, bred back to Gelderlanders in subsequent generations, would be moved back into the main stud book. In actual practice, the outcross program became the focus rather than a means to upgrade the existing breed. In 1969 the Gelderlander and Groninger registries merged to form the Royal Warmblood Horse Studbook of the Netherlands (KWPN).

Gelderlander owners were urged by the KWPN to cross their mares with foreign stallions to produce horses of the desired riding type, but over the years pressure from breeders has led to various schemes designed to preserve the Gelderlander. Currently there is a section for Gelderlanders in the KWPN. To qualify, horses must be sired by an approved Gelderlander stallion and out of mare with Gelderlander, Harness, Hackney or Saddlebred blood. Only 6.25 percent of the pedigree can be from the two improvement breeds, for a maximum of 12.5 percent Hackney or Saddlebred blood.

There is also a section for Classic Gelderlander horses in the International Heavy Warmblood stud book. Horses qualify if they have at least 75 percent Gelderlander lines for mares, and at least 87.5 percent for stallions. For a brief time the *Noordeuropees Warmbloed Paard* (NeWP) was another registry that accepted classic Gelderlander horses, but it was absorbed by the Groninger Horse Society (*Het Groninger Paard*) in 2010.

Population

The Dutch Foundation for Rare Animal Breeds (*Stichting Zeldzame Huisdierrassen*) reports that there are 500 mares and 8 stallions. An additional five stallions have frozen semen stored in a gene bank. The organization classifies the Gelderlander as Threatened, which means there are fewer than 1000 animals.

Colors

The color most closely associated with the present-day Gelderlander is chestnut, although bay and black are not uncommon. Among the eight

---

Summary

Current colors: Gelderlanders are most commonly chestnut, but bay and black are also found. Grey is uncommon, but can still be found. There is one remaining silver line and another that carries cream.

Historical Colors: Sabino-1 and roan were once present in the breed. It is thought that the type of sabino still found in Gelderlanders is caused by a different gene.

Markings/Patterns: Most Gelderlanders are liberally marked with white, though extensive body spotting is not typical. Individuals with more onservative markings can be found. There is one remaining tobiano line.

Eye color: Typically the eyes are dark, though there have been a handful of individuals with blue eyes. There are descendants of a golden-eyed smoky black stallion, but none are known to have his pale eyes.

Dutch Registry Abbreviations

FPS	Friesian Horse Studbook	1879-pres.
B.FrPS	Section of the FPS for the Bovenlander breeds	1879-1907 1915-1942
GrPS	Groninger Horse Studbook	1879-1942
DrPS	Drenthe Horse Studbook	1879-1942
GPS	Gelder Horse Studbook	1890-1915 1925-1939
NWP	North Netherlands Warmblood Horse Studbook (merger of GrPS and DrPS)	1942-1969
NSTg	Dutch Harness Horse Studbook	1912-1939
VLN	Association for the Promotion of Agricultural Horse Breeding in the Netherlands (merger of NSTg and GPS)	1939-1970
Sglt	Section within the VLN for Gelderlanders	
Sgrt	Section within the VLN for Groningers	
KWPN	Royal Warmblood Horse Studbook of the Netherlands (merger of the VLN and NWP)	1969-pres.

The history of the Dutch registries is complicated, with many overlapping breed populations. Prior to the formation of the KWPN, it was not unusual to find Dutch horses with offspring in more than one stud book.

remaining stallions, six are chestnut, one is bay and one is black. Among the mares, 64 percent are chestnut, while 17 percent are bay and 15 percent are black.

In shade the chestnuts tend toward bright, clear colors that are fully pigmented; mealy colors are not found and strongly contrasted flaxen manes

and tails are uncommon. Bays typically have fully dark points and are often counter-shaded. Brown is far less common than with the other older coaching breeds. In most cases, Gelderlanders have sabino markings of the flashy white variety, with blazes that often extend to the lips and chin and stockings. Horses with belly spots are sometimes seen, but loud body-spotting is not typical.

Black Gelderlanders usually descend from AHOY (1982), a black stallion with sabino markings. In color and markings he was much like his own sire, MONARCH. Another influential black sire was WALSER (1980), who was marked with the same blaze and stockings that AHOY had. It is not surprising then that many black Gelderlanders have more flamboyant white that is usually associated with that base color.

Although chestnut, bay and black have always been the most common, color in the Gelderlander has historically been quite varied. The presence of so many unusual colors in the Gelderlander, and indeed in so many of the other fine carriage breeds, can be explained by the prevailing attitude that riding horses and harness horses were governed by different rules of fashion. In *The Book of the Horse*, one of the most comprehensive texts on horses from the nineteenth century, Samuel Sidney writes:

"For harness all distinct colours are good, even piebalds, but bays, browns, and dark chestnuts are most in favour: greys are not fashionable; but those who fancy a pair of good greys, whether mottled or iron-grey, have to pay an extra price for them. In 1872 there were only two grey thoroughbred stallions advertised in the annual list. Where horses are to be ridden by men any extraordinary colour is objectionable."

This view, which was quite commonly held, allowed unconventional colors to persist within some of the coaching breeds for a bit longer than in the European riding breeds. Bay or brown teams were still the height of style, but for a time allowances were made for "distinct" colors. It is also interesting to note that fashion dictated some color combinations as attractive that most modern horsemen would consider woefully mismatched. It was, for instance, considered a flattering contrast to pair a grey with a bay or chestnut tobiano. Both of those colors were found in the original Gelderlander, and both persist in low numbers within the current population. Among the mares, greys account for 2 percent of the population, while tobiano is just over 1 percent.

Most of the greys are the descendants of the stallion BATELLO (1983). As his name might suggest, he is a great-great-grandson of the influential grey East Friesian, TELLO (1927). BATELLO was approved for breeding Dutch Harness Horses, but he was a purebred Gelderlander with no Hackney outcrosses. The other grey line still seen is that of the stallion GEOLOOG. He traces his color back to the other famed grey East Friesian, LANDESSOHN (1927). GEOLOOG's daughter, LEEUWA, produced the well-known North American Gelderlander stallion PATRICK (1974). Both LANDESSOHN and TELLO got their grey coloring from the original TELLO (1903), and the vivid dappling associated with this particular family is still common among their modern relatives.

Tobianos

There is a surviving tobiano family that descends from the mare VICKYROSE (1979). Her pattern can be traced back to the black tobiano mare ARAMA I, foaled in 1913. ARAMA was sired by the brown Groninger stallion, CICERO III and was out of an unregistered tobiano mare. She had seven registered foals, but only two are known to have inherited her tobiano pattern. The first of these was the stallion KOEKOEK (1923) and the second was the mare OURBONNI (1927); both were black tobianos. OURBONNI did not leave any registered foals, but KOEKOEK has 21 recorded foals, of which 12 were colored.

The most prolific of his offspring was the black tobiano stallion PETERHEAD (1928). None of his line survive in the Gelderlander population, though he has solid Dutch Warmblood descendants. PETERHEAD is interesting in that his colored daughters were often crossed with the blue roan stallion HIMBO to produce black roan tobianos, which was an unusual combination for that time.

It was another male descendant, however, that continued the line. That was the black tobiano

JOPINTO (1957), a great-grandson of the KOEKOEK daughter, HEMMIE. Her tobiano son, LEMMIE, was said to have been given to Queen Elizabeth as a gift by Prince Bernhard of the Netherlands, to thank her for the hospitality shown to the Prince during World War II. It was from JOPINTO, a stallion never officially approved for breeding, that the color came to VICKYROSE, a Dutch Warmblood mare of mostly Gelderlander lines that had been graded for breeding Harness Horses. Her tobiano daughter GONDAROSE was bred to the Gelderlander stallion UNITAS to produce the chestnut tobiano stallion JAMES BONT (1991). While he is a Gelderlander, JAMES BONT is not approved for breeding within the KWPN. He is an approved sire with the International Heavy Warmblood Horse Breeders Association. There are other tobiano mares from this family within the KWPN, but most are being used in Dutch Warmblood or even pinto sport horse breeding programs, rather than ones specifically for Gelderlanders.

There was another tobiano line unrelated to KOEKOEK that was briefly introduced through URBANA, a daughter of the tobiano Groninger stallion HELLAS. When crossed on the Groninger mare URBENA, he produced the tobiano mare URBANA (1932). URBANA was registered as a Gelderlander. She had one daughter, DRONIA (1939), with the KOEKOEK son PETERHEAD. DRONIA inherited the pattern but did not produce any recorded offspring.

There were other pinto mares registered in the early Gelderlander stud books. Most were registered as *bont*, which would indicate that they had significant amounts of white on the body. Some, like OTJETJE I (1927), regularly passed along their spotting, which would be consistent with a simple dominant pattern like tobiano. Unlike the line to HEMMIE, these pinto lines had all disappeared by the middle of the twentieth century.

Cream

In 1823, the state stallion depot in Borculo purchased four mares and eight stallions from Poland, all described as yellow with white manes. It does not appear that the palomino color persisted after the founding of the original Gelderlander (GPS) stud book.

The cream mutation was later reintroduced through the descendants of RHEINFELD. The smoky black Oldenburg stallion (discussed in the section on Groningers) had at least one foal accepted into the Gelderlander studbook. That was the palomino mare VROUWTJE, foaled in 1956.

A buckskin daughter, MAGDALENA (1949), registered as a Groninger, was crossed on the Thoroughbred stallion PERSIAN FLAG. The resulting filly, BRIGITTA (1960), was registered in the Gelderlander section of the studbook. While her color is not given, she produced a buckskin Dutch Warmblood daughter from a brown Selle Francais stallion.

There is also a small family of cream Gelderlanders that descend from the buckskin RHEINFELD son, REBUS (1942). These are CLAUDIA (1984), EDELWEISS (1986), and FABIOLA (1987). All three were daughters of RAMONA, whose buckskin dam K. FRIEDA was entered in the auxiliary studbook. Most of her descendants are registered as Dutch Warmbloods, but the *Noordeuropees Warmbloed Paard* (NeWP) recorded them in the section of their stud book for Gelderlanders. The palomino stallion CASTELEYN is a grandson of FABIOLA.

Silver

There is at least one line with the silver dilution in the Gelderlander, although this was subject to controversy before it was possible to test for the mutation. That is because the horse originally identified, the stallion IREGON (1967), looks like an ordinary bay horse in photos. Since that time, at least one of his descendants has been confirmed silver by testing. To understand how a horse could hide the silver mutation, it is important to understand that the blonde mane so closely associated with the silver mutation is somewhat temporary. As silvers age, the mane and tail tend to darken. Older red silvers often have manes and tails that do not look very different from a bay horse that has faded in the sun, and the distinctive paler ends of the mane would not be visible when the horse was braided in the style typical of Dutch coach horses. It must also be mentioned that the published photos of the stallion are black and white, and none show his mane clearly.

Although IREGON may have appeared to be a bay in photographs, he was not registered as a bay. He was registered as *koffievos*, or coffee chestnut, which suggests that as a younger horse his mane and tail were paler than they appear in later photos. Likewise his dam, granddam and tail line female ancestors were all registered as dark chestnut, dirty chestnut, or coffee chestnut. In conversations with his breeder, J. K. Wiersema was told that the mares were all colored like IREGON. It is also true that his great-granddam, DROMA (1939), produced a brown filly from the chestnut stallion DOMBURG. DROMA's color can be traced back to her grandmother, NINI, who was registered as dark chestnut. NINI had another chestnut granddaughter who produced a brown foal when bred to a chestnut stallion. When bred together, chestnut horses only produce chestnut, so the appearance of bay or brown foals from chestnut parents can be a sign that one of the parents is actually a red silver. That is especially true when this recurs within a family over generations.

That was very much the case with the descendants of NINI. In addition to producing a brown foal from a chestnut sire, DROMA had another daughter, JONITA (1945), registered as dark chestnut with a grey tail. JONITA also produced a bay foal when bred to the chestnut ROTAN.

A third daughter, SERONA (1953), was registered as dirty chestnut (*zweetvos*). SERONA produced a bay daughter from the chestnut NORKING. It was SERONA's other daughter, ERONA, that produced IREGON. So while his photos may not seem to argue for the presence of the silver mutation, there are a wealth of clues in his background that support the idea that it was there.

IREGON was approved for breeding Dutch Harness Horses, and his silver descendants in that breed are discussed in that chapter. He had silver offspring that were used in the Dutch Warmblood, which will be discussed in the fourth volume of this series. He also had one daughter from a Groninger mare that was registered as a Groninger. Both the mother, a black sabino roan, and the daughter, a silver dapple sabino, are pictured in the Wiersema book. The daughter, PEBERINA, shows the classic pale belly dappling of a silver along with the irregular leg and belly patches of a sabino. PE-BERINA left no recorded offspring, so her color did not continue in the Groninger.

Historical Colors

While there was not a formal effort to limit the colors of the Gelderlander, the changes the breed underwent in the mid-twentieth century narrowed the gene pool. Some Gelderlander lines were outcrossed to create the Dutch Warmblood and Dutch Harness Horse, while others were not continued at all. As a result, some colors were lost to genetic drift.

Sabino-1

Although the frequency of wide blazes, stockings and belly spots suggest that some form of sabino is quite common, this type of sabino patterning is different from sabino-1. Reiner Geurts made this connection in his book, *Hair Colour in the Horse*, which was written more than forty years before the sabino-1 mutation was identified. Of horses with the flashy white type of belly spotting, he writes:

> "Such markings are encountered regularly in increasing measure over the years among horses of the Gelderlander type (in a good 5% of the mares registered in the VLN Stud Book). These horses did not belong to the typical sabino families mentioned above, and in more than 90% of the cases, the parents had no such markings. The various stallions also, who had spots on the belly and have stood at stud over the years, seem only to have passed on the characteristic to a single foal."

The "typical sabino" families Geurts discussed prior to this passage were Groningers, and are believed to have carried sabino-1. That type of roaned, indistinct sabino was more characteristic of the early Groninger breed than it was of the Gelderlander. Since the Gelderlander stud book accepted Groninger horses, the sabino-1 mutation was introduced through outcrosses to members of these families.

One of these was stallion JAFFINO (1935), a dark bay with heavily ticked high white markings. His dam, ZONNESTRAAL, was registered as *bont* (pinto). Many of his offspring were roaned or had

white ticking. One of JAFFINO's Gelderlander descendants was the mare IFINA (1944), described as a chestnut roan with patches on her ribs, hip, and belly. Another granddaughter, UGIBLIA (1955), was registered as a dark bay roan pinto with a big white spot on the belly and a grey tail. The JAFFINO line died out sometime in the mid-twentieth century.

A second sabino-1 line originated with the stallion JOTHAM (1945). In photos JOTHAM has a broad blaze that encompasses his entire muzzle and high stockings that extend past his knees in the front and entirely up the stifle on the back. He has a pale body that suggests he was probably heavily roaned and patches on the barrel and left hip. All his markings have indistinct edges, which is typical of a horse that has the sabino-1 mutation.

His sire, ANTON, was a chestnut Gelderlander with the more common flashy white sabino pattern. His dam was the Groninger mare, ULTRUSS. ULTRUSS was by the sabino stallion PRIMO, who was known for producing white foals, so it is likely that the color came from her and not AN-TON. PRIMO was a half-brother to JAFFINO's dam, ZONNESTRAAL.

JOTHAM was then most likely heterozygous for the sabino-1 mutation. He produced at least one

The black tobiano stallion KOEKOEK was registered with the NSTg at a time when the breeding direction of the Gelderlander and Groninger were closely aligned. His sire and dam were Groningers, and his descendants can be found in the stud books for both breeds.

white-born foal from the brown sabino mare CI-
NAADJE. Her dam, NAADJE, was registered as a
bay with roaning. The dam of NAADJE was not
registered, but is described in the stud book as a
pinto. Although the white colt was discussed in
the Wiersema book, it appears he was never registered. CINAADJE had several other foals that were
registered as roans or, in one case, as a pale bay
with ticking, but her line died out after a few generations.

It is possible that the sabino-1 mutation survives
in the modern Gelderlander. JOTHAM still appears
in pedigrees of both Gelderlanders and Dutch
Harness Horses. One of JOTHAM's most successful
sons, OLEANDER (1950), had the irregular markings that often indicate the presence of sabino-1.
On the whole, populations with the sabino-1 mutation have a different appearance than those with
the flashy white form of sabino, but individual
variations in the patterns can result in horses that
look remarkably similar. This is especially true
for sabino horses that do not have very extensive
markings. Without testing—or the birth of a white
foal—it might be hard to know if such a horse was
carrying sabino-1 or the traditional flashy white
sabino pattern.

True Roan
Although outcrossing to the Hackney is often associated with the transition of the breed to the
Dutch Harness Horse, there were Hackneys used
in the early formation of the Gelderlander. One of
those was the bay roan stallion HOCKWOLD CA-
DET (1911). HOCKWOLD CADET was approved for
breeding by the *Gelders Paard Stamboek* (GPS),
and sired Gelderlanders from 1921 until 1934. In
addition to being bred to Gelderlander mares, he
also had a number of purebred Hackney daughters,
like the roans IRISIE (1921) and LIGIA (1924), registered as Gelderlanders. At least two of his purebred sons, both roans, were approved for breeding in the GPS. Those were FEU SACRE and NON
PARIEL, both foaled in 1927. A roan grandson,
HEDON BOY (1930), was double-registered as a
Hackney and a Gelderlander. Because HOCKWOLD
CADET was included in the first stud book and his
offspring were often registered as Gelderlanders,

HOCKWOLD CADET *was a dark-headed roan Hackney
used in the early development of the Gelderlander breed.
His line continued in the Hackney, Dutch Harness Horse
and Dutch Warmblood.*

he and his descendants are not generally viewed in
the same way as later Hackney outcrosses.

As for his coloring, Dutch color researcher Reiner Geurts suggested that HOCKWOLD CADET may
have been a sabino, and he did have four white
socks, but there is little question that whatever else
he might have carried, he was a true, dark-headed
roan. Photos of him show a very dark, unroaned
head, and many of his foals have studbook entries
that indicate they were dark-headed (*moorkop*).
Some of his descendants were said to have strange
and capricious markings, particularly those by
FEU SACRE. It may be that FEU SACRE was more
wildly marked, in addition to being a true roan,
but at least one of his roan daughters was out of a
mare by the sabino-1 stallion, PRIMO. Whether the
source of the unusual markings were introduced
by HOCKWOLD CADET, or whether they came from
the local mare population, it was unrelated to his
roan color.

HOCKWOLD CADET got his coloring from his
dam, HOCKWOLD SIGNORETTA (1907). She traces
back in an unbroken line of roan mares to the roan
stallion YOUNG GUN (1874), who was linebred to
the original bay roan Hackney, NORFOLK PHE-
NOMENON (1825). Descriptions of him might ex-

plain why his descendant found acceptance among breeders of heavy coach horses, as PHENOMENON was said to be big boned, and able to add both depth of girth and quality to lighter mares. Pictures of CADET show a horse more old-fashioned in type than the Hackneys used in later decades.

None of the many roan descendants of HOCK-WOLD CADET remain in the Gelderlander breeding pool, but his color does continue in the Dutch Warmblood with the recently approved chestnut roan stallion, EL ROSSO (1986). That is the line of HOCKWOLD CADET's chestnut roan grandson, KILLA'S BOY (1927). Like his grandsire, KILLA'S BOY is sometimes called a sabino, but he did have true roan offspring so his color was either misidentified or he was both sabino and true roan. In this particular branch of the Cadet family, roan is more commonly seen on chestnut horses than the bays and blacks.

There were other true roans in the early stud books. Among those are:

CORRIE XV   (Alex – red roan mare)
              1904 roan mare
EMINE I   (Xenophon II – unknown)
              1917 blue roan mare
SOMORA I   (Domburg – roan mare)
              1930 roan mare
CIMAROSE   (Wodanus – unknown)
              1938 blue roan mare

The first three were all NSTg helpbook mares, while the last was a Groninger used for breeding Gelderlanders. In all four, the lines died out after a few generations, taking the roan color with them. There was also a stallion, LOUIS (1904), registered as blue roan. He sired a number of blue and bay roan daughters, but like the roan mares his line died out after a few generations.

There were other lines that did not die out, at least not completely. One comes from the Groninger stallion EDMUND (1900). His offspring were registered as Gelderlanders, and little over half were recorded as grey or roan (schimmel). His later descendants are sometimes described as dark-headed (moorkop), so it seems clear that he was roan rather than—or perhaps in addition to—grey.

One of his descendants was the stallion HIMBO (1943), described as blauwmoorkop, or blue roan. HIMBO left no recorded sons, but his daughters were often noted as being dark-headed. His blue roan daughter, FAVORITE (1964), has a line that continues in both the Dutch Warmblood and the Dutch Harness Horse, but it is unclear whether or not the roan coloring is still there.

Another roan line with modern descendants is the one from GRADA III, foaled in 1919 and registered as bay roan (bruinschimmel, moorkop). Her line continues through her daughter, DO. Although her base color was not recorded, DO must have been a bay roan since she produced bay and black roans from a chestnut sire. It was a black roan daughter of DO, ROELANDA (1952) that carried the color forward into the Dutch Warmblood. Four of her roan daughters, EDELVROUWE, HOF-DAME PETERNELLA, and KOLLANDA PETERNELLA, were registered as Dutch Warmbloods or were used to produce them. ROELANDA had one son, the blue roan VIZIER (1956). He was registered as a Gelderlander and has a number of descendants with a high percentage of Gelderlander blood. The color could be reintroduced through this line, if those horses were bred to Gelderlander sires.

Eye Color

Despite the fact that most Gelderlanders have extensive white markings, the majority are dark-eyed. That is pretty typical for breeds that have the flashy white version of sabino. There is at least one bay mare, MONIEK (1994), with a completely white face, high white stockings and blue eyes. Her bay daughter ALEXIA (2005) is almost identical in markings. MONIEK has a minimally marked sire and a dam that comes from flashy white sabino bloodlines. Blue eyes and this type of pattern have occurred in other breeds, often within families that were previously known for producing fairly ordinary, dark-eyed sabinos. In each case, the extremely white face and blue eyes have led to speculation that the horses were splashed whites. It is possible that MONIEK and ALEXIA are classic splashes, since a single copy of the mutation (SW1) is not always obvious unless it is paired with another white pattern. That seems unlikely because no evidence has yet surfaced of a Gelderlander with the classic splash pattern. In fact, MONIEK and her daughter are the only two Gelderlanders this author has found with this type of marking. If there are no others, that might suggest that MONIEK carries a splashed white mutation that has not yet been formally identified, perhaps one that originated with her.

Markings
The broad blazes, white noses and high white stockings of the sabino pattern are strongly associated with Gelderlanders, but there are horses with less white and even a few individuals without white markings of any kind. Unbalanced markings, where there is little or no white on the face even though the legs are marked with high socks or stockings, are occasionally seen. Belly spots occur, but large areas of white on the sides of the horse are unusual. Relatively few Gelderlanders with flashy white have produced foals so dramatically patterned that they were registered as pintos, despite the fact that many Gelderlanders have generations of sabino breeding on both sides of their pedigree. The relative rarity of white on the body suggests that the flashy white sabino pattern may have a limited range of expression in its pure form.

Groninger

Origin: Groningen region, Netherlands

The Groninger is a heavy warmblood originally developed for general purpose agricultural work. The stronger build was needed to work the heavy clay found in the Groningen region.

Stud Book

Horses from Groningen and Drenthe were accepted for registration in the Bovenlander (Book B) section of the Friesian stud book starting in 1883. The breed split from that registry in 1896, and from 1897 to 1942 Groningers were registered in the *Groningsch Paarden Stamboek* (GrPS). In 1942 those horses merged with the Bovenlanders (FPS) and the horses from Drenthe (DrPS) to form the North-Netherlands Warmblood Horse Studbook (NWP). At the time, crossing to Oldenburgs and East Friesians was still common.

In 1939, responding to the rising interest in equestrian sports, the Gelderlander stud book set up the *Vereeniging tot bevordering van de Landbouwtuigpaardenfokkerij in Nederland* (VLN) with a section for the Gelderlander type (Sgldt) and another for Groningers (Sgrt). In 1964 both the VLN and the NWP set up sport horse registries, which allowed outcrossing to Thoroughbred stallions with the aim of producing lighter riding horses. Offspring from these crosses could then be bred back to native stock and registered as pure Gelderlanders or Groningers. The crossbred program quickly overtook the native breeds, and was particularly devastating to the Groninger.

In 1969 the NWP merged with the Gelderlander registry to form the Royal Warmblood Horse Studbook of the Netherlands (KWPN). The new registry had three sections: riding horses, coach horses, and the Gelderlander. With the merger, the existing Groninger stallions were labeled redundant and lost their breeding approval, and owners of Groninger mares were encouraged to outcross.

In 1978 the last remaining NWP stallion, BALDEWIJN, was saved from slaughter. With that stallion and twenty mares, the Groninger Horse

Society (*Het Groninger Paard*) was formed in 1982. The breed was then rebuilt using heavier East Friesians, Silesians, East Germans, and Holsteiners. One Cleveland Bay stallion, MANINGFORD HERMES, was also used. In 2010, this group merged with the *Noordeuropees WarmbloedPaard* (NeWP), another organization promoting horses of the older Groninger type. Horses in the NeWP stud book were automatically granted inclusion in the Groninger Horse Society stud book, a move that was intended to expand the limited gene pool for the breed.

Another preservation registry was formed in 1994. Originally called the *Vereniging Oud-Groninger Paard* (VOGP), it split from the Groninger Horse Society over the use of Holstein blood. The registry was later renamed the International Heavy Warmblood Horse Breeder's Association. In addition to Groningers, the International Heavy Warmblood stud book accepts Alt-Oldenburger, Silesian and East Friesian horses into its main stud book. There are also separate sections for the Gelderlanders and Dutch Harness Horses that have been bred using classic lines. For all three

Summary

Current colors: The most common colors are black, brown and dark bay. Chestnut is less common, but can be found among the mares. A single grey stallion has been approved for breeding, and there is one roan line.

Historical Colors: Cream and silver were once present in the breed. There was one mare suspected of having been a dominant white.

Markings/Patterns: Groningers vary in the markings, though most are relatively conservative. There are at least two tobiano mares, and sabino-1 is present in at least one line. One sabino-1 stallion was recently approved for breeding.

Eye color: The eyes are typically dark. One smoky black stallion had golden eyes, but it is not clear if he passed the trait to his offspring. The single suspected dominant white mare had blue eyes.

sections, mares must have at least 75 percent classic breeding, and stallions must have at least 87.5 percent classic breeding.

Population

The Dutch Foundation for Rare Animal Breeds (*Stichting Zeldzame Huisdierrassen*) reports that there are 36 approved stallions and 420 mares. Within the stud book for the International Heavy Warmblood, there are less than half as many stallions and approximately the same number of mares. The breed is classified as Threatened, which means there are fewer than 1000 animals.

Colors

The predominant color of the Groninger is black or dark brown. There are some owners and breeders who feel this is the only proper color for the breed, and there is a certain prejudice among some traditionalists regarding other colors, particularly chestnut. When the original breed formed in the late nineteenth century, the color that predominated was bay, though widespread outcrossing to Oldenburgs quickly increased the percentages of black and brown. Unlike the Friesian breeders that once shared their stud book, the Groninger breeders never adopted rules requiring or restricting specific colors. As a result, the breed has a long history of varied colors, a fact that is noted by the Groninger Horse Society.

Among the stallions approved by the Groninger Horse Society, the majority are evenly split between bay, brown and black. With only a few exceptions, the bay stallions are dark enough that they could be mistaken for brown, so the overall impression is of a very dark horse. There are not currently any approved chestnut stallions, although several of the approved stallions are known to carry the red gene. Chestnut stallions have been approved in the past, including WOLDKONING (1961), ROTAN (1954) and the premium stallion REFLEX (1950). It is believed that a modern chestnut stallion would be approved, were he of sufficient quality.

There is an approved grey stallion, TRISTAN-B (1999). TRISTAN's bay sire, TEST, is of Polish Silesian lines, and his grey dam KEIZERIN was a Dutch Warmblood approved by the NeWP. Her color traced back through the grey Holsteiner stallion RIGOLETTO (1960), who had been approved for breeding Groningers. RIGOLETTO's grey color traces back to both Thoroughbred and Shagya lines.

The varied colors once seen in the breed are reflected more accurately in the mares. Evidence suggests that the colorful nature of the mare population was not especially unique, and that many of the European coaching breeds were somewhat varied, but in the case of the Groninger these horses were more thoroughly documented thanks to the interest of two Dutch researchers: Reiner Geurts, author of *Hair Colour in the Horse* (1973) and J. K. Wiersema, author of *Het Paard in Zijn Kleurenrijkdom* (1977). In some cases the color has been preserved along with the family that introduced it, and in others the situation is a bit more like that of the grey stallion TRISTAN-B, where a historic color has been reintroduced from a different source.

Sabino

Sabino was preserved in the older Groninger type through the stallion OTTO (1984). The continuation of this line, and the color, was made more likely by the recent approval of the OTTO great-grandson MERLIJN (2005). MERLIJN is a very pale bay sabino roan, almost white in appearance. OTTO also left a number of daughters, including the black sabino GEKA (1989), the sabino roan ZESKE (granddam of MERLIJN) and the body-spotted sabino NURISHA-T (1990), which will also help ensure the color remains a part of the breed.

OTTO was a black sabino roan with an even mix of dark and light hairs, along with a broad blaze and hind stockings. In this he was much like his granddam, VEBERINA. She is one of the sabino mares pictured in the Wiersema book, and her lovely blue-grey coloring makes it obvious why such horses were once called Drenthe Blues.

Although it never made up a majority of the Groninger population, this type of coloring has a long history in the breed. As the name might suggest, many came from the earlier Drenthe stud book. The appearance and breeding records of the horses give little doubt that most, if not all, of these horses were carrying sabino-1.

As Reiner Geurts noted in his book, the sabino pattern found in the Groninger behaved differently from the one commonly seen in the Gelderlander. It also looked quite different, being more diffused and roaned in appearance. Of the sabino mares, he noted that two-thirds were registered as ticked or roan. He also noted that of those that were registered as pintos, 90 percent were described as roaned or ticked. Of those that were marked with white beyond the face and legs, only 18 percent had large white patches across their entire body, while 59 percent had white only under the belly. That distribution of roaned and patched individuals matches pretty closely to the proportions found in the early Tennessee Walking Horse stud books where the sabino-1 gene was extremely common. Even the name Drenthe Blue suggests that many of these horses were genetically black, which is another characteristic of sabino-1. While many of the sabino patterns have a higher incidence of heavy roaning with chestnut, sabino-1 tends to add significant roaning even to black horses. The strongest clue, however, was that the horses were known to produce white-born foals.

Wiersema speculated on the link between white-born horses and the sabino pattern. He pointed out that even before the founding of the Dutch stud books, breeders had known that crossing sabino horses together could produce white foals, and that at least two breeders, Mr. A. Starke and Mr. D. E. Nanninga, were actively breeding for white in the 1930s. Mr. Stark used the Drenthe stallion Koos (1926) with sabino mares, while Mr. Nanninga used a young son of Heridon. Neither his name nor a recorded line of descendants remain, but a black and white photo of the stallion shows a pattern typical of the sabino-1 mutation. The descendants of these earlier breeding programs could have contributed sabino-1 to the lines later registered in the Groninger stud book.

In addition to those early breeding programs, Wiersema documents numerous instances of sabino x sabino crosses that resulted in white foals within the Groninger breed. The first example he gives is the white Groninger gelding Prins Ajax (1942). His sire, Ajax, was said to have been sired by a brown Barb stallion and out of a white-born

The recently approved stallion Merlijn *(above) probably carries the sabino-1 gene, inherited from his grandsire* Otto. *The black sabino mare* Veberina *(below) was the granddam of* Otto. *Because the coloring was closely associated with the horses of the Drenthe region, it was sometimes called Drenthe Blue.*

mare. Pictures of Ajax show a bay sabino with an evenly roaned body, a broad blaze, white chin, high hind stockings and a detached knee patch. In addition to the white Prins Ajax, he also produced a daughter, Wipaja, that was registered as *bruinschimmel bont*, or bay roan pinto.

The dam of Prins Ajax, Osilva, was a brown sabino with a broad blaze, stockings and spotting on her barrel. Her color could be traced back through successive generations of brown or black sabino Drenthe mares.

Prins Ajax appears to have been the only offspring of his dam, but Ajax sired at least three other white-born foals. One was out of a daughter of the chestnut sabino Gelderlander JOTHAM, and the other two were out of one of his own daughters. This would support the idea that the sabino-1 mutation was present, since two copies of the mutation are necessary to get a white foal.

JOTHAM's sire, PRIMO (1928), is another horse suspected of carrying the sabino-1 mutation. In a photo taken as an older horse, PRIMO appears to be a light dapple grey with a blaze and high stockings that rise up the stifle. PRIMO was registered in both the Groninger and Friesian (Book B) stud books, and had an unusually complete pedigree for his day. His sire was the brown Oldenburg GUNTBERT, and his dam was a mare named JESSELINA. Her coloring is not known, but her dam OLMINA and granddam ELARIA were both registered as pintos (*bont*). ELARIA was described as white and light blue with brown hairs. Her dam MIDANTE was registered as *schimmel*, which can mean roan or grey; in the case of MIDANTE it would seem it meant both grey and sabino roan. The line ends with her dam, FRITSJE (1892), a roan mare said to have been out of a pinto mother.

PRIMO sired more than one white foal, including the filly UNIFLORA. She was born white with dark eyes and a black spot between her ears. PRIMO also had a pinto half-sister, ZONNESTRAAL. She was the dam of the bay sabino JAFFINO discussed in the chapter on Gelderlanders.

Another stallion that contributed to the spread of the sabino-1 mutation in the years prior to the absorption of the breed into the Dutch Warmblood was NOORDERLICHT (1953). NOORDERLICHT was a black sabino with a broad blaze, stockings over the knees and hocks, and ticking throughout his coat. When crossed with the descendants of PRIMO and JAFFINO, he produced a number of white foals.

The sabino stallion OTTO pulling a traditional farm cart known as a 'wipkar'. Pictured at 18 years old, he is participating in a yearly event known as the 'wipkarrentocht' where harnessed horses make a 25 mile tour of the Groningen countryside.

There were mare lines with patterns that suggested they, too, were carrying sabino-1. The bay sabino mare ESAMIA (1945) had the evenly distributed roaning, broad blaze and hind stockings that are typical of many sabino-1 horses. She gave the color to her daughter, ZONDERLING, although she was patched with white as well as roaned. Another foal, SARINA, was registered as blue roan, so was likely marked more like her dam. SARINA has descendants in the modern warmblood population, but it appears her coloring was lost along the way.

So far all the families mentioned can trace their color to native Drenthe horses. An unrelated line that carried sabino-1 came from the stallion MARKIES (1963). MARKIES was a Holsteiner, which suggests that sabino-1 may have been more widespread in Europe at one time. MARKIES was a grey (born chestnut) as well as a sabino. The grey came from his Thoroughbred sire, MANOMETER. The sabino color came from his chestnut Holsteiner dam, EVA. She got the sabino pattern from her sire, KOLLMAR. KOLLMAR's sire was the bay Arabian, KOHINOOR. While some strains of Arabians are known for producing sabinos, none have yet been shown to carry sabino-1, and the Hungarian lines that produced KOHINOOR—known for little or no white markings—would be an unlikely source for any sabino pattern. Instead it came through KOLMAR's dam, IDA. Wiersema identified the color in IDA and traced it back three more generations to the brown sabino Holsteiner mare, AHNE 7688.

MARKIES produced two known white-born foals. The first of these was an unnamed colt from the NOORDERLICHT daughter, SANORA, born in 1973. He was described as pure white with dark eyes. The second was the colt PAUL, also foaled in 1973. He was out of the bay sabino mare, LIONNE. She was the granddaughter of WELFALICHT, a daughter of NOORDERLICHT. Like WELFALICHT, who she greatly resembled in color, she was pictured in the Wiersema book. PAUL is the foal at her side in that photo.

Although the color line from MARKIES did not continue in the Groninger, he does have sabino descendants in the Dutch Warmblood breed. His grandsire, KOLLMAR, has Holsteiner descendants as well.

One thing must be noted about the homozygous sabino-1 Groningers. Both Geurts and Wiersema took a strong interest in white-born foals, and many of the horses they describe were ones they personally observed and, in the case of Wiersema, photographed. Both men note that the eyes color of white-born foals could vary. Geurts wrote:

> "These white-born foals have dark, but also some have blue, eyes and sometimes dim blue spots or some pigmented hair in the head or in the ears."

This matches the stud book records for homozygous sabino-1 Tennessee Walking Horses, where most were dark-eyed but still a portion had one or both eyes blue. Blue eyes are uncommon in sabino horses, but they are found upon occasion, and seem somewhat more frequent when sabino-1 is homozygous. Whether horses like this represent a common expression of the sabino-1 pattern, or carry some additional genetic factor, is not yet known.

Tobiano

There is a tobiano line in the modern Groninger through the mare CONCHITA and her daughter SCARA (2006) by BARTUS. CONCHITA's pattern comes from the well-known Dutch Warmblood stallion, SAMBER. His pattern came from his dam, TINA. TINA (1964) was registered in the Groninger stud book, as was her dam ASTRID, but after that point the color goes back through the female line in the Gelderlander stud book. The sire of CONCHITA, ISAM (1990), is a double-grandson of TINA, once through his sire SAMBER, and once through his mother RINA.

Another tobiano line originated in the Groninger, but is now found in colored sport horses. The source of the color is the tobiano mare LUCI, registered in auxiliary section of the North-Netherlands Warmblood Horse Studbook (NWP). When bred to the bay Groninger stallion SINAEDA, LUCI produced SONJA. She in turn produced one foal, the Dutch Warmblood stallion ICO (1967). ICO was only half-Groninger by blood, though his Trakehner sire had been approved for breeding by the NWP. ICO was not approved in the Netherlands, but he was used at stud there for a few years

The tobiano mare CONCHITA traces twice to TINA, the black tobiano dam of the Dutch Warmblood sire SAMBER. TINA was a registered Groninger. In the bottom photo, CONCHITA is pictured with her bay tobiano filly SCARA by BARTUS.

before being exported to Germany where he became a well-known sire of jumpers.

Ico stands out from the other Dutch tobianos in that his irregular pattern and broad face marking makes him more immediately recognizable as a tovero. His Trakehner sire was a chestnut with a broad blaze and solid legs, but it seems more likely that the extra flash in his pattern came from SINAEDA, who was a brown horse with a broad blaze and white chin, one small hind sock and a tall hind stocking.

Historically, there have been other tobiano lines. The most prolific was that of the black tobiano stallion HELLAS (1928). The markings on HELLAS suggest that he carried another pattern. He had an extremely broad, top-heavy star on his forehead and a small snip on his nose. The dark area on his neck also skewed down the top of his neck, which is sometimes seen in tobianos that inherit one of the splashed white patterns. With no information beyond a handful of old photographs of HELLAS himself, the nature of any additional pattern is open to speculation.

HELLAS was originally registered as a Friesian, as was his dam, ANNIE. She had been registered in Book B of the *Friesch Paarden-Stamboek* (FPS), so would have been referred to at the time as a Bovenlander. His sire GERHARD was a black Oldenburg that had been approved and rated preferred for the Friesian stud book. While GERHARD was also registered in Book B of the Friesian stud book, he technically had no recorded Friesian blood, and neither did HELLAS.

HELLAS had six recorded foals, all daughters. Only two are known to have inherited his tobiano pattern: URBANA (1932) and FAVORIET (1933). URBANA was included in the early Dutch Harness Horse studbook (NSTg), which at that time contained the Gelderlanders. Her descendants are discussed in the chapter on Gelderlanders.

FAVORIET, a chestnut tobiano, was included in the Groninger stud book. She had one daughter, the black tobiano YLA (1942) by the black Oldenburg stallion GRUNEWALD. YLA had one daughter, MARIANNE (1949), and she inherited the color as well. At that point the color line was lost. MARIANNE had only one daughter, a dark brown, and that daughter did not produce.

A 1932 photo of HELLAS harnessed with the tobiano Gelderlander stallion KOEKOEK shows how very similar the two breeds were even as they maintained separate stud books. HELLAS lived at a time when the coaching breeds were in transition, and this is reflected in the stud book entries of his offspring. Two of his daughters were registered in the Friesian stud book, while three others were entered in the Groninger stud book (GrPs). One last foal was entered in the old Dutch Harness

Horse (Gelderlander) stud book (NSTg). Most of their offspring were transferred into the North-Netherlands Warmblood Horse Studbook (NWP), although some were entered into the Groninger section of the Gelderlander stud book (Sgrt). In the case of KOEKOEK, almost half his foals were entered into the Groninger books, while the other half were entered as Gelderlanders. It is tempting to wonder if some of their foals, as well as the foals of other coaching horses, were lost to the stud books during this time. What is certain is that most were lost entirely when the heavier coach horses were abandoned in favor of sport horses.

This definitely came into play a few decades later with a stallion that looked remarkably like HELLAS in type and coloring. That was the black tobiano NICO (1957), sometimes called BONTE NICO or NICO VAN FRIESLAND. NICO is sometimes referred to as a Friesian, though like HELLAS he would have more accurately been termed a Bovenlander. NICO created a bit of a sensation when he was denied a breeding permit. There may have been prejudice against his color, though it had been approved in other instances. Perhaps more problematic was that he embodied the old Groninger type which has been deemed inappropriate in a breeding stallion. (It could be argued that his rather conspicuous coloring, which undoubtedly enhanced his notoriety, did not help the situation with inspectors.) Although it was illegal to use him without a breeding permit, his offspring were in high demand and sold for much higher prices than those of approved Friesians, so his owner was willing to pay the fine. Officials tried to seize the horse, or force him to be gelded or destroyed, but his owner was able to mobilize popular opinion. Prince Bernhard of the Netherlands intervened with the Ministry of Agriculture to grant the stallion a special exemption.

Unlike HELLAS, NICO was not registered. In 1965, officials with both the warmblood stud book (NWP) and the Friesian stud book (FPS) took out an ad warning mare owners that the stallion's offspring would not be accepted for registration. His line did continue through his sons, but the strain existed outside the official Dutch stud books. In recent years, efforts have been made to establish the Barockpinto (Baroque Pinto) as a breed using NICO descendants and modern Friesians, though this has been met with some resistance from both Friesian breeders and those who question to accuracy of the pedigrees. Those familiar with photos of NICO, HELLAS and KOEKOEK will note there is considerable difference between their type, which was that of the old Bovenlander horse, and a Friesian with a tobiano pattern.

Roan

The blue roan Dutch Harness Horse mare JOLANDA (1968) has a great-granddaughter that has been included in the Groninger breeding population. That is the black roan mare SINY, foaled in 1993. This was the same female line that produced the successful black roan Dutch Harness Horse gelding ZOMOOI. The JOLANDA grand-daughter EBONY was of pure Gelderlander breeding, but when bred to EXPERIMENT MONSTERGARD, the resulting foal was accepted into the Groninger stud book. EXPERIMENT MONSTERGARD was a Danish Oldenburg approved for breeding by the Groninger Horse Society. Bred to the black BASCAL, SINY produced the chestnut roan mare SANNE, dam of the successful colt EDO-H.

Although the current roan line came from the Gelderlander, there were older roan lines that were

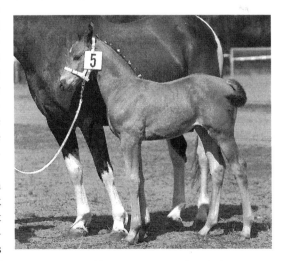

The Groninger filly ESTHER pictured with her tobiano dam. Although not registered, the mare is said to be a daughter of the tobiano stallion ISAM.

lost over time. The blue roan East Friesian stallion MOOR (1934) was used for breeding Groningers, and left numerous roan foals. MOOR is notable to color researchers not only because of his own unusual color, but because he was often crossed with colorful mares. One of these was the silver mare that produced BICA, a black silver roan. BICA produced the chestnut roan mare ABICA who went on to produce both roans and silvers.

MOOR also had a red roan tobiano daughter, RIEKJE, out of a daughter of KOEKOEK. RIEKJE produced a grey tobiano daughter, GLORETTE, from the dapple gray RINKO. GLORETTE combined three of the colorful Dutch lines: roan from MOOR, grey from TELLO, and tobiano from KOEKOEK. She was among the few descendants of MOOR to continue in the Dutch Warmblood studbook, though by that point the line had lost all three colors.

That was the case for most of his descendants. Very few still existed when the Groninger was absorbed by the Dutch Warmblood, and those few that did were not roans. It is possible that this had more to do with his type, which was heavy even for a horse of his era, rather than his uncommon color.

Another roan East Friesian stallion used in the early years of the Groninger stud book was MUSSOLINI (1925). MUSSOLINI was registered in the Friesian studbook (Book B) and the Drenthe studbook, as well as the one for the Groninger, and he left both roan and non-roan foals in each of them. Like MOOR, his line remains in a few modern Dutch horses, but the roan color was lost in the mid-twentieth century.

Historical Colors

Although many of the colors originally found in the Groninger population have been preserved, a few were lost when the breed was folded into the combined Dutch Warmblood stud book.

Cream

One smoky black Oldenburg stallion introduced the cream dilution into the Groninger studbooks. RHEINFELD was a premium stallion for the NWP from 1941-1948, and later for the VLN from 1949-1960. He was recorded in the stud book as black

and was sometimes described as mouse dun. In photos he appears black, though his coloring is somewhat faded. Wiersema referred to him as a smoky black, which was his true color. His pedigree and his own production record confirm this.

His coloring comes through his smoky black dam, PEPITA II. Oldenburg records show that PEPITA II had at least three dilute foals; two buckskin colts and a smoky black or very dark buckskin daughter, PEPA. From her the color extends back through two more generations of smoky black mares until it reaches the dam of the Oldenburg founder mare WALLY II 118, who was described as dark isabella. Her dam WALLY was the daughter of the premium mare THUSNELDA (1871), who was remembered as a yellow mare with a white mane and tail. THUSNELDA was said to trace back to the golden horses of Hanover.

RHEINFELD also possessed an unusual trait in that he had very pale yellow eyes. Lighter eyes are occasionally seen in horses with the cream dilution, but his were striking even by those standards. Like his diluted coat, they were inherited in an unbroken line from WALLY. RHEINFELD'S sister, PEPA, had them, as did her daughter, PEPA II. Eye color was often overlooked in early stud book descriptions, so to see it mentioned so consistently suggests that the trait was equally pronounced in the other members of the family. Reiner Geurts indicated that it was also present in some of the offspring of RHEINFELD. The one palomino daughter pictured in *Het Paard in Zijn Kleurenrijkdom* has pale eyes. It is not clear if the trait, like the golden eyes found in some lines of Paso Finos and Highland Ponies, was ever inherited independent of the cream dilution. Geurts seems to suggest that it was connected in some way, since the golden-eyed foals were all cream dilutes.

It may be that RHEINFELD carried another dilution in addition to cream. If he truly did descend from the cream horses of Hanover, he may have carried whatever was responsible for the golden eyes said to have been a part of their coloring. Or perhaps he was a dilute black, as well as being a smoky cream. Dilute black horses, which are called *globrunn* in Iceland, have been documented in breeds as diverse as the Arabian and the Icelandic, and many of them have golden or hazel eyes. This might explain why so many of RHEINFELD's foals are recorded as mouse-colored. Some smoky black horses fade more readily than black horses without the cream dilution, but the frequency, paired with the consistent nature of the golden eyes in the generations behind him, does raise the question whether an additional dilution might have been present.

Regardless of whether or not he carried some as-yet-unidentified dilution, it is clear that RHEINFELD carried cream. Genetically he was a black horse (*aa*) carrying chestnut (*Ee*), so he was capable of producing palominos, buckskins and smoky blacks. RHEINFELD sired 94 recorded foals with the following colors: black–33, brown–19, bay–3, chestnut–11, grey–2, palomino–14, buckskin–4, smoky–8. This gives a ratio of 26 diluted to 68 undiluted colors. The expected 50 percent split was most likely skewed by the fact that RHEINFELD was black, and was primarily crossed with black and dark brown mates. Since many smoky black horses are visually indistinguishable from an ordinary black horse, it is probable that some of his black foals were in fact smoky black. This is borne out by the fact that several of his black daughters went on to produce palomino or buckskin foals.

Most of the RHEINFELD foals that had the cream dilution were not used in breeding. He did have a smoky black son, GUSTAAF (1942), that produced a number of palomino and buckskin daughters, but his male line continued through his chestnut son REFLEX. One buckskin daughter that did reproduce was MAGDALENA (1949). Unfortunately MAGDALENA was crossed with a Thoroughbred, and her line and color continued in the Dutch Warmblood rather than the Groninger. Another son, the buckskin REBUS (1942) has a line that continued through his daughter K. FRIEDA (1969), though her descendants are either Dutch Warmbloods or Gelderlanders.

Silver
If photos of the Gelderlander IREGON caused skepticism about whether or not he carried silver, the situation was much more clear in the case of the Groninger mare JOBICA (1959). Her color was the

PEBERINA *was a silver dapple sabino. She inherited the sabino-1 gene from her mother* VEBERINA, *who is visible in the picture behind her. The silver dilution came from the Gelderlander stallion* IREGON.

subject of debate when she was presented at two years of age for grading, and observers could not decide if she was chestnut or bay. That is a common reaction to red silvers with darkly pigmented legs, because they look like a bay horse with a flaxen mane and tail, or like a flaxen chestnut with black legs. This is especially true with younger silvers, since they have their adult coloration, but their manes and tails are at their palest. The controversy about JOBICA prompted the Dutch color researcher, J. K. Wiersema, to investigate her extended family and the results convinced him that the horses were silver dilutes and that the color came from the female line.

Many Groningers from this family are pictured in the Wiersema book. JOBICA is shown in color pictures, both as a young mare and as an older broodmare. In both cases she has nearly black legs, dark countershading (typical of a genetic bay) and a dark-rooted flaxen mane and tail. Her grandam ABICA is also pictured as a foal alongside JOBICA's great-granddam BICA (1939). BICA is recorded as *blauwschimmel*, or blue roan. In the black and white photo in the book, BICA is quite obviously a true roan, which is not surprising given that she is by the black roan stallion MOOR. Her tail is not visible in the picture, but her pale forelock can be seen. It can be assumed that she inherited the silver from her unregistered dam, who was a grey daughter of TELLO, and the roan from her sire, MOOR.

Her daughter ABICA was registered as a chestnut roan, though that aspect of her coloring is not obvious in the picture of her as a foal. She looks much darker than her mother and shows faint dappling on her sides. She may have been more obviously roaned as an adult, as the coloring is not always visible in foals. She did pass on the roan coloring to another daughter, JEADA (1947). The silver she gave to JOBICA's chestnut dam, OBICA.

In addition to JOBICA, OBICA had two other daughters. One, named ABICA like her granddam, was registered as roan. (Although registered as chestnut, OBICA must have been a chestnut roan since she had the roan ABICA with a brown sire.) This second ABICA had no foals, so it is impossible to know if she also carried silver.

The second daughter, DOBICA (1956), was registered as brown but is believed to have been a brown silver. DOBICA's red silver daughter, FITA, is also pictured in the Wiersema book. Like a lot of red silvers, FITA was registered as chestnut. Wiersema identified two other daughters, NOBICA and PRICA, as being red silver. After this point the DOBICA mare line was absorbed into the Dutch Warmblood studbook, where her descendants were outcrossed rather than bred to Groninger stallions.

As for the descendants of JOBICA, only her son BALTUS was included in the Groninger stud book. Her later foals, the mare LIDA and the stallion MENNO, were part of the Dutch Warmblood breed. BALTUS (1963) is also pictured in the Wiersema book. It is just a face shot, and his mane has darkened enough that the presence of silver is not as obvious as it is with JOBICA. There are pictures of his foals, however, including red silver colts from a black Friesian and a dark brown Groninger mare. There are also two adult daughters pictured, both obvious red silvers. The only one named is ELBRICH, but she does not appear in the NWP stud book.

The BALTUS sire line was incorporated into the Dutch Warmblood and he does have modern descendants. It is possible that the mutation has survived in that breed through him, just as it may have survived through his aunt DOBICA.

A second silver line existed briefly with the vividly dappled IREGON daughter PEBERINA (1973). IREGON was a Gelderlander, but when he was bred to the Groninger mare VEBERINA, the resulting foal was registered as a Groninger. PEBERINA does not appear to have left any registered foals.

Dominant White

Wiersema and Geurts noted that some breeders were using horses with the sabino pattern to produce white-born foals. It is now clear that those horses were most likely carrying the sabino-1 mutation, which is incompletely dominant. Horses with two copies of sabino-1 are born white.

But there were white horses that did not fit the pattern of inheritance seen with the other sabino families. One of these was SNEEUWWITJE, a white Groninger mare with blue eyes foaled in 1952. Her sire, NOVUM, was registered as dark brown. Her dam, SCHOONTJE, was a grey. Both Geurts and Wiersema speculated that SNEEUWWITJE was carrying a different mutation from the other white-borns. Not only were her parents not marked, but she did not produce like a sabino white. Had she been a homozygous sabino like the other white-born Groningers, she would have produced the sabino pattern every time, and her own white color only when bred to another sabino. Instead she had white or broken-colored foals roughly half the time.

Her production record was:

1955 WITTEKIND	white mare sire: Juwelier, bay
1956 CURIOSA	black mare sire: Ornament, chestnut
1957 EDELWEIS	white mare sire: Ornament, chestnut
1958 unnamed	black stallion sire: Lutsen, black Friesian
1959 MARMORA	black sabino roan mare sire: Lutsen, black Friesian
1960 KWIKZILVER	white mare sire: Ornament, chestnut
1962 PRINSES	white mare sire: Belami, chestnut
1963 SCHEEWIESZ	white mare sire: Belami, chestnut

1964 TRIBLANCA   white mare
                     sire: Belami, chestnut
1965 VERRASSING   black sabino stallion
                     sire: Belami, chestnut
1966 ZELLI   black mare
                     sire: Belami, chestnut
1967 BLANCHE   white mare
                     sire: Belami, chestnut
1968 CHARMANTE   black mare
                     sire: Belami, chestnut

This gave her a production record of seven of thirteen foals white, so roughly half. This would suggest that she carried a simple dominant gene, but yet she also produced two sabino foals, including one from an unmarked black Friesian stallion. She also produced black horses from chestnut mates, so she had to be genetically black.

SNEEUWWITJE was most likely a dominant white. She was the source of the initial mutation, and gave it to a little more than half her offspring. Two of those foals, like many other dominant whites, had a leaky expression of the mutation, which allowed some color to bleed back into the coat. This gave them an appearance much like that of the sabino-1 horses found in the same breed, although genetically they were quite different.

SNEEUWWITJE's foals by JUWELIER, ORNAMENT and BELAMI (called ZEELANDER in the Gelder-

lander stud book) were registered with the NWP. None appear to have been used for breeding, though most would have come of age as the traditional Groninger was being phased out to make way for the Dutch Warmblood.

Eye Color

The stallion RHEINFELD had light golden eyes, but the genetic mechanism behind them remains unknown. The trait was said to have passed down consistently through his maternal line, and he gave it to some portion of his own offspring. Gold or hazel eyes have not been noted in the modern Groninger population.

Some of the homozygous sabino-1 foals had blue or partially blue eyes, and the suspected dominant white mare SNEEUWWITJE was blue-eyed. Given the relative rarity of the sabino-1 mutation in the current population, it seems unlikely that there will be many sabino whites. So far the recorded heterozygous sabino-1 Groningers have all been dark-eyed, though blue-eyed sabino-1 horses have occurred in other breeds.

Markings

The majority of Groningers are marked with white. The amount of white varies from just a star to a full blaze and four stockings. The most common face marking on the approved stallions is a star, but the second-most common is a blaze. The most common leg marking among those same stallions were two hind socks. Those horses carrying the sabino-1 mutation have irregular white markings with roaning, while the others tend to have clean, unroaned markings. Groningers with the sabino-1 gene often have irregular markings, including disconnected patches on the knees and stifle.

The mare SNEEUWWITJE is suspected to have been a dominant white. She is pictured here with her foal by the Friesian stallion LUTSEN. The fact that she produced minimally marked horses like this colt suggests that she was not homozygous for sabino-1.

Hackney Horse and Pony

Origin: England

The Hackney was developed in the eighteenth and nineteenth centuries from the earlier Norfolk Trotter and Yorkshire Roadster, with additional blood from the Thoroughbred. The modern Hackney is known as a showy carriage horse with high action at the trot.

Stud Book

In 1878 a group of horsemen at the Royal Show in England decided a trotting horse register was needed to record the pedigrees of "hackneys, roadsters, cobs and ponies." The Hackney Horse Society was formed in 1883 and the first Stud Book was published shortly afterwards. The first volume was, as was common at the time, primarily a retrospective listing of the stallions used for breeding these types of horses and ponies. It contained information on 880 stallions born between 1755 and 1881. Mares were added in the second volume published two years later. At that time, mares were admitted that had been sired by the stallions already in the Hackney stud book, or by Thoroughbred stallions if their dam was by a Hackney stallion. Mares could also be entered based on show wins in any Hackney, Roadster, Cob or Pony class. Horses with two generations of Thoroughbred breeding—that is, a mare by a Thoroughbred stallion and out of a half-Thoroughbred mare—were not permitted. At the time it was common to use Thoroughbred blood for refinement, but breeders did not want to lose the character of the breed to excessive outcrossing.

Crossbred horses were not considered fully registered, but rather were simply "entered" in the stud books. They were not granted numbers, but could be bred to produce fully registered, numbered offspring. Unlike the grading schemes in most other breeds, which were used only for the female line, the rule applied to both genders. Mares could also be inspected for inclusion. Crossbreeding was closed for stallions by 1891 and for mares a bit later.

Entry of Hackney Horse mares by the inspection process was closed in 1892, after it was abused

to get around the American tariffs on imported horses. At the time, pedigreed horses imported for breeding programs were exempted from the tariff. This rule led to the formation of stud books in many of the countries and among many of the breeds that enjoyed a strong export business. The exemption also created an economic incentive for foreign stud books to allow horses that before might not have been included. This changed in 1891 when the American Secretary of the Interior ordered the pedigree rule to be interpreted more strictly. This pushed many of the existing registries to close their books to inspected stock in order to preserve their favored trade status. Most did not return to the use of inspection schemes until war and mechanization left breeds with populations too small to continue without new blood. Hackney Pony mares could still be registered by inspection up until 1900, at which point that section was also closed.

The American Hackney Horse Society was formed around this same time, and featured prominently in many of the editorials about inspection schemes and "mongrels". The first vol-

Summary

Current colors: Bay, chestnut and black are common. There is one dark-headed roan line in the Netherlands.

Historical Colors: Grey, tobiano, cream and dun were once present. Silver is suspected in a few instances.

Markings/patterns: Sabino markings are common, as is white ticking. Body spotting does occur and is not penalized. Two manchado overos have been recorded in Argentina. Unbalanced markings, with extensive white on the legs but little on the face, are common. Unmarked horses do occur, but are less common.

Eye color: The eyes are consistently dark, though there are historical records of a handful of blue-eyed Hackneys.

ume of the American Stud Book—with only a few previously-imported mongrels—was published in 1893. The American stud book used almost identical rules, although the term "half-registered" was used in place of "entered" for those horses with non-Hackney blood. These partbreds were issued numbers and appeared alongside fully-registered horses in the stud books, with the notation "half-registered" appearing in parenthesis. The American stud book also had its own inspection procedure for admitting non-Hackney mares. Perhaps it was just British mongrels that were objectionable! The half-registry continued into the early twentieth century, although the requirements changed so that the non-Hackney horses used had to be of recognized saddle or harness blood.

In both the British and American registries, Hackney Ponies have been included in the stud book from the beginning, although they make up a very small portion of the earlier stud books. They would, of course, come to dominate the American stud books. The British stud book registers them in a separate section, whereas the American stud book lists both together, with the notation "Horse" beside those animals that are not ponies.

Hackneys became a distinct breed with a closed stud book, but for the first few decades many still considered them to be a type rather than a breed. This explains why outcrosses continued, and also why horses of other breeds were registered. Because the Hackney Society began with the stated mission to record cobs and ponies as well as Hackneys and Roadsters, a number of the early entries could more accurately, at least by modern understanding, be considered Welsh Cobs. Over time the breeders of these horses migrated over to the Welsh registry and the two breeds became quite distinct from one another, but in the early Hackney and Welsh stud books there was a fair bit of crossover.

Population
The American Livestock Breeds Conservancy estimates the worldwide Hackney Horse population to be around 3,000 horses. A detailed census done by the OakBriar Hackney Stud estimated there to be only 583 living Hackney Horses in the United

Variation in Early Breed Type

These two ponies illustrate how the lines between breeds were often blurred at the beginning of the stud book movement. CAFÉ-AU-LAIT, the red dun tobiano at the top, was a registered Shetland Pony bred by the Ladies Hope of South Park. She was also inspected and accepted as foundation stock in the Hackney stud book in 1896. There were a number of registered Shetland Pony mares entered as foundation stock in the early volumes of the Hackney stud books.

The chestnut pony with the docked tail would be more readily identified by most horsemen as a Hackney. He is LLWYN CHIEF, a registered Welsh Pony stallion. Many horses and ponies of Welsh descent were registered in the early Hackney stud books, and a number of ponies in the Welsh stud books were registered Hackneys. In the early twentieth century Welsh Ponies were often turned out in the same style as Hackneys.

States. The Hackney Pony is far more numerous, with 600 to 800 ponies registered annually in the United States. Ponies account for an estimated 95 percent of the activity with the American registry. In contrast, there are an estimated 30 to 40 Hackney Horses registered annually. In 2009, only 8 Hackney Horses were recorded.

Hackney Horses are slightly more numerous in the United Kingdom, where a detailed census gave a total of 1,450 living horses. The Hackney Horse is also popular in the Netherlands, where there are 2,300 mares and 23 stallions. There are 350 horses in Canada, and another 200 in Argentina.

Colors

Bay and chestnut are the most common colors, followed pretty closely by brown and black. Among the ponies, and particularly among the American

HEARTLAND'S BLIZZARD *displays the unusual form of sabino body-spotting sometimes seen in Hackneys. Note the large areas of clear white relative to her fairly narrow blaze, and also the placement of the white more towards her hindquarters than her girth.*

ponies, the predominant color is bay. In almost all cases the colors tend towards the darker range, without a tendency toward mealy or faded colors. Flaxen manes and tails in chestnuts are unusual, although they are occasionally seen.

Sir Walter Gilbey asserted that brown Hackneys all descended from the stallion PERFORMER through his grandson LORD DERBY II (1871). Brown Hackney mares of this breeding were in high demand with both French and German purchasers in the mid-nineteenth century, and it is thought that they played an important part in the development of both the French Coach Horses and the Oldenburg. Gilbey was writing in the early twentieth century, and it is likely that brown in the Hackney came from many sources and not just the one male line, but the horses of that specific strain probably did reinforce the tendency towards dark brown in many of the European breeds.

Gilbey also attributed the chestnut color to the influential stallion DANEGELT (1979). Like the situation with brown, it is likely that chestnut has many sources, but there is no doubt that the widespread influence of DANEGELT helped to popularize the chestnut coloring. He probably contributed to the prevalence of dark chestnut with a self-colored mane and tail, since he reliably passed that to his descendants as well.

Sabino

Sabino is extremely common among both Hackney horses and ponies. Flashy white was not uncommon for most of the history of the breed, and body spots were present on some of the most successful Hackneys, including HOPWOOD VICEROY (1904), ANTONIUS (1907), ADBOLTON KINGMAKER (1912) and BLACK MAGIC OF NORK (1939).

It does not appear that Hackneys carry the sabino-1 mutation. In fact, aside from those Hackneys with flank roaning, which may or may not be related to sabino patterning, most have the cleaner, less roaned sabino patterns.

It is also common to see unbalanced sabino patterns, where the level of white on the legs is far greater than that on the face. Stockings on Hackneys with nothing more than a star are not unusual, and it is even possible to see fairly large areas of body white on horses with very little white on the

Unbalanced Sabino Patterns in Hackneys

Figure 13. Examples of the body-spotting associated with unbalanced markings as found in some Hackney bloodlines.

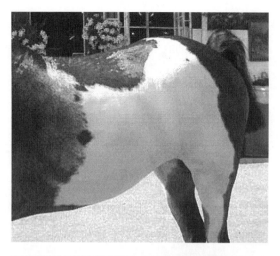

Some of the Hackneys with unbalanced patterns have areas of isolated roaning, as is seen here on the flank of HEARTLAND'S BLIZZARD. Roaning like this is more commonly seen on tobianos like the Paint Horse pictured below. This adds the the impression that horses like BLIZZARD are tobianos, but that pattern has been gone from the Hackney gene pool since the early twentieth century.

face. The stallion BROOKEBOROUGH FLASH JACK (1994) is a good example, having socks and a large area of white visible on both sides of his barrel, yet he has only a star and snip on his face. FOREWOOD NIATROSS (1986), a popular American stallion, is similarly marked. NIATROSS has hind stockings, high front stockings including one that extends to the elbow, and white on both sides of his body, yet he has an unmarked face.

On many of these Hackneys, even the nature of the spots on the body are unusual for sabino. The patches are fairly large with even, crisp edges rather than ragged or roany outlines. Sometimes there are areas of even roaning, like those seen on some tobianos. Body white is sometimes placed further back on the barrel, or even on the hips, instead of the girth area favored by the more typical forms of sabino.

This seems to be the more common expression of sabino in the breed, but there are more traditional sabino patterns, too. Hackneys with both blazes and stockings can certainly be found, as can the loud, patchy version of the sabino pattern.

True Roan

Roan was once quite prevalent in the breed. One of the influential founders, NORFOLK PHENOMENON (1824), was a bay roan with a star, hind socks and a right front ankle. He is said to have lived to thirty years of age, and many of his roan sons and grandsons were used for breeding. Among the roans registered in the early stud books of England, America and Canada, it is unusual to find a dark-headed roan Hackney that does not have a recorded line to him. His widespread influence during the years prior to the formation of the studbook make it likely that even when he is not officially included in the pedigree, as when the color traces to an unregistered roan mare, the color probably originated with him.

His most influential male descendants were his grandson HAIRSINES ACHILLES (1854) and his great-grandson BAXTER'S PERFORMER (1850). Both stallions were bay roans, and both produced in such a way that suggests that in this line, roan was linked to black rather than red. BAXTER'S PERFORMER sired the bay roan stallion JACKSON'S QUICKSILVER (1855). This was the line that eventually produced the bay roan HOCKWOLD CADET. Purchased by Baron van Voorst and brought to the Netherlands, HOCKWOLD CADET was used extensively in the formation of the Gelderlander breed. He also had purebred descendants, and some inherited his roan coloring.

A roan Hackney of this line was brought back from the Netherlands to England. That was BROWN'S CADET (1943), a chestnut roan that traced back to HOCKWOLD CADET through both his sire CHESTNUT BROWN and his dam BROWN'S

QUEENY. CADET sired the chestnut roan stallion WINESTEAD MARMADUKE in 1950. His daughter STRAWBERRY FAIR (1962) is among the last of the true roans registered in the English stud books.

The one roan line known to remain traces back to a half-sister of BROWN'S CADET. That is MIMIE, the great-granddam of the bay roan stallion DUTCH HANKY PANKY (1979). HANKY PANKY won numerous championships until he was retired in 1997. Photos of him show an extraordinarily beautiful horse, even in advanced age. Although he does not appear to have been widely used at stud, he has at least one granddaughter that carries his coloring. That is the blue roan TRIANGEL'S SILVER SHADOW (2005), out of the HANKY PANKY daughter LADY BRIGHT MOON.

HOCKWOLD CADET illustrates how an influential stallion can ensure that a rare color is preserved. When he was born in 1911, the roan coloring had already become rare. In the time that he served at stud, from 1921 until 1933, true roan had practically disappeared in England and North America. It does not appear that the color was disliked, or that breeders selected against it. The chestnut roan mare LYRIC 513 (1892) was used to illustrate the second volume of the American stud book. Her registry entry lists six first placings, and she was twice named Junior Champion Mare at Madison Square Garden. The bay roan FAKENHAM PRINCESS was another famous shower during that era.

Less common colors are often lost when breeds undergo a genetic bottleneck, even when those colors are not penalized. Roan died out in North American Hackneys some time in the mid-twentieth century. Among the last true roans was the mare GLENWOOD LASSIE (1936). She was registered as an aged mare in 1949 and was recorded as roan with no white. It is not clear where her coloring came from, and she appears to have left no offspring.

White Ticking
Although true, dark-headed roan is rare in the modern Hackney, horses with roaning in their coat are reasonably common. Some of these that are more extensively marked are registered as roan, though they can usually be identified as something

other than dark-headed roan by the fact that their immediate ancestors are not roan. True roans are rarely mistaken for anything other than what they are, but it usually takes a dramatic amount of roaning in the coat for a non-roan to be registered as roan. For that reason, in pedigrees white ticking will seem to appear from nowhere, or to skip generations. This is usually a sign that the roaning is something other than true, dark-headed roan.

Just what causes the roaning is open to speculation, and it is complicated by the fact that not only is subtle roaning not always mentioned in stud book descriptions, it is often not even visible in photographs. This makes study of white ticking difficult.

The fact that many Hackneys have roaning, particularly on the flanks, is obvious. Whether there is just one form of roaning, or more than one, is not known. It is also hard to know if the trait is related to the sabino patterning that is quite common in the breed, or if it is something separate. Because the roaning can take on a number of different characteristics, it is quite possible that there is more than one genetic mechanism at work, or that the presence of sabino in the breed influences the appearance the roaning. It is also possible that, if there is more than one type of roaning, that the two patterns influence one another.

This photo of the chestnut roan mare LYRIC appeared in the second volume of the American stud book. Although roan is extremely rare, it has a long history in the breed.

White ticking and flank roaning are particularly common among Hackneys found in the Netherlands.

true roan, although the overall impression is of a slightly darker shade of roan with less contrast between the head and neck. Horses with this kind of roaning invariably have some kind of leg markings, which suggests that the roaning has some connection to the presence of sabino, though this may simply be a reflection of how common sabino is in the Hackney population.

Belly roaning: Of the types of roaning, this one is the least common. Whereas the classic rabicano pattern originates at stifle fold and spreads upward towards the flank, this type of roaning radiates upward from the underside of the horse. Roaning is often concentrated under the forearms and up the chest as well as along the fold of the stifle. There is more contrast, in some cases enough that the horse can appear patterned rather than just roaned, but the underlying skin is dark and the edges are less distinct than with a true sabino. The Dutch Hackney stallion BROOK ACRES SILVERSUL (1969) and the Hackney Pony PERRYBRIDGE CHALLENGER (1996) are good examples of this kind of roaning.

Whatever the genetic causes, roaning in the coat of Hackneys tend to fall into three different categories, with a certain amount of overlap between them and also with the stippled form of sabino:

Rabicano: This pattern features roaning that originates at the fold of the stifle and forms vertical bands along the flanks, white hairs to either side of the dock (known as a skunk tail or coon tail), and no significant face or leg markings. In more extensively marked horses, additional roaning originates under the front legs and spreads upward on the chest. This type of roaning is rare, or at least is difficult to confirm, because sabino is present in most Hackneys and some forms of that pattern also produce flank roaning and coon tails.

Diffused flank roaning: This is the most common form of roaning seen in Hackneys. Diffused roans do not have the brindled appearance that is typical of rabicano. The roaning extends to the tail head as well, so that the entire top of the tail appears frosted. In more extensively marked individuals, the effect looks a great deal like a

Manchado

There have been at least two Hackneys with the rare manchado pattern; LA BARRANCOSA ECLAT (1970) and her grandson GREENMEADOWS PRINCE CHARLY (1993). In this regard the two are unique among those horses studied by Alberto Martin Labiano, author of *Overos Manchados*. Labiano wrote that the distinctive pattern was occasionally seen in Argentinian horses, but seemed to appear unexpectedly with no indication of unusual markings among the ancestors or the other offspring. ECLAT and CHARLY were the one instance where the color was found more than once within a given family.

LA BARRANCOSA ECLAT came to the attention of some American Hackney breeders when it was suggested that there was an Argentinian Hackney with an appaloosa pattern. Because the pattern is concentrated along her topline, and because she happened to have fewer and more distinct dark spots than other manchados, it was an easy mistake to make. Neither her mane nor her tail are especially visible in the single photo available, and the fact that she has little in the way of ordinary leg or face white also adds to the impression that she has a large spotted blanket. As closer look, however, shows that the arrangement of the white, and of the colored spots, is not quite the same as would be seen with an appaloosa.

Her grandson GREENMEADOWS PRINCE CHARLY, is more strangely marked. Like the famed manchado Arabian mare, TRABAG, he looks quite unlike any of the known overo or appaloosa patterns. Even though he does have a fair bit of face white that covers his nostrils and dips over to the left side of his face, he does not look like any sort of sabino. The positioning of the white along his topline, including a fully white mane and tail, is unlike the ventral origins of the sabino family of patterns. But perhaps even more striking are the round spots set within the white areas. Like a leopard appaloosa pattern, the white areas are densely spotted, but in this case they overlap wildly to form larger splotches.

The pattern of inheritance, if it was in fact inherited and not the result of two separate (but highly coincidental) mutations, is also quite unlike that of the known overo patterns. CHARLY traces back to ECLAT through her son LA BARRANCOSA SPOT. Despite his name, Labiano describes SPOT as being *alazán tapado*, or self-colored chestnut. This

would suggest that the pattern is recessive. ECLAT was likewise said to have descended from generations of chestnuts with ordinary markings.

If the pattern is indeed recessive, it is possible that it came to Argentina through the Hackney. There are nineteenth-century paintings of Hackneys with patterns that are said to resemble those of the known manchado horses. Evidence of this sort is only somewhat reliable, since artists misinterpret coat patterns from time to time, but it is an interesting clue. It is known that there was at that time great demand in Argentina for colorful horses, and that a great number of pinto Hackneys were exported to the country. Perhaps those horses, brought over at a time before stud books were commonplace, passed the pattern along not only to the Argentinian Hackney population, but to the native population as well. As registries formed, mares descended from the imports might then be used in a top-crossing program. That might explain the presence of the color in such diverse breeds as the Argentinian Thoroughbred, Anglo-

This is the manchado pattern found on the Hackney stallion GREENMEADOWS PRINCE CHARLY. A less extensive form of the pattern occurred on his granddam, LA BARRANCOSA ECLAT.

Norman and Criollo. Exportations of colorful horses to Argentina, where they were in high demand, might also have removed the rare pattern from the English population, just as American demand for silver dapple ponies largely eliminated the color from the native Shetland population.

Historical Colors

The early Hackney stud books reflect the wide variety of colors found among the English roadsters and trotters of the early nineteenth century. This was especially true among the ponies and the cobs. Most of the less common colors were lost when the Welsh stud book was formed, though others simply fell from fashion.

Greys

Although never common, grey was once found in the breed. A portrait of Fulwar Craven painted in 1834 by John Frederick Herring Sr. shows him on a lovely white-grey Norfolk Hackney. An engraving of COPEMAN'S NORFOLK HACKNEY was one of the two stallion portraits to appear in the second volume of the British stud book, published in 1885. The text explains that the illustration was chosen to represent the "type of horse in favour sixty years ago." That same volume has six grey stallions and twelve grey mares listed. One additional mare is listed as white, but her dam was grey and she is herself the dam of one of the twelve grey mares.

Even so, the color was already in decline. In the first sixteen volumes of the English stud book, there were 116 grey stallions for a ratio of approximately two for every 300. By 1907, Sir Walter Gilbey wrote in *Horses—Breeding to Colour* that the number of grey stallions had dropped to eight. Gilbey attributes this to the low demand for greys, which in turn lowered the number of mare owners interested in breeding to a grey stud.

The color survived in low numbers into the 1920s. The best known of the remaining greys was the Prince of Wales' stallion FINDON GREY SHALES (1908), by the grey MONSONS WALPOLE SHALES and out of the grey mare MONSONS MIRABELLA. The Monson family had maintained a line of grey Hackneys that were used as hunters. For many years FINDON GREY SHALES won the award offered at the London Hackney Show for stallions suited to

producing Army horses. He also produced ROYAL SHALES, purchased by Mrs. Elizabeth Colquhoun in 1922. ROYAL SHALES was used to found the Shales Horse, a breed that claims descent from ORIGINAL SHALES and the Norfolk Trotters.

There was one particularly unusual grey entered as an inspected mare in the third volume of the British stud book. That was the Lipizzan mare ARNICA. Her sire is given as "Siglavy, Arab and Spanish" and her dam as "Sacramosa, Arab and Spanish." Arabians were rare when the Hackney Society was formed and were, like the Thoroughbred, registered in the General Stud Book, so it is not surprising that they were occasionally used for breeding Hackneys just as the Thoroughbreds were. ARNICA is the only recorded instance of Spanish blood being included. She was owned by the Prince of Wales, who had received her as a gift from the Emperor of Austria. While her breeding may have been unconventional by Hackney standards, her connections were impeccable. She does not appear to have left any offspring.

Dun and Cream

Professor C. J. Davies, writing in the *Live-Stock Journal Almanac* in 1907, used the breeding record of an unnamed Hackney mare and the stallion TROUBADOUR to illustrate the prepotency of chestnut. Although his conclusions are flawed, what most present-day readers would notice was the unusual color of the mare, described as having dark points and a dorsal stripe. Around that same time debate raged in some of the scientific journals about dun and reversion, which is the theory that the traits of domestic animals sometimes revert back to those of their wild ancestors. Among the horses in question was the Hackney mare FANNY GORDON, described as light yellow with a black dorsal band. Although dun is not present among modern Hackneys, these early color studies, along with stud book records, suggest that at one time lineback dun was present, if very rare.

Two suspected dun mares are recorded in the second volume of the English stud book. The first of these is HOT SCOTCH, listed as blue dun. The second is LADY TRAQUAIR, listed simply as dun. Both mares were foaled in 1883 and were bred and owned by John A. Hays of Esheils Farm. It is possible that either mare might be the one in Professor Davies' anecdote, since their foaling dates make them contemporaries of the stallion mentioned.

There are also a number of horses and ponies registered as cream or dun in the first few decades of the Hackney breed, although it is not always possible to know whether they were cream dilutes or lineback duns. In early British stud books the term dun is often used for both true duns and for buckskins and even palominos. In a few cases, dorsal stripes are noted, which would suggest that some were dun. In others, like the inspected mares NIMBLE (1883) and MOUSE (1886), the horses were listed as slate or silver dun. When the line of dilute color skips a generation through a black horse, that usually points to cream since cream does not show on a black horse. When it skips a

generation through a chestnut horse, that can indicate the horse was a dun, since red duns were often registered as chestnut in early British stud books. Another clue that dun is involved is the unexplained appearance of grey offspring, since many early breeders registered grullas by their literal color, which is gray. Still, while these things can provide clues, they are not absolute proof and with so much distance it is just guesswork. One thing is clear, however, and that is that there were a fair number of cream-colored dilutes among the early Hackneys, and most particularly among the inspected mares.

In at least one case the dilution was pretty clearly cream, even though the horses are recorded as dun, because the likely source of the color would suggest that the horses were creams. That source

Dilute Mares in the First Ten Volumes of the Studbook - Ponies

Volume 3				
1881	Psyche 580	Bay Trotting Pony - Joan, dun cob	Yellow dun, black points	main register
Volume 4				
~1876	Canary 918	Connemara xx - Countess	Dun	main register
Volume 6				
1882	Daisy	ancestry was not recorded	Yellow	inspected
Volume 7				
1883	Nimble	ancestry was not recorded	Silver dun, black points	inspected
1879	Queen Bess	ancestry was not recorded	Cream	inspected
Volume 8				
1880	Rhum Bay	ancestry was not recorded	Dun, two fetocks and one heel white	inspected
1888	Crafty	Kingfisher 1294 - Rhum Bay (inspected)	Cream	entered
Volume 10				
1886	Judy	ancestry was not recorded	Dun	inspected

Chart 1. Cream and dun pony mares registered in the early British Hackney stud books (1883-1890)

Dilute Mares in the First Ten Volumes of the Studbook - Horses

Volume 2

| 1883 | Hot Scotch 142 | Hay's Prince Charlie 637 - Barmaid | Blue dun | main register |
| 1883 | Lady Traquair 213 | Hay's Prince Charlie 637 - Kailzie | Dun | main register |

Volume 3

| 1880 | Creamy 537 | Platt's Blazeaway 89 - Juxies | Cream | main register |

Volume 4

| 1878 | Jennie 934 | Young Bedford Phenomenon 1685 - dun mare, dam Welsh | Red roan (produced dun) | main register |

Volume 5

| 1885 | Birdie 1016 | Perfection 543 - Jennie 934 | Dun roan | main register |

Volume 6

Aged	Alice	ancestry was not recorded	Cream	inspected
1869	Die	ancestry was not recorded	Dun, with black stripe down back	inspected
1887	Onyx	Hadeed, Arab - Die (inspected)	Dun	entered

Volume 7

| ? | Fabric | ancestry was not recorded | Dun | inspected |

Volume 8

1872	Flame	Little Wonder 409 - Dun pony	Dun	inspected
1887	Grace	Abeyan (imported Arabian) - Gipsy	Dun, white blaze, three white pasterns	inspected
Aged	Stuntney Daisy	ancestry was not recorded	Cream, whole colour	inspected
1877	Verbena	Sired by Prickwillow 623	Dun	inspected

Chart 2. Cream and dun horse mares registered in the early British Hackney stud books (1883-1890)

was the pony stallion GOLDEN PIPPIN 8489 (1895), who got his coloring from his maternal great-grandsire, ANCIENT BRITON (1857), registered as "dun or cream." ANCIENT BRITON was a grandson of the famous buckskin Welsh Cob, CYMRO LLWYD. Lacking their own stud book at the time, many Welsh Cobs were entered in the early Hackney Stud books and there was a fair bit of intermixing in the early days of the two breeds. GOLDEN PIPPIN was listed in the British stud book as dappled dun, which is itself a little unusual because the color descriptions in the Hackney books tend to be quite spare. The mention of the dappling suggests that GOLDEN PIPPIN may have inherited the sooty dappling found in many of CYMRO LLWYD's linebred Welsh Cob descendants—horses like the buckskin CARADOG LLWYD (seventeen crosses) and the palomino LLANARTH BRAINT (sixteen crosses).

Inspected Pony Mares 1894-1900 - Creams and Duns

1884	Sweet Cream	ancestry was not recorded	cream, white mane and tail
1888	Valentine	ancestry was not recorded	dun, black points
1888	Acrobat	ancestry was not recorded	cream, black points, white strip on face
1890	Ethel	ancestry was not recorded	cream, white blaze
Aged	Matron	from the Marquis of Londonderry	cream, star, line along back
1891	Princess	ancestry was not recorded	dun, black legs
Aged	Lilly	ancestry was not recorded	dun, black points
1891	Nordelph Creamy	ancestry was not recorded	cream
1894	Bantam	Little Wonder 2nd 1610 - mare by Cleverlegs	dun, black stripe down the back
1891	Beauty	ancestry was not recorded	dun, black points, star, hind feet
1888	Taffy	ancestry was not recorded	dun, black points, white near hind heel
Aged	Topsy	ancestry was not recorded	dun, black points, white off hind stocking
1890	Dainty	ancestry was not recorded	dun, white off hind fetlock
1892	French Marino	ancestry was not recorded	dun, blaze, white mane and tail
1891	Cherie	ancestry was not recorded	dun, black mane and tail, white off hind heel
1890	Coco	ancestry was not recorded	whole cream[1]
1876	Cwmelydin	ancestry was not recorded	dun, black points, star
1877	Dusty Polly	ancestry was not recorded	cream, no marks
1891	Emlyn Beauty	Imported Arab - dun Welsh Pony by Lion Express[2]	dun, star, white hind leg
1892	Fanny	ancestry was not recorded	dun, white near hind heel
1894	Friallen	Emlyn Fireaway 5993 - Mettle by King Jack	chestnut cream, star, snip down nose, white off hind coronet, flaxen mane and tail
1885	Polly Elphick	ancestry was not recorded	dun, black mane and tail, white star, nose, near fore and off hind fetlocks
1895	Primrose	ancestry was not recorded	dull cream, black points
1886	Silver	ancestry was not recorded	cream, grey mane and tail, white stockings
1894	Welsh Maid	ancestry was not recorded	dun, star, white hind heels
1893	What Is It	ancestry was not recorded	dun, star, silver mane and tail

[1] whole-colored, or without markings   [2] pedigree as given in the later Welsh Pony stud book

Chart 3. Cream and dun pony mares registered after the foundation books for horses were closed.

GOLDEN PIPPIN had three cream foals, all mares: LADY LOVERULE (1900), VENUS LOOKING GLASS (1902) and HERA (1904). Both VENUS LOOKING GLASS and HERA were imported to the United States and registered in Volume VI of the American Stud Book. Both are recorded as dun, but VENUS LOOKING GLASS' entry in the British stud book lists her as cream with black legs. HERA was imported with her buckskin daughter FAIRVIEW ROSALIND, who was also registered alongside her dam. VENUS LOOKING GLASS was imported with her buckskin son, FAIRVIEW TOMTIT. None of these horses appear to have bred forward.

One daughter, LADY LOVERULE, remained in England, but her only cream foal, FAIRVIEW GOLDEN PIPPIN, was exported to Canada in 1912. It is unclear whether she was registered in the Canadian herd book or not; there is no record of her in their database. The GOLDEN PIPPIN line does continue forward through another LOVERULE daughter, FAIRVIEW FIREFLY, but the cream coloring was lost.

There were other cream Welshes registered in the Hackney stud books. One of them was the pony mare EMLYN BEAUTY (1891), registered as dun but most likely a cream dilute. When she was registered as a Hackney, her pedigree was not given, but in the later Welsh books her sire was said to be an imported Arabian and her dam a dun Welsh Pony by the cream LION EXPRESS. That same volume—the last one before the books were closed for inspected pony mares—had the mare FRIALLEN (1894), registered as chestnut cream. It is quite likely that she was a cream, since the dilution came from her dam. That mare, METTLE, was registered as brown, from the chestnut KING JACK and out of the cream RUBY. RUBY was probably a buckskin, which were often registered in early British stud books as cream, since METTLE was a brown horse from a chestnut sire. Smoky black horses were often registered as brown, which could explain the palomino FRIALLEN. Both mares were frequent prize winners in their day, but after the formation of the Welsh stud books their foals were registered there and they did not have an impact on the Hackney.

Even when the dilutes were not double-registered as Welsh Ponies, their color often came from Welsh Ponies through the female side of the pedigree. The dun TYDRAW PRINCESS (1903) is a good example. She was by a dark bay son of DANEGELT, and out of an unregistered dun mare. That mare, MAGNET, was by the bay roan LORD BANG and out of an unregistered dun mare named POLLY. By breeding POLLY was Welsh, as her sire was the great Welsh Cob founder CARDIGAN COMET. POLLY's dam was listed as a Welsh Pony, and it is likely that she was the source for the dilution. It does not appear that TYDRAW PRINCESS left any offspring, so it impossible to know whether she was a true dun or a buckskin, though the latter would have been more likely since cream was more common in the Welsh breeds.

There were also dilutes registered through the American inspection process. The Shetland Pony breeder Charles Bunn was able to get the mare GOLDEN GLOW (1901) approved. She was registered as dun, and could have been either dun or buckskin. Her sire was STAATER'S GOLDDUST and her dam was FAIRY II by DAN HAZARD. Dilutes were less common in the American books, perhaps because there was not a large population of Welsh Pony and Cob mares to draw upon at the time.

Silver

The inspected mare MANILA (1894) was registered as chestnut with black points and a gray mane and tail. She would have been six years old when registered, so that would have been an accurate description of a bay silver pony at that age. She was a smaller pony, only 11.2 hands, but nothing is know of her background. Silver is found throughout the northern European breeds and prior to the wave of exportation to the United States, when the color became popular with Shetland breeders, it was not uncommon among the British pony population.

There was at least one red silver stallion, GOLD AWARD (1962) sold at an American sale as a registered Hackney Pony. His pedigree gave no clue as to the source of his unusual color. His breeder also produced fine harness Shetlands, so it is possible that his color was the result of a cross, known or unknown, between the two breeds. His line did not continue into modern Hackney Ponies.

Tobiano

One of the most celebrated Hackney Ponies of the nineteenth century was the tobiano mare MAGPIE

Pinto Mares in the First Ten Volumes of the Studbook - Ponies

Volume 2

1878	Magpie 228	Youngman's Confidence 158 - Spot 327	Black & White	main register

Volume 5

1881	Hiya 1141	Black Prince - skewbald pony mare	Skewbald	main register

Volume 6

1879	Jinnie	Sire, an Arab	Skewbald	inspected
1873	Nellie	Little Ben - Welsh Pony	Skewbald	inspected
1884	Miss Wentworth	Delight 175 - Nellie (inspected)	Bay and white	entered

Volume 8

1883	Thora	ancestry was not recorded	Piebald	inspected
1890	Ice Girl	Hadeed, Arabian - Thora (inspected)		entered

Volume 9

1887	Maxima	Sired by New Times 472	Skewbald	inspected

Volume 10

1883	Gaiety	ancestry was not recorded	Skewbald	inspected
1887	Patchwork	ancestry was not recorded	Grey, white patch on shoulder, white legs	inspected
Aged	Peggie	ancestry was not recorded	Piebald	inspected
1892	Sadie	Shah 3946 - Peggie (inspected)	Piebald	entered

Chart 4. Pinto pony mares registered in the early British Hackney stud books (1883-1890)

(1878). Major prizes were often mentioned in stud book entries at that time; her list took an entire page. She is said to have garnered more than 400 first prizes and was a ten-time winner at the Royal Agricultural Show. Her larger sister, MOVEMENT, was almost as successful. Both mares were out of the tobiano mare SPOT. The sire of SPOT was the unregistered Hackney stallion GANT'S PREMIER. Her dam was said to have been out of a skewbald mare who was herself from a skewbald part-Arabian mare.

MAGPIE was registered as a piebald, and illustrations of her show a black and white tobiano marked with a star. Her sister was registered as a skewbald, and in an illustration she is marked with a blaze and her pattern has the lacey edges typical of a tobiano pattern paired with sabino. MOVEMENT was larger than MAGPIE, and was bred quite differently. Her sire, WASHINGTON, was by an American trotting horse, SHEPHERD F. KNAPP, that had been exported to England. That may have been the source for her sabino patterning as well, since SHEPHERD F. KNAPP was a chestnut with white markings.

There were at least thirty-five pintos entered in the British stud books using the inspection process. A handful more were entered in the main register. Without photos it is impossible to know for a fact that they were all tobianos, but the terms used—piebald and skewbald—were typically reserved for horses with that pattern. Sabinos, even those with fairly large body spots, were usually registered as their body color with the specifics of their markings given as part of the description.

There is a chance that some had the homozygous version of the classic splash pattern, since these are often categorized as piebald or skewbald when they occur, or perhaps a combination of tobiano and splashed white. Many of the inspected mares had Welsh breeding, and splashed white has a long history in that population. The detailed description of the pattern of the inspected pony mare, MAGPIE 1622 (1893), sounds like a classic splashed white. She was registered as white with the top of her head and ears dark. Most entries from that era do not describe the pattern of the white, and most did not leave patterned descen-

dants, so it is impossible to know for sure which patterns were involved.

There were also a handful of tobianos inspected and entered as foundation stock in the American stud books. One of these was the skewbald mare ATTRACTION (1898), registered in Volume 5. Her sire was JEFF and her dam was an F. C. Edwards mare. She was registered by Charles E. Bunn, an influential breeder of Shetland Ponies. The name of the sire is interesting because Mr. Bunn owned another pony sired by a "Jeff": the famed silver dapple Shetland mare, TROT (1886). At one time TROT was suspected of being the originator of the silver dapple color, until it was discovered that the color was not limited to Shetland Ponies. She does have the distinction of being the first Shetland of that color recorded.

JEFF was never registered in the American Shetland Pony stud book, but was simply listed as "Im-

Pinto Mares in the First Ten Volumes of the Studbook - Horses

Volume 2				
~1864	Spot 327	Gant's Premier (v.I) - skewbald mare	Skewbald	main register
Volume 3				
1877	Movement 792	Washington 852 - Spot 327	Skewbald	main register
Volume 6				
1881	Fakenham Lady	ancestry was not recorded	Skewbald	inspected
1879	Nancy	ancestry was not recorded	Piebald	inspected
Volume 8				
1884	Cosette	ancestry was not recorded	Piebald	inspected
1883	Ladylike	ancestry was not recorded	Piebald	inspected
1884	Penelope	ancestry was not recorded	Skewbald	inspected
Volume 9				
1891	Cottered Bell	Cadet 1251 - Penelope (inspected)	Skewbald	entered

Chart 5. Pinto horse mares registered in the early British Hackney stud books (1883-1890)

Inspected Pony Mares 1894-1900 - Piebalds and Skewbalds

1888	Miss Fewson	Lord Durham 1825 - Welsh Pony	piebald, bay and white
1878	Lancaster Mona	ancestry was not recorded	chestnut skewbald
1890	Lancaster Patchwork	ancestry was not recorded	chestnut skewbald
1891	Cafe-au-Lait	by Lodinn (double registered Shetland Pony)	piebald, dun and white (red dun tobiano)
1891	Nena	ancestry was not recorded	piebald
1890	White Socks	bred by the Marquis of Londonderry	skewbald
1886	Fashionable	by Yorkshire Fashion 1599	piebald, brown and white
1891	Odd Girl	ancestry was not recorded	skewbald, brown head, little white on forehead and nose, white legs
Aged	Nordelph Judy	ancestry was not recorded	skewbald, roan and white
Aged	Lilac	ancestry was not recorded	roan and white
Aged	Magpie	ancestry was not recorded	piebald, white face, part white mane and tail, white spot on near side of neck and body, four white legs, white mark on withers and rump
1890	Magic	by Wildfire 1224	skewbald, four white legs
1894	Grace Darling	ancestry was not recorded	piebald, bay and white
1879	Kitty	ancestry was not recorded	odd-coloured, brown and white
1890	Lady Dash	ancestry was not recorded	skewbald
1892	Crawdom Skewbald	ancestry was not recorded	skewbald
1893	Magpie	ancestry was not recorded	white, dark patch on near flank, dark ears and top of head
1890	Nelly	ancestry was not recorded	skewbald, star, snip, four white legs, white tail
1890	Patchwork	ancestry was not recorded	piebald

Chart 6. This is a list of pony mares registered after the foundation books for horses were closed. It is impossible to know with certainty which patterns some of these ponies carried, but piebald and skewbald were most commonly used to describe horses with the tobiano pattern.

ported Jeff." The Jeff that sired ATTRACTION was also unregistered, but was described in her entry in the Hackney stud book as a Welsh Pony. At the time a Welsh Pony stallion probably would have been imported since there were very few Welsh Ponies in the United States and there was not yet a registry to record them. "IMPORTED JEFF" and "JEFF, A WELSH PONY" could be the same animal. It seems unlikely that the same breeder might have two mares born twelve years apart from two different imported ponies named Jeff. Nothing is known of ATTRACTION, beyond the fact that she was bred by the Shetland breeder, F. C. Edwards. If ATTRACTION had Shetland breeding, it is probable that she was a tobiano.

It might seem odd, to a modern horseman, that a Hackney registry would take a pinto Shetland on inspection, or that the Shetland Pony might have a Welsh Pony sire. In 1911, when that particular volume of the Hackney stud book was published, the three breeds were not as far apart as they are today. Prior to having their own stud book, Welsh Ponies were used by breeders in both Britain and America to produce Hackneys. Meanwhile the Shetland breeders of America began their registry with the intention of refining the native Shetland to create a pony more suited to fine harness. In fact, when Shetland and Welsh Ponies were first imported many were turned out much like Hackney Ponies, with braided manes, spoon cruppers and, in the case of Welsh Ponies, docked tails.

"Imported Jeff" left only TROT in the Shetland stud book, but "Jeff, a Welsh Pony" left two more Hackney daughters besides ATTRACTION. These were the roan ALERT and the chestnut COLLEEN, both entered as inspected mares. ATTRACTION produced two daughters, OAK LASSIE and NATTY, but neither inherited her pinto coloring. The roan line from ALERT continued for a time, but eventually the Bunn Hackney program moved away from the use of inspected mares and uncommon colors.

It is tempting to think of the crossing between the pony breeds as uniquely American, standing in contrast to the British tradition of keeping its mountain and moorland breeds separate and more rustic in appearance. A look at the register for inspected mares, especially during the eight years it was open exclusively for pony mares, shows that both American and British breeders experimented

with crossing Shetlands and Hackneys. Welsh Ponies, which are believed to have been used more extensively in the formation of the early American Shetland Pony than the official documents reflect, appear even more extensively in background of the English inspected mares.

One of the Shetland Ponies in the British stud book was CAFÉ-AU-LAIT, a dun and white Shetland mare owned by Lady Estella Hope of South Park. CAFÉ-AU-LAIT had lasting influence in the Shetland registry as the dam of the red dun stallion CAFE CLOCHE (1918). Tobiano and solid colored Shetlands owned by the Marquis of Londonderry were also included among the inspected mares. The Marquis of Londonderry was one of the founders of the Shetland Pony Stud Book Society, and it was his focus on the production of pit ponies that set the direction of the British Shetland towards a lower, heavier pony than those bred in America. From the heights given, it appears the ponies he registered in the Hackney stud book may have been too large to be suitable for his Shetland breeding program.

In the same volume as ATTRACTION, a piebald mare named STHOREEN BAWN was entered as half-registered. She had been imported to America by the Truman Pioneer Stud in 1910, and was by the brown Hackney pony stallion TOM GORDON and out of the inspected mare NENA, registered as a piebald. STHOREEN BAWN did not leave a lasting line, but there are many modern Hackneys that trace back to NENA through her solid descendants GLENAVON TORCH BELLE and DUN-HAVEN EMPEROR.

While there were a number of pinto Hackneys in the early stud books, they were not part of an organized attempt to produce colored Hackneys. That was done a bit later with the breeding program of Cole Ambrose of Stuntney Hall. Cole Ambrose was one of the founders of the Shire Horse Society, and his farm at Stuntney covered over 1,500 acres. For a brief while after the turn of the last century, Ambrose also produced tobiano Hackneys. At least ten tobiano mares and thirteen tobiano stallions were registered under the Stuntney prefix, but it is believed that many more were produced. Because the main market for them was export to Argentina, rather than the United States where registration status affected the tariff rate, there was not the same economic incentive to enter the horses in the stud book.

Those horses that were recorded descend from the piebald mare STELLA. Her color came from her dam, an unregistered daughter of HOWELL'S QUICKSILVER. STELLA was bred to the Thoroughbred NATIONAL GUARD to produce the skewbald mare WALSOKEN QUEEN. The tobianos of Stuntney Hall trace back to WALSOKEN QUEEN through her skewbald great-grandson STUNTNEY PARAGON (1895). PARAGON had two tobiano sons, STUNTNEY BENEDICT and STUNTNEY ROLLO, and three tobiano daughters, STUNTNEY AGATHE, STUNTNEY RHEA and STUNTNEY ROXANA. BENEDICT and ROLLO were both used at Stuntney, as was RHEA.

STUNTNEY BENEDICT, a black tobiano, was exported to the United States in 1907. He was registered in the American stud book, but does not appear to have been used to produce purebred Hackneys. He was designated as the foundation stallion in the Moroccan Spotted Horse registry. That registry, formed in 1935, was originally established to register pinto horses of Hackney and French Coach breeding, though later it incorporated gaited and Arabian blood. The registry struggled with low numbers and eventually folded in the latter part of the twentieth century.

Appaloosa
There is one interesting pony among the last set of inspected mares. PANSY (1894) was registered as white with black spots. In an American context, it would be safe to assume that she was a pinto, and most likely a tobiano. Within the context of Great Britain, however, the term spotted is used to indicate appaloosa patterning. PANSY would be a black leopard. An appaloosa Hackney, especially a leopard, might seem extraordinary, but the color was found in the ponies and cobs of Wales at that time. The owner of PANSY, Evan Jones, lived in the same area of Carmarthenshire in Wales where twenty-two years later the leopard Welsh Cob, GWYNFE HERO, was foaled. Like PANSY, he was registered as white with black (and brown) spots.

PANSY was registered with a white colt from the previous year. His sire was the grey Hackney TOWYVALE SQUIRE, but at a year old it is unlikely that he had greyed out to white. Foals registered

This photo of the stallion KANHWA *was used by the United States Department of Agriculture to illustrate the Morocco Spotted Horse. A black tobiano Hackney,* STUNTNEY BENEDICT, *was the foundation stallion for the breed.*

alongside their dams were not given detailed descriptions, so he may have been spotted as well, since a detail like that would not have been part of his foal description.

Evan Jones had another mare a year younger than PANSY named CHESS, registered as chestnut roan with "small white spots all over." He also registered a number of dun, cream and piebald mares. All came from Wales, but beyond that fact no other information is given on their ancestry. It should be noted that these colorful ponies belonged to one of the original founders of the Welsh Pony and Cob Society. Mr. Jones trained DYOLL STARLIGHT, the famed grandfather of the Welsh Mountain Pony, for the show ring. He bred the undefeated GREYLIGHT, who was often used to illustrate perfection in pony type. Although appaloosa colors eventually disappeared from the Hackney, and the broken colors were banned in later volumes of the Welsh stud books, at the time PANSY was registered they were still present and acceptable to a breeder of Mr. Jones' stature.

Dominant White
Older papers mention the Hackney stallion ACTIVE GOLDFINDER (1904) as having been suspected of carrying a recessive mutation for albinism

because he sired two blue-eyed white colts. True albino horses have not yet been documented, and most unexpected white foals are presumed to be some type of dominant white mutation. Not all dominant white individuals are completely white. Some look a great deal like sabinos, particularly sabino roans, but to date none could have been described as having ordinary markings. ACTIVE GOLDFINDER, if he had been a dominant white, would have been the exception in that he was a chestnut with seemingly ordinary markings. His registry entry states that he had a white spot on his forehead, white leg markings on his near side and white on his off fore coronet. Looking at his five-generation pedigree, his ancestors were also chestnuts and bays with ordinary markings.

ACTIVE GOLDFINDER was not, however, some kind of cryptic dominant white. Information about the family was originally published in a study focusing on albinism. Blame for the white foals fell on him in part because the color was presumed to be albinism, which as a recessive would have had to come from both parents. There was also a certain bias at the time towards the influence of sires. This sometimes caused mares to be overlooked as a source for color, which was what had happened with the two white foals. Both colts were sired by ACTIVE GOLDFINDER, but they also had the same dam, a white mare with dark eyes and roan patches. The fact that she was bred twice to the dark brown DIAMOND CITY, and produced brown foals, and then twice to ACTIVE GOLDFINDER to get two white foals made it seem that GOLDFINDER contributed to the coloring. This would be the expected ratio of solid versus white foals when a white mare was bred to solid mates.

The mare, who was sold a London auction of coach horses, was of unknown parentage. She died shortly after the original study was published, as did ACTIVE GOLDFINDER. Neither of the two white foals were registered, so their coloring did not enter the stud book. The mare was largely forgotten, but the rumors about the stallion remained.

Eye Color
Although Hackneys were once a colorful breed, and can still be found with loud pinto patterns, the majority of Hackneys have dark eyes. A hand-

Unbalanced markings in the form of four white feet and little or no white on the face may have originated with the Hackney founder stallion DANEGELT (top). Even if he was not the sole source for these type of markings, his widespread influence insured that it would be passed along to horses like his grandson KING'S PROCTOR (bottom).

ful of exceptions to this general rule have been recorded in the past.

CRESSIDA was registered as an inspected mare in Volume 8 of the British stud book. She was a black mare with a blue eye on her off side. No other markings are indicated in her description, although markings were not consistently reported by breeders at that time. No information was given about her ancestry, and it is not known if she ever produced blue-eyed foals.

Another inspected mare, LADY PATRICK, was chestnut with two blue eyes, along with a white face and low white on all four feet. She had a roan son, ST. PATRICK SHOT (1887), by the roan stallion GREAT SHOT. His markings were not mentioned and the line disappeared from the stud book.

At least one of the colorful horses bred at Stuntney Hall was blue-eyed. That was the stallion STUNTNEY RUFUS (1903). Rufus was originally registered as roan, but was later re-entered with an amended description that included a large white face, wall eyes and four white legs. Although his description would lead many to assume he had a splashed white pattern, it is not known if it was the existing classic splash (*SW1*) or a new mutation. His sire, STUNTNEY ALROY, was a minimally marked chestnut. There is not any indication that any of ALROY's other foals were blue-eyed, though at the time detailed descriptions of markings were only intermittently provided, sometimes even from the same breeder. Eye color was even less consistently reported; when RUFUS was entered into the American stud book, his markings were listed but no mention was made of his eye color. His dam STUNTNEY URIAH was registered as red roan with white front feet and one hind stocking; no mention is made

of any face markings or blue eyes. Both she and RUFUS did have roan foals with minimal white, which suggests that both were true roans rather than—or at least in addition to—sabino roan. Whatever the cause for his blue eyes, RUFUS did sire a handful of pinto patterned foals from solid mares, so he carried some kind of white pattern. RUFUS was exported to the United States in 1907, but his line did not continue.

Markings

Because sabino is so common, most Hackneys are marked with white. Unbalanced patterns are common, so white on the face tends to be somewhat conservative. Really broad blazes are less common, even on loudly marked Hackneys. Conversely, dark legs are less common that white ones. Hackneys without any white markings are rare, though they do occur, particularly in the American pony lines.

Facial depigmentation unrelated te greying has been seen in a few Hackneys. In each case, the horse was either brown or black and, with the exception of the patches on the face, were deeply pigmented. Although pigment loss like this is widely believed to be environmental in nature, its cause is not fully understood.

Hanoverian Creams
(Extinct)

Origin: Hanover, Germany

The Hanoverian Creams were large cream-colored coach horses of distinctly Spanish type bred at European royal stud farms in the eighteenth and nineteenth centuries. Although the breed is extinct, the mystery of the Royal Hanoverian Creams continues to fascinate those interested in horse color.

Stud Book

Records were kept at the royal studs where the Hanoverian Creams were bred, but these were institutional records rather than published stud books of the type used for privately owned horses. The Creams were not recorded in the early Hanoverian stud books, and were kept and bred separately from the Hanoverian warmblood.

Population

The last known Hanoverian Creams were dispersed to an unknown fate in 1921, so the breed is considered to be extinct. Even before that time, their numbers were always few and infertility was a problem throughout the history of the breed.

Colors

Although the Hanoverian is known today as a warmblood with more typical, conservative coloring, the original Memsen Stud in Hanover was founded in 1653 with the intention of breeding *weißgeborenen*, or white-born, horses. These horses, which predated the Hanoverian Creams, were brought to England in 1714 when the Elector of Hanover became King George I. At that time the white horses were bred at the royal studs of Frederiksborg, Schaumburg-Lippe and Gotha, as well as the one in Hanover.

There are some indications that white and cream horses had already been assembled by the Electress Sophia (1630-1714), but it is her son, the future King George I, that is usually credited with developing the Hanoverian Whites and later the Hanoverian Creams. These early efforts depended heavily upon the white horses of Frederiksborg.

In Hanover, there was already an established group of white-born mares at the stud in Memsen when the first cream horses were acquired. The mares were said to have descended from the white Barb stallion AUGUSTE and light grey or pale isabella mares. In 1746 the white-born Frederiksborg stallion LE BLANC was brought to the stud to cross with the descendants of AUGUSTE. These were known as the White Breed, or the Hanover Whites.

The creams originated with the stallion EUTINER, purchased in 1728 from the Bishop of Eutin. A second stallion of the same coloring was given to the King by the Duke of Brunswick in 1733, and was called BUTINER. Other horses came from Brunswick, including the stallion ADMIRABLE. All later Creams were said to trace back to his descendant SHAMHAFTE (1798), though other cream horses were acquired afterwards, including seven stallions and five mares from Weimar.

At some point the cream-colored horses eclipsed the white, and the breed was simply known as the Hanoverian Cream, although it is not really clear when this happened or even how much separation there was between the two breeding programs.

Summary

The Hanoverian Cream breeding program ended in the early twentieth century. The last horses connected to the breed were dispersed in 1942.

Historical colors: The Hanoverian Creams were pale-skinned cream horses with darker manes and tails. The gene or genes involved remain a mystery.

Markings/patterns: Markings are not mentioned in descriptions of the breed, though there was once a white variety that may have had one or more of the pattern mutations.

Eye color: Accounts differ widely about the color of the eyes, with witnesses describing them as pink, blue, or light brown. It may be that the eye color varied among individuals, which suggests that at least for a time there were multiple dilution genes present in the population.

Given that cream-colored mares were part of the white breeding program from the start, it seems likely that the two groups were often intermixed, especially as time progressed and fewer royal houses produced ceremonial coach horses.

Both the Hanoverian Whites and the Hanoverian Creams were used as coach horses. They also served as personal mounts for the royal family. One white stallion, ADONIS, was said to have been the favorite charger of King George III. ADONIS was foaled in 1784 at the Herrenhausen Stud in Hanover, by the stallion BLONDIN and out of the mare CIGNE. He was already a favored stallion there when the King requested four riding horses be sent to England, one of which needed to be a stallion of at least 8-9 years old. Accounts of the King riding ADONIS after recovering from an illness in 1811 suggest that the stallion lived to a relatively old age.

There was a brief gap in the ceremonial use of the Hanoverian Creams when Napoleon seized Hanover in 1803. As an insult to the King of England, the Emperor had eight of the cream-colored horses harnessed to the gilded state carriage used in his coronation. The infuriated English King ordered that the Royal Mews use black horses for state occasions until Hanover's independence was restored. The order remained in force until the fall of Napoleon in 1814, at which point the monarchy reclaimed the stud from the French government. It was said that the cream horses taken by Napoleon were lost without a trace.

Cream-colored horses continued to be bred in Hanover until Queen Victoria ascended the throne in 1837. At that point the Crown of Hanover passed to her uncle, the Duke of Cumberland, and many of the cream horses were moved to the Hampton Court Stud in England. A year later Memsen was closed and the horses in Hanover were moved to Neuhaus, and then later consolidated at Herrenhausen. The English program still imported horses from Hanover, but not at the levels prior to the French Revolutionary Wars. The Queen also sought additional blood from Schaumburg-Lippe where, like Hanover, white and cream horses had been bred since the early sixteenth century. Dr. William Goodwin, the Queen's veterinarian, mentions procuring four more cream mares from the Grand Duke of Saxe-Weimar in 1839.

This illustration of the "Queen's Creams" appeared in <u>*Horse World of London*</u>*, published in 1893.*

By the late 1800s, it was clear that the breed was in danger of extinction. Sir George Maude, the Royal Master of the Horse, wrote to the stud manager in Hanover expressing the Queen's concern that the creams in England had become "very much inbred" and required a cross of fresh blood. His concerns were shared by those at Herrenhausen, and exchanges were made. Two more creams were acquired from Schaumburg-Lippe in 1893 and another three from Allstedt in Saxe-Weimar in 1901.

Wallace's Monthly, published in 1893, stated that twenty to thirty creams remained at Herrenhausen in Hanover. At that time the horses were maintained by the Prussian government, which had annexed Hanover almost thirty years prior. Just four years later, the stud at Schaumburg-Lippe was sold, so the horses at Herrenhausen and Hampton Court were all that remained. Herrenhausen was closed in 1897 and the horses there dispersed. Most were believed to have been purchased by the Wulff Circus in Brussels. That left only a small group at Hampton Court.

A visitor to the Royal Mews in 1891, writing for the *English Illustrated Magazine*, describes seeing eleven Hanoverian Cream stallions. The oldest stallion of the group, MOLTKE, was then nineteen and was said to have sired most of the younger stallions then present. Among the other stallions were OCCO, who was pictured in full dress harness in the article, the eleven-year old MONARCH, and AMERONYEN. Two four-year old stallions, as yet unnamed, were mentioned as being of a lighter build than the older horses. In nineteenth-century England at least, the Roman noses and heavier Spanish build common to many of the coach breeds were already falling out of fashion, so undoubtedly the writer saw the change in type as proof of the refinement brought about by prudent breeding. In actual fact, both breeding programs struggled with maintaining both the color and the size of the horses. Fertility, originally an issue with the white-born horses, was once again a problem, most likely due to the levels of inbreeding necessary with such a small population.

It was not long after that, due to financial constraints following World War I, the creams in Eng-

This portrait of the Hanoverian Cream stallion OCCO accompanied an article about the Royal Mews in the English Illustrated Magazine in 1892.

land were dispersed. Some of the older horses were put down, while others were gelded and assigned to cavalry regiments as drum horses. Three were given to Garrard Tyrwhitt-Drake, who had been breeding cream ponies at his Cobtree Manor Stud. Others were auctioned off, and three of those were purchased by Tyrwhitt-Drake. Drake intended to use this nucleus of four mares and two stallions to preserve the breed, hoping that they might once again serve the monarchy. Sadly, his efforts seem to have come to naught. In crossbreeding the color proved elusive, and the horses continued to lose size. The situation was further complicated by the fact that all four mares had difficulty conceiving. In 1942, the last surviving horses from the Cobtree breeding program—two mares and two stallions— were given to the Whipsnade Zoo. Whether or not those horses actually carried the blood of the old Royal Creams is not known.

Mystery Color

While the fate of the last Hanoverian Creams is not known, this is not the only mystery surrounding the breed. It is also unclear just which dilution was responsible for their distinctive coloring. The author of the Royal Mews article described the stallion OCCO as having bright pink eyes. In his 1877 book *The Horse*, William Youatt describes the eyes of the Hanoverian Creams as having a white iris and a red pupil. He distinguishes the color from the wall-eye of a pied horse, which has a "white iris and a black pupil." Descriptions of pinto Shetlands from the same era sometimes refer to white eyes, so that appears to have been a common term for what modern horsemen would call blue eyes. According to these observers, the eyes of the Cream horses were either pink or pale blue with red pupils.

This does not match the description of the eyes of any of the known equine dilutions. It also contradicts statements made by the former breeding director at Herrenhausen, who stated that there had never been red-eyed albinos at the stud. It is possible that each description compounded upon an error of a single observer, since many of the various accounts use almost identical wording; it was not uncommon at the time for publications to recycle older articles, with slight alterations, and publish them as if they were current. Given that practice, it is also possible that the description was an editorial embellishment, based more on assumptions about albinos than on actual observations.

Tyrwhitt-Drake, speaking of the horses from the Hampton Court, did not mention pink eyes, but instead described them as blue. A historian familiar with the white horses of Frederiksborg also mentioned the tendency in that breeding group towards wall eyes. The painting by James Ward of King George III's stallion, ADONIS, shows a nearly white horse with pink skin and bluish eyes.

Still others described the eyes as being golden. The idea that not all the eyes were blue is supported by the painting of "Beauty", described as one of King George III's cream-colored chargers. The stallion is quite clearly cream with a somewhat darker mane and tail. He has the large, luminous eyes often seen in equine portraits of that era, and those eyes are quite clearly golden. Paintings are not empirical proof, of course. But on a painting where the coat is rendered in such detail, and with such accuracy, it is intriguing.

The painting is a closer match to the descriptions given by Professor Adolph Reul, the only direct observer with a scientific background to describe the Hanoverian Creams. He had originally encountered the Hanoverian Creams at Hampton Court, and years later saw the horses purchased by Mr. Eduard Wulff for his circus. At the time he was

Hanoverian Cream Time Line

1653   The Electress Sophia establishes the Memsen Stud and begins to breed cream-colored coach horses.

1728   The stallion EUTINER founds a line of cream-colored horses at Herrenhausen. He is joined five years later by another cream stallion, BUTINER.

1784   ADONIS is foaled. In a painting by James Ward, he is creamy white with blue eyes.

1798   The cream stallion SCHAMHAFTE is used at Herrenhausen.

1803   Napoleon takes Hanover and the cream horses that remain.

1814   King George III reclaims Hanover from Napoleon. Cream horses are acquired from the Duke of Saxe-Wiemar to aid in the rebuilding of the herd.

1838   The stud at Memsen is dissolved, leaving only Herrenhausen and Hampton Court breeding cream-colored coach horses.

1887   Queen Victoria arranges an exchange of bloodstock with the government in Hanover, and the stallion OSWALD and the mare BONA come to Hampton Court.

1893   It is believed that only twenty or thirty Creams remain at Herrenhausen.

1897   The Creams in Hanover are dispersed at auction, with many going to Circus Wulff. That same year, the Schaumburg-Lippe Stud is also dispersed.

1919   As part of the post-war austerity measures, the Crown Equerry forms a committee to determine the viability of the Cream breeding program.

1921   The Hanoverian Creams at Hampton Court are dispersed. Several are acquired by Sir Garrard Tyrwhitt-Drake.

1942   Sir Garrard Tyrwhitt-Drake gives the remainder of the cream-colored horses at his Cobtree Manor Stud to the Whipsnade Zoo.

The stallion PISTACHIO was one of the last Hanoverian Cream stallions to reside at Hampton Court.

writing, the horses had been acquired from the dispersal of Herrenhausen and were the focus of a great deal of attention in Belgium. His observations were published that same year in the *Belgian Annales de Medecine Veterinaire* in an article titled "A Curious Point of Horse Ethnography." Unlike previous writers, he does not mention blue eyes in connection with the creams, but rather refers to their color—which he indicates as being strange in appearance—as *bois de noyer*, which is a golden brown color. He also notes that the bodies of the horses are cafe-au-lait and that the manes and tails are considerably darker, a description that fits more closely with what few photographs exist of the horses. He does note that the horses are extensively pink-skinned, although it is not clear whether he means that the skin is mottled or all-over pink.

Unraveling the Mystery
It seems clear that in the eighteenth century the Royal Hanoverians, much like Count Günther's Oldenburgs before them, carried a mixture of genes that resulted in very pale coats. Within that mix were genes for white patterns (most likely dominant white) and for dilutions. At some point in the nineteenth century, the white patterns were lost and what remained were the diluted colors. The mystery, then, is which dilutions were involved.

Although the specifics vary, what observers agree upon is that the Hanoverian Creams had di-

luted skin and eyes. Three of the known dilutions affect both the skin and the eyes: cream, champagne and pearl. Of these, the least likely is champagne. Champagne foals are born with pale blue eyes, but these darken to amber with age. They are also born with darker coats that lighten with age. It seems unlikely, then, that such foals would be mistaken for albinos, which is what many contemporary writers called the Hanoverian Creams. Indeed, Vero Shaw in *The Encyclopaedia of the Stable* (1901) says that the foals were always born perfectly white.

Along with the eyes, champagne skin tends to darken with age, so it would have been unlikely that an aged coach horse like the nineteen-year old MOLTKE would have looked like an albino to observers. There is also the fact that champagne is a simple, non-lethal dominant. Were the highly-inbred Hanoverian Creams carrying champagne, their color would not have been difficult to reproduce. Many would have been homozygous and would therefore have bred true to their color even when outcrossed. But perhaps the best argument against the Creams being champagnes is that the mutation has not, to date at least, been found in any Old World breeds, leading to the suspicion that it may be a New World mutation.

The cream mutation is perhaps the most likely candidate based on sheer numbers: cream is fairly common in the equine population. It is also true that of all the dilutions, homozygous creams have the palest, and most truly blue, eyes. Hanoverian Creams were also said to have tails that had a reddish tinge. Certainly some of the photographs of the later Hanoverian Creams in ceremonial settings show horses that have pale skin and only slightly darker manes and tails, just as one might expect from a group of perlinos.

What has thrown some researchers are photos, particularly of the stallion PISTACHIO, but also of a group of stallions at the Royal Mews, that show horses with somewhat darker legs and considerably darker manes and tails. While perlinos do have darker points than cremellos, the horses pictured show an unusual amount of contrast for a homozygous cream. Perhaps underneath the dilution, the original color of the horses was black, making them smoky creams rather than perlinos. Black horses were part of both the breeding programs at both Oldenburg and Frederiksborg, and the horses that replaced the Creams during the reign of Napoleon are sometimes referred to as the Hanoverian Blacks, so it would not be surprising.

The other possibility is that some of the later, darker-pointed horses were carrying a copy of pearl along with cream. A single pearl mutation, when paired with a single cream mutation, results in a horse that can be hard to distinguish from an ordinary cremello or perlino. Some of these horses, however, are a bit darker. Homozygous pearls can have quite a bit more pigment, though they still retain the dramatically diluted appearance of the double creams and the cream-pearls. This is particularly true of black homozygous pearls, which often have quite dark manes and tails. In fact, the modern horse that most closely resembles the dark-maned Creams in their later photos is the Iberian stallion AVISPADO, tested to be a black homozygous pearl.

Pearl is a mutation at the same site (MATP) as cream. That is why a horse can carry two cream genes, or a cream and a pearl gene, or two pearl genes. In a population with both dilutions, and with a variety of underlying base colors, the horses would range from milky-white with blue eyes (chestnut plus two copies of cream, or cremello) to cream with a golden mane and tail and golden eyes (bay plus a copy of cream and a copy of pearl, or bay pearl cream) to a cafe-au-lait with a dark mane and tail and golden-brown eyes (black plus two copies of pearl, or black pearl).

Although the eye and even hair color descriptions vary with different observers, the other characteristic consistently mentioned in connection with the Hanoverian Creams is a convex profile. Descriptions of the horses almost always mention their Spanish type, especially in regards to the shape of the head. It was all the more notable because roman noses had become unfashionable by the nineteenth century, and had been mostly eliminated in other horses of the same era. Such a pronounced Spanish trait is interesting because the pearl dilution is strongly connected with horses of Iberian descent. The mutation has been identified in Lusitanos, Andalusians, Peruvian Pasos and American stock horses, which descended in part from Spanish horses shipped to the colonies during the same time the Hanoverian Cream breeding program was developed.

The presence of pearl along with cream would explain the range of coat and eye colors. It would also explain why producing the color proved to be elusive. Photographs show that whatever colors were once present among the earlier Creams, the later horses were darker in tone, which would be consistent with either cream pearls or homozygous pearls. Since a single pearl gene, unlike cream, does not dilute the coat at all, outcrossing the Creams to unrelated horses would result in a high percentage of non-diluted foals. In fact, if the Cream was a homozygous pearl, any cross made on a non-diluted mare would only give dark foals, since the offspring would carry a single recessive pearl gene. That is consistent with a report that when Tyrwhitt-Drake bred his Cream stallion PRINCE to Exmoor ponies, the resulting foals were all brown. When his brown daughters were bred back to him, cream foals resulted. The presence of the pearl gene might explain why, as the numbers of surviving Creams dwindled, the only consistent way to get the same color would be to inbreed them.

Because the Creams were dispersed to an unknown fate, this is all likely to remain little more than speculation. With few photographs and conflicting written descriptions, the potential for error is certainly there. Using the available information, and assuming that no unknown dilutions were involved, the most plausible theory seems to be that the population began with a range of patterns and dilutions which eventually narrowed to cream and pearl, and possibly to just pearl towards the end.

Kladruber

Origin: Czech Republic (Bohemia)

The Kladruber is among the oldest of the European breeds, and is the sole surviving representative of the old Baroque coach horses, or *galakarossiers*. The Kladruby Stud is on the Tentative List to be classified as a World Cultural Monument by the United Nations.

Stud Book
Established in 1562 and granted Imperial Court Stud status by the Holy Roman Emperor in 1579, Kladruby is one of the oldest state studs in Europe. Much of its earliest history was lost when the stud and all its records burned during the Seven Years' War. The stud was rebuilt in 1770, using horses that had been evacuated to Slovakia and Hungary. The breed became endangered again with the fall of the Austro-Hungarian Empire in 1918. Through an organized effort by the Research Institute for Horse Breeding, outside blood was introduced through the Arabian SHAGYA X and the Orlov Trotters LEGION and MIKROB. Lipizzans from the Favory line, which originated at Kladruby, were also used. RUDOLFO, a Lusitano exported from Portugal, was added in the 1960s, as was a Friesian stallion, ROMKE. In 2002 the regeneration of the breed was considered successful and the stud book was closed to outside blood.

Although a variety of breeds have been used in the recent past, the Kladruby Stud considers the horses bred within their program to be purebred Kladrubers regardless of the origin of the ancestors. The original male Kladruber lines of Generale, Generalissimus, Napoleone, Favory, Sacramoso, and Solo are referred to as the classic lines, whereas the male lines from other breeds are referred to as non-classic. This approach of strengthening the gene pool with individuals from historically related and physically similar types is considered a model for the conservancy of rare breeds.

Population
According to the National Stud, there are approximately 1,000 Kladrubers in the Czech Republic, of which 500 are owned by the state. There are estimated to be an additional 200 purebreds in other countries.

Colors
Few uses effect breed color like carriage work. The need to assemble a large team of matched horses means the vast majority of coaching breeds, like the Cleveland Bay and the Friesian, come in a single, true-breeding color with little or no markings. The Klabruber breed followed a similar path until it narrowed down to two colors: white (technically mature grey) and black. Both varieties were used for ceremonial purposes, with the black teams serving for somber occasions and the white teams for most others. The current population at the Kladruby Stud is evenly split between the two colors, with a total of 250 blacks and 250 greys.

Black
Throughout the formation of the breed, Italian horses were favored because they tended to be larger and stronger than those of Spanish breed-

Summary

Current colors: Grey and black are the two official colors of the Kladruber. Greys are bred to turn white relatively young. Bays and chestnuts occur very rarely.

Historical Colors: A dilution gene, probably cream, was present in the early formation of the breed. It is suspected that pinto and appaloosa patterns were present in the sixteenth and seventeenth centuries.

Markings/patterns: White markings are common on the grey Kladrubers, and are at times somewhat flashy. The preference in black Kladrubers is for a solid horse, though some have moderate markings. Depigmentation is common in the greys and can involve the face extensively.

Eye color: The eyes are usually dark, although there have been a few blue-eyed individuals. Visible sclera is seen in some Kladrubers.

A comparison of an engraving of the original SACRAMOSA *and a modern black Kladruber foal show how little the breed has changed over the last two centuries.*

ing, making them more suited for the production of coach horses. One of the Italian breeds used was the extinct Polesinian. The Polesinian, which was bred near Venice, had a mixture of Neapolitan and Spanish blood. It was noted for its arched profile and for its black coloring, both of which are reflected in the modern Kladruber.

The black coloring inherited from the Italian horses was common in the early history of the breed. During the time the Kladruber herd was at Enyed, where it stayed until its restoration at Kladruby in 1771, the black stallions PESSADORO (1744) and POMPOSO (1755) were used. Most of the stallions used after the breed returned to Kladruby were black, including PEPOLI (1764), grandsire of GENERALE. Even the grey Kladrubers are most often born black.

Two black sire lines, Sacramoso and Napoleone, were used in the nineteenth century. The oldest is that of the stallion SACRAMOSO. There were two stallions of that name foaled just a year apart, but the first sire line died out in 1861. The second SACRAMOSO was foaled in 1800 at the stud of the Archbishop of Olmütz. Both horses were said to be of Spanish-Italian origin. The second black line originated with NAPOLEONE, foaled in 1849. His specific ancestry was not known, but he was believed to be of Italian descent.

The two lines were often crossed, with SACRAMOSO daughters going to NAPOLEONE sons and NAPOLEONE daughters going to SACRAMOSO sons. NAPOLEONE is credited with adding size and length of leg, while the convex profile—often more pronounced in the blacks than in the greys—is usually attributed to SACRAMOSO.

In 1918, Czechoslovakia declared its independence from the Austro-Hungarian Empire. The Kladruber horses were a casualty of the growing hostility towards all things Hapsburg. The first to be removed was the secondary black sire line of NAPOLEONE. The last remaining NAPOLEONE stallion, NAPOLEONE VI-SOLA was destroyed in 1922 at twenty years of age. The purging that

followed from 1925 and 1931 fell disproportionately on the black horses, so that only a handful remained.

In 1939 a project was initiated by Professor Frantisek Bilek to restore the black line. Two black stallions of the Sacramosa line, SACRAMOSO XXX and SOLO, were located for the program. Both were foaled in 1927 and were aged stallions when they entered stud service. A third stallion, SACRAMOSO XXIX-3 AVAR (1930), was used but died shortly after the program began. Of the mares, only two purebreds remained: 13 SABINA (1926) and 28 AJA (1928). Twenty-three purebred mares from the white breeding program were also used, along with eighteen Lipizzan mares, three Orlov

This modern black Kladruber stallion is a product of a restoration project undertaken in the 1940s.

Trotters and a small number of mares of unknown origin that fit the desired type.

The three black stallions were all closely related. Outcrossing to the grey lines was problematic because many of the greys were marked with white, and the preference with the black horses was that they be solid. Rather than increase the inbreeding by using the black Kladrubers exclusively, the decision was made to add stallions from breeds that shared a common history.

The first of these was the black Lipizzan stallion SIGLAVI PAKRA (1946). SIGLAVI PAKRA was a grandson of TULIPAN MARADHAT, founder of the Tulipan line. Known for their size and black color, the Tulipan line is thought to descend from the same Neapolitan stock as the Kladruber, so the cross was in many ways a return to the roots of the breed. SIGLAVY PAKRA was used at the Slatiňany Stud from 1958 until 1967. His line was continued through his son, SIGLAVY PAKRA FAVORINA I.

The second outcross was to the Friesian stallion ROMKE (1966), used at the stud from 1974 until 1985. It was believed that the Friesian was distantly related through Spanish stock used in the Netherlands, and they are also one of the few remaining large coaching breeds. ROMKE had three sons that were used at stud, ROMKE ELEONA II, ROMKE ELE-

USINA I and ROMKE ELEVATA IV, but his primary influence was through his daughters.

A brown Nonius stallion, NONIUS MAJMONA XLV (1965), was also used from 1969 until 1973. He produced four daughters used in the breeding program, but his line was eventually discontinued because of a high incidence of brown horses.

It took approximately thirty-five years to restore the black line at Kladruby. At the present time there are sixteen mature black breeding stallions representing five sire lines. The most numerous line is Solo with six stallions, followed by Sacramoso with five. There are two each from the Romke and the Siglavi Pakra line, and one stallion from the grey Generalissimus line.

Grey

Unlike the black Kladrubers, the grey lines were maintained continuously. At the time the black horses were dispersed, it was believed that the grey Kladrubers were more nobly bred and more attractive in appearance. Despite this, they suffered a drop in numbers and were reduced to a single sire line. That was the line to the grey stallion GENERALE, foaled in 1787. His sire was IMPERATORE, a grey son of the black foundation stallion PEPOLI. His dam must have also been grey, since he is believed to have been homozygous for grey. Modern grey Kladrubers of the Generale line descend from one stallion, GENERALE ALATA XXX, foaled in 1905.

There was a second grey line from the stallion GENERALISSIMUS. The original stallion of that name was a son of GENERALE foaled in 1797. The last stallion of that direct male line, GENERALISSIMUS ALMADA XXII, was born in 1920. The line was later continued through his daughter, 407 GENERALISSIMUS XXII (1929). Although by a Generale-line stallion, her son GENERALISSIMUS XXIII (1938) is designated as the founder of the modern Generalissimus line. The female line of 407 GENERALISSIMUS XXII is also interesting because she was out of a Shagya mare. The use of Arabian blood through Shagya mares is sometimes credited with introducing fleabiting into the Kladruber gene pool.

Because the descent is through a daughter, that line is sometimes referred to as the Generale-Generalissimus line. There is also a more recent Generalissimus line known as the Favory-Generalissimus line, founded in 1965. Like the older Generalissimus line, the Favory-Generalissimus line comes down through the female side of the pedigree. The male side goes back to the grey Lipizzan, Favory IV-K (1953). Lipizzans of the Favory and Maestoso lines, both of which originated in Kladruby, were used to broaden the gene pool after World War II. There is also a separate Favory line going back to a different Lipizzan stallion, Favory XI CK (1960).

One grey outcross line was added with the Lusitano stallion Rudolfo (1968). He joined the stud a few years after the Friesian Romke, and was also used up until 1985. He left behind one son, Rudolfo I, and a number of daughters.

A grey Orlov Trotter, Legion (1950) was also used from 1954 until 1963. He left behind two daughters, both named Legion, that have descendants in the modern grey Kladruber. Another Orlov, the grey stallion Mikrob, was used from 1978 until 1981. He left a single daughter, Aqua, who produced the current breeding stallion Generalissimus Aqua XXXIV (1990). Neither horse has a direct male descendant, so are not included among the sire lines.

Most grey Kladrubers grey rapidly and are white grey at maturity. Historically this has been a breeding goal. In recent years there has been an increase in dappled Kladrubers due to crossing with the black Sacramosa line. Because most Kladrubers are genetically black, the dappled varieties are often dramatic and are favored by some private breeders. The disadvantage is that sometimes such horses do not grey out to a uniform white color.

There is at least one fleabitten grey stallion in use at the Kladruby Stud. That is Generalissimus Aqua XXXIV (1990), a stallion from the Favory-Generalissimus line. His pedigree is interesting because it illustrates the use of outcross blood to supplement the traditional Generale line. Coming from the Favory-Generalissimus line he carries a percentage of Lipizzan blood. His dam is a daughter of the Orlov Mikrob, and she also carries a cross to the Nonius breed through her fe-

Known as the Old White Breed in the Czech Republic, white Kladrubers are actually grey. Some, like the lead horse, look white-born due to extensive depigmentation.

Like the closely related Lipizzan, Kladrubers have been selectively bred for early and complete greying.

male line, along with additional lines to Lipizzans. He is a stallion of unmistakable breed type, and is a good illustration of how intelligent use of outcross blood, even extensive outcrossing, can be used to reduce inbreeding in rare breeds.

Bay

There were a number of bays among the stallions used prior to the 1771 restoration. These included:

CERTOSO	1729 bay of Italian breeding
VIGOROSO	1730 bay from the Schwarzenberg Stud
BRUTONBONO	1742 bay from Liechtenstein
GALLIARDO	1747 bay from Count Batthyan
PRINCIPE	1760 bay from Tuscany

For a time after Kladruby was restored, bays were still used, but by the end of the eighteenth century the official colors were black and white (grey). Some sources state that after that time no bays were used at the stud, but at least one bay Lipizzan stallion, NEAPOLITANO GRATIA (1904), was used in the early part of the twentieth century. One of the original female lines, that of the mare CARIERA (1894), was also bay.

Most Kladruber greys are genetically black, but this is not uniform. Grey, especially grey selected for rapid progression to white, can easily hide the presence of bay so the color was preserved in some lines. Grey stallions from other breeds also brought the possibility of bay with them. When the black Sacramosa line was crossed with the grey lines, that insured that a portion of the greys would be heterozygous, which has allowed the occasional bay to appear. When Kladrubers are born an unexpected color they are recorded in the stud book and are not automatically removed from breeding. Mares that are otherwise suitable have been used.

A good example of this is the bay mare 937 FAVORY VI, foaled in 1971. She left behind one foal, the stallion GENERALE XLV (1975). Three of his sons and three of his daughters were used at the stud. Two of his sons, GENERALE ALATA XLVI and GENERALE PROXIMA XLVIII, established families of their own. At least one grey son of ALATA, GENERALE ESPERA L (1993) was born bay, since he has sired at least three bay foals, two of which were out of black mares.

It is likely that 937 FAVORY VI got her bay coloring from her Lipizzan grandsire, FAVORY (1938). He was a grey, but was described as having red bay fleabites. Both his sons, FAVORY IV-K (1953) and FAVORY VI-K (1954) figure frequently in the pedigrees of bay Kladrubers.

Chestnut

In recent years no fewer than eight chestnut Kladrubers have been born. Just as grey can hide bay, it can also hide chestnut. And just as with other black breeds, the recessive chestnut color can hide for generations and appear unexpectedly.

Many of the chestnuts trace back on both sides of their pedigree to the mare 164 ROMA (1955). ROMA was a black mare by a black Lipizzan stallion and out of a black daughter of SOLO. There are no obvious links to the color chestnut in her pedigree, but she does have an Arabian outcross which might have given her the red gene. Of the male and female lines that have produced known chestnuts, she is found in twelve of the sixteen.

At least one chestnut stallion, SACRAMOSO EUCLIDA XLVI-94, is privately owned and has been kept a stallion. He is a striking dark chestnut with a flaxen mane and tail that is often shown in side-saddle and in harness. He is by Sacramoso Romana XLVI, who is also the sire of the chestnut mare Banderilla. Euclida traces back to Roma on both sides of his pedigree, while Banderilla does so through their sire. Banderilla also had a chestnut daughter, Baronka. She traces to Roma both through her sire and through Banderilla.

It is possible that the chestnut gene is found in other lines yet to be discovered. Both of the Orlov outcross stallions carried chestnut. The dam of the Legion (1950) was the chestnut mare Guinea. The sire of Mikrob (1972) was the liver chestnut stallion Bokal. It is also possible that some of the mares with Shagya blood might carry chestnut, although chestnut is less common in Shagyas than in the pure Arabian strains.

Historical Colors

Like the closely related Lipizzan, the Kladruber was once found in a wide variety of colors and patterns. The Kladruby Stud was established by the Holy Roman Emperor Maximilian II to provide the Austrian court with Spanish horses. The stud at Lipica was created a few years later by the Emperor's brother, Archduke Charles II. Both farms were stocked with horses from Spain, which were then known for flamboyant colors and patterns. The exact nature of the patterns found in the early Kladruber are not known, but paintings from that era suggest tobiano and leopard patterns were among them.

Early in their history, Kladruby and Lipica exchanged breeding stock. One of these transfers was the Kladruber stallion, Favory (f. 1779), who is often described as dun. The Czech word for his color is *plavák*, which typically means buckskin. That seems the most likely possibility, given that palominos and buckskins appear quite frequently in portraits of Spanish horses of that time.

Some books contain references to a more recent breed known as the Kladruby Dun. That is the *Chlumecko-Kladrubský Plavák*, better known as the Kinsky. Although the horses, which are often palomino or buckskin, come from the same region they are unrelated to the Kladrubers. The Kinskys are said to get their coloring from a distant Spanish ancestor, but it was not the original Favory.

As this stallion shows, some grey Kladrubers have extensive areas of depigmentation on their face and bodies. Pigment loss, including loss concentrated on the face, have been studied in the breed. It is also possible for pinto and appaloosa patterning genes to hide in a breed like the Kladruber, since pink skin is not unusual.

Eye Color

Kladrubers typically have dark eyes. Among the greys, it is not uncommon to see visible white sclera. In a 1897 paper weighing the benefits of outcrossing native Criollo horses with Lipizzan and Kladruber horses, the Department of Agriculture in Argentina describes visible sclera as typical,

The stallion FAVORY ROMA XXI-27, pictured at the top, has a blue eye on his left side. SOLO SACRAMENTA XVIII - 3, pictured with a blaze and a hind ankle, is more extensively marked than is typical for black Kladrubers.

saying that it gives "much expression to the eyes." Many horses with sabino markings have noticeable eye whites, but because mottled skin is common among the greys, it is hard not to wonder if the leopard complex mutation (*Lp*) once common in the Baroque breeds could have been preserved somewhere in the grey Kladruber population.

In 2007 the grey stallion FAVORY ROMA XXI-27 was born with a single blue eye, a trait known as *oko rybí* or "fish eye" in Czech. He has a large blaze partially covering both nostrils and extending to his bottom lip and four stockings. His muzzle already shows the soft mottling seen on some of the grey Kladrubers. His sire, FAVORY RAVA XXI, has fine mottling all over his face, but does not show any unusual markings.

The same year a grey mare, ROICA-8, was born with two partially blue eyes and a large irregular blaze that skewed over her left nostril. Her breeding is remarkably similar to the dam of the blue-eyed FAVORY ROMA XXI-27.

To date no Kladrubers have been tested for the splashed white mutation. That pattern has not been noted in any historical accounts, nor is it currently known to exist in any of the closely related breeds. Even so, testing ROMA and ROICA for splashed white might help shed light on other possible causes of blue eyes in horses.

Markings

It is preferred that the horses of the black line not have markings, but some are moderately marked. Two of the current black stallions, SACRAMOSO MANTOVA X and SOLO SIRIA XXIX, have a white hind foot. Recently a black stallion with a full blaze and one white hind foot was offered for sale. Those are the exceptions, though, and most black Kladrubers are unmarked.

Grey Kladrubers are seen with a much wider range of markings, from solid to marked with wide blazes and stockings. Most tend towards the more moderate amount of white, with some white on the face and one or two white feet.

Many grey Kladrubers have pigment loss around the mouth, eyelids, udder, testicles and anus. In some cases the facial depigmentation is little more than fine pink mottling around the edges of any white markings on the muzzle, while for others it can cover much of the muzzle and around the eyes. Others lose pigment in large, clear patches around the muzzle and eyes. Depigmentation increases with age and is more common in horses that are homozygous for grey. There is also evidence that depigmentation of the face is more pronounced in males than females.

It is also thought that depigmentation of the face may be genetically separate from the depigmentation of the underside of the horse; depigmentation of the latter is correlated with increased incidence of melanomas, whereas the connection between facial depigmentation and melanomas is less clear. There is also a family connection between the two different types. Depigmentation of the undersides has been shown to have its highest incidence in the Generale line. Among the classic families, facial depigmentation is more strongly associated with the Favory line. Oddly enough, the highest correlation with facial depigmentation in the outcross lines is not with the Lipizzans, which is a breed often asso-ciated with facial depigmentation, but with the Lusitano RUDOLFO.

A small number of Kladrubers have faces that appear so completely pink-skinned that they might easily be mistaken for a dominant white or homozygous sabino-1 horse. It can be difficult to determine whether that is due to pigment loss or the presence of a patterning mutation in an adult grey horse.

Heavy Draft Breeds

The story of the American horse industry in the late nineteenth century is in many ways the story of the draft breeds. Although purebred breeding began with the English Thoroughbred in the eighteenth century, it evolved into a widespread system within the heavy horse breeds of the late nineteenth century. This was largely driven by American demand for heavy horses and their insistence that such horses have recorded pedigrees. Farm equipment was getting heavier and required teams of larger animals. Railways and urban transportation likewise needed size that American horses lacked, and a lucrative import business grew to fill the need. In an attempt to protect buyers from fraudulent dealers, the American Treasury Department ruled that only pedigreed breeding stock could be imported duty free. Many of the older draft registries were established as a result of that market pressure.

Ironically the same Industrial Revolution that gave birth to the modern draft horse eventually created the automobile and the tractor. The gasoline engine ended the heavy horse boom not long after it began, leaving many of these once-popular breeds endangered.

American Belgian

Origin: Foundation stock from Belgium

Although the American Belgian descends exclusively from the Belgian Brabant and is not a truly separate breed, selective breeding has changed its appearance. American Belgians have less feather and are more upright and lighter of build than the original imports.

Stud Book

The American Association of Importers and Breeders of Belgian Draft Horses was formed in 1887, making it one of the oldest American registries. The first volume of the stud book, published in 1905, was open to any draft horse imported from Belgium, or the offspring of two imported parents. In subsequent volumes, that rule was changed to permit only those horses born to registered parents, or imports registered with the Belgian national stud book. Belgian imports were prevalent in the years leading up to the first World War, and then again in the late 1920s and 1930s. After World War II, the preferred type in the two countries began to diverge, and importation halted. The American stud book was never closed to imports, however, and in the latter part of the twentieth century a few breeders began importing European Brabants.

In 1936, it was necessary to change the association by-laws to remain in compliance with Indiana state laws. At that time the organization was renamed the Belgian Draft Horse Corporation of America.

Population

The North American Livestock Census, conducted on behalf of the American Livestock Breeds Conservancy in 1990, estimated the global population of Belgian Drafts at 24,000. The Belgian Draft Horse Corporation registered 3,445 horses that same year. Although the breed was once overshadowed by the Percheron, it is now considered the most populous draft breed in the United States, with more registered horses than the other draft breeds combined.

Colors

On the home page of the Belgian Draft Horse Corporation website, the registry states that American Belgians are "much a one-color breed", and points out that this makes it easier to assemble a matched team. That one color is chestnut. In fact the majority of Belgians are not only chestnut, they are pretty consistently the same shade of medium to light chestnut with flaxen points. Flaxen chestnut was popular with American breeders during the postwar period, and became the signature color for the breed at a time when draft breeders were beginning to use color as a quick way to identify and promote their specific breed. Just as grey and black had become part of the image of the Percheron, light chestnut with a flaxen mane and tail came to identify the Belgian breed.

In addition to flaxen chestnuts, there are mealy chestnut Belgians, which are often called blonde by breeders. In some blonde individuals the paler undersides are quite pronounced, particularly on winter coats. The palest of these appear creamy white with a slightly darker cream topline, and could be mistaken for palomino by those unfamil-

Summary

Current colors: The majority of American Belgians are flaxen chestnut. Bay, bay roan, chestnut roan and blue roan are all rare. Frosty roans occur, especially among horses bred from recent Brabant imports. The silver dilution is suspected.

Historical Colors: At one time black and grey were present, though they were never common. Both colors could be reintroduced through Belgian imports, if they were wanted.

Markings/patterns: Many individuals have sabino markings, though flashy body spotting is rare. Sabino roans, including those that closely resemble true roan, occur and are not uncommon.

Eye color: Most Belgians are dark-eyed, but occasionally blue-eyed individuals are seen. When blue eyes occur, they are usually paired with more extensive white markings or heavy roaning.

iar with how dramatically the mealy pattern can alter chestnut.

Dappling occurs on some Belgians. This is somewhat unusual for the color chestnut, which usually does not show pronounced dappling. Often the dappling happens in conjunction with the mealy pattern, and like that pattern it is more pronounced in winter. The 1963 Ohio State Fair Champion Mare, CONSELLA, was a particularly striking example of a dappled mealy chestnut. Dappling is also seen on some light chestnut Belgians that have a more dusty, muted tone.

Sabino

In addition to being chestnut, a large portion of American Belgians carry some form of sabino. Many could be classified as having the flashy white type of patterning. Body spots are uncommon, though they do occur. The mare BRITT DU MARA-

IS (1973) had a white patch on the left side of her barrel. Another mare, MISS MELODY (1985), had a large, lacey patch on her left hip. The marking did not prevent her from being named the 1990 All-American Aged Mare. There was also a stallion, DIAMOND S. PAUL (1995), loud enough to be double-registered with the North American Spotted Draft Horse Association. One of his purebred daughters, SEDOR LADY DIVA (2001), was also double-registered as a Spotted Draft. Her pattern was more extensive, but also less distinct in outline, than that of her sire.

There are also a wide variety of sabino roans. Some of these can be difficult to tell apart from dark-headed roans, especially in a breed where frosty roan and facial roaning are found. The Canadian stallion PRINS VIEW CONGRESSMAN (1999) is a good example of this kind of pattern. His coat has an even mix of white and colored hairs, but

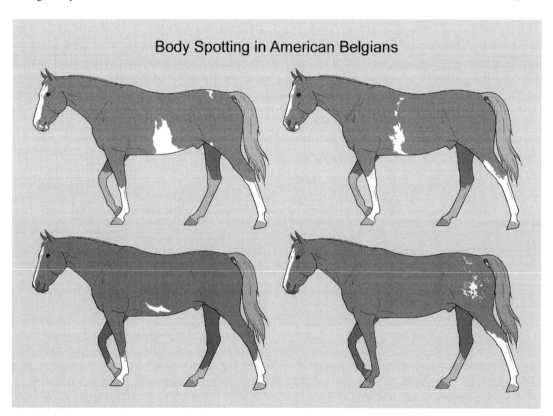

Figure 14. Examples of body spotting on Belgians (clockwise from the top left): Diamond S. Paul, left side; Diamond S. Paul, right side; Britt du Marais; Miss Melody.

his face and legs lack the strong constrast with the body that is typical of a true roan. He does have a broad blaze and pink on his lower lip, but no white on his legs.

Other sabino roans are more obvious, with extensively roaned coats that fade into white markings on the face and the legs. The mare DOUBLE O GLOW (1998) is a good example of this kind of sabino patterning. Some sabino roan Belgians are pale enough that they appear almost white, while others have a smaller percentage of white hairs that tend to concentrate on the hindquarters. Darker patches set within the roaned areas are also quite common, and can give the coat an uneven or patchy appearance.

Sabino roans have long been found among the American Belgians. It is likely that many of the original Belgians with these kinds of patterns were registered simply as roan, just as many still are today. Yet even among the early imports, and among the early stud books in Belgium, there were horses entered as chestnut with white hairs (*alezan rubican*). Because the horses were invariably chestnut with white face markings, it seems likely that these *rubican* horses were sabino roans of some kind.

Although many of the sabino patterns found in Belgians are the softer, more roaned variety, sabino-1 is not thought to be present in the gene pool. To date the testing lab at the University of California in Davis has not recorded a Belgian with the mutation.

True Roan

At one time more Belgians in the American stud books were registered as roan than chestnut. The most celebrated stallion in the early twentieth century was the chestnut roan FARCEUR (1910). FARCEUR was the Overall Grand Champion Stallion at the 1913 International Livestock Exposition, and was undefeated for the next three years at the Iowa State Fair, which was then one of the largest venues for draft horses. In 1917, he sold for $47,500, matching the previous record set by the Clydesdale BARON OF BUCHLYVIE.

FARCEUR sired a large number of roan foals, including OAKDALE FARCEUR (1921) and SUPREME FARCEUR (1922), the two sons that succeeded him

Some American Belgians registered as roan are sabino roan rather than dark-headed roan. Both of these Belgians have the blazes and stockings associated with the sabino patterns.

at stud. By the 1930s, though, buyers were only interested in chestnut, and owners of roan stallions found they could not compete for mares. One of the last roans garner a lot of attention in the show ring was the chestnut roan FAIRVIEW CHIEF (1965). Some of the modern roans trace to him, including his blue roan great-grandson, DAKOTA STEVE (1989).

True roan is still found in American Belgians, though many of them get their color from more recent Brabant imports rather than from American bloodlines. The relatively high percentage of roaning from the sabino patterns makes it difficult to determine just how common true roan is within the American bloodlines.

Many roan Belgians have the frosty manes and tails that are often seen on Brabants. It may be that the American roans carried the same trait, hidden because their base color was flaxen chestnut. It is also possible to find roans where the white hairs extend to the face, either on the cheeks and across the bridge of the nose. A few are roaned over most of the face. These horses are different from the sabino roans, which also have roaned faces, but also have extensive face markings. This type of roan, with the light face and frosty mane and tail could be mistaken for the early stages of greying.

Black-based Colors

When Belgians were imported into the United States in the early twentieth century, the majority were bay or brown. In the first volume of the American stud book, 67 percent of the stallions and 76 percent of the mares were some shade of bay or brown. Judging from pictures taken at the time, most were dark bay or brown. The shift to chestnut with flaxen points began within the first decade of the registry, with the percentage of bay

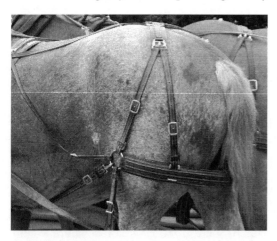

This gelding has the irregular patches seen on many sabino roan Belgians.

and brown horses dropping steadily. In the last printed stud book, published in the 1930s, the percentage of bay and brown had dropped to 5 percent for stallions and 4 percent for mares.

Black was also present, although the number of black horses as a percentage of the population dropped even more rapidly than that of the bays. By the end of twenties, black accounted for 3 percent of horses in the stud book. A decade later, it had virtually disappeared.

Chestnut came to dominate the breed so thoroughly that the black-based colors were practically unheard of in American Belgians from the postwar period until 1973, when Albert Stankewitz imported three bay roan Brabants. These were the stallion BABAR DE WOLVERTEM (1971) and the mares ETOILE VAN RINGVAART (1972) and MOLDA D'IMPDE (1972). When they arrived, horses had not been imported directly from Belgium in more than thirty years. Although bay had all but disappeared in the United States, they were not imported for their color. The intent was to improve the working qualities and soundness of the American Belgians. Because the registry had never closed the books to further imports, the horses were accepted into the stud book and crossed with existing American bloodlines.

BABAR DE WOLVERTEM was later joined by another bay roan import, BLOC VAN VELZEKE, at Anne and Henry Harper's Milkwood Farm. Other imports followed, all carrying the dominant form of Extension (E), sometimes called the black gene, along with their roan coloring. Brabant crosses still only represent a small portion of the total American Belgian population, but these later imports did succeed in reintroducing bay, brown and even black, although the latter has not yet been recorded on a non-roan. That is likely a function of the relatively small numbers of blue roans in the breed at the moment; it would be possible to get a black Belgian, especially if the popularity of blue roan continues to rise.

Bay is found separate from roan, at least among those horses carrying Brabant blood. It is less common because of the linkage of the black gene (E) with roan, which means that the two tend to be inherited together. The linkage is not absolute, however, and a small percentage of non-roan bays are born to bay roans. In shade many are light or mealy bay, and some have the reduced point coloring typical of wild bay.

Silver

There has been speculation that some portion of the American Belgian population carries the silver dilution. Because the breed is primarily chestnut, and because silver only dilutes black pigment, the presence of the mutation would not be obvious in a purebred breeding program. It is among crossbreds that red and even black silvers have been reported. Some have come from warmblood breeding programs, where the outcross is to Thoroughbreds, a breed that does not have the silver dilution. Others have come out of Pregnant Mare Urine (PMU) programs that utilized Belgian mares and black and white Paint Horse stallions.

Silver is suspected to have been present in the draft horses in Belgium, and it is known to still exist in the Ardennes. There are also clues that silver was present among the American Belgians before

the breed became uniformly chestnut. In the first volume of the American stud book, the stallion PANTALON (1885) was registered as a bay with a light gray mane. He was a Belgian import and like many horses from that time his ancestry was not documented.

In the second volume, there is a stallion, JUPITER WYT (1900), registered as "bay sorrel." Not knowing which color to call a red silver, older breeders have sometimes combined the two terms to describe their horse. In that same volume, the stallion SACRATIF (1899) was registered as a "dapple chestnut sorrel with silver colored mane and tail." At the time the term dapple chestnut was commonly used by American breeders to describe silver dapples. Dappling was occasionally noted in the description of bays or browns, but SACRATIF is the only instance in the early stud books of a chestnut noted as being dappled.

In Volume 3 of the stud book there is a stallion, YPROIS (1906), entered as a black chestnut with a white mane and tail. Like the other suspicious entries, he did not have a lasting influence on the

Color Percentages in the Early Belgian Studbooks - Stallions

	bay	black	chestnut	roan	grey
Volume 1	1203	213	202	160	26
(percentage)	67%	12%	11%	9%	1%
Volume 2	749	92	284	176	21
(percentage)	57%	7%	21%	13%	2%
Volume 3	781	78	417	257	19
(percentage)	51%	5%	27%	16%	1%
Volume 4	687	57	422	247	16
(percentage)	48%	4%	30%	17%	1%

Chart 7. Colors of Belgian stallions registered in the American stud books from 1905 until 1912.

Color Percentages in the Early Belgian Studbooks - Mares

	bay	black	chestnut	roan	grey
Volume 1	173	32	14	8	2
(percentage)	76%	14%	6%	3%	1%
Volume 2	200	20	43	50	4
(percentage)	63%	6%	14%	16%	1%
Volume 3	457	75	169	160	21
(percentage)	52%	9%	19%	18%	2%
Volume 4	426	48	232	254	23
(percentage)	43%	5%	24%	26%	2%

Chart 8. Colors of Belgian mares registered in the American stud books from 1905 until 1912.

breed, so it is difficult to know for sure if he was in fact a silver. Entries like his do suggest that the color may have been present among some portion of the early imported horses, and may have survived, hidden by the more popular chestnut color.

Historical Colors
The early Belgian imports were far more colorful than their present day descendants might suggest. While most of these colors can still be found, at least among the horses carrying the blood of recent Brabant imports, there is one color that, for the moment at least, is not present among American Belgians.

Grey
Grey was more common at the time of the initial American imports than it is now. Although even then importers favored chestnuts, a few greys were imported. One of these was the white grey mare ROSA (1904), sired by LA FLEUR and out of SARAH D RECKEM. ROSA was named Champion Belgian Mare at the 1910 Iowa State Fair and Exposition.

The state of Iowa was home to many of the influential Belgians of that era, so the State Fair was an important show.

Another grey Belgian had taken the championship at the Chicago International two years earlier. That was the stallion PERCE (1901), by MARSALA and out of LUCIE DE BUERINNIS. A painting of PERCE from Volume IV of the stud book shows a vividly dappled, massively built horse that many would have found difficult to tell apart from a Percheron. It was that fact that probably doomed the color: grey was a "Percheron color." Unlike Percherons, the Belgian Draft was new to the buying public. Grey soon fell out of favor as the American breeders sought to differentiate their breed from its better known and more popular competitor.

Because grey can still be found, if only rarely, among the Brabants, grey could be brought into the American population through importation. This is unlikely, since the same dynamic that prevented the color from gaining traction a century ago is still true today. A grey Belgian would likely be mistaken for a Percheron or a Percheron cross, and those interested in a grey draft horse are more likely to purchase a Percheron than go to the expense of acquiring a grey Brabant from Belgium.

Eye Color

The overwhelming majority of Belgians have dark eyes., though blue and partially blue eyes are occasionally seen in combination with sabino markings and patterns. There is not a specific family known for producing blue eyes, which would suggest that the blue eyes that have occurred in recent years are not necessarily linked to the presence of the classic splashed white pattern.

The first American Belgian registered with a blue eye was LOUIS 19, foaled in 1881 and recorded in the first volume of the stud book. He was described as bay with a star. Another bay with a blue eye, CONGO 3672 (1908), was listed in the third volume of the stud book. He had a blaze and a white left hind foot. LOUIS is particularly interesting because a blue eye on a horse with very little white is more typical of horses with the classic splashed white pattern. Neither stallion has recorded descendants.

At least one blue-eyed Belgian has produced a blue-eyed foal. That is the mare DOUBLE O GLOW (1998). She is a very pale flaxen chestnut sabino roan with two blue eyes. Her son, DOUBLETAIL HB's SUNDANCE (2006), is a sabino roan with a blue eye. DOUBLE O GLOW has a broad blaze and white stockings, and her foals have been marked similarly, but the cause of her blue eyes is not yet known.

Markings

Blazes and white socks have long been popular with American Belgian breeders, which helped to ensure that some type of sabino patterning was preserved in the American horses even though it

The grey stallion CARON DE BAU *(1905) was a successful show horse in the early twentieth century. Grey was once more common among winners in Belgium, too.*

appears to have been largely lost in the native Brabants. The markings came from the original Brabants, though, and not from outcrossing to American stock. Unlike many of the draft horses bred in the United States, the Belgian registry began with both male and female imports, and required American-born horses to have two imported parents from the start. Many horses in the early volumes of the stud books are noted as having white faces and white leg markings.

Among the modern American Belgians, wide white blazes are common. Horses with more moderate face markings are found, but some kind of facial white is typical. Leg markings are less common, and it is not unusual to see a Belgian with a broad face marking and no white on the legs. Those horses with white on the legs most often have hind socks or stockings. Four white legs and a blaze are less common, but can be found. Among the horses with Brabant breeding, white markings tend to be minimal, or are absent altogether.

American Cream Draft

Origin: Midwestern United States

The American Cream Draft has the distinction of being the only draft breed developed in the United States. Although the breed has been thought of as closely related to the Belgian Draft, genetic testing shows that the Cream Draft is unique and that it is no more similar to the Belgian than it is to any of the other draft breeds. This discovery has lent credibility to the effort to preserve the breed.

Stud Book

The American Cream Draft began with a single amber-eyed cream mare, OLD GRANNY. Several breeders began linebreeding her descendants and in 1944 the American Cream Horse Association of America was formed. By 1957 there were 200 horses in the stud books and the registry set the date of 1962 for closing the breed to outside blood. Before that could happen, the registry went dormant. It remained that way until 1982, when renewed interest led to a reopening of the books. In 1994 the registry changed its name to the American Cream Draft Horse Association.

Working closely with livestock conservation experts, American Cream Draft breeders have established a grading scheme that gives more horses a path to full registration. Horses with two registered parents are granted full registration. Foals with one American Cream Draft parent and one registered Belgian, Clydesdale, Percheron, Shire or Suffolk parent are eligible for the Appendix Tracking Register. Horses in the tracking register can produce fully registered foals if bred to a registered American Cream Draft, provided the foal meets the color requirements. The Appendix Tracking Register is also used for mares that do not meet registry's skin color requirements.

In 2004, the registry added the requirement that all breeding stallions be tested for junctional epiclermolysis hulbsa (JEB), a genetic disease associated with Belgian and French draft breeds. Carriers have their status noted on their registration papers and in the stud book. Sample tests done in 2004 showed that five of the ten stallions and three of the thirteen mares were carriers. Because the population is so small and maintaining genetic diversity is important, carriers are not automatically removed from breeding.

Population

The American Cream Draft was already a small breed when the market for draft horses collapsed. Efforts to restore the breed have brought the 2011 population up to 407 fully registered horses, split between 208 mares and 199 stallions. An additional 50 mares and 27 stallions are recorded in the Tracking Register. Approximately 30 horses are registered annually.

The American Livestock Breeds Conservancy lists American Cream Drafts as Critical, which is reserved for those breeds with fewer than 200 an-

---

Summary

Current colors: The definitive color for the breed is golden champagne. Three traits are required for full registration of males: cream coat, pink skin and amber eyes. The cream dilution is found in addition to champagne, but it does not reliably produce the three necessary traits, and is considered undesirable unless paired with champagne.

Historical colors: Because the Cream Draft was defined by the champagne dilution from the start, the color has not changed significantly over time.

Markings/patterns: White markings are considered desirable and many Cream Drafts have blazes and white legs.

Eye color: As champagnes, Cream Drafts are typically born with blue eyes that darken to amber with maturity. Horses that carry both the cream and the champagne gene have amber or hazel eyes. Palomino and sorrel Creams have dark eyes, and horses with two copies of the cream gene have blue eyes, neither of which is desirable.

Restrictions: Stallions must have pink skin and amber or hazel eyes. Dark-eyed, dark-skinned mares, and off-colored mares can be entered in the Tracking Register.

nual registrations in the United States and a global population that is estimated to be less than 2,000. The Equus Survival Trust also lists the breed as Critical, which means that there are between 100 and 300 active breeding mares.

Colors
The American Cream Draft breed standard calls for a cream coat, pink skin and amber eyes; in other words, gold champagne. The distinctive coloring first appeared in an unregistered draft mare named OLD GRANNY. She was purchased at a farm sale in Iowa in 1911, and is thought to have been foaled some time between 1890 and 1905. Her background is unknown.

OLD GRANNY is sometimes credited as the first instance of champagne in American horses. The estimated foaling dates place her just a little older than the original champagne Tennessee Walking Horse, GOLDEN LADY. Just as with OLD GRANNY, the exact foaling date for GOLDEN LADY is not known but it is estimated to be around 1910. GOLDEN LADY is different from OLD GRANNY in that she has a recorded pedigree stretching back four generations. Likewise the color line for the champagne Saddlebred stallion THE HARVESTER (sire of BAMBOO HARVESTER, better known as the MR. ED) can be traced back to a golden mare named QUEEN, foaled around 1900. It seems likely then that the color, which is thought to be a New World mutation, originated some time prior to the formation of these three breeds.

While the champagne color did not originate with OLD GRANNY, the American Cream Draft breed did. When bred to a black Percheron, GRANNY produced the cream stallion NELSON'S BUCK in 1920. BUCK was used at stud for one year before he was gelded, and sired his only registered foal, the cream stallion YANCY. The dam of YANCY was also a black Percheron. Both BUCK and YANCY were gold champagnes, which might seem odd since most Percherons do not carry chestnut. That early in the twentieth century, it is quite possible that the horses used were not purebred Percherons by modern standards. Defining the breed of a horse by the top-crosses was quite common then, so it is possible that the Percherons carried local blood,

Many American Cream Drafts are marked with white. This stallion, JOKER'S GOLDEN BOY, has particularly extensive markings.

and the red gene, through the female side of their pedigree.

YANCY sired two golden champagne foals, a daughter EUREKA and a son KNOX 1ST. Foaled in 1926 and out of a bay grade Shire mare, KNOX had lasting influence as the sire of the gold champagne stallion SILVER LACE (1931). Although he took after his sire in color, in form SILVER LACE was said to greatly resemble his Farceur-bred Belgian dam.

SILVER LACE was the horse that brought attention to the descendants of OLD GRANNY. At the time he was used at stud, the state of Iowa required that publicly offered stallions be registered with a recognized breed organization. In order to offer SILVER LACE without the required permit, his owner G. A. Lenning formed the Silver Lace Horse Company. Those wishing to breed to SILVER LACE bought shares in the company. Since the mare owners were technically joint owners of the stallion, his services were not being offered to the public. The situation was controversial, however, and in 1939 the stallion died under suspicious circumstances.

Although he lived only eight years, SILVER LACE made an impression in that short period of time. One of the men who sought out his offspring was C. T. Rierson of Ardmore Stock Farm. Rierson was instrumental in the formation of the registry and

American White Drafts

The American White Draft is unrelated to the American Cream Draft. American White Drafts are a strain of white-born horses of draft type that have traditionally been registered with the American White and Creme Horse Association, formerly known as the American Albino Association.

Unlike the Cream Drafts, which are gold champagne, the White Drafts are dominant white. The color comes from SILVER CHIEF, a stallion from the White Horse Ranch in Nebraska. SILVER CHIEF traced his color back to OLD KING (1906), one of the earliest recorded dominant white stallions.

In 1973 David McCafferty crossed one of his SILVER CHIEF sons on the registered Belgian mare DOTTIE. The resulting white filly was named SILVER BELL. From there McCafferty set about developing a strain of white horses of draft type. His breeding program was featured in an article in the *Draft Horse Journal* in 1983. The accompanying picture showed a team of six white drafts, four stallions and two mares. When a breed survey was conducted by the white registry five years later, there were fifteen White Drafts registered. More recently horses from the program have appeared on calendars and book covers thanks to the beautiful photography of Mark Barrett.

The Old King family of whites were known for producing a high percentage of uniformly white foals, and the drafts are no exception. They do not breed true, though, as some dark foals are born each year. One of the unusual aspects of the American White Draft is that they often have blue eyes. OLD KING himself was described as brown-eyed, and that is the color most often attributed to his descendants. In the interview in the *Draft Horse Journal*, McCafferty states that his horses do not have the pink eyes of an albino, but have blue eyes. This does not appear to be linked to any of the other patterns, as the non-white foals are only moderately marked.

then in popularizing the new breed. By the late 1950s, there were 200 American Creams entered in the stud books and almost all were descendants of SILVER LACE.

Due in large part to the fame of Roy Rogers and Trigger, the early twentieth century saw a surge in the popularity of golden horses. These new golden draft horses arrived at just the right time to take advantage of that market. From the start, what set the descendants of OLD GRANNY apart from the other gold and cream horses of the era was their ability to consistently pass along their color. Unlike palomino, which is incompletely dominant, champagne will breed true. As early breeders began linebreeding their Cream Drafts, they would have had foal crops with a high percentage of the desired color.

Cream

In many ways the Cream Draft breeders had it more simple than their contemporaries breeding golden saddle horses because their outcross breeds lacked the cream dilution. It was the presence of the two separate dilutions, cream and champagne, that muddied the waters for those interested in breeding golden horses.

In fact, it was not until 1974, when Stefan Adalsteinsson's paper "The Inheritance of the Palomino Color in Icelandic Horses" was published in *The Journal of Heredity*, that the scientific community understood cream and lineback dun as separate mutations. Pink-skinned palominos were not mentioned in these studies, but they were the focus of controversy among palomino breeders from the start. The two palomino registries were split on the issue. The oldest registry, the Palomino Horse Association (1936), accepted golden horses regardless of skin color. The Palomino Horse Breeders of America (1941) originally permitted pink-skinned horses, but began requiring dark skin in 1943.

Golden horses with pink skin were mentioned in the 1983 book *Horse Color* by Dr. Phillip Sponenberg and Bonnie Beaver. A picture of the pink-skinned palomino Saddlebred, SO PROUDLY WE HAIL (1977), was included in the color plates. Many still classified the color as a variation of palomino. That did not change until the paper "Cham-

pagne, a Dominant Color Dilution in Horses"
(Sponenberg and Bowling) was published in 1996.

With that discovery a long way off, breeders of
golden horses were left to draw their own conclusions about the inheritance of the golden coat coloring they sought. At the time, the theory that breeding golden horses together resulted in progressively
lighter skin and eyes was common. This idea that
the traits of the parents were blended together in
the offspring, known as blending inheritance, was
a common theory as late as the nineteenth century.
Scientists rejected blending inheritance when the
work by Mendel was rediscovered in the 1890s, but
many animal breeders continued to hold the idea
well into the twentieth century.

For breeders of golden horses, it seemed somewhat logical that these pink-skinned palominos
were an intermediary step between dark-skinned
golden horses and blue-eyed creams. Champagnes
with the cream dilution, known today as ivory
champagnes, fall between gold champagnes and
blue-eyed creams in terms of eye and coat color.
That aspect of the two colors would have made
blending seem even more plausible. That was why
pink skin was considered undesirable by many
golden horse breeders; it was thought to be proof
that one had gone too far in concentrating the
golden coloring, and that cremellos were not far
behind.

This did not concern the early Cream Draft
breeders, because they both wanted the pink skin
and found that their horses were true breeding.
It could be speculated that had there been more
communication between the draft breeders and
those working with the saddle breeds, the separate
nature of the two colors might have come to light
sooner. As it was, the confusion between cream
and champagne worked in reverse for the Cream
Draft. Instead of including champagnes in a palomino breeding program, they eventually included
palomino in what had been a champagne breed.

By the middle of the twentieth century, the
breed faced extinction. The combined effect of the
death of longtime breeder and promoter C. T. Rierson and the dramatic collapse of the draft horse
market left the registry dormant. When it was revived in 1982, few enough horses remained that

The mare Rose Hill's Cream of Wheat Bess, *showing
the old-fashioned draft type that sets the Cream Draft apart
from other heavy breeds bred in the United States.*

the stud book had to be reopened. Not knowing
that the cream coloring was the result of a specific
mutation, horses were entered into the stud book
that were not champagne.

Some of these horses carried the cream mutation. Although not truly pink-skinned, some palominos do have lighter than normal skin. Likewise,
very pale coats—traditionally called isabella in
America—and lighter eyes are also found in some
horses with the cream mutation. Although not
champagne, this type of horse could be mistaken
for a cream horse with pink skin and amber eyes.

It is also possible for a very pale blonde sorrel
to look cream-colored. This kind of color is not
that uncommon among American Belgians and
grade draft horses of Belgian breeding. Pale blonde
horses do not have pink skin, nor do they typically
have amber eyes, but they could look close enough
to the right body color to be mistaken for cream or
be thought of as capable of producing cream.

Once the genetics of the original Cream Draft
coloring was understood, it was clear that the isabella and pale blonde horses did not have the right
genes to produce the desired color. On the advice
of conservation experts, off-colored mares were
retained for breeding purposes. Champagne remained the desired color, and stallions must have
the correct color to be used for breeding, but mares
with the cream dilution can still be used while the
breed seeks to broaden its genetic base.

Because they are champagne, American Cream Draft foals are born with pink skin and blue eyes. As the horse matures, the skin becomes more freckled and the eyes darken to amber.

While the cream dilution does not produce the desired color by itself because the skin and eyes are usually too dark, ivory champagnes—horses that have both the cream and the champagne dilution—meet the breed requirements because their skin is pink and their eyes are hazel or amber. Because ivory champagnes have paler coats than gold champagnes, they are called "light cream" by breeders. The stallion JD WILL'S PRIDE (1997) has been tested to carry both champagne and cream, and many others are pale enough that it is likely they would test as ivory champagnes.

Pearl

Because the color was only recently identified, it is not known if any Cream Drafts carry the pearl dilution. The pearl dilution could produce the desired color, though. Horses with one cream and one pearl gene look like cremellos, but often have eyes that are closer to hazel or gold than blue. Homozygous pearls have pinkish skin and eyes that range from pale tan to light brown. Either could

fit the breed requirements for coat, eye and skin color. Whether or not the color was present would depend on the background of some of the outcross horses used to expand the gene pool. If horses of Spanish descent, like the American stock horse breeds, were used then it is possible that the pearl gene is present.

Eye Color

The breed standard calls for amber eyes, which are part of the defining characteristics of the champagne dilution. Champagnes are usually born with bright blue eyes that darken as the horse matures. Since palomino is permitted in the mares, some of those may have dark eyes. Horses that inherit both the champagne and the cream dilution often have paler eyes than horses with just the champagne mutation, usually tending towards green. As far as the author is aware, bright blue eyes like those found in pintos have not been noted in any specific individual, but given the flashy nature of the markings, it could conceivably occur.

Markings

White markings have always been common in the breed, particularly blazes. When present, leg markings are often more moderate, but flashy white trim has long been considered desirable by breeders of golden horses, and the American Creams are no exception. A few horses have had white that extended up the stifle, typical of the flashy sabino pattern, but extensive body-spotting has not yet been seen.

Ardennes

Origin: Ardennes region of Belgium and France

The Ardennes is one of the oldest of the heavy horses, and has been used extensively to improve other draft horse breeds. The reason for its popularity is clear in this description given by an American consul in 1908:

> "Much smaller than the smallest Flemish horse, the Ardennes horse is robust, long-necked, and broad shouldered; he resists fatigue and supports privations better than the horse of other races."

The Ardennes is still bred in Belgium and France, with slight variation between the two breeding groups. There is also a Swedish version of the breed as well, which is quite similar but that also carries the blood of native Swedish country stock.

Stud Book

The Ardennes has stud books Belgium, France and Sweden. The oldest is in Belgium, where the *Société Mutuelle Pour l'élevage du Cheval Ardennais* (The Mutual Society for Ardennais Horse Breeding) was founded in 1841. The Belgian Draft Horse stud book consolidated the breed with the Brabant and the Flemish Horse in 1886. Although all three of the Belgian Draft breeds were included in the book, the Ardennes were recorded in a separate section. The three books were later combined, and then split again in 1936 when the Belgian Ardennes and the Belgian Brabant were given separate books. The two breeds remained separate until 2011, when four Brabant stallions were approved for breeding to Ardennes mares.

In the last ten years, the Belgian Ardennes stud book has also experimented with outcrossing to Arabians to bring back the more active type found prior to its transition from work horse to meat animal. The grading up scheme allows the descendants of the original cross full registration status as an Ardennes when the percentage of Arabian blood is 12.5 percent or lower. Another program is utilizing Norman Cobs. In those crosses, full registration status is granted after two generations

rather than the three used for Arabians. Just as with the Arabians, the intent is to bring back the utility the breed once had.

The first Ardennes were brought to Sweden in 1873, and a stud book was established there in 1901. Outcrossing to native Swedish stock was permitted up until 1925, after which it was phased out. Horses are occasionally imported from Belgium, but the majority of the horses are of Swedish breeding, and trace back through uniquely Swedish lines.

The French stud book is the youngest of the three, having been established in 1909. It permits the use of approved Trait du Nord (the French version of the Belgian Brabant) and Auxois horses for breeding Ardennes. As with several of the other French draft breeds, there is an grading up process that allows for the use of draft mares of unknown background.

Summary

Current colors: Bay and bay roan are the most common colors. Ordinary and wild bay are both found. Mealy bays are common, especially among the Swedish Ardennes. Chestnut, chestnut roan, black and black roan are less common. Flaxen manes are common on chestnuts, and occasionally seen on bays. Grey and the silver dilution are found in the Swedish Ardennes, but are rare.

Markings/patterns: Most Ardennes are solid or minimally marked. Some do have white on the face or legs. White markings are more common in the Swedish Ardennes. There has been one suspected dominant white foal born in France.

Eye color: At least one bay foal was born with blue eyes, and the one dominant white foal had blue eyes. Those two were exceptions in what is otherwise a dark-eyed breed.

Restrictions: Only bay, roan, and chestnut are permitted in France. Although it does occur, black is not an accepted there, although very dark bay and brown are tolerated. Sweden and Belgium allow the color black.

Population

Haras Nationaux reported that in 2008, there were 1,564 mares and 224 stallions in France. In 2007, there were 729 foals registered. The European Farm Animal Biodiversity Information System (EFABIS) estimates there are 1,500 mares and 85 stallions in Belgium, and another 485 mares and 72 stallions in Sweden.

Colors

The three different breeding populations of Ardennes have a slightly different distribution of colors, and the stud books in the three countries each have different policies regarding color. In general, the French horses have the most restrictive policies and the smallest range of colors, while the Belgian horses have the most permissive stud book and the Swedish horses have the widest range of colors.

Bay is common in all three groups. The body color can range from pale buff to a shade so dark that the horse appears black, but a clear medium bay is the most common. There is an even mix between horses that have the fully black points of an ordinary bay, and those that are wild bays with minimal black on their legs. Mealy markings are common, particularly among the Swedish Ardennes. Sooty dappling is sometimes seen, also most frequently in the Swedish horses.

Chestnut is less common than bay, but is an accepted color in all three countries. Twelve of the approved stallions in France, or slightly less than 7 percent, are chestnut. The color is more common in Belgium, where 11 percent of the licensed stallions are chestnut. Sweden has the highest proportion of chestnuts, with almost one in four stallions chestnut. Sweden also has the greatest variation in color among its chestnuts. Like the chestnuts in France and Belgium, most have flaxen points, but the shade can range from a mealy blonde to a dark liver. Dappling is sometimes seen on the paler chestnuts.

Black is rare in the Ardennes and is not accepted in France. It does occur there on rare occasions, but stallions of that color cannot be licensed. In some cases it appears black horses are registered in France as brown, which is not a preferred color

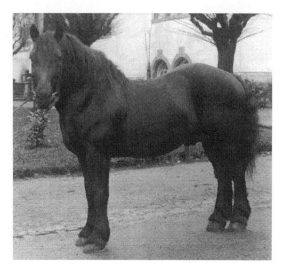

The black Ardennes AUDAX (1931) was an influential sire of Black Forest Horses. Black is no longer an accepted color in France, though it does occur on rare occasions.

but is tolerated. The black Ardennes stallion KING DU DOL (1998) was registered in France as brown, but was later exported to Poland and registered as black. In photographs he appears to be solid black.

Black is accepted in both Belgium and Sweden. There are no black horses among the current licensed stallions in Belgium, but in Sweden there is a licensed black stallion, HERKULES (2003). Black Ardennes, notably the stallion AUDAX, have been used in the past to improve the Black Forest Horse.

Roan

Roan is the second-most common color in France and Belgium. Almost a quarter of the approved stallions in France are roan, and a similar portion of roans are found in Belgium. The majority of these are bay roans, in part because bay is such a common color, but also because roan in the Ardennes is most likely linked to the black-based colors (*E*). There is one chestnut roan stallion in France, PEPSI DU VALLON (2003), and at least two chestnut roan stallions in Belgium, WINNI DE LE VIERRE (1994) and the approved Brabant outcross OWEN VAN HET HERMESHOF (2007). Black is not considered objectionable when paired with roan, so black roans are found. The stallion TOUT NOIR DU VALLON is a black roan.

Roan Ardennes can be of the traditional variety with dark points, or they can be frosty with silvered manes and tails. Some roan Ardennes are very pale and even the head is extensively roaned, making them difficult to distinguish from greys, especially in old photographs. Reverse dappling occurs on some of the roans, and in some cases can be quite pronounced.

Roan is less common among the Swedish Ardennes. There are currently four licensed chestnut roan stallions: CARLANG (2005), ROLANG (2000), ULLTAN (1996) and EVER (2004). Three of the four are related; CARLANG and EVER are sons of ROLANG. There are three bay roans: FREJ (1990), KUNO TE ZANDE (2001) and VERMOT (2001). KUNO TE ZANDE is a Brabant outcross, and has the frosty roan coloring common in that breed. Because the four chestnut roans are all flaxen chestnut, it is not clear if they are frosty roans.

Grey

A photograph of a grey Ardennes stallion was included in Count C. G. Wrangel's book *Die Rassen des Pferdes*. It is perhaps fitting then that the Swedish Ardennes, which began with imports made by Count Wrangel in 1873, still has rare grey individuals. Included among them is one licensed stallion, the rose grey AKRON (2000). His color comes from his dam, AKLEJA. AKRON has a grey half-brother, ARKTIS, and a grey half-sister ANEMONE. The color goes back to the mare AKJA (1977), the dam of AKLEJA. AKJA also produced the grey mare ANEMONA, but she did not leave any recorded foals.

Although grey was viewed favorably by Count Wrangel, who saw it as proof of oriental influence, it was not a common color even in the early days of the Swedish registry. Grey is no longer found in either the Belgian or French Ardennes, and in France the color is not accepted.

Silver

Silver is present in the Swedish Ardennes, where it was previously called *läderfux*. It is now called silver with the base color designated: *silverbrun* (red silver) and *silversvart* (black silver). The original source of the mutation is not known, though

Ardennes Color Restrictions

Each of the three countries where Ardennes are bred have a slightly different breed standard, including different requirements regarding color.

France

The French stud book is the most restrictive. The standard states that the following colors are preferred: bay, bay roan, chestnut, black roan and chestnut roan. Dark bay and brown are tolerated, but all others are excluded.

Sweden

The Swedish stud book adopted a standard in 1925 that required "clean" colors, which was defined as anything other than yellow or dun. The current Swedish standard lists the following accepted colors: bay, brown, black and chestnut, bay and black silver (formerly *läderfux*) and grey and roan variations in these colors.

Belgium

There are no specific restrictions in the Belgian stud book. The standard states that coat color not important, and then goes on to list aspects of temperament like bravery and calmness that are considered necessary.

historically silver has been present in a variety of French and Belgian draft breeds. Its presence in the Swedish horses, but not the French or Belgian, may be the result of genetic drift; that is, once the populations diverged, it died out in France and Belgium but survived in Sweden. It is also possible that it came from the native Swedish mares, and is not present in the other Ardennes because of this difference in the founder populations.

However it got there, the silver dilution can be found in the descendants of the red silver stallion VERONG (1992). His red silver grandson TOXID (2003) is currently listed among the licensed stallions. In addition to giving the silver dilution to VIRA, the dam of TOXID, VERONG sired eleven oth-

This grey Ardennes appeared in the 1908 edition of the Graf C. G. Wrangel book Die Rassen des Pferdes. *The author felt that the stallion, exported to Russia, illustrated how use of oriental blood had refined the breed.*

er foals registered as red silver. He also has a red silver roan daughter, MIKAN.

Another silver is the stallion DACKE (1993). He is registered as a dark chestnut, but his body color is truly difficult to categorize. He is dark enough that he could be mistaken for a black chestnut, though a chestnut that dark would be quite unusual in the Ardennes. He has pronounced dark shading on his lower legs and fetlocks, and pale areas along his cannon bones. His mane and tail are the same color as his body, though that may be due to age. He cannot be a chestnut, though, because he sired a red silver mare, HÖGSHULTS DAISI (1999), with the chestnut mare SANNI. That same year he also sired the black silver mare MISS DECIBEL, also from a chestnut mare.

A third stallion believed to be a silver is IB MUNTER (2002). His color comes from his dam FANNY II, who is registered as red silver. To date IB MUNTER is her only silver foal. There are likely other silver families in the Swedish Ardennes, but identifying them is complicated by the fact that many of the bay Ardennes have an unrelated factor that causes flaxen manes.

Flaxen-maned Bays
Although they look a bit like red silvers, some bay Ardennes have flaxen manes. They are unlike red silvers in that only the long hair is altered, so the legs remain black. In many of these horses, the

mane can seem variegated, almost to the point of being striped with flaxen and black. This is different from silver, where the roots of the mane are often dark but the hair is light. Like the mane of a silver dilute, the pale color is most pronounced when the horse is a young adult, and tends to darken with age.

Most of these horses are wild bays. It is not unusual for wild bays to have paler hairs mixed in their manes or tails, but the flaxen-maned bays are much more dramatic in appearance. Often it is just the mane, though some horses do have flaxen in their tails as well. As wild bays there is not as much black on the points, but what black the legs retain is a true black that does not change with the seasons like black that has been diluted by silver. The stallion BONAIR, recently exported to Poland for use in breeding Polish Coldbloods, is a particularly striking example of a flaxen-maned bay.

White Ticking
A few horses have been registered with white ticking. The dark silver stallion, DACKE, is faintly ticked with white throughout his coat and even in his mane. The chestnut stallion PIRAT is so extensively ticked that he might be mistaken for roan, but his parents and grandparents were all bays. He has a blaze, but no leg white, much like some of the more minimal sabino roans. DACKE passed his ticking on to a small percentage of his offspring, though it may be that the trait was under-reported. PIRAT has yet been used extensively for breeding, so it remains to be seen how consistently he passes along his ticking.

Blue-Eyed White
In 2009 a white colt named VERY WHITE DU VALLON was born in France. His father was the dark bay Brabant FELIX VAN DE WAAIENBERG and his dam was the bay roan Ardennes MAJESTEE DU VALLON. Neither parent was marked with white, and both came from generations of plain bay or roan ancestors. The most likely explanation is that he is a new dominant white mutation, although recessive dilutions cannot be completely ruled out. Any time a foal is born pink-skinned and blue-eyed there is a possibility that he carries some kind of recessive dilution. This is particularly true in this

case because an unexpected dilute foal, MARINKA VAN'T HEEREINT, was born the previous year in a closely related breed. Unlike MARINKA, though, VERY WHITE DU VALLON does, as his name suggests, appear very white and not cream or taupe. He has also remained blue-eyed and pink-skinned. Unlike double-diluted creams, which retain their pink skin and blue eyes as adults, the newer dilutions like champagne and pearl have skin and eye colors that to darken with age.

If VERY WHITE DU VALLON is a dominant white mutation, the commercial tests would not detect it since each new dominant white mutation is slightly different. He could still be confirmed as a dominant white, but his particularly mutation would have to be specifically identified. Test breeding could also help determine his color, since a dominant white would give either white coats or sabino-type patterns to half their offspring. VERY WHITE DU VALLON was registered, but it is unlikely that he will be used for breeding because white is not among the accepted breed colors in France.

Eye Color

A bay French Ardennes foal with a blaze and blue eyes was born in 2007. There have been suggestions that he was a splashed white. White markings of any kind are unusual among the French horses, and there are no indications that classic splash has

been a part of any of the Belgian and French draft breeds. It would be slightly more plausible for the Swedish Ardennes, where native mares were used for a time, because classic splash is found in both the Gotland Pony and the North Swedish Horse. Without more background information on the foal, and a more complete understanding of the causes behind blue eyes in horses, he remains a mystery.

The white-born colt VERY WHITE DU VALLON also has blue eyes. Dominant white horses sometimes have blue eyes, and can produce dark or blue eyes or a combination of the two.

Markings

White markings are uncommon among the Belgian and French Ardennes, but do occur. Stars are the most common, but blazes are occasionally seen, particularly on chestnuts. White markings on the legs are rarer than white on the face, but some individuals do have white on one or both hind feet.

Swedish Ardennes are much more commonly marked with white. Most do have some amount of white on the face, ranging from stars to broad blazes. Almost a third of the licensed stallions have at least a white foot, but extensive white on the legs is still less common than in many light horse breeds. As with most breeds, chestnut horses are often more extensively marked than bays or blacks.

Belgian Brabant
Belgian Heavy Draft, Brabacon

Origin: Belgium

The Belgian Brabant is one of the oldest and most widespread of the heavy draft breeds. In addition to providing the basis for the American Belgian, there are versions of the breed in many countries, all with different names. In the southern part of Belgium, it is the Cheval de Trait Belge, while in northern Belgium is it the Belgisch Trekpaard. In France it is the Trait du Nord and in the Netherlands it is the Nederland Trekpaard. Along with the Ardennes, the Brabant has often been used to improve the heavy breeds of other countries.

Stud Book
The Brabant stud book was established in 1879. The National Draft Horse Society of Belgium was founded in 1886, although a Ministry of Agriculture committee for improvement of the breed had existed since 1854. The stud book published at that time combined the Ardennes, the Brabant and the Flemish Horse. The last two eventually merged to form the Belgian Draft, while the Ardennes was moved to a separate stud book in 1936.

Some of the incentive for developing a public stud book could be found in the American import tariff policies. Pedigree animals destined for breeding programs were exempted from the tariffs, but for a horse to be considered pedigreed there needed to be a public register. The first two decades of the twentieth century were the golden age of the draft horse. Because America did not have a native heavy breed, horsemen were forced to import suitable stock in order to meet the demand. Foreign breeders needed to be able to supply recorded pedigrees to compete in that market.

The Belgian Draft was widely exported, not just to America but across much of Europe. In some cases, the breed continued in its pure form in the importing country. One of those countries was France, where the breed is called the Trait du Nord. The French stud book was established in 1910. The Dutch Draft is almost entirely derived from the Belgian Draft and looks quite similar. The American Belgian is purely Belgian, although it has evolved quite differently from the Brabant. Even in those countries that did not maintain the breed in its pure form, the Brabant often had a great deal of influence on the breeds that were developed.

Brabants are still accepted for registration in the American Belgian registry. A handful have been imported and registered in recent years. There is also the American Brabant Association which was formed to promote the original Brabant type.

Population
At the turn of the last century, the breed was at the height of its numbers. From 1900 to 1910, an average of 38,000 foals were born and 26,000 horses were exported annually. It is tempting, given the current popularity Belgians enjoy, to imagine that many of these horses were exported to the United States. In fact the majority were sent to Germany;

Summary

Current colors: Bay roan is the most common color, followed by bay and brown. Black, chestnut, blue roan and chestnut roan are uncommon, and grey is rare. Homozygous roans are known to exist in the breed, and many roans are frosty. Recently a dilute black filly was born, but she died before reaching maturity.

Historical Colors: Duns were said to have existed in the breed prior to 1886, though the exact nature of their color is not known. Two white fillies were born in the middle of the twentieth century.

Markings/patterns: Solid or minimally marked horses are most typical, though white marking do occur occasionally on the face and legs. Chestnuts with more extensive white were known to occur in the past.

Eye color: The modern Brabant is dark-eyed. A few individuals with blue eyes were recorded in the past, but the trait is not typical of the breed. The dilute black filly had blue eyes, but it is likely they would have darkened to amber had she lived to adulthood.

of the 26,551 horses exported in 1903, 21,235 were imported by Germans compared to 245 by Americans. American imports did increase sharply after 1905, but they never reached the German levels. France and the Netherlands also imported Belgians by the thousands during this time.

These numbers dropped during World War I when it was estimated that the German army seized as much as 60 percent of the horses in Belgium. But as with most of the heavy horse breeds, the real damage was done by the tractor and the automobile. In 1997 the European Farm Animal Biodiversity Information System reported that the breed had reached a low of 1,500 registered mares and 65 stallions, with an overall population of less than 3,000. Since that time, the breed's numbers have been increasing, with new registrations approaching close to 1,000 annually.

Colors

Color in the Belgian draft horse has been subject to changing fashions over the years. In more recent years, the registry in Belgium has stated the importance of preserving and encouraging the production of all the colors found in the breed. As a result there are representatives of most of the different colors even among stallions.

Roan

For much of the last century, the most common color for Brabants has been dark-headed roan. One of the original foundation stallions, BAYARD (1864), was a chestnut roan. He came from a family of roans that traced back to the blue roan OLD MIN DE LA COZETTE, foaled in 1855. A descendant of BAYARD, ALBION D'HOR (1916), popularized the roan color. ALBION D'HOR was the National Champion stallion in 1923. His sons and grandsons took every national title from 1925 until 1936. Most of those years, his daughters or granddaughters also took the mare title.

ALBION D'HOR was a bay roan, as was his most successful son, AVENIR D'HERSE. Both they and their descendants produced almost exclusively bay roans, despite that fact that AVENIR D'HERSE must have inherited the red gene from his chestnut mother, CARMEN D'HERSE. That is because roan in

The production record of the bay roan COSTAUD DE MARCHE *has be used to refute the theory that homozygous roan is lethal.*

Brabants is linked to the black gene (*E*). This was shown in a 1984 study by Dr. Phillip Sponenberg. Using the production records of a bay roan Brabant stallion crossed on chestnut American Belgian mares, the study showed that roan was consistently inherited with the bay coloring. The foals usually inherited both bay and roan, or chestnut and not-roan. The linkage was not absolute, though. Of the fifty-seven foals, thirty were bay roan and twenty-five were chestnut, but there was a bay an a chestnut roan foal. Although the study only looked at the production record of one bay roan stallion, the distribution of the colors in the Brabant population support the conclusion. Among the current group of approved stallions standing in Belgium, fully half are bay or black roan. Currently 13 percent of the stallions are chestnut, but there are no chestnut roans on the list. The percentages are even more striking in the Netherlands, where 64 percent of the approved stallions are roan, and 15 percent are chestnut. As in Belgium, there are no chestnut roans on the list. This does not reflect a particular bias against chestnut roan; it simply is a rare combination.

The study outlining the linkage to the black-based colors is not the only roan study that focused on the Brabant. That is because such a high incidence of roan is unusual. While roan occurs

The blue roan MILKWOOD TERRY BLUE has the pale mane and tail associated with frosty roan. Silver manes and tails are quite common in bay and black roan Brabants.

in a wide range of breeds, it tends to be rare. The Brabant and the breeds closely related to it offer a chance to examine the production records of a large numbers of roans. It was an analysis of those records that prompted H. F. Hintz and L. D. Van Vleck to suggest that roan was lethal in its homozygous state. That conclusion was based on the ratio of roan to non-roan foals among American Belgians. The authors did note that rare homozygous stallions had been reported. Later both Reiner Geurts and J. K. Wiersema questioned the theory that roan is a homozygous lethal using the Brabant stallions QUARRE, a blue roan, and COSTAUD DE MARCHE, a bay roan, as examples.

Researchers have been puzzled by these conflicting results. There seems to be little doubt that some Brabant stallions are homozygous for roan, but this does not explain the ratios found in the Hintz and Van Vleck study. It is possible that some portion of the roans in the study were misidentified. That is always a possibility when using stud book records rather than living animals. Many American Belgians identified as roan are in fact sabinos with roaning in their coat. That, coupled with base color linkage, might skew the results.

There is also a chance that there is more than one mutation responsible for the roan phenotype. This is particularly interesting in the case of Brabants because roans in the breed sometimes vary

in appearance. The most notable are the frosty roans. Whereas traditional dark-headed roan produces a uniformly light body with dark points, frosty roans often have roaning in the mane and tail. Some frosty roans also have white concentrated along the topline, although that does not seem to be the case with most Brabants.

The other difference is the amount of roaning on the face. It is not unusual to see Brabants with roaning that extends past the cheeks and even along the bridge of the nose. In rare individuals, the entire head can be roaned, leaving just the ears and possibly the area immediately around the eyes dark. The stallion ROB VAN'T KOUTERHOF is a good example of pronounced facial roaning.

Some Brabant roans show dappling. In most instances the dappling is reversed, with darker spots against a paler background. Some photos of the stallions AVENIR D'HERSE and AVARE D'EMPTINNE show them with reverse dappling, though it would appear that such markings are not permanent from year to year. More rarely roan Brabants have light dappling on a dark background similar to a grey. Like the reverse dappling, such variations in coat color appear to be seasonal and temporary.

Bay and Brown
The next most common colors in Brabants are bay and brown. Nineteen of the eighty-four approved stallions in Belgium, or 21 percent, are bay or brown. Most of the roans are also bay or brown, so the incidence of the bay color is even higher than that percentage suggests.

In shade many bay Brabants are quite dark, so it can be difficult to determine which horses are bay and which are brown. Bright and light bays can be found, but are less common than the dark, especially among the stallions. Mealy markings are common, and many bay and brown Brabants have pronounced goggles and muzzle contrast. Often the legs are not fully black, though with the abundant feathering found in the breed it can be difficult to determine if this is from the mealy pattern or the allele for wild bay. Vivid dappling is uncommon, which suggests that most of the horses have an inherently dark shade rather than the sooty mutation.

Chestnut

While chestnut is the color most closely associated with the Belgian in America, in the breed's native country it is far less common. As of 2011, 13 percent of the stallions approved for breeding in Belgium were chestnut. Among those is the 2002 National Champion stallion IGOR VAN GAASBEEK (1998). He has a chestnut son, ZEUS RUPELMONDE, approved for breeding in the Netherlands. Prior to IGOR, a chestnut had not been named Champion since VADROUILLE D'ENÉE won in 1950.

Chestnut was not always an uncommon color in the Brabant. The two most influential sons of OR-ANGE I were the chestnuts BRILLANT (1863) and JUPITER (1880). JUPITER was widely considered the best son of ORANGE I, and from 1894 until 1909 all but three of the male winners in Brussels were his sons or grandsons. His most famous son was the 1898 Champion RÊVE D'OR, who went on to be named Champion over all breeds in Paris in 1900. Photos of RÊVE D'OR were often used to illustrate the breed in the early twentieth century.

A chestnut grandson of JUPITER, GAMBRINUS DU FOSTEAU, was Champion in 1905. He was followed by another chestnut grandson, INDIGÈNE DU FOS-TEAU, the next year. INDIGÈNE DU FOSTEAU held the title from 1906 until 1909. He sired the chestnut INDIGÈNE DE WISBECQ, Champion in 1914. At the time the owners of INDIGÈNE DE WISBECQ turned down an offer of $40,000—an outrageous sum for the time. INDIGÈNE DU FOSTEAU was reported to have been killed along with his owner by German soldiers during the 1914 invasion of Belgium. Atrocities committed during that offensive were used as propaganda to generate American sympathy, and the story of the stallion's death was reported widely in the American agricultural press.

Shortly after the Championship shows resumed in Brussels in 1919, the predominant color of the winners changed from chestnut to brown and then to roan. Chestnuts could still be found, but the color never regained its prominent place among the horses winning top honors. It is far more closely associated by most horsemen with the American version of the breed than with the Brabant.

As for the chestnuts that do remain in the Brabant, in shade they often resemble the darker American Belgians. Their body color tends more towards red than to blonde, though they do have uniformly flaxen points. Mealy chestnuts are found, though they are not as common as ordinary flaxen chestnuts.

Black

Flanders was known as far back as the Roman times for producing massive black horses. The first volume of the American stud book describes the Brabant as the product of crosses between the large Flemish horses with slightly smaller horses of Ardenne. Judging from the large number of black Belgians that were imported into the United States during the formation of the American stud book, it is clear that the black coloring of the Flemish horses was still present despite outcrossing. One manuscript from the early nineteenth century had this to say about color in the Brabant:

> "Though we have horses of every color we reduce them to three principal coats,—the black, the most common; then comes the light and dark bay, and lastly the gray of several shades."

The manuscript is mentioned in an article published in the May 1911 *Breeder's Gazette*. The author, E. Mueleman, notes that there has been a steady decline in the numbers of black horses.

The chestnut BRILLANT *(1868) was the International Champion of Paris in 1878. Today he bears a stronger resemblance to the American type than to the Brabant.*

During that time, black went from being the most common color in the breed to making up less than 3 percent of the entries at the National show in Brussels.

Although it is still one of the less common colors in the breed, black has been making a bit of a comeback. Eight of the stallions approved for breeding in Belgium are black, making up close to 10 percent of the list. In 1997 the black stallion SULTAN VAN WOOLDINK was named National Champion of Belgium. Being black or carrying black is increasingly seen as a selling point in breeding stallions.

Grey

Grey is found only rarely in the modern Brabant. There is one grey stallion, KARLO VAN DE VLAMINGWEG (2000), approved for breeding in Belgium. His sire is the black DORUS VAN DE ZANDSLAGEN. His grey coloring comes from his dam, KARLA VAN DE WIELLEKEN. His approval for breeding increases the chance that grey will remain in the gene pool.

There was a time when the color was found among some of the most successful breeding and show horses in Belgium. The sire of ORANGE I, the stallion to which all modern Belgians trace, was the grey stallion ALFRED, also known as FORTON OF APPELTERRE (1851). ALFRED lived to be twenty-six years old and was an influential sire. Had ORANGE I been grey rather than bay, the frequency of grey in the Belgian breed might have turned out very differently.

Another influential grey was the stallion MERCURE (1882). He was the second stallion to win the title of National Champion of Belgium, and sired close to forty National winners at that show during the late nineteenth century. A majority of the grey Belgians imported to America in the late nineteenth and early twentieth century were descendants of MERCURE, including his grey sons MERCURE II (1899), FORBAN (1894), TUDOR (1889), LATOUR (1888) and TRIBOULET (1896).

The grey stallion BLANQUI was named National Champion in 1893. Two National Champion mares were also grey. The MERCURE daughter BRILLANTE won the title in 1896 and 1897. She was followed in 1898 and 1899 by the grey mare FAUCILLE.

Dilutes

When discussing the decline in certain colors among Belgian drafts in *Types and Breeds of Farm Animals*, Charles Sumner Plumber states that dun had not been recorded in the breed since 1886. Like many of the earliest stud books for draft horses, duns were recorded in small numbers but which specific dilution or dilutions were involved is not known. It is possible that they were not true dilutes at all, but were very pale mealy bays. Even now these colors are occasionally misidentified as buckskin or dun.

In 2008 breeders in the Netherlands were surprised by the birth of a diluted filly, MARINKA VAN'T HEEREIND. She had dusky pink skin, bright blue eyes and a dark taupe-colored coat. Within a few months her skin darkened, though it still did not appear truly black. Her lower legs were chocolate, while her head, mane and tail were a lighter shade of the same color. Her body was significantly paler, which suggests that she may have inherited her mother's roan color. Her eyes remained blue. Unfortunately she died of colic while still a foal, so her adult coloration will never be known.

Shortly after she was born tests were done and it was determined that she was genetically black (*Eeaa*) and that she did not carry cream, pearl or silver. Because her dam CLARA was an unmarked

During the late part of the nineteenth century, many of the National Champions of Belgium were grey. PERCE was bred in Belgium and exported to the United States in 1906.

bay roan from a long line of known roans, questions arose about her sire, the bay Brabant Baron van't Zeegat. He also tested negative for pearl, and was genetically bay (*EeAa*). Whatever color Marinka was, it was a dilution that is not currently identifiable by testing. It may be that she would have continued to darken as she matured, and her eyes develop more pigment. If that were the case, she would likely look a great deal like the diluted black horses found in some of the primitive pony breeds, as well as in the Arabian horse. Her circumstances are also very similar to those of the unidentified dilute Alt-Oldenburg mare, Gaja.

Silver

Because silver is thought to be present in the American Belgian, as well as in some of the other European draft breeds, it is possible that the Brabant once carried the silver dilution. Gerd Eriksson, whose family bred Belgians in Sweden, tells a story of his grandfather being fined by inspectors for falsifying a pedigree when he presented a black colt from two chestnut parents. According to Eriksson, while the Swedish Board of Agriculture might not have known, the breeder's association was aware that two chestnut Belgians occasionally produced unexpected colors. Because red silvers can be mistaken for chestnut, bay or black foals from two chestnut parents raise the possibility that silver is involved. In most of the Swedish cases, one of the parents was registered as *läderfux*, which would now be called red silver. One suspected red silver roan stallion, Willembroux, exported to Sweden from Belgium, has descendants noted as being black with a light mane and tail and dappled brown with a white mane and tail.

It is not known if silver is still present among the Brabants. Silver manes and tails on bays are the usual indicator that silver is present in the gene pool, but frosty roan turns the manes and tails on many Brabants silver. In some individuals where the roaning is less pronounced, either due to seasonal changes or aging, this can give the horse the appearance of being bay with a gray mane and tail. Upon close inspection, the manes on these horses look somewhat different, having a fairly even silver gray color rather than the dark-rooted flaxen appearance of a red silver. Nonetheless, the high frequency of silver manes on Brabants would make it possible for the silver dilution to remain in the breeding population, especially at low levels, without attracting much attention.

Historical Colors

There are two known cases of white-born Brabant foals. The first of these was a filly named Blanche Neige born in 1943. She was pure white with just a spot of black on her eye. Her dam was chestnut and her sire and grandsire were both bay. She was registered in the stud book, but does not appear to have been used for breeding. The second was an unnamed filly born in 1950. She is pictured alongside her solid brown dam in J. K. Wiersema's *Het Paard in Zijn Kleurenrijkdom*, and looks completely white. She was described as having black eyes. The mother came from a line of plain brown horses, and the sire was a roan. It is not known if she was ever registered. Although there is not much information for either filly, the pattern of inheritance for both fits the profile of a dominant white mutation.

Eye Color

The modern Belgian Brabant is a dark-eyed breed, which is not surprising given the fact that most Brabants have only minimal amounts of white. The one oddly diluted Dutch filly Marinka was born with pale blue eyes, though her premature death meant that their final color will never be known. Some dilutes, like pearls and champagnes, are born with blue eyes that darken with age.

It is also clear that something that causes blue eyes was present, at least rarely, among the early Brabant population. Two of the early American imports from Belgium, the stallions Louis 19 and Congo 3672, each had a blue eye. Congo was marked with white, but Louis had only a star along with the blue eye. There are also modern blue-eyed American Belgians born from time to time.

Markings

The majority of modern Brabants are solid or only minimally marked with white. More than three-quarters of the current approved stallions have no leg white and no more facial white than a small star. There are Brabants with a little more white on the face, and even horses with white on the feet, but these are less common. As with many breeds the chestnuts have slightly more white than non-chestnuts, but flashy markings are not typical even among the chestnuts.

There was a time when more extensive white markings were found. The foundation stallion BRILLANT was marked with a blaze and white feet. RÊVE D'OR also had a blaze and socks, and some of his descendants were even more flamboyantly marked. His grandson GAMBRINUS DU FOSTEAU had an extremely broad blaze. His great-grandson INDIGÈNE DE WISBECQ had a bald face and hind stockings. These kinds of white markings became less common over time, though they did continue in the American Belgian.

Black Forest Horse
Schwärzwalder Füchse

Origin: Black Forest of Germany

The Black Forest Horse is closely related to the Noriker, and looks much like a lighter version of that breed. It is best known for its distinctive chocolate coloring and its abundant blonde mane and tail.

Stud Book

The Black Forest Horse dates back to the Middle Ages. A breeding association was formed in 1896. In the late nineteenth and early twentieth century stallions from a variety of heavy breeds were used, including Norikers, Ardennes, Rhenish-Germans and Belgians. Many of those same breeds were used again to rebuild to breed after the Second World War.

Following its revival after the war, the Black Forest Horse reached a second low point in 1973 with only four stallion lines: Deutschritter (D), Mittler (M), Raith-Nero (R) and Wirts-Diamant (W). The last two lines were founded by Norikers. Because inbreeding depression was a real concern, an experimental program was started in 1978 to develop additional sire lines. Initially two Freiberger stallions, HAUENSTEIN and DAYAN, were crossed on Black Forest mares. DAYAN's great-grandson FELDSEE (1994) established the F-line. Another line was added with the Schleswiger stallion VARUS (1980). His great-grandson, VOGTSBERG (1998) established the V-line. Another outcross to Norikers was done in 1992 using the stallion RIFF-VULCAN (1989). In 2002 the stud book was closed, though a few outside stallions have been approved for limited breeding experiments.

Population

The European Farm Animal Biodiversity Information System reports there are 949 mares and 62 stallions. More than a third of the breeding stallions belong to the State Stud at Marbach. The breed is considered endangered by the Society for the Conservation of Old and Endangered Livestock Breeds in Germany (*Gesellschaft zur Erhaltung alter und gefährdeter Haustierrassen e.V.*).

Colors

The color most closely associated with the Black Forest Horse is dark chestnut with a very pale flaxen mane and tail. The name of the breed in its native country, *Füchse*, means fox and refers to the chestnut color. The most common shade is a deep chocolate brown with a nearly white mane and tail. Although that is the most desired color, the coat can vary from a rich red chestnut to almost black. As is usually true for chestnuts, most are not dappled. Pale manes are typical, and are almost uniformly present on the stallions. Mares and geldings sometimes have sooty manes and tails, and some red chestnuts have striking dark gray manes.

The breed has been the focus of studies to determine the cause of the dark body and contrasting mane and tail, though so far there have been no conclusions. Because the body color can be so dark that the horses appear black, and because the manes and tails are light, it is often assumed that the breed is composed of black silvers rather than dark chestnuts. Genetic testing has so far shown

Summary

Current colors: The color most closely associated with the Black Forest Horse is dark, undappled liver chestnut with a pale flaxen mane and tail. Bay, black and grey occur only rarely.

Historical Colors: Roan was present in the early formation of the breed due to use of Ardennes stallions. There were dilute and pinto mares in the early stud books, but the exact type are not known.

Markings/patterns: White markings are common, particularly blazes. White leg markings are also seen, but many have facial white without white on the legs. Flank roaning in seen occasionally. Unmarked horses are unusual, but do occur.

Eye color: Dark eyes are typical, though there have been rare blue-eyed individuals.

Restrictions Stallions that have blue eyes or large belly spots are not accepted for breeding.

Flaxen manes and tails are a distinctive characteristic of the breed. Unlike silver dilutes, which have manes and tails that darken with age, the contrast between the body color does not typically change with age. Pictured is the Noriker RAITH-NERO, founder of the R-line.

all to be genetically chestnut (*ee*) and not black or brown with the silver dilution. Interestingly enough, of those horses tested, almost a third were carrying a rare alternate form of chestnut, referred to by scientists as *e^a*. To date no visible difference has been noted between horses with this form of the red gene, so it does not explain the unusual contrast between the body color and the mane and tail seen in many Black Forest Horses. It does raise interesting questions about the origins of the breed and its relationship to other breeding groups since the alternate allele has not yet been found in the breeds known to have been used in the development of the Black Forest Horse.

The color distribution in the breed gave clues that the horses were dark chestnut rather than silver. The absence of black individuals makes silver less likely. Black silvers would produce a certain number of undiluted black foals. This would particularly be expected when the existing lines were outcrossed to the two Freiberger stallions, since there is no indication that breed has the silver dilution. Even if the Black Forest Horses been uniformly silver, those first generation Freiberger crosses would have been heterozygous. Once there were heterozygous silvers, some portion of their descendants should appear with the black base color, but without the silver dilution.

There would also be the possibility of bay silvers. That would be expected were the breed made up of ordinary red chestnuts and black silvers, since crossing a chestnut with a genetically black horse can produce bay. Bay is a common color in the Freiberger, and the Noriker WIRTS-DIAMANT had numerous bay ancestors.

The absence of blacks and bay silvers is a good argument that the majority of Black Forest Horses are chestnut. It is still possible that silver is present, if not as common as dark chestnut. Heavy selection for chocolate bodies and pale manes and tails would make it likely to survive if it is was present, but to date it has not been confirmed.

Bay
Although the preferred color has always been dark chestnut, at one time bay was more common that it is today. Bay mares made up almost 13 percent of the original mares, and by the end of World War II almost 20 percent of the registered mares were bay. A much smaller portion of the stallions were bay. The last bay stallion to stand in the Black Forest area was the Ardennes CENSOR, who served from 1949 until 1952. The last bay Black Forest stallions were NACHBAR (1955), DIKTATOR (1958), and MUNTER (1961). None served in the Black Forest region, however, so they left no recorded offspring.

Bay did continue through two mare families. The first of these is that of the mare AFRA (1975). AFRA was by the Black Forest stallion MILLIONÄR from a Trakehner mare. AFRA was bred to the Black Forest stallion MORITZ to produce the bay mare ANABELL in 1989. ANABELL left two bay daughters, ARIELLE and DISTEL.

The second bay family traces back to the mare ANGERIA (1958). She was bay, but she came from two chestnut parents, so it is thought that her sire was recorded incorrectly. The bay color continues through her granddaughter ANJA. She produced two bay colts, but neither has been used for breeding. Instead her line continues through her bay daughter, ANETTE (1991) by MORITZ. ANETTE is a bright bay with a blaze and four stockings. She also has the distinctive silvered mane that is seen in some bay coldbloods. It is a trait that can be seen in a number of her descendants.

ANETTE produced three bay daughters, ARIANNA (1999), AMELIE (2000) and ALINA (2001), for her breeder Werner Blattert. With her daughters,

ANETTE won the prestigious award for mare families at the 2004 Rossfest. Since that time, an experimental cross was approved to reinforce the bay coloring. AMELIE was crossed with the bay Welsh Cob stallion UNICORN LANCELOT, and produced the bay colt LEONHARD. It is hoped that through this family, a new sire line carrying the bay coloring will eventually be developed.

Black

To get bay or black, it is necessary to have the dominant form of the Extension gene (*E*), sometimes called the black gene. That is what chestnut horses lack; they have the recessive form of Extension (*e*), sometimes called the red gene. Even though chestnut horses lack the black gene, they still have the Agouti gene, which tells the black pigment where to go. Since a chestnut has no black pigment, the effects are not visible, but the instructions are still there.

That is the explanation for the single black Black Forest Horse in the modern population, the mare ATLANTA (2005). She was born to the mare DISTEL (1998), a granddaughter of the bay AFRA. As a bay, DISTEL could give her daughter the black gene (*E*). She also carried the recessive form of Agouti (*a*), most likely from her dark chestnut sire, DIRK, who was tested to be heterozygous at Agouti (*Aa*). When bred to MODUS, who must also have carried the recessive form of Agouti, the components for

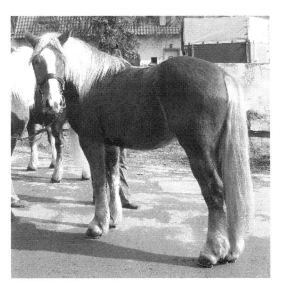

black coloring—one dominant Extension (*E*) and two recessive Agouti (*aa*)—were possible.

Were bay, and therefore the black gene, to become more common in the Black Forest, it is likely that more black foals would be born. In addition to DIRK, the stallions at Marbach tested to carry black (*a*) are DACHSBERG, DIFLOR, DONNERGROLL, MERAN, MODUS, REMUS, REVISOR and RIEMER.

Those are the known carriers, but it is likely that there are more. When the breed was founded, 53 of the 184 original Black Forest mares were black. The numbers were even higher among the Ardennes mares used to breed Black Forest horses. In that group, 89 of the 209 mares were black. Another 38 black mares of unknown origin were also used. There was also a black stallion, AUDAX (1931). The number of black mares had dropped to just over 3 percent by the end of World War II, but the use of black horses during the formative years make it quite likely that many chestnut Black Forest Horses carry black.

Grey

Only one grey line remains in the breed, that of the grey AUDAX daughter, FLORA. Her dam, also named FLORA, was a grey of unknown breeding. FLORA had a grey daughter, FORTUNA (1966), by the chestnut stallion DEISS. FORTUNA then produced two grey daughters, FLORENTINE (1972) and FAMINA (1977).

FLORENTINE was bred to the Freiberger stallion DAYAN and produced the chestnut stallion FREYER. It was FREYER's grandson, FELDSEE, that founded the F-line. FLORENTINE had a grey colt by WIRT, but at the time, preserving the grey coloring had not been given a priority and he was gelded. Although the line to FLORENTINE continues through FELDSEE, the grey color was lost.

The color was maintained in the line from FORTUNA's second grey daughter, FAMINA. When bred to her sister's son FREYER, she produced a grey filly named FLORA in 1985. FLORA produced two grey colts, but like the grey colt from FLORENTINE these

In addition to the dark liver chestnut, there are red chestnut Black Forest Horses. Even though the darker variety could easily be mistaken for silver dapple, so far all the horses have tested to be genetically chestnut.

were gelded. She also had a single grey daughter, FORTUNA, in 2000. FORTUNA, a state premium mare, is the only remaining grey Black Forest Horse still breeding. In 2006 she was bred to the Andalusian stallion HONROSO XIV in hopes of reinforcing the grey coloring and potentially creating a new sire line much like was done with FELDSEE. The breeding did not result in a live foal, but there are plans to repeat the cross.

White Ticking

White hairs on the flanks are not uncommon in Black Forest Horses, and can be quite pronounced in some individuals. The mare GOLDINE, described in detail in the section about eye color, had enough white hairs that she could have been described as a stippled sabino. Others have had the false-roan sabino pattern. The most common form, though, is white ticking on the fold of the stifle or flanks.

Among the current state stallions, FELDSEE has white ticking on his flanks, as well as flashier markings than the average Black Forest, which suggests the roaning may be part of the sabino pattern rather than a separate form of white ticking like rabicano. The fact that FELDSEE is known for

Many descendants of the stallion FELDSEE have white ticking on the flanks and irregular markings. The mare FELI has a blaze and ticking across her flanks and hindquarters, but no leg white. Her foal, JOLLI, has white on her legs and ticking, but much of the white on her face is hidden by an occluding spot.

siring foals with more extensive white markings as well as roaning supports that theory.

One FELDSEE colt, FRIDOLIN, could be classified as an stippled sabino with a pattern quite similar to the one on GOLDINE. He has pronounced white ticking on his undersides and flanks that blends into high hind stockings. He also has a very broad blaze and high front stockings with irregular edges.

Among the false-roan sabino Black Forest Horses is the mare SARAH (1990). She is a daughter of the grey mare FLORA, who is by FELDSEE's grandsire FREYER. As is typical of this kind of pattern, SARAH is evenly roaned throughout her coat. It is not thought that she inherited her mother's grey coloring, though, because the percentage of her white hairs has remained stable over her lifetime. Like many false-roan sabinos, she had solid, unroaned legs and a blaze. Two more mares, the half-sisters HERA and HERBA, have the same kind of fully roaned appearance. They also have dark legs and blazes. Their mother, HEIDI, comes from the same sire line that produced FELDSEE.

Historical Colors

Although flaxen chestnut has always been preferred, horses in the Black Forest region were initially more varied in color; only 56 percent of the Black Forest mares born between 1880 and 1990 were chestnut. When mares from Ardennes and Underbaden are included, the percentage drops to just over 40 percent. Photos taken of horses gathered for evaluations during the post-war period show that this was still true then. By that time, the percentage of chestnuts had risen to 72 percent, but there were still mares registered as black, bay, grey and roan. There was even one recorded as isabelle and one recorded as a pinto, though the exact colors of the two mares are not known.

Among the stallions, unusual colors were far less common. Even so, quality non-chestnut stallions like the blacks AUDAX and TELL and the bay CENSOR were used at stud as late as 1952. Some of these colors have been preserved through the mares, or are the focus of programs to reintroduce them through new sire lines.

Roan

It is likely that many of the horses recorded in the early stud books as *schimmel* were in fact roan. When evaluating the working horses of the region in 1887, a district veterinarian described them as predominantly chestnut roan in color. Use of Belgians and Ardennes to improve the local stock brought more roan horses into the breeding population of the Black Forest.

One of the earliest of these was the red roan Belgian stallion CARTHAGO. He was purchased at the World Exhibition in 1893 and brought to the Black Forest region. His lasting influence came through his son MARQUIS. Although not a roan, MARQUIS was interesting in that he had obvious sabino markings. Although no longer common in the Belgian Brabant population, flashy white markings were found among earlier horses.

MARQUIS came from the neighboring region of Underbaden, where farmers had also formed a co-

operative to improve the native work horses, primarily by outcrossing to Belgians. Another roan stallion, BUFALO-BILL (1929) was used there. One of his chestnut sons, BUNKER, was used in the Black Forest region. His roan son, BUFFO, sired two stallions registered as Black Forest Horses: BRUNOLD and BUSSARD. Neither inherited his roan coloring.

During the late 1940s there were a number of roan Ardennes stallions used. These include the chestnut roan stallions URBAN, KILIAN and KARLOS and the bay roan ECKSTEIN. Another

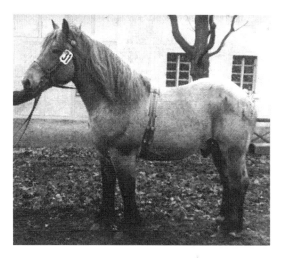

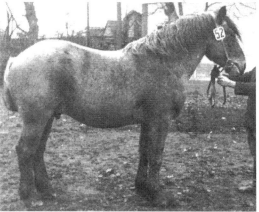

Horses from the nearby Underbaden region were used in the early formation of the Black Forest breed. The roan Underbaden stallions, BUFALO-BILL and his son BUFFO, had Black Forest descendants. The light manes on both horses are most likely due to the frosty roan gene, which is common in both Belgians and Ardennes.

Ardennes, EMIR, was listed simply as *schimmel*. None of these stallions had a lasting impact, and no dark-headed roan Black Forest Horses remain. Unlike bay, black and grey, there are no current plans to reintroduce the roan coloring.

Eye Color

Black Forest Horses typically have dark eyes, but there have been a few blue-eyed individuals. Probably the best known of these was the mare GOLDINE (1946). GOLDINE was named Champion Mare at the first Rossfest in 1949. Rossfest was established to celebrate the Black Forest Horse after the losses of World War II, and that first year more than 300 horses attended.

Like the other blue-eyed Black Forest Horses, GOLDINE had extensive white markings. She was bald-faced with white that completely covered her lower face. The areas around her eyes, which were both blue, were dark. She also had high stockings with roaned edges, and her body had extensive white ticking.

Despite the success of GOLDINE, blue eyes have never been common. In more recent years, they have become unpopular and are thought to be a sign of bad character. Stallions with blue eyes cannot be licensed, but they do occur upon occasion. German photographer Lothar Lenz captured a pair of blue-eyed Black Forest Horses. Both had unusually large amounts of white on the face and legs. Because some Black Forest Horses have broad

GOLDINE, the Champion mare at the first Rossfest in 1949, had two blue eyes and coat extensively stippled with white. Blue eyes are not considered desirable by modern Black Forest Horse breeders.

white face markings, it is not entirely unexpected that blue eyes might occur upon occasion. The exact cause for them has not yet been identified.

Markings

The majority of Black Forest Horses are marked with white. Blazes are particularly common, and many are broad and encompass the upper and lower lip. Occluding spots, particularly located on the forehead are also seen. Solid, unmarked faces can be found, but they are less common than horses with markings.

Leg markings do occur, though they are currently less fashionable than dark legs. Of the twenty-four stallions standing at Marbach, eleven have four dark legs. This is despite the fact that most of the stallions—twenty-one of the twenty-four—have blazes. In most breeds, white on the face and white on the legs are usually found together, but in some lines in the Black Forest Horse, white face markings occur separately from leg markings. In this regard the situation with the black Black Forest Horse is similar to that of the Haflinger, where white blazes are desired but white legs are not.

The stallions that do have white on the legs tend to have fairly moderate markings, and all have at least one dark leg. Tradition in many breeds has been that breeders use a stallion with one or more dark feet to lessen the chance of body spotting. This could be a consideration with Black Forest Horses, since stallions with large areas of white on the belly cannot be licensed for breeding.

There was a time, however, when more extensive white markings were popular. The bald-faced mare GOLDINE has already been discussed. Long before her show ring success there was the influential stallion MARQUIS (1896). He lost his breeding license after losing an eye, but was popular enough with breeders that they pressured the state to return him to stud service a few years later. His male line died out after several generations, but he was an influential sire of broodmares and most modern Black Forest Horses trace back to him in at least one line; many trace back multiple times.

The founder of the M-line, the stallion MILAN (1927), had high white hind stockings that traveled up the front of his stifle. Somewhat later, the Noriker stallion NACHKOMMEN was used. He had four stockings and, like MILAN, his hind stockings extended up the front of his leg. His left foreleg had the dramatic drop in height that is often seen in horses with flashy sabino markings. A similar type of leg marking was found in the on the surviving stallion of the D-line, DIKTATOR (1968). His marking, which was on a hind leg, almost split his leg vertically when viewed from the side, leaving the back of his fetlock dark but trailing up almost to his stifle on the front. Among the current stallions, the white ticked stallion FELDSEE is often credited with siring foals with more than the average amount of white. He also tends to throw a fair number of foals with spots that occlude some portion of their face markings. Sometimes this is subtle, as it is on FELDSEE himself, and the top of the blaze looks scalloped. In other individuals it can erase the top portion of the blaze entirely, or split the blaze into two pieces. Horses with the larger occluding spots can appear to have oddly shaped or placed stars and snips, when in fact a full blaze is hidden beneath one large spot.

High white leg markings are no longer common, and the younger stallions are even more likely to have dark legs. Among those with dark legs, it is not unusual to see pronounced dappling along the cannons and pale hair at the fetlock. Although that look is often associated with the silver mutation, in these horses it appears to go along with whatever factor is darkening the coat.

Flashy white, particularly on the legs, was more common in the early twentieth century. The stallion at the top, MARQUIS (1896) was an influential sire of broodmares. He was of Belgian breeding, which is interesting given how much he resembles a modern American Belgian. The stallion below is the Noriker NACHKOMMEN (1931). Like MARQUIS, he has the lighter build preferred by Black Forest breeders.

Boulonnais

Origin: Boulogne, France

Like the more familiar Percheron, the Boulonnais is a French heavy draft breed descended from heavy chargers that had been further refined by the addition of Arabian blood. It is generally larger and heavier of bone than the Percheron. Once used in agriculture and transporting fish, the breed is now primarily raised for meat production.

Stud Book

Heavy horses have been bred in the Boulogne region since the seventeenth century. In his 1888 book *Les Races de Chevaux de Trait*, H. Valleé de Loncey wrote that the Boulonnais was the most famous of the large draft breeds of France.

Boulonnais were imported in fairly large numbers to the United States during the late nineteenth century. These imports were originally registered—along with Percherons, Bretons and other regional varieties of French draft horses—in the National Register of Norman Horses. The book was published by the National Association of Importers and Breeders of Norman Horses. Formed twenty-six years prior to the French Boulonnais association and seven years before the French Percheron association, the organization was the first American registry established to record draft horses.

Almost as soon as the registry was off the ground, controversy erupted over whether the different French Drafts were separate breeds, or merely regional strains of what was essentially the same breed. Because formal stud books were not yet maintained in the parent country for "common" horses (that is, anything other than "blood" horses), the situation was vague enough that each side could claim to be correct. The battle raged across the editorial pages of livestock magazines like *Wallace's Monthly* and *The Breeder's Gazette*.

Some breeders left to form what would eventually become the Percheron Society of America, while those that remained continued as the National Norman Horse Association. The latter group, which advocated for a unified French draft

stud book, published its first stud book in 1881, then published two more volumes before changing the name to the National Register of French Draft Horses. Eleven more volumes were published before the group dissolved. However accurate the group may have been in its original position, in the thirty years that followed breed differences became more pronounced and separate stud books were established in France. The Percheron became the preeminent draft horse in America for the first half of the twentieth century, while the other French draft breeds remained in France.

It is impossible to now know just how many Boulonnais were imported during the time that the French Draft registry was active. True to their stated belief that the heavy horses of France were all part of the same breed, no breed is given with the stud book entries. Information provided in the first few volumes was absolutely minimal, with just the animal's name, basic color and owner. Because stud books were a recent innovation, the lack of information on the parents was not especially surprising. What is a bit surprising, given the high level of interest in just where in France the horses originated, is that no import information is given either. There are no breeders, no sell-

Summary

Current colors: The majority of Boulonnais are grey, and the breed has a tendency for early and complete greying. Chestnuts are occasionally seen and it is likely that most of the greys are genetically chestnut. A single stallion was used to reintroduce the black color.

Historical Colors: Bay and black were one more common, and at one time roan was present.

Markings/patterns: White markings are common and can be flashy, although it is not clear if individuals have had body markings. Stippled sabinos have occurred. Depigmentation is common and can involve the face extensively.

Eye color: The eyes are dark.

ers and no places given, although some entries do state that sire or dam were "from the Boulonnais tribe." Later volumes did designate those horses already registered in French stud books with a letter after their number: Percherons (P), Boulonnais (B) and Nivernais (N). After the Percherons, the Boulonnais were the most numerous, so it is a reasonable assumption that the breed did contribute to some extent to the North American heavy horse population.

Whatever effect the breed may have had on the early development of draft breeds in the United States, it is now bred almost exclusively in France. The French stud book was established in 1885 and the *Syndicat Hippique Boulonnais* was formed in 1902. In 2009 the French government instituted a recovery plan for the breed that involved the creation of an outcross register, called Book B. Boulonnais mares may be crossed with an Arabian stallion, and the offspring entered into Book B. Horses from Book B may be crossed with horses from the main stud book (Book A). Horses from Book B that have no more than 25 percent Arabian blood and conform strictly to the breed standard can be entered in the main stud book.

Population

Haras Nationaux reported that in 2008, there were 578 mares and 61 stallions in the breed. There were 234 foals recorded in 2007. The Boulonnais is considered critically endangered and has been the focus of a government recovery plan.

Colors

In *The Historie du Cheval Boulonnais* (1883), the breed is described as characteristically grey, but the author also acknowledged that this hampered the breed, particularly when it came to marketing the horses to American purchasers. Grey was a less desired color, one considered difficult to keep clean. This preference for darker colors led breeders to outcross to Flemish horses, which were mostly dark bay. These were the same Flemish horses that were behind the strains of Belgians preferred by American importers a few decades later. By 1911 the breed was described in the *Cyclopedia of American Agriculture* as being "dapple gray, dark iron-

Preserving Genetic Diversity

This nineteenth-century Boulonnais shows the breed's strong visual resemblance to the Percheron. Writers from that era claimed the Percheron was created by crossing the smaller, more active Breton with the heavier Boulonnais.

Even for those who claimed that the Percheron was a distinct breed, there was always the assumption that the two breeds were closely related. This has only recently been called into question. In 2009, an analysis of genetic diversity in the French horses showed that the Boulonnais was genetically distinct from not only the Percheron, but from the other French draft breeds. The results showed a closer relationship between the Percheron, the Comtois and the Norman Cob than to the Boulonnais. Given the genetic distance between the two breeds, it seems unlikely that the Boulonnais played a primary role in the development of the Percheron.

In light of the findings, it was recommended that steps be taken to preserve the Boulonnais, along with the other genetically distinct draft breed, the Poitevin Mulassier. Because the Boulonnais and the Mulassier are significantly different from the other draft breeds, as well as the light and pony breeds, ensuring that their genes are not lost contributes to the overall diversity of the equine population.

gray, black, brown and chestnut." The author went on to say that the grey color had been increasing in recent years, and was now more often seen in the Boulonnais than in the Percheron. This probably reflected the importance of American exports to breeders of Percherons, and the fact that once the French Norman registry dissolved, foreign preferences no longer carried weight with the other French breeds. Boulonnais were more likely to keep their preferred color because market forces in America no longer affected them.

Grey is still the predominant color in modern Boulonnais. Of the sixty-one approved stallions, forty-seven are grey. Most of these are white-grey,

These two stallions show the most common colors of the Boulonnais. At the top is the grey TIMIDE DE L'ECURIE, *and below is the flaxen chestnut* MARECHAL 7.

which is why the breed is sometimes referred to as the White Marble Horse. Dappling is less common and tends to have less contrast than in greys born black or bay, but it does occur. Many Boulonnais grey quickly, and it is not uncommon to see nearly white weanlings.

The vast majority of the greys are genetically chestnut, which is the second-most common color. Twelve of the current approved stallions are chestnut, and it is estimated that 12 percent of the mares are this color. Most are red chestnut and flaxen manes and tails are common. A few are quite dark, almost liver in color, like the stallion ROYAL DE TOURVILLE (2005). One chestnut stallion, BALISTO BP (1989) is dark enough to appear black in some photos. On the other end of the spectrum, a few mares exhibit the dusty, dappled form of light chestnut seen in other draft breeds. Although these extremes can be found, medium to dark red is the more typical shade.

Black

Black was recently reintroduced through the stallion ARTABAN (1988). His color came from the black mare MINA. She was not a registered Boulonnais, but was entered into the breeding program as a *trait d'origine inconnue*, or draft horse of unknown origin. ARTABAN sired the black stallion ESOPE, who was approved for breeding in 1996. In the years that have followed, ESOPE has been shown under harness at many of the largest exhibitions in France, bringing attention both to his unusual color and his rare breed. At first he was paired with two white-grey mares FROU-FROU and FANNIE, but later all-black teams were assembled using his descendants. One of his sons, the black stallion MAH JONG D'ABBECOURT, was approved for breeding in 2003. The registry estimates there are ten black Boulonnais as of 2011.

Sabino

Because many Boulonnais are marked with blazes, white chins and stockings, it can be assumed that the flashy white form of sabino is present. This is especially true for individuals like TOLBIAC PETIT AUTIER (2007), who have white stockings with ragged white edges extending up the stifle. To date

In the eighteenth century, black was a common color in the breed, and has recently been reintroduced with the stallion ESOPE.

none have appeared with prominent body spotting, but this could be due to selection rather than genetic limitations.

There has been at least one Boulonnais born with the stippled version of the sabino pattern. That is the gelding RUBI BRIMEUSOIS, foaled in 2005 and registered as *alezan mélange*, which means chestnut with mixed hairs. (Roan is *rouan* and chestnut roans is *aubère*.) RUBI is marked with a broad blaze with irregular edges and high stockings. Extensive white ticking cover his undersides, concentrating between his forelegs and his groin. The edges of his hind stockings blend into the roaning between his hind legs, giving him the undersides-covered-in-snow look that is characteristic of this kind of sabino.

The pattern on RUBI was not typical, but other chestnut Boulonnais have shown ticked roaning on either their stifle fold or between their legs. The pale dappled chestnut mare UNION DES TILLEULS has very noticeable flank roaning along with her sabino markings. The young stallion SESAME 3 (2006) is another horse that has pronounced ticking, in his case on the fold of the stifle and between his forelegs. SESAME is marked with a blaze and white chin, but has solid legs. His sire, NOICHOC (2001), had roaning on the fold of his stifle as well. This kind of patterning, whether it is genetically separate or just a variation of the same mutation that produces flashy sabinos, would be fairly easy

to hide in a breed that has such a high percentage of greys. For that reason it may be more common that it appears based on the visible examples.

Historical Colors

At the time the French draft breeds were being formalized, the Boulonnais was already a predominantly grey breed. This was not always the case, however. A census of stallions conducted in 1778 by the National Stud indicated that the predominant colors were black and dark bay. Less than a hundred years later grey was seen as proof of refined blood. The French hippologist Eugene Gayot, Director of the State Stud in France, wrote:

> "Towards the end of the eighteenth century, attempts were made to lighten this breed, by crossing it with Barbs and Arabs, which were plentiful in the Government studs. In this way, the black or bay colour of the Boulonnais became changed into roan or grey, which tints have been transmitted to and fixed in all French cart horses, owing to a prejudice it is difficult to explain."

Arabian and Barb crosses did not influence the size of the Boulonnais over the long term, since the breed was widely considered the heaviest of the French breeds by the late nineteenth century, but the grey coloring remained. Eventually dark colors came to be seen as proof of foreign Flemish blood, which was associated with coarseness.

Despite this prejudice, black and bay were still found in the early twentieth century. This can be seen in the National Register of French Draft Horses, which began noting those imports that were already registered with one of the French breed societies in the eighth volume of its stud book. Of the 179 registered Boulonnais recorded in the eighth volume of the stud book, 99 were black and 24 were bay. The majority of imported Boulonnais remained black until Volume 11, published in 1912. At that point only a handful of purebred Boulonnais were imported and almost all were grey. It is probable that the color of the imports was less a representation of the breed than it was a reflection of what the American market demanded. French breeders might have feared that breeding dark colors led to coarseness, but it also led to increased sales of exports. As the Percheron crowded out the other French breeds as the import of choice, the Boulonnais breeders had less incentive to breed for black instead of gray.

Roan

Writers in the late nineteenth century sometimes described the breed as being grey or red roan (*rouan vineux*). It is likely that most of the horses identified as roan were chestnuts turning grey, but some photos suggest that there may have been a few dark-headed chestnut roans.

A number of the Boulonnais imported to the United States and registered with the National Register of French Draft Horses were recorded as roan. One stallion was listed as blue roan, which was a term rarely used for anything but a dark-headed roan. That was UKASE D'ESTRUVAL, foaled in 1898 and imported to the United States in 1900. In that same volume of the stud book three Boulonnais stallions, SULTAN, UGOLIN and MAGENTA, were recorded as red roan. Two volumes later, there was the chestnut roan stallion CAVOUR. A few were listed as gray roan, but most were registered simply as roan. It is quite possible that some of these, particularly the gray roans, were in fact greys.

Eye Color

Despite the prevalence of extensive white markings, Boulonnais appear to have uniformly dark eyes. It is possible that this has been strongly controlled by selection, since the majority of male Boulonnais—by some estimates close to 95 percent—are destined for slaughter. In breeds not used for meat production, horses with undesirable color traits can still be found in private, non-breeding homes or even with smaller breeders, but routine access to the slaughter house makes culling for cosmetic faults like blue eyes more likely.

Markings

Most Boulonnais are marked with white. Blazes are extremely common, as are white marks on the lower lip or chin. Leg white is found on many horses, though the exact nature is often hard to determine with a breed that turns grey so early. Minimally marked horses are also found, especially among the black horses. The original black horse, ESOPE, is marked with a blaze and hind socks, but his offspring often have far less white.

Many of the grey Boulonnais lose pigment, and the facial depigmentation can be quite pronounced. More than a third of the approved stallions that are grey have extensively mottled skin. In some, like the stallions CELESTE (1990), IDEAL 3 (1996), and LICQUOS (1999), the face appears almost entirely pink-skinned. Although depigmentation in greys is often associated with age, in Boulonnais it is present even in relatively young horses. The heavily depigmented RIVALDO is only six years old. The exact nature of this kind of pigment loss is not known, though it is often found in breeds where the majority of the horses are grey, and seems particularly common in those breeds selected for early and complete greying. It is also interesting because it could so easily mask the presence of patterning mutations like leopard complex and dominant white. It seems unlikely that a French draft breed might carry the first, but dominant white is a mutation that is possible in any breed.

Breton

Origin: Brittany

Although the Percheron is the best known of the French draft breeds, the Breton is actually more numerous in its home country. It is bred in two types, the Heavy Draft and the lighter, more active Postier.

Stud Book

The *Syndicat des Éleveurs de Cheval Breton* established a stud book for the breed in 1909. At that time two different books were published, one for the Heavy type and one for the Postier, or lighter draft, type. In 1912 the books were combined, but the two types were registered in separate sections. In 1926 the sections were combined. In 1951 the stud books were formally closed to outside blood. In 1982 the decision was made to suspend requirement that Bretons be born in the region of Bretagne. This type of restriction, sometimes referred to as restricting a breed to the "cradle of the race" used to be a common requirement in French stud books, but has since fallen out of favor. In 1993 the books were reopened to new foundation stock through an inspection scheme. Since that time outcrosses have been made to French Trotters to strengthen the Postier type.

Population

Haras Nationaux reported that in 2008, there were 6,995 mares and 716 stallions in the breed. In 2007, there were 4,043 foals registered. The Breton is also popular in Brazil, with over 2,500 horses registered between 1989 and 2009. On average 65 purebred foals are born in Brazil each year.

Colors

The French stud book restricts the breed to the following colors: chestnut, bay, roan, black, brown and chocolate. Among these, chestnut is favored and is by far the most common. Among the stallions approved for breeding in France, 93 percent are chestnut. In shade the chestnuts tend to be dark, although some dusty chestnuts can be found. Red chestnuts are common, particularly those with flaxen manes and tails. Very dark chestnuts are especially popular, with some individuals so deeply pigmented that they could easily be mistaken for black. Chestnuts with dark points, called *tostado* in Spanish, can be found and in some cases show gray or almost black shading on their heels.

Roan is the second-most common color. A little over 4 percent of the approved stallions are chestnut roan. Bay roan horses occur, but are quite rare because bay is rare. Black roan would be possible, though none have occurred in recent times. This is most likely because black is even rarer than bay. Quite a few chestnut roan Bretons could be mistaken for black roans because the base color is so dark.

The body color on roan Bretons is often quite pale and it is not unusual to see the roaning extend to the cheeks. In rare cases, the face is completely roaned, though the legs remain dark and retain the characteristic V-shaped points on the front legs. The stallion TITAN DE QUEROU (2007) is roaned in

Summary

Current colors: The French registry accepts chestnut, bay, roan, black, brown and chocolate. Chestnut is the favored color, followed by chestnut roan. Bay and brown are rare, and black rarer still. Silvers are rare, and it is possible that some portion of the chestnuts carry silver.

Historical Colors: At one time grey was the predominant color, but it is now associated with undesirable outcrossing to Percherons.

Markings/patterns: Sabino markings of the flashy white variety are common. White ticking on the fold of the stifle and roaning in the coat are seen in some individuals.

Eye color: At least two colts have been born with blue or partially blue eyes, but they are the exception in what is an otherwise dark-eyed breed.

Restrictions: The French stud book recently ruled that horses with excessive white were not eligible for inclusion in the stud book. The Brazilian registry does not permit greys, albinos or pintos.

this way, with his head the same color as his body; only his ears, legs and tail have remained dark chestnut.

Black-based Colors

Because the majority of Bretons are chestnut, the gene for producing the black-based colors (bay, brown and black) is rare. Although chestnuts are recessive at Extension (*ee*) and cannot produce black pigment, the instructions for where black pigment should go are still present at Agouti. In

These two roan stallions were used to illustrate the differences between the Postier (top) and the Heavy Draft (bottom) in 1904. The modern Postier more closely resembles the bottom horse, while the modern heavy Breton is considerably heavier.

the case of chestnut Bretons, most are carrying the dominant form of Agouti, which is bay (*A*).

Currently there are nineteen bay stallions in France. Most trace their color through the female line, since bay stallions have been even more uncommon in the past. A few, like the Postier stallion NOUGAYORK DE COAT MAN (2001), get their color from an outcross. In the case of NOUGAYORK, it was a cross to the bay French Trotter, TRITON DU RANCH. The bay stallion SISCO DU CHAPEL (2006) carries a cross to the bay Thoroughbred stallion OUR ACCOUNT.

Brown and black are less common. Most brown or black Bretons trace back to the bay mare MIMIE (1978). She was by the chestnut Breton stallion URFOL and out of a PYRENEENNE, a bay draft mare of unknown origin. She had a brown daughter, ARDENTE, who in turn produced the brown stallion HERCULE (1995). HERCULE is the sire of ROCK AND ROLL, the only approved black stallion in France, and two of the three approved brown stallions. There is also a black stallion in Brazil. JUPITER SFB (2004) was the Brazilian Reserve Champion Young Horse in 2008. Unlike ROCK AND ROLL, who has socks and a blaze, JUPITER SFB is solid black.

There is at least one case of a stallion registered as bay born to chestnut parents. ESPOIR (1992), registered as *bai clair*, is by the chestnut stallion PEDERNEC and out of the chestnut mare J'Y RESTE. Two chestnut parents cannot produce a bay foal, so in those instances either the foal or one of the parents has been misidentified. ESPOIR is also unusual in that while he has been used extensively at stud, siring 137 recorded foals, only 19 have been bay. Because the bay color is dominant to chestnut, the portion of bays should be closer to half. It may be that the basic colors on some of the horses involved may have been misidentified red silvers, Another possible explanation is that the very dark shade and the sooty shading on the lower legs of some chestnuts can make it surprisingly difficult to identify the base color on some Bretons. That might explain the registration errors.

Silver

Because both dark chestnut and flaxen manes and tails are common, there are quite a few Bretons that look like black silvers. It is unlikely that most of them actually are, since the necessary black base color is so rare. Were most of the horses silver, rather than liver chestnut, bay and black would appear more often.

There is little doubt, though, that silver is present in the Breton. A harnessed pair of dark red silver Postiers from the National Stud at Tarbes are pictured in Elwyn Hartley Edwards' *Encyclopedia of the Horse*. Obvious red silvers can also be seen in some of the promotional material from the *Syndicat*. It is likely that most are registered as chestnut. It is also possible that the silver dilution is carried by an unknown number of chestnuts. With so few black-based horses, it is impossible to know what the incidence of silver might be in the population without testing for it.

Sabino
The markings on many Bretons suggest that the breed has the flashy white sabino pattern. Body spotting is not typical, and a recent ruling by the French breed society restricting white from the body will likely ensure that the pattern stays minimal. Although the genetic mechanisms for the different sabino patterns are not yet understood, as a general rule limiting the amount of white reduces the chances of producing a more obvious pinto.

White Ticking
White ticking on the fold of the stifle is seen on some Bretons, and the edges of some leg markings are irregular, but the overall impression is one of clear white markings rather than indistinct, roaned ones. Some Bretons do have roan hairs in their coats, though they do not have a roan parent and are not true roans.

One stallion, JOYEUX DE LA CHAUFTAI (1997), has enough roaning that he is entered in the stud book as a chestnut rabicano. He is not a true roan, since both his parents are chestnuts. His grandsire, NONVAOU (1979), is also registered as a rabicano. Without photos it is hard to know what caused his roaning, though many sabino-marked Bretons have white ticking to some degree. The designation of rabicano appears to have been more common in

The grey stallion, CADOUDAL, took first prize at the 1904 Concours Hippique in Paris. His image was used to illustrate the breed in Matthew Horace Hayes book Points of the Horse.

the past, though it is hard to know whether roaning in the coat was more common then, or more pronounced on the individual horses, or whether breeders were just more likely to report it.

Historical Colors
Grey was once common in Bretons. A correspondent for *The Farmer's Magazine*, writing of the Paris Agricultural Exhibition in June 1860, describes the eighty-six Bretons on display there as "generally of an iron-grey colour." In 1888, in response to a request from the Illinois Board of Agriculture, the Director of Agriculture in France sent a clarification regarding the different breeds of draft horses found in France. He describes the Breton as grey in color, though sometimes roan and seldom bay. This assessment is repeated in *Points of the Horse* (1904), where Matthew Horace Hayes writes that Bretons are usually grey, but can occasionally be found in bay or roan. Black is noted as occurring only rarely. Chestnut, the most typical color of the modern Breton, is not mentioned by either author. However common grey might have been at the beginning of the twentieth century, it appears to have been lost sometime during the post-war period. It is now associated with the time when Percherons were used for crossbreeding, and is perceived negatively. In Brazil grey is specifically banned, though it would appear that the only

chance to get the color would be through an out-cross, which would be unlikely to get approval in the first place.

Eye Color

Although many modern Bretons have sabino markings, the vast majority are dark-eyed. This may be because the type of sabino found in the breed, flashy white, is not associated with a high incidence of blue eyes. That is not to say that blue eyes do not occur, however. The stallion NIQUEL SFB (2008) has two partially blue eyes. NIQUEL SFB was the National Champion young stallion in Brazil in 2010. A French colt, UNEK, was born the same year with a blue eye. Both horses are red chestnut with blazes and white legs.

Markings

Many Bretons have flashy white markings. Broad blazes and three or four white socks or stockings are common among the successful show horses. The hind stockings on many horses have points that extend up the stifle, but it is rare to see white any higher on the leg. Horses with blazes and little or no leg white can be found, and are a little more common than horses with leg white and solid or minimally marked faces. Completely solid Bretons can be found, especially among the bays and blacks, but some amount of white on the face and legs is more typical.

Although flashy white markings have been popular in the recent past, steps are being taken to limit the spread of white in the breed. There is no question that Bretons have gotten significantly flashier over time, and that similar trends in other breeds have eventually led to a rise in horses that could be considered pinto-patterned. To prevent this, the current standard published by the *Syndicat des Éleveurs de Cheval Breton* states that horses should not have excessive white markings. Excessive was specifically defined in 2011 to mean white outside the head and limbs. Limits were also placed on the amount of white allowed over the hocks and knees, and around the mouth, but discretion was given to inspectors to evaluate the amount of white on the horse as a whole.

Clydesdale

Origin: Scotland

The Clydesdale was developed in the eighteenth century by crossing local mares with larger Flemish stallions. It was later improved with outcrosses to the Shire, and the two breeds remain similar in appearance.

Stud Book

The Clydesdale Horse Society was formed in 1877. The first studbook, a retrospective volume listing stallions foaled prior to 1875, was published a year later. It contained information that had been gathered from show catalogues, advertisements and stud cards. The book formed the record for what was considered Clydesdale blood.

The American registry was established in 1879, two years after the parent society in Scotland. The first American stud book was published in 1882. Horses imported from Great Britain were admitted as well as those "recognized as Clydesdales", but later volumes required all imported animals to be registered with the Scottish stud book.

In the Scottish stud book, horses were registered based on a minimum amount of recognized Clydesdale blood. In the second volume, which contained 461 mares and 338 stallions, mares were required to have a sire registered in the retrospective volume. Stallions had to have a registered sire and a dam by a registered sire. Horses born after the publication of the second volume (1879) were required to have a registered sire and dam, but older animals continued to be registered with the required number of crosses, and the prefaces to many of the early stud books noted that the rules for entry had not always been strictly enforced.

Within a very short time after the first books were published, controversy arose over the use of Shire blood through the female line. Falsification of pedigrees was common, and many of the early volumes contain notations that this or that horse (and all his descendants) had been struck from the records. Debates about the stud book and the conditions for entry were common enough that a book collecting them, *History of the Clydesdale Horse,* was published in 1884. Some breeders felt the Clydesdale and Shire stud books should be combined. The idea was rejected by Shire breeders, but in the formative years of the two breeds, proposals for some type of merger came up from time to time. None gained widespread support.

Although they did not constitute a majority, there were breeders in favor of selective outcrossing to Shires. In 1883, a competing registry called the Select Clydesdale Horse Society of Scotland was formed. Instead of entry based on blood purity, horses were eligible if they had won a prize in a draft horse class in Scotland. This was not accepted by the editors of the *Breeder's Gazette,* who warned American importers that papers from the new registry were worthless because pedigree did not factor into admission. Individual merit was

Summary

Current colors: Bay, brown and black sabino predominate, with rare chestnuts. Many bays have gray or flaxen manes and tails.

Historical Colors: There were horses registered as dun, cream and mouse in the early stud books. Dark-headed roan is suspected. Greys were present until the early twentieth century.

Markings/patterns: Modern Clydesdales are uniformly sabino and often have body spotting. Roaning is typical and is sometimes extensive. Both types of splash-like patterns—white-faced and white-dipped—are found, but it is not clear if classic splash is present. At one time unmarked and minimally marked Clydesdales were found, but in the modern population it is unusual to find a horse with a dark leg.

Eye color: Most Clydesdales have dark eyes, but a blue eyes are seen upon occasion and are not penalized.

Restrictions: Greys were briefly banned by the American registry in the late nineteenth century, but the rule was overturned before it was fully implemented.

not considered an acceptable standard if the horses were impure because they might not breed true. In 1890 the Treasury Department ruled that only purebred animals could be imported duty free, and two years later the American registry was able to get the Select Society removed from the list of accepted stud books.

The Canadian stud book for Clydesdales was first published in 1886. Although the American registry came first, Canada had a much older tradition of importing draft horses from Scotland, and for a time American breeders seeking to increase the size of their draft animals imported horses bred in Canada. American importers eventually switched to the Percheron, and sometime later to the Belgian, but in Canada the Clydesdale was the favored heavy breed.

The Clydesdale was also exported in large numbers to Australia in the early twentieth century. The first stud book for Australian Draught Horses, with separate divisions for Clydesdales, Shires and Suffolks, was published in 1907. The Australian Clydesdale Society was established in 1917, and took over publishing the stud book shortly afterwards.

Population

The Clydesdale Horse Society estimates that there are currently 700 mares and 100 stallions

Many Clydesdales show pronounced dappling, which is somewhat unusual among sabino patterned horses.

in the United Kingdom. The American stud book registers 600 foals annually. The American Livestock Breeds Conservancy estimates the global population around 5,000 and has the breed on its Watch List.

Colors

Dark colors have always been preferred by Clydesdale breeders, so dark bay, brown and black are traditional. Among those, bay is by far the most common, accounting for close to three-quarters of all horses registered in the American stud book. In shade most tend be darker. Lighter shades of bay can be found, but they are less common. The mealy pattern seen in some European draft horses does not appear to be part of the modern Clydesdale gene pool.

It seems likely that some Clydesdales are brown (A^t), though determining whether a horse is brown or just a very dark bay can be difficult without genetic testing. Brown was a more common stud book designation in the early part of the twentieth century, accounting for 10 percent of entries as opposed to just 3 percent now. This may reflect a greater use of the term brown by breeders of that time, though, and not necessarily a change in the color of the animals.

Dappling is common on bays and browns. The Clydesdale is one of the few breeds where dappling is specifically mentioned as a desirable trait in early breed literature. The "Characteristic Features and Points of the Breed", published in the first volume of the Scottish stud book, states that a deep, dark brown is preferred "all the more so if dappled." Early stud book entries often mention dappling on bay and brown horses, and a report from an American agricultural representative in Scotland during the late nineteenth century noted that presence of dapples was "almost universal."

After bay, the most frequent color seen is black. Black Clydesdales—indeed black draft horses of any kind—have long been popular in the United States. The color hit its peak in the 1940s, but the numbers fell somewhat after the draft horse market crashed in the 1950s. Since that time the color has steadily increased, although it still lags behind bay in terms of numbers.

Color Percentages in the American Clydesdale

	bay	black	sabino roan	brown	chestnut
1940-1949	281	107	53	49	2
(percentage)	57%	22%	11%	10%	<1%
1950-1959	152	51	39	32	0
(percentage)	55%	19%	14%	12%	0%
1960-1969	282	62	103	57	4
(percentage)	56%	12%	20%	11%	1%
1970-1979	833	137	220	115	14
(percentage)	63%	10%	17%	9%	1%
1980-1989	2281	434	477	181	20
(percentage)	67%	13%	14%	5%	1%
1990-1999	3912	809	528	142	41
(percentage)	72%	15%	10%	3%	<1%
2000-2010	4375	985	463	192	43
(percentage)	72%	16%	8%	3%	1%

Chart 9. Color percentages of Clydesdales registered in the American stud books from 1940 until 2010.

Chestnut

Chestnut is rare in Clydesdales, but it does occur. It is not a favored color, though it was never formally penalized in the same way that it was in the Shire; the registries simply note that the color is rare. In the American stud books, the color has remained consistent at close to 1 percent of the population.

Because many bay Clydesdales have flaxen manes and tails, and because white markings often hide the color of the points, it can be difficult to confirm that a horse is chestnut unless the mane and tail are red rather than flaxen. The three-time National Champion mare, CIE BILLIE (1980), is a good example of a Clydesdale that could be mistaken for chestnut. She was registered as a bay, but had a flaxen mane and tail. For that reason it may be that, even with such low numbers, chestnut is over-reported and is in fact even more rare.

Sabino

While the base colors vary, the breed is uniformly sabino patterned. The presence of white on the face, legs and body are part of what makes the Clydesdale immediately identifiable among the draft breeds. Early Scottish breeders believed white markings to be an indicator of purity.

There is no question that this fact cost the breed in terms of popularity during the American draft horse boom. In *The Horse Book: A Practical Treatise on the American Horse Breeding Industry as Allied to the Farm*, J. H. S. Johnstone wrote about the feelings many American breeders had regarding white markings:

> "Endless controversy has raged regarding the origin of the white markings on the Clydesdale and Shire. That they are deeply ingrained in these breeds must be conceded and that the British breeders seem to favor them admits of no doubt. This is decidedly unfortunate so far as the American trade is concerned, and not only the North American but the South American trade as well. It would serve no good purpose to enter into the merits of this controversy. The fact remains that the white seems to be on the increase and so far as this country is concerned this is all the more to be regretted. If the breeders of Britain desire to cater to the trade of the people of the United States they should breed more whole-colored horses. There is no doubt of this. We do not like them all splashed up with white, head, legs and belly."

Later he expanded on this thought. He was speaking at that point about the Shire, but he could just have easily been speaking of the Clydesdale.

The stallion CHARNOCK, *registered as dark sorrel, was named the Reserve Grand Champion at the 1912 International Livestock Exposition in Chicago.*

"Again why so many of the winners should have such splotches of white upon them is something which the American mind can not discern. White markings not only persist, but tend to spread from generation to generation and they are spreading. It does not seem to make much difference in England whether America wants a whole-colored horse or not. No spirit of cooperation in this regard has been manifested and the Shire interest in this country shows the effects of it."

The author was in a good position to understand the preferences of American importers, working as the assistant editor of *The Breeder's Gazette*. *The Breeder's Gazette* was a weekly newspaper published during the late nineteenth and early twentieth century devoted to agriculture, and its editors were widely regarded as experts on issues involving livestock. Johnstone made this statement while at the same time declaring that these same horses possessed "straightness and trueness of action at the trot" that was unsurpassed. Apparently that quality did not outweigh the desire many had for unmarked horses, because the popularity of the Clydesdale and Shire did not approach that of the other more conservatively-marked breeds.

This did not seem to deter Clydesdale breeders, who were unwilling to reduce the white in order to increase their export market. The desired look was a blaze, often called a *ratch*, and four white feet. Although creating obvious pintos was not the original intention, that was the result. Sabino is not well understood, but one thing that is clear is that breeding sabinos to sabinos increases the chance for white on the body. More than any other form of white spotting, the pattern of inheritance resembles the mixing of paint: breeding flashy parents together gives whiter offspring. As a result, the average amount of white has increased in every country where Clydesdales are bred, relative to what was typical a hundred years ago.

Part of this may be because there is more than one pattern involved. Sabino currently serves as a catch-all term for what is likely a number of different patterns. Until the different genetic mechanisms that produce sabino spotting are formally identified, it is impossible to know exactly which patterns are present, but the additive nature of the white does suggest that there is more than one factor involved.

Indeed, Clydesdales can be found in almost every visual variety of the sabino patterns except the unbalanced and the false-roan. Those two patterns are largely defined by the absence of white in areas that are traditionally white in other sabinos, so it is possible that whatever causes them could be masked by the presence of other patterns.

The desired pattern among many breeders is the more moderate form of flashy white; that is, four white socks and a blaze. But even among the horses with this type of pattern, there less of a tendency for the white to travel along the leading edge of the leg towards the stifle—the typical peaked stockings of a flashy white—than it is for the leg white to spread back across the gaskin, giving the stocking a squared-off appearance at the top.

It may be that these horses, while they resemble flashy white sabinos, are really just more minimal versions of the patchy or white-dipped patterns. Those particular forms of sabino patterning are far more likely to spread up over the gaskins and upward towards the hindquarters. Many Clydesdales have this type of patterning, where the placement of the white on the body seems skewed towards the hindquarters rather than the belly and girth. It is not unusual to see Clydesdales with what looks like a slash of white extending almost to their topline.

The prevalence of flaxen and silvered tails among bay sabino Clydesdales is visible in this class of young mares. Note also that their hind stockings have square tops rather than the more typical sabino point.

Other Clydesdales display the ragged pattern, though it is less common than the flashy white, patchy and white-dipped patterns. Because irregular patches of white on the legs are common among ragged sabinos, these are the Clydesdales most likely to have a dark foot. In some horses, the leg can appear almost completely white with just a dark patch on the lower leg or near the hoof. Clydesdales with this type of pattern often have white flecking on the withers and shoulders. This can link up with patches near the girth to give the horse a banded appearance.

There is also a wide variety of sabino roans. At one time roan was considered undesirable by many breeders. The first volume of the Scottish stud book states that while roans are occasionally seen, their color should be regarded as evidence of the "stain of impure blood." Although early breeders did not distinguish between true roans and sabino roans, perhaps the author had true roan—a color closely associated with other European heavy horses—in mind. Modern Clydesdales registered as roan are

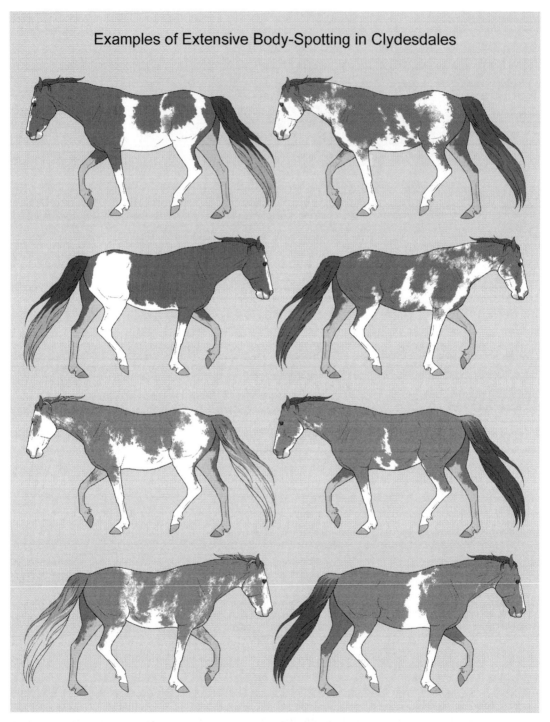

Examples of Extensive Body-Spotting in Clydesdales

Figure 15. These are four examples, showing both left and right sides, of Clydesdales with extensive body spotting. The horse in the upper left corner was also registered as a North American Spotted Draft, though as these pictures show many Clydesdales could qualify with registries that require visible pinto patterning.

clearly sabino roans. The famous American sire FAIRHOLME FOOTPRINT (1913) is a good example of a sabino registered as roan. His entry in the stud book reads "blue roan, four white legs, white on near hip, white stripe in face." His more recent relative, BARDRILL FOOTPRINT (1970), was very similar in color and was also registered as roan.

Eventually the dislike of roans was set aside and sabinos registered as roan went on to show ring success. FAIRHOLM FOOTPRINT was named Grand Champion at the 1916 Chicago International, which was the most prestigious draft show in America at the time. His sire, DUNURE FOOTPRINT, another heavily roaned black sabino, was one of the most popular sires of his era. During their day, both horses were widely held up as examples of good breeding. This helped remove whatever stigma the color had in the past.

Today many young horse lovers were first introduced to this particular color variation by the very attractive black sabino roan mare used to illustrate the breed in Dorling Kindersley's popular *Ultimate Horse Book*. Instead of sabino roan raising questions about the purity of the horse, the color has joined white-trimmed bay as the image many people have of the breed.

Sabino-1 and White
Although the patterns on many sabino roan Clydesdales resemble those of horses with the sabino-1 mutation, to date none have tested positive. It had been puzzling that white-born foals were relatively rare in Clydesdales compared to Tennessee Walking Horses, another breed where sabino roan was common. The first three volumes of the Walking Horse stud books document close to two hundred white-born horses. The absence of sabino-1, which produces white-born foals in its homozygous form, is the best explanation for the rarity of all-white Clydesdales.

There are anecdotal stories of rare white Clydesdales, though whether these were all truly white or very pale roans is not known. Jeanette Gower's book *Horse Color Explained* has a photo of a pure white Clydesdale foal alongside his flashy white sabino mother. The photo is dated 1933, but the horses are not identified by name.

Very pale sabino roans like this mare could be mistaken for white or even grey

There have also been sabino roans that were so pale as to seem white. One of these was the American stallion ANDALE FROSTY (1982). His stud book entry read "roan with broad white stripe, some color around eyes, legs and feet white, many white areas on body." In appearance his roan areas were so pale that he looked like a white horse with a dark mane and dark areas around his eyes. His son, FROSTY'S SILVER LINING, was even closer to white, although he did have some areas of dark skin as well as some darker hairs. SILVER LINING's stud book entry read "white with roan ears, mane around eyes and over hips." ANDALE FROSTY also had a daughter, GENTLE SILVER ROSE, registered as grey and white. Of his eight remaining foals, all but one were registered as roan, and all had white on the body.

More recently the mare GLENCAIRN ACRES JENNIFER (2004) was registered as "light or white roan." She is not truly white, as there are roan hairs scattered throughout her coat, but she is unusually pale. Both her eyes are dark, and there is dark skin visible under the roaned areas of her face.

Flaxen
While chestnut Clydesdales typically have red or partially red manes and tails, many bay or brown Clydesdales have flaxen manes and tails. This tendency has led to speculation that the breed might carry the silver dilution, but that seems unlikely. Flaxen manes and tails are widespread, and black base colors are common enough that were the silver dilution present, black silvers (which are often

easier to identify than bay silvers) would be expected. To date no Clydesdales have tested positive for the silver dilution.

It is more likely that the flaxen manes and tails are in some way linked to the sabino patterns. Lighter points, particularly lighter tails, have been observed in sabinos in other breeds. This is particularly true of ragged sabinos and sabino roans. Some sabinos retain this trait well into maturity, while others lose it with age. Among Clydesdales, paler manes and tails appear to be more consistently retained.

The appearance of the manes and tails does vary. Some horses have manes and tails that are truly blonde, or blonde with dark roots. Others have mixed manes and tails that are more silver than blonde. Among sabino roans, flaxen or mixed manes and tails are common regardless of base

Many Clydesdales with splash-like patterns retain color around dark eyes. It seems likely that these are sabino patterns that visually similar to splashed white.

color. With spotted sabinos, the trait is more often seen on bays or browns, though some black horses have it as well.

Splashed White

The three distinctive traits associated with splashed white are fairly common among Clydesdales. These are blue eyes, a wholly white face, and white that splashes upward from the legs and underside of the horse. What makes Clydesdales unusual, and raises questions about whether classic splash (*SW1*) is truly present, is that those three traits are not always found together on the same horse. That is, the Clydesdales with splash-like body patterns are not necessarily the ones with blue eyes or wholly-white faces. In other breeds where splashed white is known to be present, like the Gotland Pony and the Icelandic, those three traits are consistently paired in obviously patterned individuals.

The prevalence of the sabino patterns complicates the situation, since they can mimic aspects of splashed white. In breeds without sabino, heterozygous splash horses do not typically display unusual amounts of white. It is when homozygous horses are born that the presence of the pattern becomes obvious. When sabino is present, the differenced between heterozygous and homozygous splashes are not as pronounced.

There are breeds like the Welsh Mountain Pony with both sabino and splashed white, and there the classic expression of homozygous splash can still be found. To date, that specific pattern has not be observed by this author in the Clydesdale. That could be because classic splash (*SW1*) is missing, or so rare that a homozygote has not yet appeared, or because the kinds of white patterning interact differently with splashed white. Hopefully advances in the identification of the different white patterns will eventually answer the question.

Historical Colors

The basic colors present in the Clydesdale have not changed dramatically since the founding of the stud book. Bay, brown and black were prevalent then, just as they are among the present population. The biggest difference is that, with the exception of chestnut, those colors that were rare or at least uncommon then have been lost over time.

Dun

In the late nineteenth century, Clydesdales were sometimes crossed with the Highland Pony to give crofters a more substantial pony, but that was more economical to keep than a full-sized draft horse. Some of these partbreds, like the stallion MOSS CROP (1898) and the mare DUN POLLY (1902), went on to have considerable influence in the Highland Pony. It is perhaps not surprising then that a number of dun horses made their way into the early Clydesdale stud books. In the time before public stud books, the lines between different local breeds were often vague.

It should be stressed that the actual color of these horses cannot be known. In the United Kingdom, the term dun is used to describe both cream and dun dilutes. Dorsal stripes are not mentioned in the descriptions, though that may be a reflection of how color was reported within the breed, rather than the absence of the trait. As a general rule, the older the stud book, the less descriptive the entries. The fact that dun was present among the local horses, and that there were significantly more dun entries among the Clydesdales than the neighboring Shires, suggests that the horses may have been dun rather than cream.

Certainly there are entries that seem likely to have been dun. One of these was the mare JIP OF REDHOUSE (1871), registered as "mouse colour", which is the term used in the United Kingdom for grulla. She was said to have a white spot on her face and black legs. Her sire was the dark brown SCOTTISH CHIEF, and her dam was recorded as "light bay." She was registered along with her daughter ROSE OF HILLHEAD (1881), also registered as "light bay."

Others are less clear, such as the stallion recorded as "yellow bay" in the Retrospective Volume of the British Stud Book. That was POPE 593, alias YOUNG POPE, foaled in 1858. He was sired by POPE and out of a prize-winning mare by the stallion SUPERIOR 836. SUPERIOR was believed to have been a duplicate register for the stallion GLANCER 338. As SUPERIOR, the stallion's coloring was not record-

ed, but GLANCER is listed as "light bay." Whether either horse was actually diluted is open to question, but the term "yellow" would be unusual for describing even the lightest bay horse. POPE was Highly Commended at the Highland Society Show in 1868 and was a premium stallion in both 1868 and 1869. Although this predated the stud book, a number of his offspring were later registered. Aside from a few recorded as light bay, there is no indication that any were unusually colored. If POPE really was a dun, or some other diluted color, he failed to pass the coloring to his descendants.

That was not true for the stallion MIDDLETON LADDIE (1881). The entry for Laddie describes him as light dun with white hind legs, a spot of white on his foreleg and a blaze. His sire, YOUNG LOTHIAN PRINCE, was a bay, but his dam Nance was also registered as light dun. MIDDLETON LADDIE sired at least one light dun foal before being exported to Canada.

In the third volume of the Scottish stud book there is the dun mare, JESS 659 (1862). She was sired by SOVEREIGN 814, who was dark brown. No information on her dam was provided. JESS had a dun daughter, POLLY 846, by PRINCE DAVID 643, foaled in 1877. She also had a son, MARKSMAN, registered as light bay.

In the seventh volume of the Scottish stud book there was KATE OF MACHRIHANISH (1872), registered as dun. She was listed along with her daughter MALL OF MACHRIHANISH (1879), a yellow bay, and an unnamed dun colt. KATE OF MACHRIHANISH was later exported to Canada, and is also entered in that stud book as dun. She was by the stallion LORD CLYDE and out of the unregistered mare KATE.

MALL OF MACHRIHANISH was also exported to Canada and produced POLLY MCLATCHIE, registered as light bay. She in turn produced the stallion SANDY in 1886. Whether these were duns, or creams or actually light bays is not known.

NELL OF GILLESPIE (1873) is another mare registered as dun with dun offspring. Her two dun daughters BET (1880) and TIBBIE (1881) were registered along with her. Although NELL's dam is not recorded in the Scottish stud book, an extended pedigree of her bay daughter MARY EDITH gives the dam of NELL as DUN MAGGIE OF GILLESPIE.

In the eighth volume of the Scottish stud book, there is a single mare registered as dun. That is DAISY OF LUMLEY FARM (1869). Her sire was the bay CHRYSTAL'S SCOTCHMAN 4698 and her dam was the unregistered DUMPY by the brown DAINTY DAVIE 211. She was registered with two of her daughters, both bay. Since her dam's color was not recorded, and there are no further records of her maternal ancestors, it is likely that if she was correctly registered as a dilute, the color came from DUMPY.

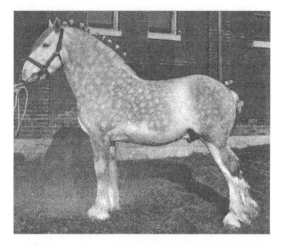

The stallion SCOTS GREY was part of an experimental program at the University of Iowa, administered by the Department of Agriculture, to create an American draft breed using grey Clydesdales and Shires. The mare, PEARLS REFINER, was a purebred Clydesdale produced by the program. Her photograph appeared in the American Clydesdale stud book.

There are a number of entries like this, where a mare is listed as dun or cream, but there is too little information available to determine if the horse was diluted, and if so which specific dilution was involved. Without indications that the horse had pale-colored relatives, it remains possible that the color was recorded in error. Solitary entries like this include:

DARROCH	f.1869	Dun
NANCY OF CRAIGENMUIR	f.1862	Dun bay
DARLING OF CULMORE	f.1873	Dun
NANCY 1651	f.1874	Dun, mark on face
NELL 1536	f.1875	Cream bay
MEG OF BLELOCH	f.1878	Dun, chestnut mane and tail
FOREST LADY	f.1888	Cream bay

Dun stud book entries do not persist past the turn of the last century. Few were exported, and the color was lost as the two Scottish breeds became more distinct from one another.

Grey
The number of grey Clydesdales had already been reduced prior to the formation of the stud book. That was because of a 1827 ruling by the Highland and Agricultural Society that Clydesdales competing for the premiums offered at their shows must be "black, bay or brown bay." In response to the rule, James Frame, one of the influential breeders at the time, made an example of gelding every grey colt born; many other breeders followed suit. The first stud book noted the obsolescence of the rule, pointing out that since 1848 grey stallions had taken top honors at Highland Society shows.

One of those stallions was GREY COMET (1849), winner of the top prize in 1856. He was described as a "handsome, well-built horse, of a dapple grey colour" and it was noted that his descendants were in great demand. That was undoubtedly true, since he appears quite frequently in the pedigrees of horses recorded in the early volumes of the stud books. He had at least two grey sons in Scotland, IRON COMET (1866) and YOUNG COMET (1865).

Another grey son, also called YOUNG COMET (1860), was exported to America.

The other influential grey stallion was MERRY TOM (1848). Like GREY COMET, MERRY TOM was a big winner at Highland Society shows in the middle of the nineteenth century. He was said to have been the best looking, but worst breeding, stallion to have won at the Highland shows. It is perhaps not surprising, then, that he left fewer foals than GREY COMET.

Around that same time, the first Clydesdale exported to Canada was GREY CLYDE (1837). An engraving of the stallion shows him to be a vivid dapple grey with white points. He was used extensively at stud and can be found in the female line of many of the early Canadian and American Clydesdales. Another influential export from that era was the grey stallion GLENELG (1839).

However successful horses like GREY COMET and MERRY TOM might have been, and however willing Canadians might have been to import greys, another shift in attitude towards the grey color was clearly underway. Looking at stud book records, it appears that many breeders were still gelding grey colts. Although Highland Society color rules were no longer enforced, owners were reluctant to send their mares to a stallion of an unfashionable color. Of the stallions listed in the first volume of the Scottish stud book, less than 3 percent were grey.

In the American and Canadian stud books, the numbers were even smaller. In 1893 the American registry passed a resolution to bar "white and grey" horses born after 1895 from registration. The rule was never implemented and was formally rescinded in 1900, but the color remained unpopular with breeders.

In 1907 a project was undertaken by the University of Iowa to develop a uniquely American draft breed based on Clydesdale and Shire blood. Because grey draft geldings were in demand, that was chosen as the color for the new breed. Eight grey horses were imported from Great Britain. Three were Clydesdales: the stallion KUROKI (1903) and the mares GREY PEARL (1902) and ROSE OF BROWNFIELD (1899). Grey could still be found, if only rarely, among some mare families, so most

The stallion FAIRHOLM FOOTPRINT *was registered as blue roan, but was a black sabino roan. Clydesdales with extensive roaning are often registered as roan, though true roan is not found in the breed.*

grey Clydesdales inherited their coloring through the female line. GREY PEARL was the exception in that her color came from PEARL OYSTER, a grey stallion owned by the Marquis of Londonderry. KUROKI was replaced as the lead sire by another grey Clydesdale, SCOTS GREY, in 1912. A third grey stallion, GREY PEARL (1910), was imported shortly afterwards. He was closely related to the original mare of the same name.

Because the program was essentially one of crossbreeding, the University of Iowa project did not produce many purebred Clydesdales. The purebreds were registered, and those were among the last greys in the American stud book. The proposed breed never got off the ground, doomed by the growing popularity of the Percheron. Not only was the Percheron grey, it had the moderate feathering that American buyers preferred. It also enjoyed the cache of being a pure breed at a time when quality was closely linked to purity of blood.

The last Clydesdale registered as grey in the American stud book was the mare CRAIGIE'S RHODA OF CLYDEHOLME, foaled in 1942. Her dam, DOLLY GREY, also produced the Canadian stallion CLYDEHOLME SILVER, registered as grey. Neither horse has any recorded offspring.

Roan

The first volume of the Scottish stud books states that while an "occasional roan is met." There is some evidence that a few of these early roans may have been true, dark-headed roans. Where horses are registered simply as roan, it is not possible to know whether they were sabinos or true roans. In some cases they may have even been grey, just as some of the horses registered as grey (particularly those listed as iron grey) may have been sabino or even roan. Later entries that detail the markings are more helpful, since those horses listed as having white legs and faces were most likely sabino roans.

It is the handful of horses registered as roan with stars and dark legs, or dark points, that suggest true roan may have once been present. These include:

MALL OF URAS	f.1872	Roan, black points
SPOT 11	f.1873	Roan, small white spot on face, white hind foot
AUNT SALLY	f.1875	Roan, black legs
VIOLET 1513	f.1880	Roan, dark points
MARY G.	f.1880	Roan, black points
STRATHERRICK	f.1881	Roan, small white spot on face, black points
MINNIE OF HILLSDALE	f.1881	Red roan, black points

The mare SPOT 11 produced the stallion STRATH-ERRICK. She was registered with an unnamed roan filly. Her entry also indicates that she took fourth prize at the Aberdeen Highland Society show. The foal entry of STRATHERRICK is even more specific, and describes him as having a small star and "black feet."

The mare MARY G. had no known roan ancestors, but hers was a top-cross pedigree so the colors of the mares, including her unregistered dam, were not known. She had two roan foals, the stallion GOODFELLOW and the mare FANCY BESS. Both had white blazes and hind feet, so it is not clear if they were true roans with white markings, which could be expected were a roan to be bred to a sabino, or if MARY G. was incorrectly described.

If any of the dark-pointed roans were true roans, the color did not continue past the first few vol-

Irregular white face markings caused by overlapping dark patches are seen on some Clydesdales.

umes of the Scottish and Canadian stud books. Sabino roan was preserved, being so closely linked to the flashy white markings that were considered to be proof of pure breeding but true roan, if it was once present, was lost.

Eye Color

While the majority of Clydesdales have dark eyes, blue eyes are not uncommon. In older judging manuals and agricultural publications it is possible to find blue eyes referred to as "Clydesdale eyes." Compared to the other common breeds of that era, blue eyes were seen more often among the Clydesdales. And while horsemen have historically viewed blue eyes as a fault, breeders of Clydesdales appear to have been less concerned about them, just as they were less concerned about extensive white markings.

Blue-eyed horses are entered and even pictured in the earliest stud books, but comparing photographs of horses to their stud book entries, it is clear that blue eyes were under-reported. This is unfortunate, since the breed could provide insight into inheritance patterns of blue eyes, particularly as they relate to the various white patterning mutations, if detailed records on eye color had been kept.

There is no clear pattern to the incidence of blue eyes, nor does it appear that Clydesdales with blue eyes consistently pass them on to their offspring. Unlike other breeds where a variety of white patterning is found, there do not seem to be families specifically associated with a high frequency of blue eyes.

Markings

White on the face and legs has always been a hallmark of the Clydesdale breed. Because the breed is uniformly sabino, most individuals have at least a blaze. In many cases the white covers one or both nostrils, the lips and the chin. On more extensively marked horses, the white can extend under the jaw and even up the cheeks. Dark occluding spots are often seen, and when they cover large areas of face the horse is said to be badger-faced. Full white faces are occasionally seen, though often such horses have some color lining the eyes, or dark spots on the muzzle. Even among the most extensively marked faces, the ears remain dark.

White legs are typical. Even more than face markings, the amount of white on the legs has become, on average, more extensive in modern times. Whereas in the early stud books it was possible to find horses with one or more dark legs, that would be difficult to do with the present population. The modern Scottish registry states that white markings are characteristic of the breed and that it is the exception to see a Clydesdale without a white face or "considerable white" on the legs. Those horses with a dark foot often have irregular white patches elsewhere on the same leg. White on all four legs is more typical, and it is not unusual to find markings on the hind legs that extend onto the hindquarters. Stockings that end on the hind legs often have a squared-off top, rather than the pointed top at the stifle that is often seen on flashy sabinos in other breeds.

Face and leg markings often have irregular, ragged or roaned outlines. In sabino roans markings often blend into the body color, making their precise outline difficult to discern.

Comtois

Origin: Jura Mountains of France

The Comtois is a descendant of the old Burgundian horses brought to France by the Germans. Though the breed was crossed with Percherons and Boulonnais in the nineteenth century, it is believed that they are little changed from their original appearance. The breed is the second-most common draft breed in France, after the Breton.

Stud Book

The *Syndicat du Cheval Comtois* was established in 1919, and the first stud book was published in 1921. Because the breed was nearly lost in the late nineteenth century, smaller Ardennes stallions were used to expand the gene pool. The stud book was closed to outside blood in 1936. Presently there is a grading up process that allows draft mares of unknown backgrounds to be used with purebred stallions.

Population

Haras Nationaux reported that in 2008, there were 8,248 mares and 1,012 stallions in the breed. In 2007, there were 4,644 foals registered.

Colors

The vast majority of Comtois are bay silver. The preferred shade is a warm red bay with a nearly white mane and tail. Darker body colors and mixed flaxen and gray manes and tails are found, but overall the shade of red silver is remarkably consistent from horse to horse.

The color is so closely associated with the breed in France that for many years bay silver was recorded in the stud book as "Comtois chestnut" (*alezan comtois*). Now most are registered as bay with a flaxen mane and tail (*bai crins laves*), chestnut with a flaxen mane and tail (*alezan crins laves*), or even just chestnut (*alezan*). There is growing awareness, however, that most Comtois are genetically bay with the silver dilution.

The silver dilution can be traced to the influence of one stallion, QUESTEUR, born in 1938. QUESTEUR is registered as chestnut, though whether he

was a chestnut carrying silver or a red silver himself is not known. His sire, JONGLEUR (1931), was also registered as a chestnut. JONGLEUR was sired by DONKE, one of the Ardennes stallions used to rebuild the breed. DONKE was described as chestnut with a flaxen mane and tail, so it is possible that the silver mutation, which is occasionally found in the Belgian as well, came from him. The dam of JONGLEUR is not recorded so that leaves her open as a possible source for the dilution as well. Likewise, the color of QUESTEUR's dam COCOTTE is not recorded, but her Comtois sire CLERVAL was bay. Whatever the source of his color, it is apparent that QUESTEUR is responsible for changing the breed from bay to red silver.

Chestnut

True chestnuts, almost always with flaxen manes and tails, are also found, though they are far less common than the red silvers. Although they do occur and can be registered, red chestnut with self-colored manes and tails are considered undesirable.

Many red silver Comtois appear chestnut at first glance because they often have very little contrast between their legs and their body color. There are a number of reasons for this. In addition to turning the mane and tail pale flaxen, silver dilutes black to

Summary

Current colors: Clear red silver is the most common, followed by brown or black silver, bay and flaxen chestnut. Pale or mealy colors, red chestnut and dappling are all considered undesirable. The preference is for bright manes and tails.

Historical Colors: Bay was once the predominant color, but is now rare.

Markings/patterns: Small amounts of white on the face are considered acceptable. Blazes, skin depigmentation and white on the legs are undesirable.

Eye color: The eyes are dark.

Champion mare MICKA 2 has the pale taupe legs that cause many Comtois to appear chestnut. The group of colts below her also look like flaxen chestnuts, but are red silvers with very pale taupe legs.

a shade somewhere between warm black and pale taupe. In the Comtois, it tends to run towards the lighter shades rather than the dark. The feathering on the heels—an area that tends to be pale on silvers—also adds the overall impression of lighter rather than darker legs. It is also likely that, due to the influence of the Ardennes, some Comtois are wild bay, and so already have less black pigment on the legs.

Comtois that appear liver chestnut (*alezan foncé*) are most often dark bay or brown horses with the silver dilution. This type of red silver is far less common than the red bay version, but it is considered an acceptable shade.

Bay

Bays without the silver dilution are found only rarely. This was the original color of the Comtois, and is considered acceptable, though it is much less common. These horses are sometimes called *bai crins noir*, or bay with a black mane and tail. Among the bay stallions are JIVAGO (1997), NESTOR 348 (2001), ORAGE DE BEAUBIER (2002), QUINTET (2004), SACHA DU MOULIN (2006), SAFRAN DES MONTANTS (2006), and TOPGUEN DU VAUDEY (2007). Although most of the bay Comtois have solid black legs, a few appear to be wild bays. The presence of wild bay in the breed would not be surprising, given the influence of the Ardennes. It also could explain why the legs on many bay silver Comtois do not show much contrast.

Bay is more common among the mares. There are also mealy bays among the mares, but the pale undersides (called *ventre de biche*) associated with the mealy coloring are considered undesirable.

Black Silver

Some Comtois are dark enough that they may be black silvers, rather than brown silvers. Usually these horses are registered as *alezan brûlé*, which is considered an acceptable, though less common, coloring.

Among the current stallions most likely to be black silver are OSCAR and OBLOGRI. Both are a uniform chocolate color with a pale mane and tail. Pronounced dapples, which are desirable in many of the other breeds with black silvers, are considered a fault in the Comtois. Dappling does occur, most often in the paler, taupe-toned silvers, but both the pale color and the dapples are considered undesirable.

Historical Colors

The formal stud book for the Comtois was established in 1919, but the breed was mentioned in veterinary texts as early 1820. Nineteenth-century writers most often describe the breed as bay or brown, though some mention the presence of roan or grey. Since Percherons were widely used to improve neighboring draft breeds during that time, it would not be surprising if there were grey Comtois, just as there were once grey Bretons. It does not appear that the color remained after the founding of the stud book. At that time, the initial stallions were small, minimally marked bay

Although there is not a lot of contrast between the body color and the legs, the mottling on the front of the cannon bones on this stallion are a good indicator that he is a red silver rather than a chestnut.

Ardennes. As a result, most of the original population was bay.

Eye Color

There is no evidence that there are Comtois with light or blue eyes. The minimal nature of their white markings makes it unlikely that the patterns known to produce blue eyes are found in the gene pool.

Markings

The preference is for no more white than a small star, but a moderate amount of white on the face is permissible. Stars, comets and snips are all common. In most cases they are small, but some individuals can be found with larger versions of those markings. Blazes do occur, but are undesirable. Most Comtois have solid, unmarked legs. Leg white is extremely rare and is considered a fault.

Comtois are occasionally found with facial depigmentation. Like excessive white markings it is counted as a fault in the show ring, though none of the marking faults bar horses from registration.

Gypsy Horses
Gypsy Cob, Coloured Cob, Tinker

Origin: United Kingdom and Ireland

The Gypsy Horse is often described as a small Shire with a colored coat. Until relatively recently it was a landrace found primarily in Britain and Ireland, though more recently efforts have been made towards standardizing the type into a recognized breed.

Stud Book

As a landrace the Gypsy Horse has not had a formal stud book. It is still bred this way in many parts of the world. In some cases the specific crosses are known, but for most Gypsy Horses only the most recent generations are known by name. It is thought that most trace back to Shires, Clydesdales, and Dales Ponies, along with native colored horses and ponies.

In the United States, where the horses have become extremely popular, a number of organizations have formed in recent years. Most have open stud books, though the procedures for entering foundation stock varies.

The oldest of these is the Gypsy Vanner Horse Society, established in 1996. The stud book is open to new horses that are passed by the Registration Committee at evaluations held in different parts of the country.

The next is the Gypsy Cob and Drum Horse Association, founded in 2002. It maintains a stud book for both Gypsy Cobs and for Drum Horses, which are defined as a cross between Gypsy Cobs and Shires, Clydesdales, Friesians or some combination of those breeds. Drum Horses may not be purebred Gypsy Cobs, but they do have to maintain a minimum of one-eighth Gypsy blood. Drum Horses are also required to reach at minimum of 16 hands by their fifth birthday.

The Gypsy Horse Association was founded in 2008. The organization recognizes the registration status of horses with the other Gypsy organizations, and also accepts previously unregistered horses based on the approval of the Registration Review Committee. This is done by a review of photographs and paperwork, including import records. Drum Horses are those horses that have between 25 percent and 75 percent Gypsy blood, with the remainder of the pedigree coming from the Sire, Clydesdale or Friesian.

There is not a stud book specifically for Gypsy Cobs in the United Kingdom. Pinto patterned Gypsies can be registered with the Coloured Horse and Pony Society (CHAPS) or in the British Skewbald and Piebald Association (BSPA). Both societies classify horses by type, with Gypsy Horses typically classed as Traditional Cobs or, for larger horses built for harness work, as Vanners. Gypsy Horses with appaloosa patterns that stand 14.2 hh or less can be registered with the British Spotted Pony Society (BSpPS), which recognizes Traditional Cobs as a native breed and therefore an acceptable outcross. The British Spotted Pony Society also maintains a Supplementary Appendix for pintaloosas, but they are not eligible for the main register.

Summary

Colors: Black is the most common base color, though bay, brown and chestnut are also found. Grey and roan are less common. The cream, pearl, dun and silver dilutions are rare.

Markings/patterns: Most are tobianos or toveros. Sabino without tobiano is less common but can be found. Sabino-1 is rare. Some kind of splashed white is suspected. Leopard complex and pattern-1 (leopard) are present, and are sometimes seen in combination with one or more of the pinto patterns. Irregular markings and bald faces are common. Minimal markings and truly solid horses are rare.

Eye color: The eyes can be dark, or blue, or any combination of the two. Gypsies with the pearl dilution are born with blue eyes that darken to amber or green.

Restrictions: The Norwegian registry bans "albinos." The German standard notes that neither albino or frame overo is found.

In Ireland there is the Irish Cob Society, founded in 1996. The Irish Cob Society accepts unrecorded horses that conform to the Irish Cob breed standard into the Supplementary Register. Offspring from the horses in the Supplementary Register are eligible for the main stud book. Outcrossing is permitted using Shire, Clydesdale and Welsh Cob mares, provided the individuals are judged to be suitable by the registry. The Irish Cob Society is recognized by the European Union as the stud book of origin for Irish Cobs, which is one of the names used for Gypsy Horses in Europe. The more common name, however, is Tinker, which the Irish society insists was a term used for a type that included horses not considered true Irish Cobs. It is their position that the Irish Cob and the Tinker are separate breeds.

As a result, some of the European countries have two associations and two stud books for Gypsy Horses: one affiliated with the Irish Cob Society, and an unaffiliated registry for Tinkers. Usually the Tinker stud books recognize horses from the various Irish Cob books, so it is possible to find Gypsy Horses that are registered with both organizations. American breeders do not use the terms Irish Cob or Tinker, and so do not differentiate between the two groups.

Population

Because so much of the Gypsy Cob population in the British Isles could still quite fairly be called a landrace, and because many imported horses in

America (the biggest importing country for the breed) are registered in multiple organizations, it is almost impossible to get an accurate population number. Those that live in Britain and Ireland will say that Gypsies are to be found everywhere, and certainly this author was struck by the prevalence of hairy, black tobiano horses along the roadside when traveling through rural England and Wales in 1995. In the United States, it is estimated that there are around 2,200 Gypsy Horses, though some breeders contend that the number is much higher, and that numbers have been manipulated to make the horses seem more rare. Part of the difficulty in getting accurate population numbers is the practice of renaming horses with each change of ownership, which is common not only among Gypsies, but American breeders as well. This means a single horse might be entered in several registries under different names.

Some European registries do provide the total number of horses registered, which given the relatively young age of the organizations, can give some sense of the Gypsy Horse population in those countries. The Swedish Tinker Horse Society (STS), formed in 1998, has approximately 1,100 horses registered. The Dutch Studbook for Tinkers (NsVt), founded in 1999, has registered over 1,500 horses. The Norwegian Tinker Association, formed in 2002, and has approximately 500 horses registered. The number of unregistered Tinkers and Irish Cobs would likely push those numbers higher.

Colors

For many, the colors and patterns found within the Gypsy Horse population are part of the attraction, and color often receives more attention from breeders of Gypsy Horses than from breeders of the other heavy breeds. In most countries, the stud books specifically state that all colors are accepted. Color testing is widely utilized by Gypsy breeders, which allows colors to be definitively confirmed. There is a fairly high level of understanding of coat color genetics in the Gypsy Horse community, which leads to more accurate stud book records.

The traditional, and most common, base color for Gypsy Horses is black, followed by bay and brown. Chestnut is somewhat less common. Bays, browns and chestnuts tend to be fully pigmented, though rare mealies are also seen. One of prominent studs in the United Kingdom, Vines, had a filly, OCTAVIA, that was a wild bay with a pronounced mealy pattern.

It is unusual to see a Gypsy Horse that is just black, bay, brown or chestnut. Typically these colors occur with at least one of the patterning genes, and often there are multiple patterns. Modifiers to the basic colors have also become popular in recent years, particularly the dilutions.

Grey

Dapple grey is a popular, but relatively rare, color among Gypsies. The black base color so common in the breed tends to produce dramatic dapple greys, which is very appealing even if the color is only temporary. Such horses are often called blue, which can be confusing since blue is also used to mean black horses that are sabino roan and even traditional roan. Grey in Gypsy Horses is often paired with tobiano and some form of sabino. This can make some horses, particularly those that grey out fairly evenly, hard to identify.

One popular grey Gypsy Horse is GREYSON. He was sired by the Dales Pony GREY BOBBIE (1966), who traces his grey coloring back to TEESDALE COMET by the Welsh Cob YOUNG COMET. In addition to his coloring, GREYSON is known for his action at the trot, which probably came from the Welsh Cob. A homozygous grey son, BLUE STEELE, was recently exported to the United States. The grey tobiano mare, SILVER BELLE, also traces back to GREY BOBBIE through her dam CANDY.

There are other grey lines, many of which trace back to horses of unknown backgrounds. It is possible that many of the grey Gypsy Horses trace back to native ponies, particularly Dales. The winning grey Dales stallion DARTDALE GREY BOBBIE II, a GREY BOBBIE grandson, is currently being used to produce traditional coloured cobs. It is

also possible that Fell Ponies, which are a slightly smaller version of the Dales, were used.

Roan

While many Gypsy Horses are roaned, true dark-headed roans are rare. There is an Elite graded bay roan stallion in the Netherlands. ICOR (2006) is a true roan with a blaze and hind stockings, so he likely carries the flashy sabino pattern as well as roan. The roan color comes from his dam, FLAME VAN DE BONTE PARELS. FLAME was a dark chestnut roan with a star and hind socks. In addition to

A Different Kind of Record

Although many Gypsy Horses exported from the United Kingdom have no recorded ancestry, breeders have begun compiling a different kind of record by creating a worldwide database of DNA profiles. In this way, relationships between horses can be determined even where no formal record exists.

This is essential information for breeders, especially those focusing on rare colors. Knowing whether or not two horses come from the same source helps to control inbreeding and maintain diversity. Although still in the early stages, a number of previously unknown parent-child and sibling relationships have already been confirmed.

At the same time, the worldwide Gypsy Horse community has embraced color testing to an extent rarely seen in other breeds. It is not uncommon to see both mares and stallions with a full panel of color tests published in advertisements. Aside from giving breeders better tools to get the results they desire, this practice makes the Gypsy Horse an invaluable resource for those interested in color genetics.

This is a different kind of historical record than those traditionally maintained by livestock registries. While unorthodox, it has the advantage of eliminating much of the human error—and occasional deceit—found in pedigree records.

ICOR, she has a dark chestnut roan daughter that was exported to Australia.

At least one true roan stallion is standing in the United States. That is the blue roan BLACKJACK, imported from SD Farms in the United Kingdom and standing at Desert Jewel Gypsy Horses. BLACKJACK is a solid, marked with only a star. There are a number of solid black roan mares at SD Farms, including SD MAGGIE and SD MISTY.

There is a single bay roan tobiano stallion in Denmark. MAX VON DE KUILENWEG (2007) is rated premium. He has a solid, unmarked face and a minimal tobiano pattern.

Cream

The desirable cream colors, palomino and buckskin, are more difficult to find in the Gypsy population because black is common. Cream primarily dilutes red pigment, so black horses do not show the effect of the gene, or at least do not show it strongly. The colors are popular, though, and are showing up more frequently among Gypsies. Often the source of the color is unknown because the backgrounds of the horses have not been documented, but the cream dilution has a long history among the ponies and cobs of the British Isles.

One of the most striking cream dilute Gypsy Horses is the solid buckskin stallion FALCON. Like many of the buckskin British native ponies, FALCON is a sooty buckskin with particularly vivid dappling, especially on his forehand. His color comes from his mother, GINGER, also called THE DUN MARE. Both were recently exported to America. Dappling is common on both palomino and buckskin Gypsy Horses.

Cream dilutes have also become popular in Europe. In the Netherlands there is a sooty buckskin tobiano Irish Cob stallion, YELLOW FELLOW VAN DE GORTERSTRAAT (2006). He was tested to be homozygous for the black gene, so he can produce 50 percent buckskins and smoky blacks, depending on the color of the dam, but no palominos. YELLOW FELLOW has an unrecorded background, but was inspected and graded premium. There is also a buckskin tovero stallion, CILLBARRA GOLDEN VALE (2002), standing in Denmark. His breeding is unknown.

There are double-diluted cream Gypsy Horses, though they are much less common than horses with just one cream mutation. Double-dilute cream stallions in the United Kingdom include the cremellos COATES TICKLED PINK and COATES THE COLOUR OF ICE. The Danish mare TOTENTINKERS BRIANNA (1998) is a tested smoky cream tobiano with pale green eyes.

The Norwegian registry bans "albinos." True albinism, where the animal is white with pink eyes, has not be documented in the horse, but rules against albino colors are sometimes used to deny registration to double-diluted cream horses.

Pearl

There are a handful of pearl Gypsy Horses. The first one identified was the filly DESERT JEWEL MYSTERY. When born she had pale skin and eyes and a tan coat. Her sire CLONONEEN ROMEO is a palomino, and her dam CLONONEEN AINE is a black tovero. She was tested, and found to be a black horse carrying one cream mutation and one pearl mutation, a combination called smoky black pearl. Because pearl acts as an intensifier for the cream dilution, her palomino sire could not have carried the mutation unnoticed. And since cream and pearl are alleles at the same locus, he could not have given her both mutations even if he was a pearl carrier. So her dam AINE is likely carrying the hidden pearl, which without cream is not visible. Because MYSTERY is a cream pearl, she has both mutations, but when bred she will only be able to give one of the two, either cream or pearl but not both, to any given foal.

Since DESERT JEWEL MYSTERY was identified, other pearls and pearl carriers have been found. Her stablemate, DESERT JEWEL CHARDONNAY, is another smoky black pearl. A buckskin pearl stallion, ERWIN DU VALLON, was recently exported from France to Australia. A buckskin pearl tobiano stallion, CAMELLA BOY WARRIOR, is standing in Norway. Another buckskin pearl tobiano stallion, SR LOVE BISCUIT, was exported to the United States.

Like many Gypsy Horses, there is very little information on the background of the currently identified pearls. Aside from its discovery among the Gypsy Horses, pearl has been a mutation primarily found among Old and New World Spanish breeds. How it came to be part of the Gypsy Horse gene pool is not known. It is interesting to speculate on the idea that theses horses, if they did not get the pearl mutation from more recent Spanish horses, might trace back to the lost Hanoverian Creams or at least to the breeding program of Garrard Tyrwhitt-Drake.

Dun

There is one known line of lineback duns descending from a grulla mare acquired by Albert Coates at the Appleby Horse Fair. COATES SHADY LADY produced the grulla mares COATES AUTUMN and COATES DUSK. The latter was exported to the United States. More recently she produced a grulla colt, COATES OLIVER'S RASCAL by the solid black stallion COATES OLIVER. Although the color is rare ar the moment, that may change as descendants of SHADY LADY are included in more breeding programs.

Many bay sabino Clydesdales have flaxen manes and tails. Because many Gypsy Horses have Clydesdale ancestors, it is often necessary to test mares like this one to be sure it is the silver dilution causing the pale mane and tail.

Silver

Many silver Gypsies trace back to a stallion known as THE BUSINESS (1990). In addition to being a black silver, THE BUSINESS also had a broad blaze, a peaked stocking on the right hind leg and irregular patches up the front of the left hind leg. He was by THE BOSS, a black sabino grandson of BOB THE BLAGDON. (At one time THE BUSINESS was also called THE BOSS, which has led to some confusion in pedigrees.) Among the American offspring of THE BUSINESS are the black silver stallions SIR ROYAL EXCALIBUR and ST. CLARINS (2002).

There is a black silver son of THE BUSINESS in the Netherlands, SILVER CASH VAN DE GORTERSTRAAT (2006). SILVER CASH tested positive for one copy of the silver dilution (Zz), and is also homozygous for the black gene (EE). He is marked with a blaze and stockings, and most likely carries some form of sabino.

There are silvers unrelated to THE BUSINESS, though their ancestry is often not recorded so they may share common ancestors. One is the silver dapple tovero mare CLONONEEN LAOIRE (2004), exported first to the United States and then to Australia. She produced the black silver colt THE CHOCOLATIER, who was also exported to Australia.

Another is the black silver tovero mare DESERT JEWEL AUBURN (2000). AUBURN is notable for having the vivid dappling often associated with silver dapple Shetland Ponies. She passed that trait on to her son AUSTIN (2007), whose eye-catching color has attracted a lot of attention and introduced the silver dilution to many who had not previously been familiar with the color.

Because black is so prevalent among Gypsies, most of the silver dilutes have been black silver. There have been red silvers, including the mare DESERT JEWEL FROSTY. Bred to THE BUSINESS, FROSTY produced the red silver stallion SILVER PHOENIX in 2006.

Silver is also found in combination with other dilutions, as well as with tobiano. The ST. CLARINS son SIR KEITH (2007) is a smoky black silver. A smoky black silver is genetically black and carries both a copy of the cream and the silver dilutions. He has a full sister, SAFFIRE, that is the same color.

The most common Gypsy Horse color is black tobiano with extensive facial white. This horse, SHAMROCK'S BILLY O'BRIEN, has two blue eyes, which are also common.

In appearance both SIR KEITH and SAFFIRE are a pale chocolate with a slightly lighter mane and tail. That is typical of smoky silvers, which often lack the more striking mane and tail contrast of an ordinary black silver. Like many smoky silvers, SIR KEITH had green eyes that darkened as he matured.

Tobiano and Tovero
The tobiano pattern, particularly black tobiano, is the one most closely associated with the Gypsy Horse. For the last few decades, it has been the color favored by traditional Gypsy breeders. Because most of the horses also have extensively marked faces, it is assumed that they carry one of the overo patterns and are what American Paint Horse breeders call tovero. Many of the influential early stallions were toveros. The OLD HORSE OF WALES (1984), THE ROADSWEEPER UK and THE LOTTERY HORSE (1994) were black toveros with extensive face white.

Because few Gypsy Horses have documented backgrounds, it can be difficult to determine exactly which of the overo patterns is involved. Because they are prevalent in the horse population in general, and in some of the foundation breeds used in the formation of the Gypsy Horse, the sa-

bino patterns are likely to be involved with many of the toveros. Splashed white is also a possibility. Should more tests become available for the different types of sabino and splashed white, the Gypsy Horse community, with its tradition of color testing, may provide the opportunity for insight into how the different patterns interact, particularly with tobiano.

It is possible to find Gypsy Horses that do not show signs of carrying any pattern other than tobiano, but these are rare. The German stallion SIR JASON DE CANTERVILLE (2003) is a black tobiano with the simple pattern and the minimally marked face of a pure tobiano.

Sabino
Although not as common as tobiano, sabino is one of the traditional colors of the Gypsy Horse, where it is called *blagdon*. Usually the term is paired with the base color of the horse, much like traditional roan. Some blagdon horses have flashy white patterns, while others are true sabino roans. The range of sabino patterning is pretty similar to that seen in Clydesdales and Shires, which is not surprising since those were among the breeds believed to have been used to develop the Gypsy Horse.

Many sabino Gypsies trace back to a black sabino stallion called THE LOB-EARED HORSE (~1976). He produced the black sabinos BOB THE BLAGDON (1997) and FLEETWOOD. He also had a son, COMANCHE (2000), that had what looks like a white-dipped pattern. THE LOB-EARED HORSE himself had a bottom-heavy blaze that covered his entire lower face, but most of his descendants have ordinary flashy sabino markings with roaned outlines.

Moderately marked sabino without tobiano is more common in European Gypsy Horses than in those in the United States, where breeders have tended to prefer tobianos, toveros and the loudly patterned sabino roans.

Sabino-1
Some portion of the sabino, or blagdon, Gypsy Horses have the sabino-1 mutation. Because other forms of sabino, particularly those found in the Clydesdale, look very similar to sabino-1, the only way to be sure that a Gypsy Horse carries sabino-1

is to test. Even predominantly white foals do not necessarily prove that a line carries sabino-1, because many Gypsies with just one copy are extremely white compared to other breeds where sabino-1 is found. This may be because other patterning mutations are present, including other sabino patterns.

Because tobiano is common in the breed, sabino-1 is occasionally paired with tobiano. Gypsies with both sabino-1 and tobiano often exhibit the classic 'tattered tissue" pattern typical of that combination. In some cases these horses could be mistaken for patchy sabinos, especially if the face is very white and the dark areas are so ragged and broken apart that the tobiano outline is difficult to discern.

Classic Splash

Because splashed white (*SW1*) is present in other British native breeds, most notably the Welsh Mountain Pony, it is possible that it is present in the Gypsy Horse. Just as the lack of documentation hampers a better understanding of the sabino patterns in the breed, it also makes it difficult to confirm that classic splash is present. The presence of the other patterns of white muddy the situation further. Splashed white is far easier to identify when the pronounced difference between the heterozygotes and the homozygotes can be seen. For that reason, it is even more important to find an unmistakable homozygous pattern to confirm that it is splashed white and not another pattern or combination of patterns.

Although the classic homozygous splash pattern has not yet been identified in Gypsy Horses by this author, there are a number of indicators that suggest the pattern may be present. The most obvious is the high incidence of blue eyes, though that trait cannot be considered exclusive to the splashed white pattern. In the 1951 paper "Die Iris- und Rumpfscheckung beim Pferd", the German researcher Ernst von Lehmann noted an increased incidence of blue eyes among tobiano warmbloods, and blue eyes have been found to some extent among dominant whites and sabinos.

There are other indicators beyond eye color. In its homozygous state, classic splash sometimes in-

cludes the ears. This is different from sabinos and dominant white, where often it is the ears that retain color even in the most extensively marked individuals. Classic splash somtimes results in white ears when paired with tobiano. The relatively high incidence of white ears among tovero Gypsies suggests that splashed white may be involved. The other tendency of splashed white is to leave color on the broad sides of the neck. This is typically a place where tobiano removes color, yet when combined with splashed white this placement often gets skewed. Likewise, colored patches on the croup that come to a downward point are also associated with the presence of classic splash.

Because the other two splashed white mutations, *SW2* and *SW3*, occurred in the American Paint Horse, it is unlikely that either form would be found in Gypsy Horses. It is possible that other splashed white mutations, not yet formally identified, are present.

Appaloosa

In Ireland and the United Kingdom, the appaloosa patterns are usually referred to as spotted. Spotted cobs have a long history in the British Isles. A royal inventory of horses from the Falkirk campaign of 1298 included a blanket-spotted Powys Horse, the predecessor of the modern Welsh Cob. He had a much higher value than was typical for a cob, pre-

Many pintaloosa Gypsy Horses are misidentified as either grey or roan pintos. The spots on the hips and mottling on the face give this horse away as both an appaloosa and a tobiano.

sumably for his unusual coloring. Appaloosa spotting could still be found in the early Welsh stud books, and spotted horses are said to have been popular with Gypsy breeders in the middle twentieth century, before they were largely replaced by the toveros, which is an easier color to breed.

One stud that preserved the appaloosa coloring is Hermit House in Yorkshire. Using the black leopard stallion KYLKENNY (~1988) and the bay near-leopard mare TANSY OF DARCY, the stud produced a number of influential appaloosas, including the fewspot leopard stallion HERMITS LONELY GHOST. Two GHOST sons have been used at Hermit House, HERMITS GHOST PALOUSE and HERMITS GHOST CHIEF. LONELY GHOST has a number of appaloosa patterned sons that have been exported to the United States, including the leopards DESERT JEWEL APOLLO and HERMITS GHOST WILLIAM. Another near-leopard son, HERMITS GHOST GLACIER, stands in Germany. Bred back to his own dam, he sired the fewspot mare HERMITS GHOST SAPPHIRE, dam of the black blanket stallion ROUGH DIAMOND. Most of the Ghost-bred Gypsy Horses are either leopards, few spots or varnish roans with extensive spotted blankets. Like many appaloosas with sabino-type markings, they have smaller spots and those with blankets have lacey edges.

Recently Hermit House added a second unrelated stallion to the stud. DIAMOND OF HERMITS is a chocolate-colored near-leopard with a blaze and hind socks. Like KYLKENNY before him, he is registered with the British Spotted Pony Society.

Although the patterns are rare, there are other appaloosa lines. In 2001 the stallion ASPERCIAL (1995) was exported from Ireland to Germany. His ancestry is unrecorded. ASPERCIAL is a black varnish with a bald face, peaked hind stockings and a large frosty blanket. It is not clear if he has any of the appaloosa patterning mutations beyond sabino. His similarly marked son, WHISPERING WINDS INDIGO (2002), was exported to the United States. Both stallions are genetically black, but show pronounced bronzing.

Occasionally appaloosa patterns are not recognized for what they are. This is especially true when the appaloosa patterns are combined with one or more of the pinto patterns. Tobiano can cover areas that might otherwise give clues with white. The

This sabino roan is so pale that he appears nearly white. Many Gypsy Horses with this type of coloring test as carrying only one copy of sabino-1, which suggests some other factor may be involved that boosts the amount of white.

sabino patterns, with their irregular white roaning and ticking and occasional skin mottling can also make accurate identification difficult.

White

White-born foals do occur in the Gypsy Horse. At least one white-born foal, SR GOOD GOLLY MISS MOLLY (2001), has tested to carry two copies of the sabino-1 mutation. Homozygous sabino-1 horses are born white. Because sabino-1 has been confirmed in the breed, it is possible that other white-born foals are homozygous for sabino-1. It is also worth noting that many Gypsies Horses that test as having a single sabino-1 mutation have more white than is typical in some of the other breeds where sabino-1 is common. This may be due to the presence of other patterning mutations or modifiers that boost the amount of white.

There has also been speculation that dominant white may be present among the Gypsy Horses. Some dominant white mutations have consistently produced all-white foals, while others have been impossible to distinguish from some forms of sabino roan. Since both all-white and sabino roans are found, such speculation is not unreasonable. Without testing, however, it is difficult to determine which patterns are involved. In breeds where parentage is documented, the occurrence of a dominant white mutation is notable because the color is an aberration; a white foal is born into a family where previously the markings were unremarkable or even non-existent. Gypsy Horses have often lacked that information, at least until recently.

Eye Color

Most of the Gypsy Horse registries have standards that specifically allow for eyes to be of any color or combination of colors. Blue eyes are common among the appaloosas as well as the pinto patterns. Pale blue or blue-green eyes are also seen in horses with two copies of the cream dilution. Horses with the pearl dilution are typically born with blue eyes that darken to green or amber. Irish breeders are said to have favored blue eyes, believing that horses with them are better color producers than horses with dark eyes.

Markings

Most Gypsy Horses have extensive white markings. Blazes and white stockings are common among the sabinos and the sabino roans. In those colors, belly spots, roaning and detached patches on the legs are also seen. Soft edges are more common that crisp or ragged edges, though the long hair so prized in the breed does tend to soften the outlines of markings and patterns.

With the tobianos, irregular white on the face is common. Sometimes the majority of the face is white, leaving only dark patches over the eyes. Oc-

cluding spots that cover part of the white face are common. When those spots are large enough, the horse is said to have a badger face. White sometimes spreads to include the ears.

There are more moderately marked Gypsy Horses, although they are uncommon. The stallion COATES OLIVER (1999) is black horse with a narrow, broken blaze and one hind sock. The mares SWF MISS AMELIA (2008) and SWF TIA'S ROYAL PRINCESS (2009) are both black with a blaze and four dark feet. SWF TIA'S ROYAL PRINCESS was unusual for a black horse in that she retained pale hairs on her lower legs and her tail for longer than expected, but she had no markings beyond a blaze and white chin. Both fillies are the product of tovero to tovero crosses, which makes their dark legs even more surprising.

Completely unmarked Gypsies are quite rare, but can be found. The mare JOSEFINE DE CANTERVILLE (2006) is black with no white markings. The stallion STARBUCK (2005) is solid black with only a star. Like the two moderately marked mares, he also comes from two tovero parents. There is also a solid dapple bay stallion, LORD FERGUS OF THE OWLISH FORTRESS (2004) marked only with a star. Horses like these are particularly unusual because breeding for loud patterns tends to concentrate the lesser modifiers believed to contribute to white markings.

Jutland Horse
Jydsk

Origin: Denmark

The Jutland is a heavy draft breed native to Denmark. Just as the Clydesdale is closely associated with the American Budweiser brewery, the Jutland is associated with the Carlsberg Brewery in Copenhagen. The typical red coat and white trim reflect the national colors of Denmark.

Stud Book
The Jutland is one of the earliest of the European breeds to adopt a formal stud book, with the first volume was published in 1881. A breeders' association followed in 1887. The first volume containing mares was issued four years later in 1891. The stud book was closed to outside blood shortly after it was established.

Population
The European Farm Animal Biodiversity Information System states that as of 2006 the Jutland breeding population is composed of 214 mares and 35 breeding stallions. The Genetic Resources Committee of the Food and Agriculture Organization (FAO) has included the Jutland in its efforts to preserve old national breeds.

Colors
In the early 1800s, the Danish crown sought to improve the native Jutland mares by crossing them with Cleveland Bays and Yorkshire Coach stallions. These crosses resulted in minimally marked bays, browns and blacks—colors that today are quite rare within the breed.

That changed with the influence of the modern breed founder, OPPENHEIM (1859). Books that speak of the Jutland history often refer to the English import as a Suffolk Punch. Many breed historians now doubt this based on the fact that he had rather extensive white markings. Some have speculated that he was actually a Shire, sold for export because his color was unacceptable. Others have suggested that he may have been a Shire/Suffolk cross. Whatever his true background, his influ-ence resulted in an almost uniformly chestnut population.

OPPENHEIM also added white markings to what had been primarily a plain breed. His great-grand-son, MUNKEDAL, had a broad blaze, white chin, and high stockings with flecked edges. Another descendant, ØLGOD, had extensive white markings and a body spot. Breeders did prefer a little less white, particularly on the legs, and the stallion eventually chosen to represent the OPPENHEIM line, ALDRUP MUNKEDAL, was a flaxen chestnut with only a blaze.

As the father of the modern Jutland, ALDRUP MUNKEDAL ensured that chestnut became the predominant color in Jutlands. Like MUNKEDAL, most have flaxen manes and tails and pale lower legs. At one end of the spectrum, the body color can approach liver, while at the other end there are very pale, mealy-toned chestnuts that could be mistaken for palomino. Pronounced dappling is seen in some of the paler chestnuts. Less common are the black and brown Jutlands, and rarer still are the bays. Most of these darker colors are strongly pigmented, as might be expected from their distant coach horse origins, but there are occasional mealy bays as well.

Summary

Current colors: Most modern Jutlands are chestnut. Black and brown are present, though much less common than chestnut. Bay is rare.

Historical Colors: The early Jutland horses varied in color. Grey and tobiano were found even among the premium breeding stock. A handful of true roan, dun and cream mares appear in the first few volumes of the stud book.

Markings/patterns: White face markings are common. White leg markings are also seen, but many have facial white without white on the legs. Unmarked horses do occur, especially among the darker colors.

Eye color: The eyes are dark.

This mare and foal are typical of the modern Jutland both in color and in type. The abundant, pale feathering can make it hard to discern white leg markings in adults.

There are a handful of Jutlands that look as if they may be red silver, though this is hard to confirm without tests. Sooty liver chestnuts can look a great deal like red silvers, especially in draft horses with heavy feathering because that gives the lower legs a much paler appearance in contrast with the darker knees and hocks. To this author's knowledge, no Jutlands have ever been tested for the silver (Z) mutation. It would not be surprising if they were to test positive, because silver is quite widespread among the European heavy draft breeds. There are also a number of horses in the early stud books described as bay or brown with gray or even white manes and tails. One such stallion, Sofus (1888), is described as copper chestnut with a variegated mane and tail and very dark legs. Because most modern Jutlands are chestnut, the silver mutation could stay hidden for generations until it was inherited by a horse that was genetically bay or black.

Historical Colors

The early stud books of the Jutland offer a rare glimpse of the colors found in a coach breed population prior to the widespread improvement schemes of the early twentieth century. The books were among the earliest recorded stud books, and are unusual for the close focus on the mares. Mares tend to be of particular interest to anyone researching the history of colors because unusual colors are most often carried through the female line. A stallion of an unfashionable color can be gelded, whereas a mare of otherwise good quality will be retained with the hope that she can produce more marketable colors if bred to the right stallion. In this way, rare colors are often preserved through a succession of mares. It also means that color fashions often lag in the female population, so that in a changing breed the mare colors give a picture of the breed as it may have been a generation earlier.

What makes the Jutland mare books particularly helpful in this regard is that the compiler, J. Jensen, used a slightly different approach to recording foundation stock than was common at the time. Most early stud books provide the names of ancestors when they are known, and fall back on stallion families or owners when they are not. Background information in these books might read something like "a Copperbottom mare" or "John Smith's mare." Jensen was unusual in that he relayed the descriptions given to him, so an entry might instead read, "brown blaze-faced mare with good legs." In many cases, these detailed descriptions go back four or five generations, so while the mares entered in the first volume of the stud book might have been born between 1864 and 1891, the information stretches back far earlier. The picture presented in those early books is one of a far more colorful breed than one might imagine for a breed that is now almost uniformly chestnut.

Grey

The prevalence of grey is particularly striking. The following grey mares appear in the plates that illustrate the first few volumes of the stud book:

Lise 124   f.1869   sire: Grensten
                      dam: "good grey mare"
Stine 228 f. 1869   sire: Grantorp
                      dam: "large, strong grey mare"

MINKA 1809   f.1891   sire: Fenris
                        dam: "a small, but very
                        good grey mare"
FROMDINE 2071 f.1894   sire: Munkedal II
                        dam: grey mare
DAGNY 2309   f. 1889 sire: Dan
                        dam: Alba by Lerbjerg

In total there were 80 grey mares in the first five volumes of the stud books. Many are daughters of the grey stallion TODBJERG II. Contemporary accounts praise the quality of TODBJERG II's offspring, mentioning only that they were sometimes small. Their color is mentioned but does not appear to have been an issue. As late as the fifth volume, there was at least one grey stallion, GREY-LOCK (1888). He has two registered full sisters who are also grey; the aforementioned MINKA and THORA 1368.

Roan
It is likely that there were a handful of true roans as well. As with many modern stud books, it can be difficult to get an exact count because many horsemen use the term roan for colors that are actually genetically distinct from dark-headed roan. Like the modern Jockey Club, it appears that many nineteenth-century Jutland breeders used the terms roan and grey interchangeably. There are also a number of horses registered as roan that were clearly sabinos with roaning. A good example of this is the stallion KJELLERUP MUNKEDAL (1891), whose picture appears in Volume V. There were, however, a few mares registered as *morenkop*, which does refer specifically to true roan. One of these was the premium mare VILLE 56, foaled in 1881 and registered in Volume I. Another premium mare, HASINE 140, was registered as brown-grey, but had a dark-headed roan mother and grandmother, so was probably also a roan.

Dilutes
There are a four mares that may have been dun. The first of these was BIANCA 319 (1878), registered as golden bay with an eel strip down her back. Another, FLORA 328 (1880), was described the same way. Both mares were said to have been

of the Frederiksborg type. A third mare, ULLA 546, was registered as light bay with an eel stripe and mealy legs. The last mare, JUTTA 1514 (1888), was also registered as a golden bay with eel mark, by a "dark brown" stallion with an eel mark. Although these mares, and a stallion in the fifth volume (HENGEST 549), are the only suspected duns in the stud books, the notation *med aal ad ryggen* ("with an eel on the back") appears in the descriptions of a number of the ancestors of stud book entries, which would suggest that the dun color was once found in at least some of the native stock.

There are three more mares, all in the first volume of the stud book, that are registered as yellow. Two are listed as yellow, and the third is listed as yellow with a black mane and tail. Since no mention is made of an eel stripe with either the mares, their ancestors or their listed progeny, it is possible that they had the cream dilution. The first mare, SIF 307 (1864), was registered posthumously, having died seven years prior to publication. She was described as having a beautiful head, a good body, a well-formed croup and plenty of bone, and had been awarded premium status. Within her entry it is noted that she produced twelve foals, seven of which are listed as yellow. Of her yellow offspring,

This illustration of the grey mare LISE 124 appeared in the first volume of the Jutland stud book. She was foaled in 1864, and was described in her entry as "being of the Frederiksborg stamp, not heavy of bone and with good movement."

two sons and one daughter were also awarded premium status. The only foal registered in the stud book, however, is her buckskin granddaughter FRIDA 312 (1880). Her entry notes that she produced quality foals, including a "good yellow mare with a white mane and tail."

The third yellow mare, GULLA 408, is not related to SIF. Her unnamed dam is listed as grey, so it is possible that the color came through her. GULLA was herself bred to the grey TODBJERG II and produced greys, but it does not appear that any were registered.

The yellow lines did not continue, and there were no more yellow horses registered after the first volume of the stud book. The last suspected dun was registered in Volume III.

Tobiano

Perhaps most surprising, however, is the presence of the tobiano pattern. The source for the pattern, which appears on at least two stallions and a number of mares in the early stud books, is not clear. For a brief time between the use of the coaching breeds and the arrival of the stallion OPPENHEIM, the Danish government experimented with a number of outcross breeds, including Hanoverians, East Prussians and Oldenburgs. The pattern may have come from the East Prussians, since tobiano is known to have been present in that breed. It is also possible that the pattern was found among the native mares, and was a remnant of the Danish baroque breeding programs.

What is clear is that the pattern was present among a small number of horses prior to the adoption of the formal stud book, and at the formation of the breed it was apparently not considered objectionable. A plate from the early 1900s showing a tobiano Jutland stallion appears in Jasper Nissen's three-volume *Enzykopädie der Pferderassen*. It is likely that it depicts the black tobiano stallion 115 STEJLBJERG-HINGSTEN or his son 137 STEJLBJERG-HINGSTEN. The parents of 115 STEJLBJERG-HINGSTEN are not recorded by name, which is not unusual for the entries in the early Jutland stud books. Instead a color and often a general description is provided. The sire of the original STEJLBJERG-HINGSTEN was a brown horse that had been awarded a premium at the cattle show in Skanderborg and sold for a high price in 1853. His dam, a black tobiano, was also a premium winner.

Most of the tobianos listed in the early stud books trace back to 115 STEJLBJERG-HINGSTEN. The first of these was GRETHE, a filly registered alongside her mother and given the same registration number, noted in the book as 5a and 5b. (The rather awkward practice of assigning shared numbers was dropped in later volumes.) GRETHE is recorded as a bay tobiano, while her mother, who is not given a name despite being assigned a registration number, is registered as black. It is unlikely

Jutland Mares registered in the studbooks 1891- 1900

	bay	chestnut	black	grey	roan	tobiano	dun	cream
Vol. I	327	143	50	21	5	2	3	5
Vol. II	326	232	68	20	0	2	1	0
Vol. III	223	157	43	10	1	3	1	0
Vol. IV	190	167	50	13	0	1	0	0
Vol. V	265	250	59	16	0	1	0	0
	1331	949	270	80	6	9	5	5

Chart 10. Colors of Jutland mares registered in the stud books from 1891 until 1900.

This was the pattern depicted in a nineteenth-century engraving of a Jutland stallion. It is likely that the image was of STEJLBJERG-HINGSTEN, a tobiano that lived during that time. Most of the tobianos in the early volumes of the stud book trace to him.

that her mother was simply black, since the color comes through her bay tobiano mother, LOTTE, who in turn was out of an unnamed bay tobiano premium mare by 137 STEJLBJERG-HINGSTEN.

Next came the black tobiano mare UNGE BROGE (1883). Her dam, GAMLE BROGE, was a black tobiano mare by 137 STEJLBJERG-HINGSTEN. Both mares were granted premium status. The last tobiano mare in Volume II was the bay tobiano DANNEBROG. Details of her parentage are not given, but she was registered with a bay tobiano foal at her side.

Five more tobianos were registered in the next three volumes of the stud books. Most were out of mares that traced back to STJELBJERG-HINGSTEN. Some traced back through STOR, an unregistered son of 137 STEJLBJERG-HINGSTEN. Those that do not have him listed in their pedigree have only limited information provided, and may have traced back to the same stock.

Silver

A few of the bay mares were noted as having gray manes and tails. SUSE 170 (1887) was registered as dark bay with a gray mane. Another mare, FRIGGA 260 (1884), also a dark bay, was noted as having gray in her mane and tail. It could be that mares like these were silver dilutes, or they could have had the silvered mane seen in some Scandinavian breeds.

Eye Color

Jutlands appear to have uniformly dark eyes. Because white markings are found, and in some cases the white on both the face and legs is extensive, it might be possible to find blue-eyed individuals. To date none have been identified.

Markings

Most chestnut-based Jutlands have face markings. Blazes, often including the upper and lower lips, are common. Leg markings are less common, even when there is a fair bit of facial white. It is not unusual to see a lot of contrast with the flaxen leg feathering, which can be mistaken for socks or stockings. Occasionally higher stockings, some extending up the gaskin, are seen. Most of the bay, brown or black Jutlands are unmarked.

Nivernais
(Extinct)

Origin: Nièvre, France

The Nivernais was a French draft breed closely related to the Percheron, though often described as somewhat smaller and more active. Although technically extinct, the situation is similar to that of some coaching breeds where the remaining horses were incorporated into an existing breed. Theoretically the genetic material necessary to recreate the Nivernais exists within the Percheron.

Stud Book
The Nivernais was created by the Count de Bouille in 1872 using native *bidet* (small) mares and heavier stallions from La Perche. A stud book was opened in 1880—three years earlier than the Percheron stud book—in response to the American Department of Agriculture policies on pedigreed livestock. American importers were particularly interested in unmarked black horses, which put the Nivernais region in competition with the breeders in La Perche. Some Percheron breeders responded by using Nivernais to increase the color within their own breed. It is also thought that some portion of the black horses exported as Percherons may well have been Nivernais.

In the United States, there were horses that were imported from Nivernais that were identified as what they were. While it was still in operation, the National French Draft Horse Association (formerly the National Norman Horse Association) registered all French coldblood horses, including the Nivernais. In later volumes, the Nivernais was one of the breeds, along with the Percheron and the Boulonnais, that was noted with a letter following the parent breed's stud book number. In Volumes 1 through 10, there were a total of 118 Nivernais registered in the American stud books. Of those, all but one were stallions. In the very early stud books, purity of blood was often defined by the number of top-crosses, so imported mares were rare.

These small numbers made the Nivernais a minority breed from the start. Unlike Le Perche, which had a long history of horse breeding, Nivernais was better known for the production of cattle. This meant that although the Nivernais got a head start on the Percheron in terms of establishing a stud book, the number of registrations were never comparable. At the height of the American export boom, twenty-five years after the stud book opened, the Nivernais stud book had recorded just over 1,000 horses. In contrast, at that same time the Percheron stud book in France had recorded over 60,000 horses. Even the Boulonnais, whose stud book began five years after the Nivernais, had recorded over 6,000. The breed was eventually eclipsed, both nationally and internationally, by the Percheron. In 1966, the Nivernais was declared a derivative race of the Percheron, and the two stud books were merged.

In 1982, the Regional Natural Park of Morvan established a conservation project for the agricultural heritage of the region which included the restoration of the Nivernais breed. In 1999 an initiative was begun within the *Societe Hippique Percheronne* to preserve what was left of the Nivernais bloodlines.

Color
The original intention of the Count de Bouille was to create a large, black breed of horse to go with

Summary

The Nivernais has been extinct since the mid-twentieth century. Efforts are being made to restore it.

Historical colors: The Nivernais was primarily a black breed, though some horses were bay, brown, grey or even roan. After 1930 only black was allowed.

Markings/patterns: Most Nivernais were solid or marked with only a small star. White on the feet was extremely rare.

Eye color: What records exist suggest that all Nivernais were dark-eyed.

The editor of <u>The Breeder's Gazette</u> considered this un-named Nivernais stallion to be a typical representative of the breed.

the white Charolais cattle raised in the region. Writers indicate that the early horses were not uniformly black, which would not be surprising since the nearest larger horses that could be used to outcross, Percherons and Boulonnais, were both predominantly grey.

This is reflected in the earliest American imports, which were much more mixed in terms of color. Among the first group were two blacks, a gray and a roan. After that, the majority (89 percent) were black. The remainder were grey (six), bay (five) and brown (two). It is likely that the black color was a big part of the reason the Nivernais were imported in the first place. American livestock writers from the time often mention the desire to breed out the lighter colors from the French draft breeds. That was the objection to the

grey coloring; it eventually resulted in a very light-colored horse. American breeders preferred darker colors, or failing that, darker greys. That made the Nivernais an attractive choice for those willing to forego Percheron papers.

In 1930, the French stud book placed a requirement that Nivernais be black. Any other color was denied registration. By that time the American French Draft stud book had folded, the Percheron reigned supreme among the French breeds, and the export market was almost non-existent.

Eye Color

There is no evidence that there were ever Nivernais with light or blue eyes. Given the minimal nature of their white markings, it seems unlikely that the patterns known to produce blue eyes were ever found in the gene pool.

Markings

Old photographs suggest that the Nivernais was marked much like the modern Percheron. That is, most of the horses were solid or had at most a star. This is reflected in the records of the imported Nivernais. Of those horses, 64 percent were unmarked and another 27 percent had nothing more than a star. Only ten horses (9 percent) had white on their legs, and those that did typically had no more than one white foot. One horse was noted as having gray hairs on his flanks, which could have been ticking such as is seen in some Suffolks, or perhaps even the rabicano pattern. It is also possible that, given the young age of most of the imports, that those registering him did not realize he was turning grey.

Noriker

Origin: Austria

The Noriker is a moderately heavy coldblood from Austria and the German Alps. Once credited as a descendant of the horses of the Roman legions, archeological evidence suggests that the horses may have been indigenous to the area long before the time of the Roman Empire.

Stud Book

In 1565, five years before the establishment of the stud at Lipica, the Archbishop of Salzburg formed the Rieß Stud using Neapolitan and Spanish stallions. In 1688, Archbishop Graf Thun issued an order requiring mare owners to use Court stallions, closing the Salzburg breeding population to the influence of other foreign outcrosses. Provisions for the licensing of private stallions were made in 1703, but the Rieß Stud continued to influence the native draft horse population until 1802. Outcrossing to heavier Burgundian stallions, as well as Kladrubers, was done during the mid-nineteenth century. From 1885 until 1893, a variety of foreign draft breeds were used to increase the size of the Noriker. Partially in response to this, the Pinzgauer Horse Association was formed in 1897 to promote the breeding of purebred native horses. The first stud book was published in 1904.

The current stud book is closed, and horses registered must have at least four generations of registered Noriker ancestry. Although current regulations require four, Norikers have unusually complete pedigrees for a draft breed, with some having as many as thirty-one recorded generations. At nine generations, 90 percent of the ancestors are still known. By comparison, nine-generation Andalusian pedigrees only have 55 percent known ancestors. This is even more remarkable given that Norikers have a relatively low level of inbreeding. Stallions must come from one of the five recognized sire lines, and take the name of the line to which they belong: Vulkan, Nero, Diamant, Schaunitz and Elmar.

There is also a separate population of Norikers in the Czech Republic. Horses of this group are called Silesian Norikers. The breed was formed using 85 stallions imported from Austria and Bavaria in the early twentieth century. From 1900 until 1930, domestic mares, some of unknown origin, were used for breeding. After 1930, mares were required to have Noriker sires and grandsires. By the middle of the twentieth century, the stud book was closed to non-Noriker blood. Although the Silesian horses share a common ancestry with the Austrian Noriker, it has been considered a separate breed by the Czech Republic since 1991. The eight sire lines of the Silesian Noriker are Hubert Nero, Bravo, Gothenscherz, Hollriegel, Neuwirth Diamant, Streiter Vulkan, Nero Diamant and Ritz Vulkan. Some of the lines are separate branches of the existing Austrian lines, while others, like Bravo, are unique to the

Summary

Current colors: Black and chestnut are the most common colors, followed by bay. Dark-headed roan is present, but is not common. Silver is suspected to be present but rare. Grey is not found in the original Noriker, but a handful of grey individuals do exist in the Silesian Noriker.

Historical: A wide variety of colors were found at the Rieß Stud in Salzburg prior to the formation of the stud book, most notably double-diluted creams. One brindle roan stallion was born in Czechloslovakia in the early twentieth century.

Markings/patterns: White face and leg markings do occur, but are usually moderate. Some Norikers are appaloosa patterned, with most being leopards or near-leopards. Suppressed leopard patterns are common, but true blanket patterns are relatively rare. Homozygous appaloosas are uncommon, and unpatterned varnish roans are not favored. There is one tobiano line. Tobianos have been crossed on the appaloosa lines, making pintaloosas a possibility. Silesian Norikers tend to have more white, and at least one has been body-spotted.

Eye color: The eyes are dark.

Czech Republic. Crosses to more recent Austrian horses have also been used.

Population

Like many European heavy breeds, the Noriker underwent a genetic bottleneck during the horse breeding crisis of the mid- to late-twentieth century brought about by the final wave of agricultural mechanization. In 1960, it was estimated that Norikers made up 80 percent of the Austrian horse population. These numbers were greatly reduced less than a decade later, when only 34,510 remained. By 1986, there were just over 7,000. The European Farm Animal Biodiversity Information System states that as of 2009 the Noriker breeding population is composed of 3,429 mares and 211 breeding stallions in Austria. A conservation program focusing on the preservation of rare lines and colors has been in place since 2007.

Within the Czech Republic the Silesian Noriker population numbers close to 1,000, with 835 mares and 40 breeding stallions. The population has a higher level of inbreeding than the Austrian Noriker, having begun with a smaller number of founders, and attempts are underway to preserve genetic diversity.

Colors

The Noriker is unusual among the older heavy draft breeds in that a high degree of color variation has been maintained. Where ease in assembling matched teams and a desire for easy recognition drove other breeds to adopt one or two defining colors, Noriker breeders preserved all three basic colors as well as some of the patterns popular during the Baroque period.

Black

Presently the most common color is black, accounting for 31 percent of the population. This number is a little misleading because a still higher percentage of horses are genetically black, but also carry one or more of the modifiers found within the breed. Roan Norikers are invariably black. Black is also the favored base color for the patterns, so a high percentage of the tobiano and appaloosa Norikers are black. If the patterned horses are added, the portion of genetically black Norikers is much closer to half.

It is likely that black was common among the horses of Salzburg prior to the formation of the stud book. Black was the favored color for ceremonial coach horses, and many of the Neapolitans used at the Rieß Stud were black. One of these, SACRAMOSO (1799), was sent to the Kladruby stud in 1809. This changed when the breed shifted to the heavier draft type of the late nineteenth century. By the middle of the twentieth century, black horses made up only 5 percent of the population. That percentage climbed to a high of 35 percent in 2000.

Chestnut

Chestnut is the second-most common color among Norikers, making up 29 percent of the population. Chestnut was less common when the stud book was formed, and made up only 10 percent of the population in 1900. The color increased fairly rapidly after that time, and since the 1920s the percentage of chestnut horses has remained stable at close to 30 percent.

One reason the color has remained stable over the years is that it has been traditional to breed chestnuts to chestnuts. It was also the color of STOISSEN-NERO (1933), a stallion considered to have embodied all the best qualities of the breed. His image is often used in logos, encouraging many to associate the color with the breed.

Chestnut Norikers range from golden chestnut to a dark liver chestnut. Chestnuts with self-colored or darker manes and tails are not typical in Austrian Norikers. Most have pale flaxen manes and tails. On darker chestnuts, the lower legs are typically flaxen and dappling is often visible on the cannons. Many of these horses could easily be mistaken for silver dilutes, though most have red tones on their body and in their manes and tails, whereas the coloring on a true silver is a cool-toned chocolate. The very pale mealy chestnut like that seen in Belgian Drafts does not appear to be part of the gene pool.

Chestnut Silesian Norikers show more variety in terms of shade and point color. Quite a few Silesian stallions are dramatically sooty with dark grey manes and tails. The stallion BRYS (1983) was a particularly striking example of this shade of chestnut. His sons BISKUP (2003) and BRYS SEZSKY (2004) are almost identical in coloring. The sooty chestnut stallion HABAS (2006) is a more clearly red-toned liver, but has a nearly black mane and tail. There are also red chestnuts with self-colored manes and tails, like the stallion RAMGOŠ (1992) and his son REGENT (2006).

Bay

Many of the source horses for the different sire lines were bay. The founder of the most numerous sire line, Vulkan, was bay. The founder of the Schaunitz line, 255 SCHAUNITZ (1896), was also bay. Today all Schaunitz-line horses trace back to him through his brown son GRUBER SCHAUNITZ (1942). All the horses from the Diamant line trace back to the red bay stallion OPUS DIAMANT (1914). It is not surprising then that when the stud book was formed, 80 percent of the horses were bay or brown. The color had a brief peak of 90 percent around 1911, but began declining to its present proportion of 25 percent afterwards.

Norikers are unusual among the Continental draft breeds in that the bays tend to be dark with fully black points. Mealy and wild bay are not typical. This may be attributed to the fact that the Belgian and Ardennes draft breeds, where that variety of bay is common, did not have a lasting influence on the Noriker. In this the Noriker probably favors its coach horse ancestors, which also tend towards brown and the darker, more richly pigmented shades of bay.

Roan

Roan in the Noriker can be traced back the influence of the Neapolitans used at the Rieß Stud. In addition to black, Italian breeders of ceremonial coach horses favored a color they called *testa di moro*, or "head of the Moor." The Austrians called it *mohrenkopf*. The Noriker, originating in Salzburg close to the Italian border, and the Italian Murgese, are the sole remaining links to these Baroque era roans.

It is fortunate that the color was preserved in the Noriker. When the breed moved away from the older Baroque type, the three roan sire lines—

Neapolitan, Bacchus and Altenberger—were lost. In the 1970s, when efforts were first made to preserve some of the older colors, the black roan stallion MUFF DIAMANT (1968) was used. He traced back through his dam, AMERIS LANDA, to the blue roans SAUL VULKAN (1930) and HINZ DIAMANT (1943). MUFF DIAMANT sired one of the most important stallions in modern roan pedigrees, MOSSLER DIAMANT (1974). He in turn sired the roan stallions MESSER DIAMANT (1980), MATTHIAS DIAMANT (1981) and MAI DIAMANT (1985), as well as a number of roan daughters.

Another roan that appears in modern pedigrees is APOLLO VULKAN (1966). Like MUFF DIAMANT, his color came through the female side of his pedigree. His line is represented by his great-grandson, the black roan STEMMER VULKAN (1989), sire of five roan breeding stallions. The third roan line is that of MAGNUS DIAMANT (1973), whose influence continues through the female side of the pedigrees of the roan stallions MARCO NERO (1999) and FERDINAND ELMAR (2005).

Presently dark-headed roan accounts for 6 percent of the Noriker population, making it slightly less common than the appaloosa patterns. It is traditional to breed roans to blacks, with the belief that true, glossy black produces the desired blue coloring along with the dark head. Fully dark heads are strongly desired by many breeders. More extensively roaned faces can be found, including 535 VULKO (1941), a Silesian stallion whose image often accompanies articles about Norikers and their coloring.

Although Austrian breeders concentrate on black roan, there are roans of other colors. The Silesian stallion STREIMUR (1994) is a bay roan, as are many of his descendants. He also has at least one chestnut roan son, STREIGUR (2006). Silesian Norikers are also more inclined to have frosty manes and tails, although those are found upon occasion in the Norikers of Austria.

Appaloosa

The Noriker shares the distinction, along with the Danish Knabstrupper, of being one of the few instances where breeders preserved the appaloosa spotting patterns of the seventeenth and eighteenth centuries. Paintings from that time clearly illustrate how popular the color was among nobility, but recent scientific studies suggest that the color was present in Germany prior to domestication. While dark-headed roan came from the Neapolitans brought to Austria to improve the local stock, the presence of the leopard complex mutation among the wild horses of Germany opens the possibility that the coloring was indigenous. That might explain the willingness of the Archbishops of Salzburg to make their valuable Italian and Spanish stallions available to peasant farmers, long before the practice was commonplace.

These two appaloosa patterned Noriker horses were used to illustrate Adolf Walther's 1912 doctoral dissertation on horse color. The first horse was a Noriker of unknown origin owned by a Viennese brewery. The mare at the bottom came from an earlier Pinzgauer stud book. Both horses are good examples of the lighter Baroque type.

Whether the prehistoric patterns remained, or were reintroduced by colorful Spanish stallions, by the seventeenth and eighteenth centuries the breed possessed the appaloosa coloring that was coveted throughout much of Europe. Unlike dark-headed roan, the appaloosa patterns were fashionable for riding horses. That makes their continued presence in what was a working farm horse breed all the more interesting. Later, after the patterns had fallen out of fashion, the color remained, particularly in the Pinzgauer region. The fact that the stud book originated there probably ensured its inclusion at a time when most registries were eliminating pinto and appaloosa colors.

Even so, the color was almost lost. Like many appaloosa breeders before them, the Austrians found the desired color difficult to obtain. There has always been a strong preference for the true, nose-to-toes leopard patterns among Noriker breeders. The difficulty with that pattern is that, just like the palomino color that was so desirable in the United States in the middle of the twentieth century, it is the product of a gene that is incompletely dominant. The sought-after coloring only happens when the horse is heterozygous; in this case, for the leopard complex (Lp) gene. Heterozygous horses do not breed true. True-breeding stallions have the color in its less desirable homozygous form. For palominos, that means a breeder would need to accept a cremello stallion. For leopards, that would have mean using a few-spotted stallion. Furthermore, a breeding program that utilized only leopards would produce a high portion of mostly white homozygous few-spots. Breeding to solids would ensure that some foals were heterozygous and therefore spotted, but it also would produce a certain number of unpatterned varnish roans.

Unlike the palomino, though, which is governed by one incompletely dominant gene, the appaloosa patterns are the product of multiple genes. For breeders in the late nineteenth century, without a grasp of Mendelian genetics, getting the desired results would have been particularly difficult. To make matters even more complicated, the breed was undergoing a shift in body type, too. The horse needed not only to inherit the right pattern, but to have the desired type as well. It is not surprising then that older type persisted among the appaloosas, or that even among the modern strains the appaloosa lines often have Baroque traits.

The surviving appaloosa line is that of 80 AR-NULF 55 (1886), founder of the Elmar sire line. Horses from this sire line descend from his post-war descendant WILLERSDORF ELMAR (1954) and his black leopard son LERCH ELMAR (1958). Two black leopard sons of LERCH ELMAR, JANK ELMAR (1963) and ACHAT ELMAR X (1966) were used to preserve the line. Most stallions from the Elmar line trace to JANK ELMAR through his sons PETER ELMAR (1968), GRUNDNER ELMAR (1980) and JAN ELMAR (1983). ACHAT ELMAR X is more often found through the female side of the pedigree, usually through his daughters FLICKA and HASENA-LONI.

Silesian Norikers have an additional appaloosa line in NEUWIRTH DIAMANT IX (1952), founder of the Neuwirth Diamant sire line. The color comes from a separate branch of the Elmar line, tracing back through his sire HEIMERER DIAMANT (1948) and his maternal grandsire 1483 ACHAT ELMAR V-49. The most influential son of NEUWIRTH DIA-MANT was NEUGOT-2 (1966), who appears in the pedigrees of the modern stallions NAVAR (1998), NACHO SALAZAR ZV (2001), and WHITE TIGER (2003).

The Elmar line carried both the leopard complex and the leopard pattern mutation (*PATN1*). That is still the most common pattern found in Norikers. Suppressed leopard patterns, often called near-leopards, are also relatively common. In some cases, the pattern is suppressed enough that the horse might be mistaken for a blanket appaloosa. There have been Norikers with a true blanket pattern and this still occurs upon occasion. It is considered acceptable by many breeders, though no blanketed stallions have been used in Austria in recent years. Appaloosas without one of the white patterning mutations, varnish roans, are not held in favor and in the past some may not have been registered. This has led to the assumption that varnish roan is not found among Norikers, which is not true. Varnish roan is present because it is a necessary component for creating the desirable patterns. It

The nose-to-toes leopard pattern on this stallion, JUDAS ELMAR, is strongly preferred by Noriker breeders. Varnish roans are not typically retained as breeding stallions.

is rarely seen, just as the mostly white few-spots are rarely seen, because males—the gender more often publicized—of those colors are not typically retained for breeding.

Breeders in the Czech Republic accept a wider range of appaloosa patterns in their breeding stallions. The stallion NEMO (1992) was a bay varnish roan, and the current stallion FALSTR (2007) is a chestnut varnish roan. The stallion NEUGAR (1989) was a chestnut with a spotted blanket, though in later years he developed vivid snow-flake-style roaning. Chestnut and bay leopards are also more common in Silesian Norikers than in the Austrian population, where black base colors are preferred.

Tobiano

Although the leopard pattern is the one most often mentioned in association with Norikers in late nineteenth-century accounts, some authors state that the breed is found in either appaloosa or pinto. In a report on the International Horse and Cattle Shows of the 1873 Universal Exhition in Vienna made to the British House of Parliament, it was noted that one of the stallions representing the Noriker was a "splendid piebald." The horse was greatly admired by the King of Italy, which caused the Emperor of Austria to make a gift of him.

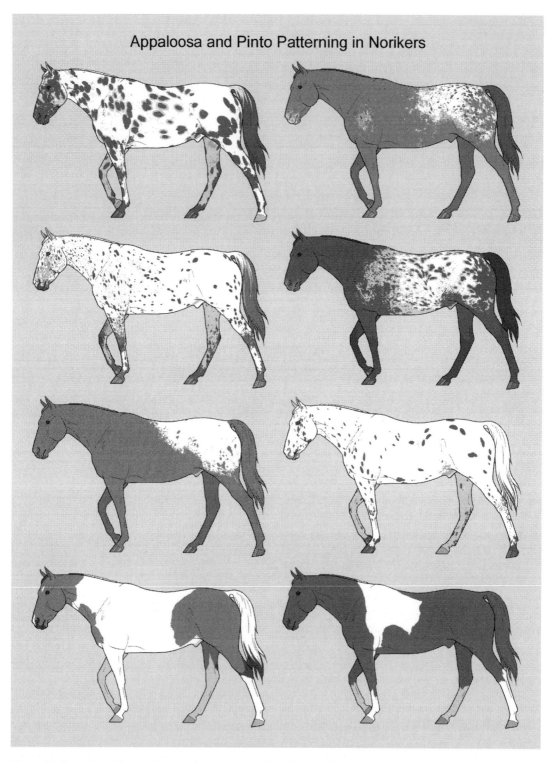

Appaloosa and Pinto Patterning in Norikers

Figure 16. Examples of the appaloosa and pinto patterns found in Norikers

The natural assumption is that the *schecke* and piebald Norikers were tobianos, since it was found among the Baroque horses and was the most common pinto pattern in Continental Europe at the time. It is also possible that the German authors were referring to different types of appaloosa patterns, since the term used for pinto, *schecke*, is sometimes paired with descriptive terms to indicate appaloosa patterns other than leopard. That is unlikely in the case of the British correspondent in Vienna, though; in that country piebald has traditionally meant tobiano. Were the stallion in question appaloosa patterned, the reporter would have referred to him as spotted, since that is British term.

Whether the early *schecke* Norikers were tobiano or not, the pattern is certainly present in the current population. There were twenty-nine living tobiano Norikers in 2008, making it the smallest color group at 1 percent of the population. All descend from HERMINE-FRIEDA, a chestnut tobiano mare foaled in 1969. Her pattern came from her dam, SUSI, who was born sometime during World War II and was said to have been of Haflinger and warmblood breeding. Her sire, KARL NERO, was a black Noriker.

HERMINE-FRIEDA was part of a program developed by the University of Vienna in partnership with the Vienna Zoo. The goal was to preserve the appaloosa and pinto colors once present in the breed. At the Zoo, HERMINE-FRIEDA produced a black tobiano son, BAJAZZO VULKAN (1976) and a chestnut tobiano daughter, HERTA (1985). BAJAZZO appears in modern pedigrees through his granddaughter VERA (1994) and grandson GAUNER VULKAN (1993). Both VERA and GAUNER VULKAN are black tobianos.

HERTA produced the black tobiano stallion LOTTO VULKAN (1992). LOTTO has two black tobiano sons, LUIGI VULKAN (2001) and LANCELOT VULKAN (2005). His daughter LENI produced the bay tobiano stallion TOMI VULKAN (2006). Bred to the BAJAZZO granddaughter VERA, LOTTO VULKAN produced VANNI, dam of the black tobiano stallion RIGO NERO (2002).

Pintaloosa

Although not a traditional color in Norikers, there has been at least one pintaloosa mare. BAROLA (2009) is a black varnish roan tobiano mare by LOTTO VULKAN and out of a granddaughter of LESSACH ELMAR. Both her sire and GAUNER VULKAN are by the leopard stallion GRUNDNER VULKAN (1986). GAUNER VULKAN has roaning along the top edge of the dark spot on his hip, but he does not appear to have any appaloosa characteristics so it is probably tobiano roaning. Neither inherited the leopard complex mutation, but it is possible that they and some of their tobiano descendants carry a hidden pattern-1 mutation. To be a leopard and not a varnish roan, GRUNDNER must have had at least one copy of the pattern-1 mutation. His tobianos sons, lacking the leopard complex mutation, would not show it but could carry it. Because it is thought that patterning genes are not visible on horses without the leopard complex mutation (*Lp*), and because Norikers have been bred for colorful patterns in the past, it is possible that individuals in the solid (and pinto) color lines carry hidden appaloosa patterning genes.

Frescoes of colorful horses decorate the Pferdeschwemme, or horse well, in Salzburg. They were painted by Josef Ebner in 1732, forty-four years after the Archbishop ruled that Salzburg mares could not be bred to foreign stallions. This horse is interesting because the white area centered on his neck is characteristic of frame overo, a pattern not thought to exist in Europe at the time.

The brindle stallion, NORBERT, was a Silesian Noriker. Now considered a separate breed, Silesian Norikers have a long history of their own, although they descend from some of the same breeding families as the Austrian horses.

Silver and Silver-Maned Bays
There are Norikers that look black silver. Doubts about whether or not they carry the silver mutation are raised by the fact that so many of the closely related Black Forest Horse also look silver, but to date have tested to be chestnut. A suspected silver Noriker stallion is pictured in the second edition of *Equine Color Genetics*, by Phillip Sponenberg. It is noted there that the horse had red silver half siblings, which would argue strongly that the mutation is present, if rare, within the Noriker.

There was at least one "white-maned" bay, the OPUS DIAMANT son 363 MAX DIAMANT III (1921). The trait was not popular among breeders, so it was likely that the horses with it were not used for breeding. It is possible that he had the same silvered mane seen in some bay Black Forest Horses, and his coloring was unrelated to the silver dilution.

There is a bay Silesian Noriker stallion, NÝR (1993), with the type of flaxen mane and tail sometimes seen in the Swedish Ardennes and the Polish Coldblood. His points appear to be true black and lack the flaxen dapples of a typical silver dilute. His son NAROK ZE SELCŮ (2002) is also flaxen-maned, though he is a mealy wild bay. NÝR is from the Nero Diamant sire line, but the connection between that line and the one to MAX DIAMANT, if there is any, is not clear.

Grey
Grey is not present in the Austrian Noriker, and is not thought to have been part of the original population. It can be found in a handful of individual horses in the Silesian population. One is the mare SHARON (2003). Her dam, MAGDA (1993), was also grey, but at that point the source of the color becomes a mystery. The sire of MAGDA, AMUR, is registered as black and her dam, LUNA, is registered as bay. No greys appear in the next five generations of her pedigree. Because greys must have at least one grey parent, either the parentage or the color designations are incorrect.

White Ticking
Several of the Silesian stallions show pronounced white ticking, including HENE (1992) and NESAN (1999). Both are chestnut with blazes and white leg markings, so it is likely that the ticking is related to one of the sabino patterns. That is probably also true of the chestnut stallion STREIGRIP (1994). He has a sprinkling of white hairs throughout his coat and a blaze with roaned edges, but no white on his legs. He is by the bay roan STREIGAR, a descendant of VULKO, but he does not appear to be a true roan. Of his sixteen registered foals, none are roan. One daughter, KARLA, was registered as chestnut with white ticking.

Historical Colors
Because Spanish horses were used during the period prior to the formation of the stud book, it is likely that the Norikers of the seventeenth and eighteenth centuries were even more colorful than the ones seen today. Frescoes painted at the height of the Baroque period around the Pferdeschwemme (horse pool) in Salzburg depict palomino, buckskin, grey, and leopard patterned horses. There is even one horse that has what looks like a loud sabino-frame pattern.

In a listing of colors found at the Rieß stud in the early nineteenth century compiled by breed historian Thomas Druml, a number of colors appear that are no longer found in the Noriker. Among these is *hermelin*, which is a term that most often meant cremello or perlino. Among the mares, it was the fourth most populous color after bay, black and roan. Nine breeding mares, two fillies and one stud colt were listed as *hermelin*. The belief that these white horses were double-diluted creams is supported by the fact that there were eight buckskins and five palominos on the list as well. A single grey mare was also included. Interestingly enough, the one color not represented among the adult horses was chestnut. Chestnut was considered undesirable by the stud, so while chestnut foals were born, they do not appear to have been retained for breeding.

There was also a Silesian Noriker, Norbert (1901), that was a brindled roan. Brindling in horses is little understood, but most pronounced brindles have proven to be chimeras. The brindling on Norbert is concentrated in the roaned areas, leaving his head and points dark. This could happen in a chimeric brindle if the two fused horses were black and black roan, since the merged coats would not be visible on the head or the legs, where both horses would have been black. Only one photo is known to exist of Norbert, and it does not appear that he has modern descendants. (The Silesian founder 41 Norbert was a different horse.)

Because colors are not known for some of the earlier Norikers, it is unclear how long these more exotic colors and patterns persisted. It is likely that many of these colors were lost long before the formation of the stud book, although some may have remained in the mare population for a time. That can be seen in the earliest volumes of many European stud books, where off-colored mares, particularly cream dilutes, were still found in small numbers.

Eye Color

To date there is no evidence of modern Norikers with light or blue eyes, and it appears that the patterns and dilutions likely to produce unusual eye colors were not, or are no longer, present in the breeding population. In some breeds where flashy markings are not found, but that have tobiano, blue-eyed or partially blue eyed foals have been born. This, along with an increase in facial white, seems to occur more frequently in breeds where tobianos are crossed—something that is not yet done with a lot of frequency in the Noriker. Should that become more common, and if there is in fact any link between blue eyes and the tobiano pattern, this might change.

Markings

While some Norikers, particularly chestnuts, do have blazes and white on their legs, breeders have traditionally preferred moderate or even unmarked horses. For this reason, white markings tend to be conservative, particularly on the legs.

Breeders of roan Norikers prefer solid, unmarked horses and not only prefer to use black horses without markings when crossing their roans, but those without chestnut breeding. The belief is that the chestnut lines increase the chance that markings will appear on the dark offspring as well as the chestnut. The absence of white markings also contributes to the more desirable expressions of the appaloosa patterns. Loudly patterned appaloosas without sabino patterning, which is closely associated with face and leg markings, tend to be more reliable color producers.

The situation is a little different in the Silesian Noriker, where white markings are more common and a wider range of them are seen. There has been at least one body-marked Silesian Noriker, the chestnut sabino mare, Dorka (1997). Dorka has a typical flashy sabino pattern with a blaze, peaked hind stockings and a large patch of white on her left side.

North American Spotted Draft

Origin: United States

If the Gypsy Cob could be referred to as a (small) Shire with spots, the North American Spotted Draft might just as easily be referred to as a Percheron with spots. Although other breeds and patterns are permitted, from the start breeders have favored black tobianos with an American Percheron build.

Stud Book

The North American Spotted Draft Horse Association was formed in 1995. Originally the registry accepted draft crosses, grades of draft type and purebred draft horses that displayed a pinto pattern. In 2000, the registry stopped accepting horses that were already registered with another breed registry. In 2010, the registry closed the Index division of the stud book, which was used to record grade horses of draft type. Prior to that decision, the Index functioned much like a grading up register in that horses in the division could be used for breeding provided they were crossed with horses from the other sections. Horses in the Index as of March 2010 were grandfathered and could be bred using the rules present when they were admitted.

The Regular division is for horses that have from one-half to seven-eighths draft horse blood. The Premium division is for horses with seven-eighths or more of draft horse blood. Parents that are not registered with the association must be from one of the six recognized draft horse breeds: Belgian, Percheron, Shire, Clydesdale, American Cream Draft, or Suffolk. Drum Horses may be used if they have a NASDHA Certificate of Identification, but Gypsy Vanners and Tinkers are not permitted. The non-draft portion can be any registered light horse breed that does not have appaloosa patterning or the tendency to gait.

A Breeding Stock division is in place for those horses that would otherwise qualify for the Regular or Premium stud book, but that do not have enough white. Only stallions and mares may be admitted since the intention is to preserve the bloodlines while breeding back the desired color.

In 2000 the founders of the registry, Gayle and Lowell Clark, split from the original organization. A second organization, the Pinto Draft Registry, was established in 2002. It accepts purebred draft horses if they are spotted, as well as draft crosses.

Population

The North American Spotted Draft Horse Association reported registering 223 horses in 2008, 130 horses in 2009 and 133 horses in 2010. The organization currently has more than 4,000 horses registered.

Colors

To qualify for full registration, North American Spotted Drafts have to have a minimum amount of white on the body. Foals must have at least four square inches, while a yearling must have eight. Adults must have fifteen square inches. In all cases the white has to occur within a proscribed area of the body beyond just flashy face and leg markings.

Summary

Current colors: Black is most common, followed by chestnut and bay. Silver, champagne, cream and dun dilutions are seen occasionally. Grey and roan are uncommon. Because the registry is not closed, and because Paint Horses are popular for crossing, almost any base color is possible.

Markings/patterns: Spotted Drafts may have any of the pinto patterns. Tobiano is most common, but frame overo and sabino are seen, as are combinations of those patterns. Because of the use of black Percherons, many of the tobianos have dark or minimally marked faces.

Eye color: The eyes may be any color. Blue and dark eyes are found on non-diluted horses, and blue, amber or green eyes are seen in some of the dilutes.

Restrictions: Horses must have the minimum amount of white, or if the pattern is primarily white, the minimum amount of color. Appaloosa patterns are not permitted.

For those horses that are primarily white, the same minimums apply to the colored spots, so an adult would have to have at least fifteen square inches of color to qualify for regular papers.

Those are the rules regarding the patterns of white. There are no limits to the base colors and modifiers that can be found. Because Percherons have been popular for crossing, black is particularly common, but bay and chestnut are also seen. Although grey is common in Percherons and roan is found in Belgians, neither is common among Spotted Drafts since the white hairs reduce the contrast of the pattern.

Paint Horses are popular for adding the desired patterns, but their use also opens the door to some of the basic colors not typically found among the draft breeds.

Silver

There are North American Spotted Drafts that have the silver dilution. One known carrier is the palomino tobiano mare BUTTERCUP KISSES. At least two of her foals, the chestnut tobiano colt MOUNTAIN VIEW SAMSON (2009) and the red silver tobiano filly MOUNTAIN VIEW GINGER KISSES (2010), have tested positive for the gene. Others, while not tested, look like good candidates for testing. The winning gelding JH's PRINCE JACKSON (2005) is a vividly dappled black silver tobiano. Because black is a common base color, black silvers of this variety would not be difficult to breed.

There are stock breeds, including Paint Horses, that carry the silver dilution. Grade horses can also be a source for the silver dilution. The other source is the American Belgian. Belgians were popular in Pregnant Mare Urine (PMU) operations, and were often crossed with black Paint Horse stallions to get large, colored riding horses. Silver-diluted tobiano horses of draft type have come from those crosses. A good example is the gelding RU PARDNER from the Young Horse Teaching and Research Program at Rutgers. A brown silver tobiano, he is by the brown tobiano Paint MCCUE TUX and out of a blonde sorrel Belgian mare. Since MCCUE TUX would have shown the silver dilution if he carried it, the color must have come from his Belgian dam.

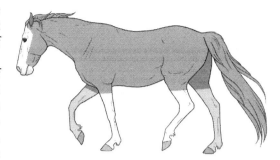

To qualify for regular registration papers, adult North American Spotted Drafts must have a total of 15 square inches of white that fall within the shaded area indicated in this illustration. Primarily white horses must have 15 square inches of color that fall within the shaded area.

Champagne

There has been at least one mare with the champagne gene registered with the North American Spotted Draft Association. MRB STORMS MYSTIC (2009) is an amber champagne tovero. Her champagne coloring comes from her American Cream Draft dam, BREHM'S SWEDE LILA. Her pattern, and the black gene (*E*) necessary for her bay base color came from her black tovero sire, MRB STORMY KNIGHT. Because the American Cream Draft is one of the approved outcross breeds, it would be possible to introduce more champagne lines into the breed. At least one Cream Draft stallion, JOKER'S GOLDEN BOY, is being used for breeding Spotted Drafts, so it is likely that more will be registered in the future.

Other Dilutions

Palomino and buckskin tobianos are seen upon occasion. One of the earliest stallions, RANGELINE BERT (1992) was a buckskin tobiano. The stallion CLARKS LAKE SCREAMING DEVIL is a very dark buckskin tobiano that carries Rangeline breeding. Like many of the buckskins from that line, he is dark enough to be mistaken for brown.

There was one stallion, CAPTAIN AVERY, advertised as a red dun tobiano, but in photos he appears to be a red silver rather than a red dun. It can be difficult to assess tobianos for dun because the white can cover the areas where the dorsal stripe and the leg barring would be. Both dilutions are

Although the most common pattern in North American Spotted Drafts is tobiano, some like this frame stallion 3B DEAKON, are overos.

found in the Paint Horse population, so it would not be hard to increase the numbers of those colors if a breeder desired.

Although none have been identified to date, it would be possible to bring the pearl dilution into the Spotted Draft using the BARLINK MACHO MAN bloodlines in the Paint Horse. His maternal granddam MY TONTIME carried the pearl dilution, and a number of his descendants have inherited it.

Tobiano

The inspiration for the formation of the registry was a black tobiano stallion named PECOS CHIEF (1980). He was purchased at a draft horse auction by Lowell and Gayle Clark and was said to have been by a Percheron stallion and out of a pinto draft mare. He attracted a lot of attention when, as a yearling, he took third place in the open draft halter class at the National Western Stock Show. He later went on to win the Supreme Champion Stallion at the New Mexico State Fair. Although some individuals kept spotted drafts, horses of draft breeding were not accepted by the Pinto Horse Association of America. The success of PECOS CHIEF and his offspring were the catalyst for the formation of a registry for pintos that had draft horse breeding or were of draft type.

It is not surprising then that tobiano remains the predominant pattern in the breed, or that the ma-

jority of the breeding stallions are black tobianos. In additional to PECOS CHIEF, who lived until 23 years of age, early black tobiano stallions include BHR BRYANT'S FLASH, WYOMING HOMBRE, and INDY PRINCE CODY.

Because it is possible to have horses that are homozygous for black and for tobiano, it is possible to get true-breeding black tobianos. That is probably part of the reason so many Spotted Draft stallions are this color. Not only is it the traditional color of the breed, but stallions like this produce 100 percent color when bred to solid draft mares. That, along with the fact that the pattern almost always produces enough white in the right places, eliminates the risk of producing less valuable Breeding Stock horses.

Sabino

The registry accepts both tobiano and overo patterns. Tobiano does not occur among the traditional draft horse breeds found in the United States, but sabino does. At least one registered Clydesdale stallion, LANDVIEW SILVER CHIEF (1998), and at least two Belgians, DIAMOND S. PAUL (1995) and his daughter SEDOR LADY DIVA (2001), were registered when the stud book still accepted purebred draft horses. (The pattern on LANDVIEW SILVER CHIEF appears in the top left corner of Figure 15, and the pattern on DIAMOND S. PAUL appears in Figure 14.)

A high percentage of Clydesdales have sabino patterns loud enough meet the patterning requirements for Spotted Drafts. Clydesdales were not used in breeding Spotted Drafts to the same extent as the Percheron or Belgian, so their eligibility went largely unnoticed by breeders. When the North American Spotted Draft Horse Association closed its books to previously registered draft horses in 2000, it cut off the possibility of Clydesdales developing into a large, dual-registered population within the registry.

Although sabino patterns can be found among the Spotted Drafts, they are most often seen in combination with tobiano. Tobianos can have the blazes and white upper lips and chins often seen on sabinos, and chestnut tobianos—particularly those with American Belgian breeding—sometimes have the ragged or lacey-edged spots often associated with sabino.

Frame Overo

Although less common than tobiano, there are frame overo Spotted Drafts. The Bryant Horse Ranch in Canada produced a number of frame overos, including the stallions 3B DEAKON and BHR BRYANT'S JAKE. Most of the time the color comes from crosses to registered Paint Horses, though like the tobianos sometimes the color comes from grade horses. Just as in American Paint Horses, sabino is often paired with frame, but there have been a few with just the frame pattern. The mares LUCKY L'S PERFECT DIAMOND and LUCKY L'S JEWEL are likely frame overos without the any of the sabino influence.

Eye Color

Dark or blue eyes are equally acceptable for registration purposes, but most Spotted Drafts have dark eyes. Blue eyes, or partially blue eyes, are more common in horses with one of the overo patterns. Spotted Drafts that carry the champagne dilution have amber eyes.

Markings

Many tobiano Spotted Drafts have solid or nearly solid faces. The absence of sabino, which is also noticeable in the simplified tobiano pattern seen on many Spotted Drafts, is probably a reflection of the influence of the minimally-marked Percherons many breeders used as outcrosses. Many of the descendants of PECOS CHIEF are marked this way. Others do have blazes or even bald faces, though compared to the Gypsy Horses or even the average Paint Horse, the amount of color that remains on the heads (on average) is notable.

Most Spotted Drafts have white legs. The kind of minimal, skewed tobiano pattern that often produces dark legs is not typical. Overos often have white on one or more legs due to the presence of one of the sabino patterns. Spotted Drafts that are pure for the frame pattern do have solid or only minimal markings on the legs, but these are less common than those with a socks or stockings.

Percheron

ORIGIN: Le Perche, France

The Percheron is one of the best-known of the draft breeds, and the second-most populous breed in America after the Belgian. Known for the beauty of its head and the quality of its movement, the breed is sometimes referred to as an Arabian that has been given draft horse proportions.

Stud Book

The first Percherons were imported to the United States in 1839. In 1848, the *American Agriculturist* ran an article titled "The Norman Horse" along with an engraving of Louis-Phillippe, a second generation stallion from those original imports. The article contained no reference to Percherons or even to the Perche region of France. At the time, draft horses from France were commonly referred to by breeders and importers as Normans. It was not a name used in France, but more likely a fanciful term coined by men who believed the horses were descendants of the ancient Norman war horse.

When fourteen men met in 1876 and formed the National Association of Importers and Breeders of Norman Horses, they laid the foundation for the oldest equine breed association in the United States, and the second oldest registry for draft horses in the world. Almost immediately there was conflict over what to call the horses. Although the organization had decided upon the more commonly accepted term "Norman", the first stud book was published in 1878 with the name "Percheron-Norman." This caused a rift between those who believed there was one breed with regional variations, and those who believed those variations were in fact separate breeds and that only the Percheron was suitable. Those believing the former split off in 1880 to form the National Norman Horse Association, while the latter formed a society for the Percheron-Norman.

The National Norman Horse Association published fifteen volumes of the National Register of Norman Horses. Its stated purpose was to establish a stud book in which "all full-blooded French draught horses can be properly registered, whether such animals be of Augeron, of Breton, of Boulonnais, of Cauchois, of Percheron, or of any other local origin." It was the position of those who supported the organization that the different draft horses found in France were only different strains of the same animal: the Norman. To a small degree, this position would later be partially validated in 1966 when the French government declared some of the minor French draft breeds (the Nivernais, Berrichon, Trait du Maine and the Augeron) to be exactly that, and merged their stud books with the one for the Percheron.

That came decades too late to help those advocating for a unified Norman breed. The nail in the coffin was the establishment of distinct draft breed registries in France, in particular the formation of the *Societe Hippique Perchonne* in 1883. Later that same year the membership of the rival Percheron-Normal society unanimously voted to issue the following decree:

> "the cumbersome and untruthful compound name Percheron-Norman, originally adopted in a spirit of compromise, should be abandoned, and that the name Percheron, which had from the first been advocated, as the only true name for this the most famous of all French breeds, should be used in its stead."

That association then dropped Norman from its name, and began to publish the Percheron Stud

A Currier and Ives print of the 1873 prize winning Percheron stallion Duc de Chartres. *Draft horses were unknown in America prior to the late nineteenth century.*

Book of America. A new stud book was printed in 1888 containing all the horses entered in the earlier Percheron-Norman books as well as the new animals scheduled for what would have been the fourth volume. After that point, only those horses originating from the French stud books could be admitted. In 1905 the organization was renamed the Percheron Society of America. In 1911 the stud books in France were closed to all but the offspring of registered parents, effectively closing the American stud books to outside blood as well. The name of the American registry changed again in 1934 to the current Percheron Horse Association of America.

Population

The European Farm Animal Biodiversity Information System states that as of 2001 the French Percheron breeding population was around 3,500 animals, with approximately 159 breeding stallions. The *Societe Hippique Perchonne* enters approximately 800 new horses in the stud book each year. In America, the breed has seen dramatic swings in population, from an estimated 10,000 horses being imported annually at the beginning of the twentieth century to 85 horses registered in 1954. Presently the Percheron Horse Association of America registers approximately 2,500 new horses annually. The Canadian Percheron Association registers approximately 500 horses annually. The American Livestock Breeds Conservancy lists Percherons as Recovering, which means the population is large enough that the breed no longer requires close monitoring to ensure its survival.

Colors

The two colors most closely associated with the Percheron are grey and black. In many countries, including France, those are the only colors accepted for registration. The American registry accepts purebred foals regardless of color, but black and grey predominate.

In France, the favored color has always been grey. At the present time, around 70 percent of the French horses are grey, while the rest are black. Just a decade ago, that percentage was closer to 90 percent. Although the base color under the grey is

Summary

Current colors: Black and grey are the most common colors, while bay, chestnut and roan are rare.

Historical colors: There was a single French mare registered as *isabelle*, though her exact color is not known.

Markings/patterns: Most American Percherons are minimally marked. European Percherons are more likely to have blazes, but as with the American horses leg white is rare. Chestnut and bays tend to have more white than the black, grey or roan horses.

Eye color: The eyes are dark.

Restrictions: The French registry does not permit bay, chestnut or roan. The American registry does not restrict color.

not recorded in the French stud books, it can be assumed that most if not all the greys are genetically black. Most of the greys are dappled, often quite strikingly so.

The widespread presence of the grey coloring is sometimes attributed to a pair of grey Arabian stallions, GODOLPHIN and GALLIPOLY, stationed at the national stud at Le Pin in the early nineteenth century. This was the oral tradition by the mid-nineteenth century, and that is reflected in the background information provided in many of the early stud book entries. However sincere those beliefs must have been at the time they were recorded, investigations of government records conducted on behalf of *The Breeder's Gazette* (a weekly paper devoted to livestock breeding) showed that while stallions of that name had stood at Le Pin during that time, neither were Arabians. One was not even grey. GODOLPHIN, foaled in 1802, was a golden chestnut of primarily English blood-horse breeding from the Meckleburg-Strelitz Stud. Instead of contributing "tone and ardor" to the Percheron, as one writer claimed, GODOLPHIN was repeatedly criticized in stallion inspection reports as having a poor croup and of being common and without quality. He was eventually removed from the stud.

GALLIPOLY, foaled in 1803, was a grey. Described as "speckled-grey" at age ten, it seems likely that he was fleabitten. He was a Turk rather than an Arabian, though it must be said that at the time the distinctions between Turks and Arabians and even Barbs were treated rather carelessly. What did strike the researchers looking at the records was that after seven years at Le Pin, inspectors recommended that GALLIPOLY be removed because he was producing horses too small to be suitable for use as remounts. Remounts being generally smaller and lighter than even the lightest varieties of Percherons bred at the time, it seemed unlikely that such a horse could be the fountainhead for a modern draft breed.

What does seem likely is that the horses native to La Perche were influenced by earlier Eastern horses, and that they were the likely source for the grey coloring. The French routed the Moslems in the Battle of Tours in 732 and it is reasonable to assume that horses were taken from the defeated army. Still others may have returned following the Crusades. Many of those horses were quite likely grey, given the frequency with which the color has always been found in the Arabian breed. In fact, grey coloring appears to have been associated with

Although draft horses are often thought of as agricultural animals, during the boom in the late nineteenth and early twentieth century it was urban use that helped fuel demand. Pictured here is a detail shot from a panoramic view of the trademark dapple grey Percherons owned by the Ringling Brothers Circus in 1914. Over 1,400 horses were utilized by the Ringling Brothers and Barnum & Bailey Circuses, many as baggage stock horses.

the horses of La Perche prior to the time GODOLPHIN and GALLIPOLY served at Le Pin. (It is equally interesting that the flashy white markings of the sabino pattern, which are also a common sign of Eastern influence, were not common among the horses of the region.)

At the time many breeders were seeking larger, heavier stallions as the market shifted away from fast trotting coach horses to true draft horses. The French government responded by stationing the first draft stallions at Le Pin in 1808. The term Percheron was not yet in use, so the stallions were listed on the rolls simply as *de trait*, or draft horse. Almost all were grays. Those of the older Boulonnais breed were listed as such, so it can be assumed that these were native Perche stallions rather than Boulonnais. That is not to say that the horses might not have carried some portion of Boulonnais blood. Such claims created a lot of controversy during the formation of the stud books, made even more charged by the politics surrounding the competing organizations. Some early breed historians were adamant that the Percheron was completely unrelated. Others from the same time insisted that this was exactly what the early Percherons were: crosses between the heavy Boulonnais and the smaller, more active Breton. This assertion has been called into question by recent genetic analysis that does not place either the Breton or the Boulonnais in an ancestral position to the Percheron. The study did show the Percheron had closer ties to some of the light horse breeds than to the Boulonnais. Because the development of the Percheron happened prior to the establishment of breed registries, any number of suitable work horses found in the area probably went into their make-up.

While dapple grey was the favored color in France, solid black was preferred by many American buyers. The winning Percheron mare Ruth and stallion Glacis at the 1911 Kansas State Fair are typical of the horses of the era.

Whether or not the Boulonnais was used, the grey color was preferred from the start. It is interesting to note that one stallion, Superior, was noted as not being in demand to the extent that his quality warranted because he sired some sorrels and "a certain shade of gray which does not please the farmers." Just what unappealing shade this might have been is not noted, but the prevalence of dapple greys among the recorded stallions suggests that the preference for vivid dappling among Percheron breeders might have a long history.

The government instituted a prize scheme for heavy draft stallions in 1820, and of the first three stallions approved, Superb, Le Curieux and Le Percheron, two were dapple grey. The third was bay. Other stallions were added and again most were dapple grey. In the years that followed, the stallions used were overwhelmingly grey. The mares, which were often listed in the books as Percherons, were mostly grey, with a smaller portion of bays and blacks. Chestnut was even less common, but there were mares of that color as well. By 1833, the approved stallions were all white, dapple grey or silver grey with white manes and tails. It was not long before most of the mares were grey as well.

It was a color in great demand at the time, particularly among teamsters who felt that grey horses were easier to see at night. Grey coloring became so associated with the Percheron that it allowed

those raising other French draft breeds to, in the words of the writers of the mid-nineteenth century, "percheronize" their horses by breeding greys and sending them to La Perche for finishing and selling. In *The Percheron Horse*, published in 1868, author Charles du Hays devotes an entire chapter to the following question: "Ought the Gray Color of the Percheron to be Inflexibly Maintained?" He confesses a long-standing preference for the traditional coloring of the breed, but speculates that broadening the color might reduce "plagiarism" by defining the breed by quality rather than by color. He also points to the declining fashion for grey horses abroad, and suggests that the time may have come to find high quality dark Percherons and use them to add color to the existing grey horses. He even goes so far as to recommend that, absent dark Percherons, breeders resort to the use of "fine, dark skin Arabs" or even "well-chosen Norfolks." There was, at least at that time, a certain prejudice among French breeders against dark colors because they were seen as the colors of an English, rather than French, horse.

By the turn of the century, black was rapidly becoming the preferred color for many breeders. This was largely a reaction to the profitable American export market, where there had always been a fairly strong preference for dark colors. This caused a certain amount of consternation among some breeders that felt the color was a sign of outcrossing to the closely related Nivernais, which was uniformly black. While that it certainly possible, it is also pretty likely that the Percherons had the color within their own breeding stock. By selecting for vividly dappled horses, the early Percheron breeders were inadvertently breeding for black, since that color tends to grey out in a more dramatic fashion. (Shetland Pony breeders a century later discovered that breeding rich, nonfading blacks to silvers gave them particularly dramatic silver dapples.)

In 1966 the Nivernais was designated as a derivative sub-race of the Percheron, and the stud books were merged, making the question of outcrossing moot. For the American stud books, however, black became the defining color of the breed almost from the start. It remains the more

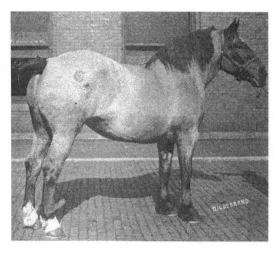

The imported blue roan mare IMPRUDENTE won numerous championships in the early twentieth century.

popular color with modern breeders, and American Percherons are almost as black as the Continental horses are grey.

So it was that the horses recorded in the early stud books were primarily grey or black. There were other colors that were preserved, however, despite the genetic bottleneck that occurred when the population was dramatically reduced following World War II. Some of this was intentional preservation on the part of a handful of American breeders, but much of it was because the greying process could mask the less popular colors and allow them to go largely unnoticed.

Roan
This was especially true of dark-headed roan, which is still found in small numbers among the American Percherons. It is a color that is often assumed by modern horsemen to have slipped in through some distant (or not-so-distant) crossings on Brabants. It is an understandable assumption, given that the color is common in Brabants and such crosses are not unusual among grade draft horses, some of which are then marketed simply as unregistered Percherons. It is, however, a color that was present from the beginning of the breed. In France one of the 1825 prize winners was AUBERT, a strawberry roan. Records show that he bred between 70 and 90 mares a year, which were

respectable numbers during that time. At the same time, a number of the mares being bred to approved stallions are listed as red roan.

The color also came the American in the form of imports. The most successful of these was the blue roan mare IMPRUDENTE (1908) who was named Champion Percheron Mare at both the Illinois and Wisconsin State Fairs, as well as taking Reserve Champion Percheron Mare at the International Live Stock Exposition in 1910 and 1911. The photograph of her that appears in the *Book of Live Stock Champions* shows a classic dark-headed roan with a star and two hind ankles.

IMPRUDENTE was registered as "blue gray." It is a designation that was found occasionally in the early volumes of the French stud books as well, along with a handful of horses that were registered simply as blue. It is possible that those horses were roans as well, but with so little information it is hard to know if the horses were roan or grey. In this regard, some of the later French Draft stud books are a little more useful because entries that were purebred Percherons (as opposed to Boulonnais or Bretons or mixes) were noted as such with a "P" beside their registration numbers, and the books have more detailed descriptions. Horses like the stallion HERISSON, recorded as "strawberry roan, black mane and tail" were probably dark-headed roans. Imported from France and registered at age eleven, it seems unlikely that he would still have a black mane and tail were he grey rather than roan.

IMPRUDENTE did have another relative registered as roan. That was the stallion PERDIX (1899), registered simply as "roan." PERDIX was a son of BEAUDOLE 34055, the paternal grandsire of IMPRUDENTE. The roan color had to have come through IMPRUDENTE's sire, since her dam PASSERELLE was black. It is not clear if BEAUDOLE was the source, since female lines at the time were often unrecorded. PERDIX had at least one roan daughter, the red roan French Draft EVANGELINE.

It was never common, and is easily hidden in a breed where most of the horses are grey. Some Percherons grey in ways that mimic roan pretty closely, which can make identification even more difficult. Even so, there are a few modern cases where unmistakable dark-headed roans can be found.

Most of these horses trace back to the mare Top-pers Justa Holly (1983). Holly is registered as a grey, but her parents, Crown Hill Justa Buddy and Toppers Topsy, are both registered as black. Since grey is dominant, grey horses must have at least one grey parent. If her parents colors are recorded properly, she cannot be a grey. Unfortunately, true roan works the same way. To get a roan, at least one parent must be roan. Her sire seems the most likely candidate for having an erroneously recorded color because he threw another grey from a different black mare. That foal was registered as having "scattered white hairs throughout the coat." Without photos it is impossible to know their true colors, but there is little question that whatever else she might have been, Holly passed along the roan coloring to some of her foals.

Another roan line comes through the mare Starlight Bonnie Laet (1971). Bonnie is registered as a dark grey, by the black Koncarhope Comet and out of the dark grey Starlight Koncar Laetta. She produced three different foals that either produced roans themselves or that had offspring that produced roans.

The first of these is the stallion Koncar Jim Laet. Like his dam, he was registered as a dark grey. He produced twenty-three foals, of which Sourdough's Blue Pearl and Jemclad Blue are registered as blue roans. His grey daughters Peggy's Laet, Mary Anne and Starlight Jodi Laet all produced blue roans.

The next of Bonnie Laet's roan producers was Jacklyn Laet. Like her half-brother Jim Laet, Bonnie was registered as grey. She produced the grey mare Bell, who in turn produced a single roan foal, Cottonwood Katie. Katie produced the roans Kate's Dandy Kandy Blue and B&C Princess Grace, who has gone on to produce roans of her own.

The last of the three was Jill Laet. Jill was a full sister to Jacklyn Laet, and like her she was registered as grey. She produced two blue roan daughters, Cottonwood Cassidy and Cottonwood Kaitlyn. She also produced a grey daughter, Cottonwood Kitt, who produced eleven foals, six of which were blue roans. Kitt belongs to Brad and Cindy Messersmith of Iowa, and is being used

in their program focusing on preserving the roan color in the Percheron breed.

Chestnut
The other less common color found in the original French horses was chestnut. It was always quite rare, and is no longer a permissible color in Europe, but it was present at the beginning. It is also a lot easier to confirm than roan because there is no confusion about the terminology used.

The first chestnut stallion appears in the first volume of the French stud book. That is Brilliant 613 (1882), listed as *alezan-brûlé*, or liver chestnut. There are four chestnut mares in the same volume: L'Amie 264, Lisette 413, Poule 255 and Rose 508. The second volume had one additional chestnut mare, L'Amie 42. There is also a stallion, Jupiter 2529, listed as *vineux* (wine-colored).

It is not surprising then that a handful of chestnut Percherons were imported to America. The color was rare, but during the height of the import craze the color was not yet associated with the Belgian breed. (Indeed, the Belgian was still largely unknown to many draft horse breeders at that point.) There was even the chestnut stallion Incluse, who took the championship at the Missouri State Fair in 1911.

Chestnut was always a rare color in the breed, but that did not prevent Incluse from taking the male grand championship at the 1911 Missouri State Fair.

Chestnuts are still found in small numbers among American Percherons. At least one breeding program, that of the Cedar Grove Stock Farm, has specialized in producing the color. One popular black stallion, JUSTAMERE SHOWTIME (1956), is known to carry the red gene. Among his chestnut offspring are BAR U SHOWTIME (1980) and BAR U PRINCE SHOWTIME (1980). The latter was used at Cedar Grove, producing twenty-three foals of which seventeen were chestnut.

A fairly high percentage of chestnut Percherons have flaxen manes and tails. Self-colored manes and even slightly darker manes are also seen. A few Percherons have had gray manes and tails, including the mare CEDAR GROVE FAN'S MEG.

Bay
Bay is the rarest of the colors found in American Percherons, but is not permitted by the French registry. That was not always the case; the first government stallion specifically listed as a Percheron was the bay DESARMÉ, foaled in 1815 and sent to the stud at Le Pin in 1821. It was even more common among the mares listed on the stallions' service

Color Percentages in the American Percheron

	black	grey	chestnut	bay	roan
1990-1992	3028	2006	44	12	5
(percentage)	*59%*	*39%*	*1%*	*<1%*	*~0%*
1993-1995	3732	2424	86	19	6
(percentage)	*59%*	*39%*	*1%*	*<1%*	*~0%*
1996-1998	4453	2424	70	15	6
(percentage)	*64%*	*35%*	*1%*	*<1%*	*~0%*
1999-2001	4909	2149	65	12	2
(percentage)	*69%*	*30%*	*1%*	*<1%*	*~0%*
2002-2004	5231	1890	39	13	2
(percentage)	*73%*	*26%*	*1%*	*<1%*	*~0%*
2005-2007	4758	1179	21	5	3
(percentage)	*80%*	*20%*	*<1%*	*~0%*	*~0%*
2008-2010	2820	551	19	2	0
(percentage)	*83%*	*16%*	*1%*	*~0%*	*0%*

Chart 11. Colors of Percherons registered in the American stud books from 1990 until 2010.

This American Percheron gelding has a narrow blaze and solid black legs. Blazes are more common on European Percherons, but white on the legs is uncommon for both groups.

rosters, but by the time the stud book was formed it was relatively uncommon. The first volume of the French stud book, published more than sixty years later in 1883, had a total of 73 bay stallions and 19 bay mares. That represented 7 percent and 5 percent respectively. (It should be noted that few mares were registered at the beginning of the stud book movement, so the early volumes of the draft breed stud books tend to be heavily skewed in terms of gender.) In the first volume of the American books, there were 87 bay stallions and 13 bay mares (10 percent and 8 percent).

There were those who liked the coloring. Alvin Howard Sanders, in his book *The History of the Percheron Horse*, wrote that Dr. J. T. Axtell was trying to establish a strain of bay Percherons, but noted that he found it difficult to obtain the color he sought. With bay rare and black so widespread in the American Percheron population, it is likely that the bays he had were heterozygous for Agouti. If his bays carried black, then bred to black mates he would still get black foals half the time. Using grey mates, which Sanders indicates he must have done, would have further reduced his chances since a portion of the foals would grey out even if they were initially born bay. It is little wonder that his program had no lasting effect.

The color did persist into the present day population, albeit only rarely, perhaps because it could be hidden under a grey coat. There was a breeder, Jack Selleck of Jemclad Percherons, attempting to preserve the bay color through the use of the stallion SWORDPOINT OOPS (1993). As his name suggests, OOPS was the unexpected result of a cross between the black EBONY OF GLYNLEA and the grey SPRUCEDALE CRYSTAL MONKARLAET. It must be assumed that the coloring came from his dam, since bay cannot hide in a line of black horses. Both parents of SPRUCEDALE CRYSTAL MONKARLAET were grey, and so were her grandparents. There do not appear to be any other bay horses born within the family, but since most are grey they might have passed unnoticed. Her only other foal was a gray mare, SWORDPOINT ABBIE. ABBIE has no foals listed in the Percheron Horse Association of America database, so it is impossible to know if she was bay or black beneath her grey coat.

The other bay line used by Jemclad was that of the dark bay mare ROCK CREST JASA (1975). JASA's sire was the black STARLIGHT KONCAR CHIEF, and her dam was the sorrel JASA HOPE WILLOWWOOD. Her dam's pedigree illustrates the role that chestnut can play in the production of bay horses. WILLOWWOOD was the product of the Cedar Side chestnut breeding program and represented several generations of chestnut Percherons. This is important because while most horsemen understand that black horses can carry a hidden chestnut gene (hence the occasional chestnut Friesian after generations of black x black crosses), it is the chestnut gene that can hide the dominant form of the Agouti gene. Black horses have the recessive form of the Agouti gene, which is why they are all-over black. The dominant form of Agouti (*A*) restricts the black to the points, creating the color bay, so black horses (*aa*) cannot carry it. Chestnut horses, however, do not have black pigment so the status of their Agouti gene is unknown. Chestnuts that appear unexpectedly from generations of black horses, like the example of the Friesians, are going to have the recessive form. They carry the recessive because the dominant gene—the one responsible for making bay—was eliminated to create the uniformly black population. But if a chestnut comes from a population where bay is found, or if the chestnut coloring is maintained over many generations reaching back to a time when bay was still present, it can be preserved.

That is what happened with ROCK CREST JASA. The bay coloring is a two-part genetic recipe, and each parent gave her one part. Her sire contributed the black gene (*E*) necessary for the bay pattern to show. Her dam gave her the Agouti instructions that sent the black pigment to the points (*A*), and not all over the body (*a*). Because the dam of ROCK CREST JASA was chestnut, she carried that color as well. JASA did not produce any chestnuts herself, but her daughter SHADY LANE BERTHA (1990) did.

It was BERTHA that was used in the Jemclad program. She was bred almost exclusively to SWORDPOINT OOPS and produced nine foals: six bays, two blacks and a chestnut. Among those the bay stallion JEMCLAD THUNDER BAY and the bay mare JEMCLAD SHIRLEY are being used in breeding programs. BERTHA's bay maternal half-brother, SHADY LANE BARN BURNER, was also used.

The other bay line came from JEMCLAD BESSIE, whose bay coloring came about in the same way as ROCK CREEK JASA. The parents were reversed in that she was by a chestnut stallion, RED DID IT (1988) and out of a black mare, WALNUT RIDGE KITT (1983). BESSIE produced two foals: one bay and one chestnut.

In total SWORDPOINT OOPS produced thirty-two foals, of which eighteen were bay. Unfortunately the death of Jack Selleck meant that the Jemclad horses were dispersed, and SWORDPOINT OOPS was gelded. Because he was bred to a number of bay mares, it may be that some of his descendants not only have the Agouti gene, but may well be homozygous for it.

Historical Colors

In the spring of 1865, John Klippart was commissioned to tour Germany and France on behalf of the Ohio State Board of Agriculture. He wrote that in France the Percheron was considered fashionable for coach and draft work, and that the most sought-after color was dappled grey. He noted that there was some question about whether the type

had been fixed because there were "so many colors". Later he stated that the horses he observed at exhibitions being called Percherons were usually "mottled", which was a term often used at that time for dapple greys, but that there were bright bays and some roans, duns and dark chestnut browns.

At least one dilute mare was registered in the early French stud books. That was CHARLOTTE 11069, foaled in 1877 and recorded as *isabelle*. Her sire, PICADOR I 7330, was a grey by the bay stallion BAYARD. Her unregistered dam, BIJOU, was not described so it is possible that the coloring came from her. Just what that color may have been, if indeed it was something other than the more typical grey, bay and black, has been lost to time. The term isabelle, much like the term dun in Britain, was used in France to describe palominos, buckskins, duns and even cremellos. CHARLOTTE left no recorded descendants, so her exact color remains open to speculation.

Eye Color

Registry records suggest that Percherons have uniformly dark eyes. Given the minimal nature of the markings found in the breed, and the absence of patterning mutations, blue eyes would be unexpected.

Markings

The markings on most of the early breeding stock remain a mystery since they were not recorded in the early stud books, and the grey coloring tends to hide whatever markings might otherwise have been visible in early portraits. It does seem that most of the foundation horses were only modestly marked with white. There was an approved stallion that stood at Loir-et-Cher in 1830 that was described as having four white feet. The fact that they were mentioned, when most of the stallions were simply grey or dapple grey, suggests that they were unusual.

In the American breeding population, little or no white is closer to the norm for the breed. White markings on the feet are quite unusual, though they can be found and have appeared on such famous stallions as CALYPSO (1897), whose photo was chosen by breeders from among twenty-five other champion stallions to represent ideal type in 1934, and the influential breeding stallion KON-CARCALYPS. It is likely that the desire to have a matched team played a part in the selection for dark legs, especially among American breeders who have historically preferred black Percherons. Unmatched leg markings are more noticeable on a black team than on a grey one.

Face markings, including blazes and white on the lower lip and chin, are more commonly seen on French and British Percherons than on horses of American breeding. Yet even among the European Percherons, it is unusual to see much leg white, even when the horses have more white on the face.

On Chestnuts

Chestnut Percherons tend to have more extensive white markings than their black siblings. White leg markings are also more typical on the chestnuts. At least one chestnut mare, GINGER LAET (1963) was marked with a broad blaze and four socks that reached her knees and hocks. The markings on her dam are not known, but her black sire, REX MONDRAGHOPE, was a black horse with a star and a white hind foot. He produced a number of flashy chestnuts.

GINGER LAET produced fourteen foals, all chestnut. Many had flashy white markings, and at least two had body white in addition to the flashy markings. The first of these was CEDAR SIDE REX'S PEARL LAET (1973) with a white spot on right flank. The other was the stallion CAPP'S IKAIKA

The Percheron stallion KEROR, showing extensive pigment loss around the muzzle and eyes. His loss of pigment did not prevent him from winning in the show ring.

Ho (1979) with a white spot on his left shoulder. Another daughter, CEDAR SIDE REX'S JESSIE LAET (1973), was marked with a blaze, hind stockings and flank roaning. Other chestnuts have had enough roaning that they were registered as roan, even though they had two chestnut parents.

Depigmentation

Some grey Percherons do show facial depigmentation, though the dramatic depigmentation seen in some Boulonnais is not typical. There has been at least one black Percheron, the stallion KEROR, who had extensive facial depigmentation. Depigmentation in non-greys is not well understood.

Poitevin Mulassier

Origin: Poitou region of France

The Mulassier is a very old breed, having been used in the production of mules since the sixteenth century. It is thought to have descended from large Flemish horses brought to help drain the marshlands of Poitou in the sixteenth century. Since the decline in the mule industry, attempts have been made to transition the breed into meat production, but it remains endangered.

Stud Book

In a French agricultural guide published in 1837, the Poitevin Mulassier was included in the chapter on "Principle Races of the Horse", taking second spot to the favored Boulonnais and followed by the Comtois, the Navarrine (now extinct), the Percheron and Breton. Although the assessment of its conformation and "lymphatic" character are not always flattering, the breed is consistently recognized as distinct by nineteenth-century writers.

The stud book was established in 1884. Like many of the French draft breeds, this event was largely motivated by the American export trade, which demanded recorded pedigrees. The breeders in the Perche region had a near monopoly, since their stud book was restricted to horses domiciled in La Perche. This effectively shut other breeding regions out of the lucrative American market. Even with the formal stud book, the Mulassier never attracted exporters. The stud book was closed in 1922, with total registrations at 424 stallions and 150 mares.

By the end of the World War II, the breed was facing extinction. Like most draft breeds, the mechanization of agriculture reduced demand for the breed. Many French draft breeds were sustained by demand for horse meat, but the Mulassier did not carry the same level of muscle mass and its slow growth rate was less suited to that industry. By the 1970s, only a few dozen horses remained. Since that time, efforts have been made to restore the breed, and an upgrading program for mares is in place to expand the gene pool.

Population

Haras Nationaux reported that in 2010, there were 265 mares of breeding age. There were 96 foals recorded that year. In 2011, there are 44 stallions being used for breeding. The Mulassier is considered critically endangered, and a plan was established in 1998 to limit inbreeding and maximize diversity. There is also an upgrading procedure for mares.

In recent years, four Mulassiers, three mares and one stallion, have been exported to the United States. Despite that fact, no purebred breeding program has been developed outside the breed's home country.

Colors

The basic color of most Mulassiers is black or dark brown, with many of the dark browns difficult to distinguish from black. Bays are slightly less common, and are often dark. The mealy pattern is found on some individuals, though the paler shades that often accompany mealy marks are not typical. Chestnuts are relatively rare.

Those colors can be found without any modifiers. Among the founding male families, RESEDA

Summary

Current colors: Black and brown are the most common base colors, followed by bay and then chestnut. The mealy pattern is seen on some horses, but in general the shades are dark. A majority of Mulassiers also have dun, grey or roan modifiers. Some roans have frosty manes and tails, and unusually light manes are occasionally noted on the duns and greys.

Markings/patterns: Most Mulassiers are solid or minimally marked. Blazes are seen on some horses, though that is less common. White leg markings are unusual, and rarely extent past the hind ankles when they do occur.

Eye color: The eyes are dark.

Restrictions: Pintos are excluded from breeding.

(1973) was a dark brown, almost black, horse. His influential son BISMARK (1989) was nearly identical in color. The dark brown stallion DARTAGNAN (1991), from the Victorieux family, was also a popular stallion for many years. While those stallions were influential, most Mulassiers have one or more of three modifiers: dun, grey and roan.

Dun

The Mulassier is perhaps best known as the heavy horse breed that has the dun dilution, and that is presently the most common of the three modifiers. Of the forty-four active breeding stallions, fourteen are some shade of dun. It is likely that under their white hairs some of the greys and roans are also dun.

It is not surprising that lineback dun came to be part of a breed used to produce mules. It was a common belief among academics of the late nineteenth century that horses and donkeys shared a common ancestor, and that the dun coloration represented a reversion to this primitive type. Having the coloration of the donkey, duns were thought to possess, in some measure at least, the qualities of their distant ancestor.

This idea was discussed in a paper by James M. Hiatt in the first volume of the National Register of French Draft Horses (1881), titled "The General History of Horse-Kind." (The article drew heavily on the ideas in Colonel Hamilton Smith's *The Natural History of Horses*.) Among the diverse breeds having the dun coloration, Hiatt notes that dun is not found among draft horses, with one exception.

> "[Dun horses] do not contain the elements of size, and have never reached, by any intermixture, the proportions of a draught animal, except in Burgundy, where, after innumerable top-crosses of the ancient chestnut leviathan of that French province, the inextinguishable dorsal stripe of the eel-back eventually marked the coat of a heavy and powerful horse."

It seems likely that the farmers in Poitou made use of these large duns from Burgundy when establishing the Mulassier, perhaps motivated by the belief that their color indicated a close relationship to the donkey. There appears little doubt that the

This unnamed Mulassier from the early twentieth century shows how little the breed has changed over time. It was a common belief in the late nineteenth century that the Poitevin mares were "internally mules", which made them less likely than ordinary mares to abort hybrid foals.

color was considered important, since selection for coat color is thought to have been one of the factors that hampered the transition of the breed from one used in mule production to that of meat production. The Breton and the Comtois rapidly eclipsed the Mulassier in that market.

Because there is a gap between the formation of the stud book and the post-war period, the original source of the dun coloring is not known. It is clear that many modern dun Mulassiers can trace their color back to the stallion ELAZUR (1948) through his grandson QUEBEC (1960). QUEBEC was a highly regarded stallion during a time when the breed population was very small, and it is estimated that he appears in 95 percent of all Mulassier pedigrees. QUEBEC is the grandsire of KEVIN (1976), who founded a family in his own right.

Although QUEBEC has widespread influence, there a number of unrelated lines that carry the dun color. One of the male family founders was the dun TITAN (1985). Like many Mulassiers, TITAN was grulla, but a shade so dark that he could be mistaken for a faded black. Many grulla Mulassiers fall on the darker end of the spectrum, with some like TITAN even darker still. This is also true for the yellow duns, some of which are dark

Most dun Mulassiers are grulla, but yellow duns occur. The yellow dun mare, GITANE, is paler than is typical, whereas very dark grullas like the mare to her left are not unusual for the breed.

THOMAS	f.1855	*gris blanc* (white grey)
LIVERSAY	f.1855	*gris pommele* (dapple grey)
JULIAN	f.1852	*gris pommele vineux* (rose grey)
LADIVE	f.1854	*gris pommele fonce* (dark grey)

The competition predated the stud book, so the idea of breed purity was not yet a factor. Even so, the descriptions of many of the entries note that the one or both parents were from the *race poitevine.*

Among the present-day Mulassiers, grey is second only to dun in numbers. Thirteen of the forty-four active stallions are grey. One of the most popular stallions in recent times has been the grey stallion PREMIER MAI (1981). He was widely praised as a stallion of rare beauty. He died relatively young, having stood at stud for only nine years, but he left behind at least five national stallions as well as several used by private owners. PREMIER MAI is also interesting in that he carried the chestnut gene, so it may be that part of his lasting legacy is to increase the number of red Mulassiers.

Another influential grey stallion from an earlier era is GITAN (1972). In photographs, GITAN is obviously grey, but also appears as if he may have originally been dun. Because so few photographs of the post-war horses are available, and because many of the color terms for grey, roan and grulla are used interchangeably, determining which horses carried which colors is often impossible.

GITAN has descendants of all colors, but one of his most successful was his grey daughter LUTTEUSE (1977). She produced eleven foals over the course of her breeding career, including six sons approved for breeding. Among those, QUO VADIS, RILT, ABSALON, and DOLLAR were grey.

Because most are genetically black or very dark brown, grey Mulassiers are often noticeably dappled. It is also quite common for them to keep their dark leg coloring for longer than might be typical for greys, most likely because many are either dun or roan. The presence of dun is also why many have dark mottled dapples down the front of their faces, since that area tends to be densely pigmented in duns.

Another unusual aspect of grey in Mulassiers is that some have manes and tails that grey out far

enough to be mistaken for bay. Although dun factors are less visible against a dark coat, the tone on the very dark yellow duns is dustier than that of a true bay, and often the dark facial mask common to duns is still visible.

Red duns are also found, though are less common because of the relative rarity of the chestnut base color. Most recently the red dun BALBUZARD (1989) was used at stud, and the popularity of his sire, PREMIER MAI, may eventually increase the portion of chestnuts, and therefore red duns.

Grey

At one time, grey was said to have been the predominant color of the horses of Poitou. That may have been a reflection of how popular grey was in France at the time, and the market in La Perche for grey draft stock. A number of late nineteenth century authors note that the higher quality Mulassiers, if grey, could be sold at a much higher profit to dealers in La Perche.

Historical records support the idea that the breed was, at least at that time, primarily grey. A catalog from the national agricultural competition in 1860 lists the following entries in the class for Mulassier stallions:

CHEVAL	f.1855	*gris pommele* (dapple grey)
MASTOC	f.1851	*blanc* (white)
MOUTON	f.1853	*gris pommele* (dapple grey)

more rapidly than their body. The stallion MIRA-BEAU DE LA POTERIE (2000) is perhaps the most dramatic example of this. At five years old, his body appeared very nearly black, with only a bit of greying visible on his face and lower legs. Meanwhile his mane was very nearly white. By eight years old, his body had begun to show some dappling and his mane and tail were creamy white. Although highly contrasting manes and tails appear to be more common in breeds that grey more slowly, variations in the greying process have not be extensively studied and the cause is not known.

Roan

Roan is the third common modifier found in Mulassiers. Among the stallions, eleven of the currently approved stallions are roan, though as with dun this number may not reflect the true extent of the color, since it is likely that some of the greys are also roan. Historically roans were often registered as grey, so tracing the color can be difficult.

Three male families were founded by dark-headed roans: HARDI (1973), KEVIN (1976) and LICK (1977). HARDI was a paternal half-brother to the grey GITAN, and was registered as a grey roan. In photos it is clear that HARDI, unlike GITAN, was a dark-headed roan and not a grey, though interestingly enough, it is GITAN that more often appears in the pedigrees of roans.

LICK was registered simply as roan, so his base color is not known. He served twenty-three years at stud, and left behind two roan sons. The first was the chestnut roan TIFARDIERE (1985). Like his sire, TIFARDIERE had a long stud career. The second LICK son, the brown roan FANFAN (1993), is still standing at stud at eighteen years of age.

The last roan line is that of KEVIN, who like LICK was registered as roan without any indication of his base color. KEVIN was only used for two seasons, 1987 and 1988. In that time he did produce the roan stallion ABSALON from the famed mare LUTTEUSE, but his primary influence is through his daughters.

Both GITAN and PREMIER MAI have roan descendants. GITAN has a bay roan grandson, UR-BAIN DU PONT (1986), sire of the grulla roan stallion INDIEN (1996). A bay roan son of PREMIER MAI, TOURBILLON (1985) was featured in the Yann Arthus-Bertrand book on European livestock, *Good Breeding*. There is also bay roan stallion, BOC BREOTIERE (1989) unrelated to the other roan lines.

Some roan Mulassiers have frosty manes and tails much like those seen in Brabants. This trait appeared in some of the stallions used in the post-war period. The bay roan stallion JUDEX (1953) had an almost silver-white mane and a nearly white tailhead. He has no direct male descendants, but his one daughter, NELLY, produced the stallion TORPILLEUR (1963), grandsire of PREMIER MAI. She was also the maternal granddam of the stallion GITAN through her daughter BARONNE, so his influence through her is widespread. The stallions GITAN DES DIEUX (1994) and MON P'TIT BOC (200) and the mare FANNY DU MARAIS (1993) have the same pale silver manes seen on JUDEX. All trace back to either PREMIER MAI or GITAN, or both, though this may simply be a reflection of the popularity of those two lines.

Brindle

During her trip to France in 2000, American Mulassier breeder Leah Patton photographed a dun gelding with brindle striping on his left hindquarter. The black stripes were only present on the one side of his body. Similar striping, which brindle researcher Sharon Batteate called "partial streaking", has been noted in other dun individuals. Most have been Quarter Horses, where at least one breeder has called them "foundation spots" because they are occasionally seen in dun horses of foundation breeding. Among these include the Quarter Horses BLUE SIERRA PINE (1997) and SILVERWOOD GOLD (1988) and the Paint Horse SBR MOONLITE STREAKER (1996). The striping on those horses is not symmetrical, and many have one-sided patterns like the one on the Mulassier.

There was speculation that these horses might be brindle carriers, or have a partially expressed brindling pattern. The more common theory now is that this type of brindle patterning is a form of dun factoring, and is not related to the full-body form of brindling. Just what causes some duns to have this kind of patterning when most do not, and why it is so often dramatically asymmetrical, is not known.

Pale manes and tails

The brindle dun gelding was also notable for his very pale mane and tail. Duns often have manes and tails that have light hairs to the outside with a pronounced darker core; the classic roaching pattern of the Fjord is designed to accent this trait. In Mulassiers, though, duns are occasionally seen with manes and tails that are completely pale. Oddly enough, among the duns this seems to often get paired with an unusually dark facial mask.

At least one yellow dun mare, FOLKA (1993), produces lighter manes with some consistency. Her daughter, LUZIE DE ROMAGNE (1999), is almost identical in terms of color. Her son KALINERO DE ROMAGNE (1998) was, at least as a young horse, a dun with an almost white mane and tail. Some of the dun foals sired by her grey son OREMYX DE ROMAGNE (2002) have also had pale manes and tails.

As noted previously, both the greys and the roans have unusually pale manes and tails. Because Mulassiers often grey very slowly, and often in an atypical pattern, it is possible that some of the pale manes and tails are in fact the result of greying. It is also possible that some are roans, since roaning can be difficult to detect on a horse with a diluted body. The exact relationship between the different modifiers, and just which play a role in creating the light manes and tails, has not be adequately studied. It has also been suggested that the silver dilution might be present, which would not be entirely unexpected given the fact that the mutation is present among some of the other French draft breeds. Whatever the source, because Mulassiers are shown with long, loose manes and tails, the effect is particularly striking.

Eye Color

To date no blue-eyed Mulassiers have been observed, and the breed appears to be uniformly dark-eyed. Because most of the horses are unmarked, and because white markings are not fa-

This unusual Mulassier gelding has partial brindling that covers his left hindquarter. It is thought that asymmetrical brindling of this type is related to dun factoring. He also has the pale mane and tail seen in some dun Mulassiers.

vored, it is unlikely that blue eyes would occur. Although lighter or golden eyes are sometimes seen in diluted horses, that has been more closely associated with cream dilutes rather than with duns.

Markings

The vast majority of Mulassiers are unmarked, and solid horses are strongly preferred by breeders. Small stars and limited leg white are sometimes seen, but more extensive white is penalized. Despite that, there have been rare Mulassiers with sabino markings. The red dun mare FALINE (1993) has a bald face and one front and one hind stocking with irregular edges. Her son TID'OR ROMAGNA (2007) is marked very similarly, with a bald face and hind stockings. Her daughter LEANE DE ROMANIER (1999) has a broad blaze, but no leg white. In 2008, she produced a red dun son, UX DE ROMAGNE, with a broad blaze, one hind stocking and a white hind ankle.

There has been at least one mare with typical flashy white sabino markings. DORINE (1991) was a red dun with a blaze, high peaked hind stockings and a small belly spot. Her sire, TOURBILLON, is unmarked, so it seems likely that the markings came through her dun dam, URSULA. In a 2000 class for mares without foals, DORINE placed sixteenth out of a group of seventeen, which is a pretty accurate reflection of breeder's dislike of white markings.

Like many breeds, sabino markings in Mulassiers are more often seen on chestnuts or chestnut-based colors. What is unusual about the Mulassier is that the legs seem resistant to white even when the face markings appear sabino-like. The chestnut mare ISABELLE DES GRAVETTE (1996) has what looks like a typical sabino blaze that encompasses her entire muzzle and chin. Her legs, however, are unmarked. The leg white common among horses that have belly spots is rare in the breed, and particularly so with stallions. White markings are not considered desirable, so horses with white are not usually crossed together.

Polish Coldblood
Zimnokrwiste

Origin: Poland

Although Poland is perhaps better known in the United States for its Arabian breeding program, the Polish Coldblood is the most numerous breed in that country; some have estimated that it makes up as much as 60 percent of the Polish equine population. It is also one of the newer heavy draft breeds, having been developed largely after World War II.

Stud Book
Unlike America and Europe, where heavy horses were among the first to benefit from selective breeding and formal stud books, in Poland the early focus was on the "noble" breeds; that is, horses descended from the Arabian and later the English Thoroughbred. The primary working breeds were the Konik and Huzul. In the early part of the twentieth century efforts were made to increase the size by using imported Ardennes from France, but this was halted by the outbreak of World War I. Although horses were sent by Germany as restitution, and more heavy horses (primarily Bretons and Belgians) were imported during the 1920s and 1930s, the working horse population was not restored until after World War II. At that time there were not enough working horses left in Poland to rebuild, so thousands of horses were brought in from Sweden, Norway, Denmark and Finland.

As a result the working horses of Poland were a very blended population. In 1955, attempts were made to establish regional breeding groups centered around provincial studs. These were Lidzbark, Sokolsky, Kopczyk Podlaski, Sztum, Lowicz and Garwolin. Each strain was slightly different in type, and often in predominant coloring, due to the mixture of breeds used. Among them, the Lidzbark is perhaps most notable from the standpoint of coloring. More than the other coldblooded strains, the horses at Lidzbark retained both the type and the dun coloring of the original stock brought by settlers from Oszmiana. The primary outcrossing was done with Scandinavian horses, rather than the Ardennes popular in most of the other regions, which more closely matched the Oszmian horses in type and color.

In 1964 a formal stud book for coldblooded horses was established with different sections for the different regional varieties. In 1972, the regional varieties were consolidated into the Polish Coldblood and horses were simply entered in alphabetical order by name. The stud book is open to horses that meet requirements of type and size, and stallions of most European draft breeds are eligible for a license if they are deemed to be of high enough quality. The most popular outcross breeds are the French, Belgian and Swedish Ardennes and the Brabants, but Bretons, Percherons and even Comtois have been licensed.

Population
The Polish Horse Breeders Association reports that there were 7,846 mares and 1,805 stallions in the stud book in 2004. That year there were 1,206 fillies and 389 colts registered. This number has been increasing, with 2,484 stallions listed in the 2011 stallion register.

Summary

Current colors: Bay and chestnut are most common, followed by black. Wild bay and mealy markings are also common. Grey, roan, dun and silver are rare. Many of the roans have frosty manes and tails.

Historical colors: Dun was once more common, particularly among the Lidzbark strain of coldbloods.

Markings/patterns: White markings are seen on some horses, though extensive white markings are uncommon. Leg markings are less common than in most breeds. Some bay horses have flaxen manes, which is a trait sometimes seen in Nordic horses.

Eye color: The eyes are dark.

Colors

The most common color in the Polish Coldblood is bay. Of the licensed stallions, 47 percent are bay. Most are clear red bays, though mealy bays are not uncommon. In some cases, the mealy bays are pale enough that they could be mistaken for buckskin. Wild bays, particularly mealy wild bays, are also seen, and can often be traced back to the influence of the Swedish Ardennes in the breed. A smaller number are dark bay or brown. Sooty dappling is sometimes seen.

Chestnut is also quite common, making up 40 percent of the listed stallions. The shade can range from dark liver to pale blonde, and flaxen manes and tails are common. One of the most popular modern stallions, the Swedish Ardennes ROLLTAN (1985), was a flaxen chestnut. Seven of his sons and over eighty of his grandsons are currently approved for breeding, so it is likely to remain common for some time to come.

Black is less common than bay or chestnut, making up only 9 percent of the licensed stallions. Dark colors are fashionable, though, and black is considered very desirable. Black Ardennes, which are not accepted as breeding stallions in France, have been imported for breeding Polish Coldbloods. Black Percherons have also been used in recent years, though that outcross has not been as popular as those with the Ardennes and the Brabants.

Grey

Grey accounts for 1 percent of the licensed stallions. The color was once more common in some of the coldblooded strains in Poland, notably the Garwolin, but has become more rare. At least two grey lines remain among the Polish mares. The first is JASIENICA, represented by the grey stallions BROSS (2002) and ŁEBEK, and the second is MOCNA, represented by the stallions GABOR and GROT.

There are also a few grey Percherons and Boulonnais that have been used in the last decade. One recent import is the Percheron stallion MANDARIN 2 (2000). With just five years at stud, he already

This dark chestnut mare, BERTA, is primarily of Polish breeding. The stud book allows outcrossing to most of the European heavy breeds.

has four grey sons approved for breeding: ASKON, ASTARIN, JORDAN and LEKTOR.

Roan

The Ardennes, Bretons and Brabants used in the early development of the Polish Coldblood were often roan, so the color has been present in the breed from the earliest days of the stud book. It has not, however, been a popular color compared to bay, chestnut and black.

Most of the true roans in the Polish Coldblood are black-based, which means they are either bay or black roan. Most are by imported Brabant stallions, or have Belgian outcross blood. Several roan Brabants appear on the current stallion list, including the bay roans WILCO VAN DE BOEKENDE KAMP and WILLEM-PAS VAN DE PLATTEWEG and the black roans ALBERIC TER DIESCHOOT and UDO VAN HET KOYENNEHOF.

There is at least one chestnut roan stallion, MAJOR (2001). He has produced two chestnut roan sons, EKWADOR and BALTON. The latter is registered as a dark chestnut roan, and he does have an almost white mane and tail, but his face is dark enough that he looks like a blue roan. Like the black-based roans, this line gets its coloring from the Brabant.

Percheron mares as well as stallions have been used for breeding Polish Coldbloods. This grey mare is the imported French Percheron SERENA 10.

Because the roan coloring comes primarily from the Brabant, frosty manes are quite common among the roan Polish Coldbloods. The Brabant outcross stallion THOBY VAN NOORDHOUT is a particularly striking example of this roan variation. Although he is a bay roan, his mane is silver-white and the hair to either side of his tail is completely white.

White Ticking

Some Polish Coldbloods have white ticking unrelated to either dark-headed or frosty roan. Among the licensed stallions, 2 percent are ticked with white. The overwhelming majority of these are some shade of chestnut. For some the ticking may be connected to the presence of one of the sabino patterns. The stallion ROLS (1993) is registered as chestnut with white ticking, and he also has a broad blaze the covers his muzzle and white leg markings. Neither his parents or grandparents were true roans. Many of his foals are also registered as chestnut with white ticking.

An even more dramatic example is the stallion OXER (2006). His coat is evenly roaned throughout, including his head, and he has a broad blaze. Because he has pale flaxen points, it is difficult to determine if he has leg markings. He fits the visual appearance of a false-roan sabino or a sabino roan. His sire, REGON, is also ticked with white, along less extensively than his son. Like ROLS, REGON traces back to the Swedish Ardennes ROLLTAN. Although ROLLTAN is registered as chestnut, and only had a white comet on his face, many of his foals are registered as having white ticking. In every case, the mares were not registered as ticked, and did not produce ticked foals when bred to other stallions. In one case a mare produced two ticked foals, one by ROLLTAN and one by his son ROLS.

Dun

Dun was the original coloring of the horses utilized by the Polish peasantry. In the early twentieth century, dun horses closely resembling the Norwegian Døle were common in both Poland and western Russia. The color is still found in the Konik and Huzul, which originated in the same area and

This photo of a dark yellow dun was used to illustrate a 1905 paper on the relationship between the Tarpan and domestic horses. He was identified as a "forest horse from western Russia." This was the type found in Oszmiana, which later was used to form the Lidzbark strain of coldbloods. Polish Coldblood type has changed dramatically from these early horses.

share common roots. In more recent times, Polish breeders have utilized a variety of European heavy draft breeds to increase the size of their horses, and dun has become increasingly rare.

Dun was still fairly common in the Lidzbark strain of Polish Coldbloods. The Lidzbarks descended from dun horses brought with immigrants from Oszmiana. These were merged with the other coldblood strains in 1972, and are no longer a separate breeding group. Only a few lines remain, and without efforts to preserve it, this historical color could well be lost within the next decade.

One of the remaining lines is to the Lidzbark horses is the stallion DESPOTYCZNY (1954). His father was the bay Belgian stallion SAMSON, and DESPOTYCZNY took after him in type. His coloring came from his dam DESMINA, a dun Polish mare. In the black and white photos of his time, he does not look obviously dun—unlike many of the Lidzbark horses which are quite obviously dun even in poor quality images—but thirty-nine of his eighty recorded foals are also entered in the stud books as *bułana*, or dun. Like the United Kingdom, the Polish language does not distinguish between buckskin and yellow dun. The difference is that in Poland, the color distribution is the other way around, so it is far more likely that a horse listed as *bułana* has the dun mutation than the cream mutation. In the case of DESPOTYCZNY, it is pretty clear that he was dun because several of his sons and daughters had offspring recorded as *myszowata*, which is the Polish term for grulla. DESPOTYCZNY had only bay and dun foals. He did not produce grulla himself, probably because he was homozygous for both Extension and Agouti (*EEAA*) and therefore could not produce black. He was often crossed on the daughters of the Døle stallion HEDDAR, who carried black. Grulla appeared with regularity in the third generation.

Of DESPOTYCZNY's dun foals, twenty were stallions and nineteen were mares. Many of his sons were used for breeding, and all produced dun foals. After the second and third generation, the color is lost in all but a few lines. At least two of his sons, STRADOM and his three-quarter brother SZALBIERZ, have dun great-granddaughters that were still producing within the last decade, so the color from the male branch of the DESPOTYCZNY line might yet be preserved.

The color has been preserved, although only tenuously, through the female line. The dun mare GRUZJA (2004) traces back to DESPOTYCZNY through her dam GAMETA. GAMETA is registered as a chestnut, which is not surprising since *bułana* is used almost exclusively for dun on a bay background. In recent years some have called chestnut horses with the dun dilution *czerwonobułana*, but historically these horses have not been differentiated from ordinary chestnuts. The color would not have come from her sire, GRIN, who was bay. GAMETA, while registered as chestnut, traces back in an unbroken line of dun mares to NIEZDARA, a DESPOTYCZNY daughter. As with the male line, there are other dun descendants of DESPOTYCZNY's daughters that might still be young enough to breed.

A third dun line that has modern descendants is that of the grulla stallion NELSON. NELSON was by the brown Døle stallion SARP, so the dun mutation must have come from his unregistered mother, NORKA. He sired four grulla mares. The first of these, SZASZKA, was also a DESPOTYCZNY granddaughter. Her only foal was the dun GIRLANDA. So

Fot. Mateusz Kaca

The Swedish Ardennes stallion BONAIR *is a wild bay with a pale flaxen mane. There are black strands mixed in his mane, which is different from silvers where the manes typically have flaxen ends and dark roots.*

far GIRLANDA has only produced one known dun foal, a daughter HOJA, though at least two of her foals were registered as light chestnuts.

Dun did not come exclusively through the native stock. A blue dun North Swedish Horse, ETER (1943) was used as an outcross prior to the formal stud book. Two daughters were recorded and went on to contribute to the breed, but neither inherited their father's coloring.

Another line came from the North Swedish stallion MEDSTUGUBLACKEN (1922). Although buckskin is more common in the modern North Swedish, the word *blacken* is the Swedish word for dun. Bred to an Oszmian mare, he produced the grulla stallion MIRTUGA (1938). It was the MIRTUGA son WARMIAK (1950), another Lidzbark horse, that was added to the Polish Coldblood breeding pool.

Like the previous family, the line to WARMIAK has dwindled dramatically in the last few decades. WARMIAK had twenty-nine daughters and twenty-six sons recorded in the stud book; thirty-eight were either dun or grulla. Of those, nine had no descendants at all and another seven had no dun offspring. That left twelve sons and nine daughters to continue the color. Of the sons, the color was lost by the second generation in all but four lines. Of the daughters, dun remained after the second generation in only two lines.

There is a WARMIAK descendant on the 2011 stallion list. CERES (1998) traces to WARMIAK through his dam CETYNIA. CERES is registered as dun, but in photos it is not clear if he is a yellow dun or just a pale mealy bay. CETYNIA and her dam CENTA were both registered as light chestnut, which could mean red dun or blonde chestnut. CETYNIA also produced a light chestnut son, CUG (1996), who has sired one daughter, BASTYLIA, registered as dun. CERES has thirteen recorded foals of which several are recorded as light bay or light chestnut, and two that are listed as dun.

Silver

The French Comtois stallion QUOQUIN DE L'ETANG (2004) was included in the 2011 stallion listing. Like most horses of that breed, he is a red silver. If he is a successful sire, the silver dilution may become a permanent part of the Polish Coldblood.

There are Polish Coldbloods that appear silver, though without testing it is difficult to know if they are merely sooty chestnuts or true silver dilutes. The most likely one is the mare GIRWANA (1998). Her body coloring is a clear red, much like a Comtois, while her points are mixed flaxen and chocolate black. Silver is present in the Swedish Ardennes, though the extent the mutation has spread in that population is not currently known. Because Swedish Ardennes have been widely used for breeding Polish Coldbloods, more lines carrying the silver dilution may be identified.

Flaxen-Maned Bays

Some bay Polish Coldbloods have mixed flaxen and black manes even though they show no other signs of carrying the silver dilution. In most cases the horses are wild bays, and often mealy wild bays, and most carry the blood of the Swedish Ardennes pretty close-up in their pedigree. At least one Swedish Ardennes stallion, BONAIR (2001), is a flaxen-maned bay. He does not have a flaxen tail, but as a young adult his mane was mostly flaxen. A number of his bay descendants also have some amount of flaxen in their manes, which suggests that whatever the cause, it is genetic with perhaps a variable level of expression. The contrast appears to diminish with age, which is typical of flaxen and mixed manes across a variety of colors.

Sabino

A sabino patterned Clydesdale stallion, Royal Command (1986), was used at stud in Poland from 1993 until 2000. He was registered as a bay pinto; in appearance he was a very roaned sabino with extensive, indistinct body spotting on his belly, loins, chest, neck and jaw. Like a lot of bay Clydesdales, he had a silver mane and tail.

He sired twenty-one foals in the Polish stud book. Of those, five were registered as bay pintos. These were the daughters Bystrzyca, Bryza, Rona, Rumba and Rosa. Two more daughters, Roksana and Riwiera, were registered as bay with roaning and one, Ramona, was registered as bay roan. Many of the mares produced foals registered as pintos, or that had roaning. One one case, one of his bay daughters, Rena, has a daughter registered as grey. Her sire is chestnut, so it is more likely that she is a very pale roaned sabino.

The daughters of Royal Command have consistently produced body-spotted sabinos, but the coloring is still not typical of the Polish Coldblood breed. The only body-spotted stallion among the licensed stallions is the black Royal Command grandson Rogan (1999). He has another black grandson, Riwer (2001), that has the kind of face and leg markings typical of a sabino, but does not have obvious white on his body. To date Riwer has not sired any body-spotted foals, though the number of his registered offspring is small. Rogan has both spotted daughters and a spotted grandson.

There is also at least one body-spotted sabino Polish Coldblood that is unrelated to Royal Command. That is the mare Bajda (2003). She is a flaxen chestnut with a blaze, white chin, hind stockings and a large white patch on the right side of her barrel.

Eye Color

No Polish Coldbloods with light or blue eyes have come to the attention of the author. Because blue eyes are occasionally found among Clydesdales, particularly among those with more roaned and patched patterns, it is possible that blue eyes might one day be seen among the descendants of Royal Command. It is also possible that those lines with more flashy markings, where they consistently crossed with one another, might one day produce an individual with blue eyes. American Belgians, using the same Brabant stock but focusing for decades on producing flashy markings, are found with blue eyes on rare occasions. Given the minimal nature of the markings on many Polish Coldbloods, however, this would be a rare occurrence, if it ever happened at all.

Markings

There are a wide range of markings in the breed, which is understandable given the diverse breeds used to improve the native stock. Pictures of the original dun working horses of Poland show animals with no white markings. This is pretty typical of many of the eastern European horses, particularly those thought to descend from the Tarpan. Many of the breeds initially used to improve the Coldblood, like the French and Belgian Ardennes and the Brabant, were likewise minimally marked. For that reason, markings have traditionally been somewhat conservative.

Descriptions of the Ardennes sometimes state that the breed can be isabella, which is often translated into English as palomino. Rio du Dol, a French Ardennes imported to Poland, is the kind of pale chestnut that is sometimes mistaken for palomino. Many bay and chestnut Polish Coldbloods have a similar pale tone, which can be credited to the influence of the Ardennes.

That is not to say that white markings cannot be found, or that white markings are penalized. The Swedish Ardennes, which is a popular outcross, is marked with white more often than not. Although bald faces and high stockings are not especially common, Polish Coldbloods can be found with blazes and white feet, Like most breeds, the chestnuts tends towards more extensive markings, while blacks and bays have less. Duns and dark-headed roans also tend to have more minimal white, but that may be due more to the markings of the breeding groups that carried those colors than a true linkage between the colors and expression of white.

Shire

Origin: England

The Shire is one of the original heavy horses native to Great Britain, and is often credited as being the tallest of the draft breeds. It descends in part from the Old English Black (sometimes called the Lincolnshire Black), which is thought by many to trace back to the medieval Great Horse. Like most of the heavy draft breeds, it was nearly lost when farming became mechanized, but it has seen a surge in popularity in recent decades.

Stud Book

The predecessor to the modern Shire registry was the English Cart Horse Society, formed in 1878, making it one of the oldest equine registries. Two years later the Society published a retrospective stud book of cart horse stallions born before 1877. The book contained pedigrees of 2,381 stallions, some of which dated back more than a hundred years.

In 1886 the name was changed to the Shire Horse Society. Originally horses were registered based on the top-cross of the pedigree; that is, the male lines had to trace back to the horses in the retrospective volume. Requirements that the female lines be recorded became stricter over time until finally in 1950 stallions had to have two registered parents. The requirements for mares were never made this strict, although in 1939 a Grade Register was established to formally record the unregistered mares being used. Prior to that time, Shires could be registered if the female line had the required amount of pure blood, but the individual mares behind the pedigree had only to be described; it was not required that they actually be registered. The Grade Register, which was typical of the grading up registers used in other British breeds, was not implemented until 1950—the same year the books on stallions were closed—due to disruptions from World War II.

There was also a brief time when Clydesdales were intentionally crossed into the breed to reduce the amount of leg feather. This had come not long after talks had broken off regarding the merger of the two breeds. Crosses between Shire stallions

These two illustrations appeared in the sixth volume of the Shire Horse stud book, and show just how much type varied in the late 19th century. The chestnut, Czarina, won the Supreme Championship for mares in 1884 and was referred to as a "wonder for her age." Modern horsemen might look at her coloring and her relatively clean legs and mistake her for a Suffolk. The thick-set grey with the bald face, Thursa, was the Champion Mare at the London Cart-Horse Show in 1882.

and registered Clydesdale mares were entered into the Grade Register "B", which essentially granted the Clydesdale mare equivalent status to a second generation Grade Register mare.

Except for the provision for Clydesdale mares, the conditions for entry remain much the same today: the Shire stud book is closed to all but mares that are used in the Grading Register. Upgraded mares can be bred to registered stallions, and their female foals are then eligible for registration.

Those second generation mares can then produce daughters whose own foals (male and female) are eligible for full registration.

One unusual provision in the Shire stud book was the process for registering "old time" sires and dams. The rule allowed horses that met requirements in the past to be registered using those older rules. It was not until 1945 that this rule was changed, and even then the dates were still unusually distant: stallions had to be foaled after 1890 and mares after 1886. It would have presumably been still possible at that point, in 1945, to register a stallion foaled fifty years prior.

Population

The European Farm Animal Biodiversity Information System states that the worldwide Shire population is around 1,800 animals. The Rare Breeds Survival Trust lists the breed as At Risk, which indicates there are fewer than 1,500 registered breeding females. The American Livestock Breeds Conservancy lists Shires as Critical, a category reserved for those breeds with fewer than 200 annual registrations in the United States and a global population that is estimated to be less than 2,000.

Summary

Current colors: Black and grey are the most common colors, while bay is less common and chestnut is rare. There is a cream dilute line in the United States.

Historical colors: True roan was found in the United States at the turn of the previous century. A handful of tobiano, dun and possibly cream individuals were once found.

Markings/patterns: The breed is uniformly sabino and occasionally extensively roaned.

Eye color: The eyes are usually dark.

Restrictions: Chestnut, large white patches on the body and excessive roaning are penalized in the show ring. Horses with blue eyes are denied registration in the United Kingdom.

For the last few years, the American Shire Horse Association has recorded a yearly average of 120 foals. The Shire Horse Society in the United Kingdom records close to 500 foals yearly.

Colors

The majority of Shires are black with flashy sabino markings. A smaller portion are grey and an even smaller number are bay. Occasionally chestnuts and sabino roans are seen, though they are subject to registration restrictions in some countries.

The restriction on color is relatively recent in the breed's long history. The Shire did not have a formal standard of points until after World War II, so there was no formal guidance on the issue of color during the formation of the breed. When a standard was adopted, it simply stated that the predominating colors were bay and brown, followed by black and grey. No mention was made at that time regarding the less common colors when describing stallions and mares, though it was noted that geldings were "occasionally chestnut and roan." This changed in 1973 when the standard was revised to read, "No good stallion should be splashed with large white patches over the body." It further added that the stallion "should not be roan or chestnut." The wording was later changed to "must not be roan or chestnut." Colors of the breed were listed as black, brown, bay and grey. Meanwhile standards of points for mares and geldings were added which allowed for roan and chestnut, though chestnut has been dropped from mention entirely in the most recent version of the standards for mares and geldings.

In many ways the 1973 revision was just formalizing preferences that had existed in Britain since the founding of the breed. The early stud books contained a number of chestnuts, even among the stallions. Some of these won notable prizes, including the two-time London Champion Mare Dunsmore Chessie (1908). It would be fair to say that in these cases the overall quality of the individual horses enabled judges to overlook what was an unpopular color.

The situation was a bit different in the United States where the breed standard was revised soon after the British one, but read, "Black, brown, bay, grey or chestnut/sorrel (rare) are the preferred col-

This striking flaxen-maned chestnut is STOCKLEY TOM, *an imported stallion that illustrated the first volume of the American Shire stud book.*

ors." In keeping with American registry traditions, no distinction was made for gender and acceptable colors. Like the British revision, the American standard was a formalization of the more permissive view breeders had towards less common colors. The color percentages for stallions in the early British and American stud books (see Charts 12 and 13) illustrate this. It was still a minority coloring, but the frequency with which engravings of chestnut stallions appear in the first ten volumes of the American stud book suggest that its presence on a horse was of far less consequence to American breeders.

Show results from the time also reflect the more permissive attitude towards color. While DUN-SMORE CHESSIE stands out for the honors she won despite her coloring, it is not difficult to find winning chestnut Shires in the early days of the American registry. One of the big winners during that era was BORO BLUSTERER (1911). A red chestnut with a broad blaze, four white legs and a belly spot, BLUSTERER was named Champion Shire Stallion at the 1914 Iowa and Illinois State Fairs. The following year he took the Championship at the Panama-Pacific International Exposition in San Francisco, winning what was then a record cash prize of $7,185.

The other color singled out as less than desirable is roan, and it is important to separate the term

into the two genetically distinct colors involved. The first of these is a true, dark-headed roan. This color once existed in the breed, but appears to have been lost over time. More information about it can be found in the section for historical colors.

What is meant by roan in the present day is sabino roan. That is, a horse with a sabino pattern that is so abundantly ticked that the impression is that the horse is roan. Like true dark-headed roan, this type of coloring has never been particularly common, nor has it ever been widely popular. Most sabino Shires have the more limited flashy white form of the pattern, with fairly clear markings restricted to the face, limbs and belly. There is no indication that the breed carries the one tested form of sabino, sabino-1, which is known to consistently produce very roaned individuals. Still, some portion of Shires are born with this type of sabino pattern, and are registered as roan.

Grey

The history of grey in the Shire tells a lot about how genetic drift, population bottlenecks and changing popularity can impact colors within a breed. Over the years, all three have had an effect on the number of grey Shires.

Chart 12 and Chart 13 show shifts in popularity of the colors during the breed's first three decades. Stallion colors have been used because they, far more than mares, tend to reflect what is popular. Mares are a better indicator of the breed as it is at a point in time, since a good mare of an unfashionable color can always be taken to a better-colored mate. A stallion that is the wrong color is far more likely to be gelded and taken out of the breeding population, so stallion color tends to reflect the breed as breeders wish it to be. The charts make it clear that what breeders wished the Shire to be was darker.

It is not surprising, then, that the breed eventually returned to its roots as a black horse with white trim. What is surprising is that the second-most common color in the modern breed became grey. In many ways, it is remarkable that grey survived at all. It came very close to being lost.

Of all the colors, the popularity of grey has fluctuated the most widely over the breed's history. As the first chart shows, the percentage of grey stal-

Shire stallions registered in the early British Studbooks

	brown	bay	black	grey	roan	chestnut	other
Vol. 1 (1877)	845	545	416	317	248	188	2
(percentage)	*33%*	*21%*	*16%*	*12%*	*10%*	*7%*	*1%*
Vol. ? (1888)	265	526	156	74	37	83	0
(percentage)	*23%*	*46%*	*14%*	*7%*	*3%*	*7%*	0
Vol. 21 (1900)	197	427	82	31	13	51	0
(percentage)	*25%*	*53%*	*10%*	*4%*	*2%*	*6%*	0
Vol. 25 (1904)	262	528	107	30	21	51	0
(percentage)	*26%*	*53%*	*11%*	*3%*	*2%*	*5%*	0
Vol. 36 (1915)	249	585	74	20	6	19	0
(percentage)	*26%*	*61%*	*8%*	*2%*	*1%*	*2%*	0

Shire stallions registered in the early American Studbooks

	brown	bay	black	grey	roan	chestnut	other
Vol. 1 (1888)	212	462	134	50	22	53	0
(percentage)	*23%*	*50%*	*14%*	*5%*	*2%*	*6%*	0
Vol. 4 (1900)	165	459	135	22	10	72	0
(percentage)	*19%*	*53%*	*16%*	*3%*	*1%*	*8%*	0
Vol. 5 (1904)	254	720	154	31	14	102	0
(percentage)	*20%*	*57%*	*12%*	*2%*	*1%*	*8%*	0
Vol. 10 (1916)	111	446	71	29	16	60	0
(percentage)	*15%*	*61%*	*10%*	*4%*	*2%*	*8%*	0

Charts 12 and 13. Colors of the stallions registered in the early British and American Shire stud books.

lions in the first volume was 12 percent. What that does not show is that, as a retrospective book, the time period covered is much longer than is typical for a regular stud book. The retrospective volume covers stallions foaled prior to 1877, with the earliest stallion foaled in 1770. During that span of more than a hundred years, grey experienced a surge (rising to a high of 22 percent during the 1820s) and then a decline in popularity. The drop in the ten years that followed Volume I was just a continuation of a decline that started in mid-nineteenth century, when the color dropped to 15 percent of the population.

Some of the decline can be attributed to a growing dislike for greys among horsemen, which reached its peak during the Edwardian era. Sir Walter Gilbey, writing in his 1907 book *Horses—Breeding To Colour*, notes with apparent regret that "we must conclude that grey is dying out more rapidly among the Shires than among the Hackneys." At the time of his writing, the stud book for 1906 had just been published and showed that of the 934 stallions registered that year, only 19 had been grey. With just 2 percent of the stallions grey, it must have seemed quite likely that the color would be lost.

It was not, of course. Thirty years later, in 1936, the color had returned to favor with greys making up 17 percent of the stallions registered that year. Less than twenty years after that the number had climbed to 25 percent. It was fortunate timing that the color should reach its all-time peak right before the decline in fortunes among the draft breeds. Had the crash come when the color made up only 3 percent of the population, the chance that it could survive the genetic bottleneck that followed would have been much lower.

Chance also played a part in the earlier fortunes of the color. One of the most successful early sires in the breed was the grey LINCOLNSHIRE LAD II. Foaled in 1872, he was born when grey had fallen out of fashion. He came into his own as a sire late in life, but he was later known as the "Father of the Stud Book." No fewer than 15 of his sons sired London prize winners, but the most famous of these was HAROLD 3703 (1881). It is thought that nearly all modern Shires trace back to HAROLD.

The smoky black mare JANE'S PRIZE ONE. The cream gene she carried came from a palomino mare entered through the Grading Register.

What if HAROLD had been born grey, rather than brown? Not only was his sire grey at a time when the color was unpopular, but so was his maternal grandsire, CHAMPION 419. By luck his dam, 47962 FLOWER, did not inherit the color from CHAMPION, thereby reducing the chance that the cross that produced HAROLD would result in a grey foal. It is possible that, had he been grey, HAROLD would never have gotten the chance to influence the breed that he had as a brown horse. Yet there are many breeds were the predominant color is forever changed when an exceptional horse is born of a rare or even unpopular color. Grey became the predominant color in the Welsh Mountain Pony despite the color almost certainly being proof of outside influence because the stallion DYOLL STARLIGHT captured the fancy of breeders. Solid black, thought of as unusual in a breed where sabino roan had always been typical, became the standard color of the Tennessee Walking Horse because of the obvious talent in the black stallion MIDNIGHT SUN.

HAROLD did not inherit the coloring from either sire or grandsire, but another piece of genetic chance did come with his rise to prominence as a sire. HAROLD was not grey, but he did carry chestnut. We know this because he produced a number of chestnut sons and daughters. In most breeds the chance that any given bay or brown horse carries chestnut is pretty high, but in those where chestnut was never common and where it is subject to negative selection, the chances are much lower. In the case of HAROLD, he probably got the gene from his unregistered maternal granddam, FLOWER, who was said to have been chestnut. HAROLD may have missed the chance to transform the breed into one that was mostly grey, but his widespread use ensured that the chestnut color would persist in spite of the wishes of the majority of Shire breeders.

Cream

Two palomino mares, +A RANCH MADALYN (1968) and +A RANCH MOLLY (1970), were entered in the American stud book Grading Register. They were both by the registered Shire stallion TATTON'S SWEDE and out of an unrecorded mare. TATTON'S SWEDE was registered as light sorrel, which is sometimes how palominos are recorded in breeds where the cream dilution is not expected. His pedigree has a number of dead ends in the breed database so he cannot be ruled out, but it seems more probable that the two mares were out of the same unknown dam and that she was the source for their unusual coloring. TATTON'S SWEDE produced a number of sorrels, but those two mares were the only ones recorded as palominos. Surprisingly enough for that time period and for a draft breed, they were registered with their true colors, as were their immediate offspring.

One of the daughters of MADALYN, +A RANCH WINONA, was registered as buckskin. She produced two registered daughters, both brown, but neither left any foals. Her sister +A RANCH MOLLY had two daughters, both of which were black. One of those mares, +A RANCH DOLLY (1984), produced the black mare HEITKAMP'S JANE who in turn produced JANE'S PRIZE ONE. Through those three generations of black mares, the original cream coloring was preserved. JANE'S PRIZE ONE was in fact a smoky black, which became clear when she had the pale buckskin filly FREEDOM'S JOLIE PRIZE in 2007. When JOLIE was registered, buckskin was no longer an option so she was registered as bay, but her true color was confirmed with a genetic test.

There are other mares that trace back to +A RANCH DOLLY, and many are registered as black or brown. It is possible that some of them may carry the hidden cream dilution as well. FREEDOM'S

JOLIE PRIZE is currently owned by Tintagel Enterprises, and is being used in their Drum Horse breeding program.

Historical Colors

Although the present-day Shire is almost uniformly black or grey with sabino markings, at one time the breed was considerably more colorful. In his book, *Heavy Horses: Breeds and Management*, Herman Biddell wrote:

> "The Shire-bred man is in no wise particular. Watching the ring at the Royal, one sees black, brown, grey, bay and chestnut; with or without white, whole-coloured, blotched and sandy roan. The breeders of these fashionable horses on this point are totally without prejudice, and stopping short of sky blue or emerald green, they apparently claim all shades as the "true colour" of the Shire-bred proper."

This was written in 1898, just twenty years after the formation of the English Cart Horse Society, and reflected the Shire horse as it existed prior to the established stud book even more accurately than it did the breed during Biddell's time. These less common colors were largely lost with the turn of the last century, but some persisted into the early stud books.

Dark-headed Roan

One of the most successful early American imports was the blue roan mare COLDHAM SURPRISE (1904). She was a dark-headed roan with a small star and hind socks. She was named Grand Champion mare at the Chicago International in 1911 and again in 1913, and her photograph was used in books to illustrate correct type in draft mares. COLDHAM SURPRISE got her roan coloring from her dam, COLDHAM VIOLET (1898). VIOLET had another roan daughter, COLDHAM FLOWER (1903).

VIOLET's coloring did not come from her dam, who was a typical bay sabino. Instead it came from her sire HORBLING HAROLD, a blue roan foaled in 1894. A direct son of the original HAROLD, he had earned a Highly Commended in the class for yearling colts at the 1895 London Show. HORBLING HAROLD's coloring came from his dam, BLUE-BELL, who was registered as a blue roan. BLUEBELL

was the daughter of the blue roan stallion LIN-
COLNSHIRE BOY, foaled in 1881 and sired by the
famed grey stallion LINCOLNSHIRE LAD II (1872).
It seems likely that LINCOLNSHIRE BOY's coloring
came from his unregistered dam METTLE. Had
LINCOLNSHIRE LAD carried the roan color under
his grey coat, it would likely have been a far more
common color than it came to be.

Other HORBLING HAROLD offspring exported
to the United States include the red roan stallions
BIRTHORPE HAROLD (1898) and FULLETBY HAR-
OLD (1900). Another roan daughter, PARKSIDE
HEROINE, was exported to Canada and was shown
successfully there.

As for COLDHAM VIOLET's branch of the family,
a younger half-sister to SURPRISE was imported by
the Truman Pioneer Stud Farm. That was COLD-
HAM JEWEL, foaled in 1905 and registered as a
red roan with a streak on her face and an off hind
fetlock. She does not appear to have been shown,
nor are there records of her offspring in the stud
books.

SURPRISE did leave foals, though only one, PI-
LOT'S SURPRISE (1915), inherited her roan coloring. PILOT'S SURPRISE was registered as a strawberry roan with a star. He placed in the stallion
class at the Chicago International but did not leave
any offspring.

Another dark-headed roan that found success in
the American show ring was the stallion TRUMAN'S
BLUSTERER (1916). The blue roan BLUSTERER stood
Reserve Grand Stallion at the 1918 Iowa State Fair.
His sire was the previously mentioned chestnut
winner BORO BLUSTERER, and his dam was the
strawberry roan EASTWOOD STRAWBERRY. Just like
his sire, his dam had been imported from England
by the Truman Pioneer Stud Farm. STRAWBERRY
was by SHELFORD DANDY, who was registered as
grey. Her dam, DOGDYKE LIVELY, seems an unlikely source for the coloring, having been a brown
from a family of bays and browns, so it appears the
color came down through DANDY either hidden by
the greying, or erroneously recorded.

*FREEDOM'S JOLIE PRIZE is the only known buckskin Shire.
Her smoky black dam JANE'S PRIZE ONE is pictured on
page 323.*

Because COLDHAM SURPRISE and TRUMAN'S
BLUSTERER were winners at important shows,
photos remain that show that they were indeed
true roans. There are other entries in both the
American and British stud books that describe
roan horses with dark legs and minimal white
markings, so it is likely there were other roan
lines beyond those of BLUEBELL and EASTWOOD

COLDHAM SURPRISE was twice named Grand Champion Mare at the Chicago International. She was one of a handful of winning roan Shires owned by the Truman Pioneer Stud.

STRAWBERRY. In *The Shire Horse*, Keith Chivers states that there was a brisk trade in late nineteenth century for roan geldings for use in the cities, which would ensure that some roans were kept for breeding. They were never common, however. As the charts listing the color frequency in the American and British stud books show, after the initial retrospective stud book, roans never accounted for more than 3 percent of the stallion population. That number would have included a fairly high percentage of horses that were not dark-headed roans, since anything that had white hair mixed in the coat might get registered as roan. In most cases, the markings described and the intermittent nature of the trait over generations suggest that some registered roans were in fact sabino roans. Still others have pedigrees that suggest they were misidentified greys, something that would not be surprising when the terms roan and grey were often used interchangeably. The percentage of true roans had to have been much lower, making it almost certain that an already rare coloring would be lost when the gene pool narrowed following the decline in draft horses.

Pintos

In some ways it is not entirely correct to include pintos in with the historic colors, since sabino patterns are still present in the breed today. While the

breed standards in both England and the United States state that excessive white markings or roaning are undesirable, the patterns necessary to produce horses readily identified as pintos are there. In fact, they have been a part of the breed from the very start.

One horse that helped ensure the prevalence of sabino was the late nineteenth century stallion ENGLAND'S WONDER. Often referred to as OLD STRAWBERRY, he was registered as roan in the first volume of the stud book. Chivers writes that while he was a sought-after sire in his day, he was hampered by a reputation for producing "roans of many hues, and chestnuts, all with or without white legs and white patches, and even varieties of skewbald." At least one son, COMING WONDER, was said to have left a "vast number of strangely coloured progeny." Like his sire, COMING WONDER was registered as roan. It seems likely that both were sabino roans, but as both lived at a time when detailed markings were not recorded as part of the stud book data, it is impossible to know for sure. It is true that even in modern times, many British horsemen do not recognize sabino patterned horses as pintos—that is, as piebalds or skewbalds—unless their patterning has large patches of clear white. The description given of OLD STRAWBERRY's descendants is in keeping with how those horsemen would describe the various forms of sabino expression.

A number of breeders may have taken exception to the colors produced by OLD STRAWBERRY, but it did not stop him from becoming the leading sire of the breed in 1881. His widespread influence undoubtedly helped to ensure that the breed would eventually be uniformly sabino, if not necessarily loud enough for most to be called pintos.

The question then is whether or not other pinto patterns were once present. Getting a definitive answer is made more difficult by the fact that white markings were not routinely included in stud book entries until sometime around 1895 (Volume 16), and even then markings were often described only in vague terms like "white on the legs" or "white in the face." Because belly spots were common and such horses were not identified as piebalds or skewbalds, it can be surmised that anything registered as such would have to be more extensively marked. Because white markings intermixed with ticking were identified as roan, it can also be assumed that the horses had more cleanly marked contrast between the coat color and the pattern. Sabino can, of course, produce exactly this kind of pattern. But because the registry was not closed and because the female lines were often unrecorded, it does open the door for the possibility that some of the piebalds in the early stud books were tobianos.

This is not so unusual an idea given that the pattern was present in cart horses when the stud book was formed. Sir Walter Gilbey, writing about color in the Shire, notes that while piebalds were "seldom seen in pedigree stock", particolors were "by no means uncommon in the Fen country" of England. He was speaking from authority, having been the President of the Shire Horse Society from 1883 until 1897.

Gilbey repeated this same claim in his book *The Old English War-Horse or Shire-Horse* (1888), where he included an engraving of two tobiano "English Shire breds" from 1810. He justifies their inclusion by saying that it "seems worthwhile to include a representation of this pattern in order to make the series of typical animals as complete as possible." In the second edition of the book, published in 1899, an additional plate was included that depicted a team of four black tobiano Shires owned by B. B. Colvin, a prominent breeder of Shorthorn Cattle in the mid-nineteenth century.

He had set about developing a strain of piebald Shires. The stud was dispersed upon his death and the color was lost to the stud book.

By the time the stud book was published in 1880, only one piebald horse was included. That was EVERETT'S HORSE. Because the horse was foaled in 1825, his inclusion was posthumous. Little information was given; even his owner is only referred to by his last name. His sire was the HOLMES'S HORSE, but beyond the town where he originated nothing else is known. Perhaps he was the source for the tobianos that Gilbey claimed were not uncommon in the Fens. Although it does seem that the author was speaking of tobianos when he mentioned piebalds and particolors, it is impossible to know if the EVERETTE HORSE was a black tobiano or just a more elaborately patterned sabino.

Pintos did not appear in the stud books again for almost two decades. Their reappearance came with a family of pintos descended from the piebald mare FLOWER, foaled in 1873. All that was known about her was the name of her breeder, and that her sire was the grey stallion DRAYMAN JUN. Like so many colorful horses, it can be assumed that the trait came from her unnamed mother. Her

A team of black tovero Shires owned by B. B. Colvin in the mid-nineteenth century. This illustration, along with that of PIRATE *and* OUTLAW *(facing page) appear in Sir Walter Gilbey's book* The Great Horse or Shire Horse.

only recorded offspring were two piebald daughters, BRISK (1886) and DAMSEL (1888). Both were registered in Volume 19 of the stud book.

DAMSEL does not appear to have left behind any registered foals. BRISK had two foals, the stallion COTHAM CAPTAIN (1898) and the mare COTHAM SMART (1901). Both were registered as piebalds. COTHAM CAPTAIN's entry read, "piebald, white below hocks and knees" and COTHAM SMART read, "piebald, white and bay patches." COTHAM CAPTAIN later sired the mare VIOLET, said to have been chestnut and white. VIOLET was never registered, but she had two pinto daughters: PICKWORTH BLOSSOM (1913) and PICKWORTH BEAUTY (1916). BLOSSOM was described as being brown with white patches and four white legs, while BEAUTY was described as having a brown and white body, a white face and four white legs. COTHAM CAPTAIN was later exported to Argentina. Of his half-sister COTHAM SMART nothing more is known.

With no known photographs and obscure animals from such a distant past, it is impossible to know for sure what pattern FLOWER carried. The fact that her descendants were described as piebald at a time when horses with visible belly spotting not generally thought of as pintos suggests that the family was, at the very least, loudly marked. The uniformity of the white legs and the consistency with which the pattern appeared in each generation does lead to speculation that this might have been a family of tobianos. It is equally possible that these were loud, high-contrast sabinos that, when crossed within a gene pool already inclined towards flashy markings, produced more of the same.

There were other pinto entries where sabino does seem the most likely explanation. The first of these is TILNEY FLASH, who appeared in the same volume of the stud book as COTHAM SMART. FLASH was described as "roan and white, white face, four white legs." It is not had to imagine a sabino roan with body-spotting being described this way. Her sire, NAILSTONE CERTAINTY, was a bay with a white face and four white legs. He produced a similar daughter, TILNEY FLOSS, that was registered as "dark roan, white face and throat, four white legs." The dam of TILNEY FLASH was TILNEY

This engraving was done from an 1810 painting by J. C. Zeitter of the geldings PIRATE and OUTLAW. Teams like these were popular with breweries.

BLAZE, registered as a roan with a white face and four white legs. Like the sire, she comes from a long line of horses with white faces and four white legs. It may be that TILNEY FLASH was not that unusual in terms of her coloring, but rather that her owner was more precise (or more like a modern breeder) in describing it.

The second of these is the mare 49710 VENTURE (1903), registered as "skewbald, lot of white." She was by LOCKINGE SAXON, a black with flashy markings, and out of 42328 JOLLY, a roan with a white face and four stockings. Like the horses in TILNEY FLASH's pedigree, it seems likely that JOLLY was not a true roan with white markings, but rather a sabino roan. A sabino roan and a black sabino with flashy markings is exactly the kind of cross that might produce a sabino with enough white, and enough contrast, to be labeled as a pinto (or in this case, a skewbald). Although VENTURE may have seemed like an unexpected surprise to her breeders, the surprise to those looking back at the history of a breed where sabino has been so common is that there were not more like her.

The situation with pinto patterned Shires speaks to a larger idea in the history of horse breeding as it relates to color. Having a registry that actively restricts certain colors is quite different from having a community that does not generally favor a color. Unpopular colors tend not to do well in competitions, and stallions of unpopular colors get few bookings. That does not mean, however, that a determined breeder like B. B. Colvin cannot go off on his own and establish a breeding program based on his own tastes. Horsemen, and horse breeders in particular, tend to be an opinionated bunch. Unless a color or pattern is specifically banned from inclusion in the stud book, it is always possible someone will perpetuate what others seek to eliminate. The downside for those that like unusual colors is that once that iconoclast breeder is gone, the coloring is likely to be lost. Add in the kind of bottleneck that Shires and other heavy draft breeds experienced after the introduction of the tractor, and the odds against retaining any but the most popular colors get pretty high.

Dun

In *Horses—Breeding to Colour*, Sir Walter Gilbey wrote that dun is "a very uncommon colour among Shire Horses." Although he wrote about the rise and fall in popularity of the standard colors within the breed, and even spoke about roans and piebalds, that single sentence was all that he has to say about dilutes. A modern reader, acquainted with present-day draft horses, would likely find the fact that there were ever any duns quite remarkable. When the buckskin JOLIE PRIZE made her surprising appearance, many assumed that her family of diluted Shires was a singular occurrence.

As the quote from Gilbey shows, that is not actually the case; there were a handful of dilute mares in the early stud books. Unlike JOLIE, however, the exact nature of the dilutions are not known. With nothing more than stud book entry descriptions, and no universal terminology for colors, it is impossible to be sure which dilutions were involved. The most common term used was dun, though in Britain that has been used for lineback duns and buckskins alike. It seems likely that either cream or dun, or possibly both, were present. The earliest of these was the mare 14761 FLOWER, foaled in 1871, and registered simply as dun. Nothing is known of her background except that she was sired by LUCKY BOY. Like many of the stallions in the first volume of the stud book, his color is not listed, but it seems unlikely that a dilution came

from him. Because that volume was a retrospective account of historical cart horse sires, it would seem an unusual color would be more likely to be remembered. Her diluted coloring probably came from her unknown dam.

Her daughter, OXTON VIOLET (1884), was registered in the same volume and was also listed as dun. The first indication that the family might have had the actual dun dilution is the entry for her daughter OXTON DUNNIE (1893). DUNNIE is described in Volume 16 of the stud book as "dun, white spot on forehead and nose, black stripe down back." It is not conclusive proof, since buckskins can have dorsal stripes, but the sparse style of the entries in the Shire stud books makes it just as possible that details like an eel stripe might have been left off from the earlier mares' descriptions. At the initial meeting of the Cart Horse Society, a speaker mentioned a stallion that produced "capital work horses" that were consistently "yellowish bay with a brown mark down the back and sometimes down the shoulders also." The horse was never registered, but it does suggest that it would have been possible to find a lineback dun cart horse mare at one time.

An unrelated dilute was listed in the same volume as FLOWER and OXTON VIOLET. The mare 14200 BONNY (1886) was registered as cream with black points. Her coloring came from her unregistered dam, SMART, who was listed as dun. The maternal grandsire was the brown NEWSTEAD, so again the color most likely came through the unrecorded maternal line.

The next volume had 19279 BEAUTY (1894), registered as cream with a white near hind leg. Her color came from her dam, BONNY, an unregistered cream daughter of HONEST TOM 3732. BONNY had another daughter, 20002 GIPSY (1891) in the same volume. GIPSY was registered as dun. BEAUTY had a daughter, PAILTON SYLVIA (1900), registered as a dun in Volume 25. The color of the points on all three mares are not mentioned, so they could have been palomino, buckskin or lineback dun. HONEST TOM had another dun daughter, SMART (1875), that was never registered, though she and her dun daughter FLOWER (1888) appear in the pedigree of the bay mare 41552 DAISY.

Another dun mare, 25696 CORWEN, was registered in Volume 20. She was foaled in 1896 and was registered as "dark buff, black stripe from shoulders to tail, black below knees and hocks." Both her unregistered dam, SEREN, and granddam, TRUE, were both listed as "buff." Like the FLOWER family of mares, it seems likely that CORWEN was a lineback dun.

There were four more duns registered in Volume 27, published in 1906. The first of these is NOTTINGHAM NORAH, foaled in 1904 and registered as "dun, blaze, white underlip, hind legs white to hocks, forelegs white to knees." Her immediate ancestors were all registered as bay or brown, as were her siblings. Her markings indicate that she was a sabino, so it is possible that she was not dilute but pale due to heavy roaning. Many breeders in that era used the term dun as a catch-all for any horse that came out paler than expected, so it seems likely she was simply misregistered.

The same explanation may serve for the second of the four. TANGMERE BELLE, also foaled in 1904, was registered as "dun, white face and underlip, hind legs white up to hocks." Both her sire, CONQUEROR XVII, and her dam, HAVANT SILVER BELL, were bays with sabino markings.

The third mare, WALLINGTON ROSEBUD, is a bit more difficult to explain. She is by a bay stallion and out of a brown mare whose markings are not recorded. ROSEBUD is herself registered as "dun, white mark down face and white off hind fetlock." With such spare leg white, it is less likely that she was a pale sabino roan. The cream dilution sometimes appears to hide for generations, especially in breeds where black is common, and black horses carrying the cream dilution are often registered as brown. With so little information, and no recorded descendants, her true color remains a mystery.

The final dun mare in Volume 27, 47946 FLORRIE, was probably a true dilute. Foaled in 1901, she was registered as "dun, black streak along back." Her sire, ROYAL GAUGER, was bay and her dam was the previously mentioned CORWEN.

Another possible dilute, OXTON LASSIE III, appeared in Volume 36. She was foaled in 1912 and was listed as "cream, blaze, white off hind leg, white near hind fetlock, forelegs black." Like WALLING-TON ROSEBUD, she was by a bay stallion and out of a brown mare. Despite the fact that she shares a prefix with the previously mentioned OXTON VIOLET, there is not any clear connection between the two mares and her color is open to speculation.

Two more duns appear in Volume 42, which was published in 1921. These were 101922 BROWN and her daughter BERTHA QUEEN. BROWN was out of the unregistered dun mare JEWEL, who was herself out of a gray mare also named (oddly enough) BROWN. Once again, the color appears to have come up through the female line. Although information is lacking to be sure which dilution was involved, it does seem possible that like the other dilute families these were also duns.

The last mention of dun in the stud books was in 1960 when the mare DECOY SILVER CLOUD was registered as "gray dun, white face, forelegs white to knees, hind legs white to hocks, white patch on belly and flecked with white hairs." Her color is thought to come through her dam, DECOY MELODY, since she was entered through the Grading Register. DECOY SILVER CLOUD is better known as the dam of the black stallion RYTON REGENT (1970), once listed in the Guinness Book of Records as the tallest horse. She had six other recorded foals, all registered as black or brown.

CRANKWELL NORA, a bay mare foaled in 1902. Although never as common as those with white markings, a small percentage of Shires were once completely solid, or marked with only a small white star.

In addition to REGENT, two of her daughters, DE-COY ANNA (great-great granddam of FOX VALLEY OLIVER) and DECOY RUBY (great-granddam of DEIGHTON BRANDMARK) bred forward into the modern Shire population. If she was indeed a grulla, which is often called "gray dun" in the United Kingdom, her unusual coloring was not passed along to her recorded offspring. She was the last dun Shire registered in Britain, and whatever dilute lines might have originally been present are lost to the modern breed.

Eye Color

The type of sabino patterning found in Shires does not usually affect the color of the eyes, so most Shires have dark eyes. Blue eyes were occasionally mentioned in the older stud books , including the mares PARKER'S PICTURE and WALL EYE, the British stallion CONEY GREY PAXTON and the American stallion WILLIAM O'DONNAL, but such occurrences were, and continue to be, rare.

The current standard stipulates that blue eyes are not acceptable in stallions. Their presence also disqualifies unregistered mares from being included in the Grading Register. This is also true of their first-generation offspring; if they are born with blue eyes they may not be registered.

Markings

The desired markings in the breed are four even stockings and a blaze. As a result, the breed is uniformly sabino. Because the standard penalizes excessive white, the average Shire has less extensive markings than the closely related Clydesdale. Belly spots are still found and are not usually believed to violate the prohibition against "large white patches over the body." Large areas of white concentrated on the belly such that it is not especially distracting when the horse is viewed from the side are often overlooked. Since the breed has never had the kind of marking diagrams once used for Quarter Horses and American Welsh Ponies, marginal cases are open to interpretation.

Although blazes and socks have always been considered typical, at one time there was greater variety in the extent of the markings. The earliest stud books do not provide descriptions of markings, so it is impossible to know what proportions the different types of markings had when the breed was founded. Detailed markings were consistently provided starting with Volume 16, and there at least 4 percent of the stallions are noted as having either no markings or only a star. Over time the preference for markings, as well as the narrowing of the gene pool, eliminated the non-sabinos from the breed.

The specific mutation for the sabino pattern or patterns found in Shires is not currently known. Shires were used in the initial sabino-1 study, and none tested positive. This was not surprising since sabino-1 in its homozygous form results in a white horse. Just as with the Clydesdale, if sabino-1 were responsible for the flashy white markings in Shires, then close to a quarter of the foals would be expected to be born white, which has not been the case.

Another trait seen in some bay and even black Shires is a flaxen or silver tail. Nothing is known about the genetic mechanism behind it, but it is associated with sabino markings. Horses that carry it can sometimes be mistaken for silvers, especially when they are younger and the tail is particularly light, but there is no real evidence that silver has ever been a part of the Shire breed.

Suffolk

Origin: England

The Suffolk is an English draft horse developed in the sixteenth century in East Anglia. It is thought to have remained quite similar in type over the many centuries it has been bred.

Stud Book
The Suffolk Stud-Book Association was formed in 1877. At that time Herman Biddell was commissioned to produce a retrospective stud book covering the animals born before 1879. Biddell's book was published in 1880 and contained 1,236 stallions and 1,125 mares dating as far back as 1760.

Like most breeds that start with a retrospective stud book, admission to the Suffolk stud book was based on pedigree rather than appearance. The breed has suffered numerous bottlenecks over the years, most recently in 1966 when only nine foals were recorded. An inspection scheme for mares was instituted following the war years, but it was discontinued soon afterwards. In more recent times, scarce numbers caused the Association to implement a four-cross grading register.

The American Suffolk Horse Association was founded in 1907 and published its first stud book that same year. The association went dormant shortly after World War II, but was reformed in 1961. To rebuild the breed, the registry accepted the female progeny from outcrosses to Belgians. This type of grading up appears to have been more widely used by American Suffolk breeders than those in the United Kingdom, where purity of the breed has been prized for centuries. In 2001, the British registry stopped recognizing horses from the American stud book, though they can be included in a separate international section of the stud book.

Population
With somewhere between 800 and 1,200 horses, there is a much larger number of Suffolks in the United States than in Britain. It is estimated that only 150 remain in the breed's native country. The British society recorded 36 foals in 2007 and 33 foals in 2008. Both the Rare Breeds Survival Trust in the United Kingdom and the American Livestock Breeds Conservancy in the United States consider their survival status Critical.

Colors
The position on color in the Suffolk was summed up by Herman Biddell, compiler of the breed's original stud book. He wrote of the Suffolk breeder: "Chesnuts all, and all chesnut, with white facings as few as possible, is his creed, and right bravely is this idea carried out." The original stud book committee was committed to maintaining the original color exclusively, keeping with the trend at the time that livestock breeds be distinguished by a uniform color. (They were also committed to the unique spelling of their chosen color, which is still used today.)

Within that one color, all shades are considered acceptable. The registry officially recognizes seven shades: bright, red, golden, yellow (once called lemon), light, dark, and dull-dark. The most popular has traditionally been the bright chestnut. A bright chestnut color with a matching mane and tail and no white markings is often considered by

Summary

Current colors: The breed is uniformly chestnut. Seven shades are recognized: bright, red, golden, yellow, light, dark and dull-dark. Flaxen manes and tails occur occasionally, but high contrast is not typical. Bright chestnut with a self mane and tail is preferred.

Historical colors: Prior to the formation of the stud book, some Suffolk-bred horses were bay.

Markings/patterns: Small amounts of white are permitted. White ticking is found in some strains and is permitted as long as it is not so pronounced as to appear roan.

Eye color: The eyes are dark.

Restrictions: No color other than chestnut has ever been accepted into the stud book.

WHITTON VIOLET showing extensive condition dappling. Vivid dappling is rare in the breed, probably because bright chestnut is favored and dark, sooty chestnut is rare.

many breeders to be the ideal for the breed. After that red and golden follow, though in the early stages of the breed a deep red color was believed to be a sign of bay ancestry. Obviously chestnut horses do not produce bay foals, unless the chestnuts are misidentified bay silvers, which seems unlikely even in the years prior to the formal stud book.

The dark chestnut is said to be a mahogany brown color approaching black, and the dull dark a slightly lighter shade than the dark. In actual practice, horses are registered simply as dark chestnut, perhaps because the word dull has such a negative connotation. Dark chestnut was favored by some early breeders who felt that the color indicated hardiness, but is rare now. Most dark chestnut Suffolks have self-colored manes and tails; very dark chestnut with a strongly contrasting pale mane and tail, such as is seen in the Black Forest Horse, does not appear to have been part of the gene pool.

Yellow, or lemon, chestnut is described as a paler shade of golden chestnut. There was at least one lemon chestnut stallion, though he predated the stud book. That was HIGHNECKED CAPTAIN, the 1841 winner at the Royal Agricultural Show. He was said to have passed his color to many of his daughters. It does not appear this designation was used by breeders after the stud book was estab-

lished. It may be that most simply listed their paler horses as light chestnut. This was considered the least desirable color by Biddell, who wrote:

"The most objectionable is the dull, mealy chesnut, fading off at the flanks, muzzle and lower extremities, to a dirty white, sugar-paper hue, indicative of a weakly constitution, and want of fire and stamina."

There is also a strong historical preference for self-colored manes and tails. Some of the older entries in the stud books list the horse as having a light, flaxen, silver or white manes and tails, but this was relatively rare. Of the 285 horses in the first volume of the American stud book, three horses were listed with white manes and tails, while two had light manes and tails. In the second volume, also listing 285 horses, there were nine horses described as having light manes and tails, and one each with flaxen and silver manes and tails. Flaxen chestnuts were extremely popular with American horsemen in the early twentieth century, but Suffolk breeders largely followed the British lead and selected for matching manes and tails.

Chart 13. The percentage of Suffolks showing white ticking has remained relatively constant over the years.

Percent of Suffolks Ticked with White

British Stud Books

date	total registered	ticked	percentage
1886	1088	39	4%
1890	435	12	3%
1895	414	13	3%
1902	478	19	4%
1908	757	33	4%
1947	1619	21	1%
1960	121	6	5%

American Stud Books

date	total registered	ticked	percentage
1907	285	9	3%
1912	285	7	2%

It is rare for British Suffolks to have white markings on their legs. This stallion, HIGHPOINT WILLIAM, has lighter lower legs, but they are not marked with white. Even with self-colored manes and tails, the lower legs on Suffolks are often quite pale.

White ticking

White ticking has been present in the breed from the very beginning. White or silver hairs are not considered objectionable so long as there are not so many that the horse appears roan rather than chestnut. The trait is thought to trace back to CATLIN'S WHITE-FACED BOXER (1835). He passed it on to his influential descendant, CUPBEARER 3RD. Most entries state that only a few white hairs are present, though a handful have been described has having many white hairs throughout the coat. Biddell called these horses "silver-haired chestnuts."

Some writers drew a connection to white ticking and white markings on the face, particularly blazes. It was also thought that bright chestnuts were more prone to ticking than the other shades. Stud book records show that most ticked Suffolks do have white on the face, though minimal markings like stars seem almost as common as blazes. Leg markings appear no more frequently with ticked horses than in Suffolks that lacked ticking. Ticking was somewhat less common in the darker shades, though the small portion of dark chestnuts might have skewed the distribution.

With only slight fluctuations up or down, white ticking has remained present in approximately 3-4 percent of the Suffolk population. It is possible that ticking, especially minor ticking, is underreported.

Bend Or Spots

At least two Suffolks have been registered with dark Bend Or spots noted in their entries. The first of these was the red chestnut RUBY (1874), listed as having "dark spots about the body." The second was the chestnut MAC LADY MARY (1947), recorded as having dark spots on the body and hindquarters.

Historical Colors

Biddell stated in his 1898 book *Heavy Horses: Breeds and Management* that it had been "between forty and fifty years since a bay horse has been advertised as a Suffolk." He further noted that the horse in question was acknowledged at the time to carry outside blood.

Other writers of the era had noted the "occasional bay" in the breed. At the time competitions held at shows for breeds and registries for those same animals were quite separate, so such horses could have appeared in classes for Suffolk drafts without ever being recorded in the formal stud books. The entry requirements for the first volume of the stud book, written in 1878, state that "all horses of chestnut colour which have hitherto been exhibited as Suffolks, and have been accepted as such by any Agricultural Society in the United Kingdom, shall be eligible for entry." This eliminated bay Suffolks from the stud book, and the fact that chestnut coloring was specified suggests that bays were occasionally exhibited prior to its formation.

It is also possible that the silver mutation was present in the Suffolk landrace in the years prior to the formation of the stud book. This might account for the reports that some mares were known to have thrown bay foals, or colts with black legs. Chestnut mares do not produce bay foals when bred to chestnut stallions unless they are misidentified bay silvers. Early Suffolk breeders selected against what they believed was the tendency towards bay, even to the point of avoiding deep red shades of chestnut. What cannot be ascertained is whether or not they had valid reasons to fear unexpected bay offspring. It was the late nineteenth century, and Mendel's theories had not yet been rediscovered, so breeders were working with a very limited understanding of color inheritance. Given their strict selection against families perceived to have a link to bay, it is unlikely that the silver mutation survived, if indeed it ever was present.

Eye Color

There is no evidence that there were ever Suffolks with light or blue eyes. Because their white markings are minimal, it seems unlikely that the patterns known to produce blue eyes were found in the gene pool.

Markings

The terms for inclusion in the 1878 stud book specifically stated that Suffolks could not be denied entry based on white on the face or legs. Some time during the early twentieth century the wording was changed so that entries could not be denied for white on the face. Leg white was no longer officially protected, though horses with leg white were still registered.

Although entry into the stud book was not made conditional based on white markings, it is true that Suffolk breeders have always favored unmarked horses, which are referred to as whole-coloured. On the subject of markings, the original Suffolk standard read "star, little white on face, or a few silver hairs, is no detriment." The same standard, with that wording, was reprinted in the first volume of the American stud book. The standard did not define what constituted a little white, nor did it mention white on the feet, though presumably white beyond what was listed would be detrimental.

Stone's Prince was a Canadian import from the early twentieth century. Suffolks brought to North America often had more white than those that remained in Britain.

The end result is an all-chestnut breed with an unusually low level of white markings. Many Suffolks have no white whatsoever, or have only a small star. Blazes are seen occasionally, but are far less common now than when the breed was first established. Small amounts of white on the hind feet occur only rarely.

In general chestnut horses have more extensive white markings than either bay or black horses. This can be seen in those breeds selected for solid, unmarked bay or black coloring. When the rare chestnut is born, they will sometimes display the white markings their bay or black relatives lack. The overall low incidence of white in what is a wholly chestnut breed is unusual. In fact, unlike most chestnuts, Suffolks tend to reduce white markings when crossed with flashier mates. This suggests that the breed may carry genetic factors that suppress white markings.

Mismarks

Some Suffolks are born with a small area of white, called a mismark, on the body. A Suffolk gelding with a mismark on his left side was used to illustrate the breed in Tamsin Pickeral's *Encyclopedia of Horses and Ponies* and the *Kingfisher Illustrated Horse and Pony Encyclopedia*. Most often the marks are relatively small and do not have underlying pink skin.

This trait is not linked to any of the patterning mutations, nor is it associated with horses that have higher levels of white markings. It does not seem to run in particularly families, nor do horses with a mismark pass it to their offspring. At least nineteen Suffolks with white body marks have been registered.

BRAG
1883 chestnut stallion with a star
white on off hip

LADY JANE 3RD
1883 chestnut mare
few white spots on the body

KING CUP
1886 chestnut stallion with a blaze
spot on each quarter, spot on near cheek

GRACE 3RD
1888 chestnut mare with a star
white spot on near hindquarter

SORCERESS
1888 chestnut mare
little white spot on back rib

SPECULATION
1891 light chestnut stallion
white spot on near hindquarter

BUNNY
1891 light chestnut mare with a strip
white spot on near side, by girth

CHARSFIELD CHARLOTTE
1892 chestnut mare with a star
white mark on lower part of neck

SUDBOURNE WINNIPEG
1893 chestnut mare
white spot on neck

LADY LOVE
1894 chestnut mare with a star
few small white spots on body

SMITH'S SATURN
1895 red chestnut stallion
white spot on left hip

VALLEY PRINCE
1907 chestnut stallion with faint star
small white spot on right side

LAUREL MADAM
1936 chestnut mare with a star
white patch on near hind quarter

GODBOLTS PATRICK
1945 chestnut stallion
silver patch on off hind thigh

BAWDSEY MEDALLION
1946 chestnut mare with blaze
white patch on near side

SANDRINGHAM SURETY
1947 red chestnut mare
small white patch on top of off hindquarter

MAC BEAU WARRIOR
1949 chestnut stallion
two small white patches on near buttock

STODY SAPPHO
1950 chestnut mare with large blaze
white spot on near side of neck

MOLLANDS PRINCESS
1953 chestnut mare
small white patch on withers

Those are the horses that had white body marks noted in their stud book entries, or that had body marks visible in photographs. It is possible that, like the Bend Or spots, white mismarks are underreported by breeders.

SMITH'S SATURN was frequent winner in the early twentieth century. Judges apparently did not hold the white mark on his left hindquarter against him.

Appendixes

Breed Formation Time Line

Here are some important dates in the formation of modern horse breeds. Events not directly related to horse breeding, but that give insight into the knowledge breeders may have had about genetic inheritance, appear in italics. Where it is not obvious, the primary breed associated with the event is noted, though in some cases that was not the original or the only breed involved.

100-1300

325 Roman Emperor Constantine gives 200 fine horses from Cappadocia to the Yemen tribe of Arabia. Contemporary writings suggest that horses were bred in Egypt, Assyria and Persia, but not Arabia.

934 A Benedictine Abbey in Switzerland establishes the Einsiedeln Stud, were the monks breed the *cavalli della madonna*, or Horses of Our Lady.

982 Icelandic Parliament passes a law prohibiting importation of the horses, sealing off the **Icelandic** equine population from outside influence.

1199 King John of England imports Flemish stallions to increase the size of the native horses. These form the basis for the later British heavy breeds.

1400-1600

1476 Carthusian monks establish a stud farm at Jerez de la Frontera in Spain.

1493 Columbus brings horses to the New World

1520 The **Kinsky** Stud is founded in Bohemia.

1540 King Henry VIII passes the second Breed of Horses Act, forbidding stallions under 15 hands and mares under 13 hands to run on common lands.

1562 The Royal **Frederiksborg** Stud is founded in Denmark and becomes known for its colorful horses.

1565 The Rieß Stud is founded in Salzburg. (**Noriker**)

1566 Queen Elizabeth I repeals the 1540 Horses Act, thereby preserving many of the mountain and moorland breeds.

1567 King Phillip II of Spain issues a royal decree that a new breed of horse be developed in Andalusia.

1570 The royal stud at Lipica is founded.

1573 Marbach is made a state stud in Germany.

1579 The **Kladruby** Stud is founded in the Czech Republic.

1616 The first documented oriental horse in England, the Markham Arabian, is bought by King James I.

1653 The Memsen Stud is founded in Germany. (**Hanoverians**)

1655 A stud book is established for the Einsidler in Switzerland.

1658 The Flyinge Stud is established in Sweden. (**Swedish Warmblood**)

1665 A state stud system is established in France.

1682 Peter the Great directs the Imperial Stud of Russia to import Arabian stallions in order to improve local stock.

1685 James II of England grants a royal charter to the Appleby Fair.

1688 The Byerley Turk is captured in the Siege of Buda in Hungary and is brought to England.
Breeding mares to foreign stallions is banned in Salzburg, Austria.

1700

1704 The Darley Arabian is purchased in Syria and is brought to England.

1714 The state stud of Le Pin is established in France.

1715 Stallion inspections begin in Ostfrisia.

1723 The House of **Kinsky** is commissioned by the Emperor of Austria to produce cavalry mounts.

1728 A stud to produce cream-colored coach horses is established at Herrenhausen in Germany.

1729 The Godolphin Arabian is exported to England from France.

1731 The Trakehnen Stud is founded in East Prussia.

1735 The Celle Stud is founded in Germany. (**Hanoverians**)

1748 The Alter Real Stud is founded in Portugal.

1755 Stallion inspections begin in **Oldenburg**.

1760 *Robert Bakewell, a key figure in the British Agricultural Revolution, experiments with inbreeding as a way to establish new breeds and fix type.*

1768 The Thoroughbred Mambarino, sire of Messenger, is born. (**Standardbreds**)

1770 The Kladruby Stud is rebuilt following the Seven Years' War.

1776 The Khrenovoye Stud is founded in Russia. (**Arabians** and **Orlov Trotters**)

1780 A group of wild **Tarpans** are captured and are placed in the Zamoyski Zoo.

1783 *Robert Bakewell founds the Dishley Society, forerunner of the modern breed registry.*

1784 The Mezőhegyes State Stud is founded in Hungary. (**Nonius, Furioso-North Star** and **Gidran**)

1789 The Royal Babolna Stud is founded in Hungary. (**Shagya Arabians**)
Justin Morgan is foaled.

1791 The *Introduction to the General Stud Book* is published in Great Britain. (**Thoroughbreds**)

1792 The Radautz Stud is established in what was Austria, but is now Romania.

1793 The first volume of the General Stud Book is published in Great Britain. (**Thoroughbreds**)

1798 The Piber Stud is established in Austria for the breeding of military horses.

1800

1808 The Zamoyski **Tarpans** are dispersed among the Polish peasant farmers.

1812 The Knabstrupgaard Stud is established with the spotted mare Flaebe.
The **Mangalarga** Farm in Brazil establishes a breeding program, with the breed initially taking the name Sublime, from the founder stallion.

1816 The **Gidran** is developed at the Mezőhegyes State Stud.

1817 The first state stud in Poland, Janów Podlaski, is established. (**Arabians**)

1817 The Weil Stud is founded in Germany. (**Arabians**)

1818 The last Warden of the Forest salvages a remnant of the **Exmoors** before the Royal Forest is sold.

1820 Inspections are made mandatory in **Oldenburg**.

1821 The second volume of the General Stud Book is published, and uses the name Thoroughbred for the first time.

1829 The Sieraków Stud is founded in Poland. (**Poznan, Maury,** later the **Wielkopolski**)

1833 The *American Turf Register* is published.
The French government establishes a stud book for **Thoroughbred** horses. **Arabians** are registered in a section for Oriental horses.

1836 Abbas Pasha becomes Viceroy of Egypt, and begins to assemble a stud of high-class **Arabian** horses.

1838 A stud book for sport horses is established by Count Oktavian **Kinsky,** founder of the Pardubice Grand National.

1841 The **Ardennes** registry is founded in Belgium.

1844 The Hjerin Stud for **Fjords** is founded by the Norwegian government.

1844 The Zemsky Sluchnoy Stud is founded in Russia. (**Vyatkas**)

1845 A trotting register is established in Russia.

1856 The **Tori** Stud is founded in Estonia.
The Luczin Stud is founded in Romania. (**Huzul**)

1858 The **Fjords** at Hjerin are dispersed in favor of **Døle-Gudbrandsdal** horses.

1860 The Abbas Pasha **Arabian** Stud is dispersed, with many of the horses going to European state studs.

1861 The **Oldenburg** stud book is established in Germany.

1865 *The American Civil War ends. It is estimated that 1.5 million horses were lost during the conflict.*

1866 *Gregor Mendel publishes his findings on plant hybridization, but his discovery goes largely unnoticed.*

1867 Wallace's American Stud Book is published, with a supplemental section for trotting horses.
A horse breeding society is formed in Hanover, Germany.

1868 *Charles Darwin publishes <u>The Variation of Animals and Plants under Domestication</u>, with a chapter devoted to horses and their coloring. He is unaware of the work of Mendel.*
The **Falabella** Stud is founded in Argentina.

1869 The **East Friesian** stud book is established in Germany.

1870 Cassiano **Campolina** establishes his farm, Fazenda Tanque, in Brazil.

1871 The Royal Frederiksborg Stud is closed and its horses are dispersed.
The first American Trotting Register is published.

1872 The Pompadour Stud is founded in France. (**Anglo-Arabians**)

1873 *The Kennel Club is formed in Great Britain.*

1874 Inspections of breeding stock begin in Sweden.

1875 The Norwegian Trotting Association is founded.

1876 A registry for French Draft horses is founded in America.

1877 The **Clydesdale** Horse Society is founded in Scotland.
The **Suffolk** Stud-Book Association is founded in England.
The first **Trakehner** stud book is published by the East Prussian Stud Book Society.
Lady Ann and Wilfred Blunt travel to Aleppo to search for stock for their Crabbet **Arabian** Stud.

1878 The English Cart Horse Society, which becomes the **Shire** Horse Society, is founded in England.
The first **Clydesdale** stud book in published in Scotland.
The American Stud Book for **Thoroughbred** horses is published.

1878 A stud book for French Drafts is published in America.

The first Australian Stud Book is published. (**Thoroughbreds**)

1879 A stud book registering both **Friesians** and **Bovenlanders** is established in Friesland.

A stud book for **Brabants** is established in Belgium.

The American **Clydesdale** registry is founded.

1880 A stud book for **Nivernais** is established in France.

1881 The first **Jutland Horse** stud book is published.

1883 A **Percheron** registry is founded in France.

The **Cleveland Bay** Horse Society is founded in England.

The **Hackney** Horse Society is founded in England.

A stud book for **Arabians** is established in Spain.

1884 A stud book for the **Poitevin Mulassier** is established in France.

The American Kennel Club is founded.

1885 A stud book for the **Boulonnais** is established in France.

A horse breeders' association is formed in Holstein, Germany.

1886 The **Yorkshire Coach Horse** Society is founded.

The **Belgian Draft** registry is founded in Belgium.

A **Clydesdale** registry is founded in Canada.

1887 The **Belgian Draft** registry is founded in America.

The Pinzgauer (**Noriker**) registry is founded in Austria.

1888 The **American Shetland Pony** Club is founded.

The first **Hanoverian** stud book is published.

1889 A **Cleveland Bay** registry is founded in America.

The Tersk Stud is founded in Russia. (**Arabians** and **Part-Arabians**)

1890 The **Gelderlander** stud book (GPS) is established in the Netherlands.

The **Shetland Pony** Stud Book Society is founded in Scotland.

1891 The **Saddlebred** registry is founded in America.

A **Hackney** registry is founded in America.

A stud book for partbred (demi-sang) horses is established in France.

A pony improvement scheme is instituted by the Congested Districts Board in Ireland to help alleviate poverty. (**Connemaras**)

The Association for the Improvement of **New Forest Ponies** is founded in England.

A stud book for **Holsteiners** is established in Germany.

1893 The first **Oldenburg** stud book is published.

The Polo Pony Stud Book Society is founded in England.

The **Fell Pony** Society is founded in England.

1893 A stud book for the **Chilean Horse** is established in Chile.

1894 Joseph Battell publishes the first **Morgan** Horse Register.

A breeders' association for the **North Swedish Horse** is founded in Sweden.

The Jockey Club is founded in America. (**Thoroughbreds**)

1895 The Polish Horse Breeders Association (PZHK) is founded.

1896 A breeders' association for the **Black Forest Horse** is founded.

1897 The **Groninger** stud book (GrPS) is established in the Netherlands.

1899 The British Polo Pony stud book adds sections for the following native breeds: **Dartmoor**, **Exmoor**, **Fell**, **Highland**, **New Forest** and **Welsh Ponies**.

Professor James Cossar Ewart publishes the results of his zebra hybrid experiments in an effort to discredit the widespread theory of telegony. The study gets a lot of attention, in part because the hybrids are a novelty.

1900

1900 A stud book for **Norikers** is established in Czechoslovakia. These are later known as Silesian Norikers for the region where they are bred.

The work of Gregor Mendel is rediscovered.

1901 The **Welsh Pony and Cob** Society is founded in Wales.

A stud book for **Ardennes** is established in Sweden.

The **Silesian** stud book is established in Poland.

1902 The first **Døle** stud book is published.

1903 *The American Breeders Association is formed. The agricultural scientists involved are committed to researching and popularizing Mendel's Laws of Inheritance. Among the committees are those concerned with the breeding of coach horses, draft horses, and hybrid horses. Unfortunately, there is also a committee for research in eugenics, which many in the organization support.*

1904 A breeder cooperative is formed for the **Haflinger** in Austria.

A horse breeders' society is formed in Iceland.

1905 The first American **Belgian Draft** stud book is published.

A **Percheron** registry is founded in America.

1906 The **Welsh Pony** Society of America is founded.

1907 A **Suffolk** registry is founded in America.

The two sections of the **Friesian** stud book merge.

1907 A stud book for the **Finnhorse** is established.

1908 The **Arabian** Horse Club of America is founded.

1909 The **Morgan** Horse Club is founded in America.
A stud book for the Ardennes is established in France.

1909 A stud book for the **Breton** is established in France.
The last living **Tarpan** dies in a Russian zoo.

1910 A stud book for the **Trait du Nord** is established in France.
The first **New Forest Pony** stud book is published.
The first **Fjord** stud book is published.
The American Breeders Association begins publication of the American Breeders Magazine. In addition to profiles on Darwin and Mendel, the first issue includes an article on breeding horses for the Army.

1912 The Dutch Harness Horse stud book (NSTg) is established in the Netherlands.(**Gelderlanders**)
A stud book for the **Pura Raza Espanola** is established in Spain. Prior to that time the horses had been called **Andalusians**.

1913 The British Polo Pony Stud Book Society becomes the National Pony Society.
The National Pony Society resumes sole responsibility for the **New Forest Pony** stud book.

1914 *The American Breeders Association changes its name to the American Genetics Association, and the name of its publication to the Journal of Heredity. For the remainder of the twentieth century, the majority of research on equine genetics is published there.*

1915 Stud book divisions between **Friesians** and **Bovenlanders** return to the stud book of Friesland.

1916 Breeders of the **Fell Pony** separate from the National Pony Society.

1917 A **Clydesdale** registry is founded in Australia.
The first **Irish Draught** stud book is published.
The National Pony Society splits the **Dales Pony** from the **Fell Pony**, giving it a separate stud book.

1918 The **Arab** Horse Society is founded in Great Britain.
A stud book for **Criollos** is founded in Argentina.
World War I ends. Of the estimated one million horses that served Great Britain on the western front, only 62,000 return home alive. It is estimated that 40 million service animals died in the course of the war, most of them horses.

1919 A breeders' association for the **Comtois** is founded in France.

1920 The **Estonian Horse** Breeders Society is founded.
The first **Haflinger** stud book is published.

1920 Dr. Ruy d'Andrade encounters a group of wild horses he believes are the ancestral stock used to create the Spanish Horse while on a hunting trip in the **Sorraia** Valley.
A registry for the **Frederiksborg** Horse is founded in Denmark.
The Piber Stud begins breeding **Lipizzans**.

1921 The first **Comtois** stud book is published.
The **Exmoor** Pony Society is founded in England.
The General Stud Book of England stops registering **Arabians**.
A stud book for **Freiberger** Horses is established in Switzerland.

1922 A stud book for the **Huzul** is founded in Czechoslovakia.

1923 The Russian General Stud Book adds a section for Central Asian breeds, which includes the **Akhal-Teke**.
The **Connemara** Pony Breeder's Society is founded in Ireland.
The **Highland** Pony Society is founded in Scotland.
A stud book for **Icelandics** is founded in Iceland.

1924 A stud book for the **Huzul** is founded in Poland.

1925 The **Dartmoor** Pony Society is founded in England.

1926 A stud book for **Arabians** is established in Poland.
A stud book for **Murgese** is established in Italy.

1927 A stud book for the restored **Orlov Trotter** is published.
The **Morgan** Horse Club acquires Battell's *Morgan Horse Register.*

1928 Ponies are introduced to **Lundy** Island.
A registry for warmbloods (ASVH) is established in Sweden.

1930 Russian authorities stop recording **Vyatkas** in district stud books.

1931 The Australian Pony Stud Book Society is founded with three sections: Shetlands, Hackneys and **Australian Ponies**. The Australian Pony section includes the other mountain and moorland breeds as well as crosses.

1932 A section is added to the Estonian stud book for the **Tori** Horse.
Zoologists at the Munich Zoo attempt to recreate the extinct **Tarpan** using domestic horses thought to have descended from them. The resulting animals are now called Heck Horses.
A section for riding type ponies (Section B) is added to the **Welsh Pony** stud book.
The Weil Stud is transferred to Marbach, and is called Weil-Marbach by **Arabian** breeders.

1934 A stud book for the **Don**, with a section for the **Budyonny**, is published in Russia.

A stud book for **Campolinas** is established in Brazil.

A breeders' association is formed for the **Mangalarga** horses in Brazil.

1935 The **Tennessee Walking Horse** Breeders' Association of America is founded.

The registry for the **Morocco Spotted Horse** is founded.

1936 Dr. d'Andrade selects 10 horses, 3 stallions and 7 mares, for a preservation breeding program of the wild Iberian horses he calls **Sorraias**.

1938 The **Appaloosa** Horse Club is founded to preserve the rapidly vanishing spotted horses of American west.

1939 The existing **Gelderlander** stud books merge, and include a section for the **Groninger**. (VLN)

Coldblooded Trotters are given a separate section in the Døle stud book.

A project is initiated to restore the Old Black **Kladruber** which had been nearly destroyed after the fall of the Hapsburg Empire.

1940 The American **Quarter Horse** Association is founded.

1941 A separate stud book for the **Akhal-Teke** is published in Russia.

1942 **Bovenlanders** leave the **Friesian** stud book for a new stud book combining Groninger and Drenthe horses. (NWP)

1943 A stud book for **Gotland Ponies** is established in Sweden.

Another stud book for **Vyatkas** is established in Russia.

The American **Welsh Pony** registry is dissolved for failure to file an annual corporate report.

The Jockey Club stops registering **Arabians**.

A registry for **Paso Finos** is founded in Puerto Rico.

1944 The **American Cream Draft** registry is founded.

A stud book for the **Mérens** is established in France.

Horses are evacuated from the stud farm in **Trakehnen** in advance of Russian troops, undertaking a grueling journey later known as *Der Treck*.

1945 Only two captive populations of **Przewalski Horses** survive, totaling thirty animals.

1946 The **Welsh Pony** Society of America is resurrected and a retrospective stud book is published covering the missing years.

A registry for **Peruvians** is founded in Peru.

1947 A registry for appaloosa patterned ("spotted") horses is founded in Great Britain.

A breeders' association for **Knabstruppers** is established in Denmark.

The East Prussian stud book is dissolved and replaced with what would become the **Trakehner** Verband.

1948 The **Missouri Fox Trotting Horse** Breeders Association is founded in America.

The **Tersk** is granted a separate stud book by the Russian government.

1949 A section for **Welsh Ponies** of Cob Type (Section C) is added to the Welsh stud book.

Breeders that disagree with the inclusion of the **Mangalarga Paulista**, a trotting strain, break away to form the Association **Mangalarga Marchador**.

A stud book is established for **Anglo-Normans** in France.

1951 A separate stud book for the **Budyonny** is published in Russia.

1953 The Michałów Stud is established in Poland. (**Arabians** and **Malopolskis**)

1954 The **Pony of the Americas** Club is founded.

1955 A stud book is established for the **Konik** in Poland.

1956 Russia instructs state stud farms to produce sport horses, retaining only minimal "samples" of the primitive breeds.

1957 The **Spanish Mustang** Registry is founded in America.

1958 The stud books for French halfbred horses are combined to form the **Selle Francais**.

1959 **Norman Cob** is separated from the French general stud book.

The first stud book for **Przewalski Horses** is published.

1960 The parent breed society reclaims the **New Forest Pony** stud book from the National Pony Society.

The Spanish **Pura Raza Espanola** stud book is closed to horses from Portugal.

1961 The **Exmoor** Pony Society takes over the Exmoor stud book, formerly maintained by the National Pony Society.

The American **Paint** Quarter Horse Association is founded.

1962 The **Highland Pony** Society takes over the Highland stud book, formerly maintained by the National Pony Society.

The Polish Horse Breeders Association grants the **Malopolski** a separate stud book.

The American **Paint** Stock Horse Association is founded.

1962 The **Poznan**, **Maury**, and German warmblood breeds are combined to form the **Wielkopolksi**.

1964 A stud book for coldbloods is established in Poland.

A stud book for **Coldblooded Trotters** is established in Sweden.

1965 The two existing registries for pinto stock horses merge to form the American **Paint** Horse Association.

A separate stud book for the **Coldblooded Trotter** is established in Norway.

1966 A registry for **Lusitanos** is established in Portugal.

1967 The American Donkey and Mule Society is founded to record donkeys, mules and zebra hybrids.

1968 Efforts are made to preserve the **Kinsky** horse at the State Stud in Chlumec.

1969 Establishment of the **Dutch Warmblood** stud book. (KWPN)

The last **Przewalski Horse** is seen in the wild.

Welsh Ponies are granted a separate section in the Australian Pony Stud Book.

1971 The American **Bashkir Curly** registry is founded.

The modern **Knabstrupper** registry is founded in Denmark.

1972 The American **Miniature** Horse Registry, part of the **American Shetland Pony** registry, is founded.

A **Paso Fino** registry is established in America.

The **Australian Stock Horse** Society is founded.

A breeders' society for **Eriskay Ponies** is founded.

1973 **Felin Pony** is created at the Felin Experimental Farm in Poland.

The National Pony Society takes over administration of the **Lundy Pony** herd.

The first stud book for the **Pottock Pony** is published in France.

1975 The North American **Tarpan** Association, a registry for Heck Horses, is founded.

1976 The British registry for appaloosa horses splits into two separate registries, one for horses and one for ponies.

A stud book for the **Lewitzer** is established in Germany.

1978 A second **Miniature** Horse registry is founded in America.

A stud book for **Camargues** is established in France.

The first **Caspian** stud book is published.

1979 The **Dartmoor Pony** Society takes over the Dartmoor stud book, formerly maintained by the National Pony Society.

The National **Spotted Saddle Horse** Association is founded.

1982 A registry for **Aztecas** is established in Mexico.

1983 Restoration of the **Vyatka** begins in Russia.

1984 The **Lundy Pony** Preservation Society is founded.

1985 The **Spotted Saddle Horse** Breeders' and Exhibitors' Association is founded.

1986 The **Rocky Mountain Horse** Association is founded.

The **Waler** Horse Society is formed in Australia.

The **Morocco Spotted Horse** registry appears in lists of livestock organizations for the last time.

1988 The **Mountain Pleasure Horse** Association is founded to include a broader range of bloodlines than the registry for the Rocky Mountain Horse.

1989 The first stud book for the **Moroccan Barb** is published by the French National Stud.

1994 A stud book for the restored **Vyatka** is published in Russia.

1995 A registry for North American **Spotted Draft Horses** is founded.

The Indigenous Horse Society of India is founded. (**Marwari**)

1996 The first **Gypsy Cob** and Drum Horse registry is founded in America.

Horse Color Time Line

In recent years, unusual colors have enjoyed renewed popularity among horsemen. Although a true understanding of many of these colors is relatively new, the colors themselves are often quite old. There is a cyclical nature to fashions in horse color, where what is thought to be rare or exotic is prized for a while, then discarded in favor of the more conservative. The accompanying chart outlines some of the history of the different colors and patterns. (For simplicity, dates before the Late Modern period are often approximations.)

Pleistocene

15000 BC   Appaloosa patterned horses are painted on the cave walls at Pech Merle in France. Other cave paintings show the mealy pattern.
The alleles that produce bay (*E* and *A*) are present and are assumed to be the original color of horses. Although not yet testable, the dun dilution is assumed to be to be present as well.

14000 BC   The leopard complex mutation (*Lp*) can be found among the wild horses of Thuringia and southern Germany.

Mesolithic-Neolithic

5000 BC   The black allele (*a*) can be found among the wild horses of the Iberian Peninsula.

Copper Age

4300 BC   Both the black (*a*) and chestnut (*e*) alleles can be found among the wild horses of Romania.

3600 BC   The black allele (*a*) can be found among the wild horses of the Ukraine.

3500 BC   The leopard complex mutation (*Lp*) can be found among the wild horses of the Ukraine.

Bronze Age

3000 BC   Both the black (*a*) and chestnut (*e*) alleles can be found in the domestic horses of Siberia.

2500 BC   The sabino-1 mutation (*Sb1*) can be found in the domestic horses of western Siberia.
The black allele (*a*) can be found in the domestic horses of Germany.

1531 BC   Kassites take control of Babylon and bring with them words for horse colors: *gun*

(skewbald), *pirmah* (parti-colored) and *dakas* (spotted or dappled).

1415 BC   A pinto patterned horse is depicted in a wall painting in the Necropolis of Thebes. The spotting does not precisely match any of the currently known pinto patterns, and may have been stylized.

1300 BC   Both chestnut (*e*) and sabino-1 (*Sb1*) are present in the domestic horses of Armenia.
A Mycenaean fresco shows two women driving a chariot pulled by a chestnut and a white horse. Only the hindquarters of the horses remain, but the peaked white stockings typical of a flashy sabino are visible on the chestnut.

1250 BC   The black (*a*), chestnut (*e*), sabino-1 (*Sb1*) and tobiano (*T*) alleles can be found in the domestic horses in Moldova.

1042 BC   Chou Ch'eng-wang is the second ruler of the Zhou Dynasty. He acquires white horses with red manes and yellow-gold eyes from the Ch'üan-jung.

Iron Age

850 BC   The tobiano mutation (*T*) is present in the domestic horses of China.
Homer writes of the immortal horses Xanthus and Balius in the *Illiad*. Balius means spotted, or piebald.

800 BC   The silver dilution (Z) is present in the domestic horses of Tuva, Siberia.

610 BC   The chestnut (*e*), tobiano (*T*) and cream (*Cr*) alleles are present among the domestic horses of Tuva, Siberia.

350 BC   The chestnut (*e*), tobiano (*T*) and cream (*Cr*) alleles are present among the domestic horses of Mongolia.

246 BC   Work begins on the mausoleum for Qin Shi Huang, the First Emperor of China. In addition to the famed Terra Cotta Army, there

are two four-horse chariots in bronze. The horses pulling the chariots were painted with leopard appaloosa patterns.

29 BC Virgil writes of a piebald Thracian horse, as well as one "dappled with white." A pure white horse appears among those of several shades of brown in the mural at the Thracian Tomb of Kazanluk.

Common Era

211 Oppian asserts in his poem *Cynegetica* that horses with blue eyes are best suited for the hunting of stags. He also describes a "beautiful race" of horses, the Orynx, with varieties both striped and covered in round spots. Later translations often indicate he was speaking of the African Zebra.

400 Roman author Palladius writes of horse color in his book *Opus agriculturae*. He urges readers to select stallions of a clear and uniform color, unless their quality "makes an apology" for their color. Along with broken and mixed colors, he considers cream and mouse less desirable. True white and several shades of buff and tan are included among the desirable colors, however.

406 Vandals, a Germanic tribe, begin raiding the Roman Empire. A mosaic shows a Vandal lord riding a leopard spotted horse.

Middle Ages

618 The Tang Dynasty begins in China. Palominos, appaloosas and pintos are common in artwork from the time. One hand scroll titled *One Hundred Horses* shows duns, palominos, tobianos, varnish roans, sabinos and what looks like a buckskin silver. (A much later painting of the same name, also showing colorful horses, is better known within the art world.)

786 Beatus of Liebana, a Spanish monk, works on the second draft of his *Commentary on the Revelation*. Although Revelations refers to the first horseman as riding a white horse, in many versions of the Commentary the rider is depicted on a leopard appaloosa.

982 Icelandic horses become isolated from the rest of the equine population, insuring that the colors found in the breed are not the result of outside influences. Mutations present include roan (*R*), grey (*G*), cream (*Cr*), dun (*D*), tobiano (*T*) and splashed white (*SW1*), as well as the standard base colors.

1070 Li Gonglin becomes a civil officer during the Chinese Song Dynasty. He is best known for his paintings of horses, including at least one very detailed sabino overo.

1086 In a copy of the *Commentary on the Revelation*, the scribe Martinus portrays the victorious Christ astride a leopard appaloosa. He is accompanied by several more riders on leopards.

1298 A royal inventory of horses from the Falkirk campaign includes a blanket-spotted Powys Horse, which is valued at a higher price than other horses of similar type.

1330 Abu Bekr al-Baytar Ibn Badr al-Din, veterinarian of the Mamluk court, writes *El Naseri*, a treatise on horses. He enumerates the colors of Arabian horses, including the cream-yellow *zarah*, and dun with a dorsal stripe.

1339 King Edward I is depicted in an illustration riding into London on a leopard spotted horse.

Early Modern

1603 Anton Günther takes control of the Oldenburg Stud. He takes a special interest in unusual colors, particularly the paler dilutions.

1610 An illuminated treatise on hunting is prepared for Sultan Ahmed Khan. One of the illustrations depicts a black and white pinto horse with a lacey frame-like pattern. All four legs and the entire topline are dark, while the face is primarily white.

1628 Shah Jahan becomes the Mogul Emperor of India. In several painted portraits he is riding the same black homozygous tobiano stallion.

1635 Anthony van Dyck paints *Charles I on Horseback*, with the king mounted on a buckskin horse of Spanish type.

1653 The Electress Sophia begins breeding cream-colored coach horses at the Memsen Stud.

1670 An illustration of King Louis XIV from the carrousel to celebrate the birth of the dauphin shows him mounted on what looks to be a red silver of Spanish type.

1672 The white-born stallion Jomfrüen is acquired by the Frederiksborg Stud.

1702 Johann Georg von Hamilton paints the *Imperial Riding School*, which features a palomino and a black leopard in the foreground. The precise rendering of the colors are a hallmark of Hamilton's work. Both horses are copied by later artists.

1712 Alcocks Arabian is foaled. All modern grey Thoroughbreds trace back to him.

1724   In Germany, Berberbeck is elevated to the status of Court Stud. Golden horses, most likely cream dilutes, are bred there.

1725   The Thoroughbred mare Silverlocks is foaled. She is believed to have been a palomino.

1727   Hamilton paints *The Imperial Stud with Lipizzaner Horses*, a painting often used to illustrate the variety once found in that breed. Among the colors are blood-marked grey, dark-headed roan, palomino, buckskin, cremello, tobiano and appaloosa.

1728   The cream-colored stallion Eutiner is brought to Herrenhaussen, where he establishes the Hanoverian Cream breed.

1735   *The Sportsman's Dictionary* states that Swedish horses are white, dun, pied and wall-eyed.

1747   The Baron Reis d'Eisenberg publishes the *Description du Manege Moderne*, with illustrations of classic equestrian movements. Among the horses pictured are leopard and blanket appaloosas, tobianos, roans, and cream dilutes.

1764   The stallion Spinola is purchased for the Trakehner Stud. He is described as *porzellanschecke*, or grey pinto.

1772   Pluto is acquired from the Frederiksborg Stud for the stud at Lipica. Accounts differ on whether he was a grey or an appaloosa.

1779   The "dun" (likely buckskin) stallion Favory is born at the Kladruby Stud in what is then part of the Austrian Empire. He is transferred to Lipica four years later, where he founds one of the six classical sire lines in the Lipizzan breed.

1799   Spottee, an African stallion imported from Spain to America stands stud in Norfolk, Virginia. His coat is said to be "richly variegated" with "four different and distinct colors." He later appears in the first volume of the American Stud Book in the section for imported Spanish Horses.

1789   Sawrey Gilpin paints a portrait of King of Trumps, a bay spotted Thoroughbred owned by King George III. His pattern resembles that of the modern dominant white Thoroughbred stallion, Sato.

Late Modern

1809   The Canadian pacer Copperbottom is born. His widespread influence lays the foundation for many of the later soft-gaited breeds. It is also likely that he carried the sabino-1 mutation, and consistently passed it to his descendants.

1825   Buckskins represent 20 percent of the Lipizzans at the Spanish Riding School.

1832   Count Oktavian Kinsky focuses on breeding golden horses at the Kinsky Stud.

1835   A tobiano trotting-bred mare, Dolly, is incorporated into the stud at Lipica. Her descendant Pluto Lina is the last known tobiano Lipizzan.

1842   Rafael Tobias de Aguiar leads the Liberal Revolution in Sao Paulo. He rides a pinto horse of a pattern previously unknown in Brazil, which then takes his name: tobiano. It is believed the pattern came from Friesian imports.

1858   John Frederick Herring Sr. paints a scene from the Barnet Horse Fair. In the foreground is a grulla heavy horse.

1862   The last white stallion is born at Frederiksborg.

1876   The grey leopard part-Arabian Khediven is born. Later he becomes the first entry in the Gotland Pony stud book.

1886   The Shetland mare Trot is born. Almost eighty years later she is mistakenly identified as the first silver dapple. Her grandson Chestnut helps to popularize the color with American breeders.

1878   The first volume of the American Stud Book is published. Among the horses in the Spanish section are Coslanian, said to have been spotted with blue eyes and of the Andalusian breed, and Apalusia, a "milk-white horse with blue ears."

1888   Coke Roberts breeds one of his running mares to a stallion known as The Circus Horse. Descendants of the resulting colt, Arab, are the source for the color in many of the early crop-out appaloosa Quarter Horses.

1894   Another Coke Roberts horse, Old Fred, is born. The palomino stallion is widely believed to have carried the splashed white mutation.

1899   The black tobiano mare Eva is acquired from Russia for the Trakehner breeding program. She produced fifteen living foals.

1902   A leopard stallion from St. Petersburg, Russia, is brought to Denmark. He renews interest in the Knabstrup breed, which is almost extinct.

        Joseph Battell compiles the American Stallion Register, which records those early stallions influential in the formation of the pacer, roadster and trotter. Spotted "Arabians" are often mentioned in the pedigrees, which may help account for later perceptions in America that exotic colors were characteristic of the breed.

1906   Kaiser Wilhelm II has a fondness for pinto patterns, and appears in public on a tovero horse, presumed to be a Trakehner.

1908   The white-born colt Old King is born. He is later the focus of the first American study of dominant white horses.

1910   Golden Lady is born. She is the first "yellow" horse registered in the Tennessee Walking Horse stud book, and is one of the earliest recorded carriers of the champagne dilution.

1911   The Tetrarch, a grey stallion with large white spots is born. He becomes known as the Spotted Wonder. His success helps to revitalize the grey color in Thoroughbreds.

Old Granny, founder of the American Cream Draft horse, is purchased at a farm sale in Iowa. She carries the champagne dilution, which becomes the defining color for the breed.

1914   The Ohlau Trumpeter Hussars are mounted on black tobianos, which was the traditional color for the parade horses of the Kaiser. A few appaloosas are also used.

1918   Black becomes a requirement for entry into the Friesian stud book.

1921   The last of the Royal Hanoverian Creams are dispersed at auction.

1923   Allen Seaby, a popular author and illustrator of children's book, paints *Skewbald the New Forest Pony*, which shows a pony with a classic splashed white pattern. A book featuring the pony follows five years later.

Contemporary

1931   Dr. Valto Klemola of the University of Edinburg publishes a paper on what he believes to be a recessive form of spotting in the equine. He calls the pattern Splashed White.

1936   The Palomino Horse Association is formed, and accepts golden horses regardless of skin color.

1937   The Pardubice Grand National is won by a palomino Kinsky mare, Norma. The event receives a lot of attention, not because of Norma's color, but because her rider is Countess Lata Brandisova, the only woman to have won the event.

1938   Roy Rogers appears in the movie *Under Western Stars* riding a palomino of unknown origins named Golden Cloud. Renamed Trigger, he went on to star with Rogers in movies and a television show. His popularity generated a great deal of interest in golden horses, particularly in the United States.

1939   The stud book for the Welsh Pony and Cob Society now states that piebalds and skewbalds are not permitted.

1941   The Palomino Horse Breeders of America is formed.

1943   The Palomino Horse Breeders of America begins requiring horses to have dark skin in order to qualify for registration.

The frame overo Saddlebred, Oak Hill Chief, is named the World Champion Five-Gaited Horse. He repeats his win two more times.

1944   Ernst Bilke photographs a homozygous splashed white stallion in East Prussia. Like many of the Trakehners that lived during the war years, his fate is unknown. Among the Trakehners that survive the political upheaval of World War II, there are a handful of tobianos.

1953   The "white" Morgan stallion Chingadero is foaled on the Cross Ranch. Later it is understood that he was a perlino.

1958   The last tobiano Trakehner, the gelding Schill II, is born in Germany.

1959   A loud frame overo Morgan stallion, War Paint, is foaled on the Cross Ranch, already home to the perlino Chingadero.

1962   In response to the Morgans at the Cross Ranch, the Morgan Horse Association passes a rule banning horses with excessive white or blue eyes.

1969   Champagne Lady Diane, a Tennessee Walking Horse, is born. At the time her unusual color, the result of the champagne mutation diluting black, was thought to be a unique mutation. The mutation responsible took its name from her.

1975   Melvin Hartley sues the American Quarter Horse Association over its "white rule", which was used to deny papers to his stallion Naturally High. The registry wins the case, and the white rule stands.

1983   The Appaloosa Horse club institutes its Certified Pedigree Option (CPO) program, which allows solid horses to be registered and compete at Appaloosa shows.

1987   Purebred descendants of the tobiano Trakehner Eva, which had been presumed lost during World War II, are found in Poland.

Tobiano is found to be linked to blood protein markers, which forms the basis of a blood test to help identify homozygous tobianos.

1996   A test is developed to identify the mutation responsible for chestnut (e).

The Morgan Horse Association rescinds the rule banning excessive white markings.

1998   The mutation responsible for the frame overo pattern, and for Lethal White Syndrome (*LWS*), is identified.

2000   The International Champagne Horse Registry is formed and makes detailed records on the horses publicly available, increasing awareness of the color and the lines that carry it.

2001   A test is developed that identifies the mutation responsible for black (*a*).

A handful of horses come to the attention of those researching the champagne mutation. While several look like champagnes, they do not fit the pattern of inheritance for the color. These later prove to have the pearl dilution.

2003   A test is developed that identifies the mutation responsible for the cream dilution (C^{Cr}).

2005   A test is developed that identifies one of the sabino patterns, which is named sabino-1 in anticipation of more sabino alleles in the future.

The American Quarter Horse Association rescinds its rules about excessive white. Blue-eyed creams are also permitted.

In response to the changes at the Quarter Horse registry, the American Paint Horse Association passes a rule requiring horses to have one registered parent, thereby ending the registration of Paint and Thoroughbred crop-outs.

The website for the Kellas Shetland Pony Stud publishes an article about ponies that look silver but appear to have a different mode of inheritance. The color is called mushroom. Tests show that the ponies are genetically chestnut, which makes the silver dilution unlikely since it does not alter red pigment.

2006   A test is developed that identifies the mutation responsible for the silver dilution (*Z*).

A test is developed that identifies the mutation responsible for the pearl dilution (C^{Prl}).

2006   The Appaloosa Horse Club discontinues the Certified Pedigree Option (CPO) program.

Solid horses are registered provided they meet bloodline requirements, but require a special permit to show.

2007   Researchers identify the dominant white mutation in Franches Montagnes horses. Additional mutations are found in the Camarillo White, Arabian and Thoroughbred.

2008   A zygosity test is developed that can identify some duns.

A test is developed that identifies the mutation responsible for the champagne dilution (*Ch*).

A test is developed that identifies the mutation responsible for grey (*G*).

A more reliable tobiano test is developed.

A test is developed that identifies the mutation responsible for brown (a^t).

2009   Seven more unique dominant white mutations are identified. Included in this group are an Icelandic, Holsteiner, Quarter Horse, South German Draft, and several families of Thoroughbreds.

A zygosity test is developed that can identify some roans.

Several mushroom ponies test negative for the silver mutation, giving further evidence that it is a separate mutation.

Scientists test ancient remains for a variety of colors, and find that many have been a present in the horse population for a long time.

2011   Researchers confirm through testing that the leopard complex mutation was present in horses prior to domestication.

2012   A test is developed that identifies three different mutations that produce splashed white patterns. The most widespread of the three is not lethal in its homozygous form, and is believed to be the original pattern described by Klemola.

Horse Color Terminology

English: Horse Color; *Czech*: Zbarvení koní; *Danish*: Hestefarve; *Dutch*: Paarden Kleuren; *Finnish*: Hevosten Värit; *French*: Robe du Cheval; *German*: Fellfarben der Pferde; *Hungarian*: Ló Színek; *Icelandic*: Hestur Litir; *Norwegian*: Hestefargar; *Polish*: Umaszczenia koni; *Portuguese*: Pelajes Criollos; *Russian*: Masti loshadyeĭ; *Spanish*: Pelajes del caballo; *Swedish*: Hästfärger

Base Colors

The basic colors of chestnut, bay, brown and black, along with some of their common variations

English: chestnut, sorrel, liver
Czech: ryzák, světlý ryzák (light chestnut), tmavý ryzák (dark chestnut), černý ryzák (black chestnut)
Danish: rød, lys rød (light chestnut), sodrød (dark chestnut)
Dutch: vos, kastanjebruin, zweetvos (flaxen chestnut), koolvos or koffievos (dark chestnut)
Finnish: rautias, vaaleanrautias (light chestnut), punarautias (red chestnut), tummanrautias (dark chestnut), mustanrautias (black chestnut)
French: alezan, alezan clair (sorrel), alezan foncé (dark chestnut), alezan brûlé (liver chestnut)
German: fuchs, hellfuchs (light chestnut), dunkelfuchs (dark chestnut)
Hungarian: sarga, vilagos sarga (light chestnut), majsarga (liver chestnut)
Icelandic: rauður, ljósrauður (light chestnut), sótrauður (dark chestnut)
Norwegian: rød, lysrød (light chestnut), mørkrød (dark chestnut)
Polish: kasztanowata, jasnokasztanowata (light chestnut), brunatnokasztanowata (dark chestnut, flaxen), ciemnokasztanowata (liver)
Russian: ryzhaya, buraya (liver), igrenevaya (flaxen chestnut)

Spanish: alazán, alazán claro (light chestnut), alazán tostado (dark chestnut), alazán ruano (flaxen chestnut)
Swedish: fux, ljus fux (light chestnut), svettfux (dark chestnut), mörkfux (dark chestnut)

English: bay
Czech: hnědák, světlý hnědák (light bay), tmavý hnědák (dark bay)
Danish: brun, lysebrun (mealy bay), mørkbrun (dark bay)
Dutch: bruin, lichtbruin (light bay), donkerbruin (dark bay)
Finnish: ruunikko, punaruunikko (red bay), vaaleanruunikko (mealy bay), tummanruunikko (dark bay)
French: bai, bai cerise (red bay), bai clair (mealy bay), bai fonce (dark bay)
German: braun, rotbraun (red bay), hellbraun (mealy bay), wildbrauner (wild bay), dunkelbraun (dark bay), kastanienbraun (mahogany)
Hungarian: pej, világos pej (mealy bay), gesztenye pej (wild bay), sötétpej (dark bay)
Icelandic: jarpur, ljósjarpur (light bay), dökkjarpur (dark bay)
Norwegian: brun, lysbrun (light bay), mørkbrun (dark bay)
Polish: gniada, jasnogniada (light bay), złotogniada (golden bay), ciemnogniada (dark bay)
Russian: gnedaya, dikaya gnedaya (wild bay), zolotisto-gnedaya (golden bay), tëmno-gnedaya (dark bay)

Spanish: castaño, zaino, colorado (red bay), doradillo (light bay), castaño oscuro (dark bay)
Swedish: brun, ljusbrun (light bay), viltbrun (wild bay), mörkbrun (dark bay)

English: brown, seal
Czech: černý hnědák
Danish: sortbrun
Dutch: zwartbruin
Finnish: mustanruunikko
French: bai brun, noir pangaré
German: schwartzbraun, rechtbraun
Hungarian: nyarfekete
Icelandic: brúnn
Norwegian: svartbrun
Polish: skarogniada
Russian: karakovaya
Spanish: zaino negro, bocifuego, castaño peceño
Swedish: svartbrun

English: black, sun-faded black
Czech: vraník
Danish: sort
Dutch: zwart
Finnish: musta, sysimusta (jet black), kulomusta (summer black)
French: noir
German: rappe, sommerrappe (summer black)
Hungarian: fekete, nyárifekete (summer black)
Icelandic: svartur, móbrúnn (summer black)
Norwegian: svart
Polish: kara, wroni (summer black)
Russian: voronaya, voronaya v zagare (summer black)

Spanish: negro, morcillo, preta
   (Portuguese)
Swedish: rapp, svart

White Hairs
Modifiers that add white hairs to the
base colors, along with some of their
common variations

English: grey
Czech: bělouš, vbělující bělouš,
   grošák (dappled grey),
   červenavý bělouš (rose grey),
   pstružák (fleabitten)
Danish: skimmel, grå, gråskimmel,
   lysgrå (white grey), blåskimmel
   (dapple grey), mørkgrå (dark
   grey)
Dutch: schimmel, veranderlijk
   schimmel, grijs, appelschimmel
   (dapple grey), vliegenschimmel
   (fleabitten)
Finnish: kimo, kärpäskimo (fleabitten grey), verijälki (blood-
   marked)
French: gris, gris porcelaine (white
   grey), gris pommelé (dappe
   grey), moucheté (fleabitten),
   gris truité (red fleabites), tache
   de sang (blood-marked)
German: schimmel, apfelschimmel
   (dapple grey), fliegenschimmel
   or forellenschimmel (fleabitten), dunkelschimmel (dark
   grey), blutmal (blood-marked)
Hungarian: szürke, ezüstszürke
   (white grey), almásszürke
   (dapple grey), szeplős (fleabitten)
Icelandic: grár, hvítgrár (white
   grey), ljósgrár (light grey), ste-
   ingrár (dapple grey), dökkgrár
   (dark grey)
Norwegian: grå, lysgrå (white grey),
   mørkgrå (dark grey)
Polish: siwa, jabłkowita (dapple
   grey), mlecznosiwa (white
   grey), dropiata (fleabitten)
Russian: seraya, svetlo-seraya (white
   grey), temno-seraya (dark grey),
   seraya v yablokakh (dapple
   grey), krasno-seraya (rose grey),
   forelevaya (fleabitten)

Spanish: tordillo, tordo claro (white
   grey), tordo vinoso (rose
   grey), tordo picazo (fleabitten),
   mosqueado (fleabitten), tordo
   atruchado (heavily fleabitten),
   tordo rodado (dapple grey),
   mancha de sangre (blood-
   marked)
Swedish: skimmel, ljus skimmel
   (white grey)

English: roan, dark-headed roan,
   true roan
Czech: nevybělující, mourek (black
   roan)
Danish: skimmel, morenkop
Dutch: roan, moorkop (usually
   black roan), onveranderlijke
   schimmel
Finnish: päistärikkö
French: rouan, aubère (chestnut)
German: mohrenkopfschimmel,
   dauerschimmel
Hungarian: deres
Icelandic: litföróttur
Polish: dereszowata, pleśniawa,
   kukurydza (corn spots)
Russian: chalaya
Spanish: rosillo, moro (blue roan),
   ruao (Portuguese)
Swedish: konstantskimmel

English: rabicano, white ticking
Czech: prokvetlost srsti
Danish: stikkelhåret
Dutch: stekelharige, als een was-
   beertje (coon tail)
Finnish: päistärkarvainen (roaning)
French: rubican, rouanné
German: stichelhaarig
Polish: dereszowatą na bokach (rabi-
   cano), siwiźnie (white hairs)
Spanish: entrepelado

Dilutions

English: dun dilution, red dun, yellow dun, grulla, mouse
Czech: grůja (grulla)
Danish: gul med ål, brunblakket,
   musegrå (grulla)
Dutch: wildkleur, wildkleur vos or
   leemvos (red dun), wildkleur

bruin (yellow dun), wildkleur
   zwart (grulla)
Finnish: hallakkoväri, punahallakko
   (red dun), ruunihallakko (yellow dun), hiirakko (grulla)
French: isabelle, souris (grulla)
German: falbe mit aalstrich (dun),
   fuchsfalbe (red dun), graufalbe
   or mausfalbe (grulla), kranich-
   falbe (pale grulla)
Hungarian: fakó, vasderes, hatujj,
   egérfakó (grulla)
Icelandic: bleikur, fífilbleikur (red
   dun), mósóttur or móálóttur
   (grulla)
Norwegian: blakk, rødblakk or
   samblakk (red dun), brunblakk
   (yellow dun), grå or musegrå
   (grulla), ulsblakk (dunskin)
Polish: bułana, czerwonobułana
   (red dun), myszata (grulla)
Russian: savrasaya (yellow dun),
   kauri (red dun), myshastaya
   (grulla)
Spanish: gateado, lobero/lobuno
   (grulla), cebruno (brown-toned
   grulla)
Swedish: black, rödblack (red
   dun), brunblack (yellow dun),
   musblack (grulla), vitblack
   (dunskin)

English: cream dilution, palomino,
   buckskin (also called dun in the
   United Kingdom)
Czech: izabela (palomino), žlutá
   (palomino), plavák (buckskin)
Danish: isabella or palomino, jord-
   farvet (buckskin)
Dutch: isabel (palomino), valk
   (buckskin)
Finnish: voikkoväri, voikko (palomino), rurnivoikko (buckskin)
French: palomino, café au lait
   (palomino, self mane and tail),
   isabelle (buckskin), louvet
   (sooty buckskin)
German: isabell, fuchsisabell (palomino), erdfarbener, falbe or
   braunisabell (buckskin)
Hungarian: aranysárga (palomino),
   szarvasbőr (buckskin), fako
   (buckskin)

Icelandic: leirljós (palomino), moldóttur (buckskin)
Norwegian: gul or gulblakk (palomino), borket or ulsblakk (buckskin)
Polish: izabelowata (palomino), jelenia (buckskin)
Russian: solovay (palomino), bulanaya (buckskin), shakałego (sooty buckskin)
Spanish: bayo/baio, bayo amarillo (pale palomino), bayo ruano (palomino), bayo cabos negros (buckskin)
Swedish: isabell or gul (palomino), bork or gulbrun (buckskin)

English: cremello, perlino, blue-eyed cream, smoky cream
Czech: albín, žlutě bílá (cremello), perleťově bílá (perlino)
Danish: albino
Finnish: rautiaspohjainen valkovoikko (cremello), ruunikkopohjainen valkovoikko (perlino), mustapohjainen valkovoikko (smoky cream)
French: crème
German: albino, perlisabell, weißisabell
Hungarian: krémszínű
Icelandic: albínói or hvítingur
Norwegian: dobbeltgule, blåøgd hvit or glassøgd hvit
Polish: kremowa (cremello), perłowa (perlino), przydymiona kremowa (smoky cream)
Russian: isabella, dymchato-kremovaya (smoky cream)
Spanish: bayo blanco (cremello), bayo huevo de pato (perlino)
Swedish: gulvit (cremello), pärlvit (perlino), rökvit (smoky cream)

English: silver dilution, silver dapple, red silver, black silver, brown silver, chocolate, taffy (Australian)
Danish: brungrå (red silver), sølvtonet (black silver)
Dutch: zilverappelbruin (red silver), zilverappelzwart (black silver)
Finnish: kanelinrautias (older term for red silver), hopeaväri, hopeanruunikko (red silver), hopeanmusta (black silver)
French: pommelure d'argent (silver dapple)
German: dunkelkohlfuchs, windfarben, silber, braunsilber (red silver), rappsilber (black silver)
Hungarian: ezüst, pej ezüst (red silver), fekete ezüst (black silver)
Icelandic: vindóttur, jarpvindóttur (red silver), móvindóttur (black silver)
Norwegian: sølvgenet
Polish: srebrna
Russian: serebristo, serebristaya v yablokakh (silver dapple), serebristo-voronaya (black silver), serebristo-gnedaya (red silver)
Swedish: silver, silverbrun (red silver), silversvart (black silver)

English: champagne, gold champagne (chestnut-based), amber champagne (bay-based), classic champagne (black-based)
Finnish: samppanjaväri, rautiaspohjainen samppanjaväri (gold), ruunikkopohjainen samppanjaväri (amber), mustapohjainen samppanjaväri (classic)
German: champagner, fuchschampagner (gold), bruanchampagner (amber), rappchampagner (classic)
Polish: szampańska, złotoszampańska (gold champagne), bursztynowoszampańska (amber champagne), klasyczna szampańska (classic champagne)

English: pearl
Finnish: pearl-väri
French: perle

English: smoky black, light black
Danish: sort med rødlig skaer
Dutch: smoky
Finnish: mustanvoikko
French: noir mal teint, noir qui roussit
German: rappisabell (smoky), erdbraun, hellrappe
Icelandic: glóbrúnn
Polish: przydymiona kara
Russian: vorono-muarovaya
Swedish: sommarblek
Note that while smoky black and light black appear to be genetically distinct colors, the same term is often used. In some languages, there is not a separate term for black horses that have faded in the sun.

Pintos
Many languages have only one word for pinto, regardless of pattern. Most often the pattern being referenced is tobiano, though the terms are used for others as well.

English: pinto, piebald, skewbald, spotted (United States after mid-twentieth century)
Czech: strakáč
Danish: broget
Dutch: bont
Finnish: kirjava
French: pie
German: schecke
Hungarian: tarka
Icelandic: skjóttur
Norwegian: skjevet
Polish: srokata, pstrokatą, łaciatą, krasą
Russian: pegaya
Spanish: pampo, pio
Swedish: skäck

English: tobiano, piebald, skewbald
Czech: strakáč
Danish: broget
Dutch: platenbont, koebont
Finnish: kirjava
French: pie
German: schecke, kuhschece, plattenschecke
Hungarian: tarka
Icelandic: skjóttur
Norwegian: skjevet
Russian: pegaya
Spanish: tobiano, tubíano (Portuguese), pio alto
Swedish: skäck

English: frame overo
German: rahmenschecke

English: Sabino, blagdon (United
  Kingdom)
Dutch: Drentse blauwen (black-
  based sabino roan)
German: sabinoschecke, weißsabino
  (sabino white)
Spanish: overo

English: splashed white, splashed
  overo
Dutch: witkopbont, finsbont
Finnish: läiskynyt valkoinen
French: balzan
German: helmschecke, nordischer
  schecke, klecksschecke,
  weißkopf
Hungarian: fröcskölt fehér
Icelandic: slettuskjóttur
Polish: plamisty biały
Spanish: pampo baixo, pio bajo,
  bajos-blancos
Swedish: bukskäck

English: dominant white, white-
  born, dark-eyed white
Czech: bílá
Danish: hvidfødt
Dutch: wit
Finnish: dominanttivalkoinen
French: blanc
German: weißgeborene
Hungarian: fehér
Icelandic: albínói
Polish: biała
Russian: belaya
Spanish: blanco puro, blanco piel-
  rosa, porcelano (white with
  dark spots on the skin)

Appaloosa

English: appaloosa, spotted (United
  Kingdom), leopard, blanket,
  varnish roan, snowflake,
  marbled
Czech: tygr, skvrnitý bělouš (varnish roan), hermelín
Danish: tigrede, plettet or blommet
  (leopard spots), agattiger (leopard), skaberaktigret (blanket)

Dutch: panterbont, deken (blanket),
  sneeuwvlokken (snowflake)
Finnish: tiikerinkirjava
French: tachetée, léopard, couver-
  ture tachée (spotted blanket)
  marmoré (varnish roan),
  marque en éclair (lightning
  marks), neigé (snowflakes),
  givré (frosted), peu de taches
  (few spot)
German: tigerschecke, volltiger
  (leopard), schabrackentiger
  (blanket), weißgeborene (fewspot)
Hungarian: tarka, párductarka
  (leopard), hópehely (snowflake)
Polish: tarantowata, derka (blanket),
  derka z plamkami (spotted
  blanket), płatki śniegu (snowflakes)
Spanish: tigrado (leopard), nevado
  (frosty)
Swedish: tigre, tigrerad, leop-
  ardtiger (leopard), schabrak-
  tiger (blanket), asnöflingetiger
  (snowflake), melerad tiger
  (varnish roan)

Other color traits

English: mealy, pangaré
Finnish: jauhoturpa
French: pangaré, ventre de biche
  (light belly)
German: mehlmaul (mealy muzzle),
  kupfermaul (copper nose),
  pangaréfärbung (mealy)
Spanish: pangaro, boca de mula
  (mealy muzzle)
Swedish: mjölmule (mealy muzzle)

English: sooty
Finnish: nokikuvio
French: mélanges de poils noirs,
  fumée, charbonné
German: rußfärbung, schmultz
Spanish: tiznado

English: dappling
Czech: grošování
Danish: blommer
Dutch: appeling
Finnish: papurikko

French: pommelé
German: äpfelung
Polish: jabłka
Russian: yablok
Spanish: rodado
Swedish: apelkastning

English: dorsal stripe, eel stripe
Czech: úhoří pruh
Danish: ål ad ryggen
Dutch: aalstreep
Finnish: siima
French: raie de mulet
German: aalstrich
Hungarian: csíkos hátú
Icelandic: með ál
Spanish: raya de mula
Swedish: ål

English: leg barring, zebra stripes
Czech: zebrování
Finnish: seepraraidat
French: zébrures sur les membres
German: zebrastreifen
Hungarian: zebracsíkok
Icelandic: kengálótt
Spanish: cebraduras, pulseras en los
  miembros
Swedish: zebratecken

English: cross, shoulder stripe,
  decussated (archaic term used
  in some naturalist texts)
Finnish: aasinristi
French: bande cruciale, croix de
  Saint André
German: schulterkreuz
Hungarian: váll csíkos
Swedish: grepp

English: flaxen mane and tail, blonde
Czech: světlohřívý
Danish: lys man og hale
Dutch: lichte manen en staart
Finnish: liinakko, hamppuharja
  (gray mane and tail)
French: crins lavés, crins argentés
  (gray mane and tail)
German: hellem behang,
  weißemähnenhaare (white
  mane hairs)
Hungarian: lenszoke soreny es farok
Icelandic: glófextur

Spanish: crin y cola claras
Swedish: flax, ljus man och svans
English: Birdcatcher spots
French: tache de l'oiseleur, neigé
German: sprenkel, schneeflocken

English: Bend Or spots
German: mandlflecken, cornflecken, königsflecken

English: ink spots, cat tracks, paw prints
French: tache d'encre, empreinte
German: tintenspritzer

English: metallic sheen
Czech: kovový odlesk
Finnish: metallinkiiltoinen
French: reflets métalliques, bronzé,
German: glänzendem

Face markings

English: star
Czech: hvězda
Danish: stjerne
Dutch: kol
Finnish: tähti, tähdenaihe (faint)
French: étoile en téte
German: flocke (small), blume, stern, flämmchen
Hungarian: tűzött homlok (white hairs), csillag
Icelandic: stjörnóttur
Polish: kwiatek, gwiazdka (larger)
Spanish: pelos blancos (white hairs), lucero, lucerillo (small), estrella, frontino (large)
Swedish: stjärn, Vita hår i pannan (white hairs), stjärnämne (large)

English: snip
Czech: šňupka, slinka, nosní lysina, bílý nos (white nose)
Danish: snip
Dutch: sneb, milkmuil (white muzzle)
Finnish: pilkku
French: grisonné
German: schnippe, milchmaul (white nose)
Hungarian: piszra, tejfeles száj (lips white), fehér felső ajak (upper

lip), fehér alsó ajak (lower lip), szárcsa (chin)
Icelandic: nösóttur
Polish: chrapka
Spanish: pico blanco, bebe (white upper lip), derrama (white lower lip)
Swedish: snopp, vit överläpp (white upper lip), vit underläpp (white lower lip), vit mule (white muzzle)

English: comet, strip
Czech: nosní pruh (strip)
Dutch: druipkol (comet)
Finnish: pyrstötähti (comet), piirto (strip)
German: keilstern (comet), strich (strip)
Polish: strzałka (strip)
Spanish: cordón (strip)
Swedish: skjuten stjärn (comet)

English: blaze
Czech: lysina
Danish: blis, halvblis (half-blaze)
Dutch: bles, halve bles (half-blaze)
Finnish: läsi
French: liste
German: blesse
Hungarian: hóka, orrcsík (narrow), orrfolt (extends to nose), megtört hóka (broken blaze)
Icelandic: blesóttur, hálfblesu (half-blaze), breiðblesóttur (narrow)
Polish: łysina
Spanish: lista (narrow), malacara (wide)
Swedish: bläs, strimbläs (narrow)

English: bald, bonnet face, apron face
Czech: lucerna
Danish: hjelm
Finnish: valkopää, lyhty (bonnet)
French: belle face
German: laterne
Hungarian: lámpás
Icelandic: glámblesóttur
Polish: latarnia
Spanish: pampa, mascarillo, cara blanca (white head)
Swedish: lykta

English: mottled muzzle, depigmentation
Dutch: krotenmuil
German: krötenmaul, depigmentierung
Hungarian: békaszáj
Polish: żabi pysk, nakrapiana skóra, niepigmentowaną
Swedish: marmorerad hud

Leg markings

English: heel, coronet
Czech: bílá korunka (coronet)
Dutch: witte bal links (heel), kroonrand (coronet)
Finnish: kanta valkea (heel), valkoinen kehä or sepel (coronet)
French: principe de balzane
German: ballen (heel), kronrand (coronet)
Hungarian: pártában kesely
Polish: piętka (heel), koronkę (coronet)
Spanish: coronilla, corona blanca
Swedish: vita ballar (heel), vit kronrand (coronet)

English: ankle, pastern
Czech: spěnka bílá (pastern)
Dutch: sokje
Finnish: vuohissukka
French: petite balzane
German: fessel
Polish: pęcina
Spanish: calceta
Swedish: vit kota

English: sock
Czech: ponožka
Danish: sokker
Dutch: sok
Finnish: puolisukka
French: balzane chaussée
German: stiefel
Hungarian: félszár kesely
Icelandic: sokkóttur
Polish: pół nadpęcia
Spanish: argel, calzado
Swedish: socka, halvstrumpa

English: stocking
Czech: podkolenka

Dutch: witbeen, witbeen voor sterk oplopend (stocking that travels up the stifle)
Finnish: korkea sukka, valkojalka (high stocking)
French: balzane haut chaussée, balzane jarret (hind), balzane genou (front), balzane très haut chaussée (high stocking)
German: hochweißer fuß
Hungarian: harisnyás, szárkesely (entire leg white)
Polish: nadpęcia, nadpęcie nad stawem skokowym (high stocking)
Spanish: calzado alta, botas con del-
antal (peaked hind stockings)
Swedish: strumpa

English: ermine spots
Dutch: zwart vlekken kroonrand
French: herminé
Hungarian: hermelinkesely
Spanish: calzado mosqueado

Eye Color

English: blue, wall or watch eyes, white eyes (archaic)
Dutch: blauw oog, glasoog
Finnish: herasilmä
French: yeux bleus (both blue), oeil
bleu (one blue)
German: glasaugen, fischaugen, blaue augen
Icelandic: hringeygur, glaseygur
Norwegian: blåøgd
Polish: niebieskie oczy
Spanish: ojo azule, zarco

English: amber eyes, tiger eyes, hazel eyes
Dutch: schaapsoog, geiteoog
Finnish: pilkku
French: yeux jaunes dorés
German: gelbe augen, hellbraune augen
Polish: orzechowe oczy

Formally Identified Colors

Although the science is progressing at a rapid pace, only a portion of the colors and patterns found in horses have been formally identified by scientists. Those colors and patterns that have been identified at the molecular level are listed along with their markers and allele symbols. When a commercial test is available, that is noted.

Category	Location	Symbol	Result
Agouti	Agouti-signaling-protein (ASIP)	A A^t a	Bay (test) Brown (test) Black (test)
Extension	Melanocortin-1-receptor (MC1R)	E e e^a	Allows Agouti colors (test) Chestnut (test) Chestnut
Cream	Membrane associated transport protein (MATP)	C^{Cr} C^{Prl}	Cream (test) Pearl (test)
Dun	Not known	D	Dun (zygosity test)
Silver	Melanocyte protein (PMEL17) (sometimes called SILV)	Z	Silver (test)
Champagne	Solute Carrier 36 family A1 (SLC36A1)	CH	Champagne (test)
Grey	Syntaxin 17 (STYX17)	G	Grey (test)
Roan	thought to involve KIT	Rn	Roan (zygosity test)
Tobiano	located close to KIT	To	Tobiano (test)
Lethal White	Endothelin receptor B (EDNRB)	O	Frame overo (test)
Sabino	Mast cell growth factor receptor (KIT)	Sb1	A form of sabino (test)

Category	Location	Symbol	Result
Splashed White	Microphthalmia-associated transcription factor (MITF)	SW1	Classic splashed white (test)
		SW3	Splashed white (test)
		–	Macchiato
	paired box 3 (PAX3)	SW2	Splashed white (test)
Leopard Complex	Transient receptor potential cation channel M1 (TRPM1)	Lp	Varnish roan
Dominant White	Mast cell growth factor receptor (KIT)	W1	White (Freiberger)
		W2	White (Thoroughbred)
		W3	White (Arabian)
		W4	White (Camarillo White)
		W5	typically Sabino-like (Thoroughbred)
		W6	White (Thoroughbred)
		W7	White (Thoroughbred)
		W8	Sabino-like (Icelandic)
		W9	White (Holsteiner)
		W10	Nearly white or Sabino-like (Quarter Horse) (test)
		W11	White (South German Draft)

Colors in Draft and Coaching Breeds

The following charts summarize the colors and patterns currently known or believed to exist in the different draft and coaching breeds, as well as those suspected to have been present in the past. While every effort has been made to make these charts as comprehensive and accurate as possible, omissions are always possible. Colors can appear unexpectedly, either because they were extremely rare, or because they were previously masked by other colors, or were the result of a recent mutation. Upgrading or outcrossing schemes also bring in new possibilities—some intentional and some not. For that reason, this information should always be considered provisional, especially in breeds with open stud books or extremely large populations.

Guide to Chart Notations

Definitive: All registered horses are this color and it is considered a defining point of the breed. This does not necessarily mean that other colors do not occur or that they are not recorded, because some registries do accept off-colors in appendix or grading registers, but usually only the definitive color is granted full registration status.

Uniform: The color is uniformly present in the population, though it is not necessarily considered a defining characteristic of the breed.

Common: These are the colors most closely associated with the breed, and could be considered most typical.

Present: These are colors that are found within the breed, but may not be as frequently seen, or may only be found in specific breeding groups.

Rare: Rare colors are those considered unusual for the breed, but that have been confirmed as present.

One horse: One modern instance of the color has been documented.

One family: The color exists in the breed, but only within a small group of related individuals. Usually this is an indication that the color is relatively rare.

Suspected: When evidence suggests that the color may be found within the breed, but questions remain and no solid proof has been found, it is noted as suspected.

Not determined: When information is not available to prove or disprove the existence of a color in the current population, it is listed as not determined. This notation does not mean the color is not present, only that the author does not have enough information to make the determination. This designation often appears on the charts when colors or patterns that mask the presence of other colors are common. Grey, for instance, can make it difficult to determine whether or not other factors that add white hairs are present. Likewise, colors that are identified by point color can be hard to see when there are patterns of white that cover the legs.

Not present: Colors not thought to exist in the breeding population are listed as not present. This is used when there is more concrete information to suggest that the color is not found in the breed.

Prohibited: This indicates that the color is specifically barred from either registration or consideration in the show ring. Unless noted, this refers to the breed as it exists in its country of origin.

Restricted: These colors are subject to official limitations by the registry. In some cases, this might mean that only minimally marked individuals can be registered while more obviously patterned horses are denied papers. In others, the color may not be permitted in stallions.

Historical: Historical colors are those known to have once occurred in the breeding population, but are believed to have been lost over time.

Historical (S): Historical colors that are suspected but not confirmed. When several similar colors are possible, but the exact color is not known, each possibility is marked this way. Dilutions and pinto patterns are the most common areas for this kind of ambiguity.

(E): This indicates the breed is considered extinct. Entries for these breeds reflect the way the breed was when it was still viable.

Tested: When test results have been made public to confirm the presence of a color, this is noted. The absence of the notation is not meant to imply that no horse has tested positive, since results are not always publicized. Obvious colors like tobiano and grey are rarely tested, and many colors and patterns cannot yet be tested.

Country notations: When a rare color is found only in one country, or is only restricted in one country, it is noted in parenthesis.

Gender notations: When colors are restricted to a specific gender, it is noted in parenthesis.

Base Colors and Factors that Modify Shade

Whatever other modifiers and patterns are present, horses are also one of the four basic colors: chestnut, black, bay or brown. In some breeds, the base colors are usually or even always modified, so the columns on this chart may not represent final colors found in those breeds. For example, American Creams are uniformly chestnut, but those in the regular registry are also uniformly champagne, so their entry on this chart only tells part of the story.

Because it is not always possible to differentiate bay and brown without a test, they are grouped together. When both the standard and the wild forms of bay are known to occur in the breed, the letter (w) appears in the Bay/Brown column. Flaxen refers to the point color on chestnuts. When chestnut is rare in a breed, or is rarely seen without modifiers like grey, flaxen may be listed as Not determined.

Breed	Chestnut	Black	Bay/Brown	Mealy	Sooty	Flaxen
Alt-Oldenburg	Rare	Common	Common	Not determined	Present	Present
American Cream	Uniform	Not present	Not present	Present	Not determined	Present
Ardennes (Belgian)	Rare	Rare	Common (w)	Common	Present	Common
Ardennes (French)	Rare	Restricted	Common (w)	Common	Present	Common
Ardennes (Swedish)	Present	Rare	Common (w)	Common	Present	Common
Belgian (American)	Common	Rare	Rare (w)	Common	Rare	Common
Belgian (Brabant)	Present	Present	Common (w)	Common	Present	Common
Black Forest Horse	Common	Rare	Rare	Not determined	Common	Common
Boulonnais	Common	Rare	Historical	Not determined	Rare	Common
Breton	Common	Rare	Rare	Not determined	Common	Common
Cleveland Bay	Rare	Not Present	Definitive	Not present	Present	Not determined
Clydesdale	Rare	Common	Common	Not determined	Common	Common
Comtois	Rare	Rare	Common	Rare (faulted)	Rare[2]	Common[3]
Dutch Harness Horse	Common	Present	Present	Not present	Present	Present
East Friesian	Rare	Common	Common	Not determined	Present	Not determined
Frederiksborg White (E)	Not determined	Not determined	Not determined	Not determined	Not determined	Not determined
Friesian	Prohibited	Definitive	Historical	Not present	Not determined	Rare
Gelderlander	Common	Present	Present	Not present	Present	Present
Groninger	Rare	Common	Common	Not present	Present	Rare
Gypsy Horse	Present	Common	Present	Not determined	Present	Present
Hackney Horse / Pony	Common	Common	Common	Not present	Present	Rare
Hanoverian Cream (E)	Not determined	Not determined	Not determined	Not determined	Not determined	Not determined
Jutland	Common	Rare	Rare	Present	Rare	Common
Kladruber	Rare	Common	Rare	Not present	Not determined	Rare
Nivernais (E)	Not present	Common[1]	Rare	Not determined	Not determined	Not determined
Noriker	Common	Common	Common	Not determined	Present	Common
N. A. Spotted Draft	Present	Common	Present	Present	Present	Present
Percheron	Rare	Common	Rare	Not present	Not determined	Present
Poitevin Mulassier	Rare	Common	Present	Rare	Present	Common
Polish Coldblood	Common	Present	Common (w)	Present	Present	Common
Shire	Restricted	Common	Present	Not determined	Present	Present
Suffolk	Definitive	Not Present	Not Present	Rare	Rare	Present

[1] *Black became definitive for the breed after 1930.*
[2] *Dapples are considered a fault.*
[3] *Self-colored manes on chestnuts are considered a fault.*

Modifiers that Dilute the Base Color

There are five formally identified dilution genes found in horses: cream, dun, silver, champagne and pearl. Cremellos, perlinos and smoky creams, also known as double-dilutes, are the result of two cream genes and are therefore possible whenever a breed has the cream gene. When double-dilutes are restricted, this is noted with an (R).

There are dilutions that have not been formally identified. Light black is less understood, and may not have the same genetic cause in each breed where it appears. Mushroom, which is currently only known to occur in British Shetlands, and the unknown dilution found in Ropers Nova are not included in this chart.

Breed	Dun	Cream	Silver	Champagne	Pearl	Light Black
Alt-Oldenburg	Historical (S)	Historical	Not present	Not present	Not present	One horse
American Cream	Not present	Restricted	Not present	Definitive	Not present	Not present
Ardennes (Belgian)	Not present	Not present	Not present	Not present	Not present	Not present
Ardennes (French)	Not present	Not present	Not present	Not present	Not present	Not present
Ardennes (Swedish)	Not present	Not present	Rare	Not present	Not present	Not present
Belgian (American)	Not present	Not present	Suspected	Not present	Not present	Not present
Belgian (Brabant)	Historical (S)	Historical (S)	Suspected	Not present	Not present	One horse
Black Forest Horse	Historical (S)	Historical (S)	Not determined	Not present	Not present	Not present
Boulonnais	Not present	Not present	Not present	Not present	Not present	Not present
Breton	Not present	Not present	Rare	Not present	Not present	Not present
Cleveland Bay	Historical (S)	Not present	Not present	Not present	Not present	Not present
Clydesdale	Historical (S)	Historical (S)	Not present	Not present	Not present	Not present
Comtois	Not present	Not present	Common	Not present	Not present	Not present
Dutch Harness Horse	Not present	Rare	Rare	Not present	Not present	Not present
East Friesian	Historical (S)	Historical (S)	Not present	Not present	Not present	Not present
Frederiksborg White (E)	Not determined	Suspected	Not determined	Not present	Not determined	Not determined
Friesian	Not present	Historical (S)	Historical (S)	Not present	Not present	Rare[1]
Gelderlander	Not present	Rare	Rare	Not present	Not present	Not present
Groninger	Not present	Historical	Historical	Not present	Not present	Not present
Gypsy Horse	Rare	Present	Present	Not present	Rare	Not present
Hackney Horse / Pony	Historical	Historical	Historical (S)	Not present	Not present	Not present
Hanoverian Cream (E)	Not present	Historical (S)	Not present	Not present	Historical (S)	Not present
Jutland	Historical (S)	Historical (S)	Not present	Not present	Not present	Not present
Kladruber	Historical (S)	Historical (S)	Not present	Not present	Not present	Not present
Nivernais (E)	Not present	Not present	Not present	Not present	Not present	Not present
Noriker	Not present	Historical	Suspected	Not present	Not present	Not present
N. A. Spotted Draft	Not determined	Present	Present	Rare	Not determined	Not present
Percheron	Historical (S)	Historical (S)	Not present	Not present	Not present	Not present
Poitevin Mulassier	Common	Not present	Suspected	Not present	Not present	Not present
Polish Coldblood	Rare	Not present	Rare	Not present	Not present	Not present
Shire	Historical	Rare	Not present	Not present	Not present	Not present
Suffolk	Not present	Not present	Not present	Not present	Not present	Not present

[1] *This type of light black appears to be different from that seen in other breeds.*

Modifiers that Add White Hairs

This group of modifiers distributes white hairs through the coat. Frosty roan is similar to dark-headed roan, but the white hairs are found in the mane and tail as well as on the body. White ticking includes any sprinkling of white hairs in the coat not related to grey or roan. Because ticking is often quite subtle and can be hard to see in photographs, this can be hard to determine for many breeds. When ticking is typically seen in conjunction with sabino markings, that is noted in parenthesis.

Pinky Syndrome is the gradual loss of skin pigment. It is included on this chart because of its close association with greying. Pigment loss unrelated to greying is noted as not grey (NG).

Breed	Grey	True Roan	Frosty Roan	Ticking	Pinky Syndrome
Alt-Oldenburg	Rare	Historical	Not determined	Not determined	Not present
American Cream	Not present	Not present	Not present	Not determined	Not present
Ardennes (Belgian)	Historical	Common	Present	Rare	Not present
Ardennes (French)	Historical	Common	Present	Rare	Not present
Ardennes (Swedish)	Rare	Rare	Rare	Rare	Not present
Belgian (American)	Historical	Present	Present	Present (sabino)	Not present
Belgian (Brabant)	Rare	Common	Common	Not determined	Not present
Black Forest Horse	Rare	Historical	Historical	Present (sabino)	Not present
Boulonnais	Common	Historical	Not determined	Present (sabino)	Common
Breton	Historical	Common	Not determined	Present	Not present
Cleveland Bay	Not present	Not present	Not present	Not present	Not present
Clydesdale	Historical	Historical (S)	Not determined	Common (sabino)	Not present
Comtois	Not present	Not present	Not present	Not determined	Rare (NG)[1]
Dutch Harness Horse	Rare	Rare	Not present	Present	Not present
East Friesian	Rare	Historical	Not present	Historical	Not present
Frederiksborg White (E)	Present	Not determined	Not determined	Not determined	Not determined
Friesian	Historical (mares)	Not present	Not present	Historical	Not present
Gelderlander	Present	Historical	Not present	Not determined	Not present
Groninger	Rare	Historical	Not present	Not determined	Not present
Gypsy Horse	Rare	Rare	Not present	Not determined	Not present
Hackney Horse / Pony	Historical	Rare	Not present	Present	Rare (NG)
Hanoverian Cream (E)	Not present	Not present	Not present	Not present	Not present
Jutland	Historical	Historical	Not determined	Not determined	Not present
Kladruber	Common	Not present	Not present	Not present	Common
Nivernais (E)	Rare	Rare	Not determined	Not present	Not present
Noriker	Not present	Present	Not present	Rare (sabino)	Not present
N. A. Spotted Draft	Rare	Rare	Not determined	Not determined	Not present
Percheron	Common	Rare	Not present	Rare (sabino)	Rare
Poitevin Mulassier	Present	Present	Rare	Not present	Not present
Polish Coldblood	Rare	Rare	Rare	Rare	Not present
Shire	Common	Historical	Not determined	Not determined	Not present
Suffolk	Not present	Not present	Not present	Rare	Not present

[1] *Pigment loss is considered a fault.*

Modifiers that Add Patterns of White - Formally Identified Pintos

Formal research into pinto patterns is still in the very early stages, so many pintos do not actually have a testable pattern. There are six categories of testable pinto patterns: tobiano, frame, splashed white, sabino and dominant white. As of this writing, there are three known forms of splash, one known form of sabino and eleven forms of dominant white. More are expected. In fact, most horses thought of as being sabino do not have the one identified form of the pattern. For a more complete picture of white patterning in a given breed, this chart should be used in conjunction with the chart for undefined patterns of white.

Because splashed white-1 (*SW1*) has a fairly broad distribution, while the other two splash mutations are believed to be more limited, it is given a separate column. Since all dominant white mutations have proven to be separate from one another, they appear under the same heading. When the circumstances fit the pattern for dominant white, but the horses have not been part of the formally identified white families, they entry is marked as suspected (S).

Breed	Tobiano	Frame	Splash1	Other Splash	Sabino-1	Dom. White
Alt-Oldenburg	Not present	Not present	Not present	Not present	Not present	Historical (S)
American Cream	Not present	Not present	Not present	Not present	Not present	Not present
Ardennes (Belgian)	Not present	Not present	Not present	Not present	Not present	Not present
Ardennes (French)	Not present	Not present	Not present	Not present	Not present	One horse (S)
Ardennes (Swedish)	Not present	Not present	Not present	Not present	Not present	Not present
Belgian (American)	Not present	Not present	Not determined	Not present	Not present	Not present
Belgian (Brabant)	Not present	Not present	Not present	Not present	Not present	Historical (S)
Black Forest Horse	Not present	Not present	Not present	Not present	Not present	Not present
Boulonnais	Not present	Not present	Not present	Not present	Not present	Not present
Breton	Not present	Not present	Not present	Not present	Not present	Not present
Cleveland Bay	Not present	Not present	Not present	Not present	Not present	Not present
Clydesdale	Not present	Not present	Not determined	Not present	Not present	Historical (S)
Comtois	Not present	Not present	Not present	Not present	Not present	Not present
Dutch Harness Horse	Not present	Not present	Not present	Not present	Not present	Not present
East Friesian	Not present	Not present	Not present	Not present	Not present	Not present
Frederiksborg White (E)	Not present	Not present	Not present	Not present	Not present	Suspected
Friesian	Not present	Not present	Not present	Not present	Not present	Not present
Gelderlander	Rare	Not present	Not determined	Not present	Historical	Not present
Groninger	Rare	Not present	Not present	Not present	Rare	Historical (S)
Gypsy Horse	Common	Not present	Not determined	Not present	Tested	Not determined
Hackney Horse / Pony	Historical	Not present	Historical (S)	Not present	Not present	Not present
Hanoverian Cream (E)	Not present	Not present	Not present	Not present	Not present	Historical (S)
Jutland	Historical	Not present	Not present	Not present	Not present	Not present
Kladruber	Historical (S)	Not present	Not present	Not present	Not present	Not determined
Nivernais (E)	Not present	Not present	Not present	Not present	Not present	Not present
Noriker	Rare	Not present	Not present	Not present	Not present	Not present
N. A. Spotted Draft	Common	Rare	Not determined	Not present	Not present	Not present
Percheron	Not present	Not present	Not present	Not present	Not present	Not present
Poitevin Mulassier	Not present	Not present	Not present	Not present	Not present	Not present
Polish Coldblood	Not present	Not present	Not present	Not present	Not present	Not present
Shire	Historical	Not present	Not determined	Not present	Not present	Not present
Suffolk	Not present	Not present	Not present	Not present	Not present	Not present

Undefined Patterns of White

The group of pinto patterns on this chart do not represent formally identified mutations, but rather groupings based on visual similarities. Horses with these types of patterns are often called sabino, though it is not known if they are caused by the same type of mutation as the one known form of sabino (sabino-1) or something completely different. For more information on this group, and the differences between the six pattern types, please refer to the chapter on other white patterns. It should also be noted that there is a certain amount of overlap between the different groups, so the determinations used to compile this chart are a lot more subjective than those in the other charts.

Breed	Flashy White	Ragged	Patchy	Splash-like[1]	Stippled	Sabino Roan[2]
Alt-Oldenburg	Present	Not present	Not present	Not present	Not present	Not present
American Cream	Present	Not present	Not present	Not present	Not present	Not present
Ardennes (Belgian)	Rare	Not present	Not present	Not present	Not present	Not present
Ardennes (French)	Rare	Not present	Not present	Not present	Not present	Not present
Ardennes (Swedish)	Rare	Not present	Not present	Not present	Not present	Not present
Belgian (American)	Present	Rare	Rare	Not present	Not present	Present
Belgian (Brabant)	Historical	Not present	Not present	Not present	Not present	Not present
Black Forest Horse	Present	Rare	Not present	Not present	Rare	Rare
Boulonnais	Present	Not present	Not present	Not present	One horse	Not present
Breton	Common	Not present	Not present	Not present	Not present	Not present
Cleveland Bay	Not present	Not present	Not present	Not present	Not present	Not present
Clydesdale	Common	Common	Present	Common (D,F)	Rare	Present
Comtois	Not present	Not present	Not present	Not present	Not present	Not present
Dutch Harness Horse	Common	Rare	Rare	Not present	Rare	Rare
East Friesian	Present	Not present	Not present	Not present	Not present	Not present
Frederiksborg White (E)	Not determined	Not determined	Not determined	Not determined	Not determined	Not determined
Friesian	Not present	Not present	Not present	Not present	Not present	Not present
Gelderlander	Common	Historical	Historical	Rare (F)	Not present	Not present
Groninger	Rare	Rare	Not present	Not present	Not present	Not present
Gypsy Horse	Present	Present	Present	Present (D)	Not determined	Present
Hackney Horse / Pony	Common	Not present	Rare	Historical (F)	Rare	Not determined
Hanoverian Cream (E)	Not present	Not present	Not present	Not present	Not present	Not present
Jutland	Rare	Not present	Not present	Not present	Not present	Not present
Kladruber	Present	Not present	Not present	Not present	Not present	Not present
Nivernais (E)	Not present	Not present	Not present	Not present	Not present	Not present
Noriker	Rare	Not present	Not present	Not present	Not present	Not present
N. A. Spotted Draft	Present	Not determined	Rare	Rare (D)	Not determined	Rare
Percheron	Rare	Not present	Not present	Not present	Not present	Not present
Poitevin Mulassier	Rare	One horse	Not present	Not present	Not present	Not present
Polish Coldblood	Rare	Not present	Not present	Not present	Not present	Not present
Shire	Common	Rare	Rare	Rare (D, F)	Not present	Rare
Suffolk	Historical (rare)	Not present	Not present	Not present	Not present	Not present

[1] The two types of splash-like patterns are white-dipped (D) and white-faced (F). Time will tell if either type proves to be a form of splash.

[2] Although heterozygous sabino-1 horses are sabino roan in appearance, the presence of that gene in a breed is not counted for the purposes of this chart. This column is for horses that are some type of sabino roan but that do not test positive for sabino-1, or that do not fit the pattern of inheritance for sabino-1.

Modifiers that Add Patterns of White - Appaloosas

The mutation in the first column, leopard complex, makes the rest of the appaloosa patterns possible. Alone, it produces varnish roan. When pattern-1 is present, it produces leopards and near-leopards. Other pattern genes are thought to work with leopard complex to produce the range of smaller white patterns like frosty hips and blankets. Because some registries restrict combinations of pinto and appaloosa patterns (pintaloosas), that is given a separate column. Base color shift refers to the dilution of black pigment seen in some appaloosas.

Breed	Leopard Complex	Pattern-1	Other Patterns	Pintaloosa	Base color shift
Alt-Oldenburg	Historical	Not determined[1]	Not determined[1]	Not present	Not determined[1]
American Cream	Not present	Not present	Not present	Not present	Not present
Ardennes (Belgian)	Not present	Not present	Not present	Not present	Not present
Ardennes (French)	Not present	Not present	Not present	Not present	Not present
Ardennes (Swedish)	Not present	Not present	Not present	Not present	Not present
Belgian (American)	Not present	Not present	Not present	Not present	Not present
Belgian (Brabant)	Not present	Not present	Not present	Not present	Not present
Black Forest Horse	Not present	Not present	Not present	Not present	Not present
Boulonnais	Not present	Not present	Not present	Not present	Not present
Breton	Not present	Not present	Not present	Not present	Not present
Cleveland Bay	Not present	Not present	Not present	Not present	Not present
Clydesdale	Not present	Not present	Not present	Not present	Not present
Comtois	Not present	Not present	Not present	Not present	Not present
Dutch Harness Horse	Not present	Not present	Not present	Not present	Not present
East Friesian	Not present	Not present	Not present	Not present	Not present
Frederiksborg White (E)	Suspected	Suspected	Not determined	Suspected	Not determined
Friesian	Not present	Not present	Not present	Not present	Not present
Gelderlander	Not present	Not present	Not present	Not present	Not present
Groninger	Not present	Not present	Not present	Not present	Not present
Gypsy Horse	Present	Present	Present	Rare	Present
Hackney Horse / Pony	Historical	Not determined[1]	Not determined[1]	Not present	Not determined
Hanoverian Cream (E)	Not present	Not present	Not present	Not present	Not present
Jutland	Not present	Not present	Not present	Not present	Not present
Kladruber	Historical	Not determined[1]	Not determined[1]	Not present	Not determined[1]
Nivernais (E)	Not present	Not present	Not present	Not present	Not present
Noriker	Present	Present	Rare	Rare	Present
N. A. Spotted Draft	Not present	Not present	Not present	Not present	Not present
Percheron	Not present	Not present	Not present	Not present	Not present
Poitevin Mulassier	Not present	Not present	Not present	Not present	Not present
Polish Coldblood	Not present	Not present	Not present	Not present	Not present
Shire	Not present	Not present	Not present	Not present	Not present
Suffolk	Not present	Not present	Not present	Not present	Not present

[1] With historical accounts, it is possible to know that appaloosa patterning was present, but not have enough details to determine which specific patterns were present. Because leopard is the the most widespread of the appaloosa patterns, and because it was particularly popular in the Baroque period, it was the most likely pattern involved.

Range of Markings and Eye Color

The entries on this chart are intended to give an idea of the range of face and leg markings for each breed. These may not indicate absolute limits on either the minimal or the maximum range, but rather what is typical for the breed. Where the range is limited by registry restrictions, the entry is noted with (R) for Restricted.

For simplicity's sake, all pale eyes that are not blue in tone are included under the heading of Hazel Eyes. Entries for blue eyes do not include those associated with the cream dilution. When these entries involve horses with no modern descendants, they are noted with (H) for Historical.

Breed	Face Marking Range	Leg Marking Range	Hazel Eyes	Blue Eyes
Alt-Oldenburg	Solid faces to blazes	Solid legs to stockings	One family (H)	Not present
American Cream	Solid faces to blazes	Solid legs to stockings	Definitive	Not present
Ardennes (Belgian)	Solid faces to rare blazes	Solid legs to rare hind socks	Not present	Not present
Ardennes (French)	Solid faces to rare blazes	Solid legs to rare hind socks	Not present	Two horses
Ardennes (Swedish)	Solid faces to blazes	Solid legs to stockings	Not present	Not present
Belgian (American)	Rare solid faces to bald faces	Solid legs to stockings	Not present	Rare
Belgian (Brabant)	Solid faces to rare blazes	Solid legs to rare socks	One horse[2]	Historical (rare)
Black Forest Horse	Rare solid faces to blazes	Solid legs to rare stockings	Not present	Restricted (stallions)
Boulonnais	Solid faces to blazes	Solid legs to stockings	Not present	Not present
Breton	Rare solid faces to blazes (R)	Solid legs to stockings (R)	Not present	Rare
Cleveland Bay	Solid faces to small stars[1] (R)	Solid legs (R)	Not present	Not present
Clydesdale	Typically blazes to bald faces	Typically socks to stockings	Not present	Present
Comtois	Small star or less preferred	Leg white considered a fault	Not present	Not present
Dutch Harness Horse	Rare solid faces to bald faces	Solid legs to stockings	Not present	Not present
East Friesian	Solid faces to blazes	Solid legs to stockings	Not present	Not present
Frederiksborg White (E)	Not applicable	Not applicable	Not determined	Present
Friesian	Solid faces to small star[3] (R)	Solid legs[3] (R)	Not present	Not present
Gelderlander	Rare solids to bald faces	Rare solid legs to stockings	Not present	One family
Groninger	Solid faces to bald faces	Solid legs to stockings	One family (H)	Rare
Gypsy Horse	Rare solids to bald faces	Rare solid legs to white legs	Rare	Present
Hackney Horse / Pony	Solid faces to blazes	Solid legs to stockings	Not present	Historical (rare)
Hanoverian Cream (E)	Thought to be solid	Thought to be solid	Suspected	Suspected
Jutland	Solid faces to blazes	Solid legs to rare stockings	Not present	Not present
Kladruber (greys)	Solid faces to blazes	Solid legs to stockings	Not present	Rare
Kladruber (blacks)	Typically solid faces	Typically solid legs	Not present	Not present
Nivernais (E)	Typically solid faces	Typically solid legs	Not present	Not present
Noriker	Solid faces to blazes	Solid legs to stockings	Not present	Not present
N. A. Spotted Draft	Solid faces to bald faces	Typically legs are white	Rare	Present
Percheron	Solid faces to rare blazes	Solid legs to rare socks	Not present	Not present
Poitevin Mulassier	Solid faces to rare blazes	Typically solid legs	Not present	Not present
Polish Coldblood	Solid faces to blazes	Solid legs to stockings	Not present	Not present
Shire	Typically blazes to bald faces	Typically socks to stockings	Not present	Rare
Suffolk	Typically solid or minimal	Leg white extremely rare	Not present	Not present

[1] More white does occur on rare occasions. Mares with more white on the face are included in the Grading Register.
[2] A single foal was born with blue eyes that began to darken. She died young, but it is believed that her eyes would have been amber had she lived to adulthood.
[3] There were mares with more extensive white in the early history of the breed.

Glossary of Terms

Agouti: gene that determines where black pigment goes, when black is present

Allele: different versions of the same gene; for example, bay and black are alleles of Agouti

Appendix: *see* Grading register

Areas of exclusion: in patterns, the areas that tend to retain color even in the most extensively marked horses

Badger face: having a large occluding spot that covers the front of the face

Base colors: chestnut, black, bay and brown

Bay silver: *see* Red silver

Bend Or spots: darker spots on a red or palomino background

Birdcatcher spots: small white spots on a dark background

Black-based colors: colors that depend on the horse having the dominant form of Extension (*E*); bay, brown and black

Black gene: dominant form of Extension (*E*), makes bay, brown and black possible

Black silver: black horse with the silver dilution

Blonde: Light flaxen chestnut with the mealy pattern

Blood-marked: irregular patches of dark hair on a grey horse

Bottleneck: dramatic drop in population that narrows the gene pool

Buckskin Pearl: bay horse with one cream and one pearl gene, visually very similar to a perlino

Cat tracks: small dark spots in the white areas of a tobiano, usually a sign of homozygosity

Champagne: dilutes the skin, hair and eyes; skin is pinkish with freckles, red hair is gold, black hair is chocolate, and the eyes are amber

Chocolate: *see* Silver

Classic splash: the distinctive pattern seen in horses that are homozygous for splashed white-1 (*SW1*)

Closed stud book: registry that is no longer open to outside blood

Coon tail: white hairs at the tailhead, also called a skunk tail

Cream: dilutes red pigment to yellow, but leaves black pigment unchanged; homozygous creams have near-white hair, pink skin and blue eyes

Cream Pearl: horse with one cream and one pearl gene, visually similar to double-dilute creams

Crop-out: horse of an unexpected color or pattern

Cryptic: color or pattern that is difficult to identify as what it is

Dapples: pattern of round spots somewhat lighter than the rest of the coat

Dark-headed roan: has a mixture of white and dark hairs on the body, but not head, legs, mane or tail; does not lighten with age

Depigmentation: gradual loss of pigment in the skin, most often, but not exclusively, seen in greys

Dilution: a type of gene that lightens the coat, skin or eye color

Dominant: the version of the gene that is visible whether the horse is heterozygous or homozygous

Dominant white: type of mutation that produces white-born or sabino patterns, believed to be lethal when homozygous

Double dilute: most often used to mean a horse with two cream genes, but can mean any horse with two dilutions of any kind

Dun: dilutes the body color but leaves the points unchanged, also produces dun factors

Dun factors: dorsal stripe, zebra stripes, cobwebbing, and other traits associated with the dun coloring

Epistatic: the action of a gene masks the expression of an unrelated gene

Ermine spots: dark spots inside a white leg marking, usually near the hoof

Eumelanin: black pigment

Extension: Gene that determines if the horse can produce black pigment

False-roan sabino: white pattern featuring a white blaze and white hairs spread throughout the coat, but little or no leg white

Few-spot: horse that has both the leopard pattern and two copies of the leopard complex gene; a nearly white, unspotted appaloosa

Flashy white sabino: the most familiar form of sabino markings; blaze, white chin, socks or stockings, and small amounts of white on the belly or girth area

Flaxen: blonde hair, usually refers to the mane, tail and lower legs

Fleabitten: small dark flecks of color, usually red, that appear on older greys

Frame overo: white patterning that concentrates on the sides of the horse, leaving a dark frame around the outside of the horse, lethal when homozygous

Frosty roan: closely resembles darkheaded roan, but the mane and tail have white hairs

Grading register: process where unregistered mares can be bred to registered stallions, and over a set number of generations their offspring are accepted as purebred; variation on the older top-cross breeding system

Helpbook: *see* Grading register

Heterozygous: two different alleles for a given locus

Homozygous: two identical alleles for a given locus

Incomplete dominant: genes that give one color or pattern when heterozygous, and another when homozygous. Example: one cream on chestnut is palomino, two on chestnut is cremello

Isabella: term for pale cream or golden horses, exact definition varies in different communities

Landrace: local animal bred for a specific purpose but without a standard or stud book

Large effect: in a polygenic group, the genes that have a major effect on the final color or pattern

Leopard: pattern of small, round spots of color on a white background

Leopard complex: gene that produces varnish roan and the appaloosa characteristics; when paired with pattern genes it can produce a range of appaloosa patterns

Lethal white: *see* Frame overo

Light black: black horses that look chocolate or otherwise faded in color, but do not test positive for any known dilution, called *globrunn* in Iceland

Lightning marks: irregular white markings on the legs of appaloosas

Linkage: genes that are located close together, and so are often inherited together

Manchado: rare form of overo patterning found in Argentina

Mealy: pattern of light areas on the muzzle, eyes and undersides of the horse

Mismark: marking that is not thought to be the genetic, can be dark or white

Mushroom: dilution of chestnut that visually resembles black silver

Occluding spot: Dark patch that overlaps a white face marking

Palomino pearl: chestnut horse with one cream and one pearl gene, visually very similar to a cremello

Pattern progression: in patterns, the order in which white appears in horses with progressively more extensive patterns

Pattern-1: gene that, when paired with leopard complex, produces the leopard pattern

Pearl: recessive dilution where the homozygous horses look champagne, and horses with one copy paired with cream look cremellos or perlinos

Phaeomelanin: red pigment

Pinky syndrome: *see* Depigmentation

Points: typically the lower legs, mane and tail

Points of origin: in patterns, the areas where white begins to appear in the most minimally marked horses

Polygenic: a color that involves the interaction of multiple genes

Rabicano: form of white ticking that has flank roaning and a coon tail, but that does not produce white face or leg markings

Red gene: Recessive form of Extension (e), makes chestnut

Red silver: bay horse with the silver dilution

Recessive: genes that are visible in when homozygous, but are hidden when a dominant gene is present

Reverse dapples: a pattern of round spots that are darker than the body color, most often seen in roans and champagnes

Sabino: a group of white patterns closely associated with white on the face and legs, often used as a catchall for pinto patterns not yet formally identified

Sabino-1: incomplete dominant, with one copy producing sabino roan and two copies producing white; currently the only identified form of sabino

Sabino roan: form of sabino that is heavily roaned and ticked, with indistinct white and colored areas

Sclera: outer ring of the eye, usually mentioned when it is white

Self-colored: having the same color on the body and the points

Silver: dilutes black pigment to chocolate or taupe, but leaves red pigment unchanged

Silver carrier: chestnut horse that carries a hidden silver gene

Small-effect: in a polygenic group, the genes that have a smaller effect on the final color or pattern

Smoky Black: black horse with the cream dilution, not always visibly different from regular black, but sometimes faded in color

Smoky black pearl: black horse with one cream and one pearl gene, visually very similar to a perlino

Snowcap: horse with two copies of the leopard complex gene and the blanket pattern, resulting in white blanket without spots

Sooty: black hairs interspersed in the coat, often forming dapples

Sorrel: most often used to mean a light or flaxen chestnut, but exact definition varies in different communities

Somatic mutations: in colors, unusual colors that are not inherited from the parents, nor given to the offspring; one-of-a-kind events

Splashed white: a group of white patterns associated with blue eyes and extensive white on the face

Stippled sabino: Sabino with heavy white ticking on the body as well as white face and leg markings

Stud book: public record of the pedigrees of the members of a breed

Suppressed leopard: Form of the leopard pattern where the white areas have been reduced in size, typically with smaller, more densely spaced spots

Tobiano: white patterning that concentrates on the legs and topline, giving the impression of a white horse with round, dark patches

Top-cross: Breeding system that uses a set number of male crosses to qualify a horse as purebred, often referred to by the number required to achieve purebred status (three-cross, four-cross)

True roan: *see* Dark-headed roan

Unbalanced sabino: white pattern where the legs and possibly the body are white, but the face is minimally marked

White-dipped sabino: white pattern that looks like splashed white, but lacks the extreme white face and blue eyes, suspected to be a form of sabino

White-faced sabino: white pattern that looks like splashed white, but lacks the extensive white on the body typical of classic splash

Whole-colored: a horse that has no white markings of any kind

Wild bay: a form of bay where the legs are not fully black

Zebra stripes: the dark horizontal stripes on the legs of some dun horses

Zygosity: whether a horse has the same alleles for a trait (homozygous) or different alleles (heterozygous)

Breed Registries and Resources

The following list of organizations is included for those wishing to obtain further information about specific breeds. Parent registries are given as well as those found in countries where the breed is popular. Independent organizations, including informative breed websites, are included whenever they offer significant information not found elsewhere. Although many registries have permanent locations, some addresses are tied to the currently serving registrar or secretary, and as such may be subject to change.

Alt-Oldenburg and East Friesian

Zuchtverband für das Ostfriesische und Alt-Oldenburger Pferd e.V.
Dr. Peter Allhoff
Bahnbreede 25
33824 Werther
http://www.ostfriesen-alt-oldenburger.de

American Belgian Draft

Belgian Draft Horse Corporation of America
125 Southwood Drive
Wabash, IN 46992
http://www.belgiancorp.com/

American Cream Draft

American Cream Draft Horse Association
193 Crossover Road
Bennington, VT 05201
http://www.acdha.org/

Ardennes

Stud-Book du Cheval de Trait Ardennais
rue des Aubépines, 50
6800 Libramont
Belgium
http://www.chevaldetraitardennais.be

Union des Eleveurs de Chevaux de la Race Ardennaise
Chambre d'agriculture de la Haute Marne
26, avenue du 109ème Régiment d'Infanterie
52011 Chaumont Cedex
France
http://www.cheval-ardennais.fr/

Avelsföreningen för Svenska Ardennerhästen
Havsjö Fällhemmet
571 66 Bodafors
Sweden
http://www.ardennerforeningen.nu/

Belgian Brabant

Société Royale Le Cheval de Trait Belge
Avenue du Suffrage Universel 49
1030 Bruxelles
Belgium
http://www.chevaldetrait.be

American Brabant Association
2331A Oak Drive
Ijamsville, MD 21754-8641
http://www.theamericanbrabantassociation.com/

Koninklijke Vereniging Het Nederlands Trekpaard
Westeind 5
5245 NL Rosmalen
The Netherlands
http://www.kvth.nl/

Black Forest Horse

Pferdezuchtverband Baden-Württemberg e. V.
Am Dolderbach 11
D-72532 Gomadingen-Marbach
Germany
http://www.pzv-bw.de/de/kaltblut/

The Marbach State Stud
www.gestuet-marbach.de

Boulonnais

Syndicat Hippique Boulonnais
Mairie de Samer -2ème étage
84 Place Foch
62 830 Samer
France
http://www.le-boulonnais.com

Association pour la Promotion du Cheval Boulonnais
53 Rue de Fampoux
62223 Athies
France

Boulonnais (cont.)

Le Boulonnais Blog
http://boulonnais.canalblog.com/

Breton

Syndicat des Éleveurs du Cheval Breton
BP 30407
29404 Landivisiau Cedex
France

Associação Brasileira dos Criadores do Cavalo Bretão
R. Osvaldo Cruz
267 – Centro -13900-010-AMPARO – SP
Brazil
http://www.cavalo-bretao.com.br/

Photos from the Brazilian Breton Nationals, 2010-2012
https://picasaweb.google.com/SusanaCintra

Cleveland Bay

The Cleveland Bay Horse Society
Regional Agricultural Centre
The Great Yorkshire Showground
Harrogate, HG2 8NZ
http://www.clevelandbay.com/

The Cleveland Bay Horse Society of North America
P.O. Box 483
Goshen, NH 03752
http://www.clevelandbay.org/

Clydesdale

Clydesdale Horse Society
Mrs Marguerite Osborne MA LLB
Kinclune, Kingoldrum
Kirriemuir
Angus, DD8 5HX
Scotland, UK
http://www.clydesdalehorsesociety.com

Clydesdale Breeders of the USA
17346 Kelley Rd
Pecatonica, IL 61063
http://clydesusa.com/

Clydesdale Horse Association of Canada
2417 Holly Lane
Ottawa, Ontario
K1V 0M7

Commonwealth Clydesdale Horse Society
Mr. Rod Bowles, Secretary
P O Box 1053
Bendigo 3552
Victoria
Australia
http://www.clydesdalehorse.com.au/

Comtois

Association Nationale du Cheval de Trait Comtois
52, rue de Dole, BP 1919
25 020 BESANCON Cedex
France
http://www.chevalcomtois.com

Dutch Harness Horse

Koninklijk Warmbloed Paardenstamboek Nederland
Postbus 156
3840 AD Harderwijk
The Netherlands
http://www.kwpn.nl/

American Dutch Harness Horse Association
P.O. Box 110
Sullivan, OH 44880
http://www.adhha.com/

Friesian

Koninklijke Vereniging "Het Friesch Paarden-Stamboek"
Oprijlaan 1
9205 BZ Drachten
The Netherlands
http://www.kfps.nl/

Friesian Horse Association of North America
4037 Iron Works Parkway
Suite 160
Lexington, KY 40511-8483
http://www.fhana.com/

Gelderlander

Koninklijk Warmbloed Paardenstamboek Nederland
Postbus 156
3840 AD Harderwijk
The Netherlands
http://www.kwpn.nl/

Gelders Paard International
http://www.gelderlanderhorse.nl/

Groninger

Vereniging Het Groninger Paard
Nieuwstad 89
7201 NM Zutphen
The Netherlands
http://www.zeldzamerassen.nl/

Gypsy Horses

Gypsy Vanner Horse Society
P.O. Box 65
Waynesfield, OH 45896
http://vanners.org/

*Gypsy Cob and Drum Horse
Association*
1812 10th Street
Danville, IN 46122
http://www.gcdha.com

Gypsy Horse Association
P.O. Box 123
Plainfield, VT 05667
http://www.gypsyhorseassociation.org

The Coloured Horse & Pony Society
1 McLaren Cottage
Abertysswg, Rhymney
Tredegar NP22 5BH
United Kingdom
http://www.chapsuk.com/

British Skewbald and Piebald Association
Stanley House
Silt Drove, Tips End
Welney, Wisbech
Cambs PE14 9SL
United Kingdom
http://www.bspaonline.com/

British Spotted Pony Society
Lovaton, Daws House
Launceston
Cornwall PL157JF
United Kingdom
http://www.britishspottedponysociety.co.uk/

Irish Cob Society
Longacre, Cabin Hil
Naul, County Dublin
Ireland
http://www.irishcobsociety.com/

Pictorial database of Gypsy stallions
http://www.vannercentral.com

DNA Database for all Gypsy Horses worldwide
http://www.gypsyhorse-dna.com/

Hackney Horse and Pony

Hackney Horse Society
Mrs D. E. Hicketts, Secretary
Fallowfields, Little London
Heytesbury, Warminster
Wiltshire BA12 0ES
United Kingdom
http://www.hackney-horse.org.uk/

American Hackney Horse Society
059 Iron Works Parkway A-3
Lexington, KY 40511-8462
http://hackneysociety.com/

Het Nederlandsch Hackney Stamboek
Dhr. H. (Henk) Harmers
Roer 34
7891 MN Klazienaveen
http://www.hackneystamboek.nl/

Heavy Warmbloods

*International Heavy Warmblood Horse
Breeders Association*
Stamboekbureau
Hanestreek 6
8435 VW Donkerbroek
Nederland
http://www.ihwstudbook.com/

Jutland Horse

Avlsforeningen Den Jydske Hest
Bernth Jesper Sorensen, Secretary
Skovkrogen 3
5683 Haarby
Denmark

Kladruber

National Stud Kladruby nad Labem
NH Kladruby nad Labem, s.p.o.
533 14 Kladruby nad Labem
Czech Republic
http://www.nhkladruby.cz/

Noriker

Arbeitsgemeinschaft der Norikerpferdezüchter in Österreich
Landespferdezuchtverband Salzburg
Mayerhoferstraße 12
A-5751 Maishofen
ZVR 074589616
Austria
http://www.pferdezucht-austria.at/

Asociace Svazů Chovatelů Koní
(Horse Breeders Association of the Czech Republic)
Budejovicka 479
Pisek
397 01
Czech Republic
http://www.aschk.cz

North American Spotted Draft

North American Spotted Draft Horse Association
17594 US Hwy 20
Goshen, IN 46528
http://www.nasdha.net/

Pinto Draft Registry
P.O. Box 738
Estancia, NM 87016
http://www.pinto-draft-registry.com

Percheron

Société Hippique Percheronne de France
4, Rue Rémy Belleau
28400 Nogent le Rotrou
France
http://www.percheron-france.org/

Percheron Horse Association of America
P.O. Box 141
Fredericktown, Ohio 43019
http://www.percheronhorse.org

British Percheron Horse Society
Crockford House
New Street, Fressingfield
Eye IP21 5PG
United Kingdom
http://www.percheron.org.uk/

Poitevin Mulassier

Association Nationale des Races Mulassières du Poitou
2 rue du Port Brouillac
79510 Coulon
France
http://www.racesmulassieresdupoitou.com

Polish Coldblood

Polski Związek Hodowców Koni
(Polish Horse Breeders Association)
Koszykowa 60/62 m. 16
00-673 Warsaw
Poland
http://pzhk.pl/

Związek Hodowców Koni Ras Zimnokrwistych
(Cold-Blooded Horse Breeders Association)
Nowe Jankowice 17
86-320 Łasin
Poland
http://www.konzimnokrwisty.pl

Mateusz Kaca's Polish Coldblood Blogs
http://konie-z-zimna-krwia.bloog.pl/ (general)
http://ogiery-z-zimna-krwia.bloog.pl/ (stallions)
http://klacze-z-zimna-krwia.bloog.pl/ (mares)

Polskie Konie Zimnokrwiste Blog
http://konie-pkz.dzs.pl/

Shire

The Shire Horse Society
East of England Showground
Peterborough
PE2 6XE
United Kingdom
http://www.shire-horse.org.uk/

American Shire Horse Association
P.O. Box 408
Lake Delton, WI 53940
http://www.shirehorse.org/

Shire Horse Society Australia
245 Bridge Street
Thirlmere NSW 2572
Australia
http://www.shirehorsesociety.com.au

Suffolk

American Suffolk Horse Association
Mary Margaret M. Read
4240 Goehring Road
Ledbetter, TX 78946-5004
http://www.suffolkpunch.com/

Suffolk Horse Society
The Market Hill
Woodbridge
Suffolk
IP12 4LU
United Kingdom
http://suffolkhorsesociety.org.uk/

Rare Breed Conservancy

The American Livestock Breeds Conservancy
PO Box 477
Pittsboro, North Carolina 27312
http://albc-usa.org/

Equus Survival Trust
775 Flippin Road
Lowgap, NC 27024
http://www.equus-survival-trust.org/

Rare Breeds Survival Trust
Stoneleigh Park
Nr Kenilworth, Warwickshire
CV8 2LG
United Kingdom
https://www.rbst.org.uk/

Domestic Animal Diversity Information System (DAD-IS)
http://dad.fao.org/

European Farm Animal Biodiversity Information System (EFABIS)
http://efabis.tzv.fal.de/

Gesellschaft zur Erhaltung alter und gefährdeter Haustierrassen e. V. (GEH)
Walburger Straße 2
37213 Witzenhausen
Germany
http://www.g-e-h.de/

Associazione R.A.R.E.
Razze Autoctone a Rischio di Estinzione
Via Nemo Sottili, 1
42123 Reggio Emilia
Italy
http://www.associazionerare.it/

Stichting Zeldzame Huisdierrassen
Runderweg 6
8219 PK Lelystad
06-46150594
Netherlands
http://www.szh.nl

Rare Breeds Trust of Australia
Anne Sim, Secretary
P.O.Box 159
Abbotsford Vic 3067
Australia
http://www.rbta.org/

Bibliography

The research involved in this work was extensive, and a truly complete list of source material would be impractical. Those that might prove most useful for readers seeking further information are included here, grouped by type and subject.

Horse Color - Books

Arriens, H. *Farben und Farbvererbung beim Pferd*. Litzendorf: Tierbuchverlag Irene Hohe, 2009.

Basler, U. *Pferde aus Licht und Schatten Geschichte - Rassen - Farbvererbung der gefleckten und gescheckten Pferde*. 1. Aufl. ed. Cham: Müller Rüschlikon, 2002.

Geurts, R.. *Hair Colour in the Horse*. London: J. A. Allen, 1977.

Gilbey, W. *Horses—Breeding to Colour*. London: Vinton and Company, 1907.

Gower, J. *Horse Color Explained; A Breeder's Perspective*. North Pomfret, Vermont: Trafalgar Square, 1999.

Knowles-Pfeiffer, C. *Horse and Pony Coat Colors*. London: J. A. Allen, 2000.

Labiano, A. M. *Overos Manchados*. Buenos Aires: Editorial Dunken, 1999.

Magnússon, S. A., and F. Þorkelsson. *The Natural Colours of the Iceland Horse*. 3d ed. Reykjavík: Mál og menning, 2001.

Pearson, K., and E. Nettleship. "The Albinotic Eye." *A Monograph on Albinism in Man*. London: Dulau and Company, 1913. 372-374.

Reißmann, M. *Die Farben der Pferde; Genetik, Klassifizierung, Charakteristik*. Brunsbek: Cadmos, 2009.

Solanet, E. *Pelajes Criollos*. 10. ed. Buenos Aires: Letemendia, 2003.

Sponenberg, D. P. *Equine Color Genetics*. 3. ed. Ames, Iowa: Wiley-Blackwell, 2009.

Sponenberg, D. P., and B. Beaver. *Horse Color*. College Station: Texas A&M University Press, 1983.

Walther, A. R. *Beiträge zur Kenntnis der Vererbung der Pferdefarben*. Hannover: M & H Schaper, 1912.

Wentworth, L. "Golden Palominos and Parti-Colours." *The World's Best Horse*. London: George Allen and Unwin, 1958. 150-172.

Wiersema, J. K. *Het Paard in Zijn Kleurenrijkdoom*. The Hague: Zuidgroep B.V. Uitgevers, 1977.

Horse Color - Articles

Adalsteinsson, S. "Inheritance of the palomino color in Icelandic horses." *Journal of Heredity* 65 (1974): 15-20.

Adalsteinsson, S. "Inheritance of yellow dun and blue dun in the Icelandic Toelter horse." *Journal of Heredity* 69 (1978): 146-148.

Anderson, W. S. "Coat colour in horses: Tabulation of colour of 42,165 horses allows definite conclusions to be drawn as to value of different factors—errors in registry and in genetic description of colors—connection between gray and roan." *Journal of Heredity* 5 (1914): 482-488.

Andersson, L., and K. Sandberg. "A linkage group composed of three coat color genes and three serum protein loci in horses." *Journal of Heredity* 73 (1982): 91-94.

Bellone, R. , S. A. Brooks, L. Sandmeyer, *et al.* "Differential gene expression of TRPM1, the potential cause of congenital stationary night blindness and coat spotting patterns (LP) in the Appaloosa horse." *Genetics* 179 (2008): 1861-1870.

Belyaev, D. K., A.O. Ruvinsky and L. N. Trut. "Inherited activation-inactivation of the star gene in foxes: its bearing on the problem of domestication." *Journal of Heredity* 72 (1981): 267-274

Blunn, C. T., and C. E. Howell. "The inheritance of white facial markings in Arabian horses." *Journal of Heredity* 27 (1936): 293-300.

Bowling, A. T. "Dominant inheritance of overo spotting in Paint horses." *Journal of Heredity* 85, no. 3 (1994): 222-224.

Brooks, S. A., and E. Bailey. "Exon skipping in the KIT gene causes a sabino spotting pattern in horses." *Mammalian Genome* 16 (2005): 893-902.

Brooks, S. A., T. L. Lear, D. L. Anderson, and E. Bailey. "A chromosome inversion near the KIT gene and the tobiano spotting pattern in horses." *Cytogenetic and Genome Research* 119 (2007): 225-230.

Brunberg, E., L. Andersson, G. Cothran, *et al.* "A missense mutation in PMEL17 is associated with the silver color in the horse." *BMC Genetics* 7 (2006): 46.

Carr, G. "Few spotted leopards—a possible key to high color production." *Appaloosa News* Nov/Dec (1972): 18-20.

Castle, N. "Equine KIT gene mutations, dominant white and sabino1." Retrieved May 2009 from the Dun Central Station website: http://www.duncentralstation.com.

Castle, W. E., and F. King. "New evidence in the genetics of the palomino horse." *Journal of Heredity* 42 (1951): 61-64

Castle, W. "Genetics of the palomino horse." *Journal of Heredity* 37 (1946): 35-38.

Castle, W., and F. Smith. "Silver dapple, a unique color variety among Shetland Ponies." *Journal of Heredity* 44 (1953): 139-146.

Cook, D., S. Brooks, R. Bellone, and E. Bailey. "Missense mutation in exon 2 of SLC36A1 responsible for champagne dilution in horses." *PLoS Genetics* 4 (2008): e1000195. doi:10.1371/journal.pgen.1000195

Davies, C. L. "The Colour of Domesticated Animals." *Live-Stock Journal Almanac* (1907).

Druml, T., R. Baumung, and J. Sölkner. "Pedigree analysis in the Austrian Noriker draught horse: genetic diversity and the impact of breeding for coat colour on population structure." *Journal of Animal Breeding & Genetics* 126 (2009): 348-356.

Haase, B., S. A. Brooks, A. Schlumbaum, *et al.* "Allelic heterogeneity at the equine KIT locus in dominant white (W) horses." *PloS Genetics* 3 (2007): 2101-2108.

Haase, B., S. A. Brooks, T. Tozaki, *et al.* "Seven novel KIT mutations in horses with white coat colour phenotypes." *Animal Genetics* 40, no. 5 (2009): 623-629.

Haase, B., S. Rieder, T. Tozaki, *et al.* "Five novel KIT mutations in horses with white coat colour phenotypes." *Animal Genetics* 41, no. 2 (2011): 337-339.

Henner, J., P. A. Poncet, G. Geurin, *et al.* "Genetic mapping of the (G) locus, responsible for the coat color phenotype progressive greying with age in horses (*equus caballus*)." *Mammalian Genome* 13 (2002): 535-537.

Henner, J; PA Poncet, L Aebi, *et al.* "Horse breeding: genetic tests for the coat colors chestnut, bay and black. Results from a preliminary study in the Swiss Freiberger horse breed." *Schweizer Archiv für Tierheilkunde* 144 (2002): 405–412.

Hintz, H. F., and L.D. Van Vleck. "Lethal dominant roan in horses." *Journal of Heredity* 70 (1979): 145-146.

Hofmanová, B., I. Majzlík, L. Vostrý, and K. Mach. "Coat color of Old Kladruber horse and its diversity." *Acta fytotechnica et zootechnica* 13 (2010): 9-12.

Klemola, V. "The "pied" and "splashed white" patterns in horses and ponies." *Journal of Heredity* 24 (1933): 65-69.

Lehmann, E. von. "Beitrag zur Vererbung weißgeborener Pferde." *Zeitschrift für Tierzüchtung* 49 (1941): 191–195.

Lehmann, E. von. "Die Iris= und Rumpfscheckung beim Pferd." *Zeitschrift für Tierzüchtung und Züchtungsbiologie* 59, no. 2 (1951): 175-228.

Locke, M. M., L. S. Rugh, L. V. Millon, *et al.* "The cream dilution gene, responsible for the palomino and buckskin coat colours, maps to horse chromosome 21." *Animal Genetics* 32 (2001): 340-343.

Ludwig, A., M. Pruvost, M. Reißmann, *et al.* "Coat color variation at the beginning of horse domestication." *Science* 324 (2009): 485–485.

Marklund, S., M. Moller, K. Sandberg, and L. Andersson. "Close association between sequence polymorphism in the KIT gene and the roan coat color in horses." *Mammalian Genome* 10 (1999): 283-288.

Marklund, S., M. Moller, K. Sandberg, *et al.* "A missense mutation in the gene for melanocyte-stimulating hormone receptor (MC1R) is associated with the chestnut coat color in horses." *Mammalian Genome* 7 (1996):895–899.

Mead, B. "Mushroom - A Newly Recognised Dilution." Retrieved October 11, 2011 from the Kellas Shetland Pony Stud website: http://www.kellas-stud.co.uk/mystery.htm.

Metallinos, D. L., A. T. Bowling and J. Rine. "A missense mutation in the endothelin-B receptor gene is associated with Lethal White Foal Syndrome: an equine version of Hirschsprung Disease." *Mammalian Genome* 9 (1998): 426-431.

Pielberg, G. R., A. Golovko, E. Sundström, *et al.* "A cis-acting regulatory mutation causes premature hair graying and susceptibility to melanoma in the horse." *Nature Genetics* 40 (2008) 1004-1009.

Pulos, W. and F. Hutt. 1969. "Lethal dominant white in horses." *Journal of Heredity* 60 (1969): 59-64.

Rieder, S., C. Hagger, G. Obexer-Ruff, *et al.* "Genetic analysis of white facial and leg markings in the Swiss Franches-Montagnes horse breed." *Journal of Heredity* 99 (2008): 130-136.

Shepard, C. "The Barlink Factor: A possible new dilution gene in Paint Horses." *Champagne Horse Journal* 1 (2002): 10.

Shepard, C. "Champagne Delusions: champagne look-alike dilutions." *Champagne Horse Journal* 2 no. 3 (2003).

Sponenberg, D. P. "The inheritance of leopard spotting in the Noriker horse." *Journal of Heredity* 73 (1982): 357-359.

Sponenberg, D. P., G. Carr, E. Simak, and K. Schwink. "The inheritance of the leopard complex of spotting patterns in horses." *Journal of Heredity* 81 (1990): 323-331.

Trommershausen-Smith, A. "Inheritance of chin spot markings in horses." *Journal of Heredity* 63 (1972): 100.

Trommershausen-Smith, A. "Linkage of tobiano coat spotting and albumin markers in a pony family." *Journal of Heredity* 69 (1978): 214-216.

Wilson, J. "The inheritance of the dun coat-colour in horses." *Royal Dublin Society Scientific Proceedings* (1912): 184-201.

Woolf, C. M. "Multifactorial inheritance of white facial markings in the Arabian horse." *Journal of Heredity* 80 (1989): 173-178.

Woolf, C. M. "Multifactorial inheritance of common white markings in the Arabian horse." *Journal of Heredity* 81 (1990): 250-256.

Woolf, C. M. "Common white facial markings in bay and chestnut Arabian horses and their hybrids." *Journal of Heredity* 82 (1991): 167-169.

Woolf, C. M. "Does homozygosity contribute to the asymmetry of common white leg markings in the Arabian horse?" *Genetica* 89 (1993): 25-33.

Woolf, C. M. "Influence of stochastic events on the phenotypic variation of common white leg markings in the Arabian horse: implications for various genetic disorders in humans." *Journal of Heredity* 86 (1995): 129-135.

Woolf, C. M. "Directional and anteroposterior asymmetry of common white markings in the legs of the Arabian horse: response to selection." *Genetica* 101 (1997): 199-208.

Wriedt, C. "Vererbungsfaktoren bei weißen Pferden im Gestüt Fredriksborg." *Zeitschrift für Tierzüchtung* 1, no. 2 (1924): 231-242.

Horse Color - Other Resources

Brooks, S. A. "Studies of genetic variation at the KIT locus and white spotting patterns in the horse." Ph.D. dissertation, University of Kentucky, 2006.

Les robes du Cheval de Trait Comtois (Colors of the Comtois Horse). Poster published by the Association Nationale du Cheval de Trait Comtois. Paris, 2010.

Hofmanová, B. "Characteristics of colour in the Kladruby horse and melanoma incidence." Ph.D. dissertation, Czech Agricultural University in Prague, 2010.

Kathman, L. *Horse Color Notebooks—Draft Breeds.* Unpublished, last revision 2010.

Kathman, L. *Horse Color Notebooks—Pony Breeds.* Unpublished, last revision 2010.

Kathman, L. *Horse Color Notebooks—Coaching and Sport Breeds.* Unpublished, last revision 2011.

"Lyhenteet/Sanasto." Retrieved November 2010 from the Sukuposti website: http://sukuposti.net/lyhenteet.php.

Mead, B. "International Horse and Pony Colour Term Dictionary." Retrieved October 2011 from the Kellas Shetland Pony Stud website: http://www.kellas-stud.co.uk/mystery.htm.

Breed Formation and Early Equine History

Blew, W. C. A., W. C. Dixon, G. Fleming, and V. Shaw. *Light horses: Breeds and Management.* 2d ed. London: Vinton & Company, 1894.

British Board of Agriculture and Fisheries. *British Breeds of Live Stock*. 2d ed. London: H.M.S.O., 1913.

Curtis, G. W. *Horses, Cattle, Sheep and Swine; Origin, history, improvement, description, characteristics, merits, objections, adaptability, etc., of each of the different breeds, with hints on selection, care and management, including methods of practical breeders in the United States and Canada*. 2d ed. New York: The Rural Publishing Company, 1893.

Darwin, Charles. *The Variation of Animals and Plants Under Domestication*. London: Murray, 1868.

Denhardt, R. M. "Essay on Source Materials." *The Quarter Running Horse: America's Oldest Breed*. Norman: University of Oklahoma Press, 1979.

Dent, A., and D. Goodall. *The Foals of Epona; a History of British Ponies from the Bronze Age to Yesterday*. London: Galley Press, 1962.

Derry, M. E.. *Bred for Perfection: Shorthorn Cattle, Collies, and Arabian Horses Since 1800*. Baltimore: Johns Hopkins University Press, 2003.

Derry, M. E.. *Horses in Society: A Story of Animal Breeding and Marketing, 1800-1920*. Toronto: University of Toronto Press, 2006.

Dimon, J. *American Horses and Horse Breeding: A complete history of the horse from the remotest period in his history to date*. Hartford: John Dimon, 1895.

Duerst, J. U. *Die Beurteilung des Pferdes*. Stuttgart: Verlag von Ferdinand Enke, 1922.

Eisenberg, Reis. *The Classical Riding School: the Wilton House Collection*. New York: Vendome Press, 1978.

Forrest, J. "The Royal Mews." *The English Illustrated Magazine 1891-1892*. London: Macmillan and Company, 1892. 484-488.

Goodall, D. M. *A History of Horse Breeding*. London: Robert Hale Ltd., 1977.

Gordon, W. *The Horse World of London*. London: The Religious Tract Society, 1893.

Hale, P. H. *The Book of Live Stock Champions, being an artistic souvenir supplement*. St. Louis: National Farmer and Stock Grower, 1912.

Hayes, M. H. *Points of the Horse; a treatise on the conformation, movements, breeds and evolution of the horse*. 3d ed. London: Hurst and Blackett, 1904.

Hyland, A. *The Medieval War Horse, from Byzantium to the Crusades*. Bridgend: Grange Books, 1994.

Plumb, C. S. *Types and Breeds of Farm Animals*. 2d ed. Boston: Ginn and Company, 1920.

Plumb, C. S. *Registry Books on Farm Animals, a Comparative Study*. Columbus: Ohio State University Press, 1930.

Ridgeway, W. *The Origin and Influence of the Thoroughbred Horse*. Cambridge: University Press, 1905.

Sidney, S. *The Book of the Horse*. London: Cassell & Co., 1893.

Smith, C. H., and C. Gessner. *The Natural History of Horses The Equidae or Genus Equus*. Edinburgh: W.H. Lizars, 1841.

Trut, L. N. "Early Canid Domesticataion: The Farm-Fox Experiment." *American Scientist* 87 (1999): 161-169.

Voogt, G., and K. Wormeley. *Our Domestic Animals; their habits, intelligence and usefulness*. Boston: Ginn & Co., 1907.

Wrangel, C.G. *Das Buch vom Pferde: ein Handbuch für jeden Besitzer und Liebhaber von Pferden*. 3. verm. und verb. Aufl. ed. Stuttgart: [s.n.], 1895.

Wrangel, C.G. *Die Rassen des Pferdes*. (vol. 1). Stuttgart: Schickhardt & Ebner, 1908.

Breed Histories

Armbruster, T., W. Brodauf, and G. Schröder. *Schwarzwälder Kaltblut: Geschichte und Geschichten Band I*. Freiburg: Schillinger, 2007.

Armbruster, T., W. Brodauf, and G. Schröder. *Schwarzwälder Kaltblut: Geschichte und Geschichten Band II*. Freiburg: Schillinger, 2010.

Armbruster, T., W. Brodauf, and G. Schröder. "Raritäten: Schimmel und Braune in der Schwarzwälder Kaltblutzucht." *Schwarzwälder Kaltblut: Geschichte und Geschichten Band II*. unpublished manuscript.

Armbruster, T., and G. Schröder. "Schwarzwälder Kaltblut: Zuchtversuche mit Freiberger Hengsten." Starke Pferde 31 (2004): 55-59.

Biddell, H. *Heavy Horses: Breeds & Management*. London: Vinton & Co., 1894.

Bouma, G. J. A. *Het Friese Paard*. 2e dr. ed. Drachten: Friese Pers Boekerij, 1988. (Dutch)

Charles, H. C. *Historie du Cheval Boulonnais*. Paris: Aux Bureaux de la France Chevaline, 1883. (French)

Chivers, K. *The Shire Horse; A History of the Breed, the Society and the Men*. London: J. A. Allen, 1976.

Cornell, C. (Ed.) *Book of the Hackney; Hackney Champions 1946-1957*. London: Hackney Horse Society, 1958.

Dent, A. *Cleveland Bay Horses*. London: J. A. Allen, 1978.

Druml, T. "Die Norikerzucht – eine farbzucht? Ein kulturhistorischer ausflug." Presentation of Öngene/Vegh Seminars, Maishofen, 2003.

Du Haÿs, C., J. P. Davis, and C. W. Wright. *The Percheron Horse*. New York: Orange Judd & Company, 1868.

Frederiksborghesten og det kongelige Frederiksborgske Stutteri. Hillerød: Frederiksborgmuseet, 1981.

Gauger, G. *Das Ostfriesische Pferd*. n.p.:Tannenhausen, 2010.

Geurts, R. "Genetic analysis and breed Structure of the Friesian horse." Ph.D. dissertation, University of Utrecht, 1969.

Gilbey, W. *The Great Horse or Shire Horse*. 2d ed. London: Vinton and Company, 1899.

Grilz-Seger, G. "Über die farbzucht beim Noriker: Der mohrenkopf." Retrieved on October 2011 from the Hippo-Logos website: http://www.hippo-logos.com/main/index.php.

Hart, E. *Heavy Horses - An Anthology*. Somerset: Alan Sutton Publishing Ltd, 1994.

Hart, E. *The Coloured Horse and Pony*. London: J. A. Allen, 1993.

Jensen, J. *Det Kongelige Frederiksborgske stutteris historie fra dets første oprindelse til dets opløsning 1840*. Copenhagen: Hovedkommission, 1910.

Lizet, B. *La Bête Noire: à la recherche du cheval parfait*. Paris: Editions MSH, 1989.

Love, W. *History of the Clydesdale Horse*. Glasgow: n.p., 1884.

Mischka, J. *The Percheron Horse in America*. Whitewater: Heart Prairie Press, 1991.

Nissen, J. *Enzyklopädie der Pferderassen, Bd.1, Deutschland, Belgien, Niederlande, Luxemburg*. 2d ed. Stuttgart: Kosmos, 2003.

Nissen, J. *Enzyklopädie der Pferderassen, Bd.2, Island, Skandinavien, Großbritannien, Irland, Frankreich*. 2d ed. Stuttgart: Kosmos, 2003.

Nissen, J. *Enzyklopädie der Pferderassen, Bd.3, Spanien, Portugal, Italien, Schweiz, Österreich, Osteuropa.* 2d ed. Stuttgart: Kosmos, 2003.

The Oldenburgh Coachhorse; 300 Years Old Breed. Oldenburg i. Gr.: Ad. Littmann, Printer to His Royal Highness the Grand-Duke of Oldenburgh, 1904.

Richardson, C. *British Horse and Pony Breeds—and Their Future.* London: J. A. Allen, 2008.

Ryder, T. *The High Stepper; The Hackney Horse Yesterday and Today.* London: J.A. Allen, 1961.

Ryder, T., and R. Longstaff. "Colored Hackneys." Retrieved March 1998 from the HorseNet website: http://www.horsenet.com/hackneys/spothack.html.

Sanders, A. H., and W. Dinsmore. *A History of the Percheron Horse.* Chicago: Breeder's Gazette Print, 1917.

Telleen, M. *A Century of Belgian Horses in America.* Cedar Rapids: Mischka Press, 1991.

Theulegoet, H. D. *Monographie Cheval de Trait Belge.* Brussels: Veuve Monnom, 1911.

Weld, M. C., and C. Du Haÿs. *The Percheron Horse in America.* New York: Orange Judd Co., 1886.

Stud Books and Registry Databases

American Cleveland Bay Stud Book (vols. 1-3). Springfield: Cleveland Bay Society of America, 1889-1907.

American Clydesdale Stud Book (vols. 1-21). Springfield: American Clydesdale Association, 1882-1919.

American Hackney Horse Stud Book (vols. 1-29). New York: American Hackney Horse Society, 1893-1994.

American Hackney Horse Registry Search. Accessed in 2011 at the American Hackney Horse Society website: http://hackney.select.net/registry.php

American Shetland Club Book (vol. 1). Columbia: American Shetland Pony Club, 1893.

American Suffolk Horse Association. *American Suffolk Horse Stud Book* (vols. 1-2). Janesville: Gazette Press, 1907-1912.

Baza Koni Hodowlanych. Accessed in 2011 from Polish Horse Breeders Association (PZHK) website: http://baza.pzhk.pl/.

Burgess, C. (Ed.). *American Shire Horse Stud Book* (vols. 1-10). Chicago: American Shire Horse Association, 1888-1916.

Butterworth, T. (Ed.). *National Register of Norman Horses, a register of Norman horses imported from France, and American-bred Normans whose sire and dam are recorded* (vol. 2). Quincy: National Norman Horse Association, 1883.

Butterworth, T. (Ed.). *National Register of Norman Horses* (vol. 3). Quincy: National Norman Horse Association, 1884.

Canadian Hackney Electronic Herdbook. Accessed in 2011 from the Canadian Livestock Records Corporation website: http://www.clrc.ca/.

Clydesdale Breeders of the USA Online Studbook. Accessed in 2011 at the Heavy Horse website: http://www.clydesdale.hvyhorse.com/.

The Clydesdale Stud Book of the United States; Volume 26 to Volume 53 from 1941-1996. Pecatonica: Clydesdale Breeders of the United States, 1997.

The Clydesdale Stud-Book (vols. 2-22). Glasgow: The Clydesdale Horse Society of Great Britain and Ireland, 1888-1900.

Conner, J. D. (Ed.). *National Register of Belgian Draft Horses* (vols. 1-4). Wabash: The American Association of Importers and Breeders of Belgian Draft Horses, 1905-1912.

Crouch, J (Ed.). *National Register of the German, Hanoverian and Oldenburg Coach Horse Association* (vols. 1-2). LaFayette: German, Hanoverian and Oldenburg Coach Horse Association of America, 1901-1906.

Dijkstra, E. *Friese Stamhengsten Deel 1.* Drachten: Koniklijke Vereniging 'Het Friesch Paarden-Stamboek', 1996.

Dijkstra, E. *Friese Stamhengsten Deel 2.* Drachten: Koniklijke Vereniging 'Het Friesch Paarden-Stamboek', 2002.

Dixon, W. S. (Ed.). *The Cleveland Bay Stud Book, restrospective volume containing pedigrees of stallions foaled previous to January the 1st, 1880.* Marton: Cleveland Bay Horse Society, 1884.

Earl of Dunmore (Ed.). *The Clydesdale Stud-Book. Retrospective volume, containing pedigrees of stallions foaled previous to January the 1st, 1875.* London: Taylor and Francis, 1878.

English Cart-Horse Stud Book (vols. 1-5). London: English Cart Horse Society, 1880-1884.

Grossherzogliche Köhrungs-commission. *Stamm- u. Ahnenregister für den starken, eleganten schlag des Oldenburgischen kutschpferdes.* Oldenburg: Gerhard Stalling, 1893.

The Hackney Stud Book (vols. 1-42). Norwich: Hackney Stud Book Society, 1885-1954.

Hiatte, J. M. (Ed.). *National Register of Norman Horses with a general history of the horse-kind and a thorough history of the Norman horse* (vol. 1). Bloomington: National Norman Horse Association, 1881.

Hingstelisten 2010 — Avlsforeningen Den Jydske Hest. Retrieved April 2011 from the Breeding Association for the Jutland Horse website: http://www.denjydskehest.dk/.

Index to Stallion registered in the Clydesdale Stud Book, volumes 1-30 inclusive. Glasgow: Clydesdale Horse Society of Great Britain and Ireland, 1908.

Jensen, J. (Ed.). *Stambog over Heste af Jydsk Race, Hingste* (vol. 4). Kjøbenhavn: Foreningen Jydske Landboforeningers, 1892.

Jensen, J. (Ed.). *Stambog over Heste af Jydsk Race, Hopper* (vol. 1). Arrhus: Foreningen af Jydske Landboforeningers, 1891.

Jensen, J. (Ed.). *Stambog over Heste af Jydsk Race, Hopper* (vol. 3). Arrhus: Samvirkende Danske Landboforeningers, 1896.

Jensen, J. (Ed.). *Stambog over Heste af Jydsk Race, Hopper* (vol. 5). Arrhus: Samvirkende Danske Landboforeningers, 1900.

Lynch, W. G. (Ed.). *American Shire Horse Stud Book* (vol. 11). Bloomington: American Shire Horse Association, 1918.

National Registry of French Draft Horses (vols. 4-10). Quincy: National French Draft Horse Association (formerly the National Norman Horse Association), 1887-1908.

Nederlandsch Hackney Stamboek. Accessed in 2011 from the Dutch Hackney Studbook Society website: http://www.hackneystamboek.nl/

Norický kůň - plemenná kniha. Accessed in 2011 from the Horse Breeders Association of Unions of the Czech Republic website: http://www.aschk.cz/norik/pk/.

Ostfriesisches Stutbuch (vols. 1-2). Norden: Landwirtschaftlicher Hauptverein für Ostfriesland, 1897-1905.

Percheron Horse Association of America's Online Studbook. Accessed in 2011 at the Heavy Horse website: http://www.percheron.hvyhorse.com/.

The Percheron Register (vols. 1-2). Columbus: The Percheron Registry Company, 1904-1905.

Plemenná kniha Starokladrubského koně. Accessed in 2011 from the National Stud at Kladruby website: http://www.nhkladruby.cz/plemenna-kniha.

The Shetland Pony Stud-Book Society. *Shetland Pony Stud-Book* (vol. 18). Aberdeen: Rosemount Press, 1908.

The Shire Horse Stud Book (vols. 6- 36) London: Shire Horse Society (English Cart-Horse Society), 1885-1915.

Stud Book du Cheval Boulonnais. Accessed in 2011 from les Haras Nationaux website: http://www.haras-nationaux.fr/

Stud Book du Cheval Breton. Accessed in 2011 from les Haras Nationaux website: http://www.haras-nationaux.fr/

Stud Book du Cheval Comtois. Accessed in 2011 from les Haras Nationaux website: http://www.haras-nationaux.fr/

Stud Book du Cheval de Trait Belge. Accessed in 2011 from les Haras Nationaux website: http://www.haras-nationaux.fr/

Stud Book du Cheval Percheron. Accessed in 2011 from les Haras Nationaux website: http://www.haras-nationaux.fr/

Stud Book du Trait Ardennais. Accessed in 2011 from les Haras Nationaux website: http://www.haras-nationaux.fr/

Stud Book du Trait Poitevin Mulassier. Accessed in 2011 from les Haras Nationaux website: http://www.haras-nationaux.fr/.

Stud Book Percheron de France (vol. 1). Nogent-le-Rotrou: Société Hippique Percheronne, 1883.

Stud Book Percheron de France (vol. 6). Nogent-le-Rotrou: Société Hippique Percheronne, 1894.

Stud Book Percheron de France: Juments (vol. 4). Nogent-le-Rotrou: Société Hippique Percheronne, 1889.

The Suffolk Stud-Book; A Register of the County Breed of Cart Horses (vols. 1-54). Diss: Suffolk Horse Society, 1880-1960.

Syndicat Hippique Boulonnais. *Annuaire des Etalons Boulonnais.* 19. ed. Compiegne: les Haras Nationaux, 2009.

Syndicat Hippique Boulonnais. *Annuaire des Etalons Boulonnais.* 21. ed. Compiegne: les Haras Nationaux, 2011.

Welsh Stud Book Index, from Volume 1 to Volume 17 Inclusive. Aberystwyth: Welsh Pony and Cob Society, 1919.

Welsh Stud Book (vol. 19). Aberystwyth: Welsh Pony and Cob Society, 1921.

World Wide Shire Studbook. Accessed 2011 at the American Shire Horse Association site: http://www.shirestudbook.com/.

Photo Credits

The information contained in this book has been greatly enhanced by the many images of rare and unusual breeds and colors. This was made possible by the generosity of the photographer who kindly gave permission for their work to be included.

Historical pictures of horses—something essential to telling the story of the breeds and their histories—present a unique challenge when it comes to finding copyright holders. Every effort has been made to obtain permission for the use of material still covered by copyright protection. The publisher apologizes for any errors or omissions in the above list and would be grateful if notified of any corrections that should be incorporated in future reprints or editions of this book.

Page 263: Clydesdale gelding, photo by Christine Sutcliffe

Page 265: Comtois mare *Micka 2* (top) and Comtois colts, photos courtesy of the Association Nationale du Cheval de Trait Comtois

Page 266: Comtois stallion, photo courtesy of the Association Nationale du Cheval de Trait Comtois

Page 268: Coloured Cob, photo by Christine Sutcliffe

Page 271: Coloured Cob, photo by Christine Sutcliffe

Page 272: Gypsy Horse *Shamrock's Billy O'Brien*, photo by Cindy Evans

Page 273: Coloured Cob, photo by Christine Sutcliffe

Page 274: Gypsy Horse, photo by the author

Page 277: Jutland mare and foal, photo by Malene Thyssen

Page 278: Jutland mare *Lise 124*, from Volume V of the Jutland Horse Stud Book

Page 282: Nivernais stallion, dated 1914

Page 286: Noriker horses, dated 1912

Page 287: Noriker stallion *Judas Elmar,* photo by J. K. Wiersema

Page 289: Painting from the Pferdeschwemme in Salzburg, photo by Tammy Knight

Page 290: Silesian Noriker stallion *Norbert*, dated 1907

Page 294: North American Spotted Draft stallion *3B Deakon*, photo by Lisa Bickford

Page 296: Currier and Ives print of the 1873 prize winner, *Duc de Chartres*

Page 298: Ringling Brothers Circus horses, dated 1914

Page 299: Percheron imports *Ruth* and *Glacis*, dated 1911

Page 300: Percheron mare *Imprudente*, dated 1912

Page 301: Percheron stallion *Incluse*, dated 1911

Page 303: Percheron gelding, photo by the author

Page 305: Percheron stallion *Keror*, dated 1901

Page 307: Poitevin Mulassier stallion, dated 1907

Page 308: Poitevin Mulassier mare *Gitane*, photo by Leah Patton

Page 310: Poitevin Mulassier gelding, photo by Leah Patton

Page 313: Polish Coldblood mare *Berta*, photo by Mateuz Kaca

Page 314: Percheron mare *Serena*, photo by Mateuz Kaca

Page 315: Oszmianan stallion, dated 1905

Page 316: Swedish Ardennes stallion *Bonair*, photo by Mateuz Kaca

Page 317: Swedish Ardennes stallion *Rio du Dol*, photo by Mateuz Kaca

Page 319: Engravings of *Czarina* and *Thursa* from Volume VI of the English Cart-Horse Stud Book

Page 321: Engraving of *Stockley Tom* from Volume I of the American Shire Horse Stud Book

Page 323: Shire mare *Jane's Prize One*, photo by Cindy Knudsen

Page 325: Shire mare *Freedom's Jolie Prize*, photos by Jeffrey Anderson

Page 326: Shire mare *Coldham's Surprise*, dated 1911

Page 327: Engraving of B. B. Colvin's piebald Shire team, from Sir Walter Gilbey's *The Great Horse*, dated 1899

Page 328: Engraving of Shires Pirate and Outlaw, from Sir Walter Gilbey's *The Great Horse*, dated 1899

Page 330: Sire mare *Crankwell Nora*, from Volume 29 of the Shire Horse Stud Book

Page 333: Suffolk mare *Whitton Violet*, photo by Caroline Jones

Page 334: Suffolk stallion *Highpoint William*, photo by Caroline Jones

Page 335: Suffolk stallion *Stone's Prince*, from Volume IV of the American Suffolk Stud Book

Page 336: Suffolk stallion *Smith's Saturn*, dated 1905

All horses identified in the figures are ordered left to right, top to bottom. Figures where the horses are identified in the captions are not included.

Figure 4: Frons Balder, Coldblood Trotter; Guldhagens Ajax, Gotland; Stig-Helmer, Gotland; unknown Miniature Horse; unknown Trakehner; Barlink Ultra Lite, Paint; Allgunnens Yes, Gotland; Cindy, Gotland

Figure 6: Nadira Dream, Arabian; Awkstrukk, Arabian; unknown Criollo; unknown Criollo; Brantleys Roan Allen Jr, TN Walking Horse; Sato, Thoroughbred

Figure 7: Raffons Abida, Arabian; Moniek, Gelderlander

Figure 8: Hella V, Noriker; Mery V, Noriker; Navar, Noriker; Rubin Elmar, Noriker; Stef Elmar, Noriker; Prince Plaudit, Appaloosa; Alliance Piano Man, Miniature Horse; Xhogun Middelsom, Knabstrupper

Figure 9: Go Bar Jim, Appaloosa; Saint Plaudit, Appaloosa; Spanish Dial, Appaloosa; Lemme Go Patchy, Appaloosa; Mighty Amy, Appaloosa; Rustler Bill, Appaloosa; Thunder's Spotted Bull, Appaloosa; Boomer's Image, Appaloosa

Figure 13: unknown Hackney Pony; Dunroth Bejewelled; Forewood Niatross; Dunroth Billboard; Flamboyant ST (right); Flamboyant ST (left); Hopwood Viceroy; Ostentatious

Figure 15: (Horses are shown with left and right sides) Landview Silver Chief; Armageddon's Mistress Beulah; Arclid Scottish Lad; Great American Ben Franklin

Figure 16: Rubin Elmar, Hella V, Navar, Mery V, Neugar, Stef Elmar, Tomi Vulkan XVII, Loleila

To see more pictures from some of the talented photographers that contributed to this work, please visit their websites.

Claudia Dispa
Feel Free Photo
http://www.feelfreefoto.nl

Cristine Sutcliffe
http://www.flickr.com/photos/elrenia_greenleaf/

Cindy Evans
Cindy Evans Photography
https://www.facebook.com/CindyEvansPhotography

Martina Vannelli
http://www.flickr.com/photos/martinavannelli/

Jeffrey Anderson
http://www.jeffreyandersonphoto.com/

Dick Reed
Toskhara Arabians
http://www.toskhara.com

Horse Index

Entries in italics indicate the horse is pictured. Duplicate names have the breed in parenthesis. Where the breed is the same, duplicate names have the registration number given. Otherwise registration numbers are only given in breeds where they are considered part of the name.

General Index

Individual horses are listed in a separate index. Primary entries for a color, pattern or breed appear in boldface. Entries in italics indicate images. Page references followed by an "f" indicate a chart or figure.